Augsburg College
George Sverdrup Library
Minneapolis, Minnesota 55404
WITHDRAWN

Quantitative
International
Politics

edited by
Francis W. Hoole
Dina A. Zinnes

The Praeger Special Studies program—utilizing the most modern and efficient book production techniques and a selective worldwide distribution network—makes available to the academic, government, and business communities significant, timely research in U.S. and international economic, social, and political development.

Quantitative International Politics
An Appraisal

PRAEGER SPECIAL STUDIES IN INTERNATIONAL POLITICS AND GOVERNMENT

Praeger Publishers   New York   Washington   London

Library of Congress Cataloging in Publication Data
Main entry under title:

Quantitative international politics.

    (Praeger special studies in international politics and government)
    Includes bibliographies.
    1. International relations—Research. I. Hoole, Francis W. II. Zinnes, Dina A
JX1291.036   327   75-23971
ISBN 0-275-55650-6

PRAEGER PUBLISHERS
111 Fourth Avenue, New York, N.Y. 10003, U.S.A.

Published in the United States of America in 1976
by Praeger Publishers, Inc.

All rights reserved

© 1976 by Praeger Publishers, Inc.

Printed in the United States of America

FOREWORD
EVALUATING THE EVALUATIONS
Bruce Russett

It does indeed seem to be time to evaluate the major quantitative international relations projects and, in the process, to evaluate the progress of the "movement" as a whole. These projects have been running between ten and twenty years, and collectively they have absorbed several million dollars in resources for research and graduate training. Since the available resources palpably are shrinking, it is especially appropriate to review past large-scale efforts, in order to develop better guidelines for future work. Thus I think we should welcome this volume. It is organized around a coherent set of themes, which are subdivided by methodology, substance, and philosophy of science. It has been carried out with the full cooperation of the investigators whose work is being evaluated, by a group of evaluators who are highly competent in and sympathetic to the methods employed by the investigators, yet far from uncritical. Its comprehensiveness and the skills manifested in its pages are remarkable.

It is good to have such a formalized and well-executed set of evaluations. Scientists, and their work, are constantly being evaluated in any case, but the evaluations may vary greatly in sophistication. If the evaluations are badly conceived or ill informed, they may either let shoddy work pass with undeserved praise or stifle unorthodox research before it has had an opportunity to display its virtues effectively. It seems to me that these evaluators have judiciously avoided both extremes. While they identify some notable flaws in most of the projects, they also are alert to the real value of each, and they suggest ways in which the projects might continue with greater strength. Such constructive criticism is essential, since the quantitative study of international relations is still young and still subject to many kinds of missteps, and is still practiced by only a few hundred experienced professionals. It is also still subject to substantial criticism from outsiders who, partly because of the practitioners' failures to communicate adequately, do not entirely understand what they are criticizing. Because of this, especially while resources are so limited, the danger that promising avenues will be closed prematurely is always present. Both the evaluators and those who conceived and organized the project, Francis Hoole and Dina Zinnes, deserve full credit for having avoided the extremes of cheers and condemnation. The evaluations also can serve as useful models for students and senior researchers, who themselves will be undertaking evaluations of the work of others at a later date. Later critics should endeavor to be as competent and as conscientious.

But enough of mere praise, however well deserved. It also must be said that the role of evaluator is a seductive one; if one is unwary it can become a full-time occupation, and that should never happen. Evaluation of the research of others should be undertaken only by those who themselves engage in the hard endeavor of scientific exploration. In effect, the subject of an evaluation can and should ask of his critics, "Have you ever met a payroll?" Only those who have had the experience of trying to carry out a piece of research, like the critics in this volume, can appreciate the hazards and hard choices the practitioner must continually face, and only such an experienced critic can have much sense of how readily available the various hypothetically preferable options might really have been in the actual course of the research. In this vein I insist to my students that they should never publish critiques of the research of other scholars until they have themselves published research of their own and, coincidentally, offered a hostage to insure the probity of their own critiques.

Although research resources are no longer plentiful, it is essential that the next generation of quantitative international relations scholars should not retire into the haven of criticism alone. All of us are, I hope, sensitive to the aphorism that "those who can't, teach." Similarly, there is a story about a tomcat whose owners, tired of his nightly forays, had him altered; yet even afterward he continued to go out, no longer as a doer, but as a consultant. A generation of evaluators who are capable of penetrating criticism but who have little research output of their own would surely produce a sterile profession in short order.

This is not, I think, a purely imaginary danger. Criticism can be done cheaply; one can perform it in the armchair without the need for laboratory experiments, research assistance, data-grubbing, or computing. Anyone can play; no big grant is needed for the entry fee; all that is required is some free time and a well-honed sensitivity. If research resources are not available, quite a number of very able people will be tempted to spend most of their time as evaluators. The high productivity of the four projects reviewed in this book, as well as of several other major empirical efforts, will provide ample targets for quite a long volley of potshots; it is very important that in carrying out the necessary evaluations of past work we do not produce for the quantitative international relations profession a generation of book reviewers. The evaluations need to be performed concomitantly with, and as an immediate precursor to, new empirical analyses.

If new work is to be built on the foundations (or wreckage) of the old, we must make very intensive use of existing data collections, notably including those of the projects reviewed in this volume. On most grounds these projects are judged by their evaluators as having produced voluminous riches of relatively reliable and valid data. The editors declare that "data collection is the methodological strong suit of the projects." If there is indeed going to be a still longer period of diminished research resources, it may be a long time before the profession again has available the raw materials for as many as two or three, let alone four, such massive data-collection efforts. We need to give careful attention, therefore, to the matter of using the extant material intensively. If properly disseminated, this material provides an excellent base for further theory development and hypothesis testing by many scholars, whether they are mature professionals or graduate student apprentices. By this criterion, not all projects deserve equally high marks. The data from some projects have been available, either directly or through the Inter-University Consortium for Political Research, for a number of years, while the data from others, despite having been the subject of many published analyses, are only just beginning to be disseminated.

The reanalysis of the data of other scholars is also curiously minimized in the evaluations of this book. Very few of the reviewers have actually reanalyzed, with the computing procedures they propose, any of the data from the projects they are evaluating. As a result, some of the criticisms are obtained a bit "on the cheap," and the force of the criticisms is thereby weakened, as is the reader's sense of how deeply any methodological or theoretical flaws in the projects really run. Since I had to write this foreword without seeing the final versions of the essays in this volume, I will avoid essay-specific remarks and leave the reader to consider the applicability of my general remarks in each case.

Another limitation of some of the critiques is the tendency to primarily allow the original project directors to set the major terms of reference. Many critiques focus on relatively marginal issues, such as how appropriate the statistical tests were and whether the procedures, carried out in a factor analysis, were correct. Deeper doubts about the analysis are rarer; for example, whether factor analysis was an appropriate procedure at all or whether very different kinds of multivariate analysis or nonlinear models should have been employed. Of course some questions of this sort are raised, but there is very little of an even more fundamental sort about basic methodological and theoretical decisions. Thus there is little questioning of "level of analysis" decisions, such as whether it was wise for the researchers of the Correlates of War (COW) and Dimensionality of Nations (DON) projects to carry out their data analyses exclusively at the levels of the international system, subsystems, dyads, and national systems.

Both these projects offer and test hypotheses that make crucial assumptions about the perceptions of national decision-makers. Perhaps it was correct of the two projects to avoid detailed empirical work at that level; both projects certainly have bitten off enormous tasks as it is, and very possibly it is best, according to the principle of comparative advantage, that they have been confined to analysis of the data on nation-states or dyads, leaving work on the smaller units of analysis to others. I at least am not prepared to assert that their directors' decisions were in error. However, various essential causal inferences regarding those hypotheses cannot be fully explored with data that only covers the large units of analysis. A thoroughgoing critique of the projects would pinpoint some of those inferences and identify the relevant research that has been done by other scholars who are not associated with the projects and that applies directly to those inferences. If evidence to support or refute the hypothesized relationships cannot be found in the extant research work, then key areas for future work will have been so identified. Either way, scientific cumulation would be fostered. As only a single example, the inferences of status-field theory must be explored at the level of the decision maker as well as at the dyadic level. Key intervening variables between "objective" differences and politically relevant perceptions must be specified and their role established.

In this respect I also find it a bit surprising that the major projects generally seem to have learned so little from one another. Although there is some cross-referencing, there is sometimes a lack of any systematic effort to exploit or build upon the findings of other projects. For example—and this is not to single it out as a special offender—the excellent new Nazli Choucri and Robert North volume, though published in 1975,* cites no empirical paper, from any of the other projects with a publication date later than 1968 (one from COW is listed as 1970, but it is a reprint of an article originally appearing in 1968). Surely all of us who lead substantial empirical projects are guilty of some such behavior, being more familiar with our own work than with that of others; but it is just as clear that there has been too little cross-fertilization among the projects. There must have been something in the post-1968

---

*Nazli Choucri and Robert C. North, Nations in Conflict: National Growth and International Violence (San Francisco: W. H. Freeman and Company, 1975).

publications of the other projects that would have been relevant to the Choucri-North work. This lack becomes even more serious when cross-referencing not only across projects but across units of analysis is taken into consideration. Hardly any of the large-scale aggregate data projects at the nation-state, dyad, or international system level (and here I include my own) incorporate much of the fine crisis-perception work at the individual actor level that was done at earlier stages of the 1914 project by Richard A. Brody, Ole R. Holsti, and Robert C. North. A cumulating science must give this problem greater attention. Perhaps special mini-conferences would help; they could be arranged around particular topics such as arms races or status inconsistency and carefully organized to bring together across projects people who are working at different levels of analysis. Another valuable kind of mini-conference might be one in which the data set from one or more of the big projects was made available to users in an interactive computer mode and in which a variety of people with different methodological and theoretical orientations met to generate and immediately test hypotheses.

Finally, a work about the need for more explicit and rigorous theorizing. To my taste—and it is partly a matter of taste, despite all the conflicting claims that can be entered from a philosophy-of-science perspective—the need surely is present, at least at this stage of the development of quantitative international politics. A fairly "narrow inductivist" strategy may well have been in order for the early stages, when we knew so very little, although not all the work of the 1960s was quite as "narrow inductivist" as some of the critics imply. COW is a case in point. J. David Singer is not a formal theorist, and formal modeling was entirely absent from his project in those days. Critics have fairly accurately identified points in the project at which a more rigorous theoretical specification would have produced clearer and more appropriate empirical results; yet both the critics and Singer's own statements have often made his work appear more inductive than it really was. Though his theory has sometimes been insufficiently explicit, his empirical work has been rooted in the extensive thought and theorizing of his earlier work, which predated the COW project and which is frequently forgotten by critics dealing only with what is explicit in his current products. This has been true in other projects as well.

Overall, I find myself generally in agreement with most of the continuing critical themes of this volume, notably with the demand for more explicit and formal theorizing than in the past; with the emphasis on careful model specification; and with the call for data analysis rather than for vast new data-gathering efforts, although it is very important that certain major data sets, the holdings of which now terminate in the 1960s or early 1970s, be brought up to date soon and kept up to date. Although an emphasis on formal theory is desirable, it is equally necessary that we continue with quantitative empirical work and not retreat entirely into "mere" theory and criticism. Scientific cumulation also requires new findings.

ACKNOWLEDGMENTS

At this time we would like to acknowledge several debts incurred during the production of this volume. First, we would like to thank Henry Teune, program chairman for the 1974 Annual Meeting of the International Studies Association, for facilitating the convening of the panel sessions at which most of the first drafts of the papers in this volume were presented, and Hayward R. Alker, Jr. for his valuable participation on the 1914 panel at the 1974 ISA meeting. Next, we would like to thank Roslyn Simowitz and Marcia Prins of the Center for International Policy Studies at Indiana University for valuable editorial and secretarial assistance in the production of the final draft of the manuscript. We are extremely grateful to Steven Fraser, Karen Romano, and Richard Karz of Praeger Publishers, Inc. for their careful handling of the editing and production of this volume. Finally, we would like to thank our colleague John V. Gillespie for his inspiration and criticism.

We are grateful to the Carnegie Endowment for International Peace and the Centre de Recherches sur les Institutions Internationales for facilitating the editorial efforts and work on our own chapters by providing office space and secretarial assistance to Francis W. Hoole during his year-long stay in Geneva, Switzerland, in 1974-75. We also wish to acknowledge the support given to Dina A. Zinnes by the National Science Foundation, Grant GS 36806.

CONTENTS

	Page
FOREWORD: EVALUATING THE EVALUATIONS Bruce Russett	v
ACKNOWLEDGMENTS	xi
LIST OF TABLES AND FIGURES	xvi

PART I: INTRODUCTION

Chapter

1 INTRODUCTION   3
Francis W. Hoole and Dina A. Zinnes

PART II: THE CORRELATES OF WAR PROJECT

2 THE CORRELATES OF WAR PROJECT: CONTINUITY, DIVERSITY, AND CONVERGENCE   21
J. David Singer

3 AN APPRAISAL OF THE RESEARCH DESIGN AND PHILOSOPHY OF SCIENCE OF THE CORRELATES OF WAR PROJECT   43
Brian L. Job and Charles W. Ostrom, Jr.

4 AN APPRAISAL OF THE METHODOLOGICAL AND STATISTICAL PROCEDURES OF THE CORRELATES OF WAR PROJECT   67
Raymond Duvall

5 AN APPRAISAL OF THE SUBSTANTIVE FINDINGS OF THE CORRELATES OF WAR PROJECT   99
Harvey Starr

6 REJOINDER TO THE CRITIQUES   128
J. David Singer

Chapter		Page
	PART III: THE DIMENSIONALITY OF NATIONS PROJECT	
7	THE DIMENSIONALITY OF NATIONS PROJECT Rudolph J. Rummel	149
8	AN APPRAISAL OF THE PHILOSOPHY OF SCIENCE AND RESEARCH DESIGN INVOLVED IN THE DIMENSIONALITY OF NATIONS PROJECT Gordon Hilton	155
9	AN APPRAISAL OF THE METHODOLOGY AND STATISTICAL PRACTICES USED IN THE DIMENSIONALITY OF NATIONS PROJECT Leo Hazlewood	176
10	AN APPRAISAL OF THE SUBSTANTIVE FINDINGS OF THE DIMENSIONALITY OF NATIONS PROJECT Richard H. Van Atta and Dale B. Robertson	196
11	COMMENTS ON THE REVIEWS OF THE DIMENSIONALITY OF NATIONS PROJECT Rudolph J. Rummel	219
	PART IV: THE INTER-NATION SIMULATION PROJECT (SIMULATED INTERNATIONAL PROCESSES PROJECT)	
12	AN INCOMPLETE HISTORY OF FIFTEEN SHORT YEARS IN SIMULATING INTERNATIONAL PROCESSES Harold Guetzkow	247
13	AN APPRAISAL OF THE PHILOSOPHY OF SCIENCE OF THE INTER-NATION SIMULATION PROJECT Cheryl Christensen and Robert Butterworth	259
14	THE INTER-NATION SIMULATION PROJECT: A METHODOLOGICAL APPRAISAL Stuart J. Thorson	284
15	AN APPRAISAL OF THE SUBSTANTIVE FINDINGS OF THE INTER-NATION SIMULATION PROJECT Stuart A. Bremer	304

Chapter		Page
16	SOME INSTRUCTIVE EXPERIENCES GAINED IN SIMULATING INTERNATIONAL PROCESSES, 1957-72 Harold Guetzkow and Wm. Ladd Hollist	328

PART V: THE 1914 PROJECT (STANFORD STUDIES IN INTERNATIONAL CONFLICT AND INTEGRATION)

17	THE STANFORD STUDIES IN INTERNATIONAL CONFLICT AND INTEGRATION Robert C. North	349
18	A PHILOSOPHY-OF-SCIENCE ASSESSMENT OF THE STANFORD STUDIES IN CONFLICT AND INTEGRATION James A. Caporaso	354
19	AN APPRAISAL OF THE METHODOLOGICAL AND STATISTICAL PRACTICES USED IN THE 1914 PROJECT Karen Ann Feste	383
20	AN EVALUATION OF THE SUBSTANTIVE CONTRIBUTION OF THE STANFORD STUDIES IN CONFLICT AND INTEGRATION Mark S. Levine	407
21	A REEVALUATION OF THE RESEARCH PROGRAM OF THE STANFORD STUDIES IN INTERNATIONAL CONFLICT AND INTEGRATION Robert C. North, Ole R. Holsti, and Nazli Choucri	435

PART VI: SUMMARY, CONCLUSIONS, AND IMPLICATIONS

22	SUMMARY, CONCLUSIONS, AND IMPLICATIONS Francis W. Hoole and Dina A. Zinnes	463

PART VII: BIBLIOGRAPHIES

THE CORRELATES OF WAR PROJECT Principal Investigator: J. David Singer Prepared by: J. David Singer	481

	Page
DIMENSIONALITY OF NATIONS PROJECT Principal Investigator: Rudolph J. Rummel Prepared by: Rudolph J. Rummel	489
INTER-NATION SIMULATION PROJECT Principal Investigator: Harold Guetzkow Prepared by: Doreen R. Ellis	497
STANFORD STUDIES IN INTERNATIONAL CONFLICT AND INTEGRATION Principal Investigator: Robert C. North Prepared by: Robert C. North	514
ABOUT THE CONTRIBUTORS	521

LIST OF TABLES AND FIGURES

Table		Page
4.1	Alliances and War Occurrence in the Twentieth Century	77
4.2	Capability Concentration and War Occurrence in the Twentieth Century	78
9.1	Variables Loading on Economic Development and Size Factors	183
9.2	Alternative Matrix Configurations: The Impact of the Cases-Variables Ratio	185
9.3	Mean Inter-Item Correlations among the Key Loading Variables for Each of the Factors	186
9.4	Reanalysis of the Components of the Catholic Culture Factor	188
9.5	Within-Region Correlations among Marker Variables on Four Major Dimensionality of Nations (DON) Project Dimensions	190
10.1	Results of Analyses of Field Theory Models I and II, Using Data for 1955 and 1963	208
11.1	Comparisons of Different Models and Random Numbers	235
19.1	A Selection of Statistics Appropriate for Analyzing the 1914 Data	395
19.2	Application of Inappropriate Statistics to the 1914 Data	396

Figure		
1.1	The Evaluators	14
1.2	Authors and Essays in this Volume	15
8.1	Dimensionality of Nations Project Research Flow, 1962-72	158

Figure		Page
8.2	Levels of Studies in Political Science in Relation to the Programs Studied in this Volume	161
8.3	A Change in Paradigm in Relation to the Subject Area	164
8.4	Change in Self-Image as a Change in Paradigm	165
8.5	Change in Self-Image Producing Conflicting Theories	166
8.6	Two Conflicting Theories Tested against an Empirical Basis	169
10.1	Research Design for Field Theory Tests	205
18.1	Stimulus-Response Model of Crisis Decision Making	360
18.2	Stress, Time, and Decision Making	365
18.3	Hypothesized Lateral Pressure Dynamics	371
20.1	The S-r : s-R Model	410
20.2	Ole R. Holsti's Model: Stress, Time, and Decision Making	413
20.3	The _Nations in Conflict_ Model	415
20.4	Frequently Appearing Links in the _Nations in Conflict_ Analyses	426
20.5	Links Appearing in the British Subperiod Analyses	427

PART

I

INTRODUCTION

CHAPTER

1

INTRODUCTION
Francis W. Hoole
Dina A. Zinnes

It has often been said that a discipline can only be judged mature if proponents are willing, and indeed eager, to engage in careful self-appraisal. If this is the case, then the field variously known as Quantitative International Politics, Interpolimetrics, Systematic International Politics, or Scientific International Politics can probably be said to have gained adulthood. In the mid-1970s there has been a growing feeling that there is need to take stock of this field of study and assess where it currently stands, where it seems to be going, and what its goals ought to be.[1] The March 1974 meetings of the Interpolimetrics Section of the International Studies Association (ISA) were part of this self-appraisal movement. This volume contains an updated report of that set of meetings.

The 1974 Interpolimetrics meetings were devoted specifically to a survey and critical assessment of four major projects in the field of study that we shall call quantitative international politics (QIP). A careful appraisal of the four projects was made in the interest of determining the contribution of this field of research to the study of international politics and of identifying specific lessons that would enable scholars to improve future research. Although some may argue that other projects should also have been considered, it would probably be hard to contend that those chosen for evaluation have not provided a major impetus for the field of quantitative international politics: The Correlates of War (COW) Project under the direction of J. David Singer of the University of Michigan; The Dimensionality of Nations (DON) Project, under the leadership of Rudolph Rummel of the University of Hawaii; The Inter-Nation Simulation (INS) Project, headed by Harold Guetzkow of Northwestern University; and The 1914 Project, directed by Robert C. North of Stanford University

The age of these projects means that at one time or another each has been assessed in some form.[2] What seemed to be in order was an examination of each of the projects along dimensions that would allow for comparisons among the projects. It was decided that each project should be evaluated in terms of three dimensions that appear to be of central importance to QIP research: philosophy of science, methodology, and substance. It is recognized, however, that the demarcation line between any two of these dimensions is not always clear; indeed, each overlaps with, complements, and has implications for each of the others.

There were two obvious ways in which the meetings could have been organized. It would have been possible to compare all of the projects along a single dimension by setting up philosophy of science, methodology, and substance panels; nevertheless, the alternative approach of organizing panels around projects was adopted and the COW, DON, INS, and 1914 panels were established. By combining the discussion of all three dimensions with respect to a single project, it was hoped that the overall evaluation would be made more meaningful; furthermore, organizing each panel around one project made it easier for the head of each project to answer questions raised with respect to the studies done in connection with it.

Who should perform the evaluation of the projects? Clearly those who had been involved in a project would know its strong and weak points; yet how objective could they be? It could also be argued that it would be more valuable to the projects themselves to obtain new ideas from outside sources. However, if outsiders were to be used, it would be important to select individuals with the ability and willingness to do a careful appraisal; for instance, those who opposed the entire quantitative tradition would probably offer little that might be of value in helping the field grow and develop. Furthermore, the technical nature of much of the work made it necessary to select trained individuals, who could provide a thorough appraisal along a given dimension. The net result was that the evaluators came from what might be called the "younger generation" of QIP researchers.

Each of the panel meetings involved the presentation of three papers, plus comments by a discussant. Each paper provided a critical evaluation of a particular project from the viewpoint of philosophy of science, methodology, or substance. The discussants on the panels were the above-named principal investigators of the projects. The meetings were presided over and given direction by the panel chairmen, all of whom are established senior scholars in the field of quantitative international politics, Davis Bobrow of the University of Maryland, Charles Hermann of Ohio State University, and Charles McClelland and James Rosenau of the University of Southern California.

INTRODUCTION

As anticipated, this type of open meeting led to some heated discussion, not only between the evaluators and the project directors, but also among the members of the audience at the 1974 annual meetings of the International Studies Association, and it is probably safe to say that evaluators, project directors, and audience gained additional insights from the discussions. In light of those exchanges the evaluators revised their papers, which were then submitted to the project directors for their responses. The present volume contains the revised papers from the Interpolimetrics meetings and the written responses by the project heads. In addition, the project directors have contributed brief histories of the projects.

Before we turn to the project histories, evaluations, and responses by the project directors, it might be useful to provide some additional background. In the remainder of this chapter we will present an introduction to the field of quantitative international politics and the projects being assessed; discuss briefly the meaning and potential relevance of the philosophy of science, methodological, and substantive evaluations of the projects; introduce the contributors to this volume; and present an overview of the remainder of the volume. In the last chapter we will summarize and draw together conclusions and recommendations for research in the field of quantitative international politics.

QUANTITATIVE INTERNATIONAL POLITICS

One of the most important things to note about the field of quantitative international politics is that its substantive focal points do not differ from those found in the general field of international politics. Topics such as the causes of war, foreign-policy and national-security decision making, balance of power dynamics, international integration, and bargaining and negotiation are of equal concern to quantitative international politics and to traditional international politics: what distinguishes the QIP field is its approach. The major characteristic of this approach is the attempt to be as explicit as possible about all aspects of the presentation of an argument. It could be said that a central goal of the QIP researcher is to put his entire argument in the public domain so that others may judge, accept or reject, and build upon the research. An exact specification of assumptions used to derive hypotheses and a use of standard forms of logic and mathematics to draw conclusions from the assumptions, a precise statement of measurement rules employed in the operationalization of variables, a careful attention to possible biases in data sources, and an explicit selection of decision rules used in assessing hypotheses are all marks of QIP research.

In addition to a concern with the explicit statement of an argument, QIP research can also be distinguished from other international politics research by its use of variables and hypotheses. For example, the typical QIP researcher is not interested in the causes of the War of 1812 in themselves, but rather with the variable war. He seeks to establish hypotheses about the relationship between such variables as alliances and war. Thus QIP research focuses on general patterns and not on specific events.

The QIP research tradition has had two central branches. The first and most predominant branch has been concerned with the explicit statement of hypotheses and with careful empirical assessment of those hypotheses. Much of this research has focused on rules to measure variables, biases inherent in data sources, and a wide variety of statistical techniques to test hypotheses. The second branch, frequently identified as the mathematical modeling branch, has been less concerned with empirical assessment of hypotheses and more with providing formal arguments that allow the derivation of hypotheses that ultimately might be subjected to empirical analysis. The projects reviewed in this volume, with the possible exception of INS, represent the first branch of QIP research.

In short, QIP research approaches the familiar topics of international politics by formulating hypotheses that postulate relationships between variables. Although the emphasis may be on the empirical assessment of hypotheses or on formal derivation of hypotheses from explicitly stated assumptions, the goal is to make the entire research process as explicit as possible and to clearly state the argument so that it can become a building block in the growing structure of knowledge about international politics. Ultimately the typical QIP researcher wishes to be both theoretical and empirical, to formally derive hypotheses and to carefully and explicitly subject them to empirical tests.[3]

PROJECTS BEING ASSESSED

The projects that were examined were selected because they were of sufficient age to make a critical assessment possible, because the investigators associated with each project had produced enough published research to make an assessment generally meaningful, and because each project was well known in the field of quantitative international politics. Later in this volume the director of each

INTRODUCTION

project will present a short history of his project; therefore, in this section we will present only a brief overview. The reader who desires more information than is contained in this book is referred to the bibliographies at the end of this volume, which list the writings connected with the projects.

The Correlates of War (COW) Project was begun by J. David Singer during the early 1960s. The primary concern of the project has been the quantitative analysis of war, using data for the period from 1815 to 1965. The major effort so far has been to identify the factors that correlate with war. This project, which works in the quantitative history tradition, is especially noted for its fine collection of time-series data—undoubtedly the best collection of such data in the international politics field. These data, which have been collected on a yearly basis, have been primarily used to focus on political phenomena at the international system level. The COW Project is just beginning a second phase that will emphasize the development and testing of a theory of the causes of war.

The Dimensionality of Nations (DON) Project was begun in the early 1960s by Harold Guetzkow, Jack Saywer, and Rudolph Rummel, and after the initial phases of the project Rummel took over its direction. Initially the project was oriented around the collection and analysis of 230 attributes and behaviors of approximately 80 nations, using the period of the mid 1950s for the systematic collection of data. The emphasis then shifted to the collection and analysis of dyadic behavior for a small number of nation dyads for the same time period. Professor Rummel next developed a more formal theoretical structure called field theory, which related the attribute space to the behavior space of nations. A revised theoretical structure, called status-field theory, is currently the focus of concern for the DON Project. This project is especially known for its cross-sectional focus on various types of behavior by large numbers of nations and its use of sophisticated statistical techniques like canonical correlation and factor analysis.

The Inter-Nation Simulation (INS) Project, also known as the Simulated International Processes (SIP) Project, was begun by Harold Guetzkow in the late 1950s. By 1960 Professor Guetzkow had produced a man-machine simulation that was useful for laboratory research and educational purposes. Several revised versions of the simulation were developed in the 1960s, culminating in an enlarged international processes simulation in 1967. The Inter-Nation Simulation Project is especially noted for simulating laboratory research in the international politics field and for the variety of international political topics that it has covered. Furthermore, a large number of scholars have been involved with the project, and it has performed a valuable function as a network, or clearinghouse, for scholars and ideas in the field of quantitative international politics.

The 1914 Project, known also as The Stanford Studies in International Conflict and Integration, was begun at Stanford University in the late 1950s by Robert North. The primary concern of the project in the early years was to make understandable the conflict spiral that led to the outbreak of World War I. The data sources for the early studies were drawn primarily from the national archives of the states involved in the 1914 crisis and included diplomatic instructions and reports, consular reports, intelligence and military reports, departmental memoranda, records of meetings and debates, and memoirs and diaries. Later studies have focused on the 1870-1914 period (utilizing aggregate data) and other crises, such as the Cuban missile crisis (primarily using public statements by the governmental participants in the crisis). The 1914 Project is especially well known for its use of the stimulus-response framework to analyze conflict spirals and for the data collection technique known as content analysis.

We wish to acknowledge that there are several other major projects in the field of quantitative international politics that could have been evaluated, including The World Event Interaction Survey Project and The Yale Political Data Project.[4] Furthermore, we wish to acknowledge that a large portion of the research done in the quantitative international politics field has been undertaken by individual scholars not associated with a major research project. However, the four projects evaluated here are quite well known and seem to present adequate material for the identification of lessons that could be meaningful to the entire quantitative international politics field. We now turn to a consideration of the perspectives that were used in the assessment of the projects.

PHILOSOPHY OF SCIENCE EVALUATION

Three general philosophy of science themes appear to be especially relevant for the evaluation of work in the field of quantitative international politics. One of these concerns the definition of theory and the assessment of the extent to which a specific research endeavor has produced a theoretical statement. In short, what is theory, how do we know it when we see it, and do we see it in the research being evaluated? Within the context of research projects, the primary concern is as follows: To what extent has the project, as it has unfolded in the sequence of studies it has generated, produced an evolving line of thought that constitutes theory?

INTRODUCTION

A second related issue concerns the evaluation of theory. How can the correctness or falseness of theory be determined? Is there a logic of justification? The thinking of philosophers of science regarding concepts like empirical fit, parsimony, deductive power, scope, falsifiability, and plausibility is potentially of great use in the evaluation of theories in the field of quantitative international politics. Within the context of research projects these concerns raise issues about the manner in which a project has been sensitive to the systematic evaluation of theory.

A third theme concerns the appropriate strategy for a science. How should scholars proceed in the scientific enterprise? How is research designed and conducted? What are the major steps, if any, that ought to be followed to maximize the probability that theory will develop? What temporal order ought to be imposed upon the components of the research design? Is there a logic of discovery? Finally, and most importantly, what are the advantages and disadvantages of different research strategies?

The philosophy of science evaluators raise these and other relevant philosophy of science concerns. They were asked to step back and look at the general picture of what the researchers associated with the various projects were doing, what criteria were being used for the evaluation of theory, whether theory had been developed, and whether theory was likely to be developed. The philosophy-of-science evaluators were told to be analytical and reflective about the research strategies being pursued in the projects evaluated.

METHODOLOGY EVALUATION

By methodology we mean the full range of operational procedures involved in the systematic empirical examination of hypotheses, including research design, measurement rules, data collection, and data or statistical analysis. Some individuals may refer to these items as research techniques or quantitative research methods because they deal with techniques or methods for generating and evaluating empirical evidence. Regardless of the label, however, methodology in this context refers to the use of systematic methods in the empirical examination of hypotheses.

The research design is the vehicle by which the research enterprise is structured.[5] The evaluation of a research design involves answering a number of questions. What are the variables and how are they related? Is the level of analysis appropriate? Is the design correlational or experimental in nature? Why? Is it cross-sectional or time-series in nature? Why? What are the advantages of the research design? What are the limitations of the design? How serious are they? Perhaps the key concern is whether the best possible design has been constructed, given the circumstances of the research problem.

The evaluation of measurement rules involves a variety of considerations. What scaling and index construction techniques were used? What level of measurement was achieved? Were multiple indicators used? How were reliability and validity problems handled? Were the measurement techniques properly used? If not, how serious was the misuse? Because measurement rules provide the link between the concepts embodied in the hypotheses and the data collected from the empirical world, they are of course crucial in the empirical examination of hypotheses. Thus concern about whether or not the measurement rules are appropriate to the circumstances in which they are used is especially important.

Because the data become the evidence by which the empirical worth of a hypothesis is evaluated, the way in which the data are collected is vital in the field of quantitative international politics. Evaluating data collection techniques requires a consideration of the data sources used, of reliability and validity issues, of the proper use of data collection techniques, and finally of the extent to which a project has been innovative and creative in its use of data collection techniques. The crucial question, of course, is whether the data collection techniques and data sources were appropriate for the hypotheses being examined.

Data analysis involves the systematic summarization and evaluation of the empirical data. A number of questions regarding this aspect of the research projects are in order. What data-analytical and statistical methods were used? Were the techniques properly used? If not, how serious was the misuse? Should other techniques have been used? Did theory dictate the use of statistical techniques? Did statistical techniques impose anything on the theory? Finally, and most importantly, were the analyses appropriate for the research questions being asked?

All empirical research involves methodological dilemmas, forcing on the researcher a series of decisions involving trade-offs. The assignment of the methodology evaluators was to assess the reasonableness of these trade-offs and to evaluate the researchers' handling of their methodological dilemmas. In making their assessments the evaluators were asked to report on the methodological techniques used and to make suggestions for improvements in the methodological procedures.

INTRODUCTION

SUBSTANTIVE EVALUATION

Whereas the philosophy-of-science evaluations focused on the research strategies being pursued and the methodology evaluations focused on the techniques used in the empirical analysis, the substantive aspect of the evaluation focused on the substantive questions addressed, the research findings, and the importance of the findings. The substantive evaluations complement the philosophy-of-science and methodology assessments by examining what has been learned about international political behavior. Although a sound philosophy-of-science orientation and good methodological practices may be necessary conditions for the development of knowledge in the field of quantitative international politics, they are not sufficient conditions for understanding international politics. Therefore we must also ask about the substantive contributions of the projects.

Three general types of concerns seem relevant to an assessment of the substantive aspects of a research project. The first deals with the nature of the questions being posed as the research problem. How central to the literature are the issues raised by a project? Have the questions been asked in such a way that the project can begin to supply answers? If the substantive concerns of a project are not important and interesting, then it is reasonable to conclude that the research project is marginal.

Even if important and interesting questions are being asked, if satisfactory answers are not obtained then the worth of the research is called into question. The second general set of concerns that must be considered revolves around the identification and evaluation of the substantive findings. This would seem to involve focusing on a variety of questions. What are the findings? How much faith can be placed in them? Are the research results theoretically interesting? Were the original questions answered? What has been the substantive contribution of the project? It should be kept in mind that negative findings in answer to these questions can be worth as much as positive findings.

Finally it must be asked whether our understanding of international politics is better as a result of the project. Perhaps the really crucial question is the following: Were the time, effort, and money put into the project worth the substantive results obtained?

The substance evaluators were asked to raise these and other relevant substantive concerns. In many ways the questions regarding the substantive contributions of the projects are the really crucial ones. If the quantitative international politics movement is unable to make a substantive contribution, it is failing to meet its basic commitment. It cannot be redeemed by the use of sophisticated research strategies and techniques that produce only atheoretical, trivial substantive results.

CONTRIBUTORS TO THE VOLUME

The project directors are established researchers who are well known to the scholarly community, and we will not attempt to introduce them to the reader. However, we do want to acknowledge the honesty and openness each displayed by fully cooperating with the evaluators, who were in most cases unknown to them when the assessment process began. It would have been easy to sweep dirt under the rug by closed-files policies or by refusing to discuss certain sensitive subjects, but this did not happen. Furthermore, it takes courage to travel to International Studies Association meetings and publicly debate the worth of one's own professional work of the last decade: regardless of what is thought of the work of the selected projects, one must respect the openness and integrity of the project directors.

At this point let us briefly discuss the instructions we gave to the project directors for the preparation of their essays. First, we asked each to prepare a brief history of the project, explaining its origins and goals and identifying its major accomplishments to date. These brief histories have been placed at the beginnings of the sections of this volume concerning the projects and should help to provide perspective on each research enterprise. In their general comments, which have been placed at the ends of the sections of the volume concerning their projects we asked the project directors to respond to any aspects of the evaluations that they felt required comment and, equally important, we asked them to reflect on their experiences, identifying relevant things that have been done well or poorly, so that current and future research can be improved. Finally, we asked them to comment on where the field of quantitative international politics ought to go from here.

Because some of the evaluators may currently be known to only a segment of the community of international politics scholars, we would like to make a few comments on the process used in their selection and the characteristics of the evaluators. It was our idea that representatives of the second generation of QIP scholars should evaluate the work of the first generation of QIP scholars; we hoped that in this manner a new perspective would be brought to the evaluation of the research projects, resulting in the infusion of fresh and hopefully unorthodox ideas into the QIP field. Therefore,

INTRODUCTION

our first criterion in the selection of individuals to evaluate projects was that they be considered to be of the younger generation of research scholars in the field of quantitative international politics. A second criterion was that a potential evaluator should not have been intimately involved in the work of the project being assessed, although we viewed some association as acceptable. In this manner we hoped to set the scene for a fairly objective evaluation.

Using these criteria we tried to identify young scholars in the field of quantitative international politics who had expertise in philosophy of science, methodology, and the substantive literature of international politics. We knew many such individuals ourselves, and senior scholars from around the United States suggested others. From the list that was compiled we then invited the evaluators who have contributed to this volume to participate in the assessment endeavor.

The names of the evaluators, together with their graduate school and current institutional affiliation are provided in Figure 1.1. As can be seen from the figure, 15 individuals were involved in making the 12 project assessments. They did their graduate work at 10 different universities, and they are currently affiliated with 12 different academic or research institutions. The most senior of the evaluators received a Ph.D. in 1968, and the most junior was still working for that degree as we went to press during the summer of 1975. The average date of the receipt of the Ph.D. was 1972.

OVERVIEW OF VOLUME

The essays are presented in this volume on a project-by-project basis, with the projects arranged in alphabetical order. For each project a brief history, a philosophy-of-science evaluation, a methodological evaluation, a substantive evaluation, and comments by the project director will be presented, in that order. Some readers may prefer to read the volume on a project-by-project basis, while others may prefer to read it on a topic-by-topic basis, reading all of the project histories, then all of the philosophy of science evaluations, and so forth. Some scholars may wish to read the volume once each way. To give the reader an understanding of the organization of the volume, the names of the authors and subjects of the principal essays are presented in Figure 1.2.

Several caveats should be kept in mind by readers of this volume. First, it should be remembered that the projects being evaluated are in different stages of completion and that the research is still in progress on three of the projects. For this reason we shy away

FIGURE 1.1

The Evaluators

Name	Current Affiliation	Graduate School
Stuart A. Bremer	University of Michigan	Michigan State University
Robert Butterworth	University of Pittsburgh	University of California, Berkeley
James A. Caporaso	Northwestern University	University of Pennsylvania
Cheryl Christensen	University of Maryland	Massachusetts Institute of Technology
Raymond Duvall	Yale University	Northwestern University
Karen Ann Feste	University of Denver	University of Minnesota
Leo Hazlewood	CACI, Inc.	University of Pennsylvania
Gordon Hilton	Northwestern University	University of Lancaster
Brian L. Job	University of Minnesota	Indiana University
Mark S. Levine	Northwestern University	University of Pennsylvania
Charles W. Ostrom, Jr.	Michigan State University	Indiana University
Dale B. Robertson	American University	American University
Harvey Starr	Indiana University	Yale University
Stuart J. Thorson	Ohio State University	University of Minnesota
Richard H. Van Atta	CACI, Inc.	Indiana University

Source: This is a list of those who made the project assessments for this volume, compiled by the editors.

FIGURE 1.2

AUTHORS AND ESSAYS IN THIS VOLUME

	Correlates of War Project (COW)	Dimensionality of Nations Project (DON)	Inter-Nation Simulation Project (INS)	1914 Project
Brief history of project	J. David Singer, University of Michigan	Rudolph J. Rummel, University of Hawaii	Harold Guetzkow, Northwestern University	Robert C. North Stanford University
Philosophy of science evaluation	Brian L. Job, University of Minnesota, and Charles W. Ostrom, Jr., Michigan State University	Gordon Hilton, Northwestern University	Cheryl Christensen University of Maryland, and Robert Butterworth, University of Pittsburgh	James A. Caporaso, Northwestern University
Methodology evaluation	Raymond Duvall, Yale University	Leo Hazlewood, CACI, Inc.	Stuart J. Thorson, Ohio State University	Karen Ann Feste, University of Denver
Substantive evaluation	Harvey Starr, Indiana University	Richard H. Van Atta, CACI, Inc., and Dale B. Robertson, American University	Stuart A. Bremer, University of Michigan	Mark S. Levine Northwestern University
Comments by project director	J. David Singer University of Michigan	Rudolph J. Rummel, University of Hawaii	Harold Guetzkow and Wm. Ladd Hollist, Northwestern University	Robert C. North Stanford University; Ole R. Holsti, Duke University; Nazli Choucri, Massachusetts Institute of Technology

from any comparative or premature final judgments of the specific projects. Second, it should be kept in mind that, generally speaking, the evaluators utilized only research that had been completed and published by the end of 1973. This may mean that some of the detailed comments by the evaluators will be slightly out of date in regard to the progress of specific projects. This fact should not, however, affect the general worth of the suggestions of the evaluators; indeed, it is hoped that some of the changes suggested will have been effected immediately, perhaps even appearing in print before this volume. Third, it should be kept in mind that the limited lengths of the papers mean that the authors could only scratch the surface in their analyses. Nevertheless, they were anything but superficial, while making a number of different points about quantitative research in the international politics field.

We don't agree with everything said in the volume, and many of the contributors don't agree with each other. That is appropriate. We do respect the integrity of each writer and feel that the impersonal clash of ideas is necessary for progress in the field of quantitative international politics. Furthermore, we note there is necessarily a certain amount of overlap among the evaluations of the same project; that is appropriate, because philosophy of science, methodology, and substantive concerns naturally do overlap. We also wish to point out that the papers published in this volume represent solely the opinions of the individuals responsible for the essays. They do not reflect any group consensus or the position of the Interpolimetrics Section of the International Studies Association or, for that matter, any judgment that can be attributed to the International Studies Association.

Finally, let us note that it is easier to criticize than to do research. The evaluators have been aware of this fact and have made a special effort to be fair and constructive in their assessments. In the future they will need to report on their own continuing efforts to develop empirical theory in the international politics field. If progress is to be made, each succeeding generation of scholars must learn from and improve upon, and not just criticize, the performance of earlier generations.

NOTES

1. For example, see Warren R. Phillips, "Where Have All the Theories Gone?" World Politics 26, no. 2 (1974): 155-88; James N. Rosenau, ed., Toward Global Patterns (New York: The Free Press, forthcoming); and Harvey Starr, "The Quantitative

International Relations Scholar as Surfer: Riding the 'Fourth Wave,'" <u>Journal of Conflict Resolution</u> 18, no. 2 (1974): 336-68.

2. For example, see Gordon Hilton, "A Review of the Dimensionality of Nations Project" (London: Richardson Institute for Conflict and Peace Monograph, 1971) and J. E. Mueller, "Deterrence, Numbers and History," <u>Security Studies Papers</u>, no. 12 (Los Angeles: University of California, 1968).

3. For an extended discussion of the attributes of this field and its historical roots see Dina A. Zinnes, <u>Contemporary Research in International Politics</u> (New York: The Free Press, forthcoming).

4. See Charles A. McClelland and Gary D. Hoggard, "Conflict Patterns in the Interactions Among Nations," in <u>International Politics and Foreign Policy</u>, edited by James N. Rosenau (rev. ed., New York: The Free Press, 1969), pp. 711-24; and Bruce M. Russett, Hayward R. Alker, Jr., Karl W. Deutsch, and Harold D. Lasswell, <u>World Handbook of Political and Social Indicators</u> (New Haven: Yale University Press, 1964).

5. See Donald T. Campbell and Julian C. Stanley, <u>Experimental and Quasi-Experimental Designs for Research</u> (Chicago: Rand McNally and Company, 1966) and Adam Przeworski and Henry Teune, <u>The Logic of Comparative Social Inquiry</u>, (New York: Wiley-Interscience, 1970).

PART II
THE CORRELATES OF WAR PROJECT

CHAPTER 2

THE CORRELATES OF WAR PROJECT: CONTINUITY, DIVERSITY, AND CONVERGENCE

J. David Singer

The origins of any research enterprise tend to get lost in a welter of selective recall and vague historical traces, and the Correlates of War Project is no exception. Moreover, at the beginning of such an enterprise there is little awareness that it is likely to continue for quite a while, actually produce knowledge of value, and become an object of interest to those outside of it, and hence there is little in the way of formal record keeping. As a result, all we can do here is rely on the various traces found in our files and in the published literature, along with the memories of those who have played active roles in the project.

Another difficulty, at least in the case of the Correlates of War Project, is dating its precise beginning. In one sense the project began on December 7, 1941, my 16th birthday and the day on which war became a personally salient phenomenon for me. My experiences during World War II and the Korean War, and as a reserve intelligence officer in the years between, may also have been the original inspiration. Another critical element could have been those interwar years when I worked as a peace activist and part-time graduate student. In any event, with the end of the Korean War, with my completion of graduate school, and with my beginning of an academic career in world politics, it was nearly inevitable that I would eventually (1) discover how little we knew about the causes of war; (2) conclude that armchair analysis and polemics reflecting that very limited knowledge would not turn the nations from the road to war; and (3) try to enlarge that knowledge base myself. These same considerations probably led me to gravitate toward Michigan, with its newly-created Center for Research on Conflict Resolution, and then to decide to seek modest funding for research on something called "a longitudinal analysis of international war."

PHASE 1: EARLY THINKING AND THEORIZING

Although it is hard to say when I first began to formulate my hunches and models on the war-peace question, it is certainly true that I had read a fair fraction of the voluminous and largely speculative work on the question by the time the actual research for the Correlates of War Project was underway. As a result I had developed a distinct distaste for overly parsimonious models that rested primarily on an author's favorite explanatory variable and had acquired a strong preference for more complex causal sequence scenarios. In addition I was struck by the remarkable confidence most authors had in their personal recollection and interpretation of history, which obviated the need for anything like reproducible evidence. When evidence was adduced, it was notable that most authors were willing to generalize far and wide from a single case or a very restricted spatial-temporal domain.

On the other hand, this literature contained a few pieces of work that seemed to hold great promise. Some of the efforts indicated an awareness of the need to generalize from a long time-span and a broad global domain. Also, several of the major writers showed a keen awareness of the multiple paths by which conflicts of interest between and within nations might be transformed into disputes, crises, and wars. Most important, a handful of the earlier scholars had not only asserted the importance of reproducible evidence but had gone on to demonstrate that such evidence, in the form of quantitative data and systematic analysis, could indeed be generated. The most important of these scholars, in terms of shaping my approach to the problem, were Jean de Bloch, Lewis F. Richardson, Pitirim Sorokin, and Quincy Wright.[1]

Thus by the time the project was launched, I had written a book and about 20 speculative articles on the war-peace question.[2] I had decided that such work had to be augmented by more rigorous efforts. I had also made certain decisions about research strategy. Perhaps most critical was the decision to work from diplomatic and military history rather than from laboratory experiments or from studies of comparable situations in industrial or racial relations. The assumption was that in spite of important, but not yet measured, changes in the international system during the modern epoch, one would learn more about the problems of reducing the incidence of future wars by examining prior wars than by examining other and apparently less analogous cases.

Closely related was the decision to examine the entire international system, rather than some regional or functional subsystem or subset, and to go as far back in time as the Congress of Vienna.

As to the closing date of the era, the original plan was to end with 1945 and then, in accordance with textbook notions of good science, to ascertain how accurately the 1815-1945 regularities were obtained for the period after World War II. However, the idea of testing the theories resulting from the findings in the earlier period against the realities of the later period ultimately seemed less important than that of working from the broadest possible data base in constructing those theories. Recognizing the high probability that many of the observed patterns would change over time, that few would hold true even for the 1815-1945 period, and that these changes would themselves be critical ingredients in theory building, I soon decided to examine the entire time-period.

Equally important was the decision to work from a correlational rather than a causal point of view. Given the recurrent failure of those who had sought to ascertain or demonstrate the "causes" of all wars or some subset thereof and the at least partial success of those who were satisfied to begin with the search for covariation, it seemed prudent to recognize how near the very beginning of the search we were and how essential it was to avoid the drive for premature explanation. Given the centrality of this issue within the project and also within the social-science community, a few paragraphs of justification would seem appropriate here.

Leaving aside those who neither understand nor utilize the scientific mode in the study of world politics, there is among the rest of us a rather clear disagreement. One point of view within the scientific subculture would have us postpone systematic empiricism until a great deal more theorizing and formal articulation has been completed. Two key arguments lie behind this position, first that the formalized model will help us decide which variables to observe and measure; and second that it will enhance our ability to interpret our empirical findings. The more fully articulated (and specified) the model, the greater the confidence we can have in any causal inferences drawn from empirical findings. If the first of these propositions were true, I would be in favor of putting greater emphasis on the modeling side of our activities, but I think it is not. We still have to begin with what we think we know and on the basis of that, decide which variables to examine next. While the disciplined logic of formal modeling can help us to decide what <u>not</u> to look for, it helps us very little in identifying the variables we should attend to first.

It seems to me that the second proposition is absolutely correct, but almost irrelevant at this stage. As a matter of fact, the very invoking of the argument that a formal model will strengthen the causal inferences made from subsequent empirical findings is itself an indication of a major flaw in the deductive orientation, since it suggests that we have arrived at a stage in the growth of the discipline at which it is appropriate for us to make causal inferences. As I have argued elsewhere, we probably are not at that stage, and a search for immediate explanation is therefore quite premature.[3] The disconfirmation and/or verification of formalized explanatory models is absolutely essential, but to engage in it at this time strikes me as wasteful, diversionary, and perhaps even pretentious.

The need now is for existential and correlational knowledge. First we need to do our basic descriptive work, to find out what happened in the international system or in analogous systems in prior epochs; then we must find out what events and conditions occurred alongside one another, or at regular intervals ahead of or following one another. In the absence of a formal theory that search for regularity and covariation may seem pointless to some, but I would argue that it is the most useful and creative work we can do now. To put it another way, once we have some intuitive notions about what factors, in what combinations, might be "causing" the types or classes of wars that concern us, the next step is to operationalize those factors, generate our indicators, and try to ascertain whether they are at least associated with war. Having a good idea about which ones to examine first is crucial, and that is as likely to be the result of years of examining cases and episodes, however intuitively, as it is to be the result of speculative reasoning, however formalized. As a fair number of philosophers of science have noted, every discipline has had to go through the "natural history" phase.[4]

As one indicator of the maturity of this field, consider the number of scholar-years that have been devoted to peace research. If we begin with the work of the four pioneers mentioned earlier, de Bloch, Sorokin, Richardson, and Wright, we have about fifty scholar-years prior to the upsurge of real effort in the late 1950s. I would next estimate that the 1956-65 decade saw an annual average of perhaps 50 additional peace researchers whose work was being published, with that number reaching perhaps 100 (worldwide) since that time. This would suggest a total of 50 plus 500 plus 1000, or 1550 scholar-years devoted to a systematic search for the causes of war. Compared to the many thousands of scholar-years that have been invested in the big questions of biology, chemistry, or physics, it is probably naive to think that the research paradigms utilized by those fields today are equally appropriate to peace research, or to virtually any other social science for that matter.

Another issue concerns the rather cavalier use of the word "cause" in the social sciences. Usually implied is the notion that we do research in order to discover the cause of some particular class of event or some fluctuation in the incidence of certain conditions;

yet a moment's reflection should remind us that (1) a given event may be arrived at by any of several different paths and (2) the same set of conditions may lead to more than a single recurrent outcome. Both of these considerations, especially the former, suggest that the notion of causality may be inappropriate in the social sciences. In my mind the concept of causality assumes that one and only one causal sequence can precede one and only one outcome.

Rather than establish a "cause," what we usually try to do in social science is to look for those factors that most accurately predict the fluctuations in our outcome phenomenon in a given sequence, combination, and mix of strengths. Once we have discovered, tested, modified, and become committed to the model that best integrates those predictors, we say that it "explains" the outcome. That is, nevertheless, only half the game. What I may find to be a satisfactory explanation may leave my colleagues quite dissatisfied, because explanation is at bottom a highly subjective matter. For an explanation to satisfy, we must be persuaded that the entire sequence, from background conditions and precipitating events through perceptions and behaviors to the outcome itself, actually did or does unfold as described by the model. Thus it must be consonant with (1) what each specialist in the field thinks we know about economics and social psychology, for example, as well as about international politics and (2) what each of us believes is the way in which each set of variables links up with the preceding and succeeding ones in the entire putative chain.

Needless to say we will often differ from one another, even within a single discipline, on both of these. Furthermore we will often employ different criteria. For example, some scholars have such modest criteria that they will interpret a bivariate r^2 as "explaining   percent of the variance" in the outcome. Others will go a step further and ask for a certain agreement between the predicted fluctuations in a given outcome and the actually observed values before calling it an explanation. Still others, myself included, will demand that all of the not-obvious connections and linkages in the sequence be demonstrated empirically or logically before agreeing that we have an explanation.

These difficulties, however, are modest compared to those associated with causality. Whereas this latter term, as I understand its meaning, requires us to agree that a given state of the system, for example, causes governments to behave in a certain way, the term "explanation" merely requires us to agree that the two phenomena co-vary with appreciable regularity and strength. Put differently, there is a strong deterministic aura surrounding causality, whereas an explanation accepts the role of statements of probability in accounting for social phenomena. Needless to say, this predisposition leads me to prefer statistical models over mathematical ones, if I may be permitted the distinction, and makes me very reluctant to speak of causality at this particular stage of the game. Consequently the project studiously avoids causal models or causal inferences in the earlier investigations.

Finally, there was the decision to work from the "realist's" version of the classical balance-of-power paradigm while remaining alert to the possibilities of alternative schemes. The point here is not to accept the traditional explanations as found in the balance-of-power literature, but rather to begin with some of the constructs that are central to that orientation and to give them greater precision and combine them in models that were logical extensions of, but more complex than, the simple classical version. Thus, before the first research assistant had been hired, the commitment was made to begin with a rather familiar set of variables. At the national level these would be attributes such as industrial capability, military preparedness, diplomatic prestige, domestic stability, and the like; at the dyadic level we would attend to alliance partnerships, diplomatic bonds, shared organizational memberships, and geographical proximity as well as to similarities and differences along the abovementioned attribute dimensions. At the regional and global levels the focus would be upon alliances and diplomatic bond configurations, polarity, and capability distributions and rankings, to mention the more prominent choices. Thus, in spite of an increasing familiarity with and affinity for the concepts and models of other disciplines, my decision was not to substitute for the dominant paradigm in our field but to clarify and embellish that paradigm as prerequisite to putting it to the empirical test.[5]

PHASE 2: DATA MAKING AND INDEX CONSTRUCTION

With some of these basic decisions taken, the project's first proposal was prepared and submitted via the Center for Research on Conflict Resolution to the Carnegie Corporation. Within a few months, in the spring of 1963, a grant of $31,800 for the next two years was approved, and the recruiting of assistants could begin.*
On the assumptions that the intelligent student, regardless of major field, could learn to prepare and adhere to highly operational coding

---

*All grant figures are for direct costs only, reflecting the funds available to us for research, and not the often exorbitant "overhead" figures that go to the University bureaucracy for so-called support activities.

rules and that knowledge of the sources was needed more than conceptual or theoretical sophistication, I turned not to the social sciences but to history for these assistants. The first to be recruited was Melvin Small, then a Ph.D. candidate and now, as associate professor of history at nearby Wayne State University, one of the project's key figures. He and two fellow students were soon at work pretesting our coding rules for generating the international war and diplomatic mission data sets for the period 1816-1945.6

By the summer of 1963 we were moving along rather well on these two data sets, and since I was scheduled to spend the 1963-64 year in Oslo on a Fulbright fellowship, we decided to begin the generation of a third data set, that of formal alliances. Whereas the first two were essential to the measurement of our outcome variable and system composition, the latter would be the first of our predictor variables.7

Returning from leave in the summer of 1964 to find the data-making operation proceeding satisfactorily, I decided to begin the collection of a rather different type of data: those national attributes that might serve as a basis for quantifying each nation's basic military-industrial-demographic capabilities. During the next two years, with another grant ($24,262 in direct costs) from the Carnegie Corporation and a staff of about five part-time assistants, we concentrated on the systematic generation of a data base that should have been initiated decades earlier, but which somehow never attracted the energies of the relevant economists, demographers, and political scientists.

As the early analyses got under way, as will be discussed in the next section, our confidence in the basic research strategy increased, and in 1967 we decided to institutionalize the project and settle in for the long haul. Therefore we sought and received our first National Science Foundation support ($13,656 for two years) and began to generate such additional data sets as international trade, the system's territorial and demographic history, and the domestic political stability and ethnic composition of system members.* Needless to say, we began the generation of each data set

---

*It should be noted that the generation of each of our data sets can take perhaps four years, given the large number of nations and years, and that we seldom work with readily available and already quantified materials; much of our data is literally _made_ by converting the buzzing welter of historical traces into analytically useful indicators. The very time lag involved means that we must often make data decisions well before we know the results of those analyses that might tell us which variables ought to be examined next. Thus

only after lengthy discussion and examination of prior and current work, and always with the idea that each set would permit the derivation of indicators to serve several theoretical purposes for ourselves and for the larger research community, to which we released our data decks and later the tapes as soon as they were in reasonable condition, long before we had begun to exploit them for our own analytical and theoretical purposes.*

Let me now put the data-making and index-construction operation into a more orderly framework, emphasizing that our strategy was shaped as much by the general systems orientation as by the balance-of-power idea. This is to say that the latter usually inspired the choice of variables, while the former provided the ordering and integrating framework and suggested the approach to index construction. Thus as early as 1965 our taxonomy was rather well formulated, and it might be appropriate to summarize it here.[8]

One of the critical distinctions with which we began is that between ecological and behavioral variables. The former are used to describe the <u>background</u> conditions that might reasonably be expected to co-vary with war, and the latter represent the <u>actions</u> and <u>interactions</u> by which nations and other international actors "convert" background conditions into many disputes, some crises, and occasional wars. To be somewhat less deterministic, it might be better to think of the ecological variables as describing the systemic and subsystemic environments within which the relevant political units carry on their activities.

Among these environmental phenomena are the material, structural, and cultural attributes of the international and regional systems and the nations and pairs of nations found within them. More important, however, than such choices, discussed below, as deciding to work with an actor-oriented rather than an interaction-oriented taxonomy, treating levels of aggregation very explicitly, or to differentiating among the three classes of attributes, was the decision to focus first on the attributes of the international and regional systems. The two assumptions behind that choice were that the behavioral pattern of nations in conflict would turn out to

---

some of the rules of "normal science," while plausible, remain almost irrelevant to this type of research. See J. David Singer, "The Historical Experiment as a Research Strategy in the Study of World Politics," <u>Political Inquiry</u> 2, no. 1 (1974): 23-52.

*Most of them are available via the Inter-University Consortium for Political Research, Box 1248, Ann Arbor, Michigan 48106, and the major ones are also written up for wider use in the books and articles listed in the Part II bibliography.

be fairly uniform, with little cross-national or cross-temporal
variation and that even if the variation were considerable, it would
have less explanatory power than the conditions and attributes of
the systemic and dyadic environment. Further, we reasoned that
even if both of these assumptions turned out to be empirically wide
of the mark, nothing would be lost, since we would of necessity
have to control for such ecological variables when we later turned
to an examination of the ways in which behavior and interaction
"determined" whether certain conflicts ended up in war or not.

Coupled with this priority was the decision to focus, within
the ecological context, on structural phenomena first rather than
on the material or cultural attributes of the system, subsystem,
dyad, or nation. The assumption here was that structural conditions,
defined largely in terms of hierarchical and coalitional relationships
among the nations, would (1) manifest less variation than cultural
conditions, defined largely as the perceptions, preferences, and
predictions of elites and publics, and more variation than material
ones, defined as geography, demography, and technology; (2) reflect,
and be responsive to, the cultural and material conditions in a way
that would make for fewer short-run perturbations than the former
and less inertia than the latter; and therefore (3) directly and indirectly account for more of the variance in war and nonwar outcomes
than the other two sets of conditions. At this intermediate stage in
the project it looks as if these assumptions will indeed be borne out,
but again, even if they are not borne out, the data sets and the findings
will be essential components of the models to which we would then
turn.

Once these general decisions had been taken, the next step was
to select the more specific structural variables to begin with and
then to move on to the construction of our indicators, the pretesting
of the measures, the "finalizing" of our coders' manuals, and the
generation of the data. Since even our most severe critics agree
that our index construction and data making are more than satisfactory, we need not dwell on those matters here.* However, a brief
comment on the choice of variables seems to be in order.

---

*Or so we thought until the Raymond Duvall critique appeared
(in this volume). At this stage of the game in our field there is not
much we can say to that sort of critique. If our indicators seem to
have face validity, if they co-vary with alternative indicators of the
same phenomenon, and if their association with outcome variables
is consonant with our predictive models, there is little else we can
do to demonstrate their validity. Unlike some social scientists,
we do not use the term "auxiliary theory" to describe the reasoning

As implied above, the structural characteristics of the international system may be described along two basic dimensions, one of which reflects the ranking of the nations in the system and the other of which reflects the way in which they cluster and coalesce. The ranking of the nations may be along ordinal or interval scales, reflecting such national attributes as diplomatic importance, industrial capability, military preparedness, economic development, or diplomatic activity. They may cluster by formal alliances, by geographical proximity, by shared intergovernmental organization (IGO) memberships, or by similar diplomatic bond patterns. The range of structural concepts that may be measured on the basis of these configurations is quite broad, and that breadth is only partially evinced in the studies that have emerged to date. Suffice to say here that this particular data base also permits us to measure many national attributes and dyadic relationships as well as regional and global systemic properties. It also permits us to construct indicators of a more general and derived sort, of which the structural clarity dimension, in the context of environmental ambiguity, looks particularly promising.

Shifting from ecological to behavioral variables, we encountered a rather different set of conceptual and measurement problems. Once again, we sought to construct a data base that would be compatible with a wide variety of theoretical orientations. That consideration, plus the conviction that explanation is impossible if actions and their alleged motives are combined deductively in a given concept, led us to develop a typology of national actions that was as "theory-free" as possible. The categories in the typology also had to be not only mutually exclusive, but logically exhaustive

---

behind our indicators, since given the problems of demonstrating the validity of even the more compelling indicators, such a label seems premature. It appears in Hubert M. Blalock, Jr., <u>Theory Construction: From Verbal to Mathematical Formulations</u> (Englewood Cliffs: Prentice-Hall, 1969), pp. 151-54. Needless to say, we encourage others to construct alternative indicators, to generate the relevant data sets, and to demonstrate how much better <u>their</u> indicators are, but so far we have seen little interest in that sort of follow-up. For detailed treatments of the problem, see the several index-construction papers listed in the Part II bibliography, particularly J. David Singer and Melvin Small, "Foreign Policy Indicators: Predictors of War in History and in the State of the World Message," <u>Policy Sciences</u> 5, no. 3 (1974): 272-96.

as well. A schema that was limited to a given time, place, type of conflict, or theoretical orientation would not suffice.*

Closely related to the creation of the behavioral schema, the writing of the coders' manual, and the pretesting, was the problem of identifying the population of disputes to which it would be applied. To reiterate a point I have already made, a major objective of the entire enterprise is to systematically compare those few dispute episodes that culminated in war with the many that did not. That comparison would of course be in terms of both ecological and behavioral variables, but no such comparisons are possible until we have identified all the serious disputes that could have ended in war. That particular enterprise is now nearing completion.

Given the picture already presented, it is clear that these disputes and their associated interactions are not merely thought of as possible predictors to war. On the one hand we seek to ascertain the conditions, such as ecological factors, that best account for cross-temporal and cross-national variations in the incidence of serious disputes. Under what conditions will the system, or the regions, the dyads, and the individual nations, experience significantly more or fewer of these episodes? In that sense disputes may, like war, be thought of as outcomes to be explained. On the other hand, however, we also seek to ascertain what it is that discriminates between those that end in war and those that do not. That explanatory effort must rest on both ecological and behavioral variables. Among the former are (1) certain characteristics manifested by the regional and the global system, (2) the similarities or differences of the protagonists on key national attribute variables, and (3) the interdependencies and relationships between the conflicting opponents. As already indicated, we would not be surprised if the war or no-war outcome rested heavily on these ecological conditions. However, that outcome will also depend, to a degree that can now only be surmised, on the ways in which the

---

*The primary responsibility for constructing the typology, developing the coding rules, and generating this data set was assumed by Russell Leng of Middlebury College, who spent the year 1969-70 with us and with whom our collaboration continues. The basic scheme and its rationale are found in Russell J. Leng and J. David Singer, "Toward a Multi-Theoretical Typology of International Behavior" (mimeographed, Middlebury, Vt.: Middlebury College, 1974). Copies of the more detailed Leng and Singer, Coder's Manual for Identifying and Describing International Actions are available from Leng at Middlebury College, Middlebury, Vermont.

protagonists behave in relation to one another. In that sense, then, the dispute data serve in both a predictor and an outcome role; we seek not only to account for the onsets of disputes but for the extent to which they escalate, within a limited time period, into open warfare.

PHASE 3: EXAMINING SOME OBVIOUS HYPOTHESES

Once we had settled on the putative predictors that would be examined and had begun to acquire the data base reflecting their variation across time, place, and case, the analyses could begin. Here is one of the more controversial of our choice points; that is, having already decided that the knowledge base of the discipline was just too thin to justify the formal articulation of complex formal models, our plan was to move, quite systematically, through a brush-clearing operation of some magnitude.

With each basic variable, alliances, international organization, diplomatic bonds, capabilities, the plan was to examine the more plausible balance-of-power hypotheses associating it with war. That examination would, as already noted, take place at several levels of aggregation. To illustrate, there are several indicators of alliance patterns in the international system, and the extent to which each of them is correlated with the appropriate indicators of system-level war would first be ascertained; then the indicators of the alliance relationships between nation-pairs would be correlated with the war-proneness of the dyads; and following that, the same would be done at the national level of aggregation to ascertain the bivariate association between alliance involvement and national war experience.

It need hardly be emphasized that such analyses are clearly pretheoretical and that no one would suggest that bivariate correlations can serve as the test of a theory. Rather, the objective was to first examine the most obvious and simple propositions, whether articulated in the literature, inferred from the literature, or made out of the whole cloth. Actually, these bivariate analyses are preceded by such even more primitive efforts as examination of the time plot of each indicator, the superimposition of predictor variable time plots upon the outcome plot, and of course the examination of the scatter plots, both linear and transformed. Recognizing the limits of the ceteris paribus assumption and having no illusions whatsoever about the causal inferences that can be drawn from bivariate associations, we nevertheless reject the current tendency to dismiss such efforts as trivial. As I have argued elsewhere, we are more likely to arrive at explanatory knowledge on the basis of both correlational knowledge and intelligent speculation together than on the basis of the latter alone. The clearer the picture we have of "what goes with what," even in the absence of control variables, the less likely we are to build or believe models that are at serious variance with the referent world. Some, of course, suggest that the veridicality of a model is of minor consequence and has little effect on its scientific usefulness, but I disagree.

In this "natural history" phase of the project, then, our concern was to construct a rough and tentative overview of international realities, with particular emphasis on checking out the more prevalent folklore in the discipline. The literature is chock-full of plausible but incompatible propositions, usually expressed, I might add, in bivariate terms, and a preliminary sorting out was clearly in order.[9] This sorting out may be thought of as a "fishing expedition," but not in the perjorative sense: one of the great figures in modern social science is Emile Durkheim, whose Suicide is a systematic fishing expedition of the highest quality. Rather than generating a lot of pretentious theoretical prattle, this pioneer took some good ideas and then began to gather and evaluate the evidence for and against a variety of plausible explanations.[10] A more contemporary high-quality fishing expedition is that of the Highway Safety Research Institute at the University of Michigan. Its strategy is to gather as much of the potentially relevant data as it can about the auto crashes in its population and then systematically test a variety of hypotheses against those data. Its ingenuity in index construction and data analysis (mainly dependent on computer software) reminds us that a "fishing expedition" can be very sophisticated and creative science.

In the Correlates of War project a good many correlational propositions have already been tested, and quite a few more will be subjected to a similar scrutiny. For those that have already been published, see the bibliography to Part II as well as the summary found in Harvey Starr's critique in Chapter 5.

PHASE 4: FORMALIZING AND TESTING MORE COMPLEX MODELS

As the data-making operations went forward in parallel with the more obvious data analyses in the early 1970s and we had begun to uncover the more elementary regularities surrounding systemic, dyadic, and national war, it became increasingly feasible to move on to more complex types of analysis. Bearing in mind the extent to which the several phases of activity continue to overlap, let me now describe some of these shifts in emphasis, while noting that at about the same time that much of this brush-clearing had been completed, we were fortunate in adding to our staff Stuart Bremer, who had done graduate work at Michigan State and Northwestern. He brought to the project an innovative research orientation and a substantive and methodological competence that were very appropriate to our needs at that particular juncture.

To reiterate, our earlier preoccupation was with the association between ecological variables and war: with the extent to which systemic, dyadic, and national conditions (attributes) co-varied with the incidence of war at the systemic, dyadic, and national levels. However, in the past few years we have begun to move into the articulation and testing of models that are not only more complex, but also more dynamic. They are more complex in that they incorporate a larger number and more types of predictor-explanatory variables, and they are more dynamic in that they rest on the unfolding of events and conditions along the putative path to, and through, war.

That path may, of course, be conceived in several ways, but the scheme that seems most promising is one that marks three observation points, the first of which is the ecological conditions, and the rates and directions of change therein, that characterize the global or regional system, the dyad, or the nation in question. Once we have the ecology-war patterns reasonably well identified, those variables can be introduced into our models as environmental incentives and/or constraints or as war-inducing or war-inhibiting factors. Within that ecological context, the second observation point is that of the dispute. As noted above, the occurrence of a dispute can be treated both as an outcome to be explained and as a condition that can, in turn, lead to or away from war in the short run. Thus we next address two relevant questions: (1) which ecological factors account for the incidence of disputes and (2) which of them seem to account for the escalations of disputes into wars. The third observation point is, of course, the behavior manifested by the protagonists in the course of a dispute.

In this process we turn our attention more toward the comparative case study and less toward the straight longitudinal or cross-sectional analysis. Instead of trying to uncover the regularities of war occurrence for the system as a whole and for the individual nations that experience those wars, we now look at each war and examine the conditions and events that precede and surround it.

As we pay closer attention to the specific wars, it becomes evident that they differ markedly in several dimensions. Some are preceded by long conflicts that move "inexorably" to crisis, and others seem to arise "out of the blue." Some remain dyadic throughout, while others expand by the entry of additional nations. Some end quickly or produce relatively few casualties, while others drag on or lead to high fatality figures. Some end in a clear-cut victory while the outcome of others is ambiguous, and some lead to radical rearrangements in the stratification or clustering patterns of the system while others leave that structure largely the same as before.

Needless to say, such variations among wars and their consequences are partly a function of the conditions and events that preceded the wars and partly a function of the behavior of the belligerents and others following the onsets of the wars. In the next phase of the project, therefore, we will accelerate our investigation into these variations. With the refinement and disaggregation of the outcome variable, we can further pursue those few preliminary inquiries into what accounts for not only the onset of war but its magnitude and its consequences.

To date we have completed only a handful of analyses reflecting the unfolding ecology-dispute-behavior-war type of model, but a number of additional ones are now under way and several will appear in the forthcoming anthology of project papers. Here let me mention one of the more complex sets of analyses that is now underway, noting the extent to which it builds upon an earlier study within the balance-of-power framework.

In that earlier study we examined the effects of capability distribution patterns on the incidence of major-power war.[11] There we found that the familiar parity-fluidity model accounted for much of the fluctuation in major-power war during the nineteenth century, whereas the preponderance-stability model fit, albeit somewhat less closely, with the observed incidence of war in the twentieth century. That is, when the nineteenth-century major powers were approximately equal in capabilities and there was a fair amount of short-run redistribution in those capabilities, with a net effect toward an even greater parity during any given half-decade, the amount of war in the next half-decade tended to be quite low. In this century, however, war levels have been minimized by high concentration and very little redistribution.

Although these findings are quite interesting, they barely begin to illuminate this aspect of the balance-of-power question. Hence we moved from there to a somewhat more complex sequence of follow-up studies, the first of which examined the question from the level of the individual major power. Here we asked which particular nations experienced more or less war, as capability distributions within the entire subset fluctuated. In the nineteenth century Italy, Austria-Hungary, England, and the United States tended to get into war when concentration was <u>becoming</u> high, while France showed a very strong propensity to enter war after the concentration had risen. For the twentieth century the pattern is much weaker, with the only clear one being the U.S. tendency to experience more war when concentration is already high but very little war as it is becoming high.

These findings strongly suggest that the next step is to ascertain more about those nations whose war involvements are regularly associated with the concentration patterns. Rather than their identities, however, we now examine their own capability positions in the context of the following theoretical argument: When the capabilities of the major-power subset become highly concentrated in the hands of one or two nations, the others are likely to respond in one or both of two ways, one of which is to increase their individual capabilities by the acceleration of industrial output or by increasing the allocation of men or materiel to the military sector and the other of which is to coalesce with one another in order to create a set of countervailing capabilities.

The first response will manifest itself by a decline in the concentration indicator within a few years, and the second will produce an increase in alliance aggregation. The former will lead to a decrease in the structural clarity of the system, and the latter, usually making for greater bipolarity, will give us an increase in such clarity. If our prior findings are applicable here, the rearmament response should lead to less war in the nineteenth-century setting and more war in the twentieth, while the alliance-building response should lead to more war in the nineteenth and less in the twentieth. Another interpretation is that if the nineteenth-century disadvantaged nations rearm and/or coalesce promptly, the danger of war will usually be headed off; but if they delay too long, the nearly inevitable confrontation will probably escalate to war on the assumption that the dominant majors will press the others too far. For the twentieth century, according to this line of reasoning, if the disadvantaged nations respond quickly via capability increases or alliance formation, the probability of war will rise, but if they act slowly or not at all, war will usually be avoided.

Now, only a few of these assertions have been empirically demonstrated, but the findings to date offer sufficient grounds for asking several further questions. First, which nations usually account for increases in capability concentration? Are they centrally or peripherally located in relation to the other majors? Are they already near the top of the industrial, military, or diplomatic pecking order? Have they been rising or falling on these scales? Are they status-consistent? Can they be identified as status quo, expansionist, or revisionist nations? Second, which nations respond to the increased concentrations in which fashion? Do their relative capabilities and tendencies account for their predisposition to act on the capability-enhancing or coalition-formation fronts or to remain passive?

I think that enough has been said here to indicate in what ways a project such as this moves from the examination of the more obvious hypotheses to the articulation, testing, and rearticulation of increasingly complex models, in the hope of gradually pinning down the more important generalizations. Since that is done in several different theoretical sectors, and since the knowledge base becomes not only larger but more fully integrated, we can expect to produce (in due course) a fairly comprehensive theory of modern international war.

LOGISTICS

In concluding this brief history, let me now make explicit certain practices and arrangements that have so far only been alluded to. Since this volume should serve primarily to illuminate the ways in which our research is done, there should be elements that are logistical and procedural as well as intellectual.

Perhaps the most important point is the one that is made in the title of this chapter. Although it is certainly true that the basic conception of the project was mine and that I continue to make all the major decisions, the heterogeneity of views among the project members and the modification of my own views across time should ensure that the project is something less than a research monolith. As indicated, there have been a good many very gifted and vigorous social scientists associated with the enterprise over the years. From its very inception we have had the extraordinary guidance of Karl Deutsch, who in his affiliation with the Mental Health Research Institute at Michigan has spent several days here almost every month since 1961. Meeting with me and my colleagues and students in spur-of-the-moment sessions as well as in the regularly scheduled project seminar, he has been a sympathetic, but sharp and vigorous, critic at every turn. The reader who is familiar with Deutsch's work will appreciate how dissimilar our views are on many matters. Then there are Small, Leng, and Bremer, who—like Deutsch—have sufficiently different orientations towards matters theoretical and methodological to further assure a high degree of diversity.

Other sources of diversity in this context come from visiting scholars, faculty colleagues who attend the project's weekly seminar, and the fairly large number of graduate students who work on or are associated with the project, especially those moving toward their doctorates under the direction of my colleagues in political science or in other departments who are not part of the project. The media by which these diverse viewpoints impinge on our decision process are several. First, an inevitable amount of informal conversation arises when a dozen or so people are all working on the same general problem under one roof. Second, the lunchroom of the Institute sees about half of the team eating together on any given weekday, and on weekends and evenings a few of us will always be found at one of the local eateries. Third, we circulate within the project a large number of papers on war and peace, whether written by ourselves or by others; any one can put a paper into the circulation mill, and comments are warmly encouraged and received. Fourth, the team meets every Friday the year round, from noon to 2:30, for luncheon and the regular staff seminar. In addition to the project people, we usually have ten or so "visitors," including faculty from Michigan; faculty from neighboring Michigan State, Eastern Michigan, and Wayne State Universities; out of town scholars who are passing through or spending a term or two in Ann Arbor;* and nonproject graduate students who "take" the seminar for academic credit. As most of the above can attest, these are hardly routine sessions in which I lay down the party line. Diversity and individuality seem to be the norm whether the agenda item is big theory, data analysis methods, data management, software, coding rule details, or research priorities.

Another procedural point of importance concerns our division of labor. In general, Melvin Small oversees all data making and Stuart Bremer oversees the data management and file-building activities, while also serving as our methodological guru; all three of us, however, are in close touch with one another and with the people in all phases of the project. The student assistants play two types of roles: a few handle highly specific tasks such as

---

*The following visiting scholars have been associated with the project for one or more terms in the past decade: Leroy Rieselbach, Indiana University; Nils Petter Gleditsch, International Peace Research Institute, Oslo; Bruce Russett, Yale University; Dieter Senghaas, Frankfurt Universitat; William Coplin, Syracuse University; Urs Luterbacher, Graduate School of International Affairs, Geneva; Roderick Ogley, University of Essex; Gisela Hainke, Freiburg Universitat; Kjell Skjelsbaek, International Peace Research Institute, Oslo; Peter Harper, University of Sussex; Harald von Riekhoff, Carleton University, Ottawa; Frieder Schlupp, Frei Universitat; Andre Donneur, University of Quebec; Michael Wallace, University of British Columbia; Elaine Morton, Rutgers University; and Sandra Baxter-Bouxsein, Catholic University.

computer programming or data gathering, but since we are as
committed to education as to research, we try to give most of them
assignments that are more complex and require a fair degree of
independent judgment. Typically, as a given set of analyses is
completed, we decide which questions to investigate next and have
the assigned student write up a memo outlining how he or she would
proceed. After discussing the memo's treatment of indicators,
data base, spatial-temporal domain, time lags and spreads, statistical options, and the kinds of inferences that might be drawn from
the results, the student proceeds with minimal supervision but with
considerable input from fellow assistants and from the full staff at
the Friday seminars.

Another logistic element is that of financial support. One reason that the project has completed so much work at so little cost
(only $244,500 in direct costs since 1963) is that it is housed in a
research institute that inevitably picks up part of the bill. In our
case, the Institute pays half of my salary (since I teach only halftime), plus that of a half-time secretary, a half-time programmer,
and three half-time assistants; it also provides a modest amount of
computer support. Also worth noting is that Small and Bremer
contribute their time and effort without charge; only rarely have
they had any released time paid for out of the project budget. The
other reason, of course, is that the project is run on the assumption
that social science research money is particularly precious and
should be treated accordingly. Even leaving aside the matter of
quality and merely counting the number of books and articles produced, the number of graduate and undergraduate students we have
helped to educate, and the number of researchers whose data base
and indicators we have provided, I suspect that we would score well
in a cost-benefit analysis.

SUMMARY

In these pages I have tried to outline the origins and history of
the Correlates of War project and also articulate the considerations
behind our decisions and the resulting research strategy. At this
particular juncture in the evolution of the social sciences, that
research strategy can hardly be thought of as a popular one. In
addition to the prescientific people in the international politics field,
many of whom tend to consider the entire QIP enterprise a bootless
one, we have a number of vigorous critics from "within the fold."
In a later section of this volume I shall try to respond to some of
the more representative criticisms, as articulated by Brian L. Job

and Charles W. Ostrom, Jr.; Raymond Duvall, and Harvey Starr. Here I shall only reiterate my position on the role of theory in world politics, an understanding of which should make clear the basic research strategy behind the enterprise.

Stated simply, I see theory as what we aim for in science, rather than what we begin with at the inception of a new line of investigation. In these very early stages in the scientific study of world politics, we have a great deal of surmise, a small amount of evidence, and virtually no theory; but since theories are what provide—in "normal science"—the link between what we know, or think we know, and what we seek to know, it is natural to treat as theories those intellectual schemes that we construct for that purpose. Of course, by scientific criteria they are nothing of the kind. If we require that a theory be composed of a set of integrative propositions, all of which are logically consistent with one another, most of which are falsifiable, and many of which have been empirically supported, we would be hard-pressed to find many acceptable candidates in the literature of world politics. Of course, there are those who apply less stringent criteria and are willing to use the label of theory for anything, from a vague suspicion to a mathematical abstraction that is so divorced from the referent world as to defy falsifiability. As Wassily Leontief, a Nobel laureate economist, has observed, "the weak and all too slowly growing empirical foundation clearly cannot support the proliferating superstructure of pure, or should I say, speculative economic theory."[12]

Thus when our critics fret because our research rests on no theory, I can only remark that (1) we have looked around carefully and find nothing worthy of the name; (2) we hope to see some theories on world politics develop in the near future; and (3) when they do develop, these theories will have to rest on the existential and correlational knowledge now being generated by projects such as ours. In the interim, like the physical and biological scientists who have preceded us, we will have to proceed from intelligent surmise, creative speculation, disciplined reasoning, and whatever empirical evidence is available.

NOTES

1. Jean de Bloch, The Future of War (New York: Doubleday & McClure, 1899); Lewis F. Richardson, Statistics of Deadly Quarrels (Pittsburgh: Boxwood Press, 1960); Pitirim Sorokin, Social and Cultural Dynamics (3 vols., New York: American Book, 1937); Quincy Wright, A Study of War (2 vols., Chicago: University of Chicago, 1942).

2. Among these were J. David Singer, Deterrence, Arms Control and Disarmament: Toward a Synthesis in National Security Policy (Columbus: Ohio State University Press, 1962); J. David Singer, "Threat Perception and the Armament-Tension Dilemma," Journal of Conflict Resolution 2, no. 1 (1958): 90-105; J. David Singer, "The Strategic Dilemma: Probabilities versus Disutilities," Journal of Conflict Resolution 5, no. 2 (1961): 197-205; J. David Singer, "Stable Deterrence and Its Limits," Western Political Quarterly 15, no. 3 (1962): 449-64; J. David Singer, "Inter-Nation Influence: A Formal Model," American Political Science Review 57, no. 2 (1963): 420-30; and Karl Deutsch and J. David Singer, "Multipolar Power Systems and International Stability," World Politics 16, no. 3 (1964): 390-406.

3. See J. David Singer, "Theorists and Empiricists: The Two-Culture Problem in International Politics," in The Analysis of International Politics, edited by James N. Rosenau, Vincent Davis, and Maurice East (New York: Free Press, 1972), pp. 80-95; and J. David Singer, "Modern International War: From Conjecture to Explanation," in The Search for World Order: Essays in Honor of Quincy Wright, edited by Albert Lepawsky, Edward Buehrig, and Harold Lasswell (New York: Appleton-Century-Crofts, 1971), pp. 47-71.

4. See, for example, F. S. C. Northrop, The Logic of the Sciences and the Humanities (rev. ed., New York: World Publishing, 1971), pp. 35-58.

5. Some observers seem surprised and/or disappointed by this focus, expecting the project to reflect more fully my long interest in the concepts of other disciplines. See J. Handelman, John Vasquez, Michael O'Leary, and William Coplin, "Color It Morgenthau: A Data Based Assessment of Quantitative International Relations," paper presented at the annual meeting of the International Studies Association, New York City, 1973.

6. The coding rules, their justification, and the resulting data are found in J. David Singer and Melvin Small, The Wages of War 1816-1965: A Statistical Handbook (New York: John Wiley and Sons, 1972); J. David Singer and Melvin Small, "The Composition and Status Ordering of the International System, 1815-1940," World Politics 18, no. 2 (1966): 236-82; and Melvin Small and J. David Singer, "The Diplomatic Importance of States, 1816-1970: An Extension and Refinement of the Indicator," World Politics 25, no. 4 (1973): 577-99.

7. See J. David Singer and Melvin Small, "Formal Alliances, 1815-1939: A Quantitative Description," Journal of Peace Research 3, no. 1 (1966): 1-32; Melvin Small and J. David Singer, "Formal Alliances, 1816-1965: An Extension of the Basic Data," Journal of Peace Research 6, no. 3 (1969): 257-82.

8. A more complete description and epistemological justification is in J. David Singer, "A General Systems Taxonomy for Political Science," (Morristown, N.J.: General Learning Press, 1971).

9. Despite the recent increase in criticism of bivariate analysis, a glance at the speculative as well as the empirical work in today's social science journals will indicate the central role that these simple correlational notions continue to play. Even in fairly avant garde methods texts, bivariate theorizing is a frequent basis for methodological illustration. See, for example, Hubert M. Blalock, Jr., "Beyond Ordinal Measurement: Weak Tests of Stronger Theories," in Measurement in the Social Sciences: Theories and Strategies, edited by Hubert M. Blalock, Jr. (Chicago: Aldine, 1974), pp. 424-55.

10. Emile Durkheim, Le Suicide: Etude de Sociologie (revised edition, New York: Free Press, 1951).

11. J. David Singer, Stuart Bremer, and John Stuckey, "Capability Distribution, Uncertainty, and Major Power War, 1820-1965," in Peace, War and Numbers, edited by Bruce M. Russett (Beverly Hills: Sage Publications, 1972), pp. 19-48.

12. Wassily Leontief, "Theoretical Assumptions and Nonobserved Facts," American Economic Review 61, no. 1 (1971): 1-7. The same theme, and one that students of world politics should bear in mind when tempted to emulate the economic modelers, was noted by F. L. Hahn in his 1968 presidential address to the Econometrics Society. Remarking on the tendency of some of his colleagues to focus on modeling and abstractions while virtually ignoring the referent world, Hahn said: "There is something scandalous in the spectacle of so many people refining the analysis of economic states which they give no reason to suppose will ever, or have ever, come about. . . . It is an unsatisfactory and slightly dishonest state of affairs." Cited in Leontief, "Theoretical Assumptions," op cit., p. 2. It is one of the sad ironies in current political science and sociology that we are more and more emulating the economists, even though many of the economists themselves are beginning to realize how unsuccessful their dominant research strategy has been.

CHAPTER 3

AN APPRAISAL OF THE RESEARCH DESIGN AND PHILOSOPHY OF SCIENCE OF THE CORRELATES OF WAR PROJECT

Brian L. Job
Charles W. Ostrom, Jr.

Over the past several years J. David Singer, project coordinator of the Correlates of War project (COW), has presented a clear statement of the COW research design in a series of overview articles.[1] In these articles Singer develops the epistemological foundations and explicates the major components of the research design. Furthermore, Singer imposes a temporal order on the components of the design and asserts that the resulting "sequence of analyses" will lead to the sought-after theory of war.[2] From the emphasis he has given to the discussion and justification of the research design of the COW project, it is clear that Singer realizes the importance of philosophy of science to the construction of the design and the importance of the research design to the success of the enterprise. This paper will assess the research design of the COW project and the philosophy of science orientation underlying it by first ascertaining whether COW can be expected to attain its primary goal and then whether alterations in the original project design might facilitate the attainment of its goal.

After introducing the COW epistemology and design components, we will analyze the sequence of analyses from two points of view. First, we will discuss the assertion that by following the specified sequence of analyses it will be possible for COW to "discover" theory. After arguing that such an occurrence is unlikely, we suggest that an alteration in the temporal order of components is in order. Second, we will point out that by waiting for theory to emerge from the sequence, COW proceeds in its preliminary stages without the guidance of theory. We will then show that the lack of theory in the early analyses needlessly leads to a number of practical problems in implementing the research design, and therefore we will suggest that a change in the temporal order of the components may alleviate both the theoretical and practical problems.

Before proceeding, we acknowledge that our assessment is possible only because Singer and his associates have explicitly presented both the epistemology and the design components of their project. Also, while acknowledging that there are many other important perspectives from which to evaluate the COW project, we will confine ourselves to an evaluation of the project from the viewpoints of research design and philosophy of science.

THE RESEARCH DESIGN OF THE CORRELATES OF WAR PROJECT

The epistemological orientation of the COW project is that science, to be useful, must be both empirical and theoretical and hence capable of describing, explaining, and predicting empirical phenomena.[3] This orientation meshes with Hempel's notion of the objectives of an empirical science, that is, that "empirical science has two major objectives: to describe phenomena in the world of our experience and to establish general principles by means of which they can be explained and predicted."[4] It is thus apparent that the objective of the COW project is the advancement of the study of war to the status of an empirical science.

The primary mechanism for the realization of this objective is the COW research design, which delineates the necessary components of the research enterprise and imposes a temporal order upon them. In order to assess the COW research design it will be first necessary to develop the rationale for the temporal ordering and second to present, in detail, the research design of COW. Given the design and the objective of advancing the study of war to the status of an empirical science, the research design can then be assessed in light of how well it enables COW to achieve its goal.

Singer's belief in the temporal priority of description over explanation apparently has its foundations in the underlying relationship he perceives among the three essential types of knowledge he has identified: existential, correlational, and explanatory.[5] Existential knowledge, the "bedrock" of all other knowledge, is composed of propositions that describe regularities and patterns in a data set generated by a sequence of observations. Correlational knowledge, which constitutes the link between empirical description and explanation, is knowledge of the similarity or covariation between two or more sets of observations. Explanatory knowledge provides a theory or "causal" sequence which is "a logically consistent body of existential and correlational propositions, most of which are in operational and testable form, and many of which have been tested and confirmed."6 Singer asserts that there is no qualitative difference among the three types of knowledge;7 rather, they represent "ranges on a continuum" that has a temporal dimension. "Just as existential descriptions must precede correlational propositions, so the latter are an essential prerequisite to . . . explanatory knowledge."8

Believing that existential knowledge is a prerequisite to other knowledge, Singer has "chosen to go fairly far down the inductive road before committing [himself]...to one particular theoretical paradigm."9 Therefore the COW project has pursued a sequence of analyses consisting of the following ordered steps: (1) collection and recording of all relevant facts, (2) development of a set of bivariate hypotheses, (3) discovery by inductive inference of a set of confirmed bivariate hypotheses, (4) development of a set of multivariate hypotheses, (5) discovery by inductive inference of a set of confirmed multivariate hypotheses, and (6) construction of a dynamic causal model. Each step denotes an intermediate goal that is a necessary prerequisite to attaining the goal of the subsequent step. Successful completion of each step is to result in an incremental move towards an empirical theory of the causes of war. Singer clearly means to "move rather cautiously from the simple to the complex in order to avoid the pitfalls of ill-founded theorizing and premature closure."10

SEQUENCE OF ANALYSES

The first step is the collection of data. A necessary part of this step, of course, is a determination of what data to collect. Singer attempts to present a taxonomy that identifies the data that are relevant.11 For Singer the taxonomy is to

> be built around the concepts that are familiar as necessary, consistent only with the requirement that they reveal rather than conceal what our hunches and our knowledge lead us to believe will be the most powerful explanatory variables; at this juncture, it is largely a matter of trained intuition.12

In a belief that General Systems Theory provides such a scheme, several types of data are collected for each of the two levels of analysis, system and nation-state. The classification scheme is intentionally broad because "no coherent model of an essentially exploratory nature can emerge from . . . a restricted set of independent and intervening variables"[13] and because "no cluster of variables is likely to play a dramatic role as we gradually discover the causes of international war."[14] Thus, restrictiveness is minimized and flexibility is maximized as the General Systems taxonomy allows for "easy expansion and contraction of both the numbers of variables and the levels of analysis embraced."[15] The first step will, hopefully, result in a sufficiently broad set of data relevant to the study of war.

The second step employs correlation, to generate a series of bivariate hypotheses relating war to each of the independent variables. This step provides a measure of the association with war of each independent variable. The crucial role played by this measure of association is highlighted in the following statement by Singer:

> When all of this is said, however, there is little question in my mind that the greatest need is in the correlational sector. Our desperate requirement now is a data and findings base from which we may proceed to the systematic testing of a multiplicity of plausible explanations of war. . . . Nothing is as suggestive of hypotheses as data and correlational matrices to a scholar who is not only thoughtful, but at home with statistical methods.[16]

Thus, by computing correlational matrices, Singer asserts that he will be able to "examine the relationship between the predictor variables and war," with the major objective being to "uncover patterns" that can be used at a later juncture.[17] Therefore the second step will result in a set of relevant bivariate hypotheses.

Determining the "surviving" hypotheses, that is, bivariate correlational knowledge, requires "systematic scrutiny";[18] thus the third step involves making inductive inferences to determine which of the bivariate generalizations are confirmed. This enterprise is in the "brush-clearing category [and is] designed to help us sort out some of the dominant regularities."[19] Using standard tests of significance, the magnitude-of-correlation coefficient is judged as significant or not significant, yielding confirmed or disconfirmed generalizations respectively.

In the fourth step "the survivors of the bivariate tests are combined into a number of multivariate models."[20] The advantage of multivariate models stems from the fact that "almost every social condition or event is shaped and influenced by more than one set of conditions or events."[21] In addition, multivariate models allow the investigator to "ascertain the potency of different variables and combinations thereof."[22] Therefore the fourth step will result in a set of relevant multivariate hypotheses.

In the fifth step, the multivariate models are to be "tested via a combination of regression and dependence analyses."23 From these tests, inferences will be made about which of the multivariate models are confirmed. Essentially this enterprise is still in the "brush-clearing category." By comparing similar models in terms of goodness of fit criteria, it can be determined which models are confirmed.

In the first five steps data have been collected, hypotheses have been generated and tested, and the "best" models have been isolated. In the sixth step, "having narrowed down the field of contending models through . . . static analyses, we will move to dynamic modeling through the computer simulation strategy."24 Using this analytic tool, Singer feels that he "should achieve increasingly close approximations to an integrated and coherent theory of the causes of war."25 Thus by adopting an incremental research strategy consistent with the aforementioned epistemological view, Singer asserts that the study of war will move from description to correlation and then will "gradually shade over into explanation."26

ASSESSMENT OF THE CORRELATES OF WAR RESEARCH DESIGN

Our analysis of the COW research design leads us to conclude that Singer's conception of science is very close to what Carl G. Hempel refers to as the narrow inductivist conception of scientific inquiry.* Believing that prior theorizing only jeopardizes the objectivity of the inquiry, Singer adopts an inductive discovery procedure to enable COW to progress from the "simple to the complex" while avoiding the problems that could be caused by "ill-founded theorizing and premature closure."27 Specifically, after collecting the data and generating a large set of hypotheses, Singer proposes the use of measures of association and/or goodness of fit to distinguish the true hypotheses from the false; in more

---

*The specific ordering of steps that Hempel associates with the narrow conception is as follows: (1) observation and recording of all relevant facts, (2) analysis and classification of these facts, (3) inductive derivation of generalizations from them, and (4) further testing of the generalizations. Carl G. Hempel, Philosophy of Natural Science (Englewood Cliffs: Prentice-Hall, 1966), p. 11. These steps are very close, although not isomorphic, to those offered by Singer in "The Correlates of War Project."

formal terms, the following inductive inference pattern has been employed:*

> If the hypothesis is true, the measure of association will be "high"
> The measure of association is "high"
> ∴ The hypothesis is true

Throughout the COW research, Singer has been careful to note that no deductive conclusions can be drawn from this form of argument. He does suppose, however, that the argument is inductively correct and that the empirical support for the hypothesis in question provides enough reason to believe that a confirmed hypothesis has been discovered.

Although we find no fault with the steps in the COW research design, some controversy has arisen concerning the temporal placement of the data collection, hypothesis testing, and theory construction components. By asserting the temporal priority of data collection and hypothesis testing, Singer is at odds with others (most notably Carl G. Hempel and Wesley Salmon) who have argued for the temporal priority of theory construction.[28] This is not a disagreement between deductive inference and inductive inference; rather it is concerned with the correctness of certain types of inductive arguments. It is our contention that COW employs a form of inductive inference that is based upon two mistaken assumptions and that because of these assumptions the study of war may not be able to attain the status of an empirical science.

The first assumption underlying the temporal ordering imposed by COW is that a mechanism of discovery exists. Salmon notes as follows, however, that discovery cannot be reduced to a set of rules of procedure:

> The discovery of hypotheses requires insight, ingenuity, and originality. The process of finding answers to scien-

---

*In discussing the hazards of relying solely on goodness of fit considerations, Wesley Salmon, in The Foundations of Scientific Inference (Pittsburgh: The University of Pittsburgh Press, 1967) argues that this is a very weak form of inference as it may involve the commission of a "deductive fallacy akin to affirming the consequent" and that as a result such a method does not have "adequate credentials for admission into the class of correct induction." A major weakness of this method is that it is possible for a hypothesis to be highly supported by the data and yet not be true.

DESIGN AND PHILOSOPHY

49

tific questions cannot be transformed into a mechanical routine. Science they say, is not a sausage machine into which you feed data and by turning the crank produce finished hypotheses.[29]

It is unlikely, therefore, that COW will be able to discover true hypotheses by following its sequence of analyses.

The belief in a mechanism of discovery on the part of COW does not preclude the discovery of theory, but rather it suggests that theory will not be discovered as a direct result of this sequence of analyses no matter how careful COW is with its inference procedures. It is probable, however, that the adoption of a mechanistic approach to discovery may inhibit the discovery of theory by regimenting the enquiry to such an extent that the required insight, ingenuity, and originality are suppressed. Therefore, employing the sequence of analyses as a mechanism of discovery will even at best have no effect upon the ultimate objective; at worst it may actually impede the discovery process.

The second assumption underlying the temporal ordering imposed by COW is that inferences of type $\underline{a}$ are inductively correct. Relying solely on inferences of type $\underline{a}$ makes confirmation embarrassingly easy. Any number of hypotheses could be placed into the following form and consequently be confirmed:

If ___ is true, the measure of association will be high
The measure of association is high
∴ ___ is true

Indeed, Salmon notes that "arguments of this form are extremely weak—if not wholly incorrect."[30] The argument's weakness results from the fact that the inference pattern provides no procedure for excluding the hypotheses that are implausible and/or contradictory even though they are supported by the data. Failing to impose such controls means that at least some of the hypotheses that will be confirmed will be implausible or contradictory. In short, such a confirmation procedure is not very discriminating.

It would help to correct this shortcoming if two additional elements were incorporated into the inductive argument form, each a function of prior theorizing, plausibility and falsifiability.[31] Plausibility considerations concern the credibility of the hypothesis apart from its support in the data; the chances of confirming hypotheses that only coincidentally account for an outcome are only reduced when the number of contending hypotheses is reduced to those that are plausible. Falsifiability implies that unless the hypothesis is true its predictions are improbable; incorporating the falsifiability requirement insures that consideration will be given to the possibility that alternative hypotheses could be confirmed by the same outcome. It should be noted that a highly plausible hypothesis may also meet the falsifiability requirement. If both of these criteria are satisfied and the prediction actually obtains, then and only then will the confirmatory status of the hypothesis be high.

As a result of the temporal order imposed upon the COW research design, the following dilemma has developed: operating in the context of discovery, COW expects confirmed theory to be the final result of its sequence; however, in order to complete the sequence it will be necessary to make inductively correct confirmatory inferences, which in turn will require a certain amount of prior theorizing. Because of this dilemma it is unlikely that the study of war, under the direction of the COW project, will gain the status of an empirical science. Rather it appears that any discovery of theory by following the prescribed sequence will be largely accidental.

As an alternative to Singer's strategy, the wide inductivist conception of scientific inquiry posits a sequence that is the reverse of the COW sequence.[32] The steps in the wide inductivist sequence are (1) theory construction, (2) derivation of hypotheses from the theory, (3) operationalization of relevant concepts and the collection of data, and (4) testing and confirmation of the hypotheses. In contrast to the "narrow" view of science, which involves single-minded attention to fitting the data, the "wide" view acknowledges that the transition from theory to data requires creative imagination. Hempel asserts as follows:

> Scientific hypotheses and theories are not <u>derived</u> from observed facts, but <u>invented</u> in order to account for them. They constitute guesses at the connections that might obtain between the phenomena under study, at uniformities and patterns that might underlie their occurrence.[33]

Thus, rather than generating hypotheses to account for a set of empirical findings, this conception of inquiry presupposes that both data and tentative hypotheses are given. The task is then to assess the likelihood that, given a true hypothesis, the prediction will obtain. This is an important reorientation: the scientific objectivity of a hypothesis is a function of the rigor of its justification, not of the purity of its discovery. The problem of finding a logic of discovery is thus alleviated by moving the inquiry out of the context of discovery into the context of justification.[34] Hence, rather than wait for hypotheses to emerge, one must make creative and imaginative conjectures and then determine if they can be justified through a rigorous confirmation procedure.

DESIGN AND PHILOSOPHY 51

Viewing inductive inference as a tool to be used in the context of justification rather than as a mechanism of discovery, it is clear that the problem caused by the COW method of inductive inference can be overcome. By adopting a wide inductive orientation, the investigator will be in possession of theory prior to the hypothesis-testing phase of the analysis. As a result, the following inductively correct form of inference can be implemented:

The hypothesis is plausible
If the hypothesis is true, the observational prediction is true
The observational prediction is true
No other hypothesis is strongly confirmed by the truth of this observational prediction
∴ The hypothesis is true

This is not a deductive argument form; rather, it lays out the components of an inductively correct argument. It should be noted that this is a verbal representation of Bayes' Theorem. It will confirm a hypothesis only if the hypothesis is plausible, falsifiable, and provides an adequate fit with the available data.

Taken together, these changes in the COW sequence of analyses would allow the project to escape from the previously mentioned dilemma. Although it cannot be guaranteed that such an alteration would lead to explanatory knowledge, it is our opinion that an infusion of theory early in the sequence, a consequent move into the context of justification, and hence the possibility of developing a more rigorous form of inductive inference will markedly increase the chances that a theory of the causes of war will result from the efforts of the COW investigators.

ASSESSMENT OF THE SEQUENCE OF ANALYSES

To this point our appraisal has concentrated upon the philosophical and logical foundations of the strategy of inquiry adopted by the COW project. We have argued that Singer is mistaken in his contention that the COW sequence of analysis will proceed toward his goal of explanatory knowledge. In this section our focus changes from the theoretical to the applied. Singer's choice of the data-based, incremental approach will be accepted as a given, and we will assess the results and progress that the COW project has demonstrated in its published research. Looking ahead for a moment, we intend to show that the logical inconsistencies and the absence of theory discussed in the previous section lead to various practical difficulties for the empirical work of the COW project. While the instances and examples to be cited do not necessarily negate the value and utility of the great amount of COW work performed to date, we do believe that there is adequate evidence to support our pleas for a substantive stock-taking and appraisal of all previous COW findings and the establishment of the more explicit theoretical foundation necessary for such a large research enterprise.

Singer has sought to structure the investigation of the COW project according to the six-step sequence of analyses discussed earlier. Within this progression there are essentially three different activities to be completed prior to construction of the dynamic model of international behavior, that is, step six in Singer's sequence These three stages, which may be termed the intermediate goals of the COW project, are (1) data collection and the operationalization of indicators, (2) the formulation and testing of bivariate hypotheses and models, and (3) multivariate analyses and model construction. The discussion that follows will be organized into three segments corresponding to these headings and will attempt to assess the progress towards these goals that the COW project has demonstrated in its published research.

It is our contention that while the statements of goals and the sequencing of analyses by Singer may be necessary to ensure orderly and organized research, they are not sufficient to ensure productive and cumulative research results. At each stage of the investigation an analyst will be faced with a number of decisions that must rest on explicit, theoretically-based criteria. If this theoretical basis does not exist, questions concerning relevance of data, significance of findings, or choice of method may be decided on the grounds of expediency, availability, or convenience. This is unfortunately what we find when we examine the research design of the COW project: after consciously deciding against any prior theorizing, the COW investigators have subsequently been forced to incorporate a variety of ad hoc considerations into their analyses. Such procedures in our opinion, are problematical and make the realization of the project's intermediate goals unlikely.

DATA COLLECTION, CONCEPTS, AND OPERATIONALIZATION OF INDICATORS

Having chosen a problem with enormous scope, no less than that of the identification of the events, conditions, and interactions that cause inter-nation war, Singer and his associates sought to delimit the range of their inquiry by specifying the concepts and variables to be employed. First they restricted their investigation to incidents of inter-nation violence that occurred between 1815 and 1965 and involved at least 1,000 battle deaths.[35] This phenomenon thus became the dependent variable of the project. However, the choice of independent variables was not so easily accomplished, since the list of all possible correlates of war is virtually endless. In order to structure the investigation and to help limit the inquiry to a restricted number of promising candidate variables, Singer constructed a so-called general systems taxonomy of war.

This taxonomy, or organizational framework, successfully streamlines and categorizes a vast quantity of information concerning inter-nation violence; nevertheless, it cannot in itself solve the problem of the selection of independent variables. While the framework allows for two levels of analysis, which are the systemic and the nation-state, and four varieties of data, which are systemic attributes, nation-state attributes, inter-nation relationships, and interaction attributes, it does not indicate which level of analysis or which attributes are relevant for the COW inquiry. Practical considerations, however, necessitated that closure and selection decisions be made in order for the research to proceed. Because at this juncture the COW investigators refused to engage in what they saw as premature theorizing, or what we have earlier termed the formation of "tentative hypotheses," these decisions were often made without adequate justification. As a result the COW project has found itself faced with two problems, (1) a concern about the relevance of the data collected and (2) a concern about the validity of concept operationalizations. Each of these issues has provided a basis for criticism of their research.

The lack of specific hypotheses has caused problems in the data collection enterprise of COW because of the difficulty of selecting only the relevant correlates of war from an almost infinite number of possible correlates of war. By specifying a broad problem, Singer and his associates have limited their attention to war and its determinants, but this is not enough to guide the data collection. As Hempel notes, "Empirical facts . . . can be qualified as logically relevant or irrelevant only in reference to a given hypothesis but not in reference to a given problem."[36] Without further theoretical specification, the choices of what to examine and what to ignore are either based upon reasoning that is unclear or upon arguments of convenience rather than purpose.

Thus the first important step toward a focused inquiry is the COW decision to concentrate upon "ecological" variables in explaining warfare.[37] In terms of the general systems framework, Singer has chosen to operate largely at the systemic level and to employ national and systemic attribute variables. This determination affects all of the subsequent empirical research of the project essentially, although the matter receives only very brief consideration in the COW literature. Given the fundamental theoretical nature of the issues involved, we believe that matters such as these ought to have been treated in more detail prior to the undertaking of the actual research and analyses. It is not our contention that the COW researchers have in any way made a wrong decision; it is simply that we feel that this and other pre-data-collection issues have not been fully explicated.

As we turn more directly to the actual task of data collection, it is apparent that Singer and his associates have concentrated a great deal of time and resources in this area and have correspondingly amassed a vast amount of information about the incidence of war and the parties involved. On the one hand these operations appear to be without peer in terms of their specificity and thoroughness;[38] on the other hand, in the absence of prior guidelines for the data to be collected, it appears that the researchers have substituted criteria of accuracy or availability of data for criteria of theoretical relevancy. Occasionally, for example, one would suspect that decisions about which data to collect were made on the basis of whether or not the data available were in interval form rather than whether or not the information, regardless of measurement level, might be helpful in answering interesting substantive questions.* This appears to us to be a misplaced emphasis.

Without prior theorizing there are two pitfalls involved in such data-collection procedures. First there is a question of economy of effort. With a clear indication in mind about what is required, the investigator may be able to complete his task more quickly and more efficiently. Second, if data is collected in advance there is the danger that this availability will in turn define the investigator's research interests; that is, he will be tempted to analyze a subject because the data exists rather than acquire the data because an intriguing problem exists.

It should be noted that we remain sensitive to the argument that questions of data availability will always play some role in influencing the direction and results of a research project. Certainly

---

*For example, J. David Singer and Melvin Small, in The Wages of War, 1816-1965: A Statistical Handbook (New York: John Wiley and Sons, 1972), p. 36, do not publish fatality statistics for parties in extra-systemic wars that were not system members because of the "dubious authenticity of the figures." This immediately precludes the possibility of utilizing their data in some very interesting research on colonial war.

it would be fruitless to continue to dwell on a topic, no matter how interesting, if there obviously were no information accessible that could help to resolve the issues. This set of circumstances, however, does not appear to be true as far as inter-nation conflict is concerned, although certainly difficulties caused by biased or spotty historical record keeping abound. Our argument is that a major research enterprise such as the COW project should have as much focus and direction as possible in order to maximize the efficiency of the investigation and the relevancy of the final results.

Raw data that is collected by the investigator is not usually in a form that can be utilized directly in analyses and tests. Instead the "unrefined" pieces of information must be combined or manipulated to produce empirical indicators of complex concepts, such as the severity of war or the degree of bipolarity in the international system.[39] This process or operationalization, that is, index construction, is not simply a task in data management. The investigator must have in advance a clear understanding of the theoretical propositions he wishes to study. Otherwise, even though the indices he creates may have considerable face validity, they will run the risk of having little construct validity; in other words, they will not measure what the investigator wants measured.[40] This is precisely the problem that has occurred in the COW project. Debate has arisen concerning the construction and utility of the indicators of alliance activity used by Singer and Small, for example, and this has in turn led to a questioning of the interpretation of findings based upon these indices.[41] Such disputes could and should be precluded by more attention to the theoretical issues they intend to pursue on the part of the COW investigators, prior to undertaking ambitious but perhaps unguided efforts at operationalization.

To summarize, our argument is that operational and empirical considerations appear to have been given primacy by the COW project in its data collection and index construction activities. The absence of prior theorizing can result in concept operationalizations that are invalid or data collected that are irrelevant. Thus the COW project faces a dilemma; in an effort to infer theory it needs concepts and data; but nevertheless, theory is needed to guide the project in attaining these ends.

BIVARIATE HYPOTHESES GENERATION: A BRUSH-CLEARING ENTERPRISE?

The second intermediate goal of the COW research strategy is the assessment of bivariate relationships between the indicators of war and the various possible correlates of war. This operation involves creating a matrix of correlations between selected independent and dependent variables, determining which of the coefficients are statistically significant, and then sorting out the patterns of relationships among the indicators on this basis. Our present discussion, therefore, combines what was previously identified as two separate tasks, steps two and three in Singer's overall research program. Essentially the COW investigators are trying to bridge the gap between their data collections and the construction of multivariate models by isolating what appear to be significant bivariate linkages and by discarding insignificant relationships. Singer and his associates view this as a "brush-clearing" operation,[42] an important steppingstone in the incremental progression from data to theoretical knowledge.

However, our argument at this stage is once again that operational and statistical procedures cannot serve as substitutes for theoretically-based judgments on the part of the investigator, nor can mechanistically applied techniques by themselves lead to the discovery of theory. This in turn leads to two specific objections to the COW bivariate analysis scheme; the first concerning the distinction between theoretical and statistical significance and the second concerning the inherent failings of a "brush-clearing" operation employing a finite number of bivariate relationships.

The initial point recalls the refrain familiar in social science methodology that correlation coefficients measure the extent of shared covariance between the two variates and that significance tests indicate the improbability of such a circumstance occurring by chance, given certain assumptions. There is no foundation here for any argument that high or low coefficient values are correspondingly more or less theoretically important. Any judgment on these grounds must be based upon theoretical concerns that the analyst brings to the investigation. By focusing upon highly significant relationships, the COW researchers have no guarantee of pinpointing relevance and in fact may tend to miss much of the information presented in their correlation matrices. On the one hand, certain variables may be highly correlated with warfare indicators—but these relationships may be trivial ones, true by definition. On the other hand, a very low relationship between international violence and a certain variate may actually be very "important" from a theoretical perspective and worthy of further investigation. Unfortunately the COW procedure would tend to emphasize the wrong coefficients in such a circumstance. Admittedly the analysis and interpretation of statistical data can be a very tricky and involved procedure; but without having formulated at least tentative hypotheses in advance, the COW investigators will achieve at best a very uncertain start towards a theory of war.

DESIGN AND PHILOSOPHY 57

The second problem with Singer's correlational strategy is that it cannot serve as a "brush-clearing" mechanism. In fact, instead of helping to focus the investigator's attention, the COW approach may lead to precisely opposite results. This is because of the impossibility of applying in practice the "ideal" strategy Singer advocates. Even if presented with a matrix containing zero-order correlations between warfare and all of its correlates, the COW investigator cannot safely accept or reject a particular factor on the basis of such bivariate analysis. Although any two variables may not seem related in a bivariate manner, both could be caused by another variable or both could be connected by a series of intervening variables. Such higher-order relationships, which could be critical to the explanation of war, would not become apparent until a variety of additional partial correlations were computed among the variates. However, once the researchers are aware of these possible pitfalls, as Singer and his associates assuredly are, they are effectively prevented from discarding any factor from consideration on the basis of its simple relationship with other variables. Further analysis may always indicate the previously hidden relevance of any variable. Lacking theoretical criteria upon which to base decisions about the addition or deletion of variables, the COW investigation cannot but grow in size and complexity rather than become more focused.

Our discussion of the bivariate stage of Singer's research design has therefore shown that his stated intermediate goal cannot be achieved. Judgments about statistical significance do not coincide with judgments based on theoretical significance. Bivariate correlation evidence is not sufficient to justify the addition or deletion of variables from the investigation. Higher-order, or multivariate, analyses are necessary to do this, but again we will find that without theoretical groundwork the interpretation of such statistical findings is most difficult.

MULTIVARIATE ANALYSES AND MODEL CONSTRUCTION

A transition from bivariate to multivariate analysis is entailed in the next stage of the COW research. The development of multivariate causal models is viewed by Singer as the third of three intermediate goals prior to the development of a dynamic model of the causes of warfare. Thus at this juncture the COW investigators wish to generate a series of multivariate hypotheses in order to assess the potency of variables, individually and in combination with others, and to create multivariate models that may be compared and tested using causal modeling procedures and goodness of fit criteria. These activities correspond to steps four and five in the six-step design discussed earlier. Data-based research published by Singer and his associates in 1972 indicates that they have reached this stage in their work and are presently concentrating their efforts upon analyses of this type.[43] Although the results are interesting and the work is certainly carefully done, these articles also provide evidence that the COW project does not appear to be leading toward a theory of war. The so-called incremental strategy does not appear to be resulting in a directed and cumulative building of knowledge, nor in a refining and focusing of the COW investigation.

Our comments concerning the multivariate procedures of the project center around three points, the first of which is an extension of the bivariate analysis discussion immediately above. We argued that correlational techniques could not be used as a brush-clearing device to select the important correlation of war, and we also argued that higher-order multivariate analysis, was necessary to accurately assess the relative effects and interrelationships among variables. This means, however, that having now reached the multivariate stage, the COW investigators cannot rely upon their previous analyses for guidance. There is every reason to expect that any additions to, or recombinations of, the variables utilized in previous analyses will result in a considerable alteration of findings. The creation of multivariate hypotheses and the selection of variables must be done within some theoretical context; otherwise the investigator will be continually uncovering what appear to be new and contradictory findings without moving toward confirmation and resolution of theoretical issues.

The findings presented in a recent COW publication by Michael Wallace show the COW researchers moving from bivariate to multivariate analyses.[44] Wallace employs change in capability, intergovernmental organization (IGO) growth, and armed forces level, together with measures of status inconsistency and alliance aggregation, to explain the severity of war in the international system. Prior bivariate analyses by Wallace and others have indicated that status inconsistency, if lagged considerably; changes in capability; and alliance aggregation are related to war.[45] Wallace has also reported a significant association between the rate of growth of IGOs and the occurrence of war.[46] However, once all of these variables are introduced into a multivariate causal model, the interpretation of the bivariate results changes radically. The relationship between war and the rate of growth of IGOs is seen to be entirely spurious, as is the relationship between alliance aggregation and war. International alliance activity appears to influence the dependent variable, but only as an intervening variable between status inconsistency and change in arms levels.[47] These latter two variables are the only two seen to have a consistent, direct, positive relationship to war, but this represents the first time, to our knowledge, that arms levels factors were introduced into a COW analysis.

The point of the illustration is not that this particular analysis should not have been done or that it was performed incorrectly, although we believe it does demonstrate what will inevitably occur each time a new variable or combination of variables is investigated. Without presenting a clearer indication about where the individual bivariate, or even multivariate, analyses fit into a larger picture, the COW researchers will not appear to be progressing towards a unified and refined understanding of international warfare. What appears necessary at the moment is a thorough inventory of all previous findings and the devising of some theoretical plan of action to give direction to future efforts.

The second point about the multivariate analyses in the COW project concerns the attempts by the investigators to assess the "potency" of individual variables or combinations of variables in the various hypotheses. These assessments are to be carried out using statistical goodness of fit measures and significance tests largely in the context of multiple regression analyses. However, the same arguments cited earlier about the distinction between statistical and theoretical significance apply in the multivariate case as in the bivariate case. In fact, when there are more than two variables involved, the likelihood of relationships that are artifacts looms even larger because of the possibility of multicollinearity, spurious relationships, autocorrelation and other statistical problems. The interpretation of multivariate results, therefore, at best requires a very thorough and perceptive analyst. Unless this individual is guided by considerations of theoretical relevance and plausibility, judgments about the potency or importance of variables may be made on statistical grounds that may be technically sound but theoretically misleading. A large regression coefficient or high multiple correlation coefficient cannot be accepted without question. Without advance tentative theory in the COW project, the determination of which variables are potent, and hence which ought to be incorporated into the multivariate models, may be extremely sensitive to statistical errors and ad hoc considerations.

Finally we come to that phase in the COW project in which the alternate models themselves are to be compared in order to discriminate between competing explanations of international behavior. These procedures are essentially an attempt by Singer and his associates to construct and execute so-called "critical tests" between models.[48] However, the project's lack of theory can lead to several problems in the completion of such operations. This is evident, first of all, in the choosing of the models to be pitted against each other. The models must deal with the same phenomena and both must be theoretically plausible. If one were not plausible, and due to spuriousness or measurement error it still were to "win," an incorrect conclusion would be reached. Therefore, some advance notions of plausibility must be introduced to avoid mistaking coincidence for confirmation.

Second, the investigators must demonstrate that their models are capable of yielding different predictions, so that a decision may be reached about which performs better. However, working within the context of the COW project makes it difficult for the investigator to show logical incompatibility, since this requires prior theorizing. Furthermore, without advance conceptions of logically distinct and competing alternatives, the decision about which model will ultimately be accepted will be based upon post hoc considerations of statistical goodness of fit rather than upon sound theoretical grounds.

In an effort to highlight the above discussion, an example follows in which the COW project uses model comparison. In their article entitled "Capability, Distribution, Uncertainty, and Major Power War, 1820-1965," Singer, Bremer, and Stuckey describe two alternative models of international activity as (1) a "preponderance and stability model" based on the premise that war will increase in the system as the concentration of capabilities among nations shifts and declines and (2) a "parity and fluidity model" based on the idea that international war will decrease if resources are more equitably distributed among nations and redistribution is relatively frequent.[49] By introducing the notion of systemic "uncertainty," an unmeasured intervening systemic variable, into their arguments, the authors posit that their two models are distinct and logically incompatible. The first is to be seen as an indication that "uncertainty leads to war," while the second will presumably hold only if uncertainty leads to less rather than more violence. On this basis Singer, Bremer, and Stuckey infer the direction of the relationships between the dependent variable (war) and the independent variables (concentration, change in concentration, and "movement") that should exist in regression equations describing the international systems operating under each of the two uncertainty principles. They then find, after performing the analysis and comparing their observations and expectations, that the parity and fluidity model describes a nineteenth-century great-power environment and that the preponderance and stability model applies to the twentieth century. Their conclusions are that they have differentiated between two alternative competing models and thus have begun moving toward tentative explanatory knowledge.

This appears to be an overstatement of what is actually accomplished, and it is not clear that the authors can support the claim that one distinct model has been rejected in favor of another. They state that the preponderance and stability model predicts a "-" (concentration), "-" (delta concentration), "+" (movement) series of relationships with the war variable in a regression equation, while the parity and fluidity model predicts a "+", "+", "-" pattern, respectively. However, no argument is made that these are the only plausible models and there appear to be possible outcomes that are ignored. In fact, in two of the four regression equations for the nineteenth-century data, just such unanticipated patterns occur, but both are classified by the authors as examples of the parity and fluidity model. Without some theoretical justification this limitation of possible models seems to be overly restrictive.

There is also a question about whether these two models are logically distinct. The notion that they are logically separate is largely founded on the idea that one implies that uncertainty leads to war while the other implies precisely the opposite. These models appear, however, to be based on post hoc interpretations of the results, with an attempt to introduce the notion of "systemic uncertainty" of the decision makers as an implied intervening variable. This procedure is not sufficient to establish the logical incompatibility of the models, and in fact a plausible argument might be made to suggest that both sets of results imply only one relationship between war and uncertainty.*

In the absence of previously elaborated theory, not much faith can be placed on the COW project's comparative model assessment. Our thesis is that any testing and comparison of multivariate models requires well-developed theory. However, the COW project is then

---

*This argument could be based on the premise that "uncertainty" always leads to more war. What has changed over the years, then, is not the behavior of the decision makers but the character of the international system. National leaders have become uncertain, and war results when the status quo is altered. Thus in the nineteenth century, with a relatively equal distribution of resources, moves toward concentration caused uncertainty, while in the twentieth century, characterized by super-power dominance, moves toward parity lead to uncertainty. If this relationship is correct, the authors have but one model.

placed in another dilemma: in order to approach explanatory knowledge, the number of contending hypotheses will be distilled through a series of comparisons; to have force, however, such comparisons require fully developed theory.

To evaluate the progress COW has made in realizing each of its three intermediate goals, we assert that none of the goals has been satisfied and that none is likely to be satisfied unless theoretical direction is forthcoming. At each step the COW project faces the following dilemma: in order to incrementally proceed toward theory, theory is needed.

The project's application of its sequence of analyses seems at times to result in a vicious circle: none of the intermediate goals can be completed until the overall goal is realized, which in turn is dependent upon the realization of the intermediate goals. To break out of this, the COW project is moving on all three of its intermediate goals at once. The project seems to have abandoned its incremental approach, as noted by Singer, Bremer, and Stuckey, who state, "Even though we still have some major index construction and data generation tasks before us, we have not been completely inattentive to the possibilities of some modest theoretical analyses."[50] Although no reasons are given by Singer, the practical difficulties of following this sequence must have had a considerable impact on this decision. We must conclude that the COW project's sequence of analyses is not a mechanism of discovery.

CONCLUSION

We have thus explicated and analyzed the COW project's epistemology and sequence of analyses, and two major conclusions have emerged. First, Singer's epistemology is very close to what Hempel calls the "narrow inductivist conception of scientific inquiry" and is thus based upon the view that prior theorizing does nothing but jeopardize the scientific objectivity of the investigator.[51] The COW project proposes to proceed incrementally through a sequence of steps in order to discover explanatory knowledge, but a number of issues have been raised here that lead us to question whether relevant theory will ever emerge from the COW project's sequence of analyses. These assumptions include the following: (1) there is no logic of discovery; (2) the testing of hypotheses belongs in the context of justification; and (3) plausibility and riskiness must be considered in addition to the fit between the hypothesis and the data. Our feeling is that if explanatory knowledge were to emerge from the COW project sequence, it would be accidental rather than inevitable

Second, in an effort to assess the practical success of the COW sequence of analyses, three intermediate goals were located, each of which must be satisfied prior to the emergence of explanatory knowledge. However, an examination of the COW sequence in practice showed that none of the intermediate goals have been realized, due principally to a lack of theoretical direction. Without theoretical direction there is no sound way for the COW project to validly operationalize concepts or collect relevant data, employ bivariate correlational analysis as a brush-clearing operation, or test and confirm the multivariate hypotheses and models. In other words, at every turn in its attempt to reach explanatory knowledge, the COW project faces a need for the theory it cannot formulate until explanatory knowledge has been attained.

Solving this dilemma would require a basic alteration in the temporal order imposed upon the components of the research design, a drastic measure to be sure. Although it cannot be guaranteed that such an alteration would lead to explanatory knowledge, it is our opinion that an infusion of theory early in the sequence, a consequent move into the context of justification, and hence the possibility for the development of a more rigorous form of inductive inference, would markedly increase the chances that a theory of the causes of war would result.

NOTES

1. The reader is referred to the following articles: J. David Singer, "The Incomplete Theorist: Insight Without Evidence," in Contending Approaches to International Politics, edited by Klaus Knorr and James N. Rosenau (Princeton: Princeton University Press, 1969), pp. 62-89; J. David Singer, "From a Study of War to Peace Research: Some Criteria and Strategies," Journal of Conflict Resolution 14, no. 4 (1970): 527-42; J. David Singer, "Modern International War: From Conjecture to Explanation," in The Search for World Order, edited by Albert Lepawsky, Edward Buehrig, and Harold Lasswell (New York: Appleton-Century-Crofts, 1971), pp. 47-71; J. David Singer, "Theorists and Empiricists: The Two-Culture Problem in International Politics," in The Analysis of International Politics, edited by James N. Rosenau, Vincent Davis, and Maurice A. East (New York: Free Press, 1972), pp. 80-95; J. David Singer, "The 'Correlates of War' Project: Interim Report and Rationale," World Politics 24, no. 2 (1972): 243-70.
2. Singer, "The Correlates of War Project," op. cit., p. 249.
3. Singer, "Modern International War," op. cit.

4. Carl G. Hempel, <u>Fundamentals of Concept Formation in Empirical Science</u> (Chicago: University of Chicago Press, 1952), p. 1.

5. J. David Singer, <u>The Scientific Study of Politics: An Approach to Foreign Policy Analysis</u> (Morristown, N.J.: General Learning Press, 1972).

6. Singer, <u>Scientific Study of Politics</u>, op. cit., pp. 13-14.

7. Singer, "Modern International War," op. cit., p. 56.

8. Singer, <u>Scientific Study of Politics</u>, op. cit., p. 6.

9. Singer, "The Correlates of War Project," op. cit., p. 251.

10. Ibid., p. 249.

11. Ibid., p. 244.

12. Singer, "Modern International War," op. cit., p. 61.

13. Ibid.

14. Ibid., p. 67.

15. Singer, "The Correlates of War Project," op. cit., p. 248.

16. Singer, "Modern International War," op. cit., pp. 69-70.

17. Singer, "The Correlates of War Project," op. cit., p. 249.

18. Ibid., p. 254.

19. J. David Singer, Stuart Bremer, and John Stuckey, "Capability Distribution, Uncertainty, and Major Power War, 1820-1965," in <u>Peace, War, and Numbers</u>, edited by Bruce M. Russett (Beverly Hills: Sage Publications, 1972), p. 21.

20. Singer, "The Correlates of War Project," op. cit., p. 249.

21. Singer, "Theorists and Empiricists," op. cit., p. 14.

22. Singer, "The Correlates of War Project," op. cit., p. 251.

23. Ibid., p. 255.

24. Ibid., p. 255.

25. Ibid.

26. Singer, "Theorists and Empiricists," p. 85.

27. Singer, "The Correlates of War Project," op. cit., p. 249.

28. This is a recurring theme in Carl Hempel, <u>Aspects of Scientific Explanation and Other Essays in the Philosophy of Science</u> (New York: Free Press, 1965), Hempel, <u>Philosophy of Natural Science</u> (Englewood Cliffs: Prentice-Hall, 1966) and Hempel, <u>Fundamentals of Concept Formation</u>, op. cit. See especially Wesley Salmon, <u>The Foundations of Scientific Inference</u> (Pittsburgh: The University of Pittsburgh Press, 1967), pp. 11-53, for a discussion of the problem with using data exclusively to test one's hypotheses. After introducing the Humean account of induction, he introduces several alternatives which have been offered as solutions to Hume's problem. Note his discussion and criticism of induction by enumeration.

29. Salmon, <u>Foundations</u>, op. cit., p. 111.

30. Wesley Salmon, <u>Logic</u> (Englewood Cliffs: Prentice-Hall, 1972), p. 31.

31. Salmon, Foundations.
32. Hempel, Philosophy of Natural Science, op. cit., p. 18.
33. Ibid., p. 15.
34. See Salmon, Logic, op. cit., p. 10, for an explication of the distinction between "the context of discovery" and "the context of justification."
35. J. David Singer and Melvin Small, The Wages of War, 1816-1965: A Statistical Handbook (New York: John Wiley and Sons, 1972), pp. 17-39.
36. Hempel, Philosophy of Natural Science, op. cit., p. 11.
37. Of particular note is the 1972 article by Singer, "The Correlates of War Project," op. cit.
38. Singer and Small, Wages of War, op. cit. Also of note are J. David Singer and Melvin Small, "Formal Alliances, 1815-1939: A Quantitative Description," Journal of Peace Research 3, no. 1 (1966): 1-32; Melvin Small and J. David Singer, "Formal Alliances, 1816-1965: An Extension of the Basic Data," Journal of Peace Research 6, no. 3 (1969): 257-82; and Michael Wallace and J. David Singer, "Inter-Governmental Organization in the Global System, 1816-1964: A Quantitative Description," International Organization 24, no. 2 (1970): 239-87.
39. Indicators of the severity and intensity of war are developed in Singer and Small, Wages of War, op. cit., pp. 41-54. A bipolarity measure is utilized in J. David Singer and Melvin Small, "Alliance Aggregation and the Onset of War," in Quantitative International Politics, edited by J. David Singer (New York: Free Press, 1968), pp. 247-86.
40. Frederick Kerlinger, Foundations of Behavioral Research (New York: Holt, Rinehart and Winston, 1964). These concepts are discussed in a slightly different context in Charles Hermann, "Validation Problems in Games and Simulations with Special References to Models of International Politics," Behavioral Science 12, no. 3 (1967): 216-31.
41. See particularly Dina A. Zinnes, "An Analytical Study of the Balance of Power Theories," Journal of Peace Research 4, no. 3 (1967): 270-88.
42. J. David Singer and Michael Wallace, "Inter-governmental Organization and the Preservation of Peace, 1816-1964: Some Bivariate Relationships," International Organization 24, no. 3 (1970): 547.
43. See for example, Singer, Bremer, and Stuckey, "Capability Distribution, Uncertainty, and Major Power War," op. cit.; Michael Wallace, "Status, Formal Organization and Arms Levels as Factors Leading to the Onset of War, 1820-1964," in Peace, War and Numbers, edited by Bruce M. Russett (Beverly Hills: Sage Publications, 1972),

pp. 49-69; Michael Wallace, "Alliance Polarization, Cross-cutting and International War, 1815-1964," Journal of Conflict Resolution 17, no. 4 (1973): 575-604.

44. Wallace, "Status, Formal Organization and Arms," op. cit.

45. Michael Wallace, "Power, Status, and International War," Journal of Peace Research 8, no. 1 (1971): 23-35; Singer and Small, "Alliance Aggregation and the Onset," op. cit.; Singer, Bremer, and Stuckey, "Capability Distribution, Uncertainty, and Major Power War," op. cit.

46. Singer and Wallace, "Intergovernmental Organization and the Preservation of Peace," op. cit., p. 535.

47. Wallace, "Status, Formal Organization and Arms," op. cit.

48. Hempel, Philosophy of Natural Science, op. cit.

49. Singer, Bremer, and Stuckey, "Capability Distribution, Uncertainty, and Major Power War."

50. Ibid., p. 20.

51. Hempel, Philosophy of Natural Science, op. cit., p. 11.

CHAPTER

4

AN APPRAISAL OF THE METHODOLOGICAL AND STATISTICAL PROCEDURES OF THE CORRELATES OF WAR PROJECT

Raymond Duvall

Under what condition do international conflicts erupt into war? . . . What makes some wars short and others long? . . . Are the frequency and magnitude of war a consequence of the state of the international system?[1]

Such are the questions that have been established to guide research efforts in the Correlates of War Project, an undertaking in data collection and data analysis on the "causes" of war that has been underway since 1963.* To date the project has been marked by a tremendous amount of information gathering; data generation; and in somewhat lesser degree, data manipulation, with the intent of ultimately achieving "an integrated and coherent theory,"[2] well-founded in rigorous empirical research.

It is the purpose of this chapter to evaluate the massive project efforts and materials in terms of the methodological and statistical practices that have been utilized in them and are so fundamental to them. The evaluation is based neither on ideological nor on epistemological grounds; rather it is concerned with methodological issues in a fairly narrow sense of the term. The guiding question here is simply this: To what extent have the research procedures adopted in the project contributed to the development of scientifically meaningful answers to the guiding questions enumerated above?

---

*I place "causes" in quotes because that is a frequent practice in Project reports. For the rationale underlying the distinction accorded the term, see J. David Singer, "The Historical Experiment as a Research Strategy in the Study of World Politics," Political Inquiry 2, no. 1 (1974): 32-34.

It should be made clear at the outset that the conclusion is this: In effect, meaningful answers have so far been provided to a very limited extent, if at all. This is not meant to be either a self-congratulatory cheap shot or an indictment of the project, as such: quite the contrary, the tremendous care given to the gathering of information and the generation of data, the openness and honesty with which data and statistical results have been reported, and the very real commitment of this group of scholars to the task of untangling the causes of war make this project an admirable one. There is a very real possibility that in the not too distant future we will arrive at some definitive answers about the occurrence, severity, and duration of war through the efforts of the project. It has not arrived at that point yet, however, in spite of an apparent belief that findings have been made which are of a quality to be reported as established truths,[3] although it should be noted that the project spokesmen and members seem to recognize the tentativeness of its findings more than outsiders do.[4] The argument that is developed in this chapter is that rather serious methodological errors have been committed in COW project efforts to date, reducing or eliminating the scientific meaningfulness of the reported findings. In particular there is a pervasive lack of correspondence between the questions as posed and the strategies adopted to develop answers for them.

In writing this evaluation and in arriving at the above conclusion, I have viewed my role more as critic of that which has already been done than as spokesman for that which is left to do. In particular I do not call for any major transformations of the project for the future, partly because the project is on a largely acceptable track already, but primarily because it is too easy, and generally of very little value, for outsiders to raise the "why didn't you?" question about a research effort. More constructive are criticisms of work that has actually been done or planned. Thus this chapter nibbles at the edges, attempts to tidy an existent house. I do, however, suggest ways in which I believe the topics that are of concern here might be handled somewhat better in the future development of the project.

The presentation of this methodological evaluation is in two parts, corresponding to the two major emphases made in the project thus far in its history, the first of which focuses on measurement procedures and the generation of data, while the second deals with data analytic practices. Finally, to impose constraints on the task, I limit my attention to variables that have been central in the published works from the project: the outcome variable, which is war, and two systemic attributes or ecological predictor variables, which are structural-relational concentration and capability concentration.

MEASUREMENT: THE GENERATION OF DATA

Every scientific enterprise must at some point make an explicit attempt to link the conceptual-theoretical world to the physical-experiential world in a process of measurement. It is frequently, but mistakenly, thought that measurement is the straightforward, tedious task of quantitative description—conventionally, to measure is simply to determine how much, how large, and so on. However, measurement is not so nonproblematical; it is, in the terms of Clyde H. Coombs, an inferential process that entails critical assumptions.[5] The nature of the assumptions becomes more apparent if one considers the following restatement of a definition of measurement offered by S. S. Stevens: Measurement is the regulated assignment of numerical symbols to properties of phenomena to give to those properties some of the characteristics of the set of numbers.[6] Thus measurement is a relation, a functional mapping of numbers onto properties.

Such a formulation points to a set of potentially troublesome issues. (1) To what extent are relations among the elements of the number set structurally isomorphic to relations among the elements of the empirical property set? (2) Which relational characteristics of the set of numbers are isomorphically attributed to the set of measured properties? (3) What is the scale of numerically acceptable transformations associated with the structural isomorphism? (4) To which properties of which phenomena are numbers assigned? (5) What is the accuracy and stability of numerical assignment?

In this evaluation of the methodology of the Correlates of War Project, I attempt to make use of questions such as these. The first three are concerned with what I will refer to as precision. They are said to be the fundamental problems of measurement and to underlie the meaningfulness of answers that are produced to empirical questions. In formal terms, "[a] numerical statement is <u>meaningful</u> if and only if its truth (or falsity) is constant under admissible scale transformations of any of its numerical assignments."[7] In other words, it is the assumed precision of measurement that determines whether two numbers can be added, multiplied, ranked, and so forth. And it is in evaluating the measurement precision of the project that we ask how reasonable assumed-scale isomorphisms are, and by extension, how meaningful the resulting answers are. The fourth question raised above is concerned with what is conventionally called the problem of validity, which I decompose into two queries for the project. Do the measured properties correspond to concepts in theory? Are the phenomena to which properties are attributed the phenomena to which the properties adhere in reality? The fifth, and final, question is one of measurement reliability, which is posed cogently by M. J. Moroney, who states that "when the job is done it looks very accurate. It is an easy and fatal step to think that the accuracy of our arithmetic is equivalent to the accuracy of our knowledge about the problem in hand. We suffer from 'delusions of accuracy.'"[8] A guiding question in this evaluation, then, is whether the project so suffers.

Before turning to an evaluation of the validity, reliability, and precision of particular measurement efforts, however, a word is in order about the general measurement strategies evidenced in the project. Two points are worthy of mention. First, very detailed and precisely specified measurement rules have been developed for each variable, making measures seem highly reliable on their face. I believe it is safe to say that the basic information about war, alliances, capabilities, and so forth that is generated by the project is potentially some of the very best data available in the field of international relations. The care given to measurement assures that the project data will be used by a great many scholars. Second, it is one of the real virtues of the project that all measurement procedures are clearly and carefully detailed for interested observers. An evaluation of its validity, reliability and precision by an outsider is possible precisely because of the unusual openness of reporting that characterizes this project. If more research efforts were marked by a similar concern for measurement and open reporting, the scientific processes of adjustment to criticism and accumulation of substantive knowledge would be facilitated. However, let us now turn to our more central task, which is the raising of some of the apparent shortcomings of project measurement procedures.

War

Although one might suspect problems of validity, the first basis for evaluating measurement, to be minimal in measuring the concept of war, that is far from the case. Indeed, validity problems are consequential for this, the major outcome variable in the project. The first part of the problem is that the concept is nowhere clearly and explicitly defined in the project materials, a claim to which there are at least two potential, but largely unacceptable, responses. The first is that a definition is not required because the term war is unambiguous in conventional language. No doubt this is true in some part, but unfortunately what is unambiguous for conventional language is generally not sufficiently unambiguous for science. One gets a sense of that in the case of war by reflecting on the set of seven possible definitional criteria enumerated by J. David Singer and Melvin Small.[9] The criteria include the objectives of the participants and the legal status of the hostilities, which almost certainly could be expected to define unidentical sets. Something beyond convention is therefore required to define war for a systematic study of its causes, but as a second response, it might be said that the project does offer a definition, since the measurement procedures "define" the concept operationally. Thus, war is a deadly quarrel that involves the participation on each side of at least one member of the international system, results in at least 1,000 battle deaths, and so forth.[10]

Normally this might be quite an acceptable response, particularly in a case in which the concept is conventionally unambiguous. However, it is a more serious problem, and more fundamental than a minor definitional issue, because operations convey meanings only poorly, which is what is at issue here. In particular, the failure to specify a precise conceptual meaning for war results in a confusion over its logical and theoretical status. The confusion is evidenced in the two very distinct phrases that are found throughout the project materials: onset of war and amount of war. In the former, war is implicitly a relatively discrete phenomenon, that is, an event, an entity, a unit, to which properties, such as duration or severity, can be attributed and for which an onset can be delimited. In the latter, however, war is implicitly a property concept that is itself attributed, in varying amounts, to some entity (or, to retain consistency with the discussion of measurement presented above, some phenomenon) such as an international system.

It can be expected that these different conceptual statuses logically imply different types of analyses. The conceptualization of war as phenomenon (that is, event) is compatible with an analysis directed at questions of two types: (1) Given a war, how much of property Y, for example, severity, will be manifested under certain conditions? (2) Given a set of conditions, what is the probability that a war will occur, or slightly differently, how many will there be? There are strong indications that war is meant to be viewed conceptually as an event rather than as a variable property; in fact, in all of the explicitly theoretical works underlying the project, reference is much more clearly made to the occurrence of war than to magnitude properties. Thus the original theoretical formulation by Karl W. Deutsch and J. David Singer was concerned with structural determinants of the probability of the occurrence of war,[11] and similarly, a full ten years later Singer pointed to one of the major goals of the project to "ask whether . . . those crises that occur in periods of high polarization show a significantly higher frequency of ending up in war than those that occur in periods of medium or low polarization."[12] Similarly, in the paper that comes closest to offering a conceptual definition, war is said to be a large-scale episode of violence.[13]

If the implication is indeed that war is an event, then analysis clearly should be guided by questions of the two types enumerated in the previous paragraph. Such is not the case, however; rather, the preponderance of the project efforts has gone into an attempt to answer a quite different question of the following form: Given a set of conditions characterizing a system, how much of some other system property Y, for example, amount of war, will be evidenced in that system?[14] On its face that seems to be a reasonable guiding question, so long as the property concept is meaningfully attributed to the system in question; but therein lies the problem. The amount of war is a concept without clear meaning: it is equivalent to other statements of the form, the amount of entity x, such as the amount of cow in a farmer's field or the amount of college in a state. Such statements have at least two distinct meanings: the number of entities x, in which case the guiding question is equivalent to the second of the two previous ones, or the aggregation of some property of entities x over all such entities in the system. By implication of research efforts, the second meaning is that which is relevant to the project and its phrase, the amount of war. Such meanings are conceptually, theoretically, and hence, scientifically meaningful only if the relevant properties of entity x are approximately equivalent across each instance of x, where approximate equivalence is determined relative to the number of instances of x or where the property of x and the occurrence of x have the same or very similar determinants. The first of these is the less clear, but is the basis for expressions such as the amount of murder in a city or the amount of economic value produced in a system—the number of murderous events or economic transactions is generally very large relative to the relevant properties of each event (number of people murdered) or transaction (dollar value of exchange). Where that ratio is not large these measures also lose their meaning.

In my judgment, the concept of amount of war and its particular forms of severity, duration, and so forth, does not meet either of these conditions for meaningfulness. On the contrary, the relevant properties vary by several orders of magnitude among the small number of events that constitute the population of wars. Moreover, it seems unreasonable to expect, a priori, the determinants of the occurrence of war to be similar to the determinants of the severity or duration of war, although this is not to say that some variables may not be determinants of both occurrence and magnitude.[15] The concept contains a set of very distinct and unrelated variables,

METHODOLOGICAL AND STATISTICAL PROCEDURES 73

leaving it uncertain whether a given amount of war is the result of one war of that size or several, lesser wars and that through analysis one explains either, neither, or both poorly. If my argument is correct, then the attribution of the amount of war as a property of the international system is meaningless, and the analyses focused thereon are misdirected.

There is a second and related basis to this argument about problems of validity, and that is that properties of war are attributed to inappropriate phenomena, or entities. In particular, and without exception in project efforts to date, the operational unit, as distinct from the conceptual unit, to which war is attributed, both as event and as system property, is the system-year. There are two problems here. The first is that an excessive attribution is made to many years by the aggregation of temporal processes of some duration and the attribution of those to an initial year. The implicit assumption is that units can be freely intermixed, whether temporal snapshots or events of duration, and that the magnitude of an event of some duration is fully determined by the conditions at its inception. Such an assumption does not aid the clarity of analysis.

The second, and probably the more severe, problem is that the temporal unit, or year, does not correspond to conjecture and conception. In most cases the interest is not in the temporal ebb and flow of war but rather in the set of conditions that causes war or the aggregated property in question. Because it is believed that the amount of war is a meaningful system property and because there is only one international system, analytic comparisons are made on that system over time. The analytical model is precisely equivalent to a static cross-sectional analysis; it is simply that use is made of observations over time to provide variance on the antecedent conditions and consequent variable, the occurrence or amount of war. Time, then, is not an integral part of project analyses, at least not at the system level,[16] but instead an observational mapping convenience.

Unfortunately, the year is a rather poor surrogate for the different sets of conditions sought. It would be preferable if the creation of boundaries around units to which occurrence, or if necessary the amount, of war is attributed were based on something more nearly equivalent to altered antecedent conditions than to temporal regularity. One could use intuitive, a priori criteria, such as that international system conditions are nearly constant for these eight years but quite different from those evidenced during the subsequent two years and five months, or empirical, classificatory criteria, such as those suggested by Campbell to demark boundaries for social entities such as (temporally) different international systems.[17] The result would almost certainly be a reduction in the number of observational units but an increase in correspondence between theory and method.

A brief recommendation to the project is in order to summarize this discussion of the validity of the measurement of war. A meaningful analysis of the causes of war, one that addresses the questions reproduced at the outset of this chapter, will be an analysis in two parts. On the one hand will be an analysis of the occurrence of war, as event, under various conditions in the international system (or of participant nations, or of a conflict process). The outcome variable, war occurrence, will be given as a vector of numbers of events (or probabilities of events*), each element of which will be associated with a unit of observation, which at the systemic level will be better defined as corresponding to variation in ecological conditions than as corresponding to regular temporal slices. On the other hand will be analyses of the properties of wars, with the latter as units of analysis, measures of magnitude as outcome variables, and systemic attributes, national characteristics, and conflict process variables as predictors.

The second basis for the evaluation of measurement is the reliability of the measuring instrument. To restrict the set of events called wars to genuinely large-scale episodes of violence, a criterion of a minimum of 1,000 battle deaths was established. The major problem with this criterion is that it implies instrumental accuracy. It creates a threshold around which many cases are clustered but on the basis of which a decision is made to assign a score of zero to any case for which the instruments indicate a

---

*Bruce Bueno de Mesquita, in "The Effects of Systemic Polarization on the Probability and Duration of War: Toward an Early Warning Indicator of War," paper presented at the International Studies Association annual meeting, Washington, D.C., February 1975, claims to utilize war probabilities as the dependent variable, but as is recognized there, such are virtually impossible to specify a priori with any precision. Thus, ones and zeros are used as very crude surrogates, but such become, in effect, nominal outcome variables—whether a war did or did not occur—rather than probabilities. We simply do not know enough yet to make the assumption that war does occur when it is probable and does not when it is improbable, because probability is a sensible concept only in the context of some theory of causal processes. An outline of desirable research strategies similar to that offered here was presented previously by Dina A. Zinnes, "An Analytical Study of the Balance of Power Theories," Journal of Peace Research 4, no. 3 (1967): 280-83.

METHODOLOGICAL AND STATISTICAL PROCEDURES 75

severity of anything less than the threshold. Again, the problem has real implications. Approximately 12 percent of the 93 wars included in the project were coded as having just 1,000 battle deaths, and an additional 6 percent are within 500 deaths of that figure; that is, almost one of every five cases included in the project is at or very near this threshold. With such a concentration of cases, the researcher must be prepared to assume either that his instruments are very accurate or that he is making a substantial number of errors in classification.

To attempt an assessment of the potential effect of such classification errors, I made use of the set of wars reported by Lewis F. Richardson, and summarized in The Wages of War.[18] Using relatively restrictive criteria, I investigated the wars that had reportedly been rejected from the project on grounds only of insufficient battle deaths, and I determined that seven had apparently involved state-system actors on both sides, and therefore would be considered interstate wars, and were coded by Richardson as having 1,000 or more associated deaths.* Richardson may well have overestimated in these seven cases, but the fact that in general he underestimated deaths according to Singer and Small† leads to

---

*The seven wars are (1) England and France with the Belgians against Holland, 1830-33; (2) England with France and Holland against Japan, 1862-64; (3) France against Morocco, 1907-12 (Morocco a member of the state system from 1847 to 1911); (4) Holland against Venezuela, 1908 (Venezuela a member since 1841); (5) Haiti against the United States, 1915-20 (Haiti a member since 1859); (6) Lithuania against Poland, 1920 (Lithuania a member since 1918 and Poland since 1919); (7) China against Mongolia, 1936-37 (Mongolia a member since 1921). I am fully prepared to admit that I am no historian, and hence have no substantive knowledge of these incidents. I include them here not to argue for their necessary inclusion in the project—indeed, I would have little basis for that— but simply to show that events reportedly excluded on grounds of insufficient severity might well affect the answers that are developed about the causes of war. The point is that assumptions of accuracy might be less than entirely warranted, and that the 93 wars included in the project might not be all the wars that occurred during the period studied. They certainly would not be all the wars, were one to adopt a definition of war in terms other than of severity, a proposal that I make explicitly, below.

†Of the 93 Project wars, 68 are included by Richardson. Richardson's estimates of battle deaths are precisely the same as the COW estimates in eleven cases; smaller than the COW estimates

the suspicion that many of these seven and probably several others are sufficiently close to the threshold to cause many students of war to want to include them in analysis.

Moreover, such exclusions seem to have noticeable effects. For example, all seven of the "lesser" wars were initiated during five-year periods in which at least two other interstate wars were started. Because only 50 interstate wars are included in the project (the other 43 are extrasystemic wars, which are not relevant to this discussion) for the 150-year period from 1816 to 1965, the mean, or expected, number of wars for each five-year period is 1.6; indeed, 13, or almost one-half, of the regular five-year periods (1816-1820, 1821-1825, and so on) were marked by the initiation of fewer than two wars. Thus the fact that the seven lesser wars all occurred during periods when a relatively large number of other wars were started is an extraordinary, or improbable, circumstance. Admittedly this analysis is crude, and it is certainly dependent on cutting and clustering points in time, but it does indicate the possibility that certain periods are even more war-prone than the COW materials would have us believe and in fact that some wars during such periods may remain small precisely because so many wars are going on. The latter would be a partial answer to the question of what makes war severe.

If one continues this line of argument one can inquire what, if any, difference inclusion of the seven "lesser" wars would make on project analyses of the causes of war. In fact, the lesser wars do make a difference, although again I must emphasize that I include the analysis of these seven only for illustrative purposes and not with any presumptions of certainty about their actual status or any delusions about the definitiveness of the analyses. Consider Table 4.1, in which the relationships are presented, for the twentieth century, between the number of wars initiated during a regular five-year period and the percentage of major powers in alliance at the beginning of that period. The relationship among the 13 time periods according to the project war-count is given, and the same relationship

---

in 33 cases; and larger in 24 cases, of which 18 are extrasystem wars in which the difference can be explained partially by failure of COW to include extrasystem actor deaths. Of the six interstate wars for which Richardson's estimates are larger, five are large wars according to COW estimates (the smallest of the five is the Seven Weeks War with 36,000 battle deaths). Only the La Plata war of 1851-52 is overestimated by Richardson and considered by COW to be a small war (with 13,000 battle deaths).

TABLE 4.1

Alliances and War Occurrence in the Twentieth Century

Percentage of Major Powers in Alliance of Any Type	Number of Project Wars during Five-Year Period[a]		
	None or 1	2	3-5
Less than 50	2	0	0
50 to 85	1	1	2
More than 85	2	3	2

	Number of Project-plus-Five "Lesser" Wars during Five Year Period[b]		
	None or 1	2	3-5
Less than 50	2	0	0
50 to 85	1	0	3
More than 85	2	3	2

[a] $x^2 = 4.2$; $P > .25$
[b] $x^2 = 7.3$; $P \approx .10$

Source: The alliance bond percentages were taken from the graphical representation in Bruce Bueno de Mesquita and J. David Singer, "Alliances, Capabilities, and War: A Review and Synthesis," in Political Science Annual: An International Review, vol. 4, edited by Cornelius Cotter (Indianapolis: Bobbs-Merrill, 1973), p. 245.

after the inclusion of the five "lesser" wars that occurred in the twentieth century is also shown. Clearly the effect is to transform a highly probable, nearly random relationship into a marginally significant one. With the inclusion of the "lesser" wars, it seems somewhat safer to say that war is relatively most probable (in the twentieth century) during periods for which a majority, but less than an overwhelming majority, of the major powers have alliance bonds. Similarly, Table 4.2 involves a comparison of the two relationships, with capability concentration as the predictor variable. Again, a random pattern is transformed into a more systematic one with the inclusion of the "lesser" wars, making it a more warranted conclusion that war is most probable in periods of low

TABLE 4.2

Capability Concentration and War Occurrence in the Twentieth Century

Capability Concentration Index	Number of Project Wars during Five-Year Period[a]		
	None or 1	2	3-5
Low (less than .24)	2	1	3
High (more than .24)	3	3	1

	Number of Project-plus-Five "Lesser" Wars during Five-Year Period[b]		
	None or 1	2	3-5
Low (less than .24)	2	0	4
High (more than .24)	3	3	1

[a] $x^2 = 2.2$; $P > .25$
[b] $x^2 = 5.0$; $P < .10$

Source: The capability concentration variable was taken directly from J. David Singer, Stuart Bremer, and John Stuckey, "Capability Distribution, Uncertainty, and Major Power War, 1820-1965," in Peace, War, and Numbers, edited by Bruce M. Russett (Beverly Hills: Sage Publications, 1972), p. 29.

capability concentration. The conclusions that might be drawn are inconsequential for the present, however; what is of importance is the threat to the validity of the analyses that results from a definitional criterion that presumes as much accuracy of instrumentation as the 1,000 deaths criterion.

A related problem with this definitional criterion is that it is hazardous to define a concept or to identify an object in terms of a property that is subsequently subject to analysis. This results in the restriction of variance through the imposition of a priori bounds on variability, a restriction that is always subject to the challenge of unreasonableness. Of somewhat greater relevance is the fact that it leaves entirely unclear the conceptual status of less severe events; for instance, what is a deadly quarrel with 900 battle deaths? By the implication of the project's outlined behavioral process model the answer would be a crisis, a conflict of less severity than war.[19]

However, that is troublesome because, also according to that model, a crisis is a temporal antecedent of war and can escalate into war if the governments engage in certain actions. Thus, in some respects, the criterion of 1,000 battle deaths implies that a set of actions is distinguished solely by the consequences of those actions: a crisis escalates into a war when the 1,000th person is killed. Unfortunately, this runs directly counter to what is believed to be desirable for the project by the project participants.

> Our taxonomy requires that behavior not be classified according to the <u>consequences</u> which were either intended by those who committed the act, or observed by others. A given type of act may have a variety of consequences. . . . Thus, we distinguish between what a national government <u>does</u>, and what events or conditions did . . . result from what it does.[20]

If severity is to be analyzed as a property of war, and if war is to be thought of and analyzed as an escalation from crisis, then it would be wise to extend the application of the above principle to the concept of war. I would encourage the project to adopt alternative definitional criteria that are not tied directly to analyzed properties or to the consequences of action sequences. One possibility would be that war is the employment of military forces in direct, physical attack. Such a criterion might be felt to be too inclusive, but it would serve to clarify the conceptual boundary for war, to increase the reliability of measurement, and to increase the validity of conflict process analyses. A supportive note is offered in project materials that are concerned with a separate issue.

> [N]o matter how restricted a population of entities researchers may ultimately wish to study, any exhaustive classification should begin with all those units meeting only the most basic requirements for inclusion. Having done this, we may then select subsets of this wider population which meet more stringent criteria.[21]

I would simply add that the more stringent criteria should not be of the 1,000-battle-death kind.

Precision, the third and final basis for evaluating measurement that was enumerated above, concerns the adequacy of assumptions about the isomorphism between property relations and numerical relations.[22] On this, the project has performed admirably. With war as event, measurement is done at a nominal level and care is given to setting up such explicit criteria that like objects are assigned the same symbol (classed together) and unlike objects are not, although as indicated above, the criteria are problematic. Severity and magnitude, the properties of war, are assumed to be indexed in a manner that satisfies interval assumptions. The only apparent problem with that lies in assuming that each additional nation-month is equal to each other one, a problem the project researchers are aware of and to which they periodically give reference by retreating to a safer set of ordinal assumptions.

Structural-Relational Concentration

A major impetus to the formation of the Correlates of War project was a profound theoretical contribution by Deutsch and Singer on the destabilizing, or war-promoting, consequence of polarization in the set of relationships that determine the structure of the international system.[23] The argument presented there is that the probability of war decreases as the number and importance of cross-cutting cleavages in the system increase and that the latter are a positive function of the number of "poles," or relational centers, in the system and an inverse function of the structural clarity, or degree of relational concentration, associated with the poles. Testing this theoretical formulation has been a major concern of project participants. Attempting to test it has involved, first, attempts at the measurement of its major explanatory variables, which are polarization and cross-cutting cleavages, neither of which is directly observable. Thus measurement has been in two distinct stages, (1) a direct, or fundamental, measurement of structure-determining relationships among nations and (2) a derived measurement of the system property, polarization, through the construction of indices from the primary relationship data. Measurement in the first stage concentrated on the following three types of relationships: alliance bonds, shared membership in intergovernmental organizations, and diplomatic exchanges. The second stage has involved many persons and several indices, from the simple to the very complex. It is apparently continuing into the present.[24]

In this section I will address each of the two stages of measurement separately, but will consider the problems of validity, reliability, and precision nearly conjointly within each discussion. I limit my attention to the alliance data in order to render the discussion manageable within space limitations.

The determination of alliance bonds among nations was a task performed under the direction of Singer and Small in the mid-1960s.[25]

METHODOLOGICAL AND STATISTICAL PROCEDURES

The measurement rules that were adopted have reasonably high face reliability. They are detailed and specific; no critic can hide behind a claim of irreproducibility. Were one to systematically peruse historical diplomatic records and accounts using project directives, one would probably produce information very similar to that produced in the project. The extensiveness of search that was employed assures some degree of accuracy; the result is, I think very reliable historical data on alliance bonds over time.

However, two problems can be noted. The first is the rather arbitrary exclusion of war alliances, which lessens the validity of the measurement. Since the indexed concepts apply to international systems rather than to events, and since conceptual development specifies nothing about the nature of the system in terms of stability, a standard and universal application of measurement rules should be applied.

The second problem is an uncertainty of precision. The three alliance commitment categories have been assumed to satisfy assumptions of ordinality. Bremer and Bueno de Mesquita,[26] for example, use a scale of 1 to 4, with the latter assigned to dyads with defense pacts and the former to dyads lacking formal alliance bonds. An ordinal scale, of course, is premised on an assumed isomorphism with axioms of identity (also true for nominal scales) and monotone transitivity. The latter assumption seems problematic, especially with regard to the first category, in that all instances of nonalliance do not seem invariably less aligned than all instances of alliance. Moreover, even the basic identity axiom is of questionable validity, to the degree that different historical epochs are marked by quite different patterns; a defense pact is so common in one era that it is of questionable equivalence to a defense pact in another, more restrictive, era. On this, one project report is instructive, saying that "the non-aggression pact . . . was clearly an invention of the 1920's and 1930's,"[27] a claim based on the fact that during the nineteenth century only 11 percent of alliances were neutrality pacts, whereas during 1900-1939 fully 48 percent were of such a type. The implication of this is that the typology of alliance commitments (nonalignment, entente, neutrality, and defense) is of questionable validity and precision. More valid and precise for the concept of polarization would be a simple reliance on actual defense pact commitments and a treatment of neutrality pacts and ententes as agreements with no direct bearing on cross-cutting cleavages and relational constraint.

In the second, derived, measurement stage, indices of polarization have been constructed from the primary data on alliance bonds. Upon this base, indices for system concentration have been constructed. They have been of two types: simple, a priori indices and

statistically based, configurational indices. The former were
developed conjointly with the initial data and are of two forms;
(1) the alliance aggregation index, which is appropriately named in
that it involves a simple aggregation or summation of states belonging to at least one alliance, standardized by the total number of
states, and (2) the alliance commitment index, which is given as
the number of alliance commitments in the system relative to the
number of nations. However neither of these indices is a valid
measure of system concentration, polarization, or cross-cutting
cleavages, since these are conceptualized in terms of system configurations and the resulting structural position of individual members
of the system, while the indices are indicative only of the number of
alliance bonds in the system, a concept of very limited interest and
no apparent theoretical basis. In their present state they are simply
too crude for tests of structural models.[28]

More recently Stuart Bremer, Michael Wallace, and Bruce
Bueno de Mesquita have offered indexing procedures that do attempt
to validly assess the structural concepts. Each employs a different
clustering technique to define sets of tightly aligned nations, and
then each uses information from the resulting clusters to index the
system concentration and polarization. Bremer's is the least
adequate strategy, for six reasons.

1. His matrix of the similarity of national alignment patterns
consists of a set of coefficients, Kendall's Tau b, which are based
on the assumed ordinality of alliance categories, an assumption we
challenged above.

2. This statistical measure of similarity results in a rather
strange inflation with large numbers of ties. Since only four categories are utilized, ties are inevitable, but the result is that two
nations, both with highly similar alliance commitment patterns to
two other nations, will differ on the similarity measure to the degree
that one pair tends to have relationships of only one type while the
other pair tends to have relationships distributed evenly among all
four types. The associational statistic adopted by Bremer, in other
words, is sensitive to "skewness" in the ordinal types of relationships engaged in by a pair of nations.

3. The Tau statistic does not permit variance-covariance
interpretation, but Bremer uses it as the associational measure in
a factor analysis, from which communality estimates are discussed
in terms of explained variance.

4. He makes a direct linear transformation of Tau measures
to "standardize" them, a transformation that necessarily makes the
unfounded assumption of an interval character to the resulting
statistic.

5. He performs a factor analysis to define clusters of nations, but no clear criteria are articulated for ways in which the analysis is controlled. For example, nothing is reported about the rules for factor extraction.

6. The parity and coherence indices, or derived measures of polarity, are formed by treating national loadings on rotated factors as if they were stable and accurate (reliable) across systems of different size with similar configurations.

Thus I would not recommend adoption of the Bremer indices of system polarization, since they are based on a series of violations in their assumptions of isomorphism underlying measurement precision and as a result are not meaningful in the sense of the term given by Patrick Suppes and Joseph L. Zinnes in the general discussion of measurement above.

Similarly, Bueno de Mesquita's indices of polarization are troublesome, but somewhat less so. Like Bremer, he makes use of the Tau b statistic to indicate the degree of similarity of alliance commitments for each pair of nations, so that his indices are based on some of the same problems as Bremer's, including assumed ordinality of alliance types and sensitivity to "skewness" in types of alliance commitments. Moreover, like Bremer, he mistakenly treats the Tau b measure as if it were interval in character by calculating the mean Tau b scores for each cluster of nations. However, Tau b is not a number for which interval assumptions are appropriate. The mean scores, and hence the indices of tightness and discreteness of poles, are not meaningful information in a strict sense. However, Bueno de Mesquita's third index, that of interaction opportunities, is meaningful in terms of both precision and validity; that is, it is based on the Tau b statistic as simply an ordinal measure used to derive, through an ordinal clustering strategy (typal analysis), the number of poles in the system, the latter corresponding directly to one of the concepts in the polarization theory under test. The sole question about the interaction opportunities index, then, is its reliability, and that is largely determined by the measure of dyadic similarity on which it is based. Were a better measure of association employed, and were types of alliance not distinguished ordinally, the interaction opportunities index would be a valid, reliable, and appropriately precise measure of system polarization.

The Wallace technique, however, deserves more commendation. He refuses to accept the apparent ordinality of the initial alliance data, and he balks at violating the assumptions of isomorphism. Instead he treats alliance commitment as nominal and simply counts bonds. He then utilizes that information to create an ordinal measure of bondedness between nations according to the numbers they share in common, and he uses a clustering technique, smallest space analysis, that is appropriate to the resulting monotonic ordinal scales. Finally, he indexes polarity by measuring distances in the created multidimensional space.

The Wallace strategy is original and attractive, but unfortunately, two real problems remain. (1) The development of an ordinal bondedness scale from numbers of shared commitments may suffer on grounds of validity, since shared bonds do not necessarily make a strong alliance, and on grounds of precision, since a pair of nations with X shared bonds cannot invariably be assumed to be less tied than a pair with X + 1 shared bonds. These problems, however, inhere in the fundamental measurements of alliance bonds and are not of Wallace's doing—they are not apt to be severe. (2) The clustering technique is hampered and affected by arbitrary technical decisions. In particular, forcing a two-dimensional solution, as Wallace does, almost certainly affects the cohesiveness of clusters and the resulting polarity of the system. In many-actor worlds, what would emerge as distinct clusters in more dimensions is apt to look random in two-dimensional mapping.

In short, if one assumes that the larger and more complex world of today is apt to give rise to a variety of axes for polarization, the technique has a built-in bias against revealing the actual contemporary polarization of the international system. That problem can, however, be overcome by extending the smallest space analysis to a point where some arbitrarily reasonable fit has been realized and then utilizing a multidimensional distance metric, standardized perhaps for the number of dimensions. The Wallace technique deserves real consideration. The results from its use of data are artificial because of the arbitrariness of dimensionalizing and because of a somewhat questionable data input, but the problems can easily be rectified, and by the use of this technique the project can have a valid, reliable, and precise measure of alliance polarization. Similar strategies can be adopted for indexing system concentration in terms of shared IGO memberships and diplomatic exchanges, variables that have been analyzed relatively little in project reports as of this writing.[29]

Capability Concentration

A more recent addition to the set of Correlates of War concepts is that of concentration in the distribution of national capabilities among major powers. The degree of concentration is viewed as an unobservable system property, so that, like structural concentration, its measurement involves both fundamental and derived stages. In the first stage, indicators of national capability are measured directly. In the second stage, a national capability index is created from the separate indicators. In the third stage an index is created for the system from the separate national indices. A brief word is in order about each stage.

In the first stage, measurement is made of six indicators, which are taken to reflect the short-term and long-term power potentials of nations.[30] For these six, as for all of the primary measurement efforts in the project, the meticulous care given to measurement assures that they are among the very best indicators of historical capabilities available. Moreover, on their face they seem to be valid indicators of the concept covering military, industrial, and population bases. An extensive criticism of them would be fruitless, but one issue is worth keeping in mind. At two points a change in instrumentation is adopted: beginning in 1885 a fuel consumption indicator is added to the set, and in 1895 a shift from iron production to steel production is made for one of the industrial capability indicators.

These changes were both justified on the grounds of data availability and conceptual appropriateness and are, in these terms, defensible. What should be kept in mind, however, is that instrumentation changes often effectuate index changes and that some of the variance over time in the index may be due to methods factors rather than to changes in national capability distributions. If one examines five-year changes in the capabilities concentration index, and these are the changes that are reported,[31] one sees that the two instrumentation changes occur at times when the index changes by relatively large magnitudes. They are, in fact, the fifth and sixth largest changes in the index for the entire series from 1820 to 1913, a series of nineteen observations. The possibility of instrumentation effects should be kept clearly in mind.

In the second stage, the indicators are combined to create a national capability index, or actually three different indices based on different subsets of the indicators.[32] Of all the major concepts in the project, national capability is the only one based on the principle of multiple indicators, or what Donald T. Campbell calls multiple operationism. The potential advantages are great, since the evaluation of reliability in scoring the other concepts has rested at a face, or apparent, level, whereas reliability is subject to fairly direct testing where multiple, independent indicators are employed. That is, for other concepts, a reliance on "definitional operationism"[33] restricts reliability checks to seldom-reported inter-coder agreement, or more tenuously, probable replicability. It has been on such grounds of probable replicability that I have written above that various indicators, such as war and alliances, are seemingly reliable on their face; but for national capability, based as it is on multiple indicators, a more direct assessment of reliability is possible through the determination of the extent of inter-indicator convergence, or covariation.34 To date, the project has apparently assumed such convergence, and has used, as a result, an unweighted linear additive model to produce the aggregate index.* A more reliable, and in turn more valid, index could be generated if a careful assessment were made of indicator covariances.

In the third stage, the national capability scores are utilized to compute a measure of systemic concentration. The computational form is, as with most project indices, an a priori measure.35 On its face it seems to be a valid and reliable instrument, but its precision is of some greater doubt. In particular, it is not clear that it assigns symbols to properties in such a way that they are isomorphic to the axiom even of identity, let alone to those of some monotone transitivity or of constant intervals. The measure is sensitive in some part to the size of the system and in some part to the distribution of capabilities within systems. The argument can be seen most readily by focusing on assigned scores rather than on particular systems; for example, how many different systems can receive a score of .50? Are those systems similar enough to be assumed identical on the property of capability concentration? Are all systems scored .50 more concentrated than all systems scored .40? Are systems scored .50 as much more concentrated relative to .40 as systems that are scored .60 are, relative to .50? These are difficult questions. That even the first is a problem can be seen in an analytical comparison. For a three-actor system, a score of .50 is possible in any one of a variety of ways that satisfy two constraints:

---

*It is not entirely appropriate to say unweighted, because two of the three national capability indices do involve weights, arbitrary a priori weights rather than weights based on covariance criteria. For the various indices, see John Stuckey and J. David Singer, "The Powerful and the War-Prone: Ranking the Nations by Relative Capability and War Experience, 1820-1964," paper presented at the conference on Podor Social: America Latine en El Mundo, Mexico City, May 1973. The unweighted index is used in J. David Singer, Stuart Bremer, and John Stuckey, "Capability Distribution, Uncertainty, and Major Power War, 1820-1965," in Peace, War, and Numbers, edited by Bruce M. Russett (Beverly Hills: Sage Publications, 1972).

$$s_1 + s_2 + s_3 = 1.00$$

and

$$s_1^2 + s_2^2 + s_3^2 = 0.50$$

where s_i is the proportion of the total system capability attributed to nation i. The same score is achieved in the five-actor world if:

$$s_1 + s_2 + s_3 + s_4 + s_5 = 1.00$$

and

$$s_1^2 + s_2^2 + s_3^2 + s_4^2 + s_5^2 = 0.40$$

Three such systems are: $s_1 = .50$, $s_2 = .50$, $s_3 = 0$; and $s_1 = .66$, $s_2 = .20$, $s_3 = .14$; and $s_1 = .50$, $s_2 = .35$, $s_3 = .14$, $s_4 = .008$, $s_5 = .002$. I think that most students of behavior would expect to find very different kinds of behavior in a system of the first type, compared to a system of the second type. If so, the use of this index, questionable in precision, to predict the occurrence of war could be expected to be less fruitful than an analysis based on a more adequate index of capability concentration. I would recommend that an attempt be made to devise alternative indices.

I have not attempted, in this section, to evaluate the measurement of every variable in the project. Rather, I have attempted to point to the kinds of criticisms that might be raised about major variables in order to suggest modifications for future research and to support my claim that findings from statistical analyses have not yet proved adequate. The criticisms that I have raised can be extended, at least in terms of a similar logic, to variables not discussed here. In fact, almost every variable reported in project works to date is quite directly related to this discussion. Many recent studies, for example, focus at the nation-state level and deal with the relationship between war involvement and various indicators of national capability.[36] Thus, most of the work that has been carried out in the project is fairly directly implicated by at least some of the criticisms of measurement raised here. It is my belief that, with some revisions, the measurement of concepts in the Correlates of War Project will be sufficiently sound that meaningful, conclusive answers to questions about the causes of war will be possible. Before these answers are actually produced, however, some attention will have to be paid to considerations for appropriate statistical analysis.

DATA ANALYSIS

Given a set of symbols with some numerical properties, the COW researchers, like others of us, have manipulated the symbols in an effort to scrutinize and analyze them as data. The analysis generally involves one or both of two possibilities, the testing of bivariate hypotheses or the modeling of multivariate theories. The project efforts have involved both; at first only the former, but subsequently also the latter. In this section I offer a few evaluative comments about each of these in turn, but because the number of published statistical analyses is quite large, I do not attempt an analysis of individual works. Rather my comments here are directed at the underlying analytical logic, at what might be called, in a very general sense, the research design.

Hypothesis Testing

The first question to ask of any statistical analysis is whether it corresponds to the conjecture, the hypothesis, the theory on which it is supposed to reflect. The bivariate work offered by the project is problematic on these grounds, not because the hypothesis in question in any report is not clear—on the contrary, the test hypotheses are generally stated explicitly—but rather because the stated test hypotheses often do not correspond to the less rigorous, but guiding, verbal theorizing. Of greatest consequence is the fact that a great deal of the verbal material implies fairly complex, multiplicative hypotheses, which in the tests are translated into bivariate, linear form. The result is that the tests do not reflect on verbal conjectures; if the latter are correct, the former are providing irrelevant or even misleading answers.

A second, and ubiquitous, basis for an evaluation of hypothesis-testing research involves a statement about the use and misuse of probability models. In testing for the distributional significance or non-randomness of bivariate relations, the researcher necessarily makes use of various probability distributions. The project research involves a multiplicity of such distributions, testing for the significance of Spearman's rho,[37] Goodman and Kruskal's tau,[38] Kendall's tau,[39] and Pearson's product-moment correlation[40] and also making direct use of chi-square distributions.[41]

I will not attempt here an evaluation of each use of various statistics; suffice it for me to simply challenge the general use of such tests in the project and to object to the grounds for defense that are offered. Singer and Wallace offer three basic rationalizations for the use of significance tests: (1) one may speak of probabilities for population outcomes, and significance tests reflect those probabilities; (2) significance tests make a benchmark for the threshold of importance; and (3) the COW project observations really constitute a sample and not a population.[42] Each of these three separate statements contains an element of truth, but the implication is incorrect in each case. A benchmark of importance can be set using significance tests, but one of no real import since it is set using an assumed model that is largely irrelevant to the question being investigated. Why be locked in by a basically irrelevant mathematical model simply because it is available? The nature of that model, it should be emphasized, is one of assumptions about the way the data were generated and assumptions about the true distribution of scores. It cannot be used to test both assumptions simultaneously; one set of assumptions must be held a priori to be valid. If it is not, the result cannot be interpreted as necessarily reflecting on either set of assumptions. Since the first assumptions involve probability distributions for outcomes from independent, random samples, a test can adequately be made only where the data at hand can be safely assumed to have been generated as a random sample. That COW project observations are those of a hypothetical sample is irrelevant: the model is simply inappropriate in such a case.

The contention that the models that underlie significance tests can be used to assess the randomness of population outcomes is erroneous. What, after all, is the meaning of randomness in that case? I would strongly recommend an abandonment of this mode of inquiry—it simply facilitates no knowledge. However, I would not recommend an abandonment of the logic involved, particularly that expressed in the first clause of the first rationale summarized above. One may, and should, speak of probabilities for population outcomes, but to do so in a hypothesis-testing vein implies the creation of theoretical probability distributions rather than the adoption of null models. The research task, in other words, is turned somewhat on its head, from that of examining a distribution of data for deviation from randomness, to the fitting of data to a previously specified theoretical probability distribution. I have in mind the hypothesized connection between structural concentration and the onset of war, for which a precise functional form, or set of alternative forms, could be specified. Sampling a small number of different international systems that manifest some variance on the antecedent condition, which is structural concentration, would permit direct tests of the hypothesis. Such a strategy is, of course, possible only if a precise theory has been specified from which theoretical probability distributions can be derived. Adopting this strategy would require more intensive theorizing by the COW project participants than has been evidenced to date.

Modeling Theory

As is the case with much of contemporary social science, the project recently has been marked by a strongly increased interest in the utilization of structural equation models. One article involves the comparison of linear additive models with multiplicative models for adequacy of fit between capability concentration, changes in that concentration, and war.[43] Another utilizes linear "dependence" analysis, or path analysis, to make inferences regarding the causal linkages among status inconsistency, alliance aggregation, IGO memberships, sizes of armed forces, and war severity.[44] A third fits high-order polynomials to war data to model the causal impact of polarization in the system,[45] while a fourth makes use of spectral methods to decompose the autocovariance function of war.[46] Each of these is a variant of the basic regression model. Rather than evaluate them separately, I will attempt to point out the most important features of the regression model and indicate sources of problems in its utilization in the project.

Regression models, like tests of statistical significance, are premised on assumptions that, if violated, reduce the utility of the technique. To the extent that the intent is merely descriptive regression to generate a best-fitting hyperplane by minimizing squared deviations, the assumptions are not very restrictive. If description is the intent of the COW project, there is little to criticize in their modeling efforts, since generated equations can be interpreted as defining best-fitting forms. However, if statistical inference is or will be intended, it behooves us to consider the basic assumptions that permit inference. Basically, of course, the researcher is attempting to infer structural parameters, that is, the true "population" relationships among variables, and to infer the extent of unexplained or erroneous variance. For making these inferences, assumptions are required regarding the generation of data and either the structural parameters or the error component. For assumptions regarding the generation of data, regression models are somewhat less restrictive than are significance-test models. In order to obtain unbiased estimates, one of two assumptions is acceptable. The first assumption is that the regressor, or independent, variables are fixed in repeated samples (appropriate to controlled experiments); the second assumption is that the regressor variables are generated by a stationary stochastic process, which means that the joint probability distributions for the regressor variables are constant across all observations. A random sample defines a particular form of stationary stochastic process. Other sampling strategies, such as those employed in the COW project, can be satisfactory to the extent that they can validly assume that the joint probability distributions do not change much with time or any other observational unit.

The assumptions in the second set are quite restrictive, however, and should be fully heeded. There are five assumptions of the basic, or classical, regression model. Some of the five may be relaxed, but mostly in conjunction with alternative technical formulations, which apparently have not been utilized by the project. The assumptions are as follows:

1. Each observation on the "dependent" variable is a linear function of the observations on the "independent" variables plus the disturbance term.
2. The expected value for each disturbance is zero.
3. The expected values for the covariance matrix of disturbance terms are constant elements in the diagonal and zeros in all other cells.
4. The regressors are independent of the disturbance term for each observation.
5. There are no exact linear relationships among the regressors.

The first assumption can be relaxed to the extent that nonlinear functional forms can be translated into a linear formulation of the observations. This is done, for example, in Wallace's evaluation of the nth-degree polynomials and in the utilization by Singer, Bremer and Stuckey of multiplicative models. In the latter, log transformations of the original data permit direct assessment of multiplicativity. In such a case one also must make assumptions about the transformation of the disturbance term, which is now postulated to interact with the regressors in a multiplicative rather than additive form. In order for that to be the case, the vector of estimated residuals is given as log transforms. Corrections are required before reporting an R^2 as a measure of fit; in particular, the residuals must be translated back into raw terms. Singer, Bremer and Stuckey fail to make that translation; hence their results are essentially uninterpretable. Moreover, the logic of a direct comparison of linear additives with multiplicative models is troublesome. If two very different assumptions are made about the disturbance term, such as that it is normally distributed with mean zero or that it is log-normally distributed with positive mean, it is certain that at least one of the models is based on invalid assumptions. That, in turn, implies that at least one of the sets of parameter estimates is biased. The researcher does not know which is biased, and the decision cannot be made on grounds of best statistical fit.

The second assumption cannot be relaxed if consistency is desired. To assure its validity the project modelers, like others, have to include all important causal variables in their model and have to insure that systematic measurement error does not exist in the dependent variable. It is for this reason that I have emphasized the appropriate measurement of war in preceding sections.

The third assumption involves two implications; first, that there be constant disturbance variance across observations (homoskedasticity) and, second, that disturbances are uncorrelated across observations. The Singer, Bremer and Stuckey piece is again instructive, indicating that both implications are apt to be violated in the COW efforts. Years that have extreme war scores are shown to have noticeably larger error variances than other years. Also, estimated residuals, let alone true disturbances, are shown to be autocorrelated. As reported, then, parameter estimates are biased. Fortunately, technical alternatives are available to permit a relaxation of this assumption.

The fourth assumption implies that regressors are measured without error (again pointing up the importance of measurement), that no variable is excluded from the model that relates to the regressors in important ways, and that causation is recursive rather than reciprocal. Again, each of these can be relaxed with appropriate technical modifications. Instrumental variables can be used to replace errorful regressors, and simultaneous equation models can be developed and estimated by generalized techniques such as two-stage least-squares. I simply encourage COW personnel to ponder the adequacy of this assumption and to consider some of the alternative formulations.

The fifth assumption can be directly tested, but it does have a close relative, multicollinearity, that does not bias estimates but does reduce their efficiency; that is, if multicollinearity is high, confidence intervals around estimates are wide. Unfortunately, as of this writing the COW project researchers have not reported confidence intervals. We have no real sense of the efficiency, that is, the stability, of estimated parameters, and in that sense we have very little information about the relationships investigated through structural equation models.

CONCLUSIONS

What, if anything, can be learned from this appraisal of methodological practices? Probably the first thing that is apparent to an observer of the Correlates of War project is that very creative and instructive use has been made of historical records and documents. If one is willing to be as meticulous, as systematic, and as persevering as the COW project participants have been in perusing historical materials, one will no doubt find that there is a great potential wealth of quantitative data for students of international relations in recorded history. Indeed, the major contributions of the project thus far have been to point to precisely that fact and to act on that and create some of the very best information available on patterns of alliance commitments and national capabilities. Other information that is important to the study of international relations is certainly there in the historical record for gathering.

The second feature of the project that should be apparent, if I have been at all successful in making my arguments, is that a very careful and systematic gathering of information is not directly equivalent to good measurement of concepts. We can, as in the case in the COW project, have very good basic information but quite inadequate concept measurement, either because we impose inappropriate criteria on the basic data or because we conceptualize and effectuate poorly the rules for derived, or secondary, measurement stages in moving from basic data to concept scores.

The third feature that should be apparent is that over-time data are not directly equivalent to time-series data and that a systematic quantification of history does not necessarily result in the latter. Time-series data are scores for, or measures of, a concept for which the theoretical status is that of a process; that is, time is integral to the concept and the theory. However, many of our knowledge claims, or hypotheses, are purely in terms of conditions and outcomes of conditions—time is of no direct theoretical relevance. This is the case in the hypotheses that have been examined in the Correlates of War project. When history is used as the domain of observations for hypotheses of this type, and hence for over-time data, time becomes simply the conceptual device for drawing boundaries around different sets of conditions and is analogous to areal borders, such as those of a nation-state. Forcing the data into regular time intervals in order to make it appear as time-series data is conceptually inappropriate and probably analytically destructive. It is equivalent to spatially demarking different political conditions by scoring concepts for each 1,000 square kilometers of land surface. Theoretically relevant antecedent conditions simply are not distributed that regularly. Stated more generally, our concepts are sometimes assigned to an inappropriate observational unit.

The fourth feature that is apparent from the reports of the Correlates of War Project, to retain the parallel with previous nonequivalences, is that statistical analysis is not directly equivalent to rigorous, scientific analysis. Statistical models are scientifically useful only to the extent that they correspond fairly directly to conjecture, or postulated knowledge claim, and to the extent that they are used consistent with the mathematical assumptions on which they are based. The regression model, a path analysis, and a spectral analysis, do not themselves provide the answers, although they are tools that <u>can</u> provide useful and meaningful answers if used according to design.

NOTES

1. J. David Singer, "The 'Correlates of War' Project: Interim Report and Rationale," <u>World Politics</u> 24, no. 2 (1972): 243-70.
2. Singer, "The 'Correlates of War' Project," op. cit., pp. 255.
3. See, for example, Singer, "The 'Correlates of War' Project," op. cit., pp. 266-67.
4. Compare, for example, the statement of relationship between alliances and war given (in quite tentative terms) in Bruce Bueno de Mesquita and J. David Singer, "Alliances, Capabilities, and War: A Review and Synthesis," in <u>Political Science Annual: An International Review</u>, vol. 4, edited by Cornelius Cotter (Indianapolis: Bobbs-Merrill, 1973), pp. 271-72, with that given (in quite definitive terms) in Patrick McGowan and Howard Shapiro, <u>The Comparative Study of Foreign Policy: A Survey of Scientific Findings</u> (Beverly Hills: Sage Publications, 1973), p. 164.
5. Clyde H. Coombs, <u>A Theory of Data</u> (New York: Wiley, 1964).
6. S. S. Stevens, "Mathematics, Measurement, and Psychophysics," in <u>Handbook of Experimental Psychology</u>, edited by S. S. Stevens (New York: Wiley, 1951), p. 1. A very similar restatement to mine is offered by Bernard S. Phillips, <u>Social Research: Strategy and Tactics</u> (2nd ed., New York: Macmillan, 1971), pp. 205-206.
7. Patrick Suppes and Joseph L. Zinnes, "Basic Measurement Theory," in <u>Handbook of Mathematical Psychology</u>, vol. I, edited by R. Duncan Luce, et al. (New York: John Wiley and Sons, 1963), p. 66.
8. M. J. Moroney, <u>Facts From Figures</u> (Harmondsworth, Middlesex, England: Penguin Books, 1951), pp. 2-3.
9. J. David Singer and Melvin Small, <u>The Wages of War, 1816-1965: A Statistical Handbook</u> (New York: John Wiley and Sons, 1972), p. 18.
10. The measurement criteria are discussed at some length in ibid., pp. 14-39.
11. Karl W. Deutsch and J. David Singer, "Multipolar Power Systems and International Stability," <u>World Politics</u> 16, no. 3 (1964): 390-406.

12. J. David Singer, "The Historical Experiment as a Research Strategy in the Study of World Politics," Political Inquiry 2, no. 1 (1974): 36. For similar statements see Singer, "The 'Correlates of War' Project," op. cit., pp. 263-65, and J. David Singer, "Escalation and Control in International Conflict: A Simple Feedback Model," General Systems 15 (1970): 163-73.

13. Michael Wallace and J. David Singer, "Large Scale Violence in the Global System: Definition and Measurement," paper presented at the International Political Science Association Congress, Montreal, August 1973.

14. To my knowledge only three papers have focused analysis primarily on questions associated with war as event. They are J. David Singer and Melvin Small, "Foreign Policy Indicators: Predictors of War in History and in the State of the World Message," Policy Sciences 5, no. 3 (1974): 271-96; Bruce Bueno de Mesquita, "The Effects of Systemic Polarization on the Probability and Duration of War: Toward an Early Warning Indicator of War," paper presented at the International Studies Association annual meeting, Washington, D.C., February 1975; and, Cynthia A. Cannizzo, "The Costs of Combat: Predicting Deaths, Duration and Defeat in Interstate War, 1816-1965," paper presented at the International Studies Association annual meeting, Washington, D.C., February 1975.

15. For a study that purports to show one such variable, system polarization, see Bueno de Mesquita, "The Effects of Systemic Polarization," op. cit.

16. This point is clearly recognized by project participants. See Singer, "The 'Correlates of War' Project," op. cit., pp. 251-54.

17. Donald T. Campbell, "Common Fate, Similarity, and Other Indices of the Status of Aggregates of Individuals as Social Entities," Behavioral Science 3, no. 1 (1958): 14-25.

18. Singer and Small, The Wages of War, op. cit., pp. 82-128.

19. Singer, "The 'Correlates of War' Project," op. cit., pp. 263-65.

20. Ibid., p. 246.

21. Wallace and Singer, "Large Scale Violence," op. cit., p. 18.

22. I do not believe it necessary to discuss the relevant numerical axioms in this context. They are well developed for the interested reader in Suppes and Zinnes, "Basic Measurement Theory," op. cit.

23. Deutsch and Singer, "Multipolar Power Systems," op. cit.

24. J. David Singer and Melvin Small, "Alliance Aggregation and the Onset of War, 1815-1945," in Quantitative International Politics: Insights and Evidence, edited by J. David Singer (New York: Free Press, 1968), pp. 247-86; Stuart Bremer, "Formal Alliance Clusters in the Interstate System: 1816-1965," paper presented at American Political Science Association annual meeting, Washington,

D.C., September 1972; Michael Wallace, "Alliance Polarization, Cross-cutting, and International War, 1815-1964: A Measurement Procedure and Some Preliminary Evidence," Journal of Conflict Resolution 17, no. 4 (1973): 565-604; and, Bueno de Mesquita, "The Effects of Systemic Polarization," op. cit.

25. J. David Singer and Melvin Small, "Formal Alliances, 1815-1939: A Quantitative Description," Journal of Peace Research 3, no. 1 (1966): 1-32, and Melvin Small and J. David Singer, "Formal Alliances, 1816-1965: An Extension of The Basic Data," Journal of Peace Research 6, no. 3 (1969): 257-82.

26. Bremer, "Formal Alliance Clusters," op. cit., and Bueno de Mesquita, "The Effects of Systemic Polarization," op. cit.

27. Small and Singer, "Formal Alliances, 1816-1965," op. cit., p. 270.

28. This point was made previously in Dina A. Zinnes, "An Analytical Study of the Balance of Power Theories," Journal of Peace Research 4, no. 3 (1967): 280-83. What is somewhat surprising is that in spite of the crudeness of these indices and the greater validity of subsequently developed measures, contemporary reporting of relationships is still in terms of the earlier, crude indices. See, for example, Singer and Small, "Foreign Policy Indicators," op. cit., pp. 290-94, and Bueno de Mesquita and Singer, "Alliances, Capabilities, and War," op. cit., pp. 242-47, 270-72.

29. Stuart Bremer, "A Sociometric Analysis of Diplomatic Bonds, 1817-1940," paper presented at the Events Data Conference, (Michigan State University, 1971); Stuart Bremer, "Formal Alliance Clusters in the Inter-state System; 1816-1965," op. cit; Michael Wallace, op. cit., p. 575-604; and Bruce Bueno de Mesquita, "Measuring Systemic Polarity," Journal of Conflict Resolution 19, no. 2 (1975): 187-216. The exceptions are primarily attributable to Michael Wallace. See, for example, J. David Singer and Michael Wallace, "Inter-Governmental Organization and the Preservation of Peace, 1816-1965: Some Bivariate Relationships," International Organization 24, no. 3 (1970): 520-47, and the works on status inconsistency, one element of which is attributed status as indicated by diplomatic importance, such as Michael Wallace, "Power, Status, and International War," Journal of Peace Research 8, no. 1 (1971): 23-35; Michael Wallace, "Status, Formal Organization and Arms Levels as Factors Leading to the Onset of War, 1820-1964," in Peace, War, and Numbers, edited by Bruce M. Russett (Beverly Hills: Sage Publications, 1972), pp. 49-69; and Michael Wallace, War and Rank Among Nations (Lexington, Mass.: D. C. Heath, 1973).

METHODOLOGICAL AND STATISTICAL PROCEDURES

30. The presentation of measurement strategies for the six capability indicators is made in John Stuckey and J. David Singer, "The Powerful and the War-Prone: Ranking the Nations by Relative Capability and War Experience, 1820-1964," paper presented at the conference on Poder Social: America Latine en El Mundo, Mexico City, May 1973.

31. The capability concentration scores are reported in Singer, Bremer, and Stuckey, "Capability Distribution and Uncertainty, and Major Power War, 1820-1965," in Peace, War, and Numbers, edited by Bruce M. Russett (Beverly Hills: Sage Publications, 1972), p. 29.

32. See Stuckey and Singer, "The Powerful and the War-Prone," op. cit.

33. These terms were apparently originated by Donald T. Campbell.

34. For a clear presentation of the logic of inter-indicator correlation in assessing the reliability and validity of concept scores, see Fred N. Kerlinger, Foundations of Behavioral Research: Educational and Psychological Inquiry (New York: Holt, Rinehart, and Winston, 1964), pp. 429-62.

35. The computational formula is developed in James Lee Ray and J. David Singer, "Measuring the Concentration of Power in the International System," Sociological Methods and Research 1, no. 4 (1973): 403-437.

36. Stuart Bremer, J. David Singer, and Urs Luterbacher, "The Population Density and War Proneness of European Nations, 1816-1965," Comparative Political Studies 6, no. 3 (1973): 329-48; Stuckey and Singer, "The Powerful and the War-Prone," op. cit.; Cannizzo, "The Costs of Combat," op. cit.; and Hugh Wheeler, "The Effects of War on National Power, 1860-1965: Postwar Changes in Energy Consumption," paper presented at the International Studies Association annual meeting, Washington, D.C., February 1975.

37. Singer and Small, The Wages of War, op. cit., p. 197.

38. Wallace, "Power, Status, and International War," op. cit.

39. Singer and Wallace, "Inter-Governmental Organization and the Preservation of Peace," op. cit.

40. Singer and Small, "Alliance Aggregation and the Onset of War," op. cit.

41. Singer and Small, The Wages of War, op. cit., pp. 138 and 205.

42. Singer and Wallace, "Inter-Governmental Organization and the Preservation of Peace," op. cit.

43. Singer, Bremer, and Stuckey, "Capability Distribution, Uncertainty," op. cit.

44. Wallace, "Status, Formal Organization, and Arms Levels," op. cit.

45. Wallace, "Alliance Polarization, Cross-Cutting, and International War," op. cit.

46. Singer and Small, The Wages of War, op. cit., pp. 206-212.

CHAPTER

5

AN APPRAISAL OF THE SUBSTANTIVE FINDINGS OF THE CORRELATES OF WAR PROJECT
Harvey Starr

I sit here in my office surrounded by about 942 linear
feet of delightful and plausible speculation on the causes
and consequences of war—and there's not a damn shred
of reproducible evidence.

J. David Singer[1]

Quite simply, this essay will attempt to assess how successful J. David Singer and his colleagues on the Correlates of War project (COW) have been in meeting the challenge of developing "reproducible evidence" on the causes and correlates of war and presenting it to the academic community. In reviewing the output of COW, we will look at the significance and value of the results of this project, which has been operating continuously since 1963. We will confront these questions in two ways. First, how may we assess the research output in terms of the goals, purposes, and general context of the Correlates of War project itself? Second, to what extent have the results given us new insights into the processes of international relations? That is, "What do we know now that we did not know before?" and "So what?" In addition, the "value" of the results must include the impact the COW reports and data have had on other researchers, on the cumulative nature of the scientific process of inquiry, and on the methodological tools available to those engaged in the study of international relations.

I wish to acknowledge my appreciation to Brian Job, Charles Ostrom, Dina Zinnes, and Frank Hoole for comments on various drafts of this chapter.

A brief sketch of the organization of this review and the material to be included is in order. While there have been numerous convention papers and manuscripts of forthcoming material, this paper will only deal with articles and books that have been published. Admittedly this is somewhat arbitrary, yet it delineates the sample of COW research that is most easily accessible to the general reader. The material includes two books and twenty-two articles.[2] In the first section, which reviews COW in terms of the project context, the materials will be organized in terms of sequences in research strategy. In the analysis that is directed toward the question of new knowledge, however, the discussion will be based upon the type of "knowledge" that has been expanded by the research in question. The focus on types of knowledge produces three separate sections: descriptive or existential knowledge, correlational knowledge, and causal or explanatory knowledge. This focus will also include a variation of the "so what" question, which is the assessment of research in terms of cost. Some general impressions will be presented in the conclusion.

APPRAISAL OF THE CORRELATES OF WAR FINDINGS

Internal Criteria

Published research is most often judged by external criteria, when evaluated by readers who have been unrelated to the activities through which that research was produced. In assessing the work of the Correlates of War project, it must be recognized that the bulk of the published findings have been steps in a continuing research process—steps that, in addition, have been published to provide data and interim conclusions to the rest of the scholarly community. In this sense it is only fair that the published output be judged also by internal criteria, in terms of the research process of which each piece of research is but a part.

The Singer quotation at the opening of this chapter reflects much of the impetus behind the Correlates of War project. Singer has noted that from 1648 to the second world war there had been little change "in the quality of our knowledge regarding war and its causes."[3] The study of war had to progress beyond the mere gathering of "facts" for single case descriptions. COW thus began in the early 1960s as a "modest set of experiments in quantitative history," concerned with the causes of war and the methods by which we study war.[4]

SUBSTANTIVE FINDINGS

General descriptions of the history and development of the COW project have been provided by Singer.[5] In terms of assessing the output of the project, however, several points bear repeating here. First, as described by Singer, the research design of COW called for a flexible skeleton that was to be fleshed out by new concepts, variables, and findings, rather than for beginning with a comprehensive model. This skeleton was to be based on a general systems taxonomy.[6] Such a strategy helps to explain the variable-by-variable progression of the project. These variables have been "ecological" ones, seen as the principal bonding interactions of the system entities.

This basic, flexible design also reflects the tentativeness of the early stages of the COW project, from which, it will be argued, the project has yet to emerge. "It follows that we must indeed be tentative enough to begin with a search for the correlates of war: hence the name of the project. In other words, we are engaged in a systematic 'fishing expedition' during this phase of the enterprise."[7] This implies that the main goals of the project at this stage are description, the setting forth of data for inspection, the operationalization of key concepts, and similar activities. By these standards, the research product of COW has been useful and may be considered as achieving the basic aims of description and operationalization.

The assertion that the COW project has yet to move far beyond its opening stages is based on several observations. The output from the project to date reflects only partial completion of the research design set forth. Though the research produced meets Singer's criterion of being longitudinal, it has yet to meet, to any great extent, his criterion of being multilevel.[8] In terms of the level of analysis, almost all of the research deals with analysis of systemic aggregations, although one notable exception to this is a study of the relationship of national alliance experience and war by Singer and Small.[9] While there have yet to be any studies on the behavioral level of prewar behavior sequences, there has been one study of a relational character, Kjell Skjelsbaek's dyadic analysis of war and intergovernmental organization (IGO) membership.[10] There have been no studies at the decision-making or governmental level (what Singer has termed "cultural" variables), although the importance of the level has been explicitly recognized.[11] In sum, while data has been collected on a national level of analysis, most of the work has been performed on the systemic level and none on the decision-making level. Also, only one study moves beyond a concern with the attributes of nations to relationships, and as yet there are no studies dealing with interaction sequences.[12]

We may thus ask how far the project has progressed in terms of the skeletal sequence of analyses. J. David Singer and Melvin

Small discuss the variety of variables that were to be investigated by COW and the basic order of investigation. First are the "attribute" variables, by which we can describe nations and, when aggregated, the international system. The stages of dyadic relationships and behavioral variables, as noted, have not yet been reached.[13] The reader is directed to Singer's article, "The 'Correlates of War' Project: Interim Report and Rationale," in which he presents the variables to be dealt with by the project and the status of each in terms of the acquisition, preparation, analysis, and publication of data.[14] Of the thirty separate indicators listed, the four relating to the dependent variable have been completed, as well as four more: diplomatic representation, alliance configurations, IGO configurations, and capability distribution. Thus in terms of the phases or stages in the development of the project, only several of the structural ecological variables have been completed, leaving the bulk for future endeavor.

Given that only a small, select portion of the proposed design has been completed, an appropriate question might be why these particular variables and their indicators? Singer has written at great length on the question of why "ecological" variables should be stressed.[15] In order to deal with war, the dependent variable, one must look at the entities that take part in it, the nation-states. The focus should therefore move to those factors that provide the context within which nations behave. This is necessary, Singer argues, because until the contextual variables are identified and studied and their explanatory power discovered, it will be impossible to know how much or what type of leverage remains with the decision makers of nations. By looking first at ecological variables, we are making the distinction between the remote, fundamental, and institutional factors, on one hand, and the immediate, inciting, and behavioral "causes" of war, on the other.[16]

A second major argument for beginning with ecological variables is derived from the general systems skeleton. The idea of system requires that the units of the system be bonded in some way. War is one of the most basic of conflictual interactions or bonds, while alliances, diplomatic representation, and IGOs represent the most basic types of cooperative bonding interactions. Although other sequences could be argued, the output of the COW research has so far been consistent with the logic of this overall plan and has thus addressed the highly significant problem of the impact of the international environment on the occurrence of war. It can be argued that such a context creates an "opportunity" for war that may, through the intervening governmental level, significantly raise or lower the probability that national leaders will choose the war option over the no-war option.[17]

SUBSTANTIVE FINDINGS

The variables that have been considered by COW comprise a definite sequence of research steps. The basic problem is, of course, to study war as a ubiquitous and dominant international phenomenon; yet according to Singer, "until we can understand and explain a class of phenomena, we cannot explain a single case of that class."[18] However, in order to account for the incidence of that general class, we must first discover what its incidence has been. Therefore the first need is to describe war, to define, and to operationalize it. In doing so, the COW project has demonstrated quite clearly the cumulative aspect of the scientific enterprise, building on earlier studies in a conscious extension of the data collection projects of Quincy Wright and Lewis F. Richardson.[19]

Deriving in part from Wright's legalistic approach to the study of war, the definition of war by the COW project necessitated the inclusion of the units that engage in the activity called war. There was a need to define a population of units, or nation-states. As Bruce M. Russett, J. David Singer, and Melvin Small noted, ". . . until the population is defined, we know neither the domain about which we seek to generalize, nor the criteria for selecting a sample from that population."[20] War was to be defined in part by the nature of the units involved. Because the general systems approach requires some notion of interaction of units, diplomatic representation was used as a partial criterion for the inclusion of units into the international system. The articles presenting data on diplomatic representation patterns were necessary to delineate which units were in the system.[21] At the same time, this data also permitted a longitudinal view of the changing nature and character of the international system and subsystem, the "central system" and the major powers.

With the population of nations described, the description of war could proceed, and other COW work set out the occurrences, patterns, and trends in the activity defined as war from 1816 to 1965.[22] However, while it was indicating what war is and who fights in it and investigating several ecological correlates such as alliances and IGOs, COW was also providing another significant type of output, the presentation of a process of "data-making."[23] In explicit detail Singer and his colleagues were describing a methodology by which data could be made from historical materials and analyzed by quantitative techniques. Their concern with setting out their procedures clearly and fully was an explicit, albeit secondary, purpose in publishing accounts of the data-collecting activities.[24] The utility of describing and encouraging these research procedures rests on the intrinsic value of data-making itself. Ted R. Gurr, for example, proposes two advantages of data-making: the possibility of indexing "many important variables that cannot be indexed using available data," and the opening up for quantitative study of "the whole span of documented human history."[25]

I think it fair to conclude that, in terms of what COW has set out to do, the material published so far can be considered valuable in achieving the aims of the early stages of the project. The main problem in terms of an internal assessment is not what has been produced, but what has yet to be produced. As Gordon Hilton did in his review of the Dimensionality of Nations project, we may look at COW in terms of developmental phases.[26] (See also Chapter 8 of this book.) The COW project must still be considered, even after a decade, to be in its opening phases. One of the more recent articles, and one of the few multivariate analyses, still refers to itself as a preliminary "brush-clearing" exercise.[27] We are, then, confronted with the legitimate question of when we go further and also how we go further; that is, has COW provided the basis in terms of data, findings, and "theory" from which scholars can move toward a theory of war? (See Chapter 3.)

We must also, at this juncture, raise the question of whether the overall project design has been too ambitious. In an assessment, questions concerning the ratio of output to design are relevant. Perhaps the most useful lesson to draw from this project for others concerns the difficulties encountered in quantitative history, including the problems of assembling rigorous data sets and the pace of progress that can realistically hoped to be achieved.

External Criteria: An Appraisal in Terms of New "Knowledge"

In the above section we have already partially answered the "So what?" question as applied to the Correlates of War project. The material produced so far may be viewed as valuable in terms of criteria internal to the project itself and related to certain modes of inquiry represented by that project. However, there must also be external assessment: in what ways have the findings of the project been of use in the study of international relations? What new knowledge has it added?

There are, of course, numerous ways by which we might attempt to answer these questions. One way is to structure our review in terms of several different conceptions of "knowledge." Singer himself enumerates three kinds or levels of knowledge that may be achieved: existential knowledge, correlational knowledge, and causal or explanatory knowledge.[28] Employing this three-tiered approach, we can order and separate out the new knowledge that COW has provided us.

Existential Knowledge

By "existential" knowledge, Singer notes, "We mean nothing more than a descriptive regularity or pattern."[29] Such knowledge would give us a better idea of what the world looks like, and it is along these lines that a large portion of the COW work may be outlined and discussed. To study any phenomenon, such as war, it must first be defined, described, and set out for examination. Existential knowledge, then, is strongly tied to the process of operationalization, "perhaps the bedrock of scientific method."[30] The research product of COW has provided us with operationalizations of a number of crucial international phenomena.

For the dependent variable of war, Singer and Small, in The Wages of War, 1816-1965: A Statistical Handbook,[31] present the most explicitly developed and described listing of wars in the literature. A list of 93 wars is developed for the period 1816-1965. Given the existence of three previous war lists, those of Wright, Richardson, and Sorokin, does the COW data represent a valuable addition to descriptive knowledge? This question is addressed in full in The Wages of War,[32] where these three data sets are presented alongside the COW data to permit comparison. The COW data attempts to rectify operational deficiencies in both the Wright and the Richardson data.* There are a number of arguable operational points in the COW data, however. For example, there is the arbitrary 1,000 battle death per war figure or the 100 battle deaths per nation for every 1,000 men in battle zone figure. Still, this data set is the most clearly and carefully defined.[33] It permits the greatest degree of reliability, while getting at the large-scale organized aspects of war (the factor Richardson stressed) and the quasi-legal aspect of war concerning the status of the participants (stressed by Wright). Thus the COW definition maintains validity by including the essential dimensions of war used in other studies while at the same time being the most reliable.

---

*J. David Singer and Melvin Small note, "As the balance of this volume should indicate, neither Wright's nor Richardson's listings are adequately refined or classified for the purposes of the study which engages us here." The Wages of War, 1816-1965: A Statistical Handbook (New York: John Wiley and Sons, 1972), p. 8. Wars listed by Wright and Richardson were excluded from the COW list for the following reasons: war did not meet minimum battle death requirements (185 times), war was a civil war (75 times), participants were not qualified system members (20 times), and war continued past 1965 (5 times).

The contribution of The Wages of War is avowedly existential. "All we have done is to generate a particular set of data and then refined and systematized it into a multitude of potentially useful forms."[34] Perhaps the best indicator of this descriptive enterprise would be a list of the 88 tables that appear in the book; the reader will be spared that pleasure, but I will note that in these tables war is not the only unit of analysis considered; the international system and the individual nation are considered also. Thus all the units of the international system are listed with dates of entry and exit to and from the system, for the total system as well as for the Eurocentric, highly interactive "central" system. One section focuses on the nation, with each nation listed together with its total number of years in the system, of wars, of war months, of battle deaths per year, of wars per year, of war months per year, of battle deaths per war, of battle deaths per month. Nowhere else can such a complete description of the modern war experience by nation, or by year, be found.

For summaries of the results of this univariate analysis, see the appendixes to this chapter.[35] In The Wages of War the authors themselves ask, "More specifically, what do we and our readers know now that we did not know before?"[36] The list of answers begins with operational definitions both of the international system and of international war. War is represented not only by Richardson's original severity-of-deadliness indicator but also by magnitude in terms of nation-months and intensity, newly developed indicators of war. The variety of indicators that are developed, "multiple operationism,"[37] is another advantage of the COW data, in that it permits a variety of data aggregations. Indeed, the study of secular trends and periodicity of war could not have been undertaken without the new indicators. Findings concerning periodicity, the war proneness of nations, and the closely related study of war and major powers, reinforce the findings of Richardson and Wright.[38] The analyses of the seasonal influence on war and of the success of nations at war, including the factor of the initiation of hostilities, are new.

The relationship between victory or defeat and battle deaths is also investigated; no battle-death threshold or advantage to the winning side in terms of battle-death ratios is found. However, using 41 interstate wars from the COW list, Steven Rosen found that in 30 cases the winning side lost a smaller percentage of its population but a greater number of its people, since the winners tended to have larger populations.[39] Rosen also replicated Richardson's test to see whether there was a range of battle deaths as a percentage of population within which nations quit war. He could confirm the upper limit, 5 percent of population, but not the lower .5 percent, since in 23 of 77 cases the defeated party lost less than .5 percent of its population. This is an example of the way COW data, even when not analyzed by project researchers, has been used to confirm the development of new findings on war.

The COW findings regarding the question of traditional enmities and friendships partially reinforces Richardson, uncovering a general fluidity in choices of allies and enemies. However, the COW project researchers note that of 209 belligerent dyads, 19 percent had previously fought before and 21 percent had previously been allies. This differs from Richardson's conclusion that alliances have a pacifying effect that declines over time, a finding that is generally supported by recent analysis of war coalition dyads.[40]

Overall, Singer and Small in The Wages of War bring a great deal of new and better data to bear on such important questions as what a war is; how it is defined in terms of what happens to whom; who gets into war and where; when they get into war; and who wins. Nevertheless there are problems with these data, highlighted in the brief criticism of the operationalization of war above. It is necessary to ask how relevant the COW operationalization and definition of war will be to these questions in the future and, indeed, to the bulk of violent international conflict since World War II.

The second-largest number of wars that are excluded from the COW list but were included on the Richardson and Wright lists were variations of civil wars.[41] For the 1945-65 period, COW lists only 12 wars, six of which were interstate and six extrasystemic. For approximately the same time period, Istvan Kende lists 97 "wars,"[42] with his typology based heavily on the post-World War II phenomena of internally oriented conflict with outside intervention.* For 1945-64, Wright lists 30 "hostilities" that reached Richardson's 3.0 level of deadliness.[43] Summarizing eleven lists of postwar conflicts, researchers at the Stockholm International Peace Research Institute (SIPRI) find 53 conflicts ranging up to the 3.0 magnitude of deadliness and 43 greater than 3.0.[44] At the furthest point from the COW list of 12 is Edward Azar's discussion of 559 "wars, domestic upheavals, and large-scale hostilities" in the period 1945-70.[45]

---

*Istvan Kende, "Twenty-Five Years of Local Wars," Journal of Peace Research 8, no. 1 (1971): 5-27, also argues that the locus of war has changed, that the site of war has moved outside Europe to Asia, Africa and Latin America. For postwar conflicts he indicates that Europe is the site of the fewest wars, with 4; Asia with 29; the Middle East with 25; Africa with 16; and America with 23. For the 93 wars on the COW list, Europe is the site of the most, with 33; followed by Asia with 27; the Middle East with 19;

Quite clearly, lists of different lengths result from different operational criteria. The issue raised here is whether the criteria of the COW project will prove the most useful in the study of war in the contemporary period or whether COW will only be able to provide knowledge about a type of international phenomenon that has existed for the most part in the past. If the last is true, the future utility of this data as an important descriptive product of COW is greatly reduced.

The description of war constitutes only a portion of the existential output of the COW project, however. Briefly, we may highlight a number of additional contributions. A step that was necessarily prior to the presentation of international system membership was the development of data on diplomatic representation. These data were presented first by Singer and Small, covering 1815-1940.[46] Nations were awarded points for composite raw scores of status based on the diplomatic representation they received from others. For each half-decade from 1815 to 1940, the nations were listed by rank according to their composite raw scores and composite standardized scores (raw scores divided by the highest score for that year) and also by a "weighted status score." This latter score was based on the raw scores of nations sending missions, since an ambassador from France would be worth much more than one from say, Peru.* Data were presented for each time period, not only by international system membership, but also longitudinally for each nation. Thus the data permit a historical view of each nation and the demonstration of continuity or steady or dramatic rises or declines in the statuses of individual states through time.

These data have been brought up to date, providing scores for the 1950-70 period.[47] Ironically, the analysis performed here demonstrates that the simple number of missions received, without any form of weighting for mission type or weight of sender, is as good an indicator as any of the weighted measures, since, for example, the scores weighted by type of mission produced a rank

---

the Western Hemisphere with 16; and Africa with 8. This again argues for a change in the phenomenon under study, which would restrict the utility of the Eurocentric sample of COW wars. J. David Singer and Melvin Small, in The Wages of War, 1816-1965: A Statistical Handbook (New York: John Wiley and Sons, 1972), p. 296, note this Eurocentricity and caution the reader against cross-regional comparisons.

*It is unclear why the authors, after standardizing the raw scores, did not also standardize the weighted scores in order to control for the steady upward secular trend of the data set.

order correlation of .99 with simple number of missions received. For the period 1950-70 the nations were ranked both according to number of missions received and as normalized, by missions received as a percentage of total system members.

These data are useful not only for aid in operationalizing system membership but also to tap in some way the importance or status of states. As argued by Small and Singer, the decision to send missions reflects a number of opportunity costs, in terms both of limited resources and of political opposition, domestic and foreign.[48] The original COW data, in addition to covering far longer time periods than other studies of diplomatic representation, were also published before the appearance of other studies.[49] In addition, these data formed the basis of Michael Wallace's study of status and war.

In a similar manner, two articles by Singer and Small set out a quantitative description of international alliances.[50] The only other extensive list of alliances is that of Bruce Russett, which "draws upon and extends" the COW list.[51] However, Russett does not present his data in the body of the article. His list covers a much shorter time period (1920-57) and includes both universal and wartime alliances; thus he delineates 137 alliances, while the COW list for 1816-1965 contains 172 alliances.* Since the research interest of COW was in alliance as an independent ecological variable and as a possible correlate of war, a different set of concerns from those of Russett, all alliances formed during war or three months prior to war were excluded. Again this limits the usefulness of the COW data for a number of possible research questions on alliance. Still, for each alliance COW provides the dates of effective inception and termination of the alliance for each member and for each type of alliance based on the nature of the treaty commitment. For both, the total system and the central system alliance commitments, measured by a number of indicators, were aggregated annually, 1815-1939.†

---

*Harvey Starr, in War Coalitions: The Distribution of Payoffs and Losses (Lexington, Mass.: D. C. Heath, 1972), lists 36 wartime "coalitions" in the period 1820-1967.

†J. David Singer and Melvin Small, in "National Alliance Commitments and War Involvement, 1815-1945," Papers of the Peace Research Society 5 (1966): 109-140, present data for 12 alliance variables and 5 war indicators, with the data arrayed for the nation as the unit of analysis. Thus data for alliance, as with war, can be viewed from both the aggregated systemic perspective or from the level of the individual nation-state. A full descriptive analysis

Ole R. Holsti, P. Terrence Hopmann, and John D. Sullivan note that "Even a cursory examination of the literature reveals a distinct shortage of research that is designed to shed light on the central issues of alliance theory and is also documented with data derived by explicit and systematic methods."[52] The work of Singer and Small is explicitly cited as an exception.

Finally, Michael Wallace and J. David Singer developed a data set covering IGOs in the international system from 1816 to 1964, again presenting data that had previously been uncollected.[53] For each half decade they developed three measures of the amount of IGO in the system: (1) the number of qualifying IGOs, (2) the total number of nation memberships, and (3) a weighted index of nation memberships reflecting the diplomatic importance of each member belonging to the IGO. Given their criteria for nation memberships they were able to set out the number of IGO memberships in each period, by nation. With an additional six measures of periodic change in the amount of IGO, they were able to demonstrate the "dramatic upward trend" in growth rates in the number of IGOs, in the number of nations, and in simple and weighted nation memberships "even with the flattening effect of the logarithmic transformation."[54] Some additional descriptive data is added by Kjell Skjelsbaek in a later article.[55]

Assessing the "existential" knowledge derived from the COW project has brought to light both strengths and weaknesses. We have demonstrated a substantial increase in our knowledge of what international relations looks like. Still, the relevance of some of the operational rules has been called into question, especially in regard to war and alliance. Questions about the validity of these measures must also be taken into account in assessing the overall impact of the project. Let us simply sum up this section with a statement from the conclusion of Wallace and Singer, which may be generalized to work performed on the other independent variables.

> As is quite clear, we have tested no hypotheses, confirmed no models, and demonstrated no statistical or causal relationships. . . . This report is intended for those who have wearied of the isolated case studies and the endless speculations which have characterized much of the work in international organization [such as in wars and alliances] and who want to progress from hunches to

---

of this data is presented in Bruce Bueno De Mesquita and J. David Singer, "Alliance, Capabilities, and War: A Review and Synthesis," Political Science Annual 4 (1973): 237-80.

hypotheses and from impressions to evidence. With the data presented here, a good many propositions . . . can now be put to the test.[56]

Correlational Knowledge

Following from the above citation, we may say that a certain basis of existential knowledge must be established before we can move on to correlational knowledge, that is, the extent of covariation between two sets of indicators. Practically all of the remaining increment to our knowledge of international relations derived from the Correlates of War project falls into this category.

Overall, the contribution of the project to correlational knowledge does not appear to be as significant as its existential contribution. This opinion reflects several issues to be noted below. It would be foolhardy to attempt to review the numerous relationships, unfortunately almost all bivariate, that are discussed in the published research findings of the project. Instead the reader is directed to Appendix A for a list of the major research findings of COW organized by variable. The utility of such findings follows closely on the idea of existential knowledge and may be characterized by the aforementioned notion of "brush-clearing." Given one's view of the state of the art in international relations study and of the payoffs expected from certain research methodologies, one's evaluation of these results might range from highly useful, in the sense that induction paves the way for more complex theory and results, to disappointing, given the resources expended.

As noted, instead of reviewing the individual findings of these studies, I will raise several issues relating to their value. First, a closer and more careful examination of the dependent variables in these studies is required. As Dina A. Zinnes has noted, the dependent variable in most cases is the amount of war in the international system.[57] As Zinnes also notes, this is generally operationalized, not by a frequency count of the number of wars or the number of wars begun, but usually by the magnitude and severity of war. Michael Wallace explicitly says, "Since the frequency of the outbreak of war is hardly a sensitive indicator either of conflict or of the amount of war occurring in the international system, two more sophisticated indices . . . were employed here."[58] Since analysis usually involves systemic aggregations for the half decade, magnitude generally refers to the total months of war for all nations, resulting from all wars begun in that half decade. Similarly, severity refers to the total number of battle deaths resulting from all wars begun within a certain period. Indeed, Wallace notes that battle deaths resulting from wars begun within five-year periods has been the most sensitive of the war involvement indicators.59

This means that the indicators of the dependent variable actually represent the size and severity of war and whatever factors create large wars and keep wars going. Admittedly these are important questions, but they are different from the questions of the "incidence" or the "onset" of war or of the "war-proneness" of nations, which have been presented as the main thrust of COW research.60 Singer and Small have presented a study of alliances that is one of the few studies that actually uses "number of wars begun" as an indicator of the dependent variable.61 This indicator is found to correlate positively, but not very well, with magnitude and severity indicators for the total system (ranging from .24 to .35) and for the central system (.47 to .54). This would seem to demonstrate that these indicators represent different aspects of "war." Although all these aspects are important in the study of war, the point is that they are not the same. Despite the impression conveyed, the correlational studies produced by COW are generally not devoted to the analysis of factors associated with the onset of war. Zinnes has suggested two alternative measures for the onset of war: either a dichotomous war/no war coding for each nation (or dyad) at a certain point in time, or a crude indicator of the "probability" of war at the systemic level.62 This would involve dividing the number of dyads at war by all possible nation pairs in the system. The point is, simply, that there is difficulty in interpreting the results, given the indicators of the dependent variable employed in most of these studies. What exactly is being correlated with what? This difficulty in interpretation weakens the overall significance of the correlational findings.

A second difficulty concerns the broad question of underanalysis. With the material available, it would seem that further questions, of multivariate relationships in particular, could be pursued. Since chapter 3 and chapter 4 of this volume deal more fully with this question, suffice it to note the overwhelming bivariate nature of the analysis and the basically linear view of the world inherent in the analysis. Such operations as the use of curvilinear models, the search for thresholds, and step-level functions would have been valuable in many instances. For contrast, a useful application of curvilinear models is presented by Wallace in the investigation of alliance polarization and war.63 This point, again, is one of omission more than one of commission, but it is important given the question of cost.

The "So what?" question takes on added meaning if the enterprise producing the research has absorbed large amounts of resources. The results that are discussed under existential and correlational

SUBSTANTIVE FINDINGS   113

knowledge and summarized in Appendix A may be very useful, but
it is at least fair to raise the issue of cost in terms of time, money,
and man-hours.* One striking way to assess the findings of the project in relation to the cost of the effort is to compare its results with
those of another research effort. For simple comparison, Appendix
B presents a list of the findings summarized by Singer in "The
'Correlates of War' Project: Interim Report and Rationale"[64] and
a list of the major findings in the editor's introduction to Richardson's
Statistics of Deadly Quarrels,[65] as summarized by Quincy Wright.
Note first the approximate comparability of many of the findings
(for example, that the first item on each list notes that there has
been no increase in the frequency of war). One must then consider
the disparity in resources involved: personnel, funding, and the
opportunity costs of such funding. The question of cost—was it
worth it?—cannot be answered. There exist no suitable criteria
for an answer (published pages per dollar? findings per man-year?);
yet although the question cannot be resolved, it remains a legitimate
area of concern and must be raised.

Given the problems discussed, there are a number of positive
points to be made. The correlational results include the testing
and analysis of Galtungian status theory by Wallace, the testing of
bipolarity theories and other propositions concerning alliances by
Singer and Small and by Bueno de Mesquita and Singer, and the
testing of the effects of power distribution by Singer, Bremer, and
Stuckey. A review of Appendix A will also reveal the scope of the
findings, combining broad temporal and spacial generality with the
analysis of truncated systemic and temporal domains. Much of what
has been produced is new, while much reinforces previous work.
While the project is impressive in these and other respects, hopefully the reader has been alerted by the above discussion to issues,
such as that of the validity of indicators, that limit the impact of
the project on the current state of our correlational knowledge.

Causal Knowledge

Singer defines causal or explanatory knowledge as "the extent
to which a given class of outcomes or events was 'caused' by a
given sequence of prior conditions or events."[66] Wallace contends
that investigation must now go beyond correlation and into causal

---

*The principal supportive agencies for the project have been the
Carnegie Corporation; the Center for Research on Conflict Resolution
at the University of Michigan; and the National Science Foundation.

sequences and seeks to determine the sequences that link status inconsistency to war.[67] Again there is ambiguity over the dependent variable. In the abstract Wallace indicates he will investigate the links between status inconsistency with the "outbreak of conflict." His dependent variable as defined later in the article, however, is the number of battle deaths that result from all war begun within the half decade. This, it seems to me, is not the same as "outbreak of war."

Wallace modifies his earlier work in order to develop a multivariate explanatory model. Severity of war is the dependent variable, while there are eight independent variables, which are (1) change in population, (2) change in military personnel, (3) change in diplomatic status, (4) difference between population and diplomatic status, (5) difference between military personnel and diplomatic status, (6) number of alliances, (7) growth in IGOs, and (8) growth in armed forces. Each is aggregated for the international system by half-decade rather than by nation because of an "identification" problem.[68]

Using "dependence analysis," Wallace investigates the "causal" paths to the severity of war. The findings are quite interesting. Wallace confirms the effects of status inconsistency on both the dependent and intervening variables and confirms the link between status inconsistency and alliance aggregation. Alliance aggregation is found to affect war indirectly through the indicator of armed forces expansion (alliance ⟶ arms ⟶ war). Thus alliance commitment is important in linking status inconsistency and war. The most striking finding is the direct and powerful effect changes in armed forces levels have on war, as "the tensions generated by these structural variables [status inconsistency and alliance commitments] were translated into actual armed conflict primarily via increases in the size of armed forces."[69] This finding is of great importance in regard to the development of peace strategies; because of this, a fuller discussion of the data used is required. The forthcoming two books by Singer and Small and by Singer, Wallace, and Bremer will be useful in this regard.[70]

The problem with assessing the explanatory-knowledge aspect of COW, of course, is that we must stop here. The Wallace piece contains the only multivariate causal analysis thus far published through the COW project. Hopefully, the next time a similar review is undertaken, the section on causal knowledge will be much more extensive. This will depend upon how well the project builds upon the extant existential and correlational base. Most importantly, further causal work will depend upon how well the design of the project fulfills the tasks of theory building and cumulation.[71]

CONCLUSION

In spite of the questions and qualifications raised in the above pages, a general appraisal of the substantive findings of the Correlates of War project should be a positive one. Singer and his colleagues have provided us with many statements on war and the international system that are backed by "reproducible evidence." While the actual testing of models has not been extensive, a certain amount of "plausible speculation" has been put to the empirical test. The greatest strength of the enterprise rests in the development of the data base, from which we may test speculation with reproducible evidence. The increment to our existential knowledge of international relations has been substantial. In this sense the project has helped us see what international relations look like and how the "traces" of the international environment are distributed and patterned; that is, it has helped us "to calibrate the world."[72] In the same vein COW has not permitted the macroquantitative study of war pioneered by Wright and by Richardson to wither. While there continue to be a number of important quantitative studies of war, only COW has continued the macroquantitative, or "politimetric," approach, building upon and refining the data base of Wright and Richardson.

The overall verdict on the Correlates of War project has yet to come in, since many of the project goals have yet to be reached. However, much of the data base that is necessary for this work to be done and that will help others attack these questions is available. Singer has criticized Wright's lack of analysis, given the data that had been collected. This assertion can just as validly be applied to COW; however, just as the data enterprise of Wright was indispensable to the COW project, so is that of the COW project significant for the future study of war.

APPENDIX A

Findings of the Correlates of War Project

<u>War</u>

1. The distribution of wars by nation-months fits the log normal distribution. (g)

The letter following each item refers to the source of the finding. Sources are listed at the end of each appendix.

2. The wars that rank high on severity (battle deaths) also rank high on nation-months, or magnitude, and intensity. (g)
3. The interstate wars that engaged more nations also caused more battle deaths per nation-month, but fewer per capita. (g)
4. There have been no significant secular trends; war is neither on the rise or the decline: there has been no significant trend from 1816 to 1965, either in number of wars, in severity, or in magnitude. (g)
5. There is no periodicity in terms of war begun; which fits a Poisson distribution. (g)
6. While there is periodicity of between 20 and 40 years for amount of war underway, there is no periodicity for nations experiencing three or more wars. (g)
7. More wars begin in the spring and autumn, with April and October the most war-prone months. (g)
8. The technology of war, of communications, and of agriculture seem to have had little effect on seasonal concentrations of war beginnings. (g)
9. Most interstate war has been fought in Europe by European nations, with England, France, Turkey, and Russia the most war-prone nations; most of the war in the system has been accounted for by major powers. (g)
10. There is no demonstration of traditional enmities and friendships; a general randomness in choice of allies or enemies is shown. (g)
11. The initiators win over 70 percent of wars; the nations that have done the best in terms of war success, Britain, France, and Russia, are all among the major powers. (g)
12. Winning and losing is not related to battle fatalities ratios. (g)

Diplomatic Importance of States

13. Since 1816 the distribution of ambassadors has risen from 15 percent to 88 percent, while the distribution of ministers has fallen from 72 percent to 5 percent. (j)
14. The number of missions a nation receives relates very highly to the weighting schemes also devised. (j)
15. Diplomatic rankings generally show major powers at the top, with 'pariah' states scoring lower. (j)
16. Nonaligned nations outrank their NATO and WTO counterparts in diplomatic representation scores. (j)
17. Small but centrally placed states show up with higher rankings than expected, while the more peripheral actors score in the lowest groups. (j)
18. Peripheral states move up in diplomatic rankings as they industrialize and/or seek increasingly active roles in the system. (j)

Status Inconsistency

19. The correlations between status inconsistency and the magnitude and severity of war get higher as one moves from 5- to 10- to 15-year lags; these are positive and do better for the nineteenth century than for the twentieth. (k)
20. Using multiple regression, status inconsistency explains more variance in magnitude of systemic war for the 1850-1964 period ($r^2 = .71$) than for any other. (k)
21. For 1820-1964, a range of status inconsistency variables correlates positively with severity of war. (l)
22. There exists a positive link between status inconsistency and alliance aggregation; alliances affect war indirectly, through rate of change in size of armed forces. (l)
23. Status inconsistency has a strong negative effect on the rate of growth of membership in IGOs. (l)
24. Increases in arms levels appear to be the key factors in transforming the structural tensions of the international system, including those of status inconsistency, into a tendency toward belligerency. (l)
25. Status inconsistency was an intervening variable between national mobility and war. (l)

Alliances

26. There were 148 formal alliances discovered (1815-1965): 73 defense, 39 neutrality, and 36 ententes, with the average alliance lasting 98 months; average size at inception, 2.43 nations; average maximum size, 2.53 nations; with major powers making up over 40 percent of the average coalition. (b) (Different figures are given in j.)
27. Only a fraction of the nations chose to enter alliances, with only 30 percent of all nations joining an alliance in the nineteenth century and 38 percent in the twentieth; for major powers the equivalent figures are 65 percent and 69 percent, however. (b)
28. There has been no steady trend in the growth or decline of the percentage of nations in alliance. (b)
29. Defense pacts have accounted for the most alliances: 61 percent in the nineteenth century, 46 percent in the twentieth, and 49 percent overall. (b)
30. Alliance commitments do make a difference in how nations behave in terms of aiding nations at war, fighting them, or remaining neutral. (d)
31. Partners in defense alliances tend to honor them, and entente partners tend much more to fight alongside each other than

against each other; neutrality pact commitments are less frequently honored. (o)
32. An individual nation's alliance commitments are positively related to its war involvement; this is stronger for the twentieth century than the nineteenth and for central system members; many correlations disappear when years of system membership are included. (e)
33. For the international system in the 1815-1945 period, aggregations of alliance commitment and measures of bipolarity correlate weakly but positively with subsequent war. (f)
34. However, this relationship is negative–predicts strongly away from war–for the nineteenth century and positive for the twentieth century. (f)
35. There appears to be no relationship between the power distribution within an alliance and its durability. (b)
36. The size of an alliance seems to be positively related, especially in the nineteenth century, to the durability of the alliance. (b)
37. In the twentieth century, alliance involvement of major powers appears to be related to subsequent, 5-year lag, concentration of power. (b)
38. There appears to be no linear relationship between alliance polarization in the international system and the magnitude and severity of wars begun in subsequent periods. (m)
39. There is a curvilinear relationship between alliance polarization and conflict in the international system, with war more probable at very low and very high levels of polarization. (m)

Intergovernmental Organizations

40. For 1815-1964, measures of IGOs, as well as system size, increase in an approximately linear fashion with time, for example, for the number of IGOs and for simple nation memberships in IGOs. (n)
41. There is almost no relationship between amount of IGO and subsequent amount of war in the international system. (h)
42. There is a positive relationship between the amount of war ending in the international system and subsequent increases in IGOs, ten years following; thus while IGO does not appear to affect the amount of war, the amount of war seems to precede the development of more IGOs. (h)
43. Increases in IGO membership seem to decrease the severity of subsequent wars. (l)
44. The greater the severity of war, the greater the growth in the number and size of IGOs. (i)
45. Shared IGO memberships do not predict well to war in the 1910-1964 period. (i)

SUBSTANTIVE FINDINGS 119

46. The shared IGO memberships of opponents tend to diminish in the two decades prior to the outbreak of war; however, so do those of war partners, but not to the same degree. (i)
47. After war, shared IGO memberships of opponents stay about the same, with some decrease. (i)
48. At every point ($t-2$, t_0, $t+2$), pairs of war partners generally have more shared memberships than pairs of opponents. (i)

Power Distribution

49. An additive version of a model that predicts that there will be less war when there is approximate parity in the power distribution among nations and a relatively fluid power hierarchy works very well in explaining the variance of nation-months of war during the nineteenth century ($R^2 = .73$). (c)
50. A multiplicative version of a model that predicts there will be less war when there is a preponderance of power concentrated in few nations, and when there is a fairly stable rank order among major powers, provides the best explanation of variance ($R^2 = .46$) in the twentieth century. (c)

Population Density

51. When controlling for technological development and for nation-specific differences such as culture, no relationship is found between various measures of population density (or crowding) and measures of war participation for European nations. (a)
52. For European nations, the initiators of war were generally urbanizing faster than the nations that were attacked. (a)

Sources: (a) Stuart Bremer, J. David Singer, and Urs Luterbacher, "The Population Density and War Proneness of European Nations, 1816-1965," Comparative Political Studies 6, no. 3 (1973): 329-48; (b) Bruce Bueno de Mesquita and J. David Singer, "Alliances, Capabilities, and War: A Review and Synthesis," Political Science Annual 4 (1973): 237-80; (c) J. David Singer, Stuart Bremer, and John Stuckey, "Capability Distribution, Uncertainty, and Major Power War, 1820-1965," in Peace, War, and Numbers, edited by Bruce M. Russett (Beverly Hills: Sage Publications, 1972), pp. 19-48;

(d) J. David Singer and Melvin Small, "Formal Alliances, 1815-1939: A Quantitative Description," Journal of Peace Research 3, no. 1 (1966): 1-32; (e) J. David Singer and Melvin Small, "National Alliance Commitments and War Involvement, 1815-1945," Peace Research Society (International) Papers, 5 (1966): 109-140; (f) J. David Singer and Melvin Small, "Alliance Aggregation and the Onset of War,

1815-1945," in Quantitative International Politics: Insights and Evidence, edited by J. David Singer (New York: Free Press, 1968), pp. 247-86;

(g) J. David Singer and Melvin Small, The Wages of War, 1816-1965, A Statistical Handbook (New York: John Wiley and Sons, 1972); (h) J. David Singer and Michael Wallace, "Inter-Governmental Organization and the Preservation of Peace, 1816-1965: Some Bivariate Relationships," International Organization 24, no. 3 (1970): 520-47; (i) Kjell Skjelsbaek, "Shared Membership in Intergovernmental Organizations and Dyadic War, 1865-1964," in The United Nations: Problems and Prospects, edited by Edwin Fedder (St. Louis: Center for International Studies, 1971), pp. 31-61;

(j) Melvin Small and J. David Singer, "The Diplomatic Importance of States, 1816-1970: An Extension and Refinement of the Indicator," World Politics 25, no. 4 (1973): 577-99; (k) Michael Wallace, "Power, Status, and International War," Journal of Peace Research 8, no. 1 (1971): 23-35; (l) Michael Wallace, "Status, Formal Organization and Arms Levels as Factors Leading to the Onset of War, 1820-1924," in Peace, War, and Numbers, edited by Bruce M. Russett (Beverly Hills: Sage Publications, 1972), pp. 49-69;

(m) Michael Wallace, "Alliance Polarization, Cross-Cutting, and International War, 1815-1964: A Measurement Procedure and Some Preliminary Evidence," Journal of Conflict Resolution 17, no. 4 (1973): 575-604; (n) Michael Wallace and J. David Singer, "Intergovernmental Organization in the Global System, 1816-1964: A Quantitative Description," International Organization 24, no. 2 (1970): 239-87; (o) Melvin Small and J. David Singer, "Formal Alliances 1816-1965: An Extension of the Basic Data," Journal of Peace Research 6, no. 3 (1969): 257-82.

APPENDIX B

Summaries of Research Findings: "Correlates of War" and Statistics of Deadly Quarrels

Major Findings of the Correlates of War Project

1. There was no increase in the frequency of interstate war.
2. Extrasystemic wars increased in the nineteenth century and decreased in the twentieth.
3. There was only a modest increase in the severity and magnitude of war, 1816-1965.
4. The amount of war underway shows a strong periodicity in the 20- to 40-year range.

SUBSTANTIVE FINDINGS   121

5. The most interstate war was fought in Europe by European nations.
6. England, France, Turkey, and Russia are the most war-prone nations.
7. There is a general randomness in the choice of allies and enemies.
8. Initiators were victorious in 34 of 50 interstate wars.
9. The victors suffered fewer battle deaths than the losers in 36 cases, with several outstanding exceptions.
10. There appears to be no clear battle-death threshold at which the defeated tend to surrender.
11. When intra-European war levels are high, those involving non-European adversaries are low, and vice-versa.
12. The amount of IGO in the system has no visible effect on the incidence of war; the IGO growth rate decreases before war and increases after war.
13. Former allies show a mild postwar decline in shared IGO memberships; former enemies show a clear increase.
14. Alliances are negatively related to war in the nineteenth century and positively related in the twentieth.
15. The more alliance bonds a nation has, the more war it experiences in the next several years during either century.
16. Alliance partners are fairly likely to honor their commitments.
17. A high concentration in the capabilities of the major powers led to more war in the nineteenth century but to less in the twentieth.
18. Although major powers do account for a disproportionate share of all war activity, there seems to be no strong relationship between a given war-proneness and its power rank, share of resources, or changes therein.
19. The greater the differences between distributions of diplomatic importance and capabilities, the more war the system will experience.
20. There seems to be no relationship between the growth rate of the population of a nation and its density and war-proneness.
21. Most interstate wars are between nations that are not only close together geographically, but quite similar on most other attribute dimensions.

Major Findings of Statistics of Deadly Quarrels

1. Wars seem to have been distributed by chance in time (beginning and end), with no evidence of increasing or decreasing frequency; there is evidence of oscillation in the frequency of wars in periods of nine to 144 years.
2. From 1820-1949, loss of life from deadly quarrels accounted for 1.6 percent of all deaths.

3. The increase in world population during this period appears not to have been accompanied by a proportionate increase in frequency of war or loss of life in war.
4. Though states vary greatly in their participation in war, none can be characterized as inherently pacific or belligerent.
5. States have tended to become involved in wars in proportion to the number of states with which they have common frontiers.
6. Common citizenship has not assured peace, but there do seem to be pacifying influences in common government, intermarriage, and common culture; the actual occurrence of war has been far less than would be expected from the opportunities for war presented by geographical contiguity.
7. The longer groups have been united by a common government, the less has been the probability of war between them.
8. Alliances seem to have some influence of preventing war between former allies, but the influence declines with the passage of time.
9. Desire for revenge seems to have been an important cause of war during this period, declining with time but rising slightly after a generation.
10. Economic causes seem to have figured directly in less than 29 percent of the wars; relative wealth and poverty seem to have little influence, as opposed to Marxist assumptions.
11. Similarities or differences of language seem to have had little influence on the occurrence of wars during this period.
12. Similarity of religion does not seem to have made for peace (except perhaps for Confucianism), but differences in religion seem to have caused war.
13. The larger the number of belligerents in a war, the more neutrals have tended to be drawn in; wars with many participants have tended to be longer and less frequent.
14. Most wars have been localized; neutrals have tended to become belligerents only if two or more major powers have been involved.
15. In proportion to their possible contacts for war-making, sea powers seem to have been less belligerent than land powers.
16. International relations cannot be considered a chaotic field with all nations equally likely to be infected with war; geographical relations have exerted great influence.

Sources: J. David Singer, "The 'Correlates of War' Project: Interim Report and Rationale," World Politics 24, no. 2 (1972): 265-67; Lewis F. Richardson, Statistics of Deadly Quarrels (Chicago: Quadrangle Books, 1960), pp. ix-xiii.

NOTES

1. New York Times, May 6, 1971, p. 45.
2. Unfortunately, two books which would have added greatly to the scope of the data produced and the variables operationalized are still forthcoming at the time of this writing: J. David Singer and Melvin Small, The Strength of Nations: Comparative Capabilities Since Waterloo, forthcoming; and J. David Singer, Michael Wallace, and Stuart Bremer, A Structural History of the International System, 1816-1965, forthcoming.
3. J. David Singer, "Modern International War: From Conjecture to Explanation," in The Search for World Order: Essays in Honor of Quincy Wright, edited by Albert Lepawsky, Edward Buehrig, and Harold Lasswell (New York: Appleton-Century-Crofts, 1971), p. 56.
4. J. David Singer, "The 'Correlates of War' Project: Interim Report and Rationale," World Politics 24, no. 2 (1972): 243.
5. J. David Singer, "From a Study of War to Peace Research: Some Criteria and Strategies," Journal of Conflict Resolution 14, no. 4 (1970): 527-42; Singer, "Modern International War," op. cit.; "The 'Correlates of War' Project," op. cit.
6. See Singer, "The 'Correlates of War' Project," op. cit., p. 245, and J. David Singer, "Escalation and Control in International Conflict: A Simple Feedback Model," General Systems 15 (1970): 163-73.
7. J. David Singer and Melvin Small, The Wages of War, 1816-1965: A Statistical Handbook (New York: John Wiley and Sons, 1972), p. 376.
8. Singer, "Escalation and Control," op. cit., p. 163.
9. J. David Singer and Melvin Small, "National Alliance Commitments and War Involvement, 1815-1945," Peace Research Society, Papers, 5 (1966): 109-140. See also Singer and Small, Wages of War, op. cit., chapter 11.
10. Kjell Skjelsbaek, "Shared Membership in Intergovernmental Organizations and Dyadic War, 1865-1964," in The United Nations: Problems and Prospects, edited by Edwin Fedder (St. Louis: Center for International Studies, 1971), pp. 31-61.
11. See Singer, "Modern International War," op. cit., p. 66.
12. See Singer, "The 'Correlates of War' Project," op. cit., p. 246.
13. Singer and Small, Wages of War, op. cit., pp. 377-78.
14. Singer, "The 'Correlates of War' Project," op. cit., p. 268.
15. Singer, "From a Study of War to Peace Research," op. cit.; "Modern International War," op. cit.; and "The 'Correlates of War' Project," op. cit.

16. Singer, "From a Study of War to Peace Research," op. cit., p. 536.

17. See Lewis F. Richardson, Statistics of Deadly Quarrels (Chicago: Quadrangle Books, 1960), for an example of an attempt to measure the incidence of war against a variety of possible "opportunities" for war. See also Harvey Starr, "'Opportunity' and 'Willingness' as Ordering Concepts in the Study of War" (mimeographed, Bloomington: Indiana University, 1975).

18. Singer, "From a Study of War to Peace Research," op. cit.

19. Richardson, Statistics of Deadly Quarrels, op. cit., and Quincy Wright, A Study of War (2nd ed., Chicago: University of Chicago Press, 1965). A list of works by scholars not connected with COW who have utilized COW data would include: Steven Rosen, "War Power and the Willingness to Suffer," in Peace, War, and Numbers, edited by Bruce M. Russett (Beverly Hills: Sage Publications, 1972), pp. 167-83; Maurice A. East, "Status Discrepancy and Violence in the International System: An Empirical Analysis," in The Analysis of International Politics, edited by James N. Rosenau, Vincent Davis, and Maurice A. East (New York: Free Press, 1972), pp. 299-319; Harvey Starr, War Coalitions: The Distribution of Payoffs and Losses (Lexington, Mass.: D. C. Heath, 1972); Wayne H. Ferris, The Power Capabilities of Nation-States (Lexington, Mass.: D. C. Heath, 1973); Ole R. Holsti, P. Terrence Hopmann, and John D. Sullivan, Unity and Disintegration in International Alliances (New York: Wiley-Interscience, 1973); Brian L. Job, "Alliance Formation in the International System: The Application of the Poisson Model," paper prepared for the International Studies Association Meeting, New York, March 1973; Manus I. Midlarsky, "Power, Uncertainty, and the Onset of International Violence, Journal of Conflict Resolution 18, no. 3 (1974): 395-431.

20. Bruce M. Russett, J. David Singer and Melvin Small, "National Political Units in the Twentieth Century: A Standardized List," American Political Science Review 62, no. 3 (1968): 932.

21. See J. David Singer and Melvin Small, "The Composition and Status Ordering of the International System: 1815-1940," World Politics 18, no. 2 (1966): 236-82; Melvin Small and J. David Singer, "The Diplomatic Importance of States, 1816-1970: An Extension and Refinement of the Indicator," World Politics 25, no. 4 (1973): 577-99; Russett, Singer and Small, "National Political Units," op. cit.

22. Singer and Small, Wages of War, op. cit.

23. See J. David Singer, "Data-Making in International Relations," Behavioral Science 10, no. 1 (1965): 68-80.

24. For example, see Singer and Small, "Composition and Status Ordering," op. cit., p. 236.

25. Ted Robert Gurr, Politimetrics (Englewood Cliffs: Prentice-Hall, 1972), p. 77.

26. Gordon Hilton, A Review of the Dimensionality of Nations Project (London: Richardson Institute for Conflict and Peace Research, 1971).

27. J. David Singer, Stuart Bremer, and John Stuckey, "Capability Distribution, Uncertainty, and Major Power War, 1820-1965," in Peace, War, and Numbers, edited by Bruce M. Russett (Beverly Hills: Sage Publications, 1972), p. 21.

28. J. David Singer, The Scientific Study of Politics: An Approach to Foreign Policy Analysis (Morristown, N.J.: General Learning Press, 1972).

29. Ibid., p. 9.

30. Ibid.

31. Singer and Small, Wages of War, op. cit.

32. Ibid., Chapter 5.

33. Ibid., Appendix A.

34. Ibid., p. 374.

35. See also Melvin Small and J. David Singer, "Patterns of International Warfare, 1816-1965," Annals of the American Academy of Political and Social Science 391 (1970): 145-55, and Singer and Small, Wages of War, op. cit., pp. 374-76.

36. Singer and Small, Wages of War, op. cit., p. 374.

37. Gurr, Politimetrics, op. cit., p. 32.

38. Richardson, Deadly Quarrels, op. cit., pp. 173-174, and Quincy Wright, A Study of War, op. cit., Appendices XIX, XX.

39. Steven Rosen, "War Power and the Willingness to Suffer," op. cit.

40. See Harvey Starr, Coalitions and Future War: A Dyadic Study of Cooperation and Conflict (Beverly Hills: Sage Publications, 1975).

41. See Singer and Small, Wages of War, op. cit., p. 201.

42. Istvan Kende, "Twenty-Five Years of Local Wars," Journal of Peace Research 8, no. 1 (1971): 5-27.

43. Wright, Study of War, op. cit., pp. 1544-47.

44. Stockholm International Peace Research Institute, Year-Book of World Armaments and Disarmament, 1968/69 (Stockholm: Almqvist and Wiksele, 1970), pp. 365-72.

45. Edward Azar, Probe for Peace: Small State Hostilities (Minneapolis: Burgess Publishing, 1973).

46. Singer and Small, "Composition and Status Ordering," op. cit.

47. Small and Singer, "Diplomatic Importance of States," op. cit.

48. Ibid., p. 582.

49. For example, Chadwick Alger and Steve Brams used data only for 1963-64 in their 1967 article, "Patterns of Representation in National Capitals and International Organizations," World Politics 19, no. 4 (1967): 646-63. Bruce M. Russett and Curtis Lamb, in "Global Patterns of Diplomatic Exchange, 1963-64," Journal of Peace Research 6, no. 1 (1969): 37-55, also looked at 1963-64. Again, 1958 was the only year analyzed by Robert Bernstein and Peter Weldon, in "A Structural Approach to the Analysis of International Relations," Journal of Conflict Resolution 12, no. 2 (1968): 159-81.

50. J. David Singer and Melvin Small, "Formal Alliances, 1815-1939: A Quantitative Description," Journal of Peace Research 3, no. 1 (1966): 1-32, and Melvin Small and J. David Singer, "Formal Alliances 1816-1965: An Extension of the Basic Data," Journal of Peace Research 6, no. 3 (1969): 257-82.

51. Bruce M. Russett, "An Empirical Typology of International Alliances," Midwest Journal of Political Science 15, no. 2 (1971): 262-89.

52. Ole R. Holsti, P. Terrence Hopmann, and John D. Sullivan, Unity and Disintegration in International Alliances: Comparative Studies (New York: Wiley-Interscience, 1973), p. 42.

53. Michael Wallace and J. David Singer, "Intergovernmental Organization in the Global System, 1816-1964: A Quantitative Description," International Organization 24, no. 2 (1970): 239-87.

54. Ibid., p. 275.

55. Skjelsbaek, "Shared Membership," op. cit.

56. Wallace and Singer, "Intergovernmental Organization," op. cit., p. 284.

57. Dina A. Zinnes, Contemporary Research in International Relations (New York: Free Press, forthcoming), Chapter 9.

58. Michael Wallace, "Power, Status, and International War," Journal of Peace Research 8, no. 1 (1971): 25.

59. Michael Wallace, "Status, Formal Organization and Arms Levels as Factors Leading to the Onset of War, 1820-1964," in Peace, War and Numbers, edited by Bruce M. Russett (Beverly Hills: Sage Publications, 1972), p. 57.

60. See Singer and Small, Wages of War, op. cit., p. 377; J. David Singer and Melvin Small, "Alliance Aggregation and the Onset of War, 1815-1945," in Quantitative International Politics, edited by J. David Singer (New York: Free Press, 1968), pp. 247-86; Singer, Bremer, and Stuckey, "Capability Distribution," op. cit., p. 21.

61. Singer and Small, "Alliance Aggregation," op. cit.

62. Dina A. Zinnes, "An Analytical Study of the Balance of Power Theories," Journal of Peace Research 4, no. 3 (1967): 283.

63. Michael Wallace, "Alliance Polarization, Cross-Cutting, and International War, 1815-1964: A Measurement Procedure and Some Preliminary Evidence," Journal of Conflict Resolution 17, no. 4 (1973): 575-604.

64. Singer, "The 'Correlates of War' Project," op. cit.

65. Richardson, Statistics of Deadly Quarrels, op. cit.

66. Singer, Scientific Study of Politics, op. cit., p. 1.

67. Wallace, "Status, Formal Organization and Arms Levels," op. cit., p. 51.

68. Wallace, "Power, Status and International War," op. cit., p. 27.

69. Wallace, "Status, Formal Organization and Arms Levels," op. cit., p. 49.

70. Singer and Small, Strength of Nations, op. cit., and Singer, Wallace, and Bremer, Structural History, op. cit.

71. Job and Ostrom, "Appraisal of Research Design," op. cit.

72. Nigel Howard, The Field of Nations (Boston: Little, Brown, 1971), p. 150.

CHAPTER 6

REJOINDER TO THE CRITIQUES
J. David Singer

Given the length and imaginativeness of the three critiques, one could prepare a rejoinder of considerable size, but the editors have imposed very stringent limits. Moreover, we have considered a fair fraction of the criticisms and suggestions at one time or another in the past, and several of them are thus anticipated in earlier papers as well as in the project history. Without ceremony, then, let me take the three papers in order and respond to a few of the criticisms and suggestions that my colleagues and I found particularly salient. Of those that we ignore, some seemed so reasonable as to require no response, and some so frivolous as to deserve none.

PHILOSOPHY OF SCIENCE AND RESEARCH DESIGN

The dominant theme of Chapter 3, the Brian L. Job and Charles W. Ostrom critique, is quite obviously that of "theory versus data." It begins with the interesting assertion that we have done no theorizing prior to data collection and that I believe "that prior theorizing only jeopardizes the objectivity of the inquiry." The fact is that I

Both the project history and the rejoinder benefited from consultation with and suggestions from many of the students and faculty associated with the project; especially helpful were Stuart Bremer, Thomas Cusack, and Alan Levy. Ultimately the statement is completely my own, and not all of my colleagues would agree with everything that is said here.

REJOINDER

have been theorizing about the causes of war for about three decades and will continue to do so for some time to come. What I object to is not theorizing—understood here as a creative and disciplined speculation intended to make sense out of what we know and think we know—but the tendency to embrace the result of that speculation and to call it a theory. Theory is no more the guaranteed result of theorizing than art is the guaranteed result of drawing. A theory, as I suggested in the project history, is a body of knowledge in the form of propositions that are logically consistent with one another and falsifiable, and a fair fraction of them must also rest on reproducible evidence. In the matter of war and its causes, no such body existed at the outset of our project, and while we are closer today than we were then, there is still nothing approximating a scientific theory.

Therefore we have no choice but to commence each phase of our investigation on the basis of this rather limited, but incrementally expanding, body of findings and hunches. Put bluntly, we begin each inquiry with everything relevant that we know, but do not delude ourselves into thinking that it is a theory. As Carl G. Hempel, from whom Job and Ostrom draw heavily, puts it, the narrow inductivist, of which I am allegedly a glaring example, eschews "guesses or hypotheses . . . in the belief that such preconceived ideas would jeopardize the scientific objectivity of the investigation." When guesses and hypotheses become equivalent to a scientific theory, I will plead guilty; for the moment viva la difference! Our theoretical emperor is, of course, nearly naked and no amount of optimistic labelling can change his state of deshabille. It follows from this that we could hardly be guilty of formulating our hypotheses only after data collection.

In this connection, their assertion that I am at odds with Hempel regarding "the temporal priority of theory construction" is not supported by a careful reading of that authority. The data collection and hypothesis testing of the COW project are designed, as I have written elsewhere, to produce a body of existential and correlational knowledge essential to the development of the more powerful and desirable explanatory knowledge. The articulation of scientific theory, in the sense described above, becomes reasonable only after the establishment of those empirical uniformities. Contrary to what Job and Ostrom attribute to him, Hempel seems to agree with this research sequence, as shown by the following passage:

> Theories are usually introduced when previous study of a class of phenomena has revealed a system of uniformities that can be expressed in the form of empirical laws. Theories then seek to explain those regularities and,

> generally, to afford a deeper and more accurate understanding of the phenomena in question. To this end, a theory construes those phenomena as manifestations of entities and processes that lie behind or beneath them, as it were. These are assumed to be governed by characteristic theoretical laws, or theoretical principles, by means of which the theory then explains the empirical uniformities that have been previously discovered, and usually also predicts "new regularities of similar kinds.[1]

Hempel further elaborates this point by developing a progression of scientific inquiry, the final outcome of which is the formulation of scientific theories, as follows:

> The concepts used in a given field of scientific inquiry will change with the systematic advances made in that field: the formation of concepts will go hand in hand with the formulation of laws and, eventually, of theories. . . . The laws may at first express simple uniform or statistical connections among observables; they will then be formulated in terms of the observational vocabulary of the discipline to which they belong. Further systematic progress, however, will call for the formulation of principles expressed in theoretical terms which refer to various kinds of unobservable entities and their characteristics. In the course of such development, classifications defined by reference to manifest, observable characteristics will tend to give way to systems based on theoretical concepts.[2]

One implication of the priority of known empirical regularities to the construction of theories is that they are turned up by a number of disparate investigations, reflecting a variety of theoretical orientations and research strategies and covering a good number of years. In "normal science" as described by Thomas C. Kuhn, the work of synthesis and integration usually comes only after such a range of activities.[3] Our field, unfortunately, has seen very little of that kind of work, and one may, as a matter of fact, conceive of the early stages of the COW project as the functional equivalent of several individual investigations conducted by several research teams over a long period of time.

A second criticism is that we follow a "mechanistic approach to discovery" and that "insight, ingenuity, and originality are [potentially] suppressed."

If my broad grasp of the historical and speculative literature, the consideration of a wide range of causes of war models in my writing and teaching, and my refusal to embrace any single model now is mechanistic and inhibiting, so be it. As for the procedural aspects of discovery, Job and Ostrom quote Wesley Salmon to the effect that "the process of finding answers to scientific questions cannot be transformed into a mechanical routine"[4] and that science "is not a sausage machine into which you feed data and by turning the crank produce finished hypotheses."[5] That quote is followed by the comment that "it is unlikely, therefore, that COW will be able to discover true hypotheses by following its sequence of analyses." Leaving aside the semantically dubious proposition that one seeks to "discover true hypotheses," even the most casual perusal of our work will indicate that the "sausage machine" analogy is a bit off the mark; as a matter of fact, what could be *more* mechanistic and rigid than embracing a theoretical model in the absence of solid grounds for doing so and then staying with it long after the empirical evidence suggests a more promising direction?

Another important allegation by Job and Ostrom, extending beyond their oft-reiterated "lack of theory" issue, is that we follow the "narrow inductivist" research strategy rather than the "wide inductivist" one, virtually assuring a lack of efficiency and cumulativeness. My reading of Hempel suggests that he has in mind a continuum rather than a dichotomy; but more to the point, our strategy is clearly a mix of the two. Job and Ostrom invoke his authority to support their contention, as follows:

> Scientific hypotheses and theories are not *derived* from observed facts, but *invented* in order to account for them. They constitute guesses at the connections that might obtain between the phenomena under study, at uniformities and patterns that might underlie their occurrence.[6]

If this statement is meant to reflect the wide inductivist strategy, then it is difficult to place us in the narrow category; that is, I fully agree that theories are invented to account for observed facts and regularities, and further, I presume that this invention occurs after these facts have indeed been observed. Hempel is not suggesting that we invent theories to account for invented facts!

As to the role of hypotheses as "guesses at the connections that might obtain between the phenomena under study," no one could agree more. However, as Hempel reminds us later in that same paragraph, those guesses had better reflect something more than a plausible armchair hunch.

"Happy guesses" of this kind require great ingenuity, especially if they involve a radical departure from current modes of scientific thinking, as did, for example, the theory of relativity and quantum theory. The inventive effort required in scientific research will benefit from a thorough familiarity with current knowledge in the field. A complete novice will hardly make an important scientific discovery, for the ideas that may occur to him are likely to duplicate what has been tried or to run afoul of well-established facts or theories of which he is not aware.[7]

In sum, we follow a very catholic strategy when it comes to the heuristics of formulating hypotheses, and we are as influenced by formal reasoning as by historical anecdote, and by another's interpretation of his results as by scrutinizing our own correlation matrices. Regardless of the sources of inspiration, however, we treat our hypotheses only as guesses (happy ones, we hope) that remain to be vindicated by empirical regularity.

A further and particularly irritating allegation is that "decisions about which data to collect were made on the basis of whether or not the data available were in interval form, rather than whether or not the information, regardless of measurement level, might be helpful in answering interesting substantive questions." First, we are not engaged in the "collection" of "available" data; we are engaged in the generation and extraction of data from all sorts of historical traces. Little of that data can be thought of as available.

Second, the footnote to this asserted "suspicion" complains that our inability to extract reliable fatality estimates from the traces of colonial wars "precludes the possibility of utilizing their data in some very interesting research on colonial war." We labored long and hard in our effort to identify and then measure some of the characteristics of all types of wars (interstate, imperial, colonial, and civil), even though our primary concern has been with the former type. Further, we have made every single data set available to the entire scholarly community as soon as it was in reasonably clean condition, long before we had even begun to utilize and exploit the fruits of these labors. If Job and Ostrom care to devote several years to generating fatality figures for the nonsystemic political entities that participated in these extrasystemic wars, let them do so; but to suggest that we have shaped our theoretical focal points to the accessibility and accuracy of available interval-level figures is to seriously distort the very essence of our research strategy.

Third, it is said that we are willing to accept high correlations as confirming a hypothesis, ignoring the extent to which it may be implausible, contradictory (presumably with another hypothesis), or not falsifiable. Leaving aside plausibility, which has led all too many of us down the primrose path of premature closure, the rest of the charge hardly seems justified. Why articulate and then put to the test a number of rival hypotheses if not to ascertain their consistency with one another and with the empirical evidence? And why treat empirically-supported hypotheses as only that, and not as confirmed explanatory statements, if not to recognize that alternative hypotheses could be confirmed by the same outcome?* Having often chided others for overinterpreting coefficients of correlation or determination, it is unlikely that I would then turn around and commit that sin myself.

Turning now to some points that are less a matter of misinterpretation than of disagreement, it is suggested that we have no clear understanding of the theoretical propositions we wish to study and thus our indices "will run the risk of having little construct validity" and will not measure what we want or claim to measure. They then allege that "debate has arisen concerning the construction and utility" of our indicators and that "this has in turn led to a questioning of the interpretation of findings based upon these indices." We have noted as often as anyone, and perhaps more, since we have constructed more indices of familiar constructs than most others, that there is no final proof of the validity of one's indices and that there always will be debate about their construction and utility. This is fine with us, but it is quite inappropriate to assert that "debate has arisen" merely because one scholar made the incorrect assertion that for us "the operational measure of a perfect balance of power system is one in which no state belongs to an alliance."[8]

A key element in the incremental sequence problem concerns the order in which we examine the several levels of aggregation.

---

*One definitional source of confusion here might be the distinction between hypothesis and theory, which Hempel and Job and Ostrom occasionally use interchangeably. As I see it, a hypothesis is a very explicit, operationally stated proposition regarding the mere statistical association or covariation between or among two or more empirical phenomena, but does not necessarily imply causality. A theory, on the other hand, is a set of logically interdependent hypotheses (and assumptions), most of which have been empirically confirmed, brought together for the explicit purpose of illuminating causal patterns.

Since we are seeking to account for the amount of war experienced by each nation, each dyad, each class of nations, each region, and the larger international system, there is the inevitable issue of temporal priorities. Some members of the project team believe that accounting for the incidence of war at the systemic, aggregated level is a desirable first step, prior to focusing on the individual nations or the dyads. Others, more eager to move toward explanatory findings quickly, see the systemic level analyses as a detour with little theoretical payoff. However, since theoretically attractive questions are found at all levels, we end up articulating and testing models that are designed to account for the incidence of war at the systemic, dyadic, and national levels. Despite this mild agnosticism, we do have a rather strong commitment to the prior importance of systemic level investigations, reflecting our agreement with Herbert Simon's comment regarding "the top-down strategy that built the natural sciences over the past three centuries."[9] Simon points out that "we knew a great deal about the gross physical and chemical behavior of matter before we had a knowledge of molecules, a great deal about molecular chemistry before we had an atomic theory, and a great deal about atoms before we had any theory of elementary particles—if, indeed we have such a theory today."[10] The parallel, it seems to me, is clear. Eventually we hope to produce a complete explanation of why war occurs when and where it does, and this would by definition be a reductionist explanation; but meanwhile we can go a long way toward understanding the onset and unfolding of war without looking at the specific nations involved or examining the black boxes of the decision-making process or the minds of those who participate in that process.

The essential and recurrent theme in the Job and Ostrom critique is, of course, that because we have no theory, "the project does not appear to be leading toward a theory of war" or a "unified and refined understanding of international warfare." Virtually every point raised by Job and Ostrom proceeds from the "absence of theory" premise, and I trust that this brief rejoinder, the project's intellectual history, my earlier writings, and the work of the project itself will demonstrate that we have here little more than a caricature of the enterprise and its rationale.

METHODOLOGICAL CRITICISMS

Shifting from the general question of research strategy to the more specific issues of method and technique, we note several basic concerns in Chapter 4, by Raymond Duvall. The most general of these is that "there is a pervasive lack of correspondence between the questions as posed and the strategies adopted to develop answers for them." That lack is said to inhere in both our data-generating and data-analyzing procedures.

Looking briefly at the problems of measurement, index construction, and data generation, I fear that we are at a bit of an impasse. For example, our measurement of war and its differentiation from other forms of inter-nation conflict are seen as inadequate, primarily in terms of validity. First, Duvall is concerned about our treatment of war as both a discrete occurrence and as a phenomenon with "magnitude properties". All around us, people distinguish between occurrences and their magnitudes. The number of babies born in a given week or year is distinguished from their mean weight at birth; the number of industrial strikes in a decade is distinguished from the man-days lost through such strikes; and so on. Similarly, wars can be measured according to frequency as well as magnitude. We see no difficulty about whether the magnitude, severity, or intensity is measured as a property not only of a given war but of the nations that experience it or the system in which it occurs. It depends on the unit and level of analysis of the outcome variable in the analysis at hand.

Closely related is the concern about whether it is the frequency of war or the amount of war that is our outcome variable. Our choice of indicator(s) will vary with the theoretical question being addressed. We want to know not only under what conditions the system experiences more war or less but under what conditions disputes will result in a war, as opposed to a nonwar outcome. We also want to know under what conditions a war, once it has begun, will expand and escalate. Needless to say, it is quite possible that different conditions are at work in the occurrence of war and in its escalation.

Another criticism is that our 1,000 battle-fatality threshold is arbitrary and that it assumes greater precision than is warranted. It is, if we may make a subtle distinction, arbitrary, but not capricious. After we had drawn up our entire list of about 500 candidate wars, the question was one of identifying the "real, serious international wars," and differentiating them not only from civil wars but from episodes of armed conflict that most practitioners and observers would agree were something less than international wars. The first criterion for exclusion was the political status of the protagonists, and the second was that of severity, measured in battle-connected deaths among the combatant personnel. Very simply, it seemed obvious to us that, despite a temporal spread of a century and a half and some dramatic changes in weapons technology and military medicine, very few of those cases with fewer than a thousand battle fatalities would be called serious international wars by qualified observers; that is, the threshold was decided upon in the presence of the larger population of cases, and not in an unwarranted fashion. As for misplaced precision, no one knows better than Melvin Small and myself how difficult it is to ascertain battle death figures, and as a matter of fact, we ended up including several wars for which our earlier estimates were in the 750-1,000 range in order to be sure that no bona fide case was excluded; the 1,000 battle-death figure should be understood as meaning "at, or close to, 1,000 battle-connected deaths." Thus it is incorrect to say that we treat a deadly quarrel with 900 battle deaths as a crisis and one with 1,000 as a war.

As for the suggested solution to this measurement problem—defining a war as any "employment of military forces in direct, physical attack"—the cure is worse than the alleged illness; that is, by eliminating the fatality threshold, we would end up, like Richardson, in embracing all sorts of skirmishes, confrontations, artillery exchanges, and seizures (such as in the May 1975 Mayaguez incident), not to mention assassinations and executions. This rule would of course obliterate the crucial distinction between serious disputes or confrontations on the one hand and wars on the other and would preclude any comparisons between confrontations that do and do not end up in war.

In this connection, Duvall goes on to note (1) that we exclude seven cases that Richardson coded as entailing 1,000 or more associated deaths and (2) that including them would "have noticeable effects." Richardson, who, like Duvall, is "no historian" and who relied largely on English-language encyclopedias for most of his evidence, included not only the deaths of noncombatants but also of combatant and noncombatant personnel of nations that were not even members of the interstate system. More to the point, we find that even if those seven putative wars were included, there would not be the "noticeable effects" that are claimed. Following his illustrative comparison of the association between alliance aggregation and capability concentration on the one hand and the frequency of war in the twentieth century on the other, we can find only a negligible difference. That is, instead of the alleged transformation of a "nearly random relationship into a marginally significant one," we see merely an overinterpreted artifact. That is, we are told that the χ^2 values in his matrices rise from 4.2 to 7.3 and from 2.2 to 5.0, and that the p values improve in each case from $>.25$ to about .10. A cursory inspection shows that only one case actually moves to a different cell in each of these analyses, merely reminding us that χ^2 is highly sensitive to modest changes when working with a small N. Not only is this not exactly news, but it does seem bizarre to find in the same critique (1) a denunciation of our use of tests of statistical significance and then (2) a reliance on such a test, and an inappropriate one at that, to buttress a dubious argument.11

Shifting from the measurement problems allegedly inhering in our outcome variables, Duvall turns to those that might jeopardize the predictor variables, focusing on alliances for illustrative purposes. His first concern is that we lose measurement validity when we exclude wartime alliances; yet if the theoretical concern is with the extent to which peacetime alliance configurations predict to the onset of war, this is hardly a problem. For other purposes, of course, the wartime alliance data could be included. His second concern is that since different classes of alliance might reflect different degrees of commitment during different historical epochs, our "typology of alliance commitments . . . is of questionable validity and precision." Perhaps, but the suggestion that we look only at defense pacts and ignore neutrality pacts and ententes may help to throw away information, but hardly overcomes the problem. Once again, we are advised to make a priori decisions on measurement in the absence of any logical or empirical reason for so doing. The prudent thing, and what we do as a matter of course, is to run our analyses using data generated by varying coding rules, in order to ascertain empirically what difference it makes to include or exclude a certain set of phenomena.

I might add that since no two events or arrangements in political history are identical in every respect, we are forever in the position of lumping together somewhat disparate phenomena. While those of the idiographic persuasion find this offensive, those of us who take the nomethetic view (and this would certainly include our critic) recognize that (1) there is nothing wrong with putting somewhat dissimilar phenomena into the same category as long as they are similar along the theoretically relevant dimensions; and (2) unless we do distinguish between and classify complex phenomena that are far from easy to classify, we will never get very far in understanding world politics.

Turning from the raw data sets to the indicators derived therefrom, our critic generally appreciates what we do and why; but he nevertheless misses the key point that the admittedly crude alliance aggregation and alliance commitment indicators are not offered as "valid measure(s) of system concentration, polarization, or crosscutting cleavages." As a matter of fact, a fair number of our papers are addressed to the construction of these latter indicators, with reasonable success, and Duvall actually cites them.12 In examining some of these efforts, and thus accepting the above-noted distinction, he goes on to itemize all the things that are allegedly wrong with these efforts to get at concentration and polarization, failing along the way to distinguish between these two very different concepts. The discussion is technically correct but rather unhelpful, since it merely emphasizes that just about every technique for measuring such concepts as polarization requires some rather heroic assumptions. Again, the serious social scientist either forges ahead, constructing the most valid indices that he or she can, or surrenders to the counsel of perfection that leads inevitably to immobility. As in other sciences, no one claims that the very first indicators of gravity, friction, refraction, or spectral density; nor those of wealth or authoritarian personality, were as good as the later ones. Someone must take the plunge, and in the QIP community, all too often that task has been left to the other fellow.

Another of our indicators that comes in for criticism in Chapter 4 is that of capabilities and their distribution among the major powers. After agreeing with the basic decisions, Duvall expresses concern that our introduction of energy consumption in 1885 and shift from iron to steel in 1895 are affecting and distorting the concentration index. In support of this contention, he notes that of the 19 observations up through 1913, these two years show the fifth- and sixth-largest changes. We reply that not only are these years not very far from the median value for that artificially restricted period, but they also rank sixteenth and seventeenth among the entire 28 observations.* Are these grounds for alarm?

As to the derived indicator itself, capability concentration, he quite correctly notes that somewhat different capability distributions can give pretty much the same concentration score, merely reiterating the point made in the original index construction paper. Furthermore, if after reading that paper, which summarizes, compares, and integrates just about every indicator of concentration found in the social sciences, Duvall would like to propose "a more adequate index of capability concentration," we will await the results eagerly.

---

*In this connection, it is surprising to see it assumed that we never examined the covariation between and among the six factors that comprise the combined indicator. It hardly seems necessary to state the obvious in the analysis paper, especially since it is discussed in the paper (cited by Duvall) that addresses the construction of our capability index; see John Stuckey and J. David Singer, "The Powerful and the War-Prone: Ranking the Nations by Relative Capability and War Experience, 1820-1964," paper presented at the conference on Poder Social: America Latine en El Mundo, Mexico City, May 1973.

REJOINDER 139

A final point in this connection is (1) that we continue to have vigorous debate within the project about alternative ways of measuring not only polarization and concentration but also power, mobility, status, prestige, and so forth; (2) that we try these alternative algorithms; and (3) that it often makes little difference which ones are used. In sum, while one can admire the technical competence and verve of Duvall's criticisms on the data-making and index-construction front, one can only end up agreeing that there are difficulties, that there is room for differences of opinion about the validity of indicators, and that we need more effort to improve upon—rather than merely criticize—the pioneering efforts of those who are helping to build a cumulative science.

Before shifting from data-making to data analysis, let me briefly digress to respond to a related issue of measurement, which is our use of such fixed interobservational intervals as the year or the half-decade, reflected in the comment that the "temporal unit, or year, does not correspond to conjecture and/or conception." It is then asserted that we use the year as a poor surrogate for the different sets of conditions sought. First, the year is used as a surrogate only when one is examining secular trends and periodicities, or when it is explicitly identified as a surrogate for a changing condition such as industrial technology.[13] More often the year _is_ only a "mapping convenience," merely providing the fixed intervals for observation of the possible explanatory conditions. In place of fixed temporal intervals, one may, of course, posit historical epochs or periods, the duration of which varies. However, this requires us to articulate some ratio, constant or changing, between "diplomatic time" and "real time," and if any empirical basis for estimating that ratio exists, I am unaware of it. In the absence of evidence or of reasonable surmise to the contrary, prudence dictates that we treat all of the 150 years in our study as if they were of equal length. While we have kept a sharp eye out for really clear inflection points at which the relationships among variables show systematic changes, there is so far almost no historical evidence to suggest that we could validly demark more than two or three temporal periods of differing lengths. That is, we find no empirical grounds for specifying breaks that would justify the division of our century-and-a-half epoch into historically meaningful observational units other than those based on the revolution of the earth around the sun.

Turning next to data analysis, Duvall's first criticism is that our early bivariate empirical tests "do not correspond to the less rigorous, but guiding verbal theorizing" because our "verbal material implies fairly complex, multiplicative hypotheses, which, in the tests, are translated into bivariate, linear form." In other words, he quite fails to differentiate between the often-complex theoretical argument that leads us to articulate a hypothesis and the hypothesis itself. The essence of a cumulative and prudent research strategy is the disaggregation of our grand and ambitious models into a sequence of discrete but highly integrated submodels, each of which can and should first be examined independently. Throughout the history of the project we have made it patently clear that we are not yet testing any theories but merely testing certain of the more critical propositions that are implied by, and have been inferred from, those theoretical arguments that are all too often mistaken for theories. Thus it is very wide of the mark to assert that we translate complex verbal models into simple bivariate or multivariate hypotheses; the hypotheses flow from, but are not identical to, the complex models.

The second complaint in the data analysis section is the all-too-familiar one of "the use and misuse of probability models." After summarizing the reasons we give for using such models and the concomitant tests of statistical significance, Duvall asserts that the "implication is incorrect in each case." We are, of course, thoroughly familiar with the arguments for and against the use of significance tests under certain conditions and for certain purposes. The issues have been debated often among project members as well as within the larger University of Michigan community, which certainly has its share of competent methodologists. Moreover, we use these tests rather more sparingly than is suggested in the critique, and yet remain convinced that, when applied and interpreted prudently, they can be quite helpful.[14]

A third concern is that our theoretical analyses, which are reflected in the use of such techniques as correlation, path analysis, polynominal curve-fitting, conjoint measurement, factor analysis, and spectral analysis, all rest on one version or another of the regression model. Like virtually all other social scientists, we are limited by the range of statistical models and methods now available, and we recognize the limitations and dangers inherent in this heavy reliance on the regression mode, as nicely summarized by Duvall. Thus, although we continue to explore alternative modes that require different, and more realistic, assumptions, we have little choice but to continue using the conventional methods in a thoughtful manner. Moreover, as he perceptively notes, the threat to explanation is of minor concern to us now, since our preoccupation remains more one of "descriptive regression" than of "statistical inference."[15] As we move beyond the acquisition and codification of existential and correlational knowledge and directly attack the problem of explanation, these caveats will become more salient.

To summarize, then, we find the Duvall critique a fairly useful one, in that it reminds us of all the ways in which high-minded social scientists can be led astray. In the generation of data, in data reduction, in index construction, in data analysis, and in the resulting inferences, the number of pitfalls is alarmingly high. The very awareness of these has inhibited the purists among us in the search for systematic knowledge, while an ignorance of them has permitted many practitioners to mistake a statistical association for an explanatory theory. I would like to believe that my colleagues and I have steered an intelligent middle course, and in so doing, begun to mark the route to a coherent theory of world politics.

SUBSTANTIVE FINDINGS

The third critique, offered by Harvey Starr as Chapter 5, poses more procedural difficulties than the other two. This is partly because the more interesting criticisms are essentially the same methodological and epistemological ones to which I have already responded. Another reason is that the bulk of the substantive complaint is that we have not progressed further. All we can do is agree that progress has been slow, if the benchmark is that of our hopes or of the needs of the discipline. However, if our results to date are measured against the money that has been spent, the scholar-months invested, or some productivity norm for the entire discipline, we need not be embarrassed.*

Although there is no point in getting into a discussion of the project's quantitative or qualitative superiority vis-a-vis earlier or contemporary investigations, I cannot overlook the dubious ploy of comparing our output and costs to those of Richardson. I take second place to none in my regard for the work of our predecessors in the QIP area, but nevertheless must note the limitations of their work. While we have certainly followed in their footsteps, it can hardly be said that they built a solid foundation upon which we could safely build; rather, they demonstrated the feasibility of attacking the war-peace problem in a scientific fashion, giving us the confidence to do the same, but with conceptual and methodological tools that were not available to them.

---

*That productivity should not be underestimated by any omission of the work that is still in the "pipeline," a full list of titles for which the unpublished work is readily available.

It is of greater relevance that, with much of the more tedious and back-breaking work of data-making behind us, we can now expect to accelerate the more rewarding work of fleshing out, formalizing, and testing our theoretical models. As this shift in emphasis occurs, we need not overlook the fact that neither we nor the rest of the research community can go very far without the data base generated during these earlier years.

I could continue on to a point-by-point rejoinder to Starr, but having already taken too much time from the research enterprise itself in order to respond to our other critics in this volume and elsewhere, let me move quickly to a brief conclusion, much of which is relevant to, and stimulated by, this particular critique.

CONCLUSION

Let me now wonder aloud whether the game of responding to these criticisms has been worth the candle. While I am in full accord with the notion of open and frank criticism in the scientific arena, I nevertheless would now question the value of institutionalizing it. We already see a great deal of it in journal articles and letters to journal editors, not to mention papers and discussions at professional meetings. Since much of the criticism found in those contexts is of a rather casual and amateurish short, however, a case could be made for professionalizing the activity, and I, for one, originally found the case persuasive. Over the past several years, having observed the process and results, I have lost my enthusiasm for criticism, however. Let me summarize the reasons.

First, the chances of hearing a new criticism or suggestion that has not already been anticipated by a careful researcher or picked up early from a colleague are very close to zero. Moreover, almost all of the criticisms and suggestions heard will have already been considered carefully, and often rejected, by the thoughtful researcher. Also, the critic will have devoted a good deal of time and paper to an activity in which he or she may already have become too proficient, thanks to the emphases in graduate school, instead of attending to more constructive activities.

Second, the director of a serious research project is put into an awkward position. If he or she chooses not to reply to criticisms in journals or in unpublished papers—and that is my general policy—the director appears to be ignoring them. Even if he or she responds to these points in a subsequent paper, as I often do, and even actually finds the suggestions useful enough to follow, the time lag is long enough to give the impression of indifference. However, if I were to stop my work to respond to every paper that criticizes it, soon there would be nothing forthcoming for the next wave of critics.

Third, even if there were no opportunity costs involved, there remains the matter of style, taste, and dignity. While I have tried in this volume to respond in civil and measured tones, I have obviously not been fully successful. Some of the criticisms are bound to be just too silly and irresponsible and do not deserve a serious reply; while I have tended here to sidestep the more frivolous ones, some just could not be ignored.

Fourth, and closely related, is the fine line between scientific discourse and rhetorical debate. Whereas the former is designed to, and usually does, illuminate and clarify, a debate is usually designed to win an argument. Each of the critiques at hand is, unhappily, a mix of the two, and that mix is more or less inherent in the activity. To put it another way, one could argue that institutionalized criticism is damaging to scientific discourse. Taking on the role of critic, even in writing a book review, puts the scholar, and especially the younger scholar, in a position that is incredibly tempting. I note, for example, that this same Harvey Starr who arraigns our work so conscientiously in this volume is far from consistent: in two recent reviews, he turned time and again to the Correlates of War project as a model of how high quality research should be done.[16] The role, in effect, seems to determine the critic's response set and to override his intellectual judgment.

In sum, we in the QIP community have more important things to do than engage in debate that soon becomes repetitive and sterile. Although this particular volume may serve as a useful pedagogical tool and will certainly represent an advance over some of the earlier efforts, it nevertheless could be dangerously seductive. To educate our graduate students well in the skills of both doing research and evaluating research, and then to further institutionalize the latter, could create the wrong mix of incentives. Given the great difficulty of formulating, executing, and writing up a solid piece of research and the relative ease of criticizing such, there is little justification for then rewarding the easier activity. The need for adding to our sparse knowledge is great, and we already have all the rhetoric and free advice that we can handle.

NOTES

1. Carl G. Hempel, <u>Philosophy of Natural Science</u> (Englewood Cliffs: Prentice-Hall, 1966), p. 70.
2. Carl G. Hempel, <u>Aspects of Scientific Explanation and Other Essays in the Philosophy of Science</u> (New York: Free Press, 1965), pp. 148-49.

3. Thomas C. Kuhn, The Structure of Scientific Revolutions (Chicago: University of Chicago Press, 1970).
4. As quoted in Chapter 3 from Wesley Salmon, The Foundations of Scientific Inference (Pittsburgh: The University of Pittsburgh Press, 1967), p. 111.
5. Ibid.
6. Hempel, Philosophy of Natural Science, op. cit., p. 15.
7. Ibid.
8. Dina A. Zinnes, "An Analytical Study of the Balance of Power Theories," Journal of Peace Research, vol. 3, no. 3 (1967): 270-288. This is based on our statement that one inference from the balance of power literature is that alliances can inhibit the efficacy of the "invisible hand."
9. Herbert Simon, The Sciences of the Artificial (Cambridge, Mass.: The M.I.T. Press, 1969), pp. 16-17.
10. Ibid.
11. To reassure those who might otherwise be reluctant to use the project's war indicators, let me refer to the highly favorable evaluations of them in recent reviews: Charles Taylor, "Review of The Wages of War," in Perspective 9, no. 2 (1972): 239; Ted Robert Gurr, "The Neo-Alexandrians: A Review Essay on Data Handbooks in Political Science," American Political Science Review 68, no. 1 (1974): 243-52; Rudolph J. Rummel, "Review of The Wages of War," in American Political Science Review 69, no. 1 (1975): 390-91; and Donald McCloskey, "Review of The Wages of War," in Journal of American Statistical Association 69, no. 345 (1974): 274-274. We know of no unfavorable reviews by quantitatively oriented scholars.
12. Among these are James Lee Ray and J. David Singer, "Measuring the Concentration of Power in the International System," Sociological Methods and Research 1, no. 4 (1973): 403-437; Bruce Bueno de Mesquita, "Measuring Systemic Polarity," Journal of Conflict Resolution 19, no. 2 (1975): 187-216; Stuart Bremer, "A Sociometric Analysis of Diplomatic Bonds, 1817-1940," paper presented at the Events Data Conference, Michigan State University, 1971, and "Formal Alliance Clusters in the Inter-state System, 1816-1965," paper presented at the annual meeting of the American Political Science Association, Washington, D.C., September 1972; and Michael Wallace, "Alliance Polarization, Cross-Cutting, and International War, 1815-1964; A Measurement Procedure and Some Preliminary Evidence," Journal of Conflict Resolution 17, no. 4, (1973): 575-604.
13. Stuart Bremer, J. David Singer, and Urs Luterbacher, "The Population Density and War Proneness of European Nations, 1816-1965," Comparative Political Studies 6, no. 3 (1973): 329-48.

14. Robert F. Winch and Donald T. Campbell, "Proof? No. Evidence? Yes. The Significance of Tests of Significance," in The Significance Test Controversy, edited by Denton E. Morrison and Ramon E. Henkel (Chicago: Aldine, 1970), pp. 199-208.

15. It should be noted that J. David Singer, Stuart Bremer, and John Stuckey, "Capability Distribution, Uncertainty, and Major Power War, 1820-1965," in Peace, War, and Numbers, edited by Bruce M. Russett (Beverly Hills: Sage Publications, 1972), pp. 19-48, the article cited by Duvall to illustrate problems of valid inference, does not rest upon tests of significance; there is no effort there to exploit inferential statistics.

16. Harvey Starr, "The Quantitative International Relations Scholar as Surfer: Riding the 'Fourth Wave'," Journal of Conflict Resolution 18, no. 2 (1974): 336-68, and Harvey Starr, "Review of Geoffrey Blainey's The Causes of War," Journal of Peace Science 1, no. 2 (1975): 181-87.

PART

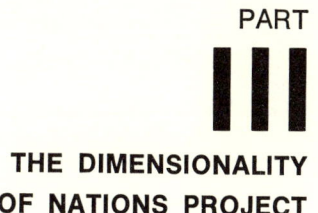

THE DIMENSIONALITY
OF NATIONS PROJECT

CHAPTER 7

THE DIMENSIONALITY OF NATIONS PROJECT
Rudolph J. Rummel

HISTORY

The Dimensionality of Nations (DON) project began in 1961 in the confluence of three interests, the first of which was provided by Harold Guetzkow. Very much involved in Inter-nation Simulation (INS), he desired an empirical-quantitative mapping of the international system that would be useful in the construction and validation of INS. Jack Sawyer, a professor of social psychology at the University of Chicago, contributed the second interest, which was to replicate the early work of Raymond Cattell on the dimensionality of nations, and especially to exploit the better data being published and the computer, which was just coming into wide use. I offered the third interest, which was that of developing a mathematical theory of war that would make possible prediction and control.[1] To that end, I saw the need for systematic data to test such a theory and for operational concepts to form its structure.

To achieve these three interests, Guetzkow, Sawyer, and I worked on a proposal to map the cross-national patterns of nations using factor analysis, which was submitted to the National Science Foundation in 1961. The proposal was approved for two years and began in 1962 with Guetzkow as principal investigator, Sawyer as technical consultant, and myself as research assistant. (I was a doctoral candidate in the international relations program at Northwestern University at that time.) The following year I accepted my first academic appointment, at Indiana University, and DON was transferred with me. In 1964 NSF approved a new two-year proposal, extending the quantitative analysis beyond the original design, with myself as principal investigator.

The research, which was directed towards mapping cross-national variation, involved collecting data on 236 attributes (such as defense expenditures, GNP, literacy, energy consumption, threats, population, and area) for 82 nations for 1955, which was the best data year as viewed from 1962, and a thorough methodological investigation of the application of factor analysis to such data. This was Phase I of DON. It ended in 1964, with significant results to be mentioned later.[2]

While Phase I was underway, I became increasingly interested in quantitatively mapping the directed behavior between nations. Phase I involved analyzing variables of attributes and behavior, with nations as the cases or observations. The new line of research entailed analyzing the behavior of specific nations to other specific nations, such as the behavior of the United States to China, of the USSR to Poland, and of France to the United Kingdom, an analysis with dyads as the observations.

This new line of research was initiated in 1965, as Phase II of the DON project. Hundreds of variables subsequently were analyzed for about 400 dyads, and the linkages between dyadic behavior and nation distances were determined cross-sectionally and across time for the years 1950-65. Moreover, the dyadic dimensions and linkages for the major actors in the international system, the United States, China, and the USSR, with all other nations were also determined for this period.[3]

During Phase II a theoretical structure called a social field theory was formulated and subsequently served to guide research. The theory is elaborated mathematically, drawing upon the theorems of n-dimensional spaces and linear algebra. Simply put, the theory states that nations are social units that interact in a social field (in some ways analogous to an electromagnetic field) and that this field can be analytically divided into two spaces, a space of behavior and a space of attributes.

Within the attribute space, nations are located in terms of their characteristics; within the behavior space, dyads (such as US → USSR) are located in terms of their behavior. A distance vector between nations located in the attribute space can be measured and treated as a force acting on the origin-of-behavior space. In other words, the locations of dyads in behavior space are a function (resolution) of the distances (forces) between nations on attribute dimensions. Mathematically, the theory has been expressed as:

$$W_{i \to j} = \sum_{i=1}^{p} \alpha_{i\ell} d_{\ell, i-j} ,$$

where

$W_{i \to j}$ = location (as a vector) of dyad $i \to j$ in behavior space,
d_ℓ = distance vector between nations i and j on attribute dimension ℓ of an attribute space of p dimensions,
$\alpha_{i\ell}$ = a parameter for actor i and dimension ℓ.

Leaving mathematical considerations aside, field theory says simply that nations will behave towards each other in terms of their socioeconomic, cultural, geographic, and political distances and that each actor will weigh these distances from its own perspective.

RESULTS

In view of the above, what are some of the accumulated findings of the project? These concern methodology, data, substance, and theory. Regarding methodology, it should be remembered that when the DON research began, factor analysis had never been applied to international relations or international behavior, although Cattell, Berry, and Schnore had separately published applications on cross-national attributes or characteristics. There had been some scattered multiple regression analyses, but no canonical analyses, no discriminant analyses, and no multidimensional scaling. Although applied here and there, the correlation coefficient was still a strange animal indeed to most students of international relations. Journals in the field spent pages explaining the nature of the chi-square and its application to a simple fourfold table. In this context, DON undertook a concerted effort to determine the usefulness and applicability of multivariate methods, particularly factor analysis, in analyzing international relations. My book, Applied Factor Analysis,[4] was one result of this effort.

DON has been continuously collecting and refining a core set of data, the characteristics of which are well known and understood through a variety of analyses. We have tried to insure that the data we collected were always in a form immediately usable by others; this entailed giving explicit definitions, coding rules, and so forth. These data have been transferred to the Inter-University Consortium for Political Research at the University of Michigan and should provide a good base for others to build upon.

Concerning substantive accumulation, which means a convergence on stable and reliable findings, I offer the following generalizations, which are based on a decade of intensive, programmatic quantitative research and on continuous comparison with the results of others. International relations is highly structured: the treaties, trade, aid, threats, GNP per capita, defense expenditures, literacy, riots, and other attributes and behavior of nations are organized into very stable and clear patterns. In the course of the DON research, correlations over .80, and indeed ranging to .89 and .99, are commonplace; and since so many correlation coefficients are above .50, I usually ignore those below this level. For example, in one study power parity between the United States and object nations statistically accounted for 88 percent of the variation in U.S. cooperative and deterrence behavior toward 81 nations, including such different object nations as Yemen, India, Japan, the USSR, and China.[5] Eventually the research community will become aware of how structured international relations are: the point here is that the fact of such structure is now core knowledge, based on accumulated scientific research.

I find that the major dimensions accounting for national variation in attributes concern wealth, politics, and power. Nations can generally be characterized as rich or poor, democratic or totalitarian, strong or weak. Every study that has included appropriate variables has shown that wealth, politics, and power are dimensions of social and political groups, whether nations, regions, provinces, cities, or small groups. The stability in findings on these three dimensions is so consistent that they could be referred to as social laws.

Moreover, the two- or three-dozen analyses containing the relevant variables also delineated Catholic culture, domestic conflict behavior, and density as secondary national dimensions, even though these studies involved different time frames, researchers, and designs. Therefore it seems that quantitative analyses have converged on a stable and reliable set of dimensions for characterizing nations, which we can rely on as empirical concepts for understanding and explaining modern international behavior.

How are these dimensions linked to behavior? Consistently through dozens of analyses, some involving all U.S. dyadic behavior, some involving all Chinese dyadic behavior, some involving samples of Soviet, Brazilian, Indonesian, Indian, Cuban, Dutch, English, Israeli, Egyptian, and Polish behavior, some involving cross-sectional data, and some involving longitudinal data, we again find that wealth, power, and politics are the most important dimensions in statistically accounting for dyadic behavior.[6] Furthermore, the relative power between two nations best explains (statistically) their dyadic conflict behavior, while cooperation is best explained in relation to conflict and on the basis of wealth, politics, and power distances jointly. Here I do not mean the usual social science multiple correlations between .30 and .50, but correlations explaining around 90 percent of the variance, with the odds of their actually being zero exceeding a billion to one!

Another set of substantive findings has to do with conflict behavior alone. Through our analyses and comparisons with other studies, we consistently found that domestic conflict behavior for nations involves a turmoil dimension, of riots and demonstrations, that is statistically independent of revolution and guerilla warfare dimensions. (This finding was first published in 1963 and has subsequently been well illustrated by American domestic turmoil.) Moreover, we consistently observed that, for all nations, domestic and foreign conflict behavior are statistically independent, whether we were analyzing events data in isolation; whether partialing out different levels of wealth, power, or density; or holding constant such different qualities as Catholic culture, Western-pluralistic democracy, or communism. Domestic conflict does not help to explain foreign conflict statistically; neither do the other national characteristics. Generalizing across several dozen separate studies to account for foreign conflict quantitatively requires us to analyze conflict dyadically and to examine dyadic differences in wealth, power, politics, culture, and geographic distances.

Our results have converged consistently with those of others in establishing the explanatory and integrating value of field theory. Most find this a strange assertion, and there are rumblings that field theory is an unsuccessful paradigm. As will be shown in the chapter giving my comments on the reviews, this much can be said: The results accumulated across 51 different and independent analyses clearly show that field theory (the Model II version) can explain the linkages between national attributes and dyadic international behavior. Moreover, the theory synthesizes a variety of diverse ideas and results in a variety of fields and thus serves as a general or broad-gauge scientific theory of international relations.

So much for our accumulated findings. I realize their controversial nature; and the style of their presentation here is incautious, surely dogmatic. I ask the reader to realize that over a decade of work has been condensed into a few generalizations. I cannot surround them here with the necessary qualifications, justifications, and evidence. However, the many details have been established in the books and reports referred to throughout the discussion. Their worth is now for others to weigh.

NOTES

1. For an intellectual autobiography, see Rudolph J. Rummel, "Roots of Faith," in In Search of Global Patterns, edited by James N. Rosenau (New York: Free Press, forthcoming).

2. Phase I results are mainly given in Rudolph J. Rummel, <u>Dimensions of Nations</u> (Beverly Hills: Sage Publications, 1972).

3. Most of the Phase II results are given in Rudolph J. Rummel, <u>National Attributes and Behavior</u> (Beverly Hills: Sage Publications, forthcoming in 1976), and Rudolph J. Rummel, <u>Field Theory Evolving</u> (Beverly Hills: Sage Publications, forthcoming in 1976).

4. Rudolph J. Rummel, <u>Applied Factor Analysis</u> (Evanston: Northwestern University Press, 1970).

5. Rudolph J. Rummel, "U.S. Foreign Relations: Conflict, Cooperation and Attribute Distances," in <u>Peace, War, and Numbers</u>, edited by Bruce M. Russett (Beverly Hills: Sage Publications, 1972), pp. 71-113.

6. These various analyses are given in Rummel, <u>Field Theory Evolving</u>, op. cit.

CHAPTER

8

AN APPRAISAL OF THE PHILOSOPHY OF SCIENCE AND RESEARCH DESIGN INVOLVED IN THE DIMENSIONALITY OF NATIONS PROJECT
Gordon Hilton

The concerns of philosophy of science were radically changed by the ideas of Thomas C. Kuhn.[1] This broader interpretation of the scope of philosophy of science now admits both the sociology of knowledge and the history of science as valid topics for discussion. Because of this and because I have commented elsewhere on the philosophical content of the Dimensionality of Nations project (DON),[2] I shall use this opportunity to present an essay comparing and contrasting competing ideas about how a science develops.

The concern with the development of science derives from a need to provide rules that govern the acceptance and rejection of theories, without which scientific growth would become anarchic. However, a theory of scientific development should be capable of two other contributions as well: it should rationally reconstruct past scientific development, and perhaps more importantly, it should provide a charter for future scientific efforts. Such a product will undoubtably have some overall concern with intellectual honesty.

There are three serious competing theories of scientific development. One of these views scientific development as a social process, governed by psychological and sociological forces. This is the theory of Kuhn. The other two theories, those of Karl Popper and Imre Lakatos,[3] suggest that science has, and should have, developed according to some dialectical process involving theory and an empirical base, and that as far as is possible other forces should be

---

In preparing this essay I was helped by James A. Caporaso, Jean Dose, and Mark Levine, Department of Political Science, Northwestern University, and John Laing, Department of Philosophy, University of Illinois at Chicago Circle.

eliminated. All three, however, hold the belief that science does not grow by accretion.

The ability of each of these three distinct theories to provide accurate reconstruction of scientific development has been discussed at length by their sponsors. Unfortunately, all the scientific endeavours used as examples by them were taken from the natural sciences, primarily physics; before we, as social scientists, adopt any of them it would be wise to gauge the ability of these theories to provide adequate reconstruction of social science development. This is where the DON project comes in. DON is a major social science research program. Begun in 1962, it has gone through various phases of theory development and articulation and has provided a training ground for a number of social scientists. In addition, it has been articulated vividly and clearly by Rudolph J. Rummel. There is an incredible amount of documentation of the project. Each stage in the development of DON has been reported in the famous research reports. Field and status-field theory are part of an axiomatic structure, a rarity in the social sciences. This allows us to pin down with some certainty the basic assumptions of the theories. DON has provided a very rigorous empirical base for testing the various models of field theory and status-field theory. What has perhaps been the most important feature of DON has been testing of the models, making it possible to determine how the project personnel responded to the successes and failure of their models.

The flow diagram in Figure 8.1 shows the development of DON, with some extra research excursions undertaken by the project. The important point, however, is that DON has a clear developmental sequence. Various models and theories have been produced as a response to confrontations with data. In this figure it is quite easy to trace the main research thrust of the project since the initial generation of field theory. DON has been no random research process, but one in which an incremental step research strategy has been adopted. It is thus capable of rational reconstruction. For a more detailed description of DON, the reader might refer to my review of the project.[4]

We shall employ DON in the same way that the sponsors of the three theories of scientific development used projects from the natural scientists. In this way we may be able to point to the strengths and weaknesses of each theory as it applies to political science. After this, the discussion moves to a meta-level at which I scrutinize each of the theories of scientific development, using the rules for acceptance and rejection that each theory advocates. If rules are provided for theory acceptance or rejection, there is no reason why such rules cannot be employed at a meta-level to look at theories about theories.

DESCRIPTIVE THESES

Kuhn's notable contribution to matters of scientific development began with his Structure of Scientific Revolutions.[5] In this offering he distinguishes between two modes of scientific activity, the first of which is normal science. In this mode scientists work within an accepted paradigm that is so designed that the scientist never questions the foundations upon which it is based. It provides the puzzles for solution, the methodology for scrutiny, and an acceptable set of solutions to the puzzles. The paradigm thus provides a common frame of reference for the researchers; as long as research takes place within this paradigm, normal science is being conducted.

The second mode of scientific activity is necessary when crisis occurs within a paradigm. There comes a time in normal science when the paradigm cannot account for a growing number of anomalies. The scientists within the paradigm become increasingly critical of the paradigm. Arguments centering around the fundamental interpretation of the rules of the existing paradigm will break out, as the scientists repeatedly fail to account for the anomalies. Scientists cannot work without an acceptable set of rules for frame of reference, and therefore a revolution to another paradigm occurs. The transference to the new paradigm is in the form of a gestalt switch—another way of looking at the same problem.

Kuhn's ideas provide a description only, although in Chapter 12 of his book he does argue that his analysis has normal implications.[6] His efforts at describing the activities of scientists derive from what he perceives as the difference between the way science really proceeds and the way it is presented in scientific textbooks. The alternative he presents, he argues, has an ability to make coherent the way in which science has developed.

He likewise rejects the thesis that paradigms are rejected by facts alone. He allows that an overload of anomalies will be significant in producing a crisis that eventually leads to revolution, but holds that the paradigm will not be overthrown unless there is another paradigm ready to take its place. Despite the fact that the extant paradigm is proving to be substantially false, scientists will stick with what they have unless there is something different and better around. This, as we shall see, differs from the rational development of science prescribed by Popper and Lakatos.

In this essay, we must be clear about what a levels problem is. It would be unfair to apply Kuhn's model and those of the other authors unless we apply them at a level of social science that corresponds to the level on which they were applied in the physical sciences. We can conceptualize the levels problem as shown in Figure 8.2.

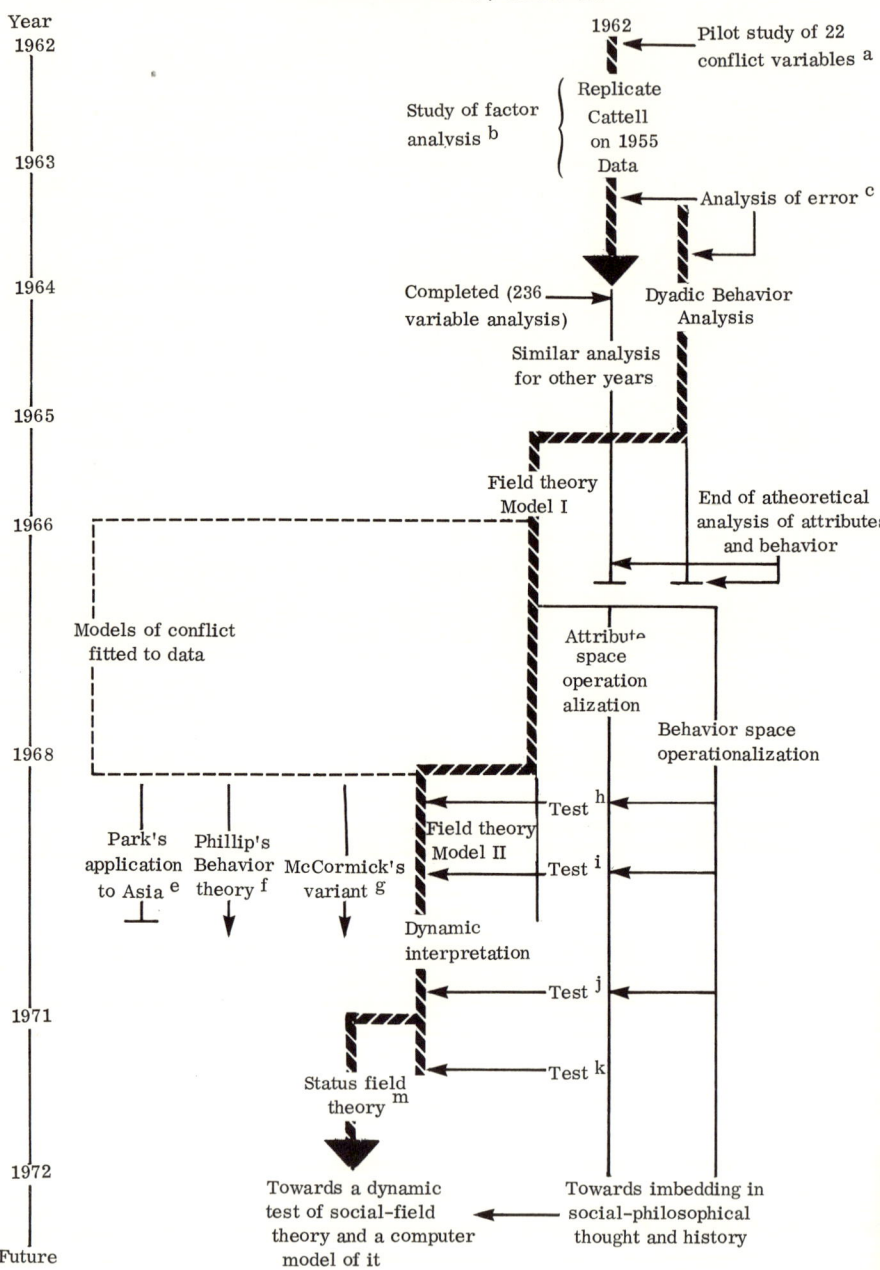

FIGURE 8.1

Dimensionality of Nations Project
Research Flow, 1962-72

[a] Rudolph J. Rummel, "Dimensions of Conflict Behavior Within and Between Nations, General Systems 8 (1963): 1-50.
[b] Rudolph J. Rummel, Applied Factor Analysis (Evanston: Northwestern University Press, 1970).
[c] Rudolph J. Rummel, "Dimensions of Error in Cross-National Data," in Handbook of Method in Cultural Anthropology, edited by Raoul Naroll and Ronald Cohen (Garden City, N.Y.: Natural History Press, 1971).
[d] Rudolph J. Rummel, "A Field Theory of Social Action with Application to Conflict within Nations," General Systems 10 (1965): 183-211.
[e] Tong-Whan Park, "Asian Conflict—Systemic Perspective: Application of Field Theory (1955 and 1963)," Dimensionality of Nations Project, Research Report No. 35 (Honolulu: University of Hawaii, 1969).
[f] Warren R. Phillips, "Dynamic Patterns of International Conflict," Dimensionality of Nations Project, Research Report No. 33 (Honolulu: University of Hawaii, 1969).
[g] David McCormick, "A Field Theory of Dynamic International Processes," Dimensionality of Nations Project, Research Report No. 30 (Honolulu: University of Hawaii, 1969).
[h] Rudolph J. Rummel, "Field Theory and Indicators of International Behavior," Dimensionality of Nations Project, Research Report No. 29 (Honolulu: University of Hawaii, 1969).
[i] Richard Van Atta and Rudolph J. Rummel, "Testing Field Theory on the 1963 Behavior Space of Nations," Dimensionality of Nations Project, Research Report No. 43 (Honolulu: University of Hawaii, 1970).
[j] Sang-Woo Rhee, "Communist China's Foreign Behavior: An Application of Field Theory Model II," Dimensionality of Nations Project, Research Report No. 57 (Honolulu: University of Hawaii, 1971).
[k] Rudolph J. Rummel, "Status-Field Theory and International Relations," Dimensionality of Nations Project, Research Report No. 50 (Honolulu: University of Hawaii, 1973).

Source: Data compiled by the editors.

There are some discrepancies among our authors about what level each is addressing. In addition, the definition of a paradigm, research program, or problem network allows for flexibility in moving up and down through the levels. We must justify our choice of level in order to show that we are providing a fair application of the author's models to the social sciences. This has been one of the major problems in the application of Kuhn and others to the social sciences.

For the purposes of this paper, we will use the "bottom" level as our test of the authors' theories, although this is not to say that this is the only level at which these theories may be applicable.[7] It is now our task to demonstrate why this level is appropriately conceptualized as a "paradigm" or "research program," as those terms are used by authors.

According to Kuhn, a paradigm "stands for the entire constellation of beliefs, values, techniques and so on shared by the members of a given community."[8] This fits in with our level of paradigm analysis. The people on the DON project entertain and share certain beliefs (the axiomatic structure), values (the goal of reducing conflict at the international level), and techniques (factor analysis, canonical correlation, and all the other linear techniques). Research programs, that is, series of theories, as defined by Lakatos,[9] are also served by our definition of a research program. We see, therefore, that by determining our paradigm at the research program level it may be possible to compare the ideas of Kuhn and Lakatos. Let us therefore return to the major effort of this section, which is to consider the ideas of Kuhn, using the DON project.

According to Kuhn there are three major focal points in the period of normal science. The first concerns "A class of facts that the paradigm has shown to be particularly revealing";[10] the second concerns predictions allowed by the paradigm; and in the case of the third, "empirical work is undertaken to articulate the paradigm theory."[11] These foci coincide with those of the DON project, in which attribute and behavior space are undeniably important and revealing facts. Moreover, in an early piece about the project Rudolph J. Rummel professed concern with prediction.[12] Much of the more recent work has been in the development of the parameters for both field theory and status-field theory, which can only be seen as articulation of the theory.

There are other areas of research behavior on DON that can be interpreted in a Kuhnian sense. People operating in the paradigm must adopt the rules of the paradigm, which are a way of prescribing the scientific behavior of the research group. Mostly these rules are built into the education of the students who choose to work in the paradigm. On the DON project there was an articulated program

FIGURE 8.2

Levels of Studies in Political Science in Relation to
the Programs Studied in this Volume

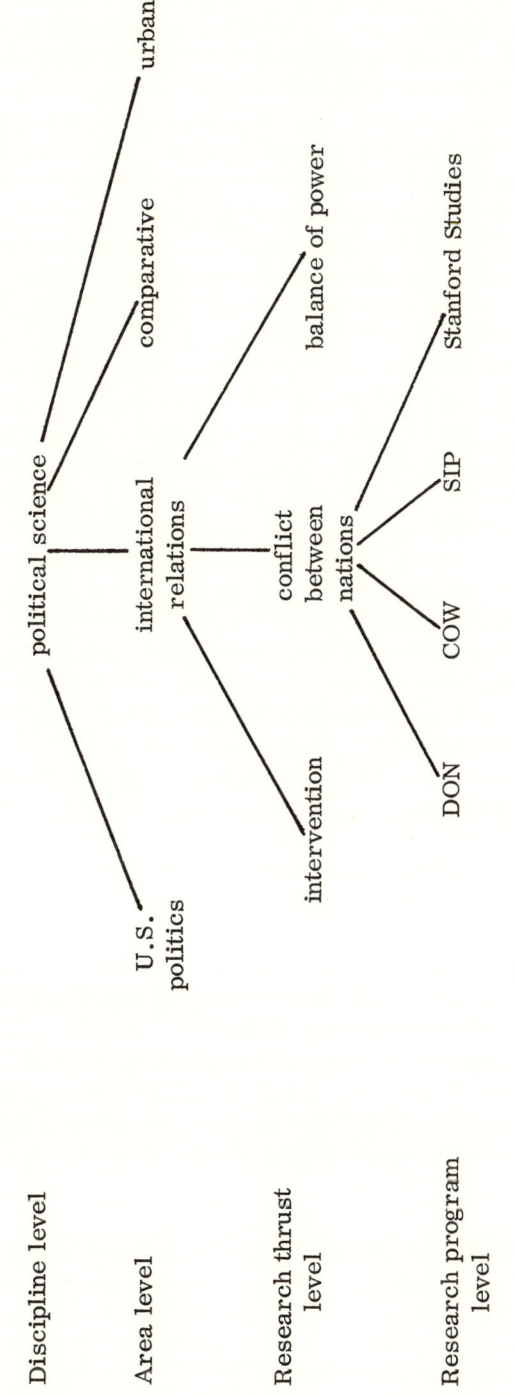

Source: Data compiled by the author.

for induction into the paradigm; this program involved four steps and was communicated to me privately by Rudolph Rummel. In the first year the student is expected to attain skills in statistics, multivariate methods, and computer usage. During this period the student also collects data for the project. During the second year, analysis rather than data collection is encouraged. In the third year the student is well versed in the appropriate methodologies and is given more discretion and less direction. In the fourth year, if the student's dissertation proposal is accepted and the research topic relates to DON, the student works alone. This educational program obviously makes a great deal of sense in terms of paradigm implementation, particularly when such students get teaching positions. Its success is obvious: most of the successful doctorates awarded to students from the DON project have been within the paradigm boundaries encompassed by field theory and status-field theory.

Other attempts at paradigm implementation and growth have been attempted by the project. There was a floating student plan, in which graduates from various other schools were invited to join the project for a time while DON students spent time in other schools. A textbook called Applied Factor Analysis was produced, which laid out the methodology of the DON project with seductive clarity.[13] The staggering number of research reports put out by the project were sent regularly to over 300 people. All of these strategies would aid paradigm implementation, a natural objective for those who had accepted the paradigm or who had been educated in it.

The manner in which anomalies are coped with during normal science has also been discussed by Kuhn.[14] Given any anomaly, the paradigm will be adjusted to make that anomaly expected by the paradigm—turning defeat into victory. The change from Model I to Model II of field theory exhibited this pattern. Testing for Model I produced quite disappointing results; but changing the model slightly so that the parameters became actor-identified produced more encouraging results. The theory was not completely rejected for its delinquency; it was simply adjusted.

We see, therefore, that there are many ways in which the DON project has conformed to the Kuhn thesis; however, there are many ways in which it has not. As Figure 8.2 suggests, there are at least three competing paradigms.* The other three projects dis-

---

*Rummel argues that there is an even more fundamental difference between his paradigm and those of the other projects discussed in this volume. While the other paradigms are based in Euclidian space with a finite number of dimensions, his theories are in Hilbertian space, in which there are an infinite number of dimensions.

cussed in this volume can also be considered as paradigms by our definition. They have training programs and produce their own students and therefore schools of thought.[15] However, this pluralism is not allowed for in Kuhn's scheme of things. There is, according to his thesis, a paradigm that remains dominant until its inability to explain occuring anomalies produces a crisis, during which fluidity another paradigm is adopted. In no way does Kuhn allow for coexisting paradigms, all of them suffering under anomalies yet all of them continuing to survive. The pluralism may very well be a function of the social as against natural science context; in trying to provide factual anecdotal support for his thesis, Kuhn invariably resorts to natural science examples. We do not, in the social sciences, have sufficient confidence in our data to dismiss a paradigm because it has failed in a confrontation with data. We are not prepared to allow the one-way sweeping aside of theory by data, and for good reason. Consider the diagram below:

	data	
paradigm	good	bad
true	paradigm support	anomaly
false	anomaly	no determination

Our testing allows only two results, paradigm support or anomaly, but both these outcomes can occur in a variety of ways. When an anomaly is obtained, is it because the paradigm is false and the data good, or is it because the paradigm is true and the data bad? This quite natural insecurity in the data used by social scientists leads us to be less dogmatic about rejection; this encourages the pluralism we have noted.

This has fundamental implications for Kuhn's thesis when applied to the social sciences. Crisis occurs, by his thesis, when a sufficient number of anomalies are generated. However, this can only happen when we are sure that these anomalies are a function of the inadequacy of the paradigm rather than of the inadequacy of the data. Thus paradigms in the social sciences can never go into crisis in the sense of Kuhn; and without crisis there can be no revolution, in his sense.

Although data in the social sciences pose large problems in applying Kuhn's thesis, the very nature of social science poses more fundamental difficulties. R. W. Friedrichs briefly mentioned this difficulty,[16] and I shall expand upon his efforts. The difficulty derives from the assertion that as social scientists we are more intimately involved with our paradigms. Friedrichs argues as follows:

Whereas atoms and cells are not in any way consequentially influenced by the image the physicist and biologist hold of themselves as scientist, social phenomena may be immediately and profoundly conditioned by the image the social scientist has internalised regarding the nature of his activity. The paradigms that order a [social scientist's] conception of his subject matter, in other words may themselves be a reflection, or function, of a more fundamental image: the paradigm <u>in terms of which he sees himself</u>.[17]

Consider Figures 8.3 and 8.4. In Figure 8.3, which relates to the natural sciences, a change in paradigm from P_1 to P_2 involves looking at the subject matter in a different way—a gestalt switch! Notice, however, in Figure 8.4 a concern with our image of ourselves as scientific agent can of itself be considered as a paradigm level and will no doubt affect the way in which we look at the subject area.

We see that in the social sciences it is possible to delineate two paradigmatic levels, both intimately linked to each other. It may be the case that a change in our image of ourselves as agent also alters our view of the subject area. This has tremendous implications for our view of Kuhn, since a change in a paradigm in the social sciences may have nothing to do with anomalies or with competing or emerging paradigms, but instead may have more to do with the way we perceive our role in society. For example, a

FIGURE 8.3

A Change in Paradigm in Relation
to the Subject Area

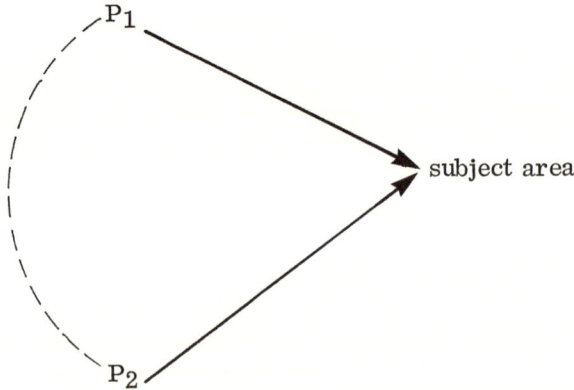

FIGURE 8.4

Change in Self-Image as a Change
in Paradigm

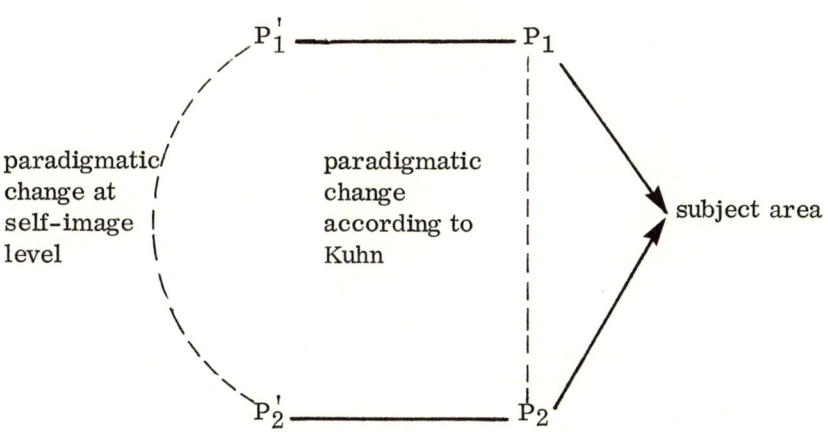

social scientist who views himself as a social engineer will bring
into his theories the variables he considers manipulable: those
that will eventually alow him to twist and turn the knobs and levers
of society. On the other hand, a social scientist who views himself
as a searcher for knowledge will select other variables for his
theory. Thus the content of the two theories will differ because of
the theorists' differing views of their roles in society. Figure 8.5
shows this.

We should also note that much of Kuhn's argument seems tauto-
logical when he discusses immature sciences. Since the social
sciences have a limited history, supporters of Kuhn may very well
point out that noncorroboration of this thesis says more about the
immaturity of political science than about any inadequacy in the
thesis. This more or less amounts to the argument that if a science
does provide support for Kuhn then it is mature, but that if it does
not provide support then it is immature and thus Kuhn is not applicable.

Finally, I want to underline two ideas that have been obtained
in this section of the chapter that may be useful in the next section.
The first idea concerns proliferation. We have seen evidence of
pluralism in social science; any useful theory of scientific development must be capable of explaining this, but Kuhn's theory did not.
The second idea concerns persistence. The ability of a scientist
to stick with his paradigm despite anomalies and discouraging
results is important if any paradigm is to be fully exercised.

FIGURE 8.5

Change in Self-Image Producing Conflicting Theories

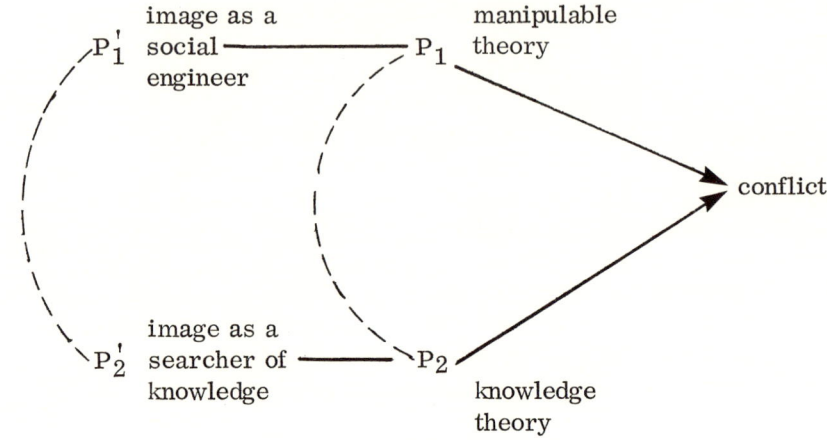

PRESCRIPTIVE THESES

Two major contributors to normative discussion of the development of science are Karl Popper and Imre Lakatos. Since the ideas of Lakatos follow from those of Popper, we shall deal with Popper first.

The whole basis of Popper is founded upon the idea of falsification.[18] His brand of falsification, which has been called methodological falsification, grew out of dogmatic falsification, which he found unacceptable.[19] Dogmatic falsification admitted the fallibility of theories but maintained an infallible empirical basis. To the dogmatic falsificationist, all theories are admissable. Science cannot, of course, prove any of these theories, but science can provide an absolutely solid empirical base that can be used to overthrow them. Thus a theory is acceptable as such, if and only if it is capable of refutation using this empirical base. Intellectual and scientific honesty are contained in the specification in advance of the experimental conditions under which one would relinquish one's theory. Therefore science grows by a succession of theory dismissals using hard facts.

There are some severe difficulties with this thesis for all sciences, not only the social sciences. It just is not the case that the empirical base is infallible. No one can ever be sure that any particular experiment or confrontation between theory and fact will be crucial in the overthrow of the theory.

Popper's methodological falsification is an attempt to overcome this difficulty. Although no facts are infallible, the scientific community is capable of generating a list of "acceptable falsifiers." This becomes the "empirical basis" for the methodological falsificationist. Theories don't become falsified; they are "falsified." Thus the methodological falsificationist distinguishes between rejection and "rejection." A theory that is "falsified" and subsequently "rejected" may be a true theory. This is not an ideal situation, but it is better than an alternative of scientific shambles. A theory is acceptable or scientific if it has an "empirical basis." Obviously this criterion is far easier to satisfy than the dogmatic falsification criterion.

The methodological falsificationist operates according to some consensus in the scientific community about what is and what is not a "test" of a given theory. In doing this, he overcomes the problem—in the social sciences, the severe problem—of arguing the infallibility of an empirical base. This approach to the development of science also accords with our requirement of theory proliferation. Nowhere in the argument is there any reference to a central paradigm or problem network. Paradigms are allowed to coexist. Those that survive encounters with the "empirical base" will survive. This approach ends up by prescribing the "survival of the fittest"; this appears to be an acceptable form of scientific honesty, despite its risky decision.

Such risky decisions can appear downright suicidal, however. As we saw earlier, a theory that is "falsified" and subsequently "rejected" may indeed be a true theory. There will be occasions when a true theory is "rejected," possibly very early in its career. This does not satisfy our requirement for persistence, which we declared in the previous section of the essay. The methodological falsificationist argues that this is the price we have to pay for scientific growth.

Despite anomalies found in field theory, Rummel did not reject the theory, although he did modify it from Model I to Model II. More anomalies with Model II and a desire to incorporate competing theories eventually culminated in a switch to status-field theory. Even despite some disappointing results with status-field theory, Rummel has not abandoned the theory. Why not? Does he lack the scientific honesty implied in the prescriptions of the methodological falsificationist? Of course not, except that he is also persistent. He knows that anomalies can be expected for a variety of reasons, only one of which is that the theory is wrong. He knows that chance results can show a theory in an inaccurate light. Should he abandon what he feels is an intuitively acceptable theory because of some chance results? Of course not; this would be too naive. Should subsequent testing of status-field theory be successful, his persistence in not reacting savagely to premature "rejection" will be seen as a sensible policy. On the other hand, should status-field theory never resolve its anomalies, it will be seen rather vindictively by his peers. Obviously the latter situation must be guarded against, simply because there has to come a time when enough testing is enough. An ideal situation would be a set of rules by which some anomalies are allowed, but in a controlled fashion. We could then eliminate the risk from acting purely as a methodological falsificationist without compromising the agreeable code of scientific honesty.

Imre Lakatos has suggested such a program, which he has called sophisticated falsification, which differs from naive falsification in both the rules for acceptance as a scientific theory and in rejection.[20] Lakatos advises that a theory should be accepted as scientific if and only if it has excess empirical content over its predecessor. By excess empirical content, one requires the new theory to predict novel facts its predecessor could not. The sophisticated falsificationist criterion for the rejection of theory T_1 is as follows: T_1 will be falsified if and only if its successor T_2 (1) has excess empirical content, (2) explains the success of T_1, and (3) has some of the excess empirical content corroborated. Thus Lakatos provides a controlled manner in which anomalies can be accommodated without the risk of "rejecting" true theories. This code for operating allows both of our previously developed requirements of proliferation and persistence, while still testing theories against a factual base.

Lakatos' sophisticated falsificationism allows us to deal with series of theories rather than individual theories. It is not only a two-way fight between a theory and a factual base, but a three-way fight between the old theory, the new theory, and the factual base. Figure 8.6 shows this. Falsification, in its generally accepted sense, is neither a sufficient nor a necessary condition for theory elimination. With this code a theory can be eliminated without recourse to any testing at all, if a successor appears that has excess empirical content that may be corroborated. Lakatos states "that no experiment, experimental report, observational statement or well corroborated low level falsifying hypothesis alone can lead to falsification. There is no falsification before the emergence of a better theory."[21]

A series of theories is considered theoretically progressive if each subsequent theory has more empirical content than a previous one. It is considered empirically progressive if some of this excess content is corroborated. If a new theory has both, it is called a progressive problem shift. Otherwise, it is a degenerative problem shift.

Sophisticated falsification provides two heuristics. The first, the positive heuristic, describes research paths to follow. The

FIGURE 8.6

Two Conflicting Theories Tested
against an Empirical Basis

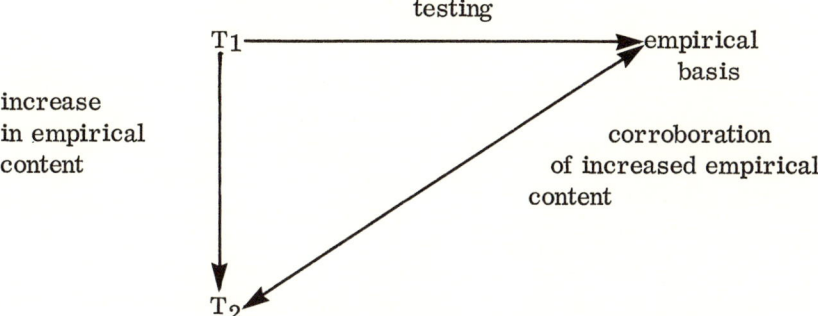

second, the negative heuristic, describes paths not to follow. A series of theories is called a research program, and each research program has two components, a hard inner core and a protective belt of middle-range hypotheses.

The negative heuristic of the program forbids any testing of the fundamental hard core of the research program. To protect this core, auxiliary middle-range hypotheses are generated and tested. If they fail, they can be adjusted or completely replaced. Using the DON example, we see that this is precisely how Rummel has acted. We can consider the hard core of the DON research program as including the axiomatic proposition that "the international field comprises a Euclidian attribute space defining all nation attributes and Euclidian behavior space defining all nation dyadic interactions."[22] Attached to this we have the methodological operator of factor analysis, which edits and controls the ways in which the international field will be discussed.

The negative heuristic will forbid the testing of this component in the hard core of the research program. Rummel has pronounced this as definitional and thus irrefutable, in some way beyond question. This axiomatic proposition has not been tested and probably cannot be; however, there has been testing of the middle-range hypotheses placed as a protective belt around the hard core. Thus the testing of Model I and II of field theory and the hypotheses generated in status-field theory provide evidence of this.

The positive heuristic provides a long-range program for coping with anomalies generated in the testing of the protective belt of hypotheses. It provides for a set of increasingly complex models. As long as each model has excess empirical content over its predecessor, a progressive problem shift is maintained. Again this is precisely how Rummel has acted. Consider Model I of field theory, which is represented mathematically by the following equation:

$$w_{i \to j, k} = \alpha_1 d_{i \to j, 1} + \alpha_2 d_{i \to j, 2} + \ldots + \alpha_p d_{i \to j, p}$$

This equation states that the behavior of nation i toward nation j on behavior dimension k, $w_{i \to j, k}$ is a linear addition of the distance vectors between i and j on all of the attribute dimensions, where there are a total of p such dimensions. The parameters α_1, α_2, and so forth, describe mathematically the precise relationship between $w_{i-j, k}$ and $d_{i-j, 2}$, and so on. For example, suppose there are just two dimensions, which we call power and economic development. In this two-dimensional attribute space we can locate all nations. Suppose further we are interested in the behavior dimension conflict; that is, we imagine only one behavior dimension. In addition, we may be mostly interested in the nation dyad U.S.→China. The equation now becomes as follows:

$$w_{U.S. \to China, conflict} = \alpha_{power} d_{U.S. \to China, power} + \alpha_{economic\ development} d_{U.S. \to China, economic\ development}$$

Model I did not test this out particularly well, and with the help of logical criticism from students, Model II was produced. In Model II the parameters were made actor-specific. Each actor nation having its own value for the parameter on each attribute distance is increased empirical content over Model I—a novel fact. Model II can be described mathematically as follows:

$$w_{i \to j, k} = \alpha_{i, 1} d_{i \to j} + \alpha_{i, 2} d_{i \to j, 2} + \ldots + \alpha_{i, p} d_{i \to j, p}$$

We can again use the U.S.→China example. Interpreting this equation to predict conflict behavior as a function of the differences between the two attributes of power and economic development, we get the following:

$$w_{U.S. \to China, conflict} = \alpha_{U.S., power} d_{U.S. \to China, power} + \alpha_{U.S., economic\ development} d_{U.S. \to China, economic\ development}$$

Thus the change from α_{power} to $\alpha_{U.S.\ power}$ is an increase in empirical content. Furthermore, since Model II tested out far better

DESIGN AND PHILOSOPHY   171

than Model I, its excess empirical content has achieved some corroboration. Thus the anomalies generated in testing Model I lead to a progressive problem shift to Model II, which vindicates Rummel's persistence. Notice also that there is no confrontation at all with the hard core; the negative heuristic forbids this.

Field theory (Model II) was finally superseded by status-field theory. Status-field theory again provided an increase in empirical content. The signs of various parameters were predicted, and the actions of certain types of nations were presumed to be a function of a particular attribute distance. Parts of status-field theory are still being tested. Tests still generate anomalies, but as we see when adopting the code of the sophisticated falsificationist, this is of little importance.

Thus we have evidence that Professor Rummel has been acting as a sophisticated falsificationist. The question that now arises is, When should he abandon the research program? Lakatos provides a guide for this too. He requires that a research program be abandoned when another research program supersedes it or when the existing program moves into a degenerative problem shift. Thus, if status-field theory tests out badly and Rummel does not come up with a model that has increased empirical content, he should abandon the research program. A sure indicator of a degenerative problem shift will be constant attention to anomalies. While there is a progressive problem shift, the researcher can virtually disregard the anomalies. In a degenerative shift he will not be able to dismiss them with the production of a new model, and therefore his attention will be absorbed by the anomalies.

To summarize, sophisticated falsificationism was generated as a safeguard against the considerable risks taken in adopting the methodological falsification of Popper. These risks involved the possible elimination of true theories, of which the scientific honesty in methodological falsification required preservation. The sophisticated falsificationist is able to combine all of this by providing rules for sets of theories. Sophisticated falsification requires that all theories have some novel empirical content over their predecessors and that some of this empirical content be corroborated. We saw that this policy allows the researcher not to be blocked by anomalies but given time to see whether he can contrive to make the anomalies disappear. We also saw that we were able to reconstruct the history of the DON research program. The sophisticated falsificationist thesis of scientific development also does not forbid the proliferation of research programs. Thus within this one thesis we have accommodated the requirements both of persistence in the fact of anomalies and of proliferation of research programs.

Lakatos' sophisticated falsificationist supersedes Popper's methodological falsificationist. Not only that, but increased empirical content is corroborated by facts. Thus, while the DON research program provided an anomaly for Popper because Rummel continued his research after the generation of anomalies on his program, the Lakatos model coped with this. However, with the Lakatos model have we really solved the problem of premature rejection or have we just postponed it? It could be argued that periods of degenerative shifts could, if left long enough, be turned into progressive problem shifts. We therefore require some other rule for determining the length of time allowed a degenerative shift. What shall we use as a guide in knowing when to abandon a research program rather than wait hopefully for a progressive problem shift? Although Lakatos does not provide adequately for this, I think the problem solves itself. A research program that has moved into a degenerative shift will eventually wither and die, particularly in the social sciences, where there are such scarce financial and intellectual resources.

META-LEVEL ANALYSIS OF BOTH DESCRIPTIVE AND PRESCRIPTIVE THESES

In determining which theories of scientific development we might use in the social sciences, we again ask the question, Why be concerned with the way science develops? The immediate response to this is that we require rules that govern the acceptance or rejection of scientific theories, paradigms or research programs. A theory of scientific development should (1) allow a reconstruction of our previous efforts in science and (2) provide us with a guide to show us which rules we should adhere to in order to achieve some form of scientific honesty. Programs should not be abandoned according to some unarticulated common sense. Let us take each of the three theories and check for these characteristics.

Kuhn's <u>Theory of Scientific Revolutions</u> attempts to describe scientific development in terms of overriding paradigms and occasional revolutions to other overriding paradigms. Evidence of the existence of at least four paradigms at the level of the Dimensionality of Nations project provides a major anomaly for Kuhn's thesis. It will be argued by his supporters (and I've gone over this in a previous part of the essay) that either my selection of the paradigmatic level is wrong and/or that political science is an immature science and thus that Kuhnian analysis is not relevant. Assuming this to be correct, Kuhn's thesis still does not satisfy the second characteristic of providing us with a chart for our future scientific efforts. In short

DESIGN AND PHILOSOPHY 173

Kuhn is not normative; his thesis will be of little use in providing rules for future use.

We now turn to the ideas of Popper and Lakatos. Since both are designed as normative theories, they instantly satisfy the second of our characteristics. We can thus restrict our discussion to their ability to reconstruct past scientific endeavors. Let us consider Popper first. Popper's methodological falsification requires that a theory be "rejected" if it is "falsified." We noted that this produces grave risks of incorrectly throwing out true theories. We also saw that the persistence of Rummel led him to carry on with his theory long after it had generated anomalies. If we apply Popper's normative theory at the meta-level; that is, if we use methodological falsification as the method for falsifying Popper's own theory, we see this one anomaly, of Rummel not acting as Popper would predict, forcing us to reject Popper's theory. Ironically, the risks that the methodological falsificationists would have us take in science have worked against themselves. Thus the argument that methodological falsification is a true theory of the growth of science is lost in our attempt to achieve scientific order.

Turning our attention to the research programmism of Lakatos, a normative theory, we found that it did provide a rational reconstruction of the DON project. The controlled avoidance of overreaction to anomalies during a progressive problem shift made sense of the activities of those involved in the project. The problem of deciding when to end a program or when to decide that a degenerating problem shift has set in permanently seems to take care of itself in the social sciences.

However, let us again exploit a meta-level analysis; let us use sophisticated falsification upon the sophisticated falsificationist theory. Sophisticated falsification deals with sets of theories and the progression from one to another. Thus we must deal with methodological falsification and sophisticated falsification in tandem. Was it a progressive problem shift from methodological falsification to sophisticated falsification? Does sophisticated falsification contain empirical content over methodological falsification? Yes it does. It predicts that despite anomalies a researcher ought to continue with his theory. Does sophisticated falsification have any of this excess empirical content corroborated? Yes it does. The activities of the DON project provide this. The sophisticated falsificationist therefore conforms to his own normative theory.

Of the three theories of scientific development, it would appear that Lakatos is the most persuasive. It satisfies both of our necessary conditions. However, it has areas of weakness when trying to reconstruct a history of a particular social science. For example, how would Lakatos explain the demise of Project Camelot? Obviously there are historical forces in operation that are external to the research program or discipline. We can thus distinguish internal and external historical forces. Internal history accounts for the professional activities of a discipline; it is concerned with the theories held. External history accounts for the relationship between the discipline and the societal and cultural environment. It is concerned with the social, political, and economic forces surrounding and acting on the discipline. Obviously the forces that destroyed Project Camelot were of the external variety.

A poor theory of scientific development will be forced to resort to external history to resolve its anomalies. For example, Rummel's persistence with field theory despite the anomalies is a serious anomaly in terms of Popper's theory. Popperists have to resort to external history to explain this. In this case they might suggest that the Advanced Research Projects Agency of the Department of Defense (ARPA) had too much money to give away or that perhaps Rummel's personality was so intertwined with and committed to DON that he was blind to the failure of field theory. I personally have heard both of these rationalizations.

However, as the theories of scientific development become improved, there is a reduced need for external history as explanation, as if external history becomes internal history. Accordingly, Lakatos with his sophisticated falsificationism completely accounts for Rummel's persistence.

We should note, therefore, that the history of science will always be richer than its internal reconstruction, particularly in social science disciplines in which external historical forces play such a large part. A better theory of scientific development will convert some of these external forces into internal forces within the control of the discipline.

Finally, what can we conclude about Rummel's approach to quantitative international politics in particular, and what can we prescribe for quantitative international politics researchers in general? It seems to me that Rummel was able to balance pragmatism with honesty: pragmatism, because he continued with his ideas despite anomalies; honesty, because he implicitly stated the conditions under which he would adjust his ideas. More than this, he has demonstrated quite clearly that we should think in terms of research programs instead of fragmented research studies. It is only when we can consider programs as a whole, as we can with the DON project, the COW project, and the Stanford Studies, that we can compare and contrast various theories in sequence. Such comparison and contrast cannot easily be achieved with the present rather fragmented approach to quantitative international politics.

NOTES

1. Thomas C. Kuhn, *The Structure of Scientific Revolutions* (Chicago: University of Chicago Press, 1970).
2. Gordon Hilton, *A Review of the Dimensionality of Nations Project* (Beverly Hills: Sage Publications, 1973).
3. Karl Popper, *The Logic of Scientific Discovery* (London: Hutchinson, 1959), and Imre Lakatos and Alan Musgrave, *Criticism and the Growth of Knowledge* (Cambridge: Cambridge University Press, 1970).
4. Hilton, *A Review of the DON Project*, op. cit.
5. Kuhn, *Structure*, op. cit.
6. Ibid.
7. See R. W. Friedrichs, *A Sociology of Sociology* (New York: Free Press, 1970).
8. Kuhn, *Structure*, op. cit., p. 175. In this edition of the book Kuhn admits to many definitions of the term paradigm.
9. Lakatos and Musgrave, *Criticism and the Growth of Knowledge*, op. cit.
10. Kuhn, *Structure*, op. cit., p. 25.
11. Ibid.
12. Rudolph J. Rummel, "DON Project: A Five-Year Program," Dimensionality of Nations Project, Research Report No. 9 (Honolulu: University of Hawaii, 1967).
13. Rudolph J. Rummel, *Applied Factor Analysis* (Evanston: Northwestern University Press, 1970).
14. Kuhn, *Structure*, op. cit., p. 52.
15. Bruce M. Russett, "Methodological and Theoretical Schools in International Relations" (mimeographed, New Haven: Yale University, no date).
16. Friedrichs, *A Sociology of Sociology*, op. cit., p. 55.
17. Ibid., p. 65.
18. Karl Popper, *The Logic of Scientific Discovery*, op. cit.
19. Ibid.
20. Lakatos, *Criticism and Growth*, op. cit., p. 91.
21. Ibid., p. 119.
22. Hilton, *A Review of the DON Project*, op. cit., p. 29.

CHAPTER

9

AN APPRAISAL OF THE METHODOLOGY AND STATISTICAL PRACTICES USED IN THE DIMENSIONALITY OF NATIONS PROJECT

Leo Hazlewood

The Dimensionality of Nations Project (DON) was originally undertaken in 1962 to help develop "a knowledge of the basic structure of cross-national data"[1] in three separate but related ways. First, since much social science theory was "based largely on intuitively grounded concepts and limited knowledge of the relations among a few variables for which data have been readily available in the past,"[2] attention was focused on "a broad mapping of the cross-national domain to serve as guidance for the choice of major concepts and variables for research on specific areas."[3] Second, once broad concept mapping was obtained, the results would also test the temporal stability of the dimensions of nations previously reported by Cattel, Berry, and others. Third, the acquisition and analysis of a large body of cross-national data would help direct the future theoretical work in international relations by empirically grounding concepts suggested in the theoretical literature and providing external validation for laboratory simulation such as Harold Guetzkow's Simulated International Processes project.

All independent states with a population of at least 800,000 in 1955 (n = 82) were included in the analysis, yielding observation points from all continents and geographical regions. Over 500 variables were initially considered for inclusion in the study.

I wish to thank the Computer Center of Florida State University for its generous grants of computer time to perform the statistical manipulations reported in this paper. I also wish to thank CACI, Inc. for staff support in the preparation and duplication of the draft of this paper.

According to Rummel, this was reduced to 230 variables (the maximum capability of existing factor analysis programs), based on (1) the spread across substantive types of variables, (2) an attempt to avoid arithmetic redundancy, (3) data availability, (4) scale properties of the individual variables, (5) prior use or recommended use from other data-based studies, and (6) their theoretical importance and policy relevance.[4]

The collection and analysis of these 230 variables, first for 1955 and later for other years, constituted the first phase of the DON project. Once this had been completed, a second phase of the project, the development and testing of field theory, occupied the attention of the DON researchers. Papers by Gordon Hilton, Richard H. Van Atta, and Dale B. Robertson in this volume, and by others elsewhere,[5] more elaborately detail the history of the DON project. In this critique we shall examine a number of methodological and data analytical practices that have been utilized in the DON project. For the most part our attention will be directed towards the creation of the attribute and behavioral space from the DON data, since it is in this phase of the project that the methodology for which the project has become known was developed. We shall also consider the procedures that are used to relate attribute space to behavior space. In each instance we will consider whether the procedures were followed and what the implications of these procedures were for the results generated in the project. We shall also be concerned with the extent to which the procedures facilitated or retarded the avowed interest of the project in concept mapping, information generation on the structure of cross-national data, and assessment of the existing theoretical frameworks in international relations. Toward these ends we shall examine the composition of the basic data matrix, the nature of the factor analyses and their interpretation, the assessment of error and missing data, and the procedures used to relate attribute space to behavior space.

CREATION OF THE DATA MATRIX

True to the initial purposes of the project, variables from both attribute and behavioral space were selected for inclusion in the DON analyses. The 230 substantive variables* were organized into

---

*Throughout the paper, a distinction will be made between the substantive DON variables and the error variables inserted as part

27 domains, 17 dealing with intranational characteristics (comprising 61.3 percent of the variables) and 10 dealing with international characteristics (comprising 38.7 percent of the variables). This matrix, plus six error measures, forms the basis of the DON analyses in the first phase of the project.

Almost one-half of the substantive variables (n = 112) were included in the DON analyses because their importance was mentioned or prescribed in theoretical literature or in textbooks on international relations. In Rummel's words, "the texts of Haas and Whiting (1956), Lerche (1959), Organski (1958), Strauz-Hope and Possony (1954), Morgenthau (1954), and Wright (1955), were searched for variables."[6] Additionally, a number of other variables (n = 88) were chosen from the results reported in the earlier dimensionalizing studies by Berry, Cattell, and others as the DON researchers attempted to replicate the previous efforts with more recent data.*

All of the variables gathered by the DON researchers were jointly considered in a factor analysis to explore the patterned relationships present in the data matrix. At this point it may be useful to distinguish between two uses of factor analysis. According to Karl Joreskog and Dennis Lawley,[7] factor analysis can be used to confirm hypotheses or to explore the total variance in a data matrix. Confirmatory factor analysis, the first of the uses, assumes that the researcher has already obtained "a certain amount of knowledge about the variates measured and is therefore in a position to formulate a hypothesis that specifies the factors on which the variates depend."[8] Contrasted with this is exploratory factor analysis, in which a priori knowledge of the internal structure of the variates is unavailable and the object of the study is to discover and interpret the underlying patterns in the data. Stated in other terms, confirmatory factor analysis emphasizes clear and explicit hypothesis testing, the hypothesis involved being a particular factor structure. Exploratory factor analysis emphasizes the discovery of relationships in the data, using factor analysis as the probing instrument.

Given the number of DON variables suggested in the existing texts or theoretical literature on international politics, we can question the emphasis on exploratory factor analysis that character-

---

of Rummel's extremely creative attempt to assess the impact of various kinds and sources of error in the analysis. There are 230 variables used in the DON analysis for 1955.

*There are 46 variables that overlap the two categories (theoretically derived and derived from previous correlational-factor analytic studies) discussed so far.

ized virtually all of the first phase of the project. If the 112 variables were actually drawn from or suggested by existing conceptual frameworks, the DON researchers could have at least as usefully explored the relationships postulated among the different types of exchanges between states. Thus, if the DON project had been oriented toward validating simulations, its analyses could have focused on testing the relationships isolated in the laboratory. If DON had been oriented toward testing existing conceptual frameworks in the international politics literature of the time, or at least what was being suggested to students enrolled in international politics courses at the time, it could have engaged in more focused analyses of these questions. Instead of systematic tests of what was hypothesized in the literature or what had been found in the simulations, the 112 variables were joined with the remaining variables in general factor analysis, which may have obscured more than it elucidated about the major concepts and hypotheses in the field.

Similarly, given this expressed objective of replicating the earlier dimensionalizing studies, it is not clear why the DON researchers chose to perform their replications on the total set of 230 variables rather than on the smaller set of 88 variables that had been selected to represent the previous studies. It would seem that the earlier studies of the dimensions of cross-national behavior had indeed provided the knowledge needed to formulate hypotheses about the factor structure to be expected in the analyses; but instead the DON analyses concentrated on exploration, which meant exhaustive searches of the variance in the complete data matrix, rather than on confirmation, which would have meant the testing of explicit hypotheses about the factor structure that was expected to emerge.

Arguments can be made for both exploratory and confirmatory factor analysis, of course, but it is reasonable to question whether the relative gains of the DON project through exploratory factor analysis would have been greater than those obtained through confirmatory factor analysis. Given the prior knowledge from earlier studies of the probable underlying factor structure for a number of these 88 variables, supplemented by the explicit theoretical justification found for a number of these indicators in the international relations literature, it seems that confirmatory factor analysis would have yielded more evidence and more numerous theoretical insights to aid the advancement of the field. The choice of exploratory factor analysis to examine such a large set of variables in the name of concept mapping only increased the probability that the field of international relations would detour away from systematic hypothesis testing toward the mapping of dimensions that had little or no relationship to existing theory.[9]

COMPOSITION OF THE DATA MATRIX

Given the decision by the DON researchers to explore all 230 substantive variables together, the potential impact of different kinds of variables on the correlation matrix (and on the factor analysis derived from it) is of interest. One area of concern is the impact of ratio or proportional variables, where one variable is "deflated" by some other one such as population, on the correlation matrix generated to create the factor analysis. Over 50 percent (123 of 230) of the substantive variables employed in the DON analysis are ratios or proportions, most frequently involving a substantive variable divided by either population or gross national product. For example, 55 of the 230 substantive variables, or 23.9 percent, have been "per capitized" with one of several forms of the population variable.

Since the covariation between the terms may be inflated, the practice of using proportional variables in associational analysis, be it correlation or regression, in which no specific hypotheses link the ratios to each other, has generally been objected to.[10] Correlations between variables, expressed as proportions in which one of the terms is shared in common (such as $r_{(x/y)\ (z/y)}$) or between a proportion and one of its component parts (such as $r_{(x/y)\ (x)}$) may inflate the variation summarized in the correlation. This problem is severe in the bivariate case and even more serious in the multivariate case. Since the factor analyses used in the DON analysis have been computed on a correlation matrix employing so many of these proportional variables, the entire correlation matrix may include much more patterned variation, some of which is spurious, than may actually be present.

An examination of the correlations for each of the 230 substantive variables suggests that proportional variables share variation more frequently than do nonproportional variables.[11] Of the 76 variables that have at least 100 correlations with other variables equal to or greater than .30, 50, or 68.8 percent, are proportions or ratios. Of the 17 variables that have 90 correlations at least equal to .30 with other variables, ten, or 58.8 percent, are proportions or ratios. Furthermore, an inspection of these correlations indicates that the proportional or ratio variables have a substantial percentage of their high correlations with other variables that contain either one of their constituent parts (for example, the ratio of gross national product to total population might have a high correlation with gross national product) or one of their constituent parts in another ratio (for example, the ratio of agricultural population to total population might have a high correlation with pieces of domestic mail to total population). Particularly problematic are the correla-

METHODOLOGY AND STATISTICAL PRACTICES 181

tions involving one or more of the forms of the population variable. Here the introduction of total population as a control for size creates systematic interrelationships among a large number of different variables.

The proportional variables share more variance with the factors extracted from the DON data and also share variance with these factors more often. For example, no fewer than 36, or 57.1 percent, of the 63 variables that load above .40 on more than one factor are proportions. Of the remaining 27 variables loading above .40 on more than one factor, 18 either are binary variables that might yield peculiar distributions for the correlations, have at least 25 percent missing data, or are a component of one or more of the proportional variables that are part of the DON data. Thus only 9 of the DON variables that do not have some obvious data constraints load more than once on the 15 DON factors.

Tables for the economic development and size factors illustrate the confounding effect of the proportional variables in the DON analysis. Of 88 variables that load over .40 on the economic development factor, 61, or 69.3 percent, are proportions, and 40 of these 61 contain either population or GNP.[12] The 27 nonproportional variables that load over .40 on the first factor include 9 with 25 percent or more missing data; 2 binary variables; 6 that either have a per-capitized version that also loads on the factor or are used with another variable to create a ratio variable; and 4 that are arithmetically redundant, since they are composed of parts of other variables, including trade and exports, and treaties and multi-lateral treaties. In short, only 6 out of 88 variables loading over .40 have no obvious affliction attached to their distribution, preparation, or composition: these are average temperature, revolutions, embassies and legations in other countries, embassies and legation in country, number of IGO memberships, and number of IGOs headquartered in the country.

Only one out of 12 variables that share at least 75 percent of their variance with economic development is not a proportion.*
All 11 of the proportional variables share population as a common term. Life expectancy at birth, with more than 33 percent missing data, is the only high-loading variable that does not include population.

If we examine the key loading items on the size dimension, as we did with economic development, the divergence between the two factors is sharply outlined.[13] Of the 10 highest loading items on

---

*Rummel's Table 9.50 excludes the ratio of illiterates to population > 10, which also loaded -.89 on the first factor. We have included it in our discussion here. Rudolph J. Rummel, The Dimensions of Nations (Beverly Hills, Sage Publications, 1972), Table 9.50.

the size factor, 9 are not proportional variables. Only the ratio of UN assessment to total assessment is a proportion, and more than 30 percent of the data for this variable is missing. In fact, only about the one-third of the variables that load over .40 (17 to 50, or 34 percent) are proportions. Instead, the most commonly loading variables on this factor are those used to compute many of the proportional variables (15 to 50) or those that are arithmetically redundant (10 to 50), such as trade and exports, two kinds of treaties, and several kinds of population and economic statistics. Of the variables that load over .40 on this factor, only 5, or 10 percent, have more than 25 percent of their data missing.

The pattern reversal, from one factor composed largely of proportional variables to another factor composed largely of the variables used to create the proportions, suggests that the economic development factor, which is marked by proportional variables, variables with appreciable missing data, and variables with curious scale properties, is in part a manifestation of the noise that would be expected in an 82 by 236 aggregate data matrix for the earliest year in which data were generally available (1955). The strong loadings of two of the error measures used in the DON analysis on this factor (missing data error measure at -.63) may further indicate the extent of the noise extracted with this first factor.

A final demonstration of the impact of the proportional variables and the components of the proportions on the economic development and size dimensions is seen in Table 9.1, in which the 22 variables that load over .40 on both factors are displayed. Of the 22 variables, 9 are proportions, and 3 of the nonproportional variables are components of proportional variables that load on the factor (total energy consumption and total energy consumption to population; railroad length and railway freight to railroad length; exports and raw material exports to exports). Five of the remaining indicators are part of a proportion that loads either on economic development or on size. Table 9.1 also presents a clear sign consistency, since variables that are positively related to one factor are positively related to the other factor, and vice versa.

THE DIMENSIONS OF NATIONS

At the heart of the DON project is the use of factor analysis to explore the dimensions of contemporary nations and to compare these dimensions with results obtained in previous dimensionalizing studies. Fifteen factors with eigenvalues greater than 4.0 were extracted from the correlation matrix of 230 substantive variables

TABLE 9.1

Variables Loading on Economic Development
and Size Factors

Variables	Economic Development	Size
Excise and customs revenue/ total revenue	-.41	-.57
Energy resources potentially available/population	.45	.49
Total energy consumption	.57	.78
Electricity generation	.65	.74
Total energy consumption/ population	.49	.67
Steel production	.59	.66
Railroad length	.40	.72
Railway freight/railroad length	.41	.58
Railway freight/population	.71	.46
Vehicles in use	.60	.69
Air passenger kilometers	.50	.53
Aid received/GNP^2 per capita	-.67	-.45
Treaties	.52	.45
Foreign mail sent and received	.54	.59
Embassies and legations in other countries	.44	.67
Embassies and legations within country	.46	.48
UN assessment/total assessment	.48	.81
Science NGO/NGO	.44	.43
Foreign college students in country	.48	.61
Trade	.57	.75
Exports	.52	.76
Raw Material exports/ exports	-.55	-.47

and 6 error measures. These factors, in turn, are divided into the three primary dimensions, which are economic development, political orientation, and size; the four major dimensions, which are Catholic culture, domestic conflict, foreign conflict, and density; and eight minor dimensions, which are Oriental culture, seaport dependency, diversity, equality, traders, sufficiency, and two factors that are unlabeled. The fifteen factors account for 76.9 percent of the total variance, although only two of the factors (economic development and size) account for more than 10 percent individually, and only one additional factor (political orientation) accounts for more than 5 percent of the total variance. Together, the remaining 12 factors account for less of the total variance than do the 3 primary factors (40.1 percent for the 3 primary factors versus 36.8 percent for the rest of the DON factors).

In this section we shall examine whether the factor analysis yields results that can be accounted for by problems in the data or in the data analysis procedures. The DON data matrix consists of 236 variables gathered for 82 countries, or a ratio of almost three variables for each case included in the study. By the usual practice in factor analysis, however, the number of cases (or rows) should exceed the number of variables (or columns) in the standard R data matrix. Some psychometricians further recommend that the number of variables should be about one tenth of the number of cases used in the analysis.[14] Thus the DON factor analysis was undertaken on a matrix that included three times as many variables as there were cases.

Table 9.2 presents the consequences of alternative cases to variables ratios for factor analysis.* Matrices ranging from 10 times as many cases as there were variables to 3 times as many variables as there are cases were factor analyzed. Using random numbers as the input data, the results show the capacity of factor analysis to generate "meaningful" factors from patternless numbers. Moreover, the generation of at least mathematically meaningful factors is increased as the cases-to-variables ratio is altered. By the time the data matrix is configured in the same form as the DON matrix, no fewer than 45 factors with eigenvalues greater than 1.0 are generated, and 14 of these have eigenvalues greater than 4.0. In other words, almost the same number of factors with eigenvalues greater than 4.0 as the DON data produced can be generated through the analysis of random numbers.

---

*I wish to thank Mark S. Levine of Northwestern University for bringing this characteristic of factor analysis to my attention.

TABLE 9.2

Alternative Matrix Configurations:
The Impact of the Cases-Variables Ratio

Cases	Variables	Number of Factors with Eigenvalues Greater than 1.0	Number of Factors with Eigenvalues Greater than 4.0
50	5	2	0
50	10	5	0
50	20	9	0
50	25	10	0
50	40	16	0
50	50	18	0
50	60	22	1
50	75	27	2
50	100	34	7
50	125	40	10
50	150	45	14

Given the apparent capacity of factor analysis to join together either the random or the patterned, it is small wonder that some of the factors isolated in the DON analysis include rather curious combinations of variables. Rummel admits that several of the factors, including one of the primary and at least one of the major factors, are poorly defined. In fact, after the few major factors, it appears that one, two, or three centrally loading and highly intercorrelated items often join together to make a factor of limited variance, dubious stability, and limited explanatory utility. Table 9.3 presents the mean inter-item correlations among the key loading items for each of the 15 DON dimensions. With the exception of diversity, only the first three factors share an average of 50 percent of their variance across all key loading items. By the time the fourth factor (Catholic culture) is reached in the rotation, less than 25 percent is shared in common in 10 of the 12 remaining factors.

On the other hand, foreign conflict and diversity, the only factors other than the major dimensions that have relatively highly correlated key loading items, illustrate combinations that are almost indistinguishable from chance, once the cases-to-variables ratio has become so distorted. Since no other variable loads above /.42/, diversity is solely a function of a strong negative correlation ($r = -.80$) between language groups with at least 1 percent of the

TABLE 9.3

Mean Inter-Item Correlations Among the Key
Loading Variables for Each of the Factors

Dimensions	Mean Inter-Item Correlations	Range of Absolute Correlations
Economic Development	.73	.94 to .31
Political orientation	.69	.91 to .57
Size	.79	.98 to .50
Catholic culture	.44	.70 to .21
Foreign conflict behavior	.49	.81 to .12
Density	.45	.75 to .01
Oriental culture	.31	.93 to .09
Domestic conflict behavior	.41	.69 to .19
(Unlabeled)	.31	.41 to .23
(Unlabeled)	.17	.52 to .01
Traders	.29	.47 to .03
Diversity	.80	.80
Equality	.32	.89 to .00
Seaport dependency	.32	.90 to .11
Sufficiency	.28	.61 to .01

Note: Only the absolute values of the correlation coefficients were used in these computations.

population and the percentage of the population in the largest language group. Foreign conflict balances several high correlations (13 of 45 correlations > .60, and 4 of 45 > .70) against a number of moderate and weaker correlations to produce a reasonably coherent pattern. However, other analysis by Rummel[15] indicates that foreign conflict decomposes into other patterns when it is examined separately.

THE STABILITY OF THE FACTORS

When used to explore a data matrix, factor analysis may produce trivial or nonsensical results, especially when the number of variables far exceeds the number of cases. In this section we shall explore whether the DON dimensions remain stable, that is, emerge in an identifiable form, when they are reanalyzed one by one. In other words, we shall examine the DON factors to see if they are

METHODOLOGY AND STATISTICAL PRACTICES 187

identifiable when each is reexamined with factor analysis performed on each one separately. Although some variation will occur from one analysis to the next, the core of the factor should remain identifiable from analysis to analysis.

Catholic culture is one dimension that is not very clearly defined, and it includes some variables that are only tangentially linked to an intuitive notion of Catholic culture. Moreover, Rummel's discussion suggests dissatisfaction with some of the loadings of this factor, leading to the conclusion that "due to the high loading of Roman Catholics/population, this cluster of attributes is named Catholic culture."[16] Thus, we tested the internal stability of Catholic culture by refactoring the correlation matrix of variables that loaded .40 or higher on the dimension.[17] If the factor is stable, at least its core loading items should remain distinguishable. If it is unstable, quite different patterns may be expected to emerge.

The correlation matrix of the variables loading on the Catholic culture factor produce three factors with eigenvalues greater than 1.00 (4.04, 1.86 and 1.22). The first two of these factors were extracted with an orthogonal rotation, varimax solution, and the results are presented in Table 9.4. Inspection of the table demonstrates that the Catholic culture factor does maintain its integrity under isolated analysis, but that one additional factor, termed Moslem culture, is also present in these variables.

The discovery of an additional factor within one of the major DON factors is not an isolated occurrence. Rather, it is generally the case that upon individual reanalysis the DON factors break into a core segment which was used to name the factor from the 236 variable analysis and one or more additional interpretable factors composed of variables which merely hung on to the core elements in the original analysis. This type of decomposition becomes a concern if the purpose of the analysis is to produce a set of empirically grounded concepts around which future research is to be based. Where the task of the analysis is to obtain factors that represent the major concepts for the development of a field, a definite regression problem exists in this type of empirical concept formation. If each of the primary and major dimensions can be decomposed into other meaningful factors, at what point does the analyst conclude that the major concepts for use in subsequent analysis have been identified?

Another difficulty stemming from the DON analysis is the stability of some or all of the 15 dimensions over sets of countries. Here we shall focus on the stability of the 15 dimensions across clusters of the 82 countries used in the DON analysis. Would all or most of the primary or major dimensions be found in either theoretically or geographically defined clusters of these 82 states? Even if the factors do exist for groups of countries, they may be

TABLE 9.4

Reanalysis of the Components of the
Catholic Culture Factor

Indicators	Catholic Culture	Moslem Culture	h^2
Typhoid deaths/population	.76	.39	.73
Monarchy or not	-.43	.31	.28
Law students/total college students	.54	.09	.30
Roman Catholics/total population	.73	-.49	.77
Mohammedans/population	-.18	.80	.68
Female students/total students	.05	-.81	.66
Government revenue/government expenditures	-.05	-.63	.40
Neutral or not	.65	-.22	.46
Air distance from the United States	-.59	.54	.64
Air distance from the United States/air distance from the United States and the USSR	-.75	.29	.65

unlikely to have the same relationships to one another within the clusters of states as observed in the complete set of 82 countries. Hence we shall ask whether the practice of considering all 82 countries without any apparent probing for variations in the 15 dimensions within sets of these countries may yield what are asserted to be general organizing concepts around which the study of international relations should be structured but which are not at all useful for studies employing specific clusters of states; two such clusters would be the Latin American and the "authoritarian" states. In other words, we shall examine whether in these data a pattern of nonadditivity exists that is masked whenever all 82 states are considered simultaneously.

Clearly, the reanalysis of all the variables used in the DON study for limited numbers of states will produce even more matrix configuration problems than we have suggested exist for the 82-nation analysis. On the other hand, we can gain some idea of how much difference there might be within groups of states if we examine correlations among the marker variables selected by Rummel for each of the 15 factors computed for all countries and for geographical sets of the original 82. The occurrence of different correlations within groups of countries may suggest that significant differences exist between the factors found for the 82 countries and those that might occur in smaller and perhaps more homogeneous geographically defined groupings of countries.

Marker variables for economic development are called energy consumption per capita (ENC-PC); political orientation is called freedom of opposition (TOTALI); size is called national income (NI); and Catholic culture is called Roman Catholics/populations (CATH). These variables are correlated with one another for 82 countries and for five general geographical regions (Western Europe and North America, Central and South America, Eastern Europe, Sub-Saharan Africa and Asia, and North Africa and the Middle East). As Table 9.5 demonstrates, quite different relationships are obtained among the marker variables across the geographical regions, and every one of the regional results is appreciably different in some way from the correlations observed in the 82-country analysis.

This pattern of differing magnitudes and signs to the coefficients from one geographical region to the next suggests that the simultaneous analysis of 82 countries may discover concepts and relationships that are quite different from those that might be observed within different clusters of states. While this is not direct evidence of the lack of spatial generality of the DON dimensions, these results clearly suggest the absence of any orthogonality between the dimensions whenever different groups of nations are examined. Hence the research utility of the DON analysis may be limited to global cross-polity studies and may be less useful for the analysis of international and intranational behavior within more restricted numbers of states.

MISSING-DATA ANALYSIS

Given the availability of cross-national data for a large number of countries, missing data is always a problem. However, as the number of blank cells in the first DON data matrix (for 1955) will testify, the decision to collect and analyze 230 substantive variables from 82 countries was not without its perils. By the estimate of the DON researchers, around 17 percent of the initial data cells were empty and 83 of the 230 variables had at least 20 percent missing data. Moreover, between 35 and 72 percent of the data for 11 countries (North Vietnam, Mongolia, North Korea, Yemen, Laos, South Vietnam, Nepal, Saudi Arabia, Afghanistan, Cambodia, and Liberia) were missing.[18]

TABLE 9.5

Within-Region Correlations among Marker Variables on Four Major Dimensionality of Nations (DON) Project Dimensions

Area	ENC-PC			TOTALI		NI
	TOTALI	NI	(CATH	NI	(CATH	(CATH
Western Europe and North America (n = 21)	.38	.71	-.23	.10	-.36	-.10
North Africa and the Middle East (n = 11)	.39	-.06	-.18	.06	.29	-.22
Central and South America (n = 21)	-.16	.35	-.48	.18	.09	.04
Eastern Europe (n = 8)	—	.05	.43	—	—	-.27
Africa and Asia (n = 21)	.05	.23	-.03	-.04	.23	-.09
All countries (n = 82)	.18	.56	.24	.06	.06	.08

ENC-PC = energy consumption per capita
TOTALI = freedom of opposition
NI = national income
(CATH = Roman Catholics to total population

Note: There was no variation in the values of the eight Eastern European states on the TOTALI measure; hence no correlations involving TOTALI are computed for that geographical region.

Missing data presented a problem serious enough that a missing data error measure was used as one of the six error measures in the DON analysis and the original data matrix for 1955 was reanalyzed for 71 countries and 153 variables to test whether the same factors would be obtained as were extracted from the initial (larger) matrix. Over 90 percent of the variance in the missing data measure was accounted for by the 15 orthogonal factors, as inverse loading were obtained for economic development (-.63), political orientation (-.52), and size (-.37). Thus at least some of the structure of the first three factors is attributable to missing data.

To test whether missing data influenced the factors derived, the DON researchers excluded all countries with more than 35 percent missing data and all indicators with at least 20 percent missing data and compared the resulting factors to those obtained in the 236 variable analysis. Since no intraclass correlation coefficient below .90 was obtained between the matching factors for the 71 by 153 matrix and the 82 by 236 matrix, Rummel concluded that missing data did not influence the major dimensions of nations but may have influenced the minor dimensions, in which considerably more instability was observed.[19]

The missing data analyses used in the DON project constitute the most advanced work available on the impact of empty data cells on the substantive results obtained in empirical political science. It is one of the few, perhaps the only, examples of an attempt to deal systematically with bivariate and multivariate error. It is also one of the few studies available that systematically deals with both random and systematic error. Indeed, of all of the methodological innovations for the analysis of cross-national data that the DON project pioneered, the handling of missing data may well be the most important. These analyses combine insight bred through necessity with multivariate statistical theory to yield a truly innovative approach to a very complex problem.

RELATING ATTRIBUTE AND BEHAVIORAL SPACE

Since the distinction between attribute and behavioral space became central only after the DON project was underway, concern about accounting for the behavior of individual variables focused on the interpretation of the factor loadings as correlation coefficients and the communality for each variable as a multiple correlation coefficient. Rummel states that "we can say that if Y is an attribute of nations then for any nation i,

$$Y = \alpha_1 X_{i1} + \alpha_2 X_{i2} + \ldots + \alpha_7 X_{i7'}$$

where X is a basic indicator of one of the fourteen dimensions."[20] For example, using the 236 variable analysis, he argues that about 80 percent of the variance in intergovernmental organizational memberships for 1955 across the 82 countries can be accounted for as follows:[21]

IGOs = .57 Economic development + .51 Political orientation + .33 Size − .33 Catholic culture

$R^2 = .80$

This is an acceptable statistical practice, and prescriptions for its use to interpret the pattern of loadings across several factors for a particular variable are conventionally found in discussions of factor analysis. However, no guidance is given in what decisional criteria should be used to select among the varying results that might arise from the use of different variables or from the use of segments of a large data set in more focused factor analyses. For example, an examination of the IGO memberships variable in the dimensions of international relations suggests the following:[22]

IGOs = .70 Participation + .25 Popularity + .24 Ideology + .33 South America + .26 Aid − .35 Factor 13 (unlabeled)

$R^2 = .77$

Other than marginal differences in the size of the coefficients of determination (R^2 = .80 versus .77), the DON researchers have not presented any criteria for selecting between competing predictions of IGO memberships. Since there was no prior theoretical guidance on what factors should emerge, we are only able to examine the signs and magnitudes of the coefficients in the equation in a descriptive sense. Hence the amount of variance accounted for is the sole critical standard available to us.

This question of decisional criteria is at least somewhat analogous to the specification problem in regression analysis. Unless we have some prior theoretical guidance regarding the behavior of the individual terms in the equation—specifically on the direction and magnitude of the coefficients—we can only select the factor analysis that has produced the largest h^2 (and thus the largest R^2) as the best means to account for the variation in a specific variable. While this type of postdictive analysis should account for large amounts of the variance, its utility for the development of systematic explanation and prediction is quite limited.

As field theory became more central to the project, the analysis turned more to canonical analysis to relate the multiple predictor variables from the dimensions of attribute space to the multiple criterion variables from the dimensions of behavior space. As is true of any other multivariate procedure, of course, canonical analysis is only as useful as the theoretical analysis that has preceded it. Given the lack of explicit theoretical specification, most of the canonical analysis reported in the DON studies has been attentive to the size of the canonical correlations and has evidenced far less concern for the canonical weights of specific variables. As long as attention remains directed solely at the canonical correlation, and on the trace correlation as a means to summarize the canonical R's produced for any predictor and criterion sets, the usual criticism that canonical analysis "on the surface seems to involve a blind empirical approach of maximizing explained variance"[23] and a rejection of parsimonious explanation will be pertinent.

SUMMARY

This discussion has focused on some of the methodological and statistical practices employed in the Dimensionality of Nations project. We have suggested a number of questions about the kinds of variables employed in the DON analysis and the impact of these variables on the factor analyses reported. We have examined the DON factors and raised questions about their composition, potential for decomposition, and stability for sets of countries. We have questioned the impact of missing data on the DON factors resulting from the 236 variable analysis. Finally, we have examined the practice of relating variables or sets of variables to one another when the only apparent criterion for selection among competing specifications is the amount of variance accounted for as summarized by the communality (interpreted as a multiple correlation) or the canonical correlation coefficient.

Although these critical questions have been emphasized, the importance of the DON project as an example for those working with cross-national data should not be underemphasized. The experience of the DON project contributed greatly to the advancement of our knowledge of the problems encountered in the analysis of cross-national aggregate data. It has contributed important examples of the utility of data transformations and the need for several kinds of error analysis. It has exposed political scientists to some multivariate statistical techniques, which are used extensively in other disciplines and which might be useful for some problems in the analysis of intranational and international politics. It was an early leader in the use of events data and dyadic analysis.

Many questions remain, of course, about the DON analysis and the utility of the direction to be taken in the future. However, whatever one's orientation toward the project there is little question that DON has had a powerful effect on the development of quantitative international politics.

NOTES

1. Rudolph J. Rummel, The Dimensions of Nations (Beverly Hills: Sage Publications, 1972), p. 12.
2. Ibid., p. 11.
3. Ibid., p. 12.
4. Ibid., pp. 13, 80-86.
5. Rudolph J. Rummel, "The Dimensionality of Nations Project," in Comparing Nations, edited by Richard L. Merritt and Stein Rokkan (New Haven: Yale University Press, 1966), pp. 109-130; Gordon Hilton, A Review of the Dimensionality of Nations Project (Beverly Hills: Sage Publications, 1973).
6. Rummel, The Dimensions of Nations, op. cit., p. 85.
7. Karl Joreskog and Dennis Lawley, "New Methods in Maximum Likelihood Factor Analysis," British Journal of Mathematical and Statistical Psychology 21, no. 1 (1968): 85-96. See also Karl Joreskog, "A General Approach to Confirmatory Maximum Likelihood Factor Analysis," Psychometrika 34, no. 1 (1969): 183-202.
8. Ibid., p. 85.
9. See John Armstrong, "Derivation of Theory by Means of Factor Analysis or Tom Swift and His Electric Factor Analysis Machine," The American Statistician 21, no. 6 (1967): 17-21.
10. Glenn Fugitt and Stanley Lieberson, "Correlation of Ratios or Difference Scores Having Common Terms," in Sociological Methodology, 1973-1974, edited by Herbert Costner (San Francisco: Jossey-Bass Publishers, 1974), pp. 128-44; Karl Schuessler, "Analysis of Ratio Variables," American Journal of Sociology 80, no. 4 (1974): 379-96.
11. Rummel, The Dimensions of Nations, op. cit., pp. 203-09, 448-67.
12. Ibid., pp. 221-23.
13. Ibid., p. 321.
14. Jim C. Nunnally, Psychometric Theory (New York: McGraw-Hill, 1967).
15. Rudolph J. Rummel, "Dimensions of Conflict Behavior Within and Between Nations," General Systems 8 (1963): 1-50.

16. Rummel, The Dimensions of Nations, op. cit., p. 230.
17. The list is from Ibid., p. 232.
18. Ibid., pp. 260-61.
19. Ibid., pp. 260-65.
20. Ibid., p.297.
21. Ibid.
22. Ibid., p. 499.
23. Hubert Blalock, Theory Construction (Englewood Cliffs: Prentice-Hall, 1969), p. 42.

CHAPTER

10

AN APPRAISAL OF THE SUBSTANTIVE FINDINGS OF THE DIMENSIONALITY OF NATIONS PROJECT

Richard H. Van Atta
Dale B. Robertson

Our concern in this presentation is to offer an appraisal of the substantive findings of the Dimensionality of Nations Project (DON). This task, if carried out completely, would necessitate a voluminous report. The principal investigator of the DON project, Rudolph Rummel, recently compiled a 49-page report entitled "A Summary and Annotated Bibliography of Research by the Dimensionality of Nations Project."[1] The substantive findings of the project have been presented in approximately 70 research reports, a score of published articles, and a book of nearly 500 pages entitled The Dimensions of Nations.[2] In order to provide an appraisal of the DON research findings in a reasonably brief fashion, we shall have to adopt a strategy that focuses our review.

As Rummel specifically states, the primary motivating force behind the DON project has been the development and testing of "field theory."[3] Therefore we shall channel our review of substantive findings to research that is directed toward this aim. This review shall proceed by first discussing the substantive research question of the DON project, the question or set of questions the project is attempting to answer. We shall next treat the problem of operationalization, what variables are used in the study and how they are measured. After that we shall consider the assessment of the research question, the testing of the proposition that the interaction between nation-states is explained by their attribute differences. Since the focus of this appraisal is upon research testing field theory as the "mainline" task of the DON project, we shall not treat all of the studies that have been produced by the project. Rather we shall concentrate on those studies that are directed at the operationalization or testing of the field theory models.[4] As we proceed with this appraisal we confront a major problem if we restrict our discussion to only the empirical findings of the DON project and avoid penetrating into questions which are more "methodological" in nature. Substantive findings, particularly of a project as deeply based upon specific methodological and theoretical presuppositions as DON, cannot be assessed in a vacuum. We shall, therefore, upon occasion raise questions regarding the theoretical specification and methodological practices which have affected the DON research findings, hoping that we do not infringe unduly upon the assigned tasks of others.

SUBSTANTIVE QUESTIONS ADDRESSED BY THE DIMENSIONALITY OF NATIONS PROJECT

The research goals and even the basic driving questions underlying a research project that has spanned a decade are bound to evolve over time. Indeed, if the questions pursued were not crystalized, made more precise, and revised over this period of time, we would probably accuse the researchers of being both unproductive and closed-minded. A major, and from our perspective, most laudable, feature of the DON project is that the basic research question has become increasingly refined and specified with the passage of time. New concerns have also entered into the analysis as the project has reached a mature status. Equally important is the fact that, although the focus of the project has evolved, there does appear to be a concentration of effort on a topic, rather than a helter-skelter jumping from one "hot" topic to another.*

The initial research concern of the DON project was "to identify the primary clusters—dimensions—of interrelationships among variables which index the characteristics of nations. . . . Once these are determined the second goal is to identify the basic variables which index the position (factor score) of each nation on the dimensions."[5] The project was initiated as an experiment in the measurement of the properties of nation-states, based upon the assumption

---

*In making this statement the authors realize that the line between dogged, closed-minded pursuit down an obviously dead-end track and the concerted devotion to developing a breakthrough on an apparently intractable question is hard to draw. What is the most "productive" approach to developing knowledge, is a question for philosophy of science and will be avoided here. The authors' personal view should be clear from this statement regarding Rummel's approach.

that while nations are "extremely complex units in complex relations with each other," they could be described by a "reasonably small number of dimensions."[6] The purpose of this pursuit was simply stated: "Such basic measurements of national characteristics . . . may provide useful data for a number of research concerns."[7]

Rummel's earliest analyses, starting with his well-known study of the "Dimensions of Conflict Behavior Within and Between Nations,"[8] demonstrate, however, that the project was driven by more than just an urge to provide measurement of national characteristics. In this work the research question put forth was "what relationship exists between the dimensions of foreign conflict behavior on the one hand, and domestic conflict behavior dimensions on the other."[9] A theme basic to the subsequent work of the project is entailed in this question: What is the relationship between domestic (internal) properties of nations and their foreign behavior? In a review of the research output of the project a decade later, Rummel asserted that "the main-line goal (of the DON project) . . . was to determine the linkage between international behavior and attributes."[10] In the interim, as the research progressed, Rummel provided and continued to revise an analytical structure that posed this question in a specific fashion. This structure he labeled "social field theory."

Field theory is a concise set of statements posing a particular form of linkage between the attributes of nation-states and their dyadic behavior. A recent presentation specifies the assumptions of this theory as follows:

1. International relations is a field consisting of all nation attributes and interactions and their complex relationships through time.
2. The international field comprises a Euclidean attribute space defining all nation dyadic interactions.
3. The attribute distances between nations in attribute space at a particular time are social forces determining the location of dyads in behavior space at that time.*[11]

In the first two assumptions Rummel specifies that there exist two different spaces of variables, attribute and behavior spaces, each analytically defined in terms of a set of basic dimensions. He then asserts in the third statement that the values for a dyad on the

---

*Originally social field theory was presented as a set of seven "propositions." Some of these were collapsed and others discarded as unnecessary, leaving the above three statements.

SUBSTANTIVE FINDINGS

behavior dimensions are a function of the differences between the two nations comprising this dyad on the dimensions of attribute space. It is this asserted relationship between attribute differences and dyadic behavior toward which the bulk of the DON project empirical research has been directed. Given the paramount importance of this assertion for the empirical research program of the project, we shall concentrate our discussion briefly on its theoretical significance and then focus upon the implications of the research results that have thus far been obtained regarding this theoretical statement.

Initially we shall explore the theoretical significance of the assertion that attribute differences are "social forces determining the location of dyads in behavior space." In this statement field theory offers a specific variation upon the rather basic contention that international behavior is explained by the internal properties of the nation-states involved. However, the presentation of the statement provides no explanation of this linkage. It does not flow deductively either from arguments regarding nation-states as actors or from assertions about the international system as a whole. The substantive and logical implications of the statement are not specified in such a way as to provide an explanation for the variety of empirical linkages that might be obtained. Field theory states simply that attribute distances determine dyadic behavior. What types of behavior are predicted by what types of attribute differences, or combinations thereof, are not explicated in the theoretical corpus. We might therefore state that field theory is a framework for analyzing linkages. It says very little about their substantive properties. When we come to evaluate the substantive significance of the findings designed to "test" this assertion of linkage between attribute differences and dyadic behavior, we shall return to this question of theoretical specification. Indeed, we shall assert that this lack of specification makes assessment of this proposition extremely problematical.

Since the initial presentation of field theory, Rummel has provided a revision, status-field theory, which is considerably richer in analytical presuppositions. Essentially what Rummel has done has been to elaborate the field theory framework with a set of axioms regarding the properties of status differentiation in the international system. From these axioms a set of propositions is then derived, predicting the cooperative and conflictful behavior of an actor towards an object in terms of the relative status position of these nations. There are some extremely important aspects of this transformation of Rummel's thinking. The field theory statement that attribute differences explain nation-state behavior, which in the original presentation was treated as an empirical proposition, has become an axiom, assumed to be true. The original breadth of field theory has been narrowed to a consideration of only a specific type of attribute, the status dimensions, and specific types of behavior, conflictful and cooperative. Thus Rummel is no longer treating the original general "linkage" assertion; rather he is focusing upon a particular attribute property, which is status differentiation as it impacts upon the mix of cooperative and conflictual interaction directed from one actor to another. In appraising the substantive findings of this project, we shall reflect upon this theoretical evolution, as it may in fact represent the true substantive importance of these findings.

Concluding this section, we can state that the general research question posed by the DON project is whether there exists a systematic relationship between the attribute differences of nation-states and their dyadic behavior. This question immediately raises other, and for Rummel intermediate, questions. What are the attributes and behaviors of nations? How can they be operationalized so as to test this proposition? Field theory, as laid out by Rummel, dictated certain approaches be taken to the operationalization of these concepts, but provided very little basis for ascertaining what ought to be the actual variables in the analysis. In the next section we shall treat the preliminary phase of DON research, which is the empirical delineation of "attribute" and "behavior" spaces, before considering the actual analyses of field theory.

OPERATIONALIZATION: ATTRIBUTE AND BEHAVIOR SPACES

In accordance with the first two assumptions of field theory presented above, the first stage in the analysis is to delineate the attribute and behavior spaces (A-space and B-space). In <u>The Dimensions of Nations</u>, Rummel presents "the major substantive results of the DON analyses . . . organized into two sections: national characteristics and dyadic international behavior."[12] These findings provide the operationalization of the two spaces for the field theory "tests."

What these results provide is an empirical taxonomy of two sets of variables. The technique for providing this taxonomy is factor analysis (principle component analysis with both orthogonal and oblique rotational procedures). At this stage of the analysis the substantive findings focus on the structural composition of two abstractly defined variable sets in terms of the basic clustering of the variables within these sets. The findings of the DON project with regard to the set of attribute variables, as succinctly summarize

SUBSTANTIVE FINDINGS 201

by Rummel, are that "nations are mostly distinguished by their economic development, power or size, political orientation, density, Catholic culture, foreign conflict and domestic conflict."[13] Regarding behavior space, Rummel states that the DON analyses "showed that the 1963 dimensions of global dyadic behavior comprised deterrence, cold war, exports, students, migrants, diplomatic, military treaties, aid, and U.N. voting,"[14] with largely the same dimensions being depicted in a subsequent analysis of 1955 dyadic behavioral variables.[15]

These findings were the result of intensive analysis and the expenditure of great amounts of effort and money. Rummel has published a book detailing most of these findings[16] and several articles in major journals that elaborate the findings, amplifying various aspects such as indicator development[17] and computerized data analysis.[18] The scope of this effort is not captured well by single-sentence summaries, since so much must be embedded in these sentences. As Leo Hazlewood states in Chapter 9, underlying the composition of the data matrices that went into these analyses was a considerable search of the literature to ascertain which variables to include, not to mention the time spent in coding the variables, processing the data, and conducting the several preparatory and final data analyses. Indeed Rummel's statements regarding the findings of this stage of the analysis are richly elaborated in the pages of The Dimensions of Nations.[19] From a purely empirical standpoint one cannot quarrel that the DON project is devoid of findings, since the correlations, patterns, mappings, factors, hierarchical clusters, and other data treatments abound to the point that they can scarcely be absorbed.

In assessing the substantive results of this stage of the project, we are torn in two directions. The first direction would lead to the appraisal that the DON project has so proliferated statistical and graphical findings that it is not possible to separate the wheat from the chaff; for example, Chapter 12 of The Dimensions of Nations presents analyses of "nation types"-"how nations group in their mutual similarity"-on the premise that "grouping nations, objects, individuals, or cases by types is a basic step in describing phenomena and building science."[20] We are led into a discussion of taxonomic methodology and then into a presentation of several figures, charts, and graphs, each depicting a grouping or clustering of nations on some set of attribute dimensions. What one finds in pursuing the perturbations of this chapter is that what it obtains as groupings is highly artifactual. It depends upon the clustering technique (Rummel uses both direct factor analysis and hierarchical clustering), on what variables one decides to input (all 14 dimensions, just the 4, 5, 6 "most important" as determined by some exogenous criteria), and if one wanted to go further, on what subset of cases versus the universe of cases one analyzes. Thus, just what ought to be construed and appraised as "substantive findings" becomes a difficult question. Our personal information processing systems are in danger of being overloaded by the ability of the computer to spew forth analyses of infinite variety. The findings as they emerge from this stage of the DON study may simply overwhelm rather than inform.

The second direction in which these results take us is more sanguine. Examining the findings of this study, correlation by correlation, factor loading by factor loading, over several data sets and time periods, obviously can distract us from the very purpose for which they were developed. What we are interested in from the DON project perspective is a set of reasonably stable dimensions, that can serve to operationalize the basic concepts of "field theory." The question here is whether Rummel has appropriately ascertained the variable sets for his subsequent analysis. Substantive appraisal at this point links inexorably with methodological considerations. Rummel has put forth a set of dimensions, his operationalization. Whether they are adequate, valid, appropriate measures is a question for open debate and hopefully for serious research. Some analysts have raised questions regarding the use of factor analysis (see Chapter 7), while others have criticized particular applications of the technique.[21] Questions can and should be raised regarding variable selection, aggregation of variables, transformation, and other data manipulations. The adequacy of the definitional criteria for separating "attribute" from "behavior" must be examined. In the next section, as we pursue our discussion regarding the testing of field theory, we shall return to some of these points.

In arriving at an appraisal of Rummel's effort, it should also be noted that the state of the art in 1962 provided very little for the DON researchers to build upon and that the extant theoretical material was only suggestive of possible concepts. Rummel's subject was bereft of analytical formulation of basic concepts. He therefore chose to engage in an effort to develop a mapping of the myriad of variables into "dimensions," which he felt would provide a basis for theoretical advancement, as well as a set of potentially useful "indicators." Rummel and others, such as Bruce Russett and his colleagues on the Yale Political Data Program[22] and Irma Adelman and Cynthia Taft Morris in economics,[23] have encountered severe criticism for taking a broad brush sweep over conceptual specification, permitting technique to dominate over thought, with results that are essentially methodological artifacts. Rummel's broad brush cannot be denied, and it must be admitted that it can provide only an initial sketch, not a detailed composition. What we have been provided with is a body of descriptive information to use and to improve upon in our attempts to array nation-states regarding their "structural" properties. This sweeping effort of Rummel and others is justified, considering the state of the art at the time it was initiated. However, the direction of our efforts should now be steered toward digesting this material and bolstering our conceptual inventory. The more stable and prominent dimensions ascertained by Rummel are logical candidates for theoretical elaboration. At the same time, efforts ought to be directed toward assessing the methodological properties of the DON research product. The DON project started out as an experiment in measurement. The experiment has succeeded to the point of showing that with concerned effort one can obtain same systematic mapping of nation-state properties. The question remains to be seen just how important these properties are in our efforts to understand international relations.

Before moving to an appraisal of the theory-testing aspect of the DON project, we shall conclude this section with our appraisal of the substantive contribution made by Rummel's measurement efforts. Our conclusions are that the DON project has been successful in demonstrating the existence, during the last two decades, of rather basic empirical regularities in the properties of nation-states. The DON project has provided a data set and empirical analyses that can permit researchers to come to grips with what might be called the structural properties of the international system. Actors can be related in terms of their values on various properties, such as ideological homogeneity, technological development, and international conflict, from which measures of concepts can be derived such as status, alignment, and dependence.

TESTING FIELD THEORY: MODEL I

At this juncture we turn our attention to the main substantive thrust of the DON project, which is testing field theory. Rummel and his colleagues set out to assess the validity of the proposition that the interaction between two nations is a linear function of their relative attribute differences. This proposition has been presented in the following mathematical expression:

$$w_{i \to j, k} = \alpha_1 d_{i-j, 1} + \alpha_2 d_{i-j, 2} + \ldots + \alpha_p d_{i-j, q}$$

In this expression, $w_{i \to j, k}$ denotes the behavior of nation i to nation j (i→j) on a particular behavior dimension k, (where the behavior dimensions are $w_1, w_2, \ldots w_k, \ldots w_p$). The right-hand portion of the expression states that the behavior of i to j on behavior dimension k is a linear sum of the differences between i and j on each of the q attribute dimensions ($d_{i-j,1}$ denotes the differences between i and j on an attribute "1"). The impact of the separate attribute dimensions upon behavior varies according to the value of the parameter α_1.

The research design that Rummel pursued to test this proposition went through a series of stages as depicted in Figure 10.1 below. The initial analyses were conducted on data on a "selected" sample of nations for the year 1955, with subsequent analysis of both a "selected" and a "random" sample of cases for 1963. The major substantive finding of this research was that the field theory model as initially formulated was nearly a complete failure from an empirical standpoint. The results of three separate data sets (1955 "selected sample," 1963 "selected sample," and 1963 "random sample") showed that with the original field theory model only 13 percent of the variance was found to be in common between the independent variable set, attribute differences, and the dependent variable set, dyadic interaction.[24] Thus the conclusion was reached that this model was an unacceptable interpretation of the relationship between attribute differences and international behavior.

These research findings, with their devastating impact on Rummel's theoretical formulation, forced an examination of the model's logical implications. Scrutiny of the formula-linking attribute differences to dyadic behavior demonstrated that the model greatly constrained the behavioral relations between nations. Indeed, as initially formulated, the linkage expression logically necessitated that the behavior from nation i to nation j be just the opposite of that of nation j to nation i. Thus if nation i directed high amounts of conflict behavior to j, j would, according to the implications of the model, direct proportionally nonconflictual behavior toward i. Such antisymmetric behavior is possible in international relations, but Rummel's original field theory statement permitted no other patterns. Thus, for example, a situation in which two actors directed high amounts of conflict behavior at one another would be inconsistent with this formulation.

A substantive result that has subsequently been of importance did emerge from the effort to assess field theory, empirically, despite the logical problems of the model. The empirical analysis of this model, utilizing data for 1955, indicated a relatively strong correlation between differences of nations on national income (a "power" indicator) and energy consumption per capita (a "development" indicator), with the behavior dimensions "salience" and "international organization." This result was interpreted by Rummel

FIGURE 10.1

Research Design for Field Theory Tests

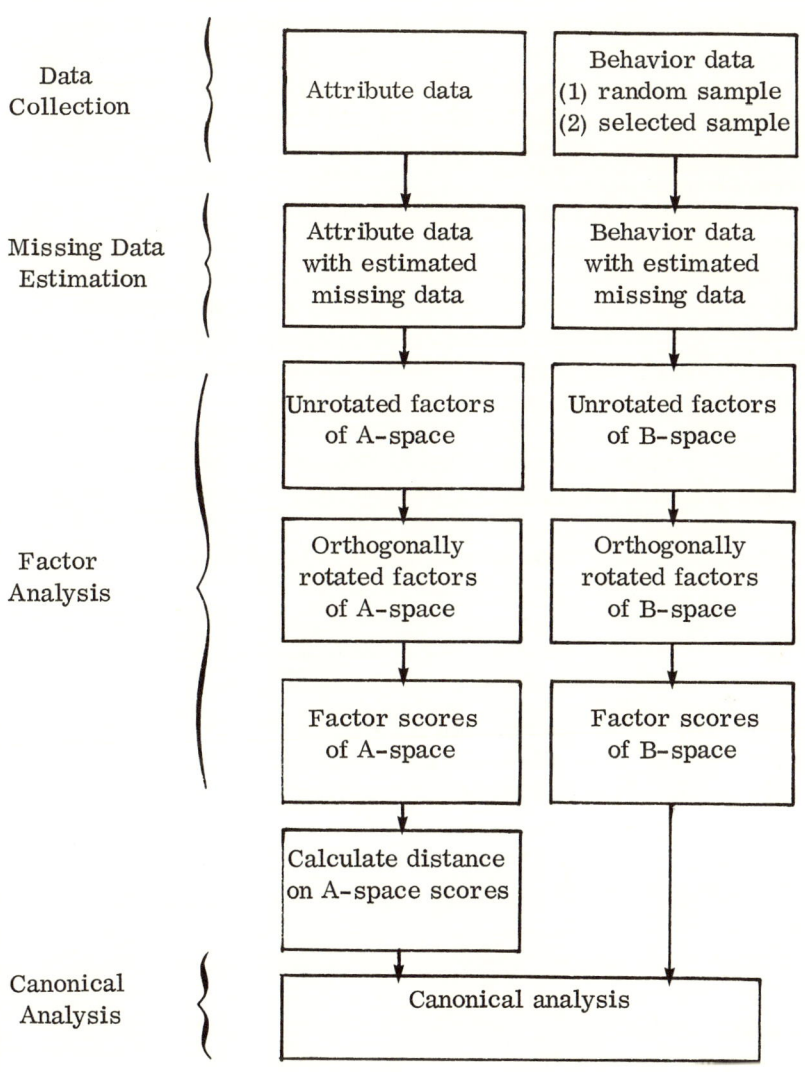

as showing that greater similarity between nations on the "power" dimension, together with greater dissimilarity between nations on the "development" dimension, is associated with greater dyadic interaction in terms of such variables as tourists, translations, treaties, and international organization comembership.[25] In a footnote he suggests that this finding is commensurate with the notions of a theory of status in international relations, stating that "if these results hold up, they give a particularly good bridge for connecting field theory and rank theory."[26] However, the empirical study for 1963 data did not reveal any correlations strong enough to bolster these findings.[27]

In retrospect it would appear that, due to its extremely restrictive and unrealistic analytical implications, this formulation of field theory should have been abandoned long before the research stage. The thrust of the project was placed upon the empirical assessment of a proposition, rather than upon analyzing its theoretical implications; yet it appears that it was the very effort to test the proposition empirically that uncovered the flaw in theoretical specification. Perhaps this experience is best viewed in a constructive light. Any model ought to be scrutinized for logical inconsistencies and patently absurd consequences, but often the best light is shed on these problems when we attempt to apply or empirically assess the model, rather than assess it in the abstract.

TESTING FIELD THEORY: MODEL II

The original proposition linking attribute differences with dyadic behavior proved to be of questionable empirical validity, as well as a highly doubtful theoretical statement on logical grounds. Rummel's response to these theoretical and empirical setbacks was to reformulate the proposition by adding a subscript to the notation, whereby the original proposition,

$$w_{i \to j, k} = \alpha_1 d_{i-j, 1} + \alpha_2 d_{i-j, 2} + \ldots + \alpha_p d_{i-j, q}$$

became

$$w_{i \to j, k} = \alpha_{\underline{i}, 1} d_{i-j, 1} + \alpha_{\underline{i}, 2} d_{i-j, 2} + \ldots + \alpha_{\underline{i}, p} d_{i-j, q}$$

This new formulation of the posited relationship was identified as Model II of field theory.

SUBSTANTIVE FINDINGS

Before going into the substantive aspects of the analyses of this revised model, something should be said regarding its theoretical properties. Replacing the coefficient α_1 of Model I with $\alpha_{i,1}$ of Model II relieves the posited relationship between the attribute differences and behavior of a severe constraint. In Model II, as opposed to Model I, it is not assumed that the forces that link attributes to behavior are uniform across actors. The model does imply, however, that the forces operating for a particular actor are consistent across all of its dyadic linkages.

The model does allow for symmetric and asymmetric behavior, as well as the antisymmetric type of behavior permitted by Model I.[28] It has been asserted that this movement to Model II is an abandonment of the pursuit of a general theory of international relations by Rummel.[29] However, only if one insists that all relationships posited to hold among nation-states do so with equal weighting over the actors would this be the case. Rummel's first model did make this assumption. Its lack of realism was demonstrated by the poor fit of Model I to the data. Model II still puts forth a general relationship between attribute difference and dyadic behavior. It is potentially more complex, yet the types of behavior that must be encompassed by a general model of international relations are themselves complex. Rather than a model with a single set of parameters, we are presented with a model that has variable parameters opening up in the development of theory a broad area that will specify the direction and relative magnitude of these parameters. Therefore we would argue that what Model II gives up is not generality, but undue simplicity.

Since this new model was devised, several analyses have been done that offer some evidence regarding the empirical basis of the relationship it puts forth. The first analyses, using data for 1955, were done on cases drawn as a sample of nations representing "the full scope of differences and similarities among nations . . . as they relate to interaction between nations."[30] The results of this study demonstrated a substantially greater explanation of the variance in the dyadic behavior of nations by this less constrained model. In 14 substudies, one for each of the nations in the sample, an average of about 53 percent of the variance in B-space was accounted for by differences between the attributes of actor and object nations.[31] A replication of this analysis, using data for 1963, showed overall a very similar degree of relationship between the two variable spaces.[32] Table 10.1 displays the results of these analyses, along with the findings of the actor-specific studies to which we now turn.

The results of the analyses of Model II were highly encouraging, particularly as compared to the disastrous outcome of the Model I

TABLE 10.1

Results of Analyses of Field Theory Models I and II,
Using Data for 1955 and 1963

	Percentage of Variance of B-space Accounted for by Attribute Differences[a]	
	1955	1963
Model I Analyses		
Selected Sample[b]	.13	.13
Random Sample	—	—
Model II Analyses		
United States (1)	.46	—
United States (2)[c]	.56	.63
China (1)[d]	.52	.49
China (2)[c]	.62	.37
USSR (1)	.31	.18
USSR (2)[c]	.59	.42
Brazil	.55	.64
Burma	.45	.53
Cuba	.59	.48
Egypt	.62	.59
India	.53	.52
Indonesia	.42	.49
Israel	.64	.53
Jordan	.50	.61
Netherlands	.40	.55
Poland	.48	.62
United Kingdom	.56	.45

[a]The percentage of variance accounted for in these studies is determined by the square of the trace correlation after canonical regression of attribute difference scores onto dyadic behavior scores. The individual studies should be consulted for differences in variable sets and analysis procedures.

[b]The results of the 1955 Model I analysis first reported by Randolph J. Rummel. These results are compared to 1963 Model I findings in Richard H. Van Atta's subsequent study, "Field Theory and National-International Linkages," in Conflict Behavior and Linkage Politics, edited by Jonathan Wilkenfeld (New York: McKay, 1963).

[c]Results of Model II studies using a selected sample of nations as objects for each actor. 1955 results were first reported by Rummel in "Field Theory and Indicators of International Behavior," op. cit.

[d]For his study Sang-Wu Rhee used a variety of research procedures resulting in squared trace correlations varying between .45 and .58. The results reported here are those used by Rhee for most of his interpretations, from "Communist China's Foreign Behavior: An Application of Field Theory Model II," Dimensionality of Nations Project, Research Report No. 57 (Honolulu: University of Hawaii, 1971).

tests. Instead of accounting for less than 20 percent of the variance in behavior, field theory Model II demonstrated a relationship in which over half of the variance in dyadic behavior was accounted for by attribute differences. Subsequent studies focusing on particular nations as actors, using the United States, the USSR, and the People's Republic of China, substantiated the findings of the "selected sample" studies. Rummel used data for 1955 on U.S. interaction for the first single-actor analysis. The results showed that approximately 47 percent of the variance in the dyadic interaction of the United States with other nations could be accounted for by the difference on the attribute dimensions between the United States and the object of the interaction.[33] Studies of Chinese and Soviet foreign behavior resulted in again approximately one-half of the variance in dyadic behavior being explained. A rather general substantive conclusion from these studies is that the revised model of field theory consistently results in about 50 percent of the variance B-space being explained by attribute differences.

Obviously Model II is a marked improvement over its predecessor; yet we have some trouble accepting these results as demonstration of the merits of field theory. It should be noted, first, that field theory was put forth as essentially a deterministic model. The equations in the model are devoid of an error term. Ostensibly, then, the fit of A-space should be perfect. Ought we then to reject field theory on the basis of the empirical results? Certainly it could be claimed that such a rejection would be premature. It could be argued that if differences in A-space do not account for all of the variance in dyadic behavior, the obvious answer is that we have not yet "captured" all of A-space. Some important dimensions remain unoperationalized in the previous analyses. However, such an assertion raises the question of falsifiability rather starkly. If such a claim can be made, can one really say that field theory can be tested at all? Even if an analysis should account for 99 percent of the variance in some B-space, could it not be asserted that there exist dimensions of B-space, not yet operationalized, that are not accounted for? The problem is that field theory specifies neither the substantive dimensions of either space nor the dimensionality of the spaces (number of dimensions). Thus the model is not adequately specified for purposes of testing. The results of the analyses are interesting and suggestive, but not a "test" of field theory, since there are no criteria by which to assert that the model can either be rejected or accepted.

The second point that should be raised is that the results of these studies hinge upon the theoretical clarity with which "attributes" and "behavior" are defined and measured. There is at least some conceptual ambiguity evident in the definitions of A-space and B-space.

Rummel gives very little attention to the defining properties of "attributes" as opposed to "behaviors." An attribute "is defined as any descriptive concept which differentiates a social unit from all other social units."[34] An interaction "is defined as a behavioral act . . . [that] couples two social units together."[35] These definitions lead to difficulties in specifying the attribute and behavior spaces. For example, the mobilization of military forces within a nation is an internal act. It does not by itself involve any other nations. Nevertheless, troop movements and mobilizations are usually treated as "behavior," since it is usually presumed that such an act is an attempt to influence or act upon another state. Should defense expenditures, then, be similarly treated, or are these merely "attributes" of the actors? Is the number of immigrants from one country, say Ireland, to another, say the United States, an interaction—"a behavioral act" of the social unit? Is it appropriate to say that Ireland "behaved" toward the United States in this context? Does not behavior connote some control, or at least a degree of purposiveness? Certain transactions, including trade, migration, and travel, are virtually uncontrolled by some governments, while others parcel out these involvements down to the most minute detail. Is there no distinction to be made here of whether the "actor" could or did have control over its "behavior?"

On a less theoretical plane it can be seen that the separation of "attribute" from "behavior" for purposes of empirical analysis contains some pitfalls. In his study of U.S. foreign relations Rummel lists negative communication, students, and exports as indicators of behavior space dimensions. At the same time, number of threats, foreign college students, and exports/GNP are listed as attributes.[36] The analysis by Rhee of Chinese dyadic interaction[37] contains similar problems. The behavior dimension "trade" is composed of import and export variables, while the attribute dimension "political orientation" contains a trade direction variable (western trade/western trade + Communist trade). Also in the Rhee study, one of the attribute variables is an aggregate foreign conflict dimension. It must be noted that the behavior-based variables that the DON researchers incorporate in attribute space are aggregations (total number of foreign students, total exports divided by GNP) and therefore not definitionally identical to the behavior space variables that are dyadic (such as foreign students from Nation A to foreign students from Nation B). The problem is that the distribution of behavior for actors frequently is so skewed toward specific objects that this distinction is obviated. If Nation A engages in 87 percent of its conflict with Nation B, any meaningful distinction to be made between dyadic conflict as behavior and total conflict as an attribute would appear to be lost.

SUBSTANTIVE FINDINGS 211

This problem would appear to be accentuated in the Model II studies, in which only a single actor is analyzed. This relationship between aggregate and dyadic behavior may lead to impressive correlations that are essentially artifactual. In the Rhee study of Chinese foreign behavior, for example, the following relationship is presented:

.75 Political Orientation + .37 Foreign Conflict
-.35 Soviet Aid→ .65 Trade + .63 Diplomacy
-.33 Negative Communication[38]

The correlation between the first set, which is ostensibly attributes, and the second set, which is dyadic behavior, is .95. The distribution of each of the "attribute" variables is extremely skewed; only a few of the cases have appreciable values, and most are zero or near zero. The aggregation is over a very small number of actual non-zero values. Even though attribute differences, and not absolute attribute values, are used, there would appear to be considerably less substantive implication to this finding than should be presumed by the high correlation. We are, in fact, largely correlating variables with themselves.

Of course a remedy to this conceptual problem would be to eliminate from attribute space all those variables that directly involve the behavior of other nations. In an analysis of Soviet foreign behavior, we expunged the following DON variables from attribute space prior to analysis: trade (western trade, Communist trade, and trade direction), bloc membership, number killed in foreign violence, U.S. aid, and U.N. voting. The results of our study rather definitely diverge from the DON analyses, indicating that the elimination of these conceptually ambiguous variables may have led to substantially less predictability. Instead of accounting for 50 percent of the variance, as in the DON studies, our studies averaged around 25 percent. The results of our analyses of Soviet behavior with the field theory model raise some problems in interpreting the findings of the earlier DON studies. Our predictive capacity was substantially and consistently lower, and we found our results not to be consistent, using alternative strategies of analysis.[39]

The results of the Model II studies of DON indicate that attribute differences may be a useful predictor of dyadic interaction. However, our results seem to demonstrate that there exist some definite problems with theoretical specification and research strategy that need to be addressed before we go much further with analysis of the model. There have been very few attempts by researchers outside of the project to apply field theory, which makes it difficult to evaluate the impact of alternative operationalizations, data sets, and

assessment techniques on the generality of the findings.* We hope
that, as familiarity with the model increases, other researchers
who are not directly connected with the project and its methods will
provide a basis for independently evaluating the findings discussed
above.

BEYOND MODEL II: ADDITIONAL SUBSTANTIVE CONSIDERATIONS

This discussion of the substantive findings of the DON project
has reviewed the effort to assess the relationship between attribute
differences and dyadic behavior that is expressed in Model I and
its revised formulation, Model II, of field theory. The research
question under consideration was whether there is a "fit" between
one set of variables and another. The technique used to ascertain
this "fit" was correlation, with percentage of variance being the
basis for assessment. The research reports dealing with "tests"
of field theory give primary focus to the overall relationship between
A-space differences and B-space, and then only secondarily evaluate
the individual linkages between variables.

---

*Jack E. Vincent and some associates have reported results for
some "empirical tests" of Rummel's social field theory. Jack E.
Vincent, Roger Baker, Susan Gagnon, Keith Hamm, and Scott Reilly,
"Empirical Tests of Attribute, Social Field, and Status Field Theories
on International Relations Data," International Studies Quarterly 17,
no. 4 (1973): 405-43. The Vincent study elaborates analyses of the
relationship between attribute distances and aggregated dyadic
"conflict" and "cooperation" behavior variables. Analyses are
separately reported for ten different actors: China, the Dominican
Republic, Ethiopia, Japan, New Zealand, Turkey, the USSR, the
United Arab Republic, the United Kingdom, and the United States.
The data base was aggregated over 1962-64 for the behavior variables.

Because of the aggregation techniques employed, the lack of
appropriate match between the years for which attribute and behavior
data were selected, and other questionable operationalization procedures, this study cannot be considered completely commensurate
with the DON studies. The correlation results reported by Vincent
show considerable variability over the several "testing" procedures
employed, making any assessment of the "validity" of field theory
from this study problematical.

For the subsequent development of field theory, a shift from concern with the overall fit of A-space and B-space to a specification and examination of particular linkages appears to be necessary. Of particular interest in this regard is Rummel's own concentration on status in the international realm. As we mentioned above, the one substantive result that emerged from the initial Model I test was the relationship of two status attributes, "development" and "power," to such behavior variables as tourists, treaties, and translations. Rummel noted that these results seemed consistent with the notions of "rank theory" in international relations. In his research treatment of U.S. foreign behavior, Rummel explicitly stated the hypothesis, following from the work of Johan Galtung[40] and Gustavo Lagos,[41] "that the actions of one state to another are a function of their relative statuses."[42] Thus, although the substantive concern was primarily with the testing of the field theory models, Rummel had begun to develop a particular interest in the relationship of certain status variables to dyadic interaction.

Rummel has recently turned his efforts toward providing a more general theoretical presentation of status properties within the context of field theory.[43] This theoretical development obviates some of the more harsh critical points that have been raised regarding field theory. Focusing on particular attribute and behavior linkages, "Status Field" theory is more specific than were his previous efforts. Rummel has maintained the basic components of field theory (Model II) and has used them as a basis for developing a series of propositions that are much more narrow in scope. The thrust of Rummel's work is toward a theory based upon a more elaborate analytical structure that is substantively more specific, and thence testable. For our appraisal of the substantive contribution of the DON project, an important point is that this theoretical development, whatever its faults, seems to have emerged at least in part from the substantive results of the field theory analyses.

The evolution of status-field theory through the years of DON project research can be briefly sketched. The earliest findings of the project demonstrated that "power base" (or "size") and "economic development" were consistently among the most prominent attribute dimensions. The analyses of behavior data separated out dimensions of dyadic "conflict" from "cooperative" interactions such as trade, investment, and aid. With the Model II analyses, attention began to focus on the relationship between particular attribute differences as predictors of the mix of cooperative and conflictful behavior directed from an actor to an object.[44] Rhee's analysis of Chinese foreign behavior was the first study that specifically treated the status relationships that Rummel had specified in the preliminary drafts of status-field theory.[45] In particular, the difference in power base was found to be highly related to the level of trade and "negative communication" that China directed to other nations (r = .97).[46] The study a year later by Choi, which analyzed U.S. and Soviet foreign behavior, was specifically subtitled "An Application of Rummel's Status-Field Theory."[47] The results of this analysis showed similarly strong relationships between the joint "cooperation" and "conflict" behaviors of the actors studied and their "power base," relative to the objects of their behavior (r = .92 for both the United States and the USSR).[48]

CONCLUSION

These analyses provide encouragement for Rummel's theoretical efforts. Status-field theory is a promising evolution that connects Rummel's very abstract spatial notions to more tangible sociological concepts. The empirical results of DON research indicate that specific attribute differences such as the status differences can be used as potent predictors to behavioral relations. Thus, our conclusion is that the DON project has demonstrated its scientific merit. It initially set out a vague, general question concerning the existence of a relationship between attribute properties and nation-state behavior and has successively pared and trimmed that question through a series of reformulations based upon empirical analyses. There is no question that because of the DON project we know much more about relationships between attributes and behaviors and know how to ask much more pointed and specific questions regarding their relationships.

We could also say that we should have sufficient experience by now to state whether Rummel is asking the "right" question. We know that differences between an actor and its object nations predict the amount of cooperative and conflictful behavior the actor will direct to the objects. We know that differences in attribute dimensions account for about one-half the variation in dyadic behavior. One could argue that while there is a certain scientific value in these findings, they are not very "useful." They have little policy relevance; they deal with "static" relations, not policy "manipulables." Our feeling is that while the more general analyses "testing" the fit between A-space and B-space probably could only remotely be attached to policy decisions, the more substantively specified the analyses become, the greater is their potential policy importance.

Still it must be admitted that field theory provides a rather large-scale relief of international relations, which blurs the subtleties of manipulation and maneuver. Its macroscopic perspective shows the basic propensities of actors in the system, and not their ability to bluff and feint or their efforts to engage in strategically contingent behavior. Nevertheless, it would seem that knowledge of the more systematic, "environmentally determined" aspects of behavior is important not just for science, but for policy as well. Rummel's work seems credible as an effort to investigate such "structural" aspects of international relations.

In conclusion we should like to raise the following points regarding the development of field theory. First, the direction that Rummel has taken, focusing upon the status properties of social distance, is only one aspect of the original field theory perspective. Other equally interesting substantive focal points remain to be considered. Field theory, as a general model, references attribute differences, such as political, social, and cultural homogeneity, that seem to be as theoretically intriguing as the notion of social hierarchy; yet these have not received commensurate attention. Second, detailed analyses of Model II of field theory* have been done for only the "great powers," the United States, the USSR, and the People's Republic of China.[49] It would be interesting to see the extent to which these findings are similar for actors located differently in the international hierarchy, such as India, the Sudan, and Bolivia. In particular, do the status-field propositions hold up for nations at lower levels of "power" and "development"? Third, at present the Model II studies have been able to account for at best one-half of the variance of dyadic behavior. What are the implications of this finding for subsequent efforts? Do we focus only upon those predictable dimensions, such as the status dimensions? Would this imply rejection of the more general field theory model? Do we redefine attribute and behavior spaces so as to eliminate the dimensions that are much less predictable? Do we combine the field theory model with other models, such as those dealing with interactive processes,[50] to produce a more general predictive model? Do we alter some of the basic assumptions, such as that of linearity, perhaps thereby increasing the variance accounted for? All of these directions are plausible, and probably most would be fruitful.

The thrust of these concluding comments obviously indicates that we feel that the DON project work does provide a basis for potentially valuable and useful future research in international relations. Clearly others can conclude that the project has asked

---

*We are speaking of "detailed" in the sense of using a complete set of object nations, rather than a small, selected sample such as that used in the initial Model II studies.

the wrong questions, employed techniques in incorrect fashion, conducted too much empirical analysis, insufficiently specified its theoretical models, and spent too much money and time to arrive at the results it has provided. It is not our intention to condone or defend the practices of the project; rather, our evaluation is that, given the state of knowledge, methodological and substantive, at its inception, the project has provided interesting and worthwhile research findings.

NOTES

1. Rudolph J. Rummel, "A Summary and Annotated Bibliography of Research by the Dimensionality of Nations Project, 1967-1973," Dimensionality of Nations Project, Research Report No. 69 (Honolulu: University of Hawaii, 1973).

2. Rudolph J. Rummel, The Dimensions of Nations (Beverly Hills: Sage Publications, 1972).

3. Rummel, "Summary and Annotated Bibliography," op. cit., p. 23.

4. These studies are as follows: Rudolph J. Rummel, "Field Theory and Indicators of International Behavior," Dimensionality of Nations Project, Research Report No. 29 (Honolulu: University of Hawaii, 1969), the initial test of field theory, using "select" and "random" samples of nations for 1955; Richard H. Van Atta and Rudolph J. Rummel, "Testing Field Theory on the 1963 Behavior Space of Nations," Dimensionality of Nations Project, Research Report No. 43 (Honolulu: University of Hawaii, 1970), a follow-up analysis using "select" and "random" samples with data for 1963; Rudolph J. Rummel, "U.S. Foreign Relations: Conflict, Cooperation, and Attribute Distances," Dimensionality of Nations Project, Research Report No. 41 (Honolulu: University of Hawaii, 1970), which uses a field theory basis for specific propositions linking attribute distances to the foreign behavior of the United States (data is for 1955); Sang-Wu Rhee, "Communist China's Foreign Behavior: An Application of Field Theory Model II," Dimensionality of Nations Project, Research Report No. 57 (Honolulu: University of Hawaii, 1971), with data for both 1955 and 1963, applies Model II of field theory to analyze Chinese behavior; and Chang-Yoon Choi, "The Contemporary Foreign Behavior of the U.S. and the U.S.S.R.: An Application of Rummel's Status-Field Theory," Dimensionality of Nations Project, Research Report No. 68 (Honolulu: University of Hawaii, 1973), an application of Rummel's status-field theory propositions to U.S. and Soviet foreign behavior using data for 1960 and 1965.

5. Rudolph J. Rummel, "The Dimensionality of Nations Project," in Comparing Nations, edited by Richard Merritt and Stein Rokkan (New Haven: Yale University Press, 1966), p. 110.
6. Ibid., p. 111.
7. Ibid., p. 112.
8. Rudolph J. Rummel, "Dimensions of Conflict Behavior Within and Between Nations," General Systems 8 (1963): 1-50.
9. Ibid., p. 1.
10. Rummel, "Summary and Annotated Bibliography," op. cit., p. 23.
11. Gordon Hilton, A Review of the Dimensionality of Nations Project (Beverly Hills: Sage Publications, 1973), pp. 29-33.
12. Rummel, Dimensions of Nations, op. cit., p. 16.
13. Rummel, "Summary and Annotated Bibliography," op. cit., p. 23.
14. Ibid.
15. Ibid.
16. Rummel, Dimensions of Nations, op. cit.
17. Rudolph J. Rummel, "Indicators of National and Cross-National Patterns," American Political Science Review 63, no. 1 (1969): 127-47.
18. Rudolph J. Rummel, "International Patterns and Nation Profile Delineation," in Computers and the Policy-Making Community, edited by Davis Bobrow and Judah L. Swartz (Englewood Cliffs: Prentice-Hall, 1969), pp. 154-202.
19. Rummel, Dimensions of Nations, op. cit.
20. Ibid., p. 299.
21. Jack E. Vincent, "Comments on Social Field Theory," Dimensionality of Nations Project, Research Report No. 58 (Honolulu: University of Hawaii, 1972).
22. Bruce M. Russett, "The Yale Political Data Program: Experience and Prospects," in Comparing Nations, edited by Richard Merritt and Stein Rokkan (New Haven: Yale University Press, 1966), pp. 95-107.
23. Irma Adelman and Cynthia Taft Morris, Society, Development, and Politics: A Quantitative Approach (Baltimore: The Johns Hopkins Press, 1971).
24. Rudolph J. Rummel, "Field Theory and Indicators of International Behavior," Dimensionality of Nations Project, Research Report No. 29 (Honolulu: University of Hawaii, 1969).
25. Rummel, "Indicators of National and Cross-National Patterns," op. cit., p. 31.
26. Ibid.
27. Richard H. Van Atta, "Field Theory and National-International Linkages," in Conflict Behavior and Linkage Politics, edited by Jonathon Wilkenfeld (New York: McKay, 1963), pp. 208-50.

28. Ibid., p. 234.
29. Vincent, "Comments on Social Field Theory," op. cit.
30. Van Atta, "Field Theory," op. cit.
31. Rummel, "Indicators of National and Cross-National Patterns," op. cit., p. 223.
32. Van Atta, "Field Theory," op. cit., pp. 234-45.
33. Rudolph J. Rummel, "U.S. Foreign Relations: Conflict, Cooperation and Attribute Distances," in Peace, War, and Numbers, edited by Bruce M. Russett (Beverly Hills: Sage, 1972), pp. 71-113.
34. Rudolph J. Rummel, "A Field Theory of Social Action with Application to Conflict within Nations," General Systems 10 (1965): 198.
35. Ibid.
36. Rummel, "U.S. Foreign Relations," op. cit.
37. Sang-Wu Rhee, "Communist China's Foreign Behavior: An Application of Field Theory Model II," Dimensionality of Nations Project, Research Report No. 57 (Honolulu: University of Hawaii, 1971).
38. Ibid., p. 158.
39. Richard H. Van Atta and Dale B. Robertson, "An Appraisal of the Substantive Findings of the Dimensionality of Nations Project," paper presented at the annual meeting of the International Studies Association, St. Louis, 1974.
40. Johan Galtung, "A Structural Theory of Aggression," Journal of Peace Research 1, no. 2 (1964): 146-77.
41. Gustavo Lagos, International Stratification and Underdeveloped Countries (Chapel Hill: University of North Carolina Press, 1963).
42. Rummel, "U.S. Foreign Relations," op. cit.
43. Rudolph J. Rummel, "Status-Field Theory and International Relations," Dimensionality of Nations Project, Research Report No. 50 (Honolulu: University of Hawaii, 1971).
44. Rummel, "U.S. Foreign Relations," op. cit.
45. Rhee, "Communist China's Foreign Behavior," op. cit., pp. 140-57.
46. Ibid., pp. 146-48.
47. Chang-Yoon Choi, "The Contemporary Foreign Behavior of the U.S. and U.S.S.R.", op. cit.
48. Ibid., p. 161.
49. See Van Atta, "Field Theory and National-International Linkages," op. cit., for the report on these studies.
50. Warren R. Phillips, "The Conflict Environment of Nations: A Study of Conflict Inputs to Nations in 1963," in Conflict Behavior and Linkage Politics, edited by Jonathan Wilkenfeld (New York: David McKay, 1972), pp. 124-47.

CHAPTER 11

COMMENTS ON THE REVIEWS OF THE DIMENSIONALITY OF NATIONS PROJECT

Rudolph J. Rummel

In this brief rejoinder I regret my inability to give each comment on DON a full response. A paragraph-long critical point often requires several pages to develop a clear counter-argument, with adequate qualifications, logic, and evidence. My approach here will be as follows, therefore.

Each critical comment will be noted and my response given, even if with unsatisfactory austerity. Be assured, however, that my brevity does not connote lack of appreciation. The points raised here and elsewhere will eventually be the focus of a volume, once I have completed preparation of the conceptual, substantive, and epistemological groundwork for understanding the efforts and results of the DON project.[1]

After these rejoinders, I will summarize and evaluate DON's theoretical perspective. This will provide more context to my rejoinders and indirectly deal with the implicit perspectives of the reviews, on the theoretical and empirical efforts of the project. There I want to confront the sense of the reviews, as apart from their details.

Finally, one more orienting comment. I appreciate the effort that went into these reviews and am sympathetic to the difficulty their authors faced in untangling the detailed, varied, and complex results of the project. To those who have not "lived" DON, trying to grapple with it is at first like starting to read a new methodological book in the middle: one is immediately lost as to framework, definitions, and intentions. DON has to be read page by page from the beginning. Moreover, some of the pages and chapters are missing (which I am now trying to fill in), and also the print on the pages previously read keeps changing. As DON has developed and as I have gained more experience and perspective, new directions have evolved and previous views have been altered. The reviewers cannot be expected to be aware of this.2 Considering this difficulty, the reviewers have done impressive work. If indeed there be errors of fact, interpretation, or logic, they no doubt are due in part to the complexity of DON and the unavailability of the full story. This notwithstanding, their reviews have been very helpful to me and will be influential in my future work. Now for my rejoinders.

METHODOLOGICAL CONSIDERATIONS

In Chapter 9 Leo Hazlewood focused on the Dimensions of Nations, published in 1972, and especially on the 236 variable factor analysis. This design was completed in 1964, and thus Hazlewood is focusing on the earliest history of DON. His specific comments and my responses are as follows.

First, Hazlewood holds that DON emphasized exploratory factor analysis when it should have used confirmatory factor analysis. However, DON actually did both: marker variables were included from all previous factor analyses so that confirmatory analyses could be done. However, many additional variables also were included to do a wider (exploratory) mapping of cross-national variance. First the mapping was completed: the primary, major, and minor dimensions of nations were defined. Then all nonconfirmatory variables were eliminated and, using only the marker variables, a factor comparison against the results of other studies was done. (See Chapter 10.) In the fullest sense of the phrase "confirmatory factor analysis," as meant by factor methodologists, these were confirmatory analyses.*

Second, Hazlewood asks why DON went beyond 88 marker variables instead of doing a confirmatory analysis with only this number. DON went beyond the marker variables in order to do a more comprehensive mapping. More data were available than heretofore. More interesting and theoretically important variables could be included, such as those on domestic and foreign conflict. Thus, from the perspective of 1962, we availed ourselves of the opportunity to go well beyond the studies of others. After this mapping was

---

*The method was Ahmavaara's factor comparison technique, which is mathematically identical to Cattell's Procustes (hypothesis testing or confirmatory) technique. See Rudolph J. Rummel, Applied Factor Analysis (Evanston: Northwestern University Press, 1970), pp. 393n, 419, and Chapter 20.

completed, however, confirmatory analyses were done with only the 88 markers, as pointed out above.

Third, the factor results are partly artifactual, according to Hazlewood, because of the many proportional variables (ratios) included. However, consider GNP per capita, for example. Dividing GNP by population is roughly like regressing GNP on population and treating the residuals as a variable. GNP per capita is GNP with the effects of population removed. Now consider another ratio, such as telephones per capita, which also has the effects of population removed. The correlation between GNP per capita and telephones per capita is then like a partial correlation, holding constant population between them. A partial correlation can go up or down, compared to the simple correlation, and which way it goes is not logically built into the partialling.

In other words, there is no necessary correlation, lack of correlation, or negative correlation produced between ratios involving the same denominator. The fact that many per capita ratios loaded the economic development dimension is not a necessary function of the denominator but a causal-functional interrelationship among all these ratios, which is known as development.* This fact is well attested by the considerable attention given to development as a social phenomena and its measurement without benefit of factor analysis by precisely those ratios highly loading on this dimension in the 236-variable analysis.

However, there is a point to be made here that Hazlewood overlooked. Although the ratios are not necessarily positively correlated, there is a necessary orthogonality between a ratio and its denominator. The linear correlation of the denominator with the numerator is removed. Therefore, the resulting ratio should have little correlation with the denominator as a separate variable. Consequently, the size dimension, as reflecting population, could be argued to be artifactually orthogonal to economic development. However, when one considers the nonpopulation variables, such as area, national income, resources, and defense expenditures, that also comprise this dimension and its interpretable meaningfulness, whatever artifactual nature it may have is insignificant. Before factor analysis was invented, size or power capability was already known and treated as a major dimension of nations.

Fourth, Hazlewood points out that variables exceed cases. In descriptive analyses, as distinct from statistical inference, it is

---

*Were Hazlewood correct, then a logical contradiction would be produced by the per capita ratios that highly load the development dimension in the negative direction, such as that of agricultural population to population.

permissible to analyze more variables than cases, however, as long as one is aware that the smaller dimensions may capitalize on random data error and that the number of dimensions cannot exceed the number of cases.

There are three ways of handling a design in which variables exceed cases, (1) by focusing on the largest dimensions, (2) by only accepting those that are substantively and theoretically meaningful, and (3) by comparing these dimensions with those found by others. We did all three. To me it seems highly unlikely that dimensions such as economic development, size, density, and political orientation would be artifacts of the number of variables. These dimensions are theoretically meaningful and well recognized in the substantive literature. Their indicators have been selected by others who were not using factor analysis; the indicators include energy consumption per capita, population, and freedom of group opposition. These dimensions are found in other factor analyses done by different people for different data (some with the cases exceeding the variables) for different years.

Hazlewood's random number test of the artifactuality of these dimensions is unpersuasive. The necessary mean eigenvalue of any factor analysis of correlations is 1.00, including random numbers. For 150 absolutely uncorrelated random numbers for 50 cases, one would get 49 eigenvalues equal to 1.0. Since random numbers always have some very small correlation, and since by chance for 150 cases we can expect around 7.5 of the correlations to be equal or greater than an absolute .195 (or at least one absolute correlation greater than or equal to an absolute .276), we can expect a number of eigenvalues over 1.00 capitalizing on random correlation. In any case, what would be useful information is the plot of the eigenvalues compared to that of the dimensions of the DON project. Substantive dimensions show sharply decreasing eigenvalues, rounding off to a linear slope near an eigenvalue of one. Random eigenvalues should show a near linear slope throughout.

For the sake of argument, assume that the plots match. Even then, are we to assume that the DON factors, which have such meaningfulness and which match those found by others, are random? Of course not. The problem is in ignoring the substance of the dimensions and in not realizing that the question of randomness not only concerns the 236-variable analysis, but also the finding that all other studies have the same major dimensions.

Fifth, Hazlewood also points out that the dimensions are unstable, since when analyzed by themselves they break into more than one dimension. This is of course true. This is not a problem of stability, but a matter of choosing the appropriate level of analysis. A dimension is defined among a matrix of variables, in a process comparable to viewing topography from 1,000 miles up and seeing only the shape of the continents. When you approach closer, as Hazlewood does by factoring only those variables highly loaded on a dimension, the valleys, mountains, and lakes become clear. When one looks closer, a cluster of intercorrelated variables in the space of other clusters is seen to have independent clusters within it. If system versus subsystem and macro-analyses versus micro-analyses will turn up different dimensions, then which are the correct ones? The answer depends on which level is most appropriate for the researcher's theoretical and substantive interests. After all, what an astronomer treats as solids, a chemist considers empty spaces, but neither denies the stability of the other's results.

Sixth, Hazlewood suggests that the subsets of nations should have been analyzed to determine stability, that factoring subsets should have been done. I agree, but not within the design of the DON project which is concerned with the global system.* Incidentally, the analyses of subsets done by Irma Adelman and Cynthia Taft Morris show development, size, and political orientation to be dimensions that are virtually invariant of region analyzed.[3]

Seventh, some of the structure of the first three dimensions, according to Hazlewood, is caused by data. He arrives at this conclusion by virtue of the correlation of a missing data measure with these dimensions and the high loadings of variables with missing data on them. However, DON did a reanalysis of a 153-variable, 71-nation reduced data matrix that had only 3 percent missing data and found that the first three dimensions correlated .95, .97, and .96 with those of the 236-variable, 82-nation results. If missing data has an effect on the dimensions, rather than being a cause of the development and political dimensions, it must be practically insignificant.

Finally, Hazlewood finds that there is a lack of theoretical specification for the canonical analysis. The primary analyses in The Dimensions of Nations were made before field theory, although I tried in the last chapter to give some idea about where DON was heading by including something on field theory. Subsequent publications have fully specified the canonical model within field theory[4] and have deduced that the canonical trace correlation would assess the fit of the theory to observations. A revision of field theory, called status-field theory, also predicts that certain status dimen-

---

*The reasons were, to match the design of the other studies against which comparisons would be done, to best fit the global perspective of Guetzkow's simulations, and to determine the most general mapping underlying the empirical concepts.

sions should exist and that distances on them would have a specified relationship to a particular combination of behaviors. DON has always used canonical analysis to test field theory, and only as dictated by the theory. After the analyses in The Dimensions of Nations, factor analysis was likewise used only as required to test field theory.

SUBSTANTIVE CONSIDERATIONS

In Chapter 10, Richard H. Van Atta and Dale B. Robertson focus on the development and testing of field theory and make the following points.

First, no explanation is given to show why attribute differences should explain behavior. In terms of the work of Quincy Wright, of the role of power differences in internal relations theory, of the role of social distance in sociology, and of the widely accepted social science belief that differences in values and norms explained behavior, this was at the time (1965) a reasonable axiom. Field theory was then partly conceived as an analytic device to squeeze the testable meaning out of this axiom, when conjoined with the others. It took years to collect and order data that would allow tests to be done. However, once a variety of tests were completed, they showed that the axiom was fruitful and empirically valid. As a consequence, I am now trying to answer this question in psychological and sociological terms in such books as The Dynamic Psychological Field, in which distance vectors are given a major role in man's psychological field,[5] and The Conflict Helix, in which these distance vectors are sociologically and culturally related to interaction and conflict in society.[6]

Second, field theory is therefore a framework. However, whether the axiom has a substantive explanation is irrelevant to whether field theory is a theory. The proper questions are whether the axiom leads to empirical tests, which it does, and whether empirical deductions from the set of axioms are falsifiable through a research program, which they are.

Third, without knowing the basis of the axiom, it is difficult to assess the proposition. It can be assessed by prior studies and analysis, which I am now doing, or by subsequent deduction and testing, which I did. I do not think either approach should stand alone.

Fourth, the original breadth of field theory is narrowed to status dimensions by status-field theory. No, status-field theory still relates dyadic behavior to all the distances in attribute space.

The only difference is that status-field theory also stipulates that there are two status dimensions of attribute space and that distances on them predict in a specified way to conflict and cooperation. Thus status-field theory entails more constraints on the theory, and more substantive richness, without losing its generality.

Fifth, the results of the test of Model I had devastating impact on my theoretical formulation. The history of Models I and II differs from what a reasonable person would deduce from the sequence of research reports and their presentation of results. Model I specifies that the α parameters in $W = \Sigma \alpha d$ are constant for all actors. Before I tested this model, a comment by Dennis Hall, a DON research assistant, at a project meeting led me to see its contra-intuitive nature, since the model predicted, for example, that U.S. behavior to the USSR on a behavioral dimension must be opposite to that of the USSR to the United States on the same dimension. This ridiculous implication had previously escaped me, but once it clicked in I could no longer accept the model. Well before any empirical testing, therefore, I sought to revise Model I in a more intuitively meaningful direction and in a way that was still subject to ultimate empirical testing and specification of the parameters. This revision became Model II, which allows the parameters to vary by actor.

The first appropriate tests of field theory were done in 1969, on Model II and not on Model I. After the Model II tests were completed on 1955 data, I then ran a Model I test out of curiosity. As intuition said should be the case, the fit to data was very poor. Both tests were subsequently reported in the same research report, Number 29.[7] For organizational purposes in the report, I put the Model I results first and Model II tests second, thus giving the appearance of a data-testing sequence that in fact had not occurred. Van Atta and Robertson could not be expected to know this history, but nonetheless it negates their point.

Sixth, Model I should have been abandoned before the research stage. As described above, it was abandoned before the data-testing stage.

Seventh, field theory is not adequately specified for purposes of testing, since there are no criteria for testing the model. Space does not allow the epistemological questions involved here to be discussed, but briefly, I believe that I have been testing field theory and that such testing is not a matter of specifying a variance figure (such as that anything above 10 percent of the variance is a positive test, but then what about 9.9 percent as opposed to 10.001 percent?) or a p-level. Rather, such testing is a program of empirical assessments, replications under different conditions, sensitivity tests, and so on, to the point at which we gain or lose confidence in the empirical validity of our theory. I do not think any theory can be falsified by any single test; nor do I believe any specific criterion is sufficient. Testing is like painting. It is art mixed with technique and a sense for the true and beautiful. One works and plays with the canvas until at some point one can step back, take a look, and say, "I like it; that's it."

Eighth, the attributes lack sufficient definition. More definition and understanding of an attribute in field theory is clearly required. This I have been sensitive to, and my current work, <u>The Conflict Helix</u>, is intended to help.[8] Briefly, the attributes of concern in the social field are social attributes, which are any characteristics of an individual or group that are relevant to or involving purposive behavior directed towards affecting or influencing other selves. Reflex behavior or the length of the hairs on one's toenails would thereby be excluded. Clearly, even this definition begs many questions, and the reader is referred to the above book for them.

Ninth, some of the canonical correlations are artifactual. Because a nation's total behavior is sometimes included on the independent variable side (such as total trade) and the same variable now treated dyadically is included on the depended side, is there not some artifactual correlation? No. The trade of the United States to the USSR, for example, is not predicted in any way by the difference in total trade between the United States and USSR. Both may be high traders without any trade between them, as happened for the United States and USSR during the height of the Cold War. Both may be low traders, but all their trade may be with each other. One may be a high trader and the other low, but the low one may send all its exports to the high trader. The relationship between the difference in total behavior of two nations and how much of their behavior they direct towards each other is fully an empirical question.*

However, even if we assume there is an artifactual correlation, the overall results still stand, since many of the high canonical correlations involve purely nonbehavioral attribute differences, such as on wealth, totalitarianism, and power, as independent variables.

---

*Even when one nation has no trade, for example, and therefore no exports to direct towards another nation, the dependency is still not artifactual. The reason is that we are dealing with differences, and the differences in level between the no-trade nation and others will vary depending on the others' total trade. Thus, while there will be no variance in the dyadic trade of the no-trade nation, the differences may have considerable independent variance.

PHILOSOPHY OF SCIENCE CONSIDERATIONS

Gordon Hilton's comments in Chapter 8 develop a philosophy of social science, using DON as an example. This is not the place to engage this philosophy, but it will be touched on indirectly in the next section as I view DON through an alternative paradigm. Here I will confine myself to Hilton's observations on DON.

First, field theory was adjusted, not rejected, after the Model I tests produced quite disappointing results. Van Atta and Robertson made the same incorrect inference. As pointed out above, Model I was rejected before I tested it. Model II was then developed and first tested. Not as a test, but out of curiosity, Model I was afterwards fitted to the data. Therefore there was no empirical anomaly here to which I had to adjust, although there certainly was an intuitively unsatisfactory deduction from Model I that caused me to revise it.

Second, anomalies in Model II and a desire to incorporate other theories culminated in a status-field theory. No anomalies in Model II are apparent to me. Model II had better tests than I had hoped, and I am still intuitively satisfied with its analytic structure and substantive-philosophical bases. What Hilton may be referring to here is its alleged bad results. On this see below, in the section on evaluating field theory.

As far as the shift to status-field theory is concerned, this was entirely due to the belief that status theory could be subsumed within field theory and thereby provide greater substantive richness. I believe this was successfully done, and the beauty of it to me is that this was done without altering Model II, making the previous tests of Model II now tests also of status-field theory.

Third, there have been some disappointing results with status-field theory. I do not know what Hilton is referring to here, and he provides no references. Indeed, I have been amazed at the consistent near 50 percent of the variance Model II has accounted for and the highly significant tests of theorem 10. (See the next section.) Theorem 11 has done quite poorly by comparison, but overall the results are positive, at least to me. In fact, except on the basis of misinformation, I would be surprised at anyone wondering why I continue with Model II. Truly, it would be an anomaly to reject this model in light of the overall results.

Fourth, my persistence led me to carry on with my theory long after it had generated anomalies. Unless he means the intuitive anomaly of Model I that led to the generation of Model II, Hilton's emphasis on anomalies is incorrect in my subjective view. However, the research program that was DON has involved much adjustment.

The adjustment has not been to empirical anomalies but to growing experience with the program; a greater appreciation of relevant humanistic insights and knowledge; a shift from a deterministic outlook to a belief in free will; a conversion in ideology from democratic socialist to libertarian; a change from a logical positivism eschewing of all metaphysics to a belief that truth is empirical, rational, and intuitive; and in short, a profound transformation of philosophical perspective, epistemology, and ethics. That field theory in its analytic ring has survived this cognitive revolution says something about field theory; but what this is I leave at this point to the philosophers of science.

ABOUT FIELD THEORY

After 1965, the heart of DON was field theory. Two of the reviews focused on field theory, and the third touched on it in the concluding part. It may be helpful, therefore, if I add my own review and critique of field theory. However biased this review may be, and I am under no illusions that a father can objectively judge his own child, it will provide a helpful perspective otherwise lacking.[9]

A Meta View

As a concept, theory is not some Platonic idea or Aristotelian essence that we must identify; neither is it some single definition; and neither is it just an interpreted analytic system of theoretical constructs, axioms, theorems, and rules of correspondence. It is not just a way of ordering observations, a set of related propositions, an explanation, or a point of view. It is a dialectical concept, taking on one or more of these meanings depending on the nature of our problems, the substantive area and its scientific development, and our long-run goals. Based as it is on physics, the philosopher's definition of theory as an interpreted analytic system is a straitjacket if applied uncritically in international relations research. However, the international relations scholar's view of theory as simply a way of ordering data would be ambiguous and misleading if applied to physics.

The point is that we should have a clear idea about what we are trying to do as scientists and how what we call theory functions to that end. This enables us to evaluate our theory as it helps achieve that goal and to avoid the scholastic and often sterile debates on theory by philosophers of physical and social science, many of whom have little practical research or theoretical experience. It enables us to direct and discipline our concern with theory by our perspectives, methodologies, and purposes.

When I originally conceived of field theory, I was concerned with developing an interpreted analytic system that would enable me to explain and predict the occurrence of international conflict. At that time I conceived of theory as a logical or mathematical system, with its primitive terms given interpretation regarding the important empirical concepts of international relations, such as nation, attribute, behavior, power, and conflict, and with universals implying falsifiable predictions. As my research and theoretical experience increased and my acquaintance with relevant methodologies, substance, and writings broadened and deepened, I began to see theory also as an orienting perspective, an intuitive framework, an artistic statement, and a balance of ideas. I perceived it as perhaps with a hard and analytic outer ring, but shading inward towards the center and outward towards the edges, into soft and slippery ideas whose insightful quality and meaning resist conceptualization and communication to others. Parts remained falsifiable, but I came to realize that the theoretical core was my philosophy and ethics, my world view, while edges beyond the analytic ring comprised my intuitive appreciation and understanding of psychology, society, and culture. As such, field theory is more of a balance of intuition, reason, and experience than it is a model or mathematical theory.

A decade ago field theory was my instrument for getting falsifiable predictions about war. I now see it as a way of looking at man. Where formerly the primary criterion for evaluating field theory was its fit to the data, there is now such a variety of criteria that it is difficult to specify any one or a combination of them as primary. These criteria form a dynamic balance, always evolving in response to experience with the theory and my own knowledge and intellectual growth.

Of course, field theory should be evaluated against explicit criteria, as I will do shortly. Nonetheless, how these criteria are weighed and the degree to which the theory satisfies each are entirely subjective. There are always other unarticulated and unarticulable criteria involved. Our final assessment of field theory will be a philosophical statement: in the current jargon, a paradigmatic assertion. I state this at the outset, because the assessment of field theory, criterion by criterion, must be in such an intuitive context.

My sense for field theory as a whole is that it constitutes a new and useful way of viewing man generally and international relations specifically. It brings a variety of prevailing theories together within one framework, unifying many diverse observations and considerable data. More importantly, its assumptions match our uncertainties about man and the quality and nature of our observations about him. I see field theory, in its assumptions and auxiliary methodologies, as manifesting a scientific and quantitative shift from a Newtonian approach to man to a quantum-theory-type perspective. The shift is from an emphasis on known variables and determinate observations and functions to one on unknown variables and indeterminate observations and functions. It moves from an emphasis on absolute characteristics and fully specified functional relations to a view of the whole, of the interrelatedness of men, groups, and characteristics; it goes from a focus on a few well-chosen variables to the system of relations between hundreds of variables; it moves from the emphasis on curve-fitting functions to the space of functions, or the function of functions; and it moves from a focus on fixed data and entities to one on probability density functions.

Intuitively, I feel that field theory is a theoretical breakthrough. This is only a feeling, of course, and it may simply reflect my single-minded preoccupation with the theory; but I have an obligation to put forth my sense of what is involved, while recognizing that such claims demand justification aside from my intuition. Here I can only say that this justification does not lie in any one report or book, nor alone in the satisfaction of the explicit criteria to be discussed, but in the whole that was DON. Ultimately, the justification of field theory will depend on whether it provides better solutions to our scientific and practical problems.

Evaluating Field Theory

Of course, to the tough-minded scientist I have said little of significance so far, and to the soft-minded humanist I have been only vague and imprudent, if not arrogant, about my own theory; but I am trying to communicate my sense of the enterprise, and with this orientation as a context, I can now turn to some specifics.

Relevant to my concerns are eight criteria on which field theory can be evaluated: specificity, elegance, richness, validity, operationalizability (unfortunately a word without substitute), testability, confirmation, and importance. I will consider each in order.

Specificity

After 1964 many of the DON reports focused on the specifiable logic of the theory: its axioms, deductions, theorems, models, methodological assumptions, auxiliary techniques, associated resear-

designs, data, and particular results. Clearly this aspect of field theory satisfies the criterion, but what about the softer inner core of philosophical assumptions and the attendant perspective on man, society, and culture? These are clarified in The Dynamic Psychological Field, which focuses on the psycho-philosophical assumptions;[10] there much of this core and the outer edges are shown to be specifiable within the field theory context.

Elegance

To me, field theory is beautiful. Its beauty lies in the numerous figures; the elegant equation $W = \Sigma \alpha d$, or its matrix interpretation $W = DP$; the derivation of the canonical test;[11] and the pleasing solution to the defining of multidimensional probability densities given by the principal axes approach.[12] Aside from the geometric perspective of field theory, which is so visually satisfying to me, its elegant equations and axioms and its ability to unify and simplify masses of variables, entities, and observations, gratify an apparent need to bring simplicity, order, and regularity to my perceptions and concepts.

An appreciation of the beauty of field theory is a matter of taste and familiarity. I can only hang this painting of man, and wait to see how its balance, simplicity, color, and perspective strike others.

Richness

Rich in concepts and ideas, field theory can lead to alternative conceptualizations, models, and applications. This is seen in the work of Brian Berry,[13] Richard Chadwick,[14] Warren Phillips,[15] and Tong-Whan Park,[16] among others. It can be seen in the various substantive divisions of Field Theory Evolving and in The Dynamic Psychological Field.[17] Particularly, the theoretical constructs of space, dimension, distance, dyadic behavior, and attributes, as they are enmeshed in the theory, are bridges to a considerable variety of substantive concepts, such as power parity, economic development, ideological and cultural differences, status, roles, goal structures, expectations, personality types, patterns of conflict, and so on. The reports and books of DON show how many of these bridges are developed.

Validity

Insofar as logical validity (logical truth) is of concern, a virtue of field theory is that it is specific enough to make it possible to track the logic from axioms and theorems to operationalization, data, and tests; and on this score, the logical whole that is the theory's analytic ring, auxiliary methodologies, and tests, are valid.

But what about face validity? Is the theory intuitively reasonable or persuasive? Restricting this question to international relations, it can be shown that the face validity of field theory is high. The theory is simply that attributes and behavior comprise interrelated wholes, within which behavior and attributes form distinct patterns or dimensions. Within this whole, the patterned behavior of any one nation is a consequence of its differences from others in the various attribute patterns nations manifest. Thus if wealth, power, and totalitarianism are such patterns, then the differences and similarities between nations in these respects will effect their patterned behavior. Substantively, this is a compelling idea that is found throughout the literature of international relations. One of its foremost scholars, Quincy Wright, has made such differences basic to his theory of international relations.

There is another kind of face validity here, and that is in terms of the operational framework. Given the diverse nature of international data, their multiple and complex interrelations, and their uncertainties and unreliabilities, it seems sensible to measure empirical patterns as multidimensional probability densities, as is done in field theory. Thus power is not some ad hoc index or specific variable, but a probability density within the diverse attributes of nations; the power parity of nations is their relative location regarding each other within this probability density space.

Operationalizability

Many of the concepts of field theory are measurable and thus allow theoretical constructs to be interpreted and auxiliary techniques to be employed to test its assertions. Various DON reports and books exemplify this quality, perhaps until recently to the point of overemphasizing measurement and data.

Testability

Are specific universal-empirical-synthetic statements made anywhere in field theory? Yes, within the analytic ring. Here the dyadic behavior of nations is explicitly given as $w = \Sigma \alpha d$, with alternative interpretations of α as general to all actors (Model I) or specific to each (Model II).

Is this universal empirically falsifiable? Yes. Since we can operationalize w and d and use canonical analysis to assess the fit between them, we can test the universal; that is, we can seek empirical examples that falsify it. Of course, we can never conclusively confirm it, no matter how often we fail to find negative evidence, since there might be falsifying evidence beyond our particular observations. However, we can find those conditions under which falsification should be easy, if indeed the universal is empirically false. If falsification fails when it is most likely to occur, then this can increase our subjective confidence in the truth of the universal.

However, this pattern of testing is an ideal that actual scientific tests only more or less satisfy. Slippage in the operationalization of constructs, inability to cover all relevant empirical conditions, random and systematic error, and exogenous variables all affect the test. Moreover, the decision must be made regarding what constitutes a falsification, and this will ultimately depend on one's subjective judgment about the reliability of the data, the adequacy of the operations, the specified conditions satisfied, and so on. In other words, between the precise analytic ring of a theory and its empirical universals are layers of methodological-operational decisions, scientific rules of thumb, and subjective evaluations.

On the one hand, therefore, is the $w = \Sigma \alpha d$ of field theory; on the other is the messy, imprecise, and ephemeral empirical world. The connection between the two is not like the engineer's bridge, which is constructed from clean and clear rules, equations, and experiences. Rather, we have between theory and data a partially explored forest of operations, methods, techniques, procedures, and data. What prevents us from being totally lost is our sense of direction, which is our wish to falsify the theory; some knowledge about the character of the forest and the lay of its underbrush and trees; and some trails hacked out by others.

Given this indeterminacy, we must recognize that no one test is sufficient to conclusively reject a theory. We must also recognize the absurdity of establishing any variance threshold or probability level at which we reject a theory. To say that a theory is to be rejected if it does not account for, say, 10 percent of the variance it predicts or if it does not significantly fit the data at, say $p \leq .05$, is absurd. Such criteria are very flexible to begin with.* They are rules of thumb that are dependent on the applied context. It would

---

*The hallowed $p \leq .05$ criterion has only the warrant of tradition. This significance criterion should really depend on the practical error a researcher can tolerate, the random error assumed in the data (the more such error, the more conservative this threshold), and the robustness of the associated statistic (such as the product moment correlation coefficient) regarding sample and population deviations from those assumed by the statistic.

be foolish to let the acceptance or rejection of a theory hang on any one such test.

To test a theory we have to work it through a variety of empirical conditions, gauge it against many alternative situations, and turn it around in our empirical fingers, always trying to put the theory through the most severe trials. To the philosopher, falsification is a logical issue; to the empirical and theoretical scientist, however, it is a self-conscious process of gaining or losing empirical confidence in a theory.

For field theory, then, what constitutes this process? In brief, it has involved the following:

1. collecting data on the most diverse range of attributes possible for all nations in order to operationalize the dimensions of attribute space upon which distances would be calculated;
2. limiting the final dimensions employed to those defining the largest probability densities in the space;
3. selecting dyads that would span the widest social, economic, cultural, political, and regional variance among nations or alternatively focusing on all the dyadic relations of one actor;
4. making the degrees of freedom as high as possible in the actual test of fit between w and $\Sigma \alpha d$; and
5. repeating the tests for as many different years, actors, dyads and alternative research decisions* as possible.

By keeping the degrees of freedom as high as possible and by maximizing the range of nations, distances, and behaviors involved in the test, field theory has been subjected to severe tests under a varity of conditions. How it has fared is the next criterion.

Confirmation

My colleagues and I have conducted hundreds of empirical tests on Model II, only a fraction of which have been published. Many of these tests were not independent, however, since they involved only a change in the number of dimensions used in the rotation from which the distances were taken, the shift to transformed data, the addition or subtraction of only one or two variables from the spaces, the change in technique from component to image analysis or from

---

*Such as, for example, regarding data transformation, choice of variables, factoring technique, and the number of factors to extract.

TABLE 11.1

Comparisons of Different Models and Random Numbers

	Number of Runs	Lowest Trace	Highest Trace	Average Squared Trace
Random Numbers	29	.14	.54	.13
Model I	4	.23	.36	.11
Model II	51	.48	.80	.49

Source: Rudolph J. Rummel, Field Theory Evolving (Beverly Hills: Sage Publications, forthcoming in 1976), Chapter 16.

multiple regression to canonical analysis, and so on. I can, however, single out 51 independent empirical tests of Model II. Moreover, there were 29 independent random-number tests of Model II. Table 11.1 presents comparative results for random numbers, runs for Model I,* and the tests for Model II.

First, Model I compared to Model II and to the random number results fares poorly, as intuitively expected. Indeed, its fit to empirical data is no better than random. Taking these into account in addition to the contra-intuitive nature of its assumptions about nations (nations are all equally influenced by the same distances, and the behavior of i↦j is the reverse of behavior j↦i for the same distance values) makes Model II the preferable interpretation of field theory. On the average we find that Model II accounts for 49 percent (squared trace times 100) of the variance in dyadic behavior, which is much greater than the 13 percent of the variance for random numbers. (See Table 11.1.)

Clearly, Model II accounts for a significant amount of the variance; how are we to evaluate this amount, given the claims for the theory? There are several approaches, which I will consider in turn.

---

*Earlier I had referred to the Model I runs as "tests," realizing how misleading the use of the word "test" is for Model I. Since Model I had long before been rejected on a priori grounds, I was in fact simply continuing to run Model I as a backboard against which to gauge Model II. See Rudolph J. Rummel, Field Theory Evolving, (Beverly Hills: Sage Publications, forthcoming in 1976), Chapter 4.

The first approach is to ask whether the variance is accounted for by artifactual or necessary correlations being introduced into the analysis. Throughout, we have tried to keep our operationalizations of attribute and behavior spaces independent and to watch our degree of freedom in assessing the dependence of behavior on distances. On this score we believe the tests to be on empirically independent data. Moreover, we assessed the possibility that the canonical analysis might have artifactual traps by redoing our analysis on random numbers, alternatively substituted on the behavior and distance sides of the equation. Consequently, I argue that our results constitute real and legitimate tests.

The second approach is to ask how the Model II results compare with other empirical results in the social sciences. I have not averaged correlations across social science tests, but my familiarity with such literature suggests that the field theory results are among the best that can be found. Consider the following analysis of psychological findings by M. D. Dunnette. He had an assistant sample

> recent issues of four APA Journals—the Journal of Applied Psychology, Journal of Abnormal and Social Psychology, Journal of Personality and Social Psychology, and Journal of Experimental Psychology. He selected randomly from among studies employing either t tests or complex analysis of variance designs, and converted the t or F values to correlation ratios (eta) in order to estimate the strength of association between independent and dependent variables.
>
> The distribution of the 112 correlation ratios ranged from .05 to .92 with a median value of .42. Five percent of the studies showed values below .20; over one-sixth were below .25; and nearly one-third failed to reach .30.[18]

With regard to sociology, Derek L. Phillips reports that

> L. K. Miller . . . examined the results of all studies published in the first three issues of American Sociological Review in the year 1961, and found that the average "significant" relationship explained about ten percent of the variance. Psychologists have been similarly unsuccessful in their attempts to account for much variance. For instance, Robert Rosenthal . . . estimates that most behavioral research accounts for something like thirteen percent of the variance by our independent variables. Clearly, an ability to account for only ten or thirteen or even twenty percent of the variance is

not very impressive and does not lead to a high degree of predictive ability.[19]

By comparison, Model II had an average multivariate correlation of .70, or 49 percent of the variance. When it is also considered that the consistent empirical results of Model II are for the greatest possible range of the behavior and attributes of nations, these tests, in the context of the general level of social science results, are indeed impressive.

The third approach to evaluating the significant amount of the variance is to ask how the results square with the theoretical ideal. Here a problem was created in the evolution of field theory. In work up to around 1970, field theory is wholly deterministic: theory behavior should be wholly accounted for by distances. Recently, as reflected in the shift from component analysis to image analysis,[20] field forces (distances) are seen to account for only the common variance in behavior, while the remaining variance is the result of unique influences and free will. Even were the deterministic view maintained, there would be both operational slippage in measuring the concepts and data error, which would enable us only to approach but not to achieve 100 percent of the variance in behavior.

Within the deterministic framework the results would be satisfactory, encouraging greater effort to isolate the operational-data problems of which the solution would further improve the empirical fit. However, within the nondeterministic perspective I now hold, the results show that field forces both account for a significant proportion of dyadic behavior (an average of 49 percent) and provide a measurement of the range of independent behavior of which nations are capable. Moreover, the canonical equations describe which behavior is largely deterministic (for some equations, on the order of 80 to 90 percent of the variance explained by distances) and which behavior is largely unique and independent of the field. Within either the deterministic or indeterministic viewpoints, then, the results for Model II are positive.

The fourth approach to evaluation is to ask whether the empirical results show wide variation depending on the conditions imposed or the severity of the tests. The answer is no. The Model II tests are consistent regardless of the sample size, actor, or nature of the data. Thus it is hard to argue that the favorable showing of field theory is the result of a particular set of conditions or an easy test.

In sum, the idea encapsulated in the analytic ring of the theory, which is that the similarities and differences among nations are forces effecting their mutual behavior, has tested out well when interpreted to allow for individual variation in the effects of distances. What about status-field theory? Since status-field theory includes the

above linkage, the results apply equally here. It says something
more, however, for it also claims that a particular equation will
be found for developed nations that will allow their conflict plus
cooperative behavior to depend on the power of the other nation.
For underdeveloped nations, such behavior will depend on the development of the others. The former is Theorem 10, and the latter is
Theorem 11. The results of these for Model II are mixed.

Overall, we find the following. The status theory equation
$w = \Sigma \alpha d$ fits the data well in a variety of situations under severe
testing conditions; Theorem 10 fits the data for developed actors
with high significance; and Theorem 11 does not fit the data at all.
In general, and taking all aspects of the multiple tests into account,
the analytic ring of field theory is supported well by the empirical
evidence, with the exception of Theorem 11.[21]

Importance

A well-confirmed theory that has not been falsified through a
variety of severe tests and conditions may be trite. It may concern
incidental scientific problems and irrelevant practical issues.
There are three ways of gauging the importance of a theory. First,
how does it relate to prevailing theories in the field? Second, how
well does it subsume the empirical findings in the field? Third,
how well does it deal with important issues? I will briefly consider
these questions in relation to field theory, one by one.

1. How is field theory related to other theories? At the analytic
and philosophical level, field theory is a type of general systems
theory. It emphasizes the whole over its parts and argues that
these parts take on their field meaning in the context of the whole,
in the field; moreover, it stresses the interdependence of aspects
of the field; and finally, it defines system states, subsystems, and
system equations. The major difference is that systems theory
employs differential equations for structuring the systems while
field theory employs linear functions, among which may be a subset
of linear differential equations.

The emphasis in field theory on principal axes provides a bridge
to mathematical communication theory, in which the eigenvalues of
the principal axes are a function of the entropy H of a discrete set
of probabilities $p_1, p_2, \ldots p_i, \ldots p_n$, in which $H = -\Sigma p_i \log p_i$.
Across this bridge much of field theory could be reinterpreted in
terms of organization, entropy, ensemble, information, channel,
noise, and so on.

Thus field theory is directly relevant and partly interpretable
in terms of two large and currently vigorous theoretical movements,
systems theory and communications theory; but what about substantiv

theory? Many of my research reports and books show the relationship of field theory to one substantive theory or another. For example, my report on U.S. foreign relations showed how the distance notion in field theory and its connection to behavior could partially subsume James Rosenau's linkage theory, Quincy Wright's distance theory, and A. F. K. Organski's power theory.[22] Moreover, <u>Field Theory Evolving</u> shows in detail how field theory can encompass status theory.[23] In total, the aforementioned book shows the usefulness of field theory for comprehending, at least, and actually enveloping in some cases, many of the prevailing scientific theories of international relations.

2. How is field theory related to quantitative findings? By virtue of the fact that the analytic structure of field theory includes the multivariate models of wide use in the social sciences, many of the empirical results gained by using these models can be directly incorporated within field theory. Various reports and books display this, and a conscious attempt is often made to test the reliability of the operationalization of field theory, such as the dimensions of attribute space, against the empirical findings of others. One of the best places to see this power of field theory illustrated is in <u>The Dynamic Psychological Field</u>, which shows how the analytic structure and philosophical core can accommodate the major empirical findings on personality by multivariate psychologists.[24]

3. How is field theory related to problems? Restricting this question to my focus on international relations, I reply that field theory and its attendant growing empirical results can specify the following: (1) the relationship of international conflict and war to other forms of international behavior and their linkages to differences and similarities in power, energy, culture, and ideology; (2) a basic set of international social indicators of past and present international behavior, and the linkages of these indicators to such national indicators as wealth, power, politics, and stability; (3) forecasts of future conflict and cooperation between particular nations in terms of their probable economic-technological growth, stability, and political change; (4) forecasts of alternative international futures, given projections about wealth, power, and so forth; (5) the manipulable aspects of international relations, which are those subject to foreign policy, as opposed to those relations ensuing from the structure of the system or the situations between any two particular nations; (6) those comparative aspects of national societies that encourage regional and global integration, as opposed to those encouraging separation and hostility.

The above claims may seem imprudent, but to the careful reader, all of the DON materials taken together provide a more than sufficient basis for them. I will not leave it at this, however. My current writing is now mainly devoted to bringing the above claims to fruition within a focus on international conflict and war.

Field theory would then satisfy the criterion of importance even if only a fraction of the above relations and claims were true. I conclude, then, that field theory is an important theory that is closely related to other theories, able to accommodate other empirical findings, and helpful in answering significant problems.

CONCLUSIONS

Field theory satisfies a number of criteria for evaluating a theory. It is specific enough for others to follow its logic and determine its validity; it is elegant (recognizing that, like beauty, elegance is a matter of taste) and fruitful; it is internally and intuitively valid; it is operationalizable and falsifiable; it has been well confirmed; and in relation to other theories and findings and to current problems, it is important.

Future Improvements

There are seven directions in which field theory, as described here, should be improved. First, the basic theoretical assumption about man's needs, attitudes, motivations, and temperaments should be clarified. From the field perspective, how is personality viewed; and specifically, how do we psychologically explain the operation of distances? What about perception, distances, and behavior? In other words, what is the nature of the psychological field? I have dealt with this question in The Dynamic Psychological Field.[25]

Second, what are the core philosophical assumptions of field theory about man and reality? How does man relate to reality? Is his will really free? What are the self and will within the field? Is the field a holist view of man, contrary to man's individualism? Is the field absolute or relative? Such questions have also been dealt with in The Dynamic Psychological Field.[26]

Third, what ethical assumptions are made about man, conflict, and war? Does a field orientation assume a status-quo or conservative view? Do the concepts of freedom and justice find expression through the field? I am especially concerned about the value assumptions and implications of field theory, and I will devote considerable time to this when I engage the practical conclusions of all this work in a subsequent volume.

COMMENTS ON THE REVIEWS   241

   Fourth, what are the dynamic sociological assumptions of
field theory? Social distance and social status are clearly part of
the theory; but what about norms, roles, expectations, and especially
the dynamics of power? As a conflict theorist who believes that a
society is fundamentally a dialectical balance of power between
competing interests and that norms and roles follow from this power
balance and not vice versa, I must make the relevance of this to the
field explicit. This is my current focus, and I hope to publish in
1976 a volume I have tentatively titled <u>The Conflict Helix</u>, a draft
of which has been completed.
   Fifth, regarding especially the international relations applications of field theory, what are the goals of nations? How are they
measured in the field, and how do they relate to the forces of the
field? In my past writings I have certainly neglected goals; indeed,
only recently have I seen the importance of explicitly dealing with
goals in the field, and I intend to consider them in the future. For
now, let me simply suggest the role of goals. I have come to see
national elites as teleologically directed, as moving towards the
satisfaction of future goals rather than simply responding to domestic
and foreign stimuli. These goals are reflected in the patterns of
behavior a nation manifests: behavior comprises goal-traces, so
to speak, and the different weights a nation gives to patterns of
diplomacy transaction, alignment, and conflict reflect its particular
goals. That is, the independent patterns of behavior mirror the
nation's distinct goal clusters. The relationship of distances to
behavior then reflects the different saliences the distances have
for a national elite in evaluating their goals in relation to another
nation. Clearly there is much to be clarified here, and such will
be done in due course.

                        Substantive Conclusions

   What, after all this theorizing and all these empirical analyses,
do I conclude about international relations? These conclusions can
be put into a series of general propositions.

   1. International relations is highly structured into clear and
      meaningful patterns of national attributes and dyadic behavior.
   2. The three dominant patterns of attributes comprise wealth,
      power, and ideology; the dominant patterns of dyadic behavior
      are transactions, alignments, international organizations,
      and negative communications.

3. About half of the variation in a nation's patterned dyadic behavior is accounted for by its similarities and differences (distances) from the object nation. The particular function relating an actor's dyadic behavior to such distances is $w = \Sigma \alpha d$, where w is the patterned behavior, d is a particular distance (vector) on one of the attribute patterns, and α is a parameter specific to the actor.
4. Although all actors are similarly affected by distances in total, it depends on the actor what distances relate to which behavior; that is, parameters generally vary by actor.
5. Although, overall, distances account for about 50 percent of the actor's patterns of dyadic behavior, some particular distance relationships explains about 80 to 90 percent of their variation in such behavior.

These five propositions are the most general I can extract from the theoretical-empirical work of DON. The reports and books themselves present a wealth of detail about specific actors, dyads, years, patterns, functions, parameters, variables, and so on; they constitute a huge reservoir of systematic-empirical-aggregate findings on nations, organized into a common theoretical framework.

NOTES

1. Two books have been completed in this effort: Rudolph J. Rummel, The Dynamic Psychological Field (Beverly Hills: Sage Publications, 1975), and Rudolph J. Rummel, Field Theory Evolving (Beverly Hills: Sage Publications, forthcoming in 1976). An additional book entitled The Conflict Helix is in first draft. Three more books are planned before the final volume: the first on international relations, the second on the epistemology of DON, and the third on international humanism, the ethical perspective within which DON's results take on their policy meaning.
2. For some of these developments see Rudolph J. Rummel, "Roots of Faith," in In Search of Global Patterns, edited by James N. Rosenau (New York: Free Press, forthcoming 1975).
3. Irma Adelman and Cynthia Taft Morris, Society, Politics, and Economic Development (Baltimore: Johns Hopkins Press, 1967).
4. Many of these theoretical-empirical reports are given in Rummel, Field Theory Evolving, op. cit.
5. Rummel, The Dynamic Psychological Field, op. cit.
6. Rummel, The Conflict Helix, op. cit.
7. Rummel, Field Theory Evolving, op. cit., Chapter 4.

8. Rummel, The Conflict Helix, op. cit.
9. See Rummel, Field Theory Evolving, op. cit., Chapter 4.
10. Rummel, The Dynamic Psychological Field, op. cit.
11. Rummel, Field Theory Evolving, op. cit., Chapter 4, Section 3.
12. Rummel, Applied Factor Analysis, op. cit., Section 14.3.4.
13. Brian Berry, Essays on Commodity Flows and the Spatial Structure of the Indian Economy (Chicago: University of Chicago Press, 1966).
14. Richard Chadwick, "International Involvement: Steps Toward the Quantitative Measurement and Explanation of International Policies," Dimensionality of Nations Project, Research Report No. 37 (Honolulu: University of Hawaii, 1972).
15. Warren Phillips, "A Mathematical Theory of Conflict Dynamics," Dimensionality of Nations Project, Research Report No. 39 (Honolulu: University of Hawaii, 1970).
16. Tong-Whan Park, "The Role of Distance in International Relations: A New Look at the Social Field Theory," Behavioral Science 17, no. 4 (1972): 337-48.
17. Rummel, Field Theory Evolving, op. cit. and Rummel, The Dynamic Psychological Field, op. cit.
18. M. D. Dunnette, "Fad, Fashions, and Folderol in Psychology," American Psychologist 21, no. 2 (1966): 345.
19. Derek L. Phillips, "Sociologists and Their Knowledge: Some Critical Remarks on a Profession," American Behavioral Scientist 14, no. 2 (1971): 569.
20. Rudolph J. Rummel, Nation Attributes and Behavior (Beverly Hills: Sage Publications, forthcoming in 1976).
21. Rummel, Field Theory Evolving, op. cit., Chapter 16.
22. Rudolph J. Rummel, "U.S. Foreign Relations: Conflict, Cooperation, and Attribute Distances," in Peace, War, and Numbers, edited by Bruce M. Russett (Beverly Hills: Sage Publications, 1972), pp. 71-113.
23. Rummel, Field Theory Evolving, op. cit., Chapter 9.
24. Rummel, The Dynamic Psychological Field, op. cit.
25. Ibid.
26. Ibid.

PART

IV

**THE INTER-NATION
SIMULATION PROJECT
(SIMULATED INTERNATIONAL
PROCESSES PROJECT)**

CHAPTER

12

AN INCOMPLETE
HISTORY OF FIFTEEN
SHORT YEARS IN
SIMULATING INTERNATIONAL
PROCESSES

Harold Guetzkow

Work on simulated international processes began during my year at the Center for Advanced Study in the Behavioral Sciences (1956-57), while I was involved in a study group with Richard C. Snyder, Karl W. Deutsch, Charles A. McClelland, and Wilbur Schram. My background of experiences as director of the Social Science Laboratory at Carnegie-Mellon University (1950-56) acquainted me with the limitations and potentials of social psychological experimentation, as well as those of all-computer simulations. The latter were pinpointed in the area of my substantive interest (international relations) by "A Simple Diplomatic Game" by Oliver Benson.[1] Hans Speier, also at the center that year from the RAND Corporation, shared insights from his use of all-manual games, which usually focused upon crisis situations.[2] The goal was to develop a creative, balanced simulation of the overall international scene, using a vehicle that would facilitate both explicitness and cumulative work.

Construction of an inter-nation simulation was begun immediately upon my arrival at Northwestern University in the fall of 1957, within the context of a broad international relations program that had been formulated by Snyder[3] and sponsored by the Carnegie Corporation of New York. One of the project's most critical decisions was taken then, which was to utilize a man-machine format for creation of the simulation, hoping thereby to combine the advantages of both all-manual and machine simulations and simultaneously to avoid their

---

Preparation of this paper was part of my activities as Gordon Fulcher Professor of Decision-making at Northwestern University.

peculiar shortcomings, as has been explained elsewhere.[4] After pilot runs,[5] including an as yet exploratory but quite critical demonstration at Asilomar with senior members of the academic community and a number of former foreign service officers, further development of the Inter-Nation Simulation (INS), as it was then labeled, was ready for outside sponsorship. Support was obtained from the Air Force Office of Scientific Research (AFOSR) in 1959. In 1964 the sponsorship shifted from AFOSR to the then newly established Advanced Research Projects Agency (ARPA) of the U.S. Department of Defense.

At this point the project became known as "Simulated International Processes" (SIP), inasmuch as the Inter-Nation Simulation (INS) was already being considered as only a "first generation" simulation. The generous support now being received made possible a succession of "in-house" assistant directors, each of whom helped elaborate the ongoing work and gave his own distinction to it. Lloyd Jensen (1965-66) implemented his interest in comparing the "output" validity of various runs of INS with the outcomes of judgments made by foreign service officers.[6] Paul L. Smoker (1966-69) emphasized the extension and reformulation of programmed aspects of the Inter-Nation Simulation, while enriching its manual components. His work represented such a quantum change from INS that it seemed wise to rechristen this modified version of the original simulation as the "International Processes Simulation" (IPS), truly a "second generation" model.[7] Throughout the participation of Smoker as well as that of Michael R. Leavitt, there was a growing interest in all-computer simulations of world affairs. As the last assistant director (1969-71), Leavitt constructed a macro-module known as "A Computer Simulation of International Alliance Behavior."[8] However, it was the initiative of Stuart R. Bremer in taking advantage of a year's student exchange privilege that crowned the effort of SIP with the construction of his "Simulated International Processer" (SIPER), an all-computer specification of a revised and updated version of the Inter-Nation Simulation, the "third generation" model.[9]*

The Simulated International Processes (SIP) project was funded from both private and public resources, the private money enabling

---

*Professor Bremer was obtaining his doctorate at Michigan State University; he became a visiting research assistant in SIP (1968-69) through the Traveling Scholar Program of the Big Ten Committee in Inter-Institutional Cooperation. Upon returning to East Lansing, Bremer built SIPER without further communication under a dissertation committee chaired by Rufus P. Browning. Bremer presented a copy of his completed dissertation to the amazed staff of the Simulated International Processes in the middle of August 1970.

us to complement the public money when federal restrictions on certain uses of the latter prevented completion of the task. Full acknowledgments, along with contract and grant numbers, are detailed elsewhere.[10] It was a tremendous privilege to participate in the stewardship of these funds. I am most grateful for the intellectual and bureaucratic aid given me in the development of the SIP project, by my government monitors as well as by our foundation aides. May I certify herewith that in no way was there ever interference in our scholarly work by anyone in the organizations from which we received funding: we worked with complete academic freedom.

The intellectual history of SIP to date has been exhibited in two contexts, as an exercise in model development[11] and by the self-assessment of its cumulative characteristics recently prepared for the National Science Foundation.[12] Bremer's evaluation, in Chapter 15 of this volume, of the substance of the project accurately develops a chronology of four phases: development of the INS as a man-machine simulation with its many variations, its applications in education and research, the study of its validity, and the forays into all-computer simulation. Another historical record is found in its products, as listed in the project bibliography. Complaint about the "relative inaccessibility of many of the studies"[13] is well taken; an attempt is being made to remedy this situation by placing some of the studies on microfilm.

Now it is possible to consider the intellectual development of the project from yet another point of view, less chronologically oriented, by noting how it confronted some of its challenges: (1) how it posed and tried to solve its underlying problems in methodology and technique, all within the framework of a day-by-day working philosophy of science; (2) how it attempted to integrate its findings; (3) how it went about meshing its development with contemporary research in the substance of international politics; and (4) how it strove to build a communication net between makers and users for policy purposes. Let us now consider each of these encounters briefly, inasmuch as they give background for the reading of the four essays on SIP that constitute its evaluation. (See Chapters 13 through 16 of this volume.)

THE PHILOSOPHIC AND METHODOLOGICAL CONTEXT OF THE SIMULATED INTERNATIONAL PROCESSES PROJECT

The central question of the project was formulated early: can one construct a simulation of international relations? The question was answered by constructing a man-machine simulation consisting of both domestic and international components, called the Inter-Nation Simulation (INS). This pragmatic style permeated our approach to problems in the philosophy of science.

The first essay that presented the INS also sketched an overall philosophic viewpoint of the effort to be undertaken and positioned its working definition of "simulation."[14] The perspective was stated with more insight and fullness in the course of the IBM Scientific Computing Symposium on Simulation Models and Gaming.[15] An earlier essay described the intellectual history of the project, it showed the development of this perspective as follows:

> [It] became increasingly clear, as we went from pilot run to pilot run in 1957 through 1959, that our participants were not serving as human subjects within an experimental situation, as it had been my custom to regard those who took part in the experiments at Michigan and Carnegie Tech. This laboratory situation was different, in that our human participants were acting as surrogates rather than as experimental subjects in their own right. In the development of our national entities it was our intention to use abstract representations, so that all participants, regardless of nationality, could man any of the nations [and] act in terms of the simulated environment with which they would find themselves. . . . Thus, our simulation was not . . . a laboratory counter-part of field behaviors. As it gradually developed the Inter-Nation Simulation was rather a theoretical construction complemented by the verbal and mathematical formulations.[16]

In an attempt to check out this phase of the project's posture, a small working conference was developed in the winter of 1964-65 to tap the philosophic wisdom of Wes Churchman, Herbert Hockberg, and Abraham Kaplan. A dissenting reaction to the conference was prepared at the time by a colleague, Paul Kress, which has been published recently but without updating its materials, thereby constituting another part of the printed historical record.[17] Inasmuch as this was the period in which the project was moving from its emanation of the INS simulation as such into checks on its veridicality, problems in validity were considered at the meeting, resulting in the essay by Charles F. Hermann.[18] This helped us recognize the Churchmanian emphasis on the fact that the purposes for the use of the simulation also help determine the selection of the methodology to be employed for the study of validity.

Although I was being rapidly socialized in the scholarship of political science at Northwestern by Richard C. Snyder and Chadwick

INTER-NATION SIMULATION PROJECT HISTORY   251

F. Alger, two colleagues with whom I was in constant and close
interaction until their lamented departure from Northwestern, it
seems to me that my sociological and psychological backgrounds
were important determinants in placing the emphasis of the project
upon validation, once a working simulation had been constructed.
However, after the findings in validity were integrated,[19] it seemed
that little would be gained by continuing such work on the INS. It
seemed that strategic advances were more likely to be made through
construction of a revised model, as was being done by Smoker[20]
in his International Processes Simulation (IPS).

Another of my colleagues at Northwestern, namely Donald T.
Campbell, was important in establishing the context in which we
worked, as he became a person of increasing charisma in our seminars and for our graduate students, especially in the application of
his notions of "proximal similarity" in support of our "quasi-
experiments." The essay by John R. Raser, Donald T. Campbell,
and Richard W. Chadwick documents this aspect of our philosophic-
methodological context.[21]

ATTEMPTS TO INTEGRATE OUTCOMES

There were at least two reasons for me, as the director of the
project, to create substantive integrations of our work as we went
along. I needed such for summing up where we stood as we developed
the guidelines for our work, and I needed ways of placing our project
within the field of other simulation efforts as well as more broadly
within the net of persons who were contributing substantive findings
each year from their nonsimulation researches in international
relations. Often the hurly-burly of project events overtook my
attempts to be more systematic and orderly in making such assessments, but on occasion it was possible to commission efforts with
common focus, even though each author usually insisted upon tailor-
ing his essay to his own perspectives. Though they were often
disjointed, parallel efforts were being undertaken by others. I tried
to always be sensitive to the academic freedoms of my collaborators,
especially since I was conducting government-sponsored research.

To make sure that the milieu in which I was operating in the
simulation field was well canvassed, Richard Dawson helped me
prepare a reader of simulation pieces in other social science disciplines.[22] This review was updated at the conclusion of the project.[23]
Although it would have been desirable for the latter book to have
included a piece surveying the overall philosophical-methodological
developments in international relations at that time, I failed to
identify anyone with such an interest. I myself was by then too

fully involved in my long-postponed leaves of absence, gaining life experiences in decision making in international affairs under Elliot Richardson in the U.S. Department of State (1969-70) and Ralph Bunche in the United Nations (1970-71).

Three pieces, focusing on simulation works in international relations as such, analyzed developments in the "manual" or "all-person" game, as exemplified by the RAND-MIT developments of Lincoln Bloomfield and his associates,[24] in the man-computer development,[25] and in the all-computer simulation.[26] These constituted another attempt at integration in the field. Hayward R. Alker and one of his students worked empirically in an effort to integrate these three simulation approaches, using the same substantive problem.[27] His efforts resulted in three case studies, tightly interwoven, using a scenario revolving around a nuclear explosion in the People's Republic of China.

Based upon this comparative work, Alker then made an appraisal of the decision makers' environments in the Inter-Nation Simulation.[28] This important piece had little impact upon developments in the project, however, inasmuch as Smoker had already formulated most of the changes involved in his International Processes Simulation. It was possible to get a critique of the Inter-Nation Simulation from Modelski, too.[29] Although it was assuring to know that Smoker had anticipated almost all of Modelski's creative suggestions, the timing was such that Modelski's essay was not used in the development of Smoker's work.

As an individual I was able to prepare an integration of our findings from some 24 different studies on the substantive validity of the man-computer simulations.[30] My inability to correlate the timing of the commissioned pieces, given the previous obligations of those involved, discouraged further attempts to develop consolidations. Perhaps the project's greatest failure was brought about in my attempt to mount a joint effort with a full-time research associate in the "Event Simulation Project," as mentioned by Bremer in Chapter 15 of this volume. This endeavor fell apart after some years of effort, largely because of exogenous factors.

MESHING DEVELOPMENTS WITHIN THE PROJECT WITH CONTEMPORARY DEVELOPMENTS IN RESEARCH BY CONTRACTING-OUT

Through the decade and a half of the project's existence, it seemed desirable to keep close contact with the developments in international relations of the more traditional variety, which were continuing apace, as well as to attempt to mesh the activities of SIP with more recent data-grounded research.[31] The funding agreements of the projects made it possible to "contract-out" portions of the research for such purposes as integration, as described above. This device was also used to induce Robert L. Pfaltzgraff, Jr.,[32] to make a check on the extent to which the concepts utilized in the three prototype simulations (RAND-MIT, the political-military exercise;[33] the Inter-Nation Simulation; and TEMPER, the all-computer simulation developed by Clark C. Abt and Morton Gordon[34]) overlapped with those used by ten prominent scholars in the verbal literature, in some ways coming full circle on the work of Denis G. Sullivan, who had early attempted to spell out concepts found in textbooks for inclusion in the original formulation of the Inter-Nation Simulation.[35]

On the other hand, there were a small number of projects commissioned in each of which the contracting investigator was asked to apply his own materials to simulation formulations in order to modify the latter conceptually in terms of his frame of reference, with later attempts to use his own empirical work to check out the adequacy of the suggested revisions in the simulation.* A stellar example of such work is found in the utilization of data from the 1914 Project by Dina A. Zinnes, in which she made an analysis of man-machine runs, using both the designs of her earlier analysis and the data obtained from historical archives on the interchange of communications during the period before World War I.[36]

BUILDING A COMMUNICATION NET WITH USERS AND PRODUCERS FOR POLICY PURPOSES

One important motivation of the U.S. government in providing the bulk of the funding for the project derived from the interest of two unusual military officers, both from the Air Force, Colonels William Thane Minor and George L. Draper, who during the existence of SIP were working intermittently within the Joint War Games

---

*This notion of attempting to mesh ongoing research in an articulated way with other researches is argued in the context of studies on disasters in an essay that was prepared by the author for the National Research Council of the National Academy of Sciences. Harold Guetzkow, "Joining Field and Laboratory Work in Disaster Research," in <u>Man and Society in Disaster</u>, edited by George W. Baker and Dwight Chapman (New York: Basic Books, 1962), pp. 350-54.

Agency of the Office of the Joint Chiefs of Staff and the Industrial College of the Armed Forces. These concerned men facilitated within their military complex the use of simulation for gaming purposes, sometimes also providing briefings for audiences on an interagency basis. In this process an extensive network of communications was built between the users of our research and the project researchers. The servicing of this network placed important demands upon our resources. My personal motivations, stemming from my high school debating experience and powerfully reinforced by my five-year period of "alternative service" with like-minded men as a conscientious objector during World War II, spurred my constant attempts to interest personnel from the U.S. Department of State in utilization of the work, but these efforts met with little success. Suggestions for such implementation are described elsewhere.[37]

Often the research subcontracts provided for the travel of the contractor to Northwestern as well as for the project director and his associates to consult at the subcontractor's home base, allowing deep exposure of both to each other's work. Field visits to the subcontractor often involved a presentation of details about SIP to colleagues and graduate students who were involved in scholarly work in international relations. In addition, many contacts were made with researchers through professional meetings, both formally through programmed panels and informally in the course of corridor contacts.

Our interaction with producers and users was not limited to the United States. In the development of a net among persons interested in simulation in Asia, the six-month visit of Hiroharu Seki to SIP eventuated in laboratory work in Tokyo as well as in a book describing the Inter-Nation Simulation and his realizations thereof.[38] On the European scene there was interest by English scholars, such as John W. Burton and his associates,[39] as well as by Canadians, through Jerome Laulicht and his colleagues in the Canadian Peace Research Institute.[40] In these ways the results of SIP were shared overseas, allowing governments of many persuasions to understand the potentials of the application of simulations to their foreign policy activities. Although for a while it looked as if the Western Behavioral Sciences Institute would spark a coordinated effort, involving Ruge from Norway, Diaz-Guerrero from Mexico, Mushakoji of Japan, and Raser of the United States, in the end this extremely important project was not executed.

This account is far from a complete history of SIP, although perhaps the foregoing materials have indicated the ways in which four central challenges of the project were met in the course of its development. It was in these efforts that the resources of the project were devoted to creating its meta-methodological postures, to maintaining some integration of its centrifugal tendencies, to reducing its insularity and provinciality, and to centering it in the mainstream of developments in the creation and utilization of knowledge about international affairs.

In the end there were at least two important items on the unfinished agenda of SIP. Early in our project discussions, the notion of executing the INS as a very abstract, highly generalized exercise without substantive international relations content had been suggested by Denis G. Sullivan. Such research would have enabled us to fathom, to some extent at least, the way in which the underlying processes of the INS were influencing the outcomes, and then it would have allowed us to consider the impact of substance-content upon its outcomes, were a comparison to be made between the INS and its abstract formulation, similar to the manner in which Pilisuk and Rapoport explored their prisoner's dilemma games in the "Michigan Disarmament" series.[41] Secondly, it is with regret that a venture in the use of very creative persons as decision makers in the INS was not undertaken, especially in the operation of an IPS. If "social scientists should not only tell it the way it is, but also tell it the way it could be,"[42] an opportunity for productive insightful men of world affairs from all cultures to help develop new "answers" to the perennial problems of international affairs would not be forgone.

Perhaps this brief history helps one understand why as director of the project I thought the 15 years of its duration were entirely too short a period in which to build an even somewhat satisfactory simulation of international relations. Little wonder, then, that I cherish the opportunities I hope will be mine during the next 15 years to work further on the simulation of international processes.[43]

NOTES

1. Oliver Benson, "A Simple Diplomatic Game," in <u>International Politics and Foreign Policy</u>, edited by James N. Rosenau (New York: Free Press, 1961), pp. 504-11.
2. Herbert Goldhammer and Hans Speier, "Some Observations on Political Gaming," <u>World Politics</u> 12, no. 1 (1959): 71-83.
3. Richard C. Snyder, "A Proposal for a Five Year Grant to the Program of Graduate Training and Research in International Relations: Proposal to the Carnegie Corporation of New York" (Evanston: Northwestern University, 1962).
4. Harold Guetzkow, "A Decade of Life with the Inter-Nation Simulation," in <u>The Process of Model-Building in the Behavioral</u>

Sciences, edited by Ralph M. Stogdill (New York: W. W. Norton, 1970), pp. 31-53.

5. Robert C. Noel, "Evolution of Inter-Nation Simulation," in Simulation in International Relations: Developments for Research and Teaching, edited by Harold Guetzkow, Chadwick F. Alger, Richard A. Brody, Robert C. Noel, and Richard Snyder (Englewood Cliffs: Prentice-Hall, 1963), pp. 69-102.

6. Harold Guetzkow and Lloyd Jensen, "Research Activities on Simulated International Processes," Background 9, no. 4 (1966): 261-74.

7. Paul L. Smoker, "An International Processes Simulation: Development, Usage, and Partial Validation" (Ph.D. diss., Lancaster, England: University of Lancaster, 1968).

8. Michael R. Leavitt, "A Computer Simulation of International Alliance Behavior" (Ph.D. diss., Northwestern University, 1971).

9. Stuart A. Bremer, "National and International Systems: A Computer Simulation" (Ph.D. diss., Michigan State University, 1970); Stuart A. Bremer, Simulated Worlds: A Computer Model of National Decision-Making (Princeton: Princeton University Press, forthcoming).

10. Guetzkow, "A Decade of Life with the Inter-Nation Simulation," op. cit., pp. 1-2; Harold Guetzkow, "Final Report: Simulated International Processes Project, Advanced Research Projects Agency, Contract No. SD 260" (Evanston: Northwestern University, 1972).

11. Guetzkow, "A Decade of Life with the Inter-Nation Simulation," op. cit.

12. Harold Guetzkow, "Sizing Up a Study in Simulated International Processes: Roughly-Hewn Surmises for a Project Autobiography," in In Search of Global Patterns, edited by James N. Rosenau (New York: Free Press, forthcoming).

13. Bremer, Simulated Worlds, op. cit., p. 14.

14. Harold Guetzkow, "Simulations in the Consolidation and Utilization of Knowledge about International Relations," in Theory and Research on the Causes of War, edited by Dean G. Pruitt and Richard C. Snyder (Englewood Cliffs: Prentice-Hall, 1969), pp. 284-300.

15. Harold Guetzkow, "Simulation in International Relations," in Proceedings of the IBM Scientific Computing Symposium on Simulation Models and Gaming (White Plains, N.Y.: International Business Machines Corporation, 1966), pp. 249-78.

16. Guetzkow, "A Decade of Life with the Inter-Nation Simulation," op. cit., pp. 42-43.

17. Paul Kress, "On Validating Simulation with Special Attention to Simulation of International Politics," International Interactions 1, no. 1 (1974): 41-50.

18. Charles F. Hermann, "Validation Problems in Games and Simulations with Special Reference to Models of International Politics," Behavioral Science 12, no. 3 (1967): 216-31.

19. Guetzkow, "Simulations in the Consolidation and Utilization of Knowledge," op. cit.

20. Smoker, "An International Processes Simulation," op. cit.

21. John R. Raser, Donald T. Campbell and Richard W. Chadwick, "Gaming and Simulation for Developing Theory Relevant to International Relations," General Systems 15 (1970): 183-204.

22. Harold Guetzkow, ed., Simulation in Social Science; readings (Englewood Cliffs, N.J.: Prentice-Hall, 1962).

23. Harold Guetzkow, Philip Kotler, and Randall L. Schultz, eds., Simulation in Social and Administrative Science: Overviews and Case-Examples (Englewood Cliffs: Prentice-Hall, 1972).

24. R. Lucas Fischer, "The RAND/MIT Political-Military Exercise and International Relations Theory," (Cambridge, Mass.: Arms Control Project, Center for International Studies, Massachusetts Institute of Technology, 1969).

25. William D. Coplin, "Inter-Nation Simulation and Contemporary Theories of International Relations," American Political Science Review 40, no. 3 (1966): 562-78.

26. Morton Gordon, "Burdens for the Designer of a Computer Simulation of International Relations: The Case of TEMPER," in Computers and the Policy-Making Community, edited by Davis B. Bobrow and Judah L. Schwartz (Englewood Cliffs: Prentice-Hall, 1969), pp. 222-45.

27. Hayward R. Alker and Ronald D. Brunner, "Simulating International Conflict: A Comparison of Three Approaches," International Studies Quarterly 13, no. 1 (1969): 70-110.

28. Hayward R. Alker, "Decision-Makers' Environments in the Inter-Nation Simulation," in Simulation in the Study of Politics, edited by William D. Coplin (Chicago: Markham, 1968), pp. 31-58.

29. George Modelski, "Simulations, Realities, and International Relations Theory," Simulation and Games 1, no. 2 (1970): 111-34.

30. Guetzkow, "Simulation in International Relations," op. cit.

31. Susan D. Jones and J. David Singer, "Beyond Conjecture," in International Politics: Abstracts of Data-Based Research (Ithaca: F. E. Peacock, 1972).

32. Robert L. Pfaltzgraff, Jr., "Simulation and International Relations Literature" (Medford: Tufts University, 1972).

33. Lincoln Bloomfield and Barton Whaley, "The Political-Military Exercise: A Progress Report," Orbis 8, no. 4 (1965): 854-70.

34. Clark C. Abt and Morton Gordon, "Report on Project TEMPER," in Theory and Research on the Causes of War, edited by Dean G. Pruitt and Richard C. Snyder (Englewood Cliffs: Prentice-Hall, 1969), pp. 245-62.

35. Denis G. Sullivan, "Towards an Inventory of Major Propositions Contained in Contemporary Textbooks in International Relations," (Ph.D. diss.: Northwestern University, 1963).

36. Dina A. Zinnes, "A Comparison of Hostile Behavior of Decision Makers in Simulate and Historical Data," World Politics 18, no. 3 (1966): 474-502.

37. Guetzkow, "Simulations in the Consolidation and Utilization of Knowledge," op. cit., pp. 289-93.

38. Hiroharu Seki, Foundations of International Systems Theory (Tokyo: University of Tokyo Press, 1969).

39. John W. Burton, "International Relations Simulation on the Cheap" (London: University College, 1966).

40. Jerome Laulicht, "A Vietnam Peace Game: Computer-Assisted Simulation of Complex Relations in International Relations," Computers and Automation 16, no. 3 (1967): 14-18.

41. Anatol Rapoport, "Games Which Simulate Deterrence and Disarmament," Peace Research Reviews 1, no. 1, (1967): 40-45.

42. Paul L. Smoker, "Social Research for Social Anticipation," American Behavioral Scientist 12, no. 6 (1969): 7-13.

43. Wm. Ladd Hollist and Harold Guetzkow, "Cumulative Research in International Relations: Empirical Analysis and Computer Simulation of International Armament Processes" (Evanston: Northwestern University, 1975). Mimeographed.

CHAPTER

13

AN APPRAISAL OF THE PHILOSOPHY OF SCIENCE OF THE INTER-NATION SIMULATION PROJECT

Cheryl Christensen
Robert Butterworth

To what extent has the Inter-Nation Simulation advanced the scientific development of international relations? The essays in this part of the volume, taken collectively, are an attempt to answer this question. Judging how well we execute that task will involve laying bare our understanding of what forms of inquiry promote an understanding of politics. Our particular aim in this essay is to show how the evaluation effort requires answers to certain questions that are essentially topics in the philosophy of science. What is scientific knowledge? How do we choose among different and competing products of the "scientific method"? How does continuity of scientific knowledge come about? Without a full exploration of such standards, we cannot systematically evaluate scientific efforts. Lacking some guiding standards, we might be unable to know whether we know more about the world because of our research endeavor or not.

In this chapter we are interested in appraising the way in which the INS research community addressed such problems within itself. How were questions of formulating scientific procedures answered? How did the project researchers expect science to progress because of the project? What impact did particular views of science have on the development of the research effort? The answers to the questions supply us with the appraisal standards that were used within INS; these standards are the data for our appraisal. Could the project have done better; and since we suggest it could have, how much did the overall effort accomplish, given what was done?

For this particular appraisal, therefore, we are concerned with INS as a prototype of scientific theorizing. Hence we focus attention on only one of the several modes in which INS could have operated, which is as a multidisciplinary research effort that could

aid the development of experimental social science. The development
of INS in this mode reflected a persuasion that social science theory
was best built eclectically, in a cumulative way. That persuasion
led to the attempt to develop simulation modules that would be capable
of being linked in flexible ways to multiple simulation efforts. This
persuasion and design has other dimensions as well, dimensions
that perhaps were unrealized by the initial INS workers but that
have deeper ramifications for the process of theory building and
knowledge growth. Once we have set forth our criteria and appraised
the INS criteria in light of them, we will make explicit some of those
deeper ramifications in an overall appraisal of the project.

HOW CAN THEORIZING BE APPRAISED?

By what kinds of evidence can we justifiably accept or reject
scientific theories? What, indeed, makes a theory "scientific"?
Before classic Newtonian physics was challenged by the theories
of special relativity and quantum physics, it seemed easiest to
assert that scientific knowledge was "proven" knowledge. "Proof"
could be provided by the evidence of the senses or by the power of
the intellect. Problems with both kinds of "proof" were long recognized. Hume, as the leading British skeptic, had convincingly
argued that empirical evidence was in and of itself insufficient to
"prove" propositions asserting causal connections.* Also, the

---

*Hume's case in point was causation, which he considered the
fundamental principle upon which the validity of knowledge depended.
His aim was to demonstrate that knowledge depended upon two things:
receiving simple sense impressions and connecting the ideas corresponding to these by the causal principle. Although constant conjunction
can be observed, Hume argued that the necessary causal relationship
cannot be given by sense data and reflects the structure of mind, not
the world. See C. R. Morris, Locke, Berkeley, Hume (Oxford:
Oxford University Press, 1931), pp. 125-39. This has generally
come down to the impossibility of creating a logic that can infallibly
increase content, as Lakatos puts it. See Imre Lakatos, "Falsification and the Methodology of Scientific Research Programmes," in
Criticism and the Growth of Knowledge, edited by Imre Lakatos and
Alan Musgrave (Cambridge: Cambridge University Press, 1970),
p. 95. Note that Kant's attempt to go beyond the skeptics' attacks
rested upon a special, a priori status for Newtonian physics and
Euclidean geometry, a position which became untenable with the

problem of certainty in inductive inferences was well known. However, such problems seemed to be merely "academic" because science seemed to speak with a single voice and gave the appearance of being a successful, cumulative effort. With special relativity, however, this image crumbled.

> Einstein's results . . . turned the tables and now very few philosophers or scientists still think that scientific knowledge is, or can be, proven knowledge. But few realize that with this the whole classical structure of intellectual values falls in ruins and has to be replaced: one cannot simply water down the ideal of proven truth—as some logical empiricists do—to the ideal of 'probable truth' or—as some sociologists of knowledge do—to 'truth by (changing) consensus.'[1]

With the earlier image destroyed, fundamental problems reopened in a very disturbing way. How can scientific knowledge be distinguished from other kinds of knowledge claims, such as religion, metaphysics, or "common sense"?[2] Moreover, there seem to be several scientific knowledge systems that compete among themselves. How can choices among their different products be made? This situation of unresolved epistemological contention is both disturbing and threatening, especially for social scientists, whose efforts to become "scientific" seem to demand a well-articulated view of exactly what becoming scientific entails and how it might occur. Moving away from an identification of scientific theories with provable theories seems to open the door to charges that scientific theories are no "better founded" than other kinds of knowledge and that holding scientific views is no different from adhering to other kinds of beliefs.*

The problem can be posed quite succinctly: How can one demonstrate the correctness or falseness of a theory? This task is quite different from that of judging whether or not a particular proposition or hypothesis is supported by empirical observation. Judging theories is more complex; the question is how an investigator can go from a

---

development and use of non-Euclidean geometry and non-Newtonian physics.

*The conflict among systems of science has not only raised questions about the methods of science but has also entailed examinations of the foundations of abstract mathematics; the foundations of logic; the role of indeterminacy in the physical world; and indeed, the kind of knowledge of nature that can be expected. See Louis Regis, Epistemology (New York: Macmillan, 1959), pp. 61-73.

particular test of a hypothesis to conclusions about the theory (set of logically interrelated definitions, axioms, and hypotheses) from which it is derived.

Suppose that an investigator has a theory from which he deduces a hypothesis and that he specifies the way in which this hypothesis can be empirically tested. The test is performed, and the result that was expected in light of the theory is obtained. Can the investigator conclude, then, that the underlying theory is correct? Obviously not. All that has been shown is that in a particular instance the hypothesized relationship holds.* Suppose, therefore, that the investigator then tests the hypothesis many times and obtains the same results. Can it then be said that the theory is proved? No, for it is possible that the hypothesized relation holds for reasons other than those suggested by the theory in question. The investigator will then try to eliminate some of the "competing hypotheses." Similarly, in choosing among competing theories, he may attempt to eliminate other possible explanations of the outcome.[3] However, for both theories and hypotheses, the potential domain of alternative explanations is infinite. From a finite number of tests, the investigator cannot prove that the theoretical deduction behind an empirical result is the right one. Each theoretical inference, that is, contains a ceteris paribus clause, which the investigator can explore by eliminating apparently plausible rival hypotheses, but which can never be fully specified; hence the investigator can never be sure that the underlying theory has been "proved."[4]

If scientific theories can never be definitively proven, does this imply that they are all equally likely or unlikely? No they are not, probabilists like Rudolph Carnap have asserted. They contend that different theories have different degrees of probability, in the sense of the calculus of probability, relative to the evidence at hand. It ought to be possible, then, to specify for any theory its probability of being correct in light of this evidence.[5] However, even this weaker notion of proof has been questioned. Karl Popper demon-

---

*In fact, even this is difficult to establish, since there are real problems in trying to prove propositions with sense data. The truth value of observational statements cannot be indubitably decided. Propositions can be derived only from other propositions; they cannot be derived from "facts." See Imre Lakatos, "Falsification and the Methodology of Scientific Research Programmes," in Criticism and the Growth of Knowledge, edited by Imre Lakatos and Alan Musgrave (Cambridge: Cambridge University Press, 1970), p. 99; and Karl Popper, The Logic of Scientific Discovery (New York: Basic Books, 1959), pp. 104-05.

PHILOSOPHY OF SCIENCE

strated that such criteria cannot be definitively established; under very general conditions, all theories have zero probability, whatever the evidence.[6] Hence Lakatos reaches the rather disturbing conclusion that "all theories are not only equally unprovable, but also equally improbable."[7]

Some philosophers argue that the inability to get at least definitive probabilistic estimates of proof means that almost everything regarded as knowledge, that is, scientific as well as common-sense knowledge, remains without foundation.[8] If one remains convinced that the confidence in scientific knowledge is confidence based upon its being proven knowledge, the situation looks rather bleak. Popper has suggested another approach that initially seems to transform the situation. He asserts that confidence in a scientific theory rests not in the volume of the positive, supporting evidence, but rather in the fact that serious attempts to falsify the theory have been unsuccessful. Where proof is impossible, according to this position, disproving is possible. Scientific theories are those that specify certain statements as potential falsifiers; that is, these statements identify conditions or experimental results that would imply giving up the theory if unfavorable outcomes were obtained.* The business of science, then, is trying hard to disprove theories. To the extent that these attempts fail, our confidence in the theories is enhanced. In its simplest form, the falsificationist approach then suggests that the objectivity of science lies not in the form of the proposed theory but in the outcome of the falsification experiments designed to disprove it. Braithwaite suggests the following:

> This objective test of falsity it is which makes the deductive system, in whose construction we have a very great freedom, a deductive system of scientific hypotheses. Man proposes a system of hypotheses: nature disposes of its truth or falsity. Man invents a scientific system and then discovers whether or not it accords with observed fact.[9]

At first glance this position is appealing, since it promises a way out of the earlier impasse. As we probe deeper, however, some of the certainty of the simple falsificationist position proves illusory. There are two especially troublesome aspects of this approach: the way in which "facts" can be separated from "theories" (demarcation criteria), and the logical certainty of falsification.

---

*This presupposes that criteria of refutation have been laid down, making it possible to agree which situations, if observed, would entail rejection. See Karl Popper, The Logic of Scientific Discovery (New York: Basic Books, 1959), p. 38.

The problem of demarcation criteria, which are standards for separating theory from data, is a complex one. The strength of the simple falsificationist position rests on its presupposition of an empirical base—a collection of "facts" that are capable of being separated from theoretical statements and hence are able to be used as independent evidence against general theories. How is this distinction between factual, or observational, statements and theoretical, or speculative, statements to be made? The simple falsificationist view is that there is a natural psychological borderline between the two kinds of statements. This assumption is highly questionable. Psychological investigations now indicate that perception involves not only sensory stimulation but also theoretical judgments that are necessary in framing perceptual images.[10] In addition, the histories of science and social science provide striking examples of the role of theory in defining what constitutes an observation. Galileo claimed, for example, that he was able to "observe" mountains on the moon with the aid of the telescope. Aristotelians claimed that the moon was a faultless body, made of a substance not found on earth. Did Galileo's observations bring the downfall of the Aristotelian view? Not in a simple sense. Galileo's sightings were observations only if one accepted the telescope, that is, a theory of optics. It was not Galileo's pure, untheoretical observations that confronted Aristotelian theory, but rather Galileo's "observations" in the light of his optical theory that confronted the Aristotelians' "observations" in the light of their theory of the heavens.[11] There was thus an observational, or instrumentational, theory without which the claim to have "observed" something was vacuous. Science today routinely uses data that count as "observations" only if certain instrumentation theories are accepted. Bubble chambers, through which particle tracks may be "observed"; electron microscopes, which permit "observation" of molecular structures; and radio telescopes, with the aid of which quasars can be "observed," are only a few conspicuous examples.

The social sciences provide similar cases, although they are not yet as unproblematic. Attempts to observe and measure attitudes provide a good example. A researcher can claim to have "observed" and measured an attitude only to the extent that the theory underlying his techniques is accepted. Those disagreeing with this "theory" can legitimately assert that nothing was being observed, but instead that artifacts were being created.[12] Psychotherapy has met an even greater resistance to its claims to be able to "observe" the operation of unconscious factors. Claims that projective tests allow one to "observe" personality traits are similarly suspect. In all these cases, "observations" cannot be admitted as observations without considering the instrumentation theory underlying them.

A second problem with the simple falsificationist view stems from the strong assumption that there is a logical asymmetry between proof and falsification: while proof cannot be logically certain, falsification can. A little more thought shows that dogmatically accepting a falsification leads to the same kinds of errors as looking for verification. Suppose that an investigator deduces a hypothesis that he contends is a "critical test" of a particular theory. A test of the hypothesis is conducted, and the result is compatible with falsifying the theory. If the test is repeated and the same result is obtained, can it be concluded that the theory is falsified? No, for the falsification is the falsification of a theoretical statement conjoined with a ceteris paribus clause. How can we be sure that the theoretical statement is wrong? Might it not be the case that there is a competing hypothesis—that some relevant ceteris paribus assumption has been ignored or violated and that if this were correctly handled, the "falsification" would be spurious? Lakatos maintains that this is the case.[13] However, here we are facing the logical twin of the verification problem. Again the ceteris paribus clause is infinite, and again, although we can eliminate plausible counter-objections, we cannot exhaustively explore the potential counter-objections. A finite number of tests will not falsify a theory either.

Certain qualifications of the simple falsificationist view yield the position Lakatos calls "naive methodological falsificationism." The most striking feature of this position is that it recognizes a number of the problems just raised and attempts to handle them by making explicit the need for scientific choice in uncertain situations. The naive methodological falsificationist recognizes that when a theory, together with a ceteris paribus clause, is tested and the conjunction is refuted, he must decide whether to take this refutation also as a refutation of the theory. A falsification of the conjunction is not an automatic falsification of the theory. According to this position, a theory may be considered rejected if the ceteris paribus clause has been tested "severely" enough to relegate it to the status of unproblematic background knowledge. This is a high-risk decision, however, for the implication of the falsificationist logic is that once a theory has been rejected, further work on it is irrational.[14] Inadequate exploration of the ceteris paribus clause, and the attendant rejection of the theory, may prematurely foreclose a whole tradition of research and exploration.

Where do we go from here? We could try to reduce the risk of bad decisions by additionally relying on nonlogical criteria for evaluating scientific theories. The aesthetic criteria of simplicity or parsimony, for example, could be used in choosing among competing theories. However, what is "simple" is not a priori obvious, and judgments about it may vary substantially over time. In physics, at one time, "simplicity" meant laws that could be expressed without using differential calculus; on these grounds it was argued that the corpuscular theory of light was "simpler" than the wave theory because the latter involved solving boundary problems of partial differential equations.[15] Alternatively, the acceptance of a theory can be based on "pragmatic" considerations of its usefulness or on some complex weighting of criteria like supporting evidence, simplicity, falsifiability, and usefulness. Carl Hempel advocates the use of multiple, weighted criteria as a promising way to proceed, although he admits that the feasibility of a rigorous and precise effort remains undecided.[16] From these views, the decision to accept one scientific theory over another is made not in terms of logical factors but in terms of informed extralogical judgments and possibly in terms of values, personal commitments, and professional consensus as well.

Thomas Kuhn suggests that the question of criteria for theory acceptance and evaluation should be considered in the context of a dual model of science. In "normal science" activity, which is primarily puzzle-solving, the scientist is not looking for criteria upon which he can "accept" the paradigm for his discipline, nor is he attempting to continuously challenge it. Working within the paradigm is simply whatever is meant by "doing" some particular science at a particular time.[17] If anomalies accumulate, then serious challenges to a paradigm may arise. In such cases of "revolutionary science," scientific practice may be characterized by choice criteria, critical experiments, and falsification attempts. The basis on which a new theory is accepted, however, may involve several factors, including judgments about which theory is better and the pressure of a building consensus or a radical change of perspective, which may resemble "conversion" more than a dispassionate assessment of potential. In its simplest form, Kuhn's theory replaces the falsificationist idea of science as perpetual challenging of theories with an intense period of revolutionary change. The emphasis that is put upon the psychology and sociology of discovery by Kuhn is relatively greater than his emphasis on the logic of discovery.[18] The certainty of scientific knowledge at some particular time is rooted in a working and workable consensus among practicing scientists.

For many reasons it is desirable to have a formulation of the philosophy of science that escapes, or at least minimizes, the problems of inference we discussed earlier, while avoiding such a heavy reliance on "psychology" or "consensus" that scientific knowledge becomes just another form of human belief. Lakatos contends that a position of "sophisticated methodological falsificationism" provides such a philosophy of science, and he offers the concept of a "research programme" as a logical and accurate way of characterizing the business of scientific practice. Before turning to his proposal, however, we need to assess the efforts of INS researchers to resolve these kinds of problems.

EFFORTS BY THE INTER-NATION SIMULATION PROJECT TO APPRAISE ITS THEORIZING

As a research effort, INS had the merit of being taken as a serious scientific enterprise by its researchers. Consequently systematic consideration was given to the epistemological problems associated with its particular style of inquiry. Such consideration, moreover, was focused precisely on the heart of the standards appraisal problem: What can be known from INS research? Within the INS community, the problems raised by this question were addressed in terms of validity.

During the course of their actual attempts to determine validity, the INS researchers proposed and explored several different philosophy of science stances, ranging from views associating scientific knowledge with "proven" knowledge, through varieties of the falsificationist approach, to Paul L. Smoker's more radical attempts to reformulate the concept of verification itself. In their practical attempts to explore the scientific worth of INS, they attempted to cope with many of the problems we discussed in the preceding section. We shall attempt to evaluate the success with which they did so and the importance of their efforts to determine the significance of INS research.

The philosophy of science under which INS was initially conceived had several features:

1. It associated scientific knowledge with valid, proven knowledge but accepted the fact that this proof could not be absolute or definitive.[19]
2. It accepted simplicity as a criterion for choosing one theory over another and as a goal to strive toward in creating theories, but it recognized that the criterion of simplicity was not a priori and itself reflected theoretical preferences.[20]
3. It admitted utility as a major criterion for judging theories, including utility for scientific theorizing, instruction, action and even normative social functions.[21]
4. It considered scientific theory to be a mixture of these criteria (utility, simplicity, and validation) that depended upon the situation existing at the time the theory was formed and the purposes for which it was to be used.[22]

There was little input from falsificationist philosophies of science to this approach, and little attention was paid to ways in which theories might be systematically attacked. INS did not even include a judgment that "scientific" theories ought to be capable, in principle, of falsifying attacks. The primary concern, instead, was with building up supporting evidence, managing complexity, and attempting to ascertain pragmatic utility. Thus the initial position was one of qualified support for the idea of scientific theory as proven theory. Within the perspective "that simulation is operating theory," Guetzkow contended that the central task was to ask, "To what extent are simulations of international processes being verified?"[23] Verification involved checking the simulation theory against an empirical base, including field and laboratory studies, international documents, and aggregate data collections.

There was, however, no supposition that these data are a theory-free empirical base. Guetzkow stated that:

> work is not done analytically with empirical materials without constructing at least implicit theories about the denotata—as events are selected from the entire population of such items and then a few reported events characterized. Sense impressions are "validated" by perceiving and then re-interpreting them in terms of individual theories of history.[24]

Such an empirical base does not meet the strict criteria that a strong verification approach would demand. Neither, Guetzkow contended, could verification expect an isomorphism between the theory and its empirical analyses; the realistic goal was a homomorphism at the level of both outputs and processes.* Nonetheless, the aim was to find a convergence of evidence to increase the credibility of the theory. "The lack of correspondences between the simulations and the empirical materials indicates the extent of nonverification," wrote Guetzkow.[25]

---

*The presumption that logical order matches natural order has been a key component in philosophies of science based on attempts to verify through deductive tests. R. Harre, in The Principles of Scientific Thinking (Chicago: University of Chicago, 1970), provides a good discussion of this attempt and its roots and problems, especially on pages 1-29. May Brodbeck provides a detailed description of the "isomorphic matching" approach to validity in her "Models, Meanings and Theories," in Symposium on Sociological Theory, edited by Llewllyn Gross (Evanston: Row Peterson, 1959), pp. 373-40

Other INS participants raised some of the problems we have already discussed in connection with this approach in the contexts of actual attempts to "verify" INS theory. John R. Raser, Donald T. Campbell, and Richard W. Chadwick, for example, drew upon Popper's simple falsification ideas and recognized an "asymmetry between logically valid rejection and logically conclusive falsifiability."[26] They argued that a positive finding could support a number of hypotheses and, as such, that validation had to include testing of alternative hypotheses. As this "winnowing" process continued and the contending hypotheses were eliminated, confidence in the theory would increase. Hence they saw simulation as a promising approach to inquiry, since it was a means of extending beyond historical experience the domain in which a theory could be falsified. The simulation provides a vehicle for testing the extent to which theories hold across different situations; but taking this view of simulation requires at least some confidence in it as an instrument that can produce results that can be generalized. They suggested that this confidence should be awarded according to "the principle of proximate similarity," the assumption that "the closer the setting of inquiry to the setting of application, the more confidently may inferences be made."[27] From this vantage point INS could, by virtue of its complexity, have considerable potential in helping to establish theories of international relations in which high confidence might be possible.

There is clearly some sense to this position: if we are trying to explain complex behavior, we may need an environment complex enough to elicit it, something a relatively controlled laboratory situation may not provide. This principle, however, does not resolve the problem of validity; the problem resurfaces, instead, as a question of confidence in the research instrument. This was a problem that Charles F. Hermann had addressed earlier. In discussing validation, he distinguished between criteria that could be used to increase confidence in propositions about international relations and those that would increase confidence in the simulation instrument itself. Validation, then, involves two questions, the first of which is, What confidence do we have in INS as a research instrument? An answer can be made by weighing three considerations: (1) internal validity, or whether the simulation's programmed relationships account for outcome variations; (2) face validity, which is an intuitive impression of the simulation's realism; and (3) variable-parameter validity, which is the adequacy of operational definitions.[28] The second question is, What confidence do we have in the research outputs of INS? An answer here involves two considerations: (1) event validity, or the degree to which simulation patterns correspond to observed historical patterns and (2) hypothesis validity, or the degree to which theoretically specified relationships correspond to

observed historical relationships.[29] Judging validity is an attempt
to get multiple measures based on these different aspects of validity.
For Hermann, confidence in the simulation increases as the results
of these multiple measures of validity show close correspondence
with empirical observations from several different positions.

Still, however, the basic problems of deriving appraisal standards
from verificationist and simple falsificationist approaches remain.
Paul L. Smoker first made that fact clear within that epistemological
context by noting that the criterion of congruing convergencies was
misconceived.[30] Why should validation be a linear function of the
number of "high" correspondences between the simulation theory
and the external environment? Smoker suggested that a complex
simulation will also be a focused one, with some parts rather finely
modeled, while other areas, of less immediate theoretical interest,
will be more coarsely modeled. How would one evaluate such a
design? Smoker argued as follows:

> A valid simulation in this case would be expected to exhibit high correspondence in some areas and low correspondence in others. Criteria of validity might well shift from demanding correspondence between a simulation and reality to defining patterns of correspondence and non-correspondence in terms of the model construction process itself. . . . The distribution of these correspondences constitutes the correspondence pattern. This correspondence pattern perspective differs from the multiple validity criteria notion where validity increases as the number of correspondences increases. . . . Validity and correspondence are no longer conceptually linked in a simple additive way such that the greater the number of correspondences the greater the validity. Nor does high correspondence necessarily imply high validity. Validity is the degree to which the predicted and actual correspondence patterns coincide.[31]

The immediate thrust of this position is to make the process of
checking correspondences "critical" to the theory one is attempting
to evaluate. It is, in many cases, too easy to "discredit" a theory
by testing it strongly in areas where it applies only weakly.

The deeper implications of this correspondence-pattern perspective are even more significant. What is it that is being validated
in this way? Asking this question leads us away from the appraisal
standards that were the roots of "mainstream" INS research and
toward an alternative philosophy of science.

Smoker developed these deeper implications within the INS context by advancing the concept of complementary validity, which has generally been ignored or misperceived by conventional INS studies. It is generally assumed that validity will be defined as a function of the predicted and actual correspondences between a theory and the "real world." The direction of the comparison is clear, as Smoker contends in the following lines:

> The "real world" is regarded as given, and the "model world" is regarded as an attempt to demonstrate or show or reveal aspects of reality. If there is a lack of validity, the model world is altered in an attempt to increase the validity of the simulation. <u>It is possible to take the complementary position and to evaluate the "real world" relative to the "model world" incorporated in the simulation.</u> With this perspective, the model world becomes an attempt to demonstrate or show or reveal the way parts of reality could, or should be (emphasis added). [32]

Within the philosophy of science operating in INS, this seems like a counter-intuitive idea; yet a moment's thought should indicate that Smoker's point may well be a crucial one. At the simplest level, once we accept the uncomfortable fact that the empirical base of a theory is not an atheoretical collection of observations but a collection of "observations" within a largely unarticulated collection of unproblematic background knowledge, it cannot be assumed that differences between theory and "data" should automatically discredit the theory. The history of science contains dramatic instances of the opposite process. Lakatos provides two excellent examples. First, he relates Sir Isaac Newton's relationship with Flamsteed as follows:

> Newton constantly criticized and corrected Flamsteed's observational theories. Newton taught Flamsteed, for instance, a better theory of the refractive power of the atmosphere; Flamsteed accepted this and corrected his original "data." One can understand the constant humiliation and slowly increasing fury of this great observer, having his data criticized and improved by a man who, on his own confession, made no observations himself.[33]

Lakatos' second example is that of Prout, who advanced the theory that the atomic weights of all pure chemical elements were whole numbers. This was in direct contradiction to the contemporary "observational evidence," but Prout contended that the means of observing was faulty and went on to revolutionize analytical chemistry, revising a large number of the experimental techniques through which the apparently disconfirmatory "data" had been produced.[34]

Smoker's research using IPS provides an intriguing substantive case that illustrates this point, one in which the deeper philosophy of science implications can be seen quite readily. In a series of IPS runs, he found evidence that the conflict style for nations apparently differed in different systemic structures.[35] This research finding could have been taken as a possibility to be explored in itself, but only if a philosophy of science different from the prevailing verificationist-simple falsificationist ideas were adopted. In terms of the dominant INS philosophy of science, was Smoker's finding a "finding" or a mistake? As a finding, it constituted a challenge to one of the presuppositions upon which a judgment of the internal validity of IPS was based. The finding

> would challenge the assumption that the conflict style for a particular nation should be invariant across simulation runs. It could be argued that only if a corresponding evolution of system state occurred in each simulation might we expect similarities of conflict style, since conflict styles might be manifestations of system states. This hypothesis would argue against the concept of internal validity in the present context on the grounds that the probabilistic causal processes at work within the simulation would be expected to produce a range of possible states from an initial starting position.[36]

What then would it mean, to argue that INS had to demonstrate "internal validity" before it could establish any "external validity?"[37] This case provides an excellent example of the operation of a ceteris paribus clause. In this case the simple across-runs constancy criterion for internal validity carries with it the tacit assumption that the system state remains significantly unchanged, or alternatively, the hypothesis that conflict style is unrelated to it. Before one decides that variation is a mark of low internal validity, this alternative hypothesis must be explored. If it is not, one might arrive at Coplin's peculiar contention that "instead of viewing a man-computer simulation such as the Inter-Nation Simulation or the World Politics Simulation as a theory of political phenomena, it would be more appropriate to say that any given run of a man-computer simulation model represents a theory of political phenomena."[38]

Here we have perhaps the logical outcome of a philosophy of science position that does serious damage to the type of "theory" that can develop. By Coplin's logic, any theory of politics that is based upon the premise of political life as an open system with a few fixed rules and flexible strategies, capable of arriving at multiple end points from a given initial position, would not be a theory of politics; each end-state might be so considered, along with the transitions that led to it, but the general contingent pattern would fail the test of internal validity under the going ceteris paribus conditions. Such judgments seem to be the danger Lakatos warns of when ceteris paribus assumptions are relegated too easily to the status of unproblematic background conditions, entailing an unwarranted rejection of a theoretical position. A far better conclusion would be that not enough is known about the branching processes that lead to different final states and that hence it is difficult to determine when implicit ceteris paribus assumptions are being misapplied.

Smoker found, however, that it was quite difficult to test the hypothesis that conflict styles vary over systemic states, with less dramatic conflict being found in more international systems, by using external referent data. He attempted to pick two groups of nations, those that showed high nation-state orientations in their behavior and those with highly international orientations, and to examine their behavior in different time periods. Comparisons with IPS runs for the two systemic states indicated some convergences compatible with a systemic transition, but the problem remained that the international system then was not, and perhaps never had been, international enough to provide a good test. Smoker concluded that a new methodological approach was necessary to try and separate significant nation-state and international differences to provide an appropriate test of the hypothesis.

There is a further complication in learning from INS-IPS theorizing. Many of the correspondence checks were conducted with aggregated run results.[39] This suggests a dual problem. If fluctuation across runs in INS-IPS indicates that internal validity is actually lacking, the external validity attempts may need to be reassessed; but it is not true that a lack of internal validity automatically means that external correspondences will be poor. Suppose the internal fluctuations happen, by luck, to match some unconsidered changes in the external environment. If, however, it is the case that a number of variables are state dependent, then the theoretical explanations based upon them, and the assumption of state-independence, will be in error, although again the error may not be quick to show itself. Either way, we see here specific manifestations of the general problems we identified in earlier philosophies of science.

Resolving such problems involves a shift to an alternative philosophy of science. If somewhat revised and extended, Smoker's complementary validity concept comes close to capturing one of the key criteria for scientific practice advanced by the philosophy of science position that we argue from in this paper. This position has been labeled a "sophisticated methodological falsificationist" position. It supplies, we argue, an understanding of science that enables us to avoid having to choose between either an uncritical acceptance of problematic standards or a premature rejection of the possibility of standards.

SOPHISTICATED METHODOLOGICAL FALSIFICATIONISM AND THE RESEARCH PROGRAM METHODOLOGY

Sophisticated methodological falsificationism contends that the focus of earlier philosophies of science is wrong. Those philosophies tried to determine whether or not a theory was scientific, and their efforts all involved "two-cornered fights"—theory versus evidence. However, Lakatos suggests that we should not focus on a single theory to see if it is "scientific," "true," or "false," but that instead we must examine a collection of theories to see the relationship among them in the light of new empirical evidence.[40] Decisions about what is scientific can be made only by considering the relationships among theories as well as the link between theory and evidence. In other words, the context in which particular theorizing efforts take place must be explicitly considered when assessing them.

How can one make this judgment? Lakatos suggests that we determine whether a collection of theories is theoretically progressive and empirically progressive.[41] Both of these concepts are best explained by referring to an illustrative situation. Consider a series of theories T_1, T_2, T_3 . . . in which each subsequent theory is built upon its predecessors by either adding auxiliary clauses or providing a semantic reinterpretation in order to accommodate some anomaly. Each theory is capable of explaining at least as much content as the one before it. This series of theories is theoretically progressive if each theory has excess empirical content than the earlier theories; that is, if it predicts some new fact that was unanticipated or even impossible in earlier theories. The series of theories is empirically progressive if at least some of this excess content is also corroborated. The series is a progressive problem shift if it is both theoretically and empirically progressive; otherwise it is a degenerating problem shift. That characterization then enables us to make the desired judgments as follows:

> We 'accept' problem shifts as 'scientific' only if they are at least theoretically progressive; if they are not we 'reject' them as 'pseudo-scientific'. Progress is measured by the degree to which a problem shift is progressive, by the degree to which it leads us to the discovery of novel facts. We regard a theory in the series as 'falsified' when it is superseded by a theory with higher corroborated content.[42]

Under this approach we still have empirical criteria, but they are different. The time-honored empirical criterion was that a theory must agree with observed facts. Now we have an empirical criterion for a series of theories, and we demand that they produce new facts. The idea of growth and the concept of empirical character are united into one.[43]

There are several important features of this position. First, the process of theorizing is now seen as "many-cornered fight," involving at least a confrontation of a theory, an observational or instrumentation theory, and evidence; often multiple competing theories are also directly involved. This is an important change. Sophisticated methodological falsificationism makes no attempt to isolate a theory and then try to validate it. Validation is part of the process of theorizing. It is empirical, but not infallible. As such, rejections are not made out of hand, but instead in relation to a better alternative. Hence this approach avoids the high opportunity costs that naive methodological falsification would have us incur. A theory is "falsified" by another theory capable of producing and corroborating new evidence, not by a process of rule application alone.

> While naive falsificationism stresses "the urgency of replacing a _falsified_ hypothesis by a better one, a sophisticated falsificationism stresses the urgency of replacing _any_ hypothesis by a better one. Falsification cannot compel the theorist to search for a better theory," simply because falsification cannot precede the better theory.[44]

A second feature of theorizing as seen from a sophisticated methodological falsificationist perspective is that it is a cybernetic process. Past theoretical experience, both positive (confirmatory) and negative (disconfirmatory), is an essential component of the process of making theoretical judgments. Past theories are not merely historical; they are not just "outputs" of some scientific method. They are part of the current attempt to learn more. The scientist does not "search" a historical data bank for rules of operation so much as he evaluates the data in light of, and on the basis of, feedback on how what is being attempted measures up to what has been achieved and what is desired.

Lakatos contends that science is characterized by a continuity that develops in the context of a research program, which is a locus of specific methodological principles. Some of the methodological rules specify paths of research to avoid (negative heuristic), while others suggest the paths to pursue (positive heuristic).[45] The positive heuristic frequently takes the form of a long-term research strategy, which attempts to handle both known anomalies and expected objections to the theoretical approach. Much of the effort is directed toward providing some confirmation for predicted "new facts," as well as toward filling in and elaborating inadequacies that researchers may be aware of—especially those arising from overly strong simplifying assumptions. The positive heuristic gives an "ordering" to the way in which yet-unexplained anomalies are handled (or, in Kuhn's terms, the way "puzzles" are solved) and often anticipates, and suggests ways to cope with, refutations. Lakatos presents substantial evidence to support his view that such activities, and not falsification attempts, dominate scientific practice.[46]

We do not conceive of INS as a full-blown research program, nor will we claim that the history of INS can be evaluated definitely as a progressive problem shift; but many features of INS, both output and developmental processes, can be usefully reexamined in light of the Lakatos criteria. We suggest that the prevailing INS standards of validation have obscured some important features of the INS effort, features that can make INS and its associated spin-offs more useful for theorizing.

THE INTER-NATION SIMULATION PROJECT REEXAMINED

This new philosophy of science reinforces Smoker's notion of complementary validity. One way of looking at his idea that the "model world" be regarded as an attempt to demonstrate something about the "real world" is to regard it, in Lakatos' terms, as a plea to look for excess empirical content within the context of our data base and the milieu of existing theories; however, the validation orientation that has infused INS theorizing makes it difficult to look for what Lakatos would identify as the most critical theoretical features, which are predicted "new facts." If validation were close correspondence with a relatively taken-as-given empirical base, potential excess empirical content would be treated as poor fit, and hence those features that might teach us most would be noticed least. Even without a systematic search of the substantive findings of INS and its associated offspring, however, at least three potential cases of specific excess theoretical content seem apparent.

The first comes from Crow's INS-based theory of deterrence. One aim of the simulation was to see what impact an invulnerable nuclear retaliatory force would have on deterrence relationships among nations. A reading of the literature on deterrence suggested that the nation with an invulnerable force would be seen as stronger, both by itself and by potential opponents. Analysis of simulation results indicated that this was the case, but provided a novel interpretation of this fact. It was found that "when the oppressor nation achieved invulnerability, it saw itself as much stronger; when it lost it again, as only a little weakened. But its opponent nation saw the possessor of invulnerability as only a little stronger when it gained invulnerability, but much weaker when it lost it."[47] This finding predicts the novel fact of systematic perceptual distortion in a seesaw arms race. Recent developments in the superpower strategic dialogue appear to be confirming this predicted new fact.

A second candidate for excess empirical content is drawn from Coplin's World Politics Simulation. It may be an important, unanticipated negative finding. He observed the following:

> In numerous runs of the World Political Simulation, the United States team has proved to be extremely isolationist by refusing to enter into trade and aid agreements. An analysis of the programmed structure of the simulation as it relates to the United States team reveals that many factors such as agricultural surplus and overseas investment which are part of the domestic political and economic environment in contemporary America are not contained in the simulation structure and may be more important than one would otherwise think.[48]

Since 1970, events have at least reduced the American agricultural surplus, questioned the status of continuing to expand foreign investment in key sectors such as oil, and threatened an intensification of such problems. There would appear to be grounds for considering this predicted "new fact" worth attempting to corroborate.[49]

The final example is drawn from the IPS, which may well constitute a progressive problem shift in relation to INS.[50] This is

Smoker's finding, which we have already discussed, that the conflict style for nations apparently differs in different systemic structures. As novel fact, it suggested some reformulations of the concept of a conflict style, and in Lakatos' framework it would also invite attempts at corroboration. The problems it posed in terms of the dominant INS philosophy of science have already been described.

In its overall development, INS has had some features that are associated with Lakatos' notion of a research program. Early in its history it developed a negative heuristic, which Guetzkow details in his account of early "avoidances." Similarly, the writings on INS and its related programs indicate the presence of a positive heuristic, which has become better developed as a commitment to moving toward more inclusive, all-machine simulations. Most of the changes made in the INS and the associated research endeavor appear to have been internally stimulated, not because the researchers were insensitive to outside criticism but because they anticipated much of the criticism in their research planning. It was the philosophy of science they worked under, rather than the processes they went through, that allowed them to judge this aspect of their research to be "pre-scientific."[51] This judgment, and not the research process, is in error from Lakatos' perspective.

CONCLUSIONS

Our aim in this final section is to present some reflections on the process of theorizing. Theorizing is a cybernetic process. It is capable not only of self-steering, a corrective use of feedback, but also of directed creative learning, an anticipatory use of feedback. Lakatos' sophisticated methodological falsificationism is the only philosophy of science, to date, that draws the full consequences of this recognition. This is not to say that it introduces a package of new ideas. We have discussed the way in which several INS investigators, working under different views of science, formulated important insights that contributed to a view of science as at least a self-correcting cybernetic process. Smoker's work was an attempt to move toward a richer conception. His insights into the way in which simulation can become an element in reality creation, and his insistence that validation itself become an endogenous part of the theorizing process, recognize vital problems that were difficult to conceptualize under more algorithmic views of science. Sophisticated methodological falsificationism not only incorporates these insights, but makes them fundamental to the process of science, locating in them the criteria for theory falsification. This reorients

PHILOSOPHY OF SCIENCE   279

our view of the "problems" facing scientific practice and the philosophy of science.

> When we decide whether it is the replacement of the "interpretative" or of the "explanatory" theory that produces novel facts, we again must make a decision about the acceptance or rejection of basic statements. But then we have only <u>postponed</u>—and possibly <u>improved</u>—the decision, not avoided it. The difficulties concerning the empirical basis which confronted "naive" falsificationism cannot be avoided by "sophisticated" falsificationism either. Even if we regard a theory as "factual," that is, if our slow-moving and limited imagination cannot offer an alternative (as Feyerabend used to put it), we have to make, at least occasionally, and temporarily, decisions about its truth value. <u>Even then, experience still remains, in an important sense the "impartial arbiter" of scientific controversy</u>. We cannot get rid of the problem of the "empirical basis," if we want to learn from experience, but we can make our learning less dogmatic.52

This philosophy of science, then, has the merit of bringing into accord important insights on the nature of the theorizing process and standards for theoretical progress. In a practical way, since this concordance was made in cybernetic terms, it raises for us the very real possibility of being able to enhance our theorizing abilities progressively: not merely through the accumulation of knowledge and the coalescence of modules of theory, but through the progressively enhanced ability to generate knowledge, modules, and coalescences. That is, with appropriate feedback mechanisms we can learn better how to learn better. Through the exploratory use of feedback data, we can expect to anticipate the kind of research programs that promise progressive problem shifts and delineate areas in which further research is required. While it may be true that we can never ultimately improve upon a "variation and selective retention" process of knowing, it may be possible to reach a point at which the search is "blind" only in a solipsistic sense.

Sophisticated methodological falsificationism does not provide an instant solution to the earlier problems, but instead it suggests that there are ways of looking at these problems that increase our ability to learn from our admittedly problematic experience. One need not avoid the words "true" and "false" when speaking of theorizing, but they need to be used within the context of a theorizing process that allows learning rather than anxiety to arise from the knowledge that these terms are, necessarily, provisional assessments. There is simply no point at which a final, definitive judgment can be made. "By regarding some observational theories as problematic we may make our methodology more flexible; but we cannot articulate and include all 'background knowledge' (or background ignorance?) in our critical deductive model. This process is bound to be piecemeal and some conventional line must be drawn at any given time."[53]

In drawing this conventional line, two errors are possible. First, we may unwittingly lock ourselves into a set of conventional distinctions, thereby increasing the possibility of theoretical closure. Second, we may be too casual about conventional distinctions, assuming that because they are to some degree arbitrary, they are unimportant. This risks an idiosyncratic and discontinuous process of investigation. Both of these errors become less likely when the research enterprise profits from a view of its progress that systematically incorporates a commitment to flexible search criteria and the exploratory use of feedback.[54]

With these considerations in mind, we have attempted to evaluate the philosophy of science in INS, not as a justification for making certain definitive statements about how good INS theory is in principle, but in terms of what it suggests about the process of social science theorizing. We have suggested that the practice of INS has been richer than the philosophy of science associated with it. We have suggested another view, Lakatos' sophisticated methodological falsificationism, that moves toward narrowing this disparity. In shifting our perspective toward Lakatos' position, we do not "solve" the problems of verification, falsification, or research design that INS had identified; rather, we suggest that such a shift in perspective makes the researcher more capable of learning in this problem-fraught environment. Moving toward a philosophy of science that guides as well as judges output seems worthwhile.

NOTES

1. Imre Lakatos, "Falsification and the Methodology of Scientific Research Programmes," in Criticism and the Growth of Knowledge edited by Imre Lakatos and Alan Musgrave (Cambridge: Cambridge University Press, 1970), p. 92.

2. Louis Regis, Epistemology (New York: Macmillan, 1959), pp. 32-61, organizes the knowledge theories of Descartes, the British empiricists, and Kant on this basis.

3. This is essentially the definition presented in Donald T. Campbell and Julian C. Stanley, Experimental and Quasi-Experiment Designs for Research (Chicago: Rand McNally and Co., 1966).

4. For a detailed development of this point, see W. V. Quine, Ontological Relativity and Other Essays (New York: Columbia University Press, 1969), pp. 30-45, and W. V. Quine, World and Object (Cambridge, Mass.: MIT Press, 1960), 51-57.

5. Rudolph Carnap, Logical Foundations of Probability (Chicago: University of Chicago Press, 1950).

6. Karl Popper, The Logic of Scientific Discovery (New York: Basic Books, 1959), pp. 387-419. For a detailed discussion of Popper's approach, see Imre Lakatos, "Changes in the Problem of Inductive Logic," in The Problem of Inductive Logic, edited by Imre Lakatos (Amsterdam: North Holland, 1968), pp. 315-417.

7. Lakatos, "Falsification," op. cit., p. 95.

8. Bertrand Russell held such a position; see Bertrand Russell, "Reply to Critics," in The Philosophy of Bertrand Russell, edited by Paul A. Schilpp (La Salle, Ill.: Open Court, 1974), pp. 681-741.

9. Quoted in Lakatos, "Falsification," op. cit., p. 97.

10. Charles M. Solley and Gardner Murphy, Development of the Perceptual World (New York: Basic Books, 1960). For the same point demonstrated from a different perspective, see Maurice Merleau-Ponty, Phenomenology of Perception (New York: Humanities Press, 1962).

11. Lakatos, "Falsification," op. cit., p. 98.

12. For a recognition of this, and an excellent discussion of the different theoretical positions underlying attitude observation and measurement techniques, see William Scott, "Attitude Measurement," in The Handbook of Social Psychology, edited by Gardner Lindzey and Elliot Arson, Vol. 2 (2nd ed., Reading, Mass.: Addison-Wesley, 1968), pp. 204-356.

13. Lakatos, "Falsification," op. cit., pp. 101-03.

14. Ibid.

15. Phillip G. Frank, "The Variety of Reasons for the Acceptance of Scientific Theories," in The Validation of Scientific Theories, edited by Phillip G. Frank (New York: Collier, 1954), p. 64. For attempts to spell out the problems more rigorously and suggest some criteria for simplicity, see Popper, Logic, op. cit., pp. 93-111; Nelson Goodman, "The Logical Simplicity of Predicates," The Journal of Symbolic Logic 14, no. 1 (1949): 32-41; and Nelson Goodman, "An Improvement in the Theory of Simplicity," The Journal of Symbolic Logic 14, no. 4 (1950): 218-29.

16. Carl Hempel, Aspects of Scientific Explanation and Other Essays in the Philosophy of Science (New York: Free Press, 1965), pp. 113-18.

17. Thomas Kuhn, The Structure of Scientific Revolutions (Chicago: University of Chicago Press, 1962). For a discussion of paradigm and scientific consensus, see Tracy Strong, "The

Activity of Political Science as Science," paper presented at American Political Science Association annual meeting, New Orleans, 1973.

18. This is a relatively accurate, although oversimplified, view of Kuhn's position. There is a strong convergence between Lakatos' position and that of the later Kuhn, as represented in Thomas Kuhn, "Reflections on my Critics," in Criticism and the Growth of Knowledge, edited by Imre Lakatos and Alan Musgrave (Cambridge: Cambridge University Press, 1970), pp. 231-78.

19. Harold Guetzkow, "A Decade of Life with the Inter-Nation Simulation," in The Process of Model-Building in the Behavioral Sciences, edited by Ralph M. Stogdill (New York: W. W. Norton, 1970), pp. 31-53. Guetzkow cites Frank, Validation, op. cit., pp. 13-31, as representative of his views; these pages are used to explicate the initial INS philosophy of science.

20. Ibid., p. 14.
21. Ibid., pp. 22-23.
22. Ibid., pp. 24-26.
23. Ibid., p. 26.
24. Harold Guetzkow, "Some Correspondences between Simulations and 'Realities' in International Relations," in New Approaches to International Relations, edited by Morton A. Kaplan (New York: St. Martin's Press, 1968), p. 208.

25. Ibid., p. 208.
26. John R. Raser, Donald T. Campbell, and Richard W. Chadwick, "Gaming and Simulation for Developing Theory Relevant to International Relations," General Systems 15 (1970): 184.

27. Raser, Campbell, and Chadwick, "Gaming," op. cit., p. 197.

28. Charles F. Hermann, "Validation Problems in Games and Simulations with Special Reference to Models of International Relations," Behavioral Science 12, no. 3 (1967): 221-22.

29. Ibid., p. 222.
30. Paul L. Smoker, "Simulation for Social Anticipation and Creation" (Evanston: Northwestern University, 1969).
31. Ibid., pp. 4-5.
32. Ibid., p. 19.
33. Lakatos, "Falsification," op. cit., p. 131, note 5.
34. Ibid., pp. 138-39.
35. Paul L. Smoker, "Analyses of Conflict Behavior in an International Process Simulation and an International System 1955-1960," Simulated International Processes Project (Evanston: Northwestern University, 1968), p. 73.

36. Ibid., p. 89.

37. Hermann appears to argue this position. See Hermann, "Validation," op. cit., p. 229.
38. William D. Coplin, "Approaches to the Social Sciences through Man-Computer Simulations," <u>Simulation and Games</u> 1, no. 4 (1970): 391-410.
39. Guetzkow, "Some Correspondences," op. cit.
40. Lakatos, "Falsification," op. cit., p. 118.
41. Ibid., pp. 116-18.
42. Ibid., pp. 118-22.
43. Ibid., p. 119.
44. Ibid., p. 122. The quotes within the quote are attributed to Popper by Lakatos.
45. The description of a research program is developed from Popper by Lakatos. Ibid., pp. 132-38.
46. Ibid., pp. 138-72.
47. Reported in Raser, Campbell, and Chadwick, "Gaming," op. cit., p. 196. The full study is described in John R. Raser and William J. Crow, <u>WINSAFE II: An Inter-National Simulation Study of Deterrence Postures Embodying the Capacity to Delay Response</u> (La Jolla, Calif.: Western Behavioral Science Institute, 1964).
48. Coplin, "Approaches," op. cit., p. 402.
49. For a discussion of the prospects for changing food reserves and international policies, see Lester Brown, "The Next Crisis? Food," <u>Foreign Policy</u>, no. 13, (1973-74), pp. 3-33. For an argument that shortages may undermine the position of international actors in favor of nation-states, see Geoffrey D. C. Best, "Middle East Oil and the U.S. Energy Crisis: Prospects for New Ventures in a Changed Market," <u>Law and Policy in International Business</u> 5, no. 1 (1973): 215-72.
50. Paul Smoker, "International Process Simulation: A Description," in <u>Experimentation and Simulation in Political Science</u>, edited by J. A. Laponce and Paul L. Smoker (Toronto: University of Toronto Press, 1972), pp. 313-65, provides a detailed comparison of the structure of IPS and INS.
51. Guetzkow, "Decade," op. cit., provides the reports of validation upon which this judgment is made.
52. Lakatos, "Falsification," op. cit., p. 131.
53. Ibid.
54. Measures for such capabilities remain to be formulated precisely, but progress is being made. Hayward R. Alker reviews some of the important achievements and suggests a strategy to develop such measures for political systems in his "Cybernetic Measures of Political Capabilities," proposal to the National Science Foundation (Cambridge, Mass.: Massachusetts Institute of Technology, 1973).

CHAPTER

14

**THE INTER-NATION
SIMULATION PROJECT:
A METHODOLOGICAL
APPRAISAL**
Stuart J. Thorson

PURPOSES AND STANDARDS

The purpose of this paper is to evaluate the methodological practices employed in the Inter-Nation Simulation Project (INS). Since INS has been described in a previous chapter, some understanding of the workings of INS will be assumed. Clearly, however, the large number of technical papers generated by INS and related research[1] prevents most everyone from being completely familiar with all aspects of INS; therefore it is especially important to draw the boundaries of any evaluation very carefully. That is, it is necessary to make clear what standards will be invoked to evaluate what aspects of INS. Such a clarification will be the task of this section.

In order to explicate standards and to then carry on an evaluation, it will be helpful to specify how certain terms will be used in this paper. The terms to be discussed, such as simulation, methodology, model, and theory, are terms that are central to this paper and that are often used in ambiguous fashion. If the evaluations to be described are to be properly understood, a large amount of the ambiguity surrounding these terms must be eliminated. The definitional discussion will lead to a brief examination of some of the

---

Support for this work was provided in part by Advanced Research Projects Agency Contract CAHC 15 73 C 0197, RF 3527-A1. Charles Hermann, Steve Holloway, Thomas Milburn, Warren Phillips, Donald Sylvan, and Dina A. Zinnes provided helpful comments on an earlier draft.

possible purposes of the INS project and the evaluation standards appropriate to these purposes. The second section will then contain the actual evaluation.

Terminology

Since in large part this paper involves "methodology," it will be useful to specify how the term will be used. Many behavioral scientists appear to employ the two terms "methodology" and "technique" as synonyms. However, it is often helpful to distinguish the two by restricting methodology to questions of justification. "The method of a science is, indeed, the rationale on which it bases its acceptance or rejection of hypothesis or theories."[2] Techniques, on the other hand, are ways of generating information that is used in evaluating a hypothesis or theory. Thus methodological positions will influence choice of technique. For example, a Hempelian scientist would probably argue that, for methodological reasons, the technique of crystal ball gazing is an inappropriate technique for the scientist. Techniques, then, are ways of generating evidence, and methodology provides the rules according to which the evidence is admitted and, if admitted, evaluated.

This distinction between methodology and technique is important for several reasons. First, from this perspective any critique of techniques requires a prior specification of the methodological perspective from which the critique is directed. Using the illustration from the previous paragraph, while crystal ball gazing is an inappropriate technique from the methodological perspective of conventional science, there may well exist other methodologies in which such a technique would be appropriate. Thus the appropriateness of a technique is generally relative, and any appraisal of techniques must include an appraisal of methodological choices. Second, as INS research illustrates, different methodological choices may be made depending upon the purpose(s) of the investigation. For example, only a portion of the objectives of the INS project are scientific in any conventional sense. As a result, it would be inappropriate to develop this critique only from the methodological perspective of science.

The next terms to be considered are "simulation," "model," and "theory." Whatever else it may be viewed as having done, INS has certainly involved the use of simulation in the investigation of international relations phenomena. Harold Guetzkow has defined a simulation as "an operating representation in reduced and/or simplified form of relations among social units by means of symbolic and/or replicate component parts."[3] The use of the adjective "social" restricts the class of simulations, and the definition can be made more general by simply removing "social." This definition suggests that there are three elements that need be specified in talking about a simulation. First, there is the system to be simulated, symbolized in this paper by s. Second, there is the representation of that system, symbolized by m. Third, there are the statements according to which the representation is described and/or "operates," symbolized by t. These statements might be in any language, be it Fortran, PL1, English, or Chinese. Any specific simulation can then be identified with an ordered triple, <s, m. t>, which identifies which referent reality (s) is being represented (m) in terms of what "operating rules" (t). If a simulation is to be completely described, all three of these must be identified. Further, changing any one of the three elements yields a new simulation. Therefore, in predicating statements to INS, care must be exercised to specify each of the three components. All too often the literature seems to equate INS only with a set of "rules," (t). As will be argued below, this has the implication of ignoring the impact that changes in s might have upon the resolution of methodological and technical questions.

However, before making these arguments, it is first necessary to explicate more completely what is included in the elements of s and m. The elements of s, the referent system to be simulated, are difficult to visualize in any concrete way, since if they were visualized they would become represented. The elements of s are the "realities" discussed by Guetzkow[4] or equivalently, the "reference systems" discussed by Charles Hermann.[5] In the case of INS, s presumably consists (loosely) of "the relations between nations." It is generally hoped that the chosen representation (m) in some way "corresponds" to the chosen s. There is no reason to require that these realities be in any sense completely known; indeed, it is precisely because they are complex, and partially or largely unknown, that they are represented as a part of a simulation effort.[6] An adequate representation consists of specification of the objects making up the representation and of the relations that are defined on these objects; that is, a representation consists of a well-specified world. This notion of representation is similar to that implicit in Guetzkow's statement that "Simulations in international relations attempt to represent the ongoing international system or components thereof, such as world alliances, international organizations, regional trade processes, etc.,"[7] and Hermann's that "a simulation or game is a partial representation of some independent system."[8]

A representation can be written as a mathematical structure (a collection of objects and relations), and one can ask questions about possible relations or correspondences between the representation and the referent reality. That is, how much like the referent reality is the representation? More precisely, is there a homomorphism between s and m? an isomorphism? or, more generally, what sorts of morphisms ("generalized mappings") might one be willing to assert as obtaining between s and m? Loosely speaking, these might be termed questions of external validity. Answers to these questions entail an examination of the possible purposes of INS and will be considered later in this essay.

Simply representing a referent reality (that is, picking an m) is not enough to yield a simulation. The representation will itself often be too complex to study directly. Therefore there will be interest in observing the behaviors produced (generated) by the representation. This objective requires developing a theory of the representation. This theory will take the form of statements "about" the representation. In the case of a simulation, the theory may be viewed as a set of "operating rules." The language in which these operating rules or statements are written will depend in part upon the mechanism chosen for use in the simulation. In an all-machine simulation, the statements might all be in Fortran, Dynamo, or Simscript, for example. In a simulation effort such as INS, which combines human subjects and a computer, the operating rules may be partly in Fortran and partly in some natural language.

The relationships between the operating rules (t) and the representation (m) are quite important. In the actual development of a simulation, m may never be made explicit. This seems to be the case in INS. Instead, m is implied* by the operating rules of t. In the case of INS, the objects of m would include such things as central decision makers, basic capabilities, and force capabilities, and the relations in m might include bureaucratic loss, and consumption satisfaction. More specifically, m is the collection of all the objects and relations that the INS operating rules are about. The "validation" of a simulation generally involves looking at correspondences between the behavior of the representation and the behavior of the referent reality. Yet, as Hermann suggests, what is actually of interest is the relation between the representation (m) and the referent reality (s).[9] This distinction between m and the behavior of m is especially significant in evaluating the "validity" of representations with "stochastic" relations. This point will be developed in greater detail in the section on evaluations. Here, however, the concern is with explicating relations between structures (m and s) and sets of sentences (t); or more generally, with the relations between sentences and the objects and relations "referred

---

*"Implied" is not being used in its strict logical sense.

to" by those sentences. Such relations may be termed semantic.[10] An example of such a semantic relation is truth. Are the sentences true of the representation? Are they true of the referent reality?

Whether or not particular sentences, or sets of sentences, are accepted as true is a question of methodology. What it means to assert them to be true is a (nontrivial) question of semantics. The particular set of sentences (t) making up the simulation is equivalent to a theory of the representation (m). The sense in which "theory" is being used here will be developed in the next few paragraphs. The purpose of the ensuing discussion is to argue that simulations belong to the subset of theories with explicit models. This result has important implications for evaluations of INS as a theoretical work.

Theories may be viewed as sets of sentences that are asserted to be true of some world. Further, these sets of sentences will generally (always, if an artificial programming language is used) have some preassigned logical framework or "rules of inference," such as first order predicate calculus or probability theory. These "rules" allow the investigation of the implications of subsets of theory statements.

When "theory" is employed in this sense, it is possible to rigorously define the related term "model" and to distinguish it from "theory." Theories are generally developed to order or account for some aspects of a referent system. For example, one of the purposes of INS was to develop a better accounting of processes underlying international relations. The question is, given a theory, or set of sentences asserted to be true, of what are the sentences true? Are they true of the "referent reality(s)?" Perhaps. However, more reasonably the theory may be asserted to be true of the representation (m) of that referent; that is, a set of sentences is true relative to some collection of objects and relations.[11] The sentences comprising Euclidean plane geometry, for example, are true of lines and figures drawn on flat sheets of paper but are not true of lines and figures drawn on a sphere (for instance, the sum of the angles in a triangle on a sphere can be greater than $180°$). That "thing," or collection of objects and relations, of which the theory is true is called a model for the theory. This notion of model can be defined more precisely,[12] but there will be no need for more precision about it in this essay.

Even the above discussion may appear to be needlessly abstract. However, the abstraction is helpful in several ways. First, it makes explicit a relationship between the simulation enterprise and the theory enterprise. To be specific, under these definitions, simulations become a subset of theory. This means, as is suggested by Guetzkow, that the kinds of critical methodological tools used to analyze scientific theories can be employed to analyze simulation efforts such as INS.[13]

Second, since one component of any simulation is an explicit representation (m) of a referent system, simulations belong to the subclass of theories with explicit models. By a result from model theory, it is known that if an axiomatic deductive theory has a model, then it is logically consistent (noncontradictory). This point is of extreme importance. It was not until the nineteenth century, for example, that model theory was able to demonstrate that negating the parallel lines axiom of Euclidean geometry did not lead to an inconsistency (assuming Euclidean geometry itself to be consistent).

Third, by making the representation (model) explicit, it is possible to efficiently investigate the results of slightly (or grossly) perturbing the representation. This kind of sensitivity testing is very difficult to do for theories without explicit models. That INS was used in such a way is documented by the number of INS "variants" that have been produced.[14]

Purposes

The preceding discussion has developed some of the basic terminology necessary to the evaluation of INS from a methodological perspective. A basic reason for using methodological rules is to decide what counts as evidence in evaluating a theory or hypothesis. Moreover, common sense suggests that what is appropriate in a particular situation is, to some extent, dependent upon contextual information and, to a larger extent, dependent upon the purpose(s) of the research. As an example of the former dependence, it would be unreasonable to criticize fifteenth-century "physicists" for failing to employ the differential calculus. The calculus was simply not available. The critique of INS in the next section will attempt to recognize this contextual problem by only mentioning the methods or techniques that were readily accessible at the time the INS project was being developed.

The problem of purpose is more pervasive. INS is not a simple research project that attempts, for example, to assess the impact of an independent variable on a dependent variable while "controlling" for some third variable. Rather, it is a large-scale research program and, as such, has a number of purposes. Guetzkow has identified three general purposes for simulations in the study of international relations:

> Simulations may serve in three ways as formats through which intellectuals may consolidate and use knowledge

about international relations: (1) simulations may be used
as techniques for increasing the coherence within and
among models, enabling scholars to assess gaps and clo-
sures in our theories; (2) simulations may be used as
constructions in terms of which empirical research may
be organized, so that the validity of our assertions may
be appraised; (3) simulations may be used by members
of the decision-making community in the development
of policy, both as devices for making systematic critiques,
through "box-scoring" its failures and successes, and
as formats for the exploration of alternative plans for
action.[15]

These three purposes might be labeled "programmatic guide to research," "description," and "policy," respectively. In the first, the concern is with integrating "islands of theory" and "organizing the division of labor more coherently among scholars working within international affairs,"[16] by examining different m and t. In the second, the emphasis is upon the degree of correspondence between the model (m) and the reference system (s), that is, the description. In the third, the primary focus is upon policy planning and the specification of alternative futures. Policy planning may be viewed as involving the specification of probability distributions over consequences of alternative (feasible) policies. For the purposes of this essay it will be helpful to separate the "policy" objective from what might be termed the "design" objective. In design the concern is less with identifying the impact of alternative (presently) feasible policies and more concerned with identifying new structures for the achievement of particular goals. This notion of design is compatible with what Guetzkow has termed "constructing alternative futures."[17] As he points out, this concern with design is one of the oldest traditions in political science; and, he argues, simulation is an important tool for the design theorist. One reason for this importance is the relative ease with which the impact of alternative representations (models) can be investigated.

A fifth purpose for simulation (and for INS in particular) that is often cited[18] is that of education. INS has been used to teach principles of international politics in high schools, colleges, and universities and various governmental bureaucracies. The studies of the effectiveness of INS as opposed to more traditional techniques have not found INS to be clearly "superior."[19] Nevertheless, in discussion with several people who have used INS in the classroom, the point was made that INS is very helpful in illustrating the meaning of various concepts, such as tradeoffs in decision making. Even if students going through INS do not know a great deal more about political "reality" as a result of their INS experience, they do appear to be better able to ask sophisticated questions about the political world. However, given a lack of agreement on appropriate educational objectives (even within the cognitive domain), the question of the relative utility of INS-type simulations for students with relevant educational objectives is still an open one.

Although it is not independent of the four purposes mentioned above, it should be mentioned that one of the great strengths of the INS project has been its continuing serious concern with problems of validation.[20]

The Hermann paper entitled "Validation Problems in Games and Simulations with Specific Reference to Models of International Politics " is something of a classic and is often cited both inside and outside of the behavioral sciences as a standard piece on the validation of simulations. Hermann argues that "validity is not a singular issue" and that "the validity of an operating model is affected by the purpose or use for which the game or simulation has been constructed."[21] Thus, for INS, validity issues are related to purpose.

Excluding education, four general purposes for INS have been identified. These were (1) as a programmatic guide to research, (2) as description, (3) as policy, and (4) as design. Since, as will become more apparent in the next section, each of these purposes may entail different research strategies and may require evaluation in terms of different methodological criteria, the evaluation will be organized around these four purposes, with special emphasis upon the validity of INS with respect to each of these purposes.

EVALUATION

This section contains an evaluation of INS in terms of each of the four purposes identified in the previous section. Since a major portion of the INS research effort appears to have been directed toward the purpose of "description," much of this section will focus upon the adequacy of the methodological practices of INS with respect to the development of descriptions of the process of international relations. The descriptive adequacy of INS is closely tied to questions of descriptive validity. Moreover, in the subsection dealing with description, it will be argued that the methodological positions entailed by the Guetzkow and Hermann views of validity are, at certain points, inappropriate to the development of a descriptively adequate INS. First, however, the adequacy of INS as a programmatic guide to research will be considered.

Programmatic Guide to Research

This purpose is potentially one of the most important for a large-scale simulation project such as INS. Reasons for this importance have been brought out in another context by Allen Newell in an interesting analysis of contemporary experimental psychology. Newell argues "that the two constructs that drive our current experimental style are (1) at a low level, the discovery and empirical exploration of [discrete empirical phenomena] and (2) at the middle level, the formulation of questions to be put to nature that center on the resolution of binary oppositions."[22] This characterization could be equally well made of the contemporary empirical study of international relations. Many recent journal articles and convention papers appear to be driven by and imbedded in such binary distinctions as internal-external, conflict-cooperation, rational-irrational, large-small, open-closed, and developed-underdeveloped. Will this approach to science, which Newell terms "playing twenty questions with nature," work? It may. However, "reality" may be too complex to yield this approach. That is, it may not be possible to simply add up answers to these "simple" questions to get a general theory of international relations. An alternative to playing twenty questions with nature is to construct large-scale simulations such as INS. INS then serves as a "complete processing model" in the sense that the model includes components (objects and relations) from a wide range of things, such as military, economic, communications, and geographic factors, that are believed to affect international politics. Thus INS allows the examination of particular phenomena, such as nuclear proliferation or public goods and alliances, as a part of the general INS model.

INS has been successful in having a wide variety of hypotheses generated and, to a lesser extent, tested, within the INS representation (in one of its versions). However, an assessment of the utility of these studies requires consideration of the related objective of description.

Description

In the "Purposes and Standards" section, three elements of a simulation—referent systems (s), representation or model (m), and theory (t)—were identified. The question of descriptive adequacy is essentially a question of the s-m relationship; that is, does the representation adequately reflect the referent system? If both the referent system (reality) and the model are viewed as "black box" systems, with input and output sets, the problem of descriptive adequacy can be posed in terms of the morphisms (mappings) that are preserved between s and m.

May Brodbeck, in her essay on models and theories, suggests that there should be an isomorphism between s and m.[23] An isomorphism is a term used to denote a mapping between two structures that involves a one-to-one correspondence between the objects and relations of the first and the second structure. As Guetzkow points out, however, such a requirement is far too strict.[24] Indeed, such a requirement may be generally undesirable. A model that was isomorphic to reality would be as intractable as reality itself. "Simulations, . . . like other models—are always a simplification of their reference system."[25] Thus, it may be asked that the relation between the reference system (s) and the model (m) be a homomorphism. Here, at an intuitive level, rather than requiring a one-to-one correspondence, the theorist maps many elements and relations of s into those of m.

However, though apparently this has not been explicitly considered in INS-related research, there are a variety of morphisms that might be said to obtain between s and m.[26] Three such morphisms can be termed "behavior preserving," "function preserving," and "structure preserving." The weakest of these is behavior preserving. Here the concern is only that equivalent inputs in s and m produce equivalent outputs. Function preserving morphisms preserve not only input-output relationships, but also internal-state changes.[27] Finally, the most restrictive morphism, structure preserving, preserves (in addition to input-output relations and state transition functions) the manner in which these relations and functions arise out of local coordinate functions.[28] Although structure-preserving morphisms will not be discussed in this paper, the set theoretical view of simulation developed in the beginning of this essay is general enough to pursue such investigations.

The first two of these morphisms, behavior preserving and structure preserving, may be formalizations of what Guetzkow meant when he wrote the following:

> Some homomorphy may exist among outputs as well as between the very processes which result in such outputs. As we analyze the correspondences between simulations and "realities" sometimes an internal process, like the representation of the decision-making within foreign offices, helps produce an outcome of some validity, such as the constellation of internal alliances. At other times less often because of lack of appropriate research an internal process will be judged to be of some validity because the very process itself has some congruence with corresponding processes in the reference data.[29]

A homomorphism among outputs only would be similar to the behavior-preserving morphism, while a morphism that preserved outputs as well as "internal processes" would be a function-preserving morphism. These different morphisms are interesting in that they suggest a variety of ways in which descriptive adequacy might be evaluated.

As was mentioned, requiring a behavior-preserving morphism is a rather weak condition, in the sense that only input-output relations are preserved. No restrictions are made on relations between the "internal" structuring of m and that of s. Much of the INS work seems to have been directed toward establishing behavior-preserving morphisms. For example, in discussing criteria for assessing the fidelity with which a model produces aspects of reality (description), Hermann suggests five standards, which are (1) internal validity, (2) face validity, (3) variable-parameter validity, (4) event validity, and (5) hypothesis validity.[30] In explicating each of these, Hermann proposes methodological rules. Therefore it will be useful to consider each of these five sorts of validity in some detail.

Internal Validity

> Any exogenous inputs introduced during the course of the game are held constant across all trials or runs. The unexplained variance between these intended replications would provide a measure of reliability or "internal validity." When the structured simulation properties are held constant, the smaller the between-run variance, the greater the internal validity is assumed to be.[31]

From the perspective of descriptive adequacy, this notion of internal validity or reliability seems to be somewhat misleading. First of all, note that the concern here is not with a relation between s and m, but rather purely in properties of m, or perhaps of relations between m and t.

Hermann seems to be asserting that it is desirable for two runs of the same simulation with equivalent input to show equivalent output (response). With input fixed, he wants to minimize between-run variance. However, if the simulation is stochastic, that is, probabilistic, as in INS, either because of the explicit use of pseudo-random-number generators or because of "noise" resulting from the use of human subjects, as in INS, the response of the simulation will itself be a random variable that will have a variance associated with it. One reason for constructing the simulation may,

METHODOLOGICAL APPRAISAL

assuming the description is accurate, be to estimate the variance associated with the INS response, under fixed initial conditions. There is no general a priori reason to desire a low between-run variance.[32] It might be counter-argued that in the case of stochastic computer simulations the pseudo-random number seed is also an input value. Therefore we would want to have a low between-run variance with the seed fixed. However, this argument loses force when the problem of internally validating the pseudo-random number generator itself is considered.

While this criticism may appear trivial, it generalizes to much of the INS validation effort. That is, reality itself (s) is seen as highly internally valid in the Hermann sense, and it therefore is expected to have very low variance; or in other words, it is hypothesized to be very unlikely that empirical events would happen in any way other than they actually did. However, the adequacy of such a hypothesis is not universal. Imagine, for example, that a "fair coin" is flipped five times with the following sequence of heads and tails:

t_1	t_2	t_3	t_4	t_5
H	H	T	H	T

Such a sequence would not be expected each time a coin was flipped five times; in fact, the probability of such a sequence, given probability theory together with the "fair coin" model, would be $.5^5$ or about .03. Quite clearly it would be inappropriate to evaluate a simulation of coin flipping by its ability to exhibit low variance over sequences. For these reasons it is not appropriate that the internal validity of INS should depend upon its having a low variance.

Face Validity

Face Validity "is a surface or initial impression of a simulation or game's realism."[33] As Hermann points out, this criterion is rather vague and is generally useful only in the early stages of simulation development. However, recent efforts suggest that face validity may be capable of being rendered more precise by identifying the mental images of individuals who "work with" the process being represented.[34] Mental images, here, refer to the ways individuals have organized at the cognitive level their information about a particular referent reality. The procedures for identifying these cognitive models are still not very rigorous; nonetheless, preliminary efforts suggest that face validity may be appropriate even beyond the early stages of simulation development.

Variable-Parameter Validity

Variable-parameter validity "involves comparisons of the simulation's variables and parameters with their assumed counterparts in the observable universe."[35] The concern is that the objects of m correspond to objects in s. There are several problems with the use of variable-parameter validity in evaluating INS. First, as Hermann noted, there is the problem of aggregation. Even a complex simulation such as INS deals with variables at a highly aggregated level. For example, most INS versions have either three or four decision makers per country. Each of these individuals represents a highly aggregated communications flow. This aggregation of "bureaucratic channels" into three or four individuals may have undesirable implications for the way communications processes are represented. Given this aggregation (and in all but the structure-preserving morphism there will be aggregation), there is no reason to expect that the INS variables will have simple "real-world counterparts."

If no simple correspondence between the variables of INS and those of the real world is asserted, then measurement problems become especially critical. Measurement theory deals with the ways in which numbers can be associated with the attributes or appearances of objects to represent the properties of the attribute as numerical properties.[36] The problem of identifying the measurement structure that is necessary to discuss variable-parameter validity in highly aggregated simulations does not appear to have been discussed within the INS research program. For example, it is doubtful that simple additive structures would suffice for an accurate movement from the physical components of weapons systems and force structures, that is, aspects of s, to numerical values for the INS variables named force capability conventional and force capability nuclear, that is, aspects of m; yet INS assumes additivity all the way up to total strength, which is a linear combination of force capability conventional, force capability nuclear, basic capabilities, and defense units. Total strength, in the INS representation, is by design defined at a high level of aggregation. In order to assess "variable-validity," it is necessary to identify a procedure for aggregating to an analogous total strength component in the referent reality. Without resolving the aggregation and related measurement problems, the idea of variable-parameter validity cannot be applied to INS in any but an intuitive manner.

Event Validity

As discussed by Hermann, event validity uses " 'natural' events as criteria against which to compare outcomes occurring in the simulation."[37] For example, Charles F. and Margaret G. Hermann used INS in an attempt to simulate the outbreak of World War I.[38] The primary purpose of their study was to evaluate the validity of INS. "One means of investigating this question is to ascertain if a simulation produces events similar to those reported in a historical situation."[39] Thus, one validity criterion being used was event validity.

For reasons analogous to those discussed under internal validity, such a use of event validity requires a commitment to a low-variance external world. Just as the "true probability" of a sequence of five coin flips was .03, suppose that the "true probability" of the specific chain of events leading to World War I was .03. Would it then be reasonable to claim that a simulation that "reliably" reproduced these events was valid? This critique of "internal validity" and "event validity" suggests that neither is necessary to or sufficient for a valid simulation.

Hypothesis Validity

The fifth and last criterion discussed by Hermann is "hypothesis validity." If X is observed to bear a given relationship to Y in the observable universe, then X' should bear a corresponding relationship to Y' in a valid operating model.[40] This criterion would seem to be identical to the behavior-preserving morphism discussed earlier. Again, the use of hypothesis validity requires the making of considerable measurement assumptions of the sort discussed earlier. These assumptions should be explicated.

Each of Hermann's last four criteria is concerned with assessing the descriptive validity of simulations, and each criterion deals with certain posited correspondences between the referent system and the simulation. The application of these criteria to INS entails a deterministic, or low variance, view of "reality" and, given the aggregated nature of INS, too simple a view of measurement. One of the luxuries of the critic is to suggest what might have been done differently. For example, it can be argued that had more attention been paid to questions of aggregation and the related problems of measurement as INS was being constructed and the operating rules written, later researchers would have found it much easier to address specific research questions within the general INS framework.

The work done with Forrester's World Dynamics simulation strongly indicates that once a complex simulation is constructed, it is often too late to disaggregate the concepts and relations in order to consider specific empirical hypotheses using simple measurement structures. The tendency then is to do experiments on the simulation model itself and to compare only broad behavior patterns in the representation with those in the referent system. For certain purposes, of course, this is perfectly adequate, but if there is a need for a simulation to serve as a "complete processing model" with which to investigate the complexity of international relations, then there is a need to consider early problems of measurement and aggregation and disaggregation. Such a purpose would seem to be what Guetzkow had in mind when he wrote that simulations "permit the coherent amalgamation of subtheories into interactive, holistic constructions of great complexity."[41] Further, he clearly recognizes the measurement problems outlined here.[42]

Policy

A third general objective according to which INS can be evaluated is "policy." There are numerous ways in which INS has been relevant to the policy community, including the pretesting of alternative policies on INS, the providing of a monitoring system, and the training of policy makers, who by their involvement in INS have learned to be aware of the complexities underlying the impacts of policies. As many of the papers coming out of the INS project have pointed out, the descriptive "validity" of INS has not been sufficiently established to encourage the policy-making community to rely upon it very heavily in the actual policy-making process. Indeed, in order to so use INS it would be necessary to be able to assert at least a function-preserving morphism between the model and the referent reality; yet as was argued earlier, the major validation efforts have centered upon establishing only a behavior-preserving morphism, that is, to preserve the input-output relationships.

With regard to the policy objective, it might have been useful to have adopted a more explicit control theoretic strategy. This would have made it far easier to address questions of policy selection using existing techniques.[43] Had this been done it would be at least theoretically, if not computationally, possible to investigate the following within INS:

   a) the relative importance of alternative policies, if different environmental conditions, or if differing parametric specifications as they affect the simular response at some point T in simular time; and,

b) that set (or combination) of policies, environmental conditions, and parametric specifications which will provide, in some sense, the optimal simular response at time T.[44]

Answering, or even posing, such questions would probably require reconceptualizing INS in response surface terms, which might not have been very difficult, since several of the "experimental designs" employed in INS reports approached doing this. More importantly, it becomes necessary to attach some sort of objective function to the simulation in order that alternative outcomes can be ordered with respect to their "desirability." The problem of identifying such functions for social systems is most difficult.[45] However, if simulation is to be seriously used in policy selection, it would seem that such problems must be addressed.

Design

While policy problems involve identifying and implementing feasible strategies to meet some goal(s), design problems deal with identifying and describing various mechanisms for the achievement of goals. The distinction being made here between policy and design is analogous to the distinction between the values of variables, including parameters, and the way these variables are related to one another. Policy changes are changes in the level of variables, whereas design changes are changes in the structure that relates to the variables.

Simulation is a very powerful technique, or means of generating data, for the design theorist. The relatively low cost of computer computation makes it possible to examine varieties of decision mechanisms in a variety of "environments." Moreover, the use of simulation allows the investigator to deal numerically with nonlinearities, time-lagged feedback, and other complications for which analytic solutions may either not exist or, if they exist, be beyond the symbol manipulation skills of most behavioral scientists.

Notice, too, a key distinction between the policy objective and the design objective. In the case of policy the representation (m) is taken as fixed and the concern is with the impact of parametric and variable value, or level, changes. However, in the case of design, the representation itself is the datum and the concern is with identifying desirable (perhaps in a constrained sense) models.

Thus experiments designed to find optimal policies within existing models will not generally serve the purpose of design, although of course they may give us an idea of the "best" a particular m can do.

Moreover, in the case of design, simulation can quite properly be viewed as a data generating technique. The data generated are, of course, the performances of various models. Under this view of design, questions of appropriate methodology again become relevant. Here, for example, there is less concern with "correspondences" between m and s; rather, the interest is in developing preference orderings over the elements of m. Perhaps, some of the methodological positions of "traditional" utopian thinkers may be applicable.

CONCLUSION

The title notwithstanding, this essay has been more a critical review of selected aspects of the methodology of INS than it has been an "appraisal." According to the Oxford English Dictionary, to appraise may be rewritten as "to estimate the amount, quality, or excellence of." The narrow scope of this essay does not permit an appraisal. Moreover, such a task requires a more experienced appraiser than I. However, and this may be more revealing anyway, I would be willing to bet that in the year 2000 it will be commonly acknowledged that the state of international relations theory owes a great debt to INS-related activities. Already, in 1975, one cannot help but notice the number of rather sophisticated projects employing simulation as a matter of course. Compare this to 1965 or 1955: had Harold Guetzkow not begun the Simulated International Processes project, a large number of us would be unable, for a wide variety of reasons, to do what we do today. Assuming that we value what we are doing, how can we do other than consider INS a success?

NOTES

1. R. Leserman, "Simulated International Process Sipfil: Bibliography of Technical Outputs with Abstracts" (Evanston, Ill.: Northwestern University, 1972).

2. Richard Rudner, Philosophy of Social Science (Englewood Cliffs: Prentice-Hall, 1966), p. 5.

3. Harold Guetzkow, "A Use of Simulation in the Study of Inter-Nation Relations," Behavioral Science 4, no. 2 (1959): 183-91.

4. Harold Guetzkow, "Some Correspondences Between Simulations and 'Realities' in International Relations," in New Approaches

to International Relations, edited by Morton Kaplan (New York: St. Martin's Press, 1968), pp. 202-09.

5. Charles F. Hermann, "Validation Problems in Games and Simulations with Special Reference to Models of International Politics," Behavioral Science 12, no. 3 (1967): 216-31.

6. An elegant argument for this point is found in Thomas Naylor, "Computer Simulation Defined," in Computer Simulation Experiments with Models of Economic Systems, edited by Thomas Naylor (New York: John Wiley and Sons, 1971), pp. 2-10.

7. Harold Guetzkow, "Simulations in the Consolidation and Utilization of Knowledge about International Relations," in Theory and Research on the Causes of War, edited by Dean G. Pruitt and Richard C. Snyder (Englewood Cliffs: Prentice-Hall, 1969), p. 285.

8. Hermann, "Validation Problems," op. cit., p. 216.

9. Ibid.

10. Alfred Tarski, "The Semantic Conception of Truth and the Foundations of Semantics," in Philosophy and Phenomenological Research 4, no. 3 (1944): 341-75.

11. Ibid.

12. Stuart J. Thorson and John Stever, "Class of Models for Selected Axiomatic Theories of Choice," Journal of Mathematical Psychology 11, no. 1 (1974): 15-32.

13. Guetzkow, "Some Correspondences," op. cit.

14. Stuart A. Bremer, "National and International Systems: A Computer Simulation," (Ph.D. diss., Michigan State University, 1970); Paul L. Smoker, "An International Processes Simulation: Theory and Description," Simulated International Processes Project (Evanston: Northwestern University, 1968); Clark Abt and Morton Gordon, "Report on Project TEMPER," in Theory and Research on the Causes of War, edited by Dean G. Pruitt and Richard C. Snyder (Englewood Cliffs: Prentice-Hall, 1969), pp. 245-62; Michael Leavitt, "A Computer Simulation of International Alliance Behavior," (Ph.D. diss.: Northwestern University, 1971).

15. Guetzkow, "Simulations in Consolidation," op. cit., p. 288.

16. Ibid.

17. Harold Guetzkow and Lloyd Jensen, "Research Activities on Simulated International Processes," Background 9, no. 4 (1966): 261-74, and Guetzkow, "Simulations in Consolidation," op. cit.

18. Harold Guetzkow, "A Use of Simulation," op. cit.

19. James A. Robinson, et al., "Teaching with Inter-Nation Simulation and Case Studies," American Political Science Review 60, no. 1 (1966): 53-65.

20. This concern has been reflected in several papers, including Chadwick F. Alger, "Use of the Inter-Nation Simulation in Undergraduate Teaching," in Simulation in International Relations, edited

by Harold Guetzkow, et al. (Englewood Cliffs: Prentice-Hall, 1963), pp. 150-89; and, Richard W. Chadwick, "An Empirical Test of Five Assumptions in an Inter-Nation Simulation, About National Political Systems," General Systems 12 (1967): 177-92.

21. Hermann, "Validation Problems," op. cit., p. 217.
22. Allen Newell and Herbert A. Simon, Human Problem Solving (Englewood Cliffs: Prentice-Hall, 1972).
23. May Brodbeck, "Models, Meanings and Theories," in Symposium on Sociological Theory, edited by Llewellyn Gross (Evanston: Row Peterson, 1959), pp. 373-403.
24. Guetzkow, "Some Correspondences," op. cit., p. 207.
25. Hermann, "Validation Problems," op. cit., p. 217.
26. Bernard Ziegler, "Towards a Formal Theory of Modeling and Simulation" (Ann Arbor: University of Michigan, 1970).
27. M. A. Arbib, Theories of Abstract Automata (Englewood Cliffs: Prentice-Hall, 1969).
28. Ziegler, "Towards a Formal Theory," op. cit., p. 6ff.
29. Guetzkow, "Some Correspondences," op. cit., p. 207.
30. Hermann, "Validation Problems," op. cit.
31. Ibid., p. 220.
32. G. Arthur Mihram, Simulation: Statistical Foundations and Methodology (New York: Academic Press, 1972), pp. 18-146.
33. Hermann, "Validation Problems," op. cit., p. 221.
34. John M. Richardson, "Quantifying 'Soft' Variables: Difficult but Essential," Modeling and Simulation 5 (1974): 186-90.
35. Hermann, "Validation Problems," op. cit., p. 222.
36. Paul F. Krantz, et al., Foundation of Measurement (New York: Academic Press, 1971).
37. Hermann, "Validation Problems," op. cit., p. 222.
38. Charles F. Hermann and Margaret G. Hermann, "An Attempt to Simulate the Outbreak of World War I," American Political Science Review 61, no. 2 (1967): 400-16.
39. Ibid., p. 401.
40. Hermann, "Validation Problems," op. cit., p. 223.
41. Guetzkow, "Simulations in Consolidation," op. cit., p. 206.
42. Guetzkow, "Some Correspondences," op. cit., p. 210.
43. See G. E. P. Box, "The Exploration and Exploitation of Response Surfaces: Some General Considerations and Examples," Biometrics 10, no. 1 (1954): 16-60; G. E. P. Box and J. S. Hunter, "Multifactor Experimental Designs for Exploring Response Surfaces," Annals of Mathematical Statistics 28, no. 1 (1957): 195-241; Norman R. Droper, "Third Order Rotatable Designs in Three Factors: Analysis," Technometrics 4, no. 2 (1962): 219-34; and D. A. Gardiner, A. H. E. Grandage, and R. J. Hader, "Third Order Rotatable

Designs for Exploring Response Surfaces," <u>Annals of Mathematical Statistics</u> 30, no. 4 (1959): 1082-96.

44. Mihram, <u>Simulation</u>, op. cit., p. 402.

45. Howard Raeffa, "Preferences for Multi-Attributed Alternatives" (Santa Monica: RAND Corporation, RM-5868-DOT/RC, 1964). Mimeographed.

CHAPTER

15

AN APPRAISAL OF THE SUBSTANTIVE FINDINGS OF THE INTER-NATION SIMULATION PROJECT

Stuart A. Bremer

An appraisal of the substantive findings of the Inter-Nation Simulation project must begin with a definition of the word "substantive." I take it to be the intention of the editors of this volume that this word refers to those contributions of the project that bear directly upon our knowledge of the world and its politics. This rather narrow definition contrasts markedly with the definition of substantive as "that part which is real rather than apparent." There is more involved here than a semantic quibble; our appraisal will be strongly shaped by the use of the narrow or the broad conception of this term.

If we accept the narrow meaning, then our focus will be restricted to cataloging and evaluating the particular hypotheses that have been tested in the course of the activities of the project. This will be done in the pages that follow; yet to do only this would omit a substantial amount of the project's real contribution. In part this is because the project was not intended to be substantive in the same sense as the Dimensionality of Nations or Correlates of War projects. There was no central set of behavior for which explanations were sought, nor was there any major effort to collect data. Hence a narrow definition of substantive findings, implying the question, What do we now know as a consequence of the project's activities? would lead one to conclude that the project's contributions have been scattered and somewhat marginal. In the evaluation that follows, I have been guided by the broader conception of substantive, involving the question, How do we think differently as a consequence of what the project did? At the outset, however, it seems necessary to acknowledge some difficulties that make such an evaluation a difficult task.

First, few people, I think, recognize the tremendous variety, scope, and magnitude of the work that has been produced by this simulation project. Even a partial bibliography of the published and unpublished materials that have been supported or inspired by the project would include several hundred entries. It is impossible in the space of these pages to adequately summarize or evaluate this decade and a half of work by scores of individuals.

Second, the boundaries of the project are difficult to define. Most scholars, I think, associate the project with the Inter-Nation Simulation (INS) work, and indeed this activity was its central concern for many years; yet even a cursory examination of the project's documentary traces reveals a large amount of research that is only indirectly related to the Inter-Nation Simulation. As one attempts to trace out the threads of development, it becomes obvious that the distinction between project "products" and nonproject "products" is by no means clear. For example, William D. Coplin's PRINCE model evolved from his World Politics Simulation (WPS), which in turn had grown out of the INS. Similarly, the Dimensionality of Nations (DON) project began as an offshoot of the Northwestern University simulation project.

Third, my own past association with the project places me in an awkward position for executing this evaluation. During eight months of 1969 I was fortunate enough to serve as a research assistant while I developed an all-computer version of the INS model. In view of this, I find myself in something of a dilemma: if I am insufficiently critical or rigorous in my evaluation, I run the risk of being accused of pulling my punches; yet if I am overly critical and unappreciative of the project's endeavors, I can be cited for biting the hand that (literally) fed me. On the other hand, as an "adopted" member of the SIP (Simulated International Processes) family, my position is also somewhat advantageous in that I have been inside the project, but not too far inside. With these factors in mind, let us turn to a survey and evaluation of the project's activities.

SURVEY AND EVALUATION

The work of the project falls into four basic categories, which correspond roughly with the given time-spans as follows: (1) development and refinement of the Inter-Nation Simulation (INS) model (1957-60); (2) application of the INS model to research and teaching (1960-63); (3) validation and revision of the INS model (1963-67); (4) construction and evaluation of new man-machine and all-computer simulation models (1968-72). In the survey that follows, each of these phases will be considered in turn.

The Development of the Inter-Nation Simulation

According to Harold Guetzkow, his conception of the Inter-Nation Simulation model developed while he attended the Center for Advanced Study in the Behavioral Sciences in 1956-57. During this time it appeared to him that a synthesis of a free-form war game and a controlled sociopsychological experiment might prove to be a useful research vehicle for investigating various hypotheses concerning foreign policy decision making.[1]

Following his year at the center, Guetzkow joined the international relations program at Northwestern University and began in 1957 to develop a man-machine simulation model through a series of pilot runs. The principal objective of these early runs was to test and improve the workability of the model. The process of incremental modification continued during 1958 and 1959, when elements such as decision latitude, programmed war outcomes, and revolution routines were added. In each case the decision to revise some aspect of the model was based on intuitive judgments about the adequacies and inadequacies of the simulation.

By 1960 these incremental modifications had produced a model that has remained, at least structurally, more or less constant for many years. The model is described in many places, but the first definitive description appeared in <u>Simulation in International Relations</u>.[2] At the conclusion of the developmental work, Guetzkow and his associates had produced (1) a number of beneficial side products, (2) a partial macrotheory of international relations, (3) a potentially useful educational tool, and (4) a method of addressing research questions in a quasi-laboratory setting. The remainder of this section will be concerned with evaluating the first two of these products, and the third and fourth will be dealt with in the next section.

One of these side products was Denis Sullivan's Ph.D. dissertation which drew together propositions concerning international relations from 10 leading textbooks.[3] Another side product was Robert C. Noel's doctoral dissertation, in which he laid out the lines of development for a more complex and realistic INS political and economic system by introducing a private economic sector and also a more highly differentiated public economic sector and a more pluralistic political sector, including political parties and interest groups.[4] Although the model was made operational, to my knowledge

SUBSTANTIVE FINDINGS   307

no simulation runs were conducted using it. The third major side
product began as an effort to find empirical measures for the "prototypic" variables used in the INS model by factor analytic techniques.
The end result of this was the Dimensionality of Nations project,
which is discussed elsewhere in this volume. All of these works
have substantial merit.

In evaluating the INS as a partial macrotheory, it should be
noted that a theory, even a partial theory, if it is to make a significant contribution to its field, must be accepted and used in various
parts of the field. In this sense INS failed to make a contribution at
this early stage. It did not serve to reorient the thinking of scholars
or policy makers on a wide scale, although it did ultimately move
beyond the confines of Northwestern in educational uses and research.
The partial theory was not taken up by those, for example, who would
be in a position to better explicate certain parts of it. Perhaps this
is because it was not often presented as a theory in the early days
of development but rather as a complex laboratory exercise. Perhaps the theory received little attention because those members of
the international relations scholarly community who were sympathetic with the macrolevel nature of the theory were alienated by the
mathematical mode of expression, while those who were sympathetic
to the effort to state theory in reasonably precise terms—the emerging
behavioralists—were primarily concerned then with micropolitical
characteristics such as perceptions, attitudes, and beliefs.

I think it may be profitable to review some of the major decisions
that were made during the developmental period, with an eye toward
assessing what impact these decisions may have had on the later
substantive contribution that the project would make to our field.
Six basic decisions that were made during this period concerning
the organization and content of the research will be examined here.

1. The use of research teams. Guetzkow has stated his preference for team research, and from the very beginning he has adhered
to the strategy of having many investigators working simultaneously
on different aspects of the project. Since 1957, scores of individuals
have been directly or indirectly associated with the project. Clearly,
the advantage of this strategy is that much more can be accomplished
in a shorter period of time, but this advantage is at least partially
offset by the inevitable problems of coordination and administration,
as well as by an apparent lack of cumulation due to equally inevitable
changes in team membership.

2. The adoption of an eclectic research strategy. The adoption
of an eclectic research strategy involved, in this case, the attempt
to strike a balance between traditional theory and empirical knowledge, drawn from a number of fields and concerning a variety of
entities, and feasibility considerations. In retrospect, no other

research strategy seems compatible with the development of the model, given the state of our knowledge.

3. The use of the man-machine format. Three major factors determined the selection of a man-machine format for the INS. First, in the judgment of the designers of INS, there was not sufficient knowledge for the complete specification of a macrotheory of world politics. Second, computer hardware and software were not developed to the stage they are now, nor were they easily accessible to the social scientist. Third, and perhaps most important, Guetzkow's abiding interest was in laboratory experimentation. The inaccessibility of real decision makers, the desire for controlled experimentation, and the initial emphasis on decision making as the central phenomenon of world politics led inevitably to the selection of the man-machine format. In one sense the selection of a "quasi-experimental" approach subjected Guetzkow and his associates to attack from two different quarters. Since the approach recognizes the trade-offs of internal and external validity with attempts to steer a middle course, it is somewhat inevitable that the strict experimentalists, who favor maximizing internal validity, would reject the results produced in "noisy" experimental situations with many uncontrolled variables. Perhaps it was equally inevitable that the external validity maximizers, who prefer to work in the "real" world, would frequently argue that the findings were irrelevant because high school students are not professional diplomats, simulated nations are not real nations, simulated wars are not real wars, and so forth.

4. Programmed and unprogrammed relationships. The choice of a man-machine format means, of course, that some of the outcomes within the simulation are determined by the logical, mathematical, and stochastic elements that comprise the programmed portion of the simulation model. The remaining elements are left free to vary according to the desires of the decision makers operating within the constraints of the programmed portion. What we wish to review here is the decision to specify the intranational aspects of the model extensively and leave the international aspects largely unspecified. George Modelski has argued that this distinction may have led the designers to neglect, at the international level, important feedback components such as "world validators."[5] The result is that the simulation produces worlds in which the individual nations are insufficiently interdependent. Robert Golembiewski, William Walsh, and William Crotty, for somewhat more obscure reasons, contend that "the absence of programmed relationships between the inter-nation behaviors and domestic core variables renders questionable the programmed relations among the core variables themselves Although I do not agree with these specific criticisms, I do think mor

SUBSTANTIVE FINDINGS   309

effort should have been devoted to the inclusion of programmed
relationships dealing with routine international transactions.

5. The selection of the nation as the basic actor. Modelski has
also criticized the Inter-Nation Simulation for overemphasizing the
role of the nation-state and neglecting various international, transnational, multinational, and supranational actors.[7] It is true, of
course, that with the exception of an occasional more or less welldefined international organization, nation-states are the major actors
within the Inter-Nation Simulation. The seriousness of Modelski's
criticism depends, I think, on one's judgment of the importance of
these organizations in the contemporary world and the degree to
which they have transformed the international system into a global
system. If we put the question another way, perhaps we can gain a
better perspective on the matter. How many of us, in a time characterized by cold-war crises, missile gaps, bipolar confrontations,
Berlin walls, espionage flights, and abortive summit meetings,
would have thought to include the whole host of nonnational actors
that were present in the system at that time? I think most of us
would have felt the need for an international organization, like the
United Nations, but not much more than that.

6. The character of the core variables. One can always disagree
with the central concepts and relationships of a particular theory,
especially if it is in the early stages of development and not of one's
own making. Although the selection of certain core variables, such
as decision latitude and basic capability, and the rejection of others
in the early stages of development had far-reaching implications for
the type of problems that INS could be addressed to and the subsequent contribution it could make to the field, there is another, more
general aspect of the core variables that I would like to discuss;
that is, the decision to use "prototypic" variables.

"Prototypic" variables, such as basic capability (BC) and
decision latitude (DL), subsume a variety of empirical referent
variables but are not directly related to any specific one. The
developers thought that their use would raise the level of abstraction
in the game and discourage "role-playing." In addition, it proved
to be useful in subsuming a great deal of complexity under a few
general concepts, not unlike the parsimony that is obtained through
the use of factor analysis. All things considered, however, I think
the use of prototypic variables was an unfortunate choice.

First, I think their use impaired communication and exchange
between the simulators and the nonsimulators. In one sense, these
variables constitute a highly specialized jargon that was not, and
is not, well understood outside the group of simulators, who have
internalized it by experience. I think this has served to restrict
communication both ways. Those not familiar with the concepts have

found it difficult, I suspect, to incorporate findings from INS studies into their work. Richard W. Chadwick developed an interesting causal model relating various intranational and international behaviors using real world data in conjunction with his validation and revision work on INS.[8] The results are reported in terms of relationships between INS concepts and are not easily incorporated into ongoing work utilizing more conventional conceptualizations. Similarly, this decision meant that important findings generated in other parts of international relations, other fields of political science, and other disciplines, such as economics, could not be directly translated into INS terms and easily incorporated into the model.

The choice also greatly compounded validation problems, in my judgment. If the prototypic variables had been specified as functions of more widely used measurement units, the cross-sectional and cross-temporal comparisons with referent systems would have been facilitated. This seems to be particularly true in the latter case, since there are very few validation studies that have dealt with the dynamic aspects of INS. From personal experience I can attest to the difficulties of trying to determine exactly, or even roughly, how much real time corresponds to one simulation period in terms of the rates of change in the prototypic variables.[9]

It should be noted that many of the criticisms considered above were recognized by Guetzkow and his associates at the end of the development period. It was decided, however—perhaps wisely, perhaps not—to slow the pace of development in order to apply the model to specific research questions and evaluate the validity of the model more systematically.

Application of the Inter-Nation Simulation Model

By 1960 the designers apparently felt that they had a reasonably complete and workable model, and accordingly they turned to the matters of application and utilization. I will differentiate between educational and research applications.

Educational Applications

As early as 1959, the Inter-Nation Simulation was used in classroom instruction at Northwestern. Chadwick F. Alger describe the early experiences in using the model in an undergraduate class in international organizations, and many of the student reactions he reported are familiar to those of us who still use it today.[10] James A. Robinson directed a comparative analysis of the use of simulation

SUBSTANTIVE FINDINGS 311

and case studies in the classroom, and the results were not heartening to those who thought simulation might produce a breakthrough in the teaching of international relations. They found no clear evidence to support the assertion that students were more interested in the course, or learned more from it, through the use of simulation as opposed to the use of case studies.[11] Cleo Cherryholmes partially substantiated these findings later, and since that time, to my knowledge, little more has been done to evaluate the INS as a teaching device.[12]

It appears that the use of the simulation began to spread to other universities during this period, but in informal ways. Often this occurred when someone who had worked in one capacity or another with the project moved to another university and carried with him the "seeds" of an INS game. The use of INS in education was greatly facilitated by the production of an improved version of the model in 1966. Cherryholmes and Guetzkow designed a college and high school version that is distributed by Science Research Associates.[13] Harry R. Targ developed and evaluated an elementary school version of the model.[14]

As far as the project itself is concerned, it does not appear that the educational applications were as central a concern as they might have been. Consider some of the things that could have been done to enhance the use of the INS as an educational tool. If effort had been directed toward developing ways in which INS could be integrated into various types of classes with different substantive focal points, including suggested readings that related the simulation to some substantive body of knowledge, it might have been more widely used. Perhaps a newsletter, in which the users of INS could have informed each other of innovations, problems, reactions, and experiences, would have been useful. If the Inter-Nation Simulation had been a more complete educational package, my suspicion is that its impact would have been substantially greater.

Research Applications

At this point in our survey of the project's activities, we come to that part of its contribution that is substantive in the narrow sense of the term. The Inter-Nation Simulation has been used to address a variety of research questions and has produced a significant number of findings. The appendix to this chapter contains a summary of the major research runs arranged in chronological order, with the most important individual studies and the major findings of each. This list should not be considered as exhaustive of the project's substantive findings, since some studies are excluded and only the major findings of the studies listed are summarized.

An examination of the appendix reveals the remarkable way in which a single run of the simulation could provide the basis for several different investigations, enabling the researchers to prorate the costs of a simulation run over several investigations. On the negative side, however, it is possible that the experimental manipulations that were introduced to study one aspect of behavior may have interfered with another aspect that was also being studied.

Not all of the studies included in the appendix were direct products of the project. The WINSAFE II runs, for example, were supported by Project Michelson. I have included them here because they utilized the Inter-Nation Simulation as a means of generating substantive knowledge, and the project should therefore receive partial credit.

As one surveys the diverse research applications of the INS model, one is struck by the fact that it has been used in interesting and innovative ways to address important questions drawn from a variety of disciplines. Certainly it is to the credit of the designers of the INS that it lends itself to so many different kinds of questions; yet if we compare these applications to some higher standards, certain shortcomings are clearly evident.

In an ideal sense, experimental studies should build on each other in a cumulative and coherent way, which the INS studies clearly do not. The very diversity of applications precludes the development of a coherent body of knowledge. If a sustained, well-coordinated set of studies had been carried out, I think the field of international relations would be much better off today. The scattering of findings across fields and levels of analysis leaves one with the impression that nothing has been nailed down and that the research potential of INS has not been fully explored. Another factor that contributes to this impression is the relative inaccessibility of many of the studies. A significant proportion of the studies is unpublished or published in ways that do not make them easily available to the scholarly community. Certainly the project is not solely to blame for this shortcoming; but the unavailability of the studies clearly has reduced the substantive impact of the INS on the field of international politics. Perhaps the principal reason why a more systematic pattern of utilization of the INS for research purposes was not undertaken is that the focus of the project shifted from application to validation, and it is to these validation studies that we will now turn.

Validation of the Inter-Nation Simulation

Between 1963 and 1968 the bulk of the project's work seems to have involved attempts to assess the validity of the INS, and clearly

SUBSTANTIVE FINDINGS 313

it is true that no other social science simulation model has received so much scrutiny from so many different angles. The methodology of validating simulations was not, and is not, well developed; yet I think it has benefited from some of the methodological studies the project encouraged or supported. Beginning with a conference in 1965 on validating simulation models, a number of project papers have wrestled with the thorny problems of validation.[15]

The validation studies themselves are quite numerous, but fortunately Guetzkow has provided us with a summary of the findings of most of them.[16] His overall assessment of 55 relationships derived from 24 different studies indicated that there was "some" or "much" correspondence between the referent and simulated worlds in about two-thirds of the cases. Modelski, after independently reviewing the same studies Guetzkow had examined, arrived at very similar conclusions.[17] The studies are too numerous for me to review here, and the interested reader is directed to Guetzkow's discussion.

One of the more ambitious attempts to assess the validity of the INS was the "Event Simulation Project" undertaken by Dorothy L. Meier in 1963 and followed up by Harry R. Targ and Terry Nardin in 1964.[18] The original intention of these runs was to match the starting conditions of the simulated world to those of the real world in 1963-64 and run the simulation forward a year or so in time, with one period of simulation time equal to six weeks of real time. After the events of 1964 and 1965 had unfolded in the real world, there was to be an assessment of the simulation's ability to predict these events in advance. This predictive power was to be compared with that of policy makers, scholars, and journalists, using predictions collected by Lloyd Jensen for the same period of time. The total venture, unfortunately, was never carried to completion. Jensen published his findings separately, and his work appears to have been the principal substantive contribution of this ambitious undertaking.[19] Terry Nardin and Neal Cutler used the data from these runs to analyze the correspondence of the dyadic interaction patterns of the simulated nations to those of referent world dyads,[20] while Patrick McGowan attempted to carry out the original intention of the designers of the predictive validity assessment. McGowan's effort represents one of the richest validation studies to date.[21]

Leaving aside the methodological aspects of the validation studies, what substantive impact have they had on the field? Since almost all of them have generated findings about the referent world as well as about the simulated worlds, there is clearly a potential substantive impact implicit in the validation strategy selected. Chadwick has provided an excellent examination of this potential, in which far more of this potential was realized than in any of the other INS validation studies.[22] As Chadwick moved through the stages of his research and validation led to theory building, the referent world increasingly became the central focus of his research. In general, however, the validation studies have been content with assessing the correspondence between the simulated and referent worlds and suggesting ways in which the simulation might be revised, rather than exploring the implications of the referent world findings. However necessary, this tendency, in conjunction with the use of "alien" prototypic variables and the limited circulation of the studies, has lessened the substantive impact of the validation studies.

These considerations are quite minor, however, compared to the much larger questions that some critics have raised concerning the use of simulation in general and validation in particular. Some argue that the validation efforts were misdirected and failed to focus on the truly critical aspects of validity, and that this failure has rendered simulation largely irrelevant.[23] The critical question is whether the behavior that results from a particular INS run or set of runs is a consequence of the structural or situational factors represented by programmed, and experimenter determined, portions of the game, as opposed to the more idiosyncratic factors that the participants bring with them. Logically, if one is to draw some inferences about the effects of a particular condition on the real world from a simulation study, it is necessary to assume that the general constraints and possibilities created by the INS framework are a realistic representation of the decision environments of real-world decision makers. Critics argue, however, that even if this assumption were correct, the results would still not be a reliable guide to action, since other factors within the simulation, such as personality characteristics, might account for the observed effects.[24] Without microvalidation studies designed to determine whether the experimental manipulations produce the postulated effect on the behavior of the participants, it cannot be said that an effective experimental research vehicle has been created.

The INS validation studies, on the other hand, have been principally concerned with the correspondence of outputs between referent and simulated systems, rather than with the isomorphism of processes, and the assumption underlying these validation studies is that if the input-output relations are similar in the simulated and referent worlds, then the processes probably are also similar. At the bottom of all this disagreement seems to reside the question of what purpose man-machine simulations such as the INS are to serve. Are they "quasi-laboratory" settings that enable us to study questions that cannot be addressed by direct observational techniques, or are they "half-way houses" between partial and complete theories of world politics? From the experimentalist view, the macrovalidity

SUBSTANTIVE FINDINGS 315

studies of INS were clearly a mistake; but the theory-building school would argue that they are precisely what was needed most. It is with the latter that I cast my vote. The validation studies, whatever their shortcomings, provided the basis for what Guetzkow has called the second- and third-generation efforts to construct simulation models of international politics, and it is to the evaluation of these efforts that I will now turn.

Beyond the Inter-Nation Simulation

Although the years 1967-68 seem to mark another shift in the project's focus, the change was not an abrupt about-face, but rather a logical extension of the validation studies. During this period a new man-machine simulation was developed by Paul L. Smoker, called the International Processes Simulation (IPS), and work was begun on a number of all-computer simulation models.

Some of the elements that were eventually incorporated in the IPS were first utilized in an earlier effort on the part of Smoker and others to use the INS in order to study the Vietnam conflict.[25] Drawing upon his own work in transnational phenomena and arms races[26] and upon the findings generated by the validation studies, Smoker created a truly ingenious simulation model.[27] A description of this very complex model is clearly beyond the scope of this paper, yet it is difficult to appreciate the richness of it without knowledge of its structure. This new model incorporates answers to almost all of the specific criticisms that were made about the INS. The economic system includes a private economic sector composed of corporations, partially programmed trade flows, a monetary unit, and diminishing marginal costs of production, as well as economic sanctions that governments can apply against each other. In the political sector, the powers of the decision makers have been restructured to make them resemble more closely those possessed by governmental decision makers. Their resources, for example, are derived from taxation of corporations and citizens, a welcome change from the INS formulation. New decision-making roles were created; each nation has a citizen who earns income, pays taxes, and may engage in demonstrations (peaceful and violent) against his own or another government as well as local and general strikes against corporations. Similarly, the corporation executive director has a variety of activities that he may engage in. The result is a much more intranationally and internationally pluralistic world. As a successor to the INS, the IPS is indeed a substantial contribution.

In order to permit a higher degree of realism, the complexity of the model was greatly increased and its operating procedures also became more complex. Part of this burden was shifted to the computer, since all the programmed portions of the simulation are truly programmed. The logistical demands of the simulation are nevertheless quite high. In spite of this, the IPS is an excellent example of the way in which theoretical insight, empirical evidence, and practical experience can be blended together in a man-machine simulation. In my opinion, the IPS is the best man-machine simulation to be found in the social sciences today.

Smoker immediately began to conduct validation studies, and he proposed eight different ones covering foreign and domestic conflict, economic characteristics, aggression and conflict, alliance formation, crises, arms races, and integration. To date, about one-half of these have been completed.

Since the simulation runs included high school participants in some and adult participants in others, a nation-state system in some and an international system in others, Smoker has been better able to separate the effects of the structure of the model from the effects of the nature of the participants. His analysis of conflict behaviors in the IPS and the referent world revealed interesting differences within the simulation runs and between these and the referent world.[28] A replication of Chadwick's work on the INS indicated that the IPS represented a substantial improvement upon the INS, and a study that was parallel to that of J. David Singer and Melvin Small[29] on the subject of alliance patterns and war revealed substantial convergence between the IPS and the Singer and Small findings.[30] Marvin Soroos examined cross-national activities in the IPS and its referent system of the period 1966-68 and some aspects of crisis behavior in the IPS, in comparison with the findings of Charles McClelland with regard to the city of Berlin.[31]

These studies give a mixed validity picture for the IPS, but on the whole the results look good, although there are areas that apparently need some revision. One of the advantages of the IPS over the INS is that it makes more predictions, and more specific predictions, and therefore is more testable and more amenable to revision that the INS. In spite of these and other clear advantages that the IPS has over the INS, I fear that it will not be widely used until a more convenient variant of the model is produced, as has been the case with the INS.

While Smoker was proceeding to enrich the environment of the participant decision makers, others were leaning more towards the elimination of human participants through all-computer simula-

SUBSTANTIVE FINDINGS 317

tion. One of the first large-scale efforts to produce such a model was the TEMPER simulation, and Guetzkow was instrumental in generating information about this model.[32] He also encouraged work outside his own "shop" along the computer simulation lines[33] and supported a comparative study of the INS, the Political-Military Exercise, and TEMPER.[34]

Within the project itself, Michael R. Leavitt, Jeffrey A. Krend, Allan L. Pelowski, and I were engaged in the construction and evaluation of computer simulation models of international politics from about 1969 until the project ended recently. Leavitt developed a computer model of alliance formation and dissolution utilizing propositions drawn from the traditional literature.[35] Krend reconstructed and updated Oliver Benson's "Simple Diplomatic Game" and worked on the development of computer modules enbodying various formulations drawn from international relations theory.[36] Pelowski experimented with an event-based simulation of the Taiwan Straits crisis.[37] My own work involved converting the INS into an all-computer simulation by the addition of decision-making and information-processing rules and comparing the resultant model, the Simulated International Processer (SIPER), with different referent systems.[38]

While it is perhaps too early to evaluate the significance of the computer simulation work, the decision to shift the project's focus from man-machine to all-computer simulations merits some discussion. Some argue that it is premature to move to computer simulation, since we have so little empirical evidence upon which to build in our field. One reply to this comes from those who take the more formal modeling approach to simulation. They view computer simulation as a way of making logical and mathematical deductions from a set of interrelated assumptions that is suitable for use by nonlogicians and nonmathematicians. Furthermore, since computer simulation involves the exploration of the implications of a theoretical structure, the principal means of evaluation involves assessing how much theoretical insight has been generated, not the amount of predictive power. The assertion is that the exploration of theory, devoid of any specific empirical content or referent, is a legitimate and necessary activity within the scientific enterprise.

Those who take a more empirical view of theory construction are inclined to consider such activities as slightly irresponsible and certainly unproductive. From their point of view, simulation is conceived as a way of integrating a variety of empirically confirmed relationships within a common context, a kind of machine-readable propositional inventory. Without these empirically supported propositions, the output is meaningless as far as the "real world" is concerned.

I take a position somewhere between these two. I personally enjoy working out the logical implications of abstract assumptions, and I think this is a legitimate endeavor in science; yet I also see a need for social scientists to be concerned with the "real" world. I think we have more knowledge in our field then we generally give ourselves credit for, and I don't think knowledge scarcity is the principal obstacle we face today. What is lacking is a framework for organizing the knowledge that we do have and for pinpointing the areas of ignorance that should be given a high priority. This is the primary function of computer simulation at this time, and I think it is a very important one. Operationally, this translates into a theory construction procedure that attempts to incorporate into a computer model the best of our knowledge, including, where necessary, judgment and intuition, until better information is available.

OVERALL EVALUATION

We began this paper by noting that the Northwestern University simulation project was fundamentally different from the other major research projects that are discussed in this volume. Our survey of its activities has revealed the breadth of its scope and the way in which it was dedicated more to the development of methods of inquiry than to the generation of substantive findings as such. Thus our overall evaluation of the project must be based on the broader conception of substantive; in other words, what were the real contributions of the project? I would suggest that the project deserves a very affirmative overall evaluation because of the following contributions: It has sensitized us to the need to be multilevel and multidisciplinary in our orientations; it has caused us to think in more rigorous and complex theoretical terms; it has provided us with an alternative way of addressing vital research questions; it has coordinated our diverse intellectual efforts to construct simulation models of political phenomena; it has served as a vital central node in one of the informal communications networks upon which we depend so much; it has supported and encouraged high-risk research, often carried out by less-than-established scholars; it has facilitated the exploration of new methods for integrating our "islands of theory."

APPENDIX: MAJOR RESEARCH APPLICATIONS OF THE INTER-NATION SIMULATION

<u>Principal Investigators</u>: Richard A. Brody, Michael J. Driver, and Harold Guetzkow
<u>Run</u>: INS-8 (1960)

Richard A. Brody, "Some Systemic Effects of the Spread of Nuclear Weapons Technology: A Study through Simulation of a Multi-Nuclear Future" <u>Journal of Conflict Resolution</u> 7, no. 4 (1963): 663-753. <u>Major findings</u>: The spread of nuclear weapons in a tight bipolar world leads to a reduction in inter-bloc conflict, an increase in intra-bloc conflict, a reduction in bloc cohesiveness, and a fragmentation of the bipolar system.

Michael J. Driver, "A Structural Analysis of Aggression, Stress, and Personality in an Inter-Nation Simulation" (West Lafayette, Ind.: Purdue University, 1965), mimeographed.
<u>Major findings</u>: A lower degree of integrative complexity in cognitive structures, whether due to stress or overall personality organization, leads to lower thresholds for aggression in decision-making behavior.

Michael J. Shapiro, "Cognitive Rigidity and Perceptual Orientations in an Inter-Nation Simulation." <u>Major findings</u>: As Holsti noted with respect to John Foster Dulles, persons with rigid cognitive styles will tend to interpret conflict in moral terms rather than instrumental terms. Persons with very rigid cognitive styles will also be resistant to attitude change.

Richard A. Brody, Alexandra Benham, and Jeffrey Milstein, "Hostile International Communication, Arms Production, and Perceptions of Threat: A Simulation Study." <u>Major findings</u>: Hostile behavior is in general a product of both the hostile behavior of another nation and the perceptions of that behavior. A variety of other elements, such as salience, capability, threat, and perceived qualities of the external nation, are involved in accounting for hostile action.

<u>Principal Investigators</u>: Charles F. Hermann and Margaret G. Hermann
<u>Run</u>: World War I (1961)

Charles F. Hermann and Margaret G. Hermann, "An Attempt to Simulate the Outbreak of World War I," <u>American Political</u>

Science Review 61, no. 2 (1967): 400-16. Major findings: There was substantial similarity between the events in the simulation and the events preceding World War I. The participants were able to identify the historical situation.

Principal Investigators: Wayman Crow and Lawrence Soloman
Run: Western Behavioral Sciences Institute (WBSI) Feasibility Studies (1962)

Wayman Crow and Lawrence Soloman, A Simulation Study of Strategic Doctrines. Major findings: Although the first study of the capacity to delay response did not work out as planned, the second study of Charles Osgood's Graduated Reciprocal Increased Tension (GRIT) strategy demonstrated that after the introduction of tension-reducing actions, tension declined in the simulated international systems as predicted.

Principal Investigator: Allen William Sherman
Run: Negotiation Simulation (1962)

Allen William Sherman, "The Social Psychology of Bilateral Negotiations," (masters thesis: Northwestern University, 1963). Major findings: In negotiations, the negotiator with the higher aspiration level will receive a larger share of the profits. Moreover, the change in a negotiator's aspiration level is positively related to how well he did in the previous negotiation session. Negotiators from smaller countries were found to have higher aspiration levels, and the aspiration levels were not related to personality characteristics.

Principal Investigators: Wayman Crow and John R. Raser
Run: WINSAFE II (1963)

John R. Raser and Wayman Crow, WINSAFE II: An Inter-Nation Simulation Study of Deterrence Postures Embodying Capacity to Delay Response. Major findings: Possession of the capacity to delay response to a nuclear attack has the following results: it increases the perceived strength of a nation and the degree of threat it poses; interest in arms control agreements tends to go down for the nation gaining this capacity, but up for others; the cohesion of a nation's alliance is not changed by CDR, while the cohesion of the opposing alliances tends to lessen; wars occur more frequently and are of greater magnitude when one nation in the system has CDR; and the probability of intended strategic war goes up when one nation in the system has CDR, while the probability of unintended war goes down.

Daniel Druckman, "Ethnocentrism in the Inter-Nation Simulation," <u>Journal of Conflict Resolution</u> 12, no 1 (1968): 45-68. <u>Major findings</u>: Decision makers tend to rate members of their own nations more favorably and rate allies more favorably than enemies. Strong enemies were "respected" more than weak enemies, but weak enemies were "liked" more than strong enemies. The more favorable the ingroup ratings, the less favorable the outgroup ratings. Decision makers with more international interaction were less ethnocentric than those with fewer such contacts.

<u>Principal Investigators</u>: James A. Robinson, Charles F. Hermann, and Margaret G. Hermann
<u>Run</u>: Crisis Simulation (1963)

Charles F. Hermann, <u>Crises in Foreign Policy: A Simulation Analysis</u> (Indianapolis: Bobbs-Merrill, 1969). <u>Major findings</u>: Action is more likely to be taken in a crisis than it is in a noncrisis, if the decision makers perceive that the precipitating agent is hostile and acting deliberately and that an important goal is threatened. In crisis situations, decision makers are no more likely to search for more alternatives, nor consider more alternatives, than they are in noncrisis situations. Affective conflict among the members of the decision-making unit does not make action more or less likely in crisis situations, and contraction of authority within the unit does not make action more likely. Decision makers concur more frequently about which are the endangered goals in times of crisis than in noncrisis. Crisis results in no less of a search for definition of the situation or for alternatives than noncrisis. In crisis situations, decision makers become less confident of their decisions and the search for support increases, as does communication among members of the decision-making unit.

Margaret G. Hermann, "Testing a Model of Psychological Stress," <u>Journal of Personality</u> 34, no. 3 (1966): 381-96. <u>Major findings</u>: The more motivated individuals are to achieve a goal, the more likely they are to perceive the goal as threatened when potentially threatening stimuli are directed toward it, and the more negative effect they experience, the greater are their efforts to cope with it.

Charles F. Hermann, "Threat, Time, and Surprise: A Simulation of International Crisis." <u>Major findings</u>: Crisis decisions engage more individuals than noncrisis decisions. When threat remains minimal, the amount of available time makes little difference in the number of alternatives discussed. At the upper levels

of threat, if decision makers possess more time, it is not used for
generating alternatives. However, in situations perceived by
decision makers as high threat and short time, more alternatives
are considered than in situations perceived as low threat and extended
time. In crisis the rate of communication by a nation's decision
makers to other international actors increases, as does the likelihood
of action. Regardless of the decision situation, nations with larger
capabilities are more likely to engage in external communication
and international activity.

Charles F. Hermann, Margaret G. Hermann, and Robert
Cantor, "Counterattack on Warning or Delay." Major findings:
Decision makers will tend to delay response to a nuclear attack if
they are confident that their own weapons will survive. However,
nations that have substantial basic capabilities but decision makers
who are low in self-esteem, perceive little ambiguity in the identity
of the attacker, interact little in making decisions, and perceive
the world to be tense, will tend to counterattack rather than delay.

James A. Robinson, Charles F. Hermann, and Margaret G.
Hermann, "Search Under Crisis in Political Gaming and Simulation,"
in Theory and Research on the Causes of War, edited by Dean G.
Pruitt and Richard C. Snyder (Englewood Cliffs: Prentice-Hall,
1969), pp. 80-94. Major findings: In crisis situations less search
for alternative courses of action will be made than in noncrisis
situations. In addition, fewer alternatives will be identified and
the search for information will not increase. The decision makers'
confidence in the ability of their decisions to protect the affected
goals is decreased.

Principal Investigators: Wayman Crow and John R. Raser
Run: WINSAFE Replication (1964)

Wayman Crow and John Raser, A Cross-Cultural Simulation
Study. Major findings: The previously noted effects of the capacity
to delay response to a nuclear attack were largely substantiated
with Mexican students. It was found that the Mexican students
tended to spend more time on international issues and less on
domestic issues than their American counterparts.

Principal Investigators: Wayman Crow and Robert C. Noel
Run: East Algonian Exercise (1965)

Wayman Crow and Robert C. Noel, The Valid Use of Simulation
Results. Major findings: Individuals high in "militarism," risk-

taking propensity, and "authoritarian nationalism" chose significantly higher levels of military response than those who were low on these factors. Group discussion of decisions tended to produce more "conservative" judgments than did individuals acting alone. Situational factors did not prove to be strong determinants, although when the opponent nation was presented as aggressive, a higher level of response was more likely.

Principal Investigators: Philip Burgess and James A. Robinson
Run: Ohio State Runs (1966)

Philip Burgess and James Robinson, "Alliances and the Theory of Collective Action: A Simulation of Coalition Processes." Major findings: As predicted by the theory of collective action, the presence of private benefits increased the cohesion among the members of an alliance and resulted in higher ratings of alliance effectiveness by its constituent members.

Principal Investigator: Dennis Forcese
Run: Alliance Cohesion Study (1967)

Dennis Forcese, "Power and Military Alliance Cohesion: Thirteen Simulation Experiments" (Ph.D. diss.: Washington University, 1968). Major findings: The manipulation of economic benefits (utilitarian power) and ideological symbols (identive power) proved to be strong determinants of alliance cohesion, while the use of threats (coercive power) did not increase the cohesion of alliances.

NOTES

1. Harold Guetzkow, "A Decade of Life with the Inter-Nation Simulation," in The Process of Model-Building in the Behavioral Sciences, edited by Ralph M. Stogdill (Columbus: Ohio State University Press, 1970), pp. 31-53.
2. Harold Guetzkow, Chadwick F. Alger, Richard C. Brody, Robert C. Noel, and Richard C. Snyder, Simulation in International Relations (Englewood Cliffs: Prentice-Hall, 1963). See also Hayward R. Alker, Jr., "Decision-Makers' Environments in the Inter-Nation Simulation," in Simulation in the Study of Politics, edited by William D. Coplin (Chicago: Markham Publishing Company, 1968), pp. 31-58.
3. Denis G. Sullivan, "Towards an Inventory of Major Propositions Contained in Contemporary Textbooks in International Relations," (Ph.D. diss., Northwestern University, 1963).

4. Robert C. Noel, "A Simplified Political-Economic System Simulation," (Ph.D. diss., Northwestern University, 1963).

5. George Modelski, "Simulations, 'Realities' and International Relations Theory," Simulation and Games 1, no. 2 (1970): 123-24.

6. Robert Golembiewski, William Welsh, and William Crotty, A Methodological Primer for Political Scientists (Chicago: Rand-McNally, 1969), pp. 291-92.

7. Modelski, "Simulations, 'Realities' and International Relations Theory," op. cit., pp. 117-20.

8. Richard W. Chadwick, "A Partial Model of National Political-Economic Systems," Journal of Peace Research 7, no. 2 (1970): 121-32.

9. Stuart A. Bremer, Simulated Worlds: A Computer Model of National Decision-Making (Princeton, N.J.: Princeton University Press, forthcoming).

10. Chadwick F. Alger, "Use of the Inter-Nation Simulation in Undergraduate Teaching," in Simulation in International Relations, edited by Harold Guetzkow, Chadwick F. Alger, Richard C. Brody, Robert C. Noel, and Richard C. Snyder (Englewood Cliffs: Prentice-Hall, 1963), pp. 150-89.

11. James A. Robinson, Leroy Anderson, Margaret G. Hermann, and Richard C. Snyder, "Teaching with Inter-Nation Simulation and Case Studies," American Political Science Review 60, no. 1 (1966): 53-65.

12. Cleo Cherryholmes, "Some Current Research on Effectiveness of Educational Simulations: Implications for Alternative Strategies," American Behavioral Scientist 10, no. 2 (1966): 4-7.

13. Harold Guetzkow and Cleo Cherryholmes, Inter-Nation Simulation Kit (Chicago: Science Research Associates, 1966).

14. Harry Targ, "The Inter-Nation Simulation: An Elementary School Exercise" (Evanston, Ill.: Northwestern University, 1967), mimeographed.

15. See, for example, Charles F. Hermann, "Validation Problems in Games and Simulations with Special Reference to Models of International Politics," Behavioral Science 12, no. 3 (1967): 216-31; Richard W. Chadwick, "An Empirical Test of Five Assumptions in an Inter-Nation Simulation, About National Political Systems,' General Systems 12 (1967): 177-92; Richard W. Chadwick, "Theory Development through Simulation: A Comparison and Analysis of Associations among Variables in an International System and an Inter-Nation Simulation," International Studies Quarterly 16, no. 1 (1972): 83-127; and John R. Raser, Donald T. Campbell, and Richard W. Chadwick, "Gaming and Simulations for Developing Theory Relevant to International Relations," General Systems 15 (1970): 183-204.

16. Harold Guetzkow, "Some Correspondences between Simulations and 'Realities' in International Relations," in New Approaches to International Relations, edited by Morton A. Kaplan (New York: St. Martin's Press, 1968), pp. 202-69.
17. Modelski, "Simulations, 'Realities' and International Relations Theory," op. cit., pp. 111-34.
18. Dorothy L. Meier, "Progress Report: Event Simulation Project," Simulated International Processes Project (Evanston: Northwestern University, 1965); Dorothy L. Meier and Arthur Stickgold, "Progress Report: Analysis Procedures," Event Simulation Project (St. Louis: Washington University, 1965); and Harry R. Targ and Terry Nardin, "The Inter-Nation Simulation as a Predictor of Contemporary Events," (Evanston: Northwestern University, 1966), mimeographed.
19. Lloyd Jensen, "Foreign Policy Elites and the Prediction of International Events," Peace Research Society, Papers 5 (1966): 199-209, and Lloyd Jensen, "Predicting International Events," Peace Research Reviews 4, no. 6 (1972): 1-65.
20. Terry Nardin and Neal E. Cutler, "Reliability and Validity of Some Patterns of International Interaction in an Inter-Nation Simulation," Journal of Peace Research 6, no. 1 (1969): 1-12.
21. Patrick McGowan, "Some External Validities of the Inter-Nation Simulation," (Evanston, Ill.: Northwestern University, 1972), mimeographed.
22. See, for example, Richard W. Chadwick, "Theory Development through Simulation," op. cit.
23. See, for example, Charles Powell, "Validity Issues in Complex Experimentation" (Los Angeles: University of Southern California, undated), mimeographed.
24. Wayman Crow and Robert C. Noel found that personality characteristics were strong determinants of participants' behavior in the East Algonian Exercise. See Wayman Crow and Robert C. Noel, The Valid Use of Simulation Results (La Jolla, Calif.: Western Behavioral Science Institute, 1965).
25. John MacRae and Paul L. Smoker, "A Vietnam Simulation: A Report on the Canadian/English Project," Journal of Peace Research 4, no. 1 (1967): 1-25, and Jerome Laulicht, "A Vietnam Peace Game: A Computer Assisted Simulation of Complex Relations in International Relations," Computers and Automation 16, no. 3 (1967): 14-18.
26. Paul L. Smoker, "Nation-State Escalation and International Integration," Journal of Peace Research 4, no. 1 (1967): 60-75, and Paul L. Smoker, "Trade, Defense, and the Richardson Theory of Arms Races: A Seven Nation Study," Journal of Peace Research 2, no. 2 (1964): 65-76.

27. Paul L. Smoker, "International Processes Simulations: A Description," in Experimentation and Simulation in Political Science, edited by J. A. Laponce and Paul L. Smoker (Toronto: University of Toronto Press, 1972), pp. 315-65.

28. Paul L. Smoker, "Analyses of Conflict Behavior in an International Processes Simulation and an International System, 1955-60," Simulated International Processes Project (Evanston, Ill.: Northwestern University, 1968).

29. J. David Singer and Melvin Small, "Alliance Aggregation and the Onset of War, 1815-1945," in Quantitative International Politics, edited by J. David Singer (New York: Free Press, 1968), pp. 247-86.

30. Paul L. Smoker, "International Processes Simulation: An Evaluation," paper presented at the Events Data Conference, Michigan State University, East Lansing, Mich., 1970.

31. Marvin Soroos, "International Involvement and Foreign Behaviors in the International Processes Simulation and a Real World Reference System," (Ph.D. diss.: Northwestern University, 1972).

32. Morton Gorden, "International Relations Theory in the TEMPER Simulation," Simulated International Processes Project, (Evanston, Ill.: Northwestern University, 1967).

33. Hayward R. Alker, Jr., "Computer Simulations, Conceptual Frameworks, and Coalition Behavior," in The Study of Coalition Behavior, edited by Sven Groenings, E. W. Kelley, and Michael Leiserson (New York: Holt, Rinehart and Winston, 1970), pp. 369-95; Dina A. Zinnes, Douglas E. Van Houweling, and Richard H. Van Atta, "International System Structure and the Balance of Power Propositions: A Computer Simulation Study" (Bloomington: Indiana University, 1972); and G. Matthew Bonham, "A Computer Simulation of Non-Crisis Information Processing by Foreign Policy Decision Makers," (Berkeley: University of California, 1970), mimeographed.

34. Hayward R. Alker, Jr., and Ronald D. Brunner, "Simulating International Conflict: A Comparison of Three Approaches," International Studies Quarterly 13, no. 1 (1969): 70-110.

35. Michael R. Leavitt, "A Computer Simulation of International Alliance Behavior," (Ph.D. diss.: Northwestern University, 1971).

36. Jeffrey A. Krend, "A Reconstruction of Oliver Benson's 'Simple Diplomatic Game'," Simulated International Processes Project (Evanston, Ill.: Northwestern University, 1970), and Jeffrey A. Krend, "Computer Simulations of International Relations as Heuristics for Social Status, Action and Change," Simulated International Processes Project (Evanston, Ill.: Northwestern University, 1972).

37. Allan L. Pelowski, "An Event-Based Simulation of the Taiwan Straits Crisis," in <u>Experimentation and Simulation in Political Science</u>, edited by J. A. Laponce and Paul L. Smoker (Toronto: University of Toronto Press, 1972), pp. 259-79.

38. Stuart A. Bremer, "National and International Systems: A Computer Simulation," (Ph.D. diss.: Michigan State University, 1970).

CHAPTER

16

SOME INSTRUCTIVE EXPERIENCES GAINED IN SIMULATING INTERNATIONAL PROCESSES, 1957-72

Harold Guetzkow
Wm. Ladd Hollist

Most of the comments of our critics in Chapters 13 through 15 of this volume strike positive, responsive chords. They tempered their retrospections by realizing that most of the critical decisions about the work of the project were made during its initial seven years (1957 to 1964), when the work of Imre Lakatos, among others cited in the three critiques, was unknown. We view our responses as an effort to clarify and explicate rather than to rebut the positions advanced in the three pieces. Seldom is one privileged to have serious, considered criticism of one's work.

This essay also provides a useful setting for elaborating on the way our present simulation research in international affairs can be

---

Preparation of this paper was part of the activities of the Gordon Scott Fulcher Chair of Decision Making at Northwestern University. Wm. Ladd Hollist is associated with the effort begun in 1973 at Northwestern to develop computer simulations for decision making in international affairs (CS-DM-IA). See, Harold Guetzkow, "Collaboration in Computer Simulation for Decision-Making in International Affairs," International Studies Notes 1, no. 1 (1974): 8-9. During his early months of affiliation with the activities of the Gordon Scott Fulcher Chair in the fall of 1974, Dr. Hollist studied the files of the Simulated International Processes (SIP) project with care. He heard the presentations of the critics and the ensuing panel discussion during the International Studies Association's annual meeting in St. Louis in 1974. His insights into the work of SIP are shared in these comments on the critiques and in the reflections on the future of rigorous, systematic research in international relations—and he profits with the senior author in the advantages obtained from retrospective vision.

expected to benefit from the past efforts in the Simulated International Processes (SIP) project and from constructive criticisms of the work. As we realign our postures for future work, we build on their insightful discussions as the latter are informed by advances in scholarly work in international studies.

Because the observations of our critics overlapped a bit, despite their different emphases, it may be more useful to present our responses by topic rather than sequentially by author. In order to avoid the repetition that would be involved in restating each commentary made by the critics, it will be assumed that our reader has studied their three pieces. We will first address issues of methodology, then philosophy of science considerations, and finally we will describe our realigned postures as we proceed now in the post-SIP work of building all-computer simulations for decision-making in international affairs.

META-METHODOLOGY

In developing his essay, Stuart J. Thorson refines the frames of reference within which he evaluates the project. Since SIP focused upon the use of simulation as its methodology, Thorson centers his comments thereon. Inasmuch as SIP was a user rather than a generator of empirical materials, it seems appropriate that Thorson gave less attention to the techniques or "methods" involved in data collection and its analysis as such. Although Thorson seems to point to no fatal flaws in the project's work, he highlights, along with other critics, three areas in which we have profited from our experiences in SIP, namely (1) the isolation of components in our model building, (2) the utilization of "prototypic" variables, and (3) the handling of the ever-present problems involved in gaining greater validity. It seems to us that valuable lessons were learned in these facets of the meta-methodology of SIP.

Experience with the Overall Components of a Model

Thorson's development in Chapter 14 of "an ordered triple, $<s, m, t>$, which identifies which reference reality (s) is being represented (m) in terms of what 'operating rules' (t)" conceives of a simulation as it was defined in the work of SIP, as has been recently reviewed in the context of "models" and "theories" by two of Guetzkow's students.[1] Over the years there has been some wobble in denotation of terms by SIP, as, for example, in its emphasis that the referent materials of SIP are not the "real" world of Thorson's (s) but merely data observations. This distinction was symbolized by Harold Guetzkow when he used quotation marks in the title of his integrative essay on the validity problem, "Some Correspondences between Simulations and 'Realities' in International Relations."[2]

This perspective is also apparent in the partial validation studies of Paul L. Smoker's International Processes Simulation (IPS)[3] and Stuart A. Bremer's Simulated International Processer (SIPER).[4] No <u>direct</u> check was made, nor could be made, of correspondences between the "real" world and the simulated representation of that world. The validation studies checked the correspondences between simulated outputs and sensory observations (data representations of the "real" world).

In project usage, the operating rules (t) often were considered as part and parcel of the representation (m), which also included the "behaviors produced (generated) by the representation" (Chapter 14). It may be useful in the long run to maintain the distinctions introduced by Thorson, as well as to specify explicitly "variables" as part of (m), along with objects ("entities" or "actors") "making up the representation and . . . the relations that are defined on these objects." Later in his essay Thorson himself seemingly misclassifies such variables as bureaucratic loss and consumption satisfaction by including them in his listing of "objects." But these quiverings neither vitiate the basic agreement that Thorson has with the SIP formulations* nor our agreement with his derivative consequences that "this means, as is suggested in Guetzkow, that the kinds of critical methodological tools used to analyze scientific theories can be employed to analyze simulation efforts such as INS";

---

*As an ever-present but supportive critic throughout the development of SIP, because of his full-term membership and then directorship of the Northwestern International Relations program within which SIP operated, Chadwick F. Alger often noted that the categorization of simulations as "all-man," "man-machine," and "all-machine" or "all-computer" misled many as the catch-phrases spread into wide usage. The project's terminology was presented with this caution: "The man-machine base for distinguishing the three varieties of constructions used for simulation of the international system is not to be taken any more seriously than other dichotomous classifications." Harold Guetzkow, "Simulation in International Relations," in <u>Proceedings of the IBM Scientific Computing Symposium on Simulation Models and Gaming</u> (White Plains, N.Y.: International Business Machines Corporation, 1966), pp. 252-54. In spite of this

RESPONSES TO CRITICS 331

and also that "since one component of any simulation is an explicit representation (m) of a referent system, simulations belong to the subclass of theories with explicit models"; and furthermore that "by making the representation (model) explicit, it is possible to efficiently investigate the results of slightly (or grossly) perturbing the representation." (See Chapter 14.)

Lessons Learned in Using "Prototypic" Variables

Thorson, Christensen and Butterworth, and Bremer all question the usefulness of specifying "prototypic" or aggregate constructions of key concepts as variables in SIP. Do criteria of abstraction and simplification justify such loosely derived variable groupings, at least until empirical findings or other decisional criteria suggest otherwise? However, to assert without the benefit of research that variables are gathered into specifiable configurations may not be preferable to hypothesizing that variables are grouped in certain prototypic concepts, the "network" of which then needs to be examined further.

In retrospect, such a methodological decision certainly seems suspect, now that both Smoker and Bremer have demonstrated how more adequately operationalized variables can be employed in their simulations. Yet as the years changed from the 1950s to the 1960s, it seemed the better part of valor to move ahead less assertively, as Guetzkow explained when presenting the "guideposts" used in developing the Inter-Nation Simulation (INS). "In constructing the simulation, whole sets of variables in the complex of national and international life are represented by simplified, generic factors, supposedly the prototypes of more elaborate realities."[5] It is interesting to speculate how this decision would have been taken had the findings of the "Dimensions of Nations" effort[6] been received

---

warning, few persons realized that an alternative categorization of simulations as "unprogrammed," "part-programmed," and "all-programmed" would perhaps have conveyed the essential ideas more adequately, as Alger suggests. Others, surely will find it useful to place simulations within a broader context of "techniques for studying object systems," as did Richard F. Barton when he contrasted "1. Analysis, 2. Man-Model simulation, 3. Man-computer simulation, [and] 4. All-computer simulation." Richard F. Barton, A Primer on Simulation and Gaming (Englewood Cliffs: Prentice-Hall, 1970), Chapter 2.

earlier, enabling its factors to have been incorporated into the INS, as they later were, to an extent, into the IPS. In making comparisons of 14 domestic and foreign conflict variables adapted from Rummel's work for inclusion in IPS, Smoker found that the overall ("TOTAL") factor structure for his IPS simulations was a close approximation to Rummel's 1955-57 findings,[7] suggesting that the original intuitive decision to incorporate the Dimensions of Nations as the backbone of INS had empirical validity of sorts.[8]

However, if the elaboration of variables were carried further, it may be that the participants in INS or IPS would not have been able to react to this added detailing. In fact, Harold M. Schroder, Michael J. Driver, and Siegfried Streufert, in analyzing empirical findings from both their own Tactical Game Task and the Inter-Nation Simulation, found that with greater informational inputs, "we witness a decline in perception," indicating an impaired ability to handle extra materials, that is, additional input variables.[9] Guetzkow's observations of the dozen runs of IPS suggested to him that a saturation point may have been reached and that further additions to the complexity of the situation would simply have overwhelmed many participants.

The programmers of computer simulations can be overloaded, too, just as the participants in a very rich environment are sometimes overwhelmed. In Guetzkow's early discussion of "Granularity Puzzles in Simulating International Behavior," explicit attention was given to the problem of the abstractness of generality with which both entities and variables might be represented in simulations.[10] On the basis of additional experiences in working with all-computer formulations, it seems that the same pressure for "complete" specification arises in the programming process, too.[11] In order to avoid overloading computer program designers, it may also be necessary to evolve a way of changing the focus of detail from time to time.

Thorson's skeptical statement that "without resolving the aggregation and related measurement problems, the idea of variable-parameter validity cannot be applied to the INS in any but an intuitive manner," is well taken, inasmuch as it was only occasionally that the prototypic materials were probed deeply. However, when such variables were examined against empirical materials, incremental improvements in the model could be made in an explicit and rigorous way. The important critiques of the INS by Charles D. Elder and Robert E. Pendley are landmarks in the probing of prototypic variables. For example, in working with economic variables in the INS, the two researchers found, among other things, that "those aspects of the INS model relating to CS_{min} to CS_{max} (CS = Consumption Standards) as stated in Programmed Assumptions 11 and 12 and as reformulated in this paper are empirically tenable."[12] In working with political variables, the two found that "INS theory is in fact a fairly good predictor of stability, of particular officeholders that the theory explains."[13] Inasmuch as these probes were already available in 1966, even though they were essayed into final manuscript in 1970, it was possible for Smoker to utilize the Elder-Pendley findings in the reformulations constituting his International Processes Simulation (IPS).[14] However, such an intensive exercise was seldom undertaken with prototypic variables, substantiating Bremer's comment that the use of prototypic variables "impaired communication and exchange between the simulators and the nonsimulators," as well as having "greatly compounded solidation problems." (See Chapter 15.)[15]

A major thrust in our current efforts to "modularly" expand existing all-computer simulations of international affairs is to disaggregate some of these black-box, prototypic variables and to specify relationships among their component parts. The data-based research of numerous scholars, as well as our own data-analysis efforts, which are aimed at facilitating incorporation of modules into existing, more comprehensive simulations of international relations, make such specifications possible. The core variables of SIP project simulations do not occupy some inviolate status; they, like all components of a usable simulation, exist as starting points open to modification and elaboration.

The Validity Problem

Thorson makes an evaluation of Charles Hermann's criteria for assessing simulation validity,[16] as do Christensen and Butterworth in Chapter 13. The latter two critics argue that three of Hermann's criteria (internal validity, face validity, and variable-parameter validity) jointly confront the issue of how much confidence can be placed in the Inter-Nation Simulation (INS), and by extension both the International Processes Simulation (IPS) and the Simulated International Processer (SIPER), as a research methodology.

The Christensen and Butterworth definition of internal validity, "the degree to which variations among runs can be accounted for by identifiable relationships within the game of simulation," is consistent with the project's interpretation. Confidence in the internal validity of a model is a necessary criterion for simulation validation.

Yet, internally valid models do not a priori assume that "reality itself (s) . . . is expected to have very low variance." (Chapter 14.) A model is internally valid if it allows one to track the variance in the referent system, knowing how similar changes in a simulation result in changes in simulated outputs. A model incorporating stochastic processes, or a model with the "noise" of human surrogates, can be internally valid if the effects of such stochastic changes can be traced to changes in the model inputs. Thorson's contention is repudiated in the empirical work of Terry Nardin and Neal E. Cutler who found that, in the six INS runs of Meier and Stickgold[17] with four INS runs of Nardin, the interrelationships among their seven variables were reproduced in 19 out of 21 cases.[18] Nardin and Cutler also checked the external validity as well as the internal validity variables in the two sets of runs. They "find more correspondence in the realm of reliability (internal validity) than in the realm of (external) validity. That is, while the magnitude of the inter-correlations for all pairs of variables is relatively well predicted from one series of simulation runs to the next, the predictions of reference system relationships generated by the Inter-Nation Simulation are less accurate."[19]

Thorson applies this same line of thought to his critique of the Hermanns' event validity, namely that "such a use of event validity requires a commitment to a low-variance external world." Events were searched at the microlevel by Hermann and Hermann in their study of the outbreak of World War I, matching 18 simulation events with reported historical events.[20] Does it not increase one's confidence in the simulation when the Hermanns report that "For half of simulation events (9 out of 18), they were able to find historical actions which seemed to be equivalent in physical format" but then decrease confidence when they further indicate only "four of the 18 simulation events took place at approximately the point in time that the simulation was intended to replicate?"[21] Of course, one is not restricted to a search for punctiform isomorphisms in analyzing events; Donald T. Campbell noted in the 1960s that one may also gain confidence in one's theory through "pattern matching,"[22] as the Hermanns then demonstrate in their following discussion of "hypotheses."[23] Although Thorson is correct in stating that neither internal nor event validity is either necessary or sufficient, the validity of a simulation would seem greater if it has both punctiform and pattern homomorphisms. The question is whether a simulation can represent the events and patterns thereof more adequately as one progressively modifies simulation inputs and parameters. This seems to be the situation when one compares the validity studies of the three generations of the constructions developed in the study of Simulated International Processes.[24]

Thorson points out that SIP's validation studies focused primarily on "behavior-preserving morphisms," while largely overlooking questions of "function-preserving morphisms" and "structure-preserving morphisms" yet the Inter-Nation Simulation (INS) does represent process functions and process structures, and such features are even more explicitly simulated in the International Processes Simulation (IPS). (See Chapter 15.) However, it would be a misunderstanding of Thorson if one attached ordinary, nonmathematical definitions to Thorson's use of Bernard P. Ziegler's Language.[25] In the vernacular of the social sciences, behavior-preserving morphisms emcompass both structural features and the interactive processes involved in the simulation of an international system. In fact, if one examines the validity findings on INS from 1957 through 1968, as are presented in Tables 5, 8, and 17 of the integrative essay on "Correspondences,"[26] one notes that of the 33 studies of the "articulated, systematic variety," a quarter at most are merely descriptive, while all others seem to contain one or more components in which structural features and dynamic processes are involved, since the researchers have studied the relationships among the variables, not merely describing inputs and outputs. This is somewhat remarkable, in that Susan D. Jones and J. David Singer report that of the 158 data-based studies in the QIP field which appeared through 1969, almost half are substantially limited to descriptive materials.[27] As Modelski notes, "for purposes of global simulation and replication of overall complexity the INS as then constituted was more successful in simulating small-group than large-scale multiple interdependent worlds."[28] In Smoker's redevelopment of INS as IPS there is a shift from the emphasis on entities of the Inter-Nation Simulation to an emphasis on structure and functions in International Simulated Processes (emphasis ours). Bremer's SIPER, (Simulated International Processer) as symbolized in the acronym, explicitly embodies variables in flux, eschewing static descriptions.

SIP'S IMPLICIT PHILOSOPHY OF SCIENCE

Christensen and Butterworth (Chapter 13) provide a useful comparative discussion of philosophies of science, with an introduction to the thinking of Imre Lakatos.[29] These authors view the actions taken in SIP as more defensible in terms of its operating philosophy of science than in its words. A converse conclusion would be more worrisome: it would seem that changes in the philosophy of science guiding SIP project work and current efforts have metamorphosed in much the same way and direction that philosophies of social science have generally been evolving.

We fundamentally agree with Christensen and Butterworth's view of the process of theorizing. "Theorizing is a cybernetic process.

It is capable not only of self-steering, a corrective use of feedback, but also of directed creative learning, an anticipatory use of feedback." These authors note that SIP project investigators have contributed insights into how this cybernetic process unfolds, at least as a self-correcting cybernetic process. We yet today view the key element in the applied philosophy of science of SIP project efforts, and in the now ongoing work in Computer Simulations for Decision-making in International affairs,[30] as developing operating models of international relations theory that are open to modification in accordance with corrective and anticipatory feedback. We see the evolution from Guetzkow's original Inter-Nation Simulation (INS) through Smoker's International Processes Simulation (IPS) and Bremer's Simulated International Processer (SIPER) occurring as a function of this cybernetic feedback process, whereby model components are modified and newly incorporated in subsequent simulations of international relations theory. As mentioned above, simulations are operative theories, and they evolve in much the same ways as verbal theories do. Indeed, perhaps the central contribution of the models coming out of the Simulated International Processes (SIP) project is that they specify roughly hewn blocks of theory that are amenable to refinement and consolidation.

Despite continuing loose usage of the term "data" to describe the outputs of simulation exercises, there seems to be an emerging consensus that the results of simulation can hardly be thought of as empirical. The distinction between data-grounded material and simulation outputs becomes even clearer when one moves from man-computer to all-computer formats, despite the predilection of the social psychologist working with human subjects in experiments to overlook his problems in extrapolation from laboratory to "natural" situations, as has been emphasized by William J. McGuire.[31] Nevertheless, it may be that the working development of this distinction, now understanding that it is fruitful to treat simulation, be it manual, man-computer, or all-computer, as simply another form of theory, subject to all the difficulties involved in the use of analytical models (including the formal mathematico-deductive ones), as well as traditional verbal speculation in vernaculars, is the project's most fundamental contribution to the development of our philosophies about social science.

The project's most "speculatular" development in the context of the philosophies of science is Paul Smoker's illumination that the validity problem is double-faced, as is appreciated by Christense and Butterworth (Chapter 13), consisting not only of an obligation to check out the correspondences between the simulation and the "real" world, thereafter modifying the former, but "to take the complementary position and to evaluate the 'real world' relative to the 'model world' incorporated in a simulation."[32] Inasmuch as the project could not even recruit ambassadors or foreign secretaries for participation in our runs, it is little wonder that Smoker's important insight could not be implemented by securing the cooperation of heads of state, say in the weeks before their appearances in New York at the opening of a General Assembly of the United Nations, to consider the policy and design implications of our simulation research. In a less euphoric mood, Smoker himself warned that "complex models have complex properties and it is wise not to take the findings of this study [his IPS analyses] too seriously."[33]

A REALIGNMENT OF RESEARCH DIRECTIONS

Bremer concludes Chapter 15 with an evaluation of the computer simulation work associated with SIP project activities and suggests directions in which such endeavors might fruitfully proceed. He notes the contention of some scholars that computer simulations of international relations are premature, "since we have so little empirical evidence upon which to build in our field." He also notes that one response to this criticism comes from those employing a formal, more mathematical modeling approach to simulation. Such persons consider the exploration of theory, "devoid of any specific empirical content or referent, . . . legitimate and necessary activity within the scientific enterprise." Those who take a more empirical view of theory, notes Bremer, consider simulation to be productive when used as a vehicle for "integrating a variety of empirically confirmed relationships within a common context, a kind of a machine-readable propositional inventory." To such scholars, "Without these empirically supported propositions, the [simulation] output is meaningless as far as the 'real world' is concerned."

Bremer takes a position somewhere in the middle. He argues the need for a "framework to organize the knowledge that we do have and pinpoint the areas of ignorance which should be given high priority," and asserts that computer simulations of international affairs serve this function in part. He also confirms the need for ongoing data-based research. He then writes, "Operationally, this translates into a theory construction procedure that attempts to incorporate into a computer model the best of our knowledge, including, where necessary, judgment and intuition, until better information is available."

We come to similar conclusions, but we wish in our final remarks in this essay to go further in suggesting specifically how this research strategy might unfold. Guetzkow has long been an advocate of trying to be cumulative in the generation of knowledge for decision making.[34] Eclectic research has been a recurrent theme in SIP project goal statements and objectives. Bremer, however, notes that because of the use of techniques of "contracting out," certain tasks or subprojects may have hindered this overall effort in SIP, suggesting that some of these products may yet merit greater integration. This general indictment may hold even if the more comprehensive SIP products (Guetzkow's INS, Smoker's IPS, and Bremer's SIPER) are viewed as successfully moving in a cumulative direction.

One sees a gradual shift in project emphasis, from an initial interest in simulations dominated by human surrogates of decision-makers and some decision-making processes, to an interest in those in which actor interactions and relationships became more formally explicated and programmed in all-computer exhibitions of relationships. Nigel Howard, a mathematician and operations researcher with considerable experience in the British Foreign Office, noted that "many theorists including Guetzkow himself believe that the mixed (man-computer) simulation is no more than a stepping-stone to the fuller automatic simulation."[35]

We offer three explanations of these trends from experience in SIP, the logic of which continues to condition the present focus of our work.

1. The employment of the Inter-Nation Simulation (INS) as a quasi-experimental laboratory setting was seen as having only a secondary usefulness,[36] especially in light of failures to consistently attract "real-world" policy makers as simulation participants. It became more and more clear that the long-term utility of INS-type simulations lay in the provision of vehicles for mounting macrotheory representations of international affairs. Guetzkow and many of his associates enrolled in the "theory-guiding school" for purposes of furthering model explication and exploration in international relations. (See Chapter 15.) For these purposes the macrovalidity studies of INS seemed to be needed more than the microvalidity studies, the absence of which Charles A. Powell laments.[37]

2. The growing number and the improving quality of empirical researches in international relations[38] have made us more confident of hypothesized relationships among the variables. The speculative foundations of the original INS model can now be reinforced or changed in light of such researches. Research in international relations is gradually moving us "beyond conjecture."

3. Advances in computer hardware and software, including the development of languages suitable for simulations, have lessened the technical difficulties of mounting mathematically specified, programmed models of international affairs on computers.

Each of the critical essays that make up Chapters 13-15 ends with an overall assessment of SIP. Perhaps because they wanted to compensate for their negative comments, the critics were overly generous. Thorson argues that "had SIP not existed, a large number of us would be unable, for a wide variety of reasons, to do what we do today." (Chapter 14.) In their section on "INS Reexamined" Christensen and Butterworth show dramatically that we were actually working in terms of a "sophisticated methodological falsification," in the term of Imre Lakatos, even though his work was published in 1970* after almost all of the commitments had been made and the work of the project was wrapped up, but for our final report to our chief sponsors.[39]

After having developed the third-generation simulation in the context of SIP, it is remarkable that Bremer still was able to appreciate the achievements of the second-generation construction. In Chapter 15 he indicates, "In my opinion, the IPS is the best man-machine simulation to be found in the social sciences today," although we would be more inclined to agree with his judgment were it limited to studies within international relations. It is interesting to note that Bremer, who was assigned the task of making the substantive evaluation, failed to include such a facet of the evaluation in his final list of seven contributions. It is hoped that this phase of the critique of IPS may be undertaken at another time, after the papers of the project are available in a more convenient and accessible medium.

It just may be that scholars in the latter part of the twentieth century are too busy reading the ever-increasing mountain of preprints, prints, and reprints that crosses their desks from their multiple memberships in our informal "colleges" to have time left to study their colleagues' work with care, let alone write critiques thereof as have Thorson, Christensen and Butterworth, and Bremer, thanks to the good offices of Francis W. Hoole and Dina A. Zinnes, the editors of this volume. It was possible to commission critiques as SIP developed; although an attempt has been made in this essay to incorporate the perspectives given by the earlier critiques as part of our learning experiences in SIP, it may be useful to at least mention the persons by name, with citation of their critical essays: Hayward R. Alker,[40] William D. Coplin,[41] Karl W. Deutsch and W. Dieter Senghass,[42] George Modelski,[43] and Robert L. Pfaltz-

---

*My colleague, James A. Caporaso, confirms my judgment that none of us in the International Relations Program at Northwestern University had contact with Lakatos until his work appeared in print in 1970.

graff, Jr.[44] Every so often one gets another surprise or two, in addition to that unexpected delivery of SIPER by Bremer.[45] One day Ernest-Otto Ezempiel of Frankfurt wrote that Reimund Seidelmann, one of his students, had completed his dissertation, giving a detailed and exhaustive critique of INS.[46] It is to be hoped that Seidelmann's monograph, which has been developed in the tradition of thoroughness of German scholarship, will soon be translated so that all of us who are concerned with the simulation of internation affairs may learn yet further lessons for our future work together.

It may be too soon to evaluate the project's main contributions to the study of international relations. In the teaching arena many have plunged ahead in the use of the INS and versions thereof, such as The Industrial College of the Armed Forces (ICAF) in its World Processes Simulation (WPS)[47] and its International Relations Exercise,[48] the more recent PRINCE simulation (A Programmed International Computerized Environment) at Syracuse University,[49] and Robert C. Noel's Political Institutions Simulation (POLIS).[50] In terms of substantive validity, there has been improvement in the degree of correspondence between the outputs of the model and data from the "real" world (referent system) as one moves from the Inter-Nation Simulation (INS) to the International Processes Simulation (IPS) and Simulated International Processer (SIPER). Dependin upon the criteria one uses, INS presents encompassing correspondences in IPS, increasing the base INS figures some 5 percent to 15 percent.[51] The comparison of INS and SIPER by Bremer reveals that in the 42 relationships examined, SIPER yields correspondence in "just under two-thirds of the relationships" while INS presents correspondences in "just under one-half."[52] The central lesson to be drawn from this experience seems to be that gains were realized as Smoker and Bremer refined both their simulations and the analyses of the referent variables. In terms of the ongoing and accelerating arms race, perhaps the most significant "project contribution" is found in Richard A. Brody's piece on nuclear proliferation.[53] His forecast of deep changes in the alliance system occurring with the spread of nuclear capability coincides with the "realities" of the world of the 1970s. The most important, overall contribution of the project, however, may well be in stimulating and setting the pace for the development of simulations, within both the government and academia.

We and others sense a need to "add up" and hopefully synthesize the expanding pockets of knowledge of international affairs. We wonder whether this endeavor can be furthered through the modular expansion and refinement of existing all-computer simulations of international relations, such as Bremer's Simulated International Processer (SIPER) and Coplin and O'Leary's Programmed Internati

Computerized Environment (PRINCE). With these objectives, our research plan proceeds in roughly four interrelated phases to be applied in various substantive areas. An initial phase (Phase I) concentrates on identifying "mini-models" that specify certain hypothesized relationships postulated as operating in a given arena of interest. Effort is made to probe for alternative explanations of phenomena considered relevant to global affairs. These "mini-models" are explicitly formulated in equations suitable for both empirical analysis and computer simulation (Phase II). Each "mini-model" is then confronted by empirical data in a regression analysis framework. From this analysis model parameters are estimated. The resultant models are next programmed as independently operable computer simulations. Comparative analysis of these computer models provides a useful means for exploring "alternative futures" (Phase III). As a further step in adding up these "mini-model" theories, each modular computer simulation is incorporated into and explored within one or both of our comprehensive simulations of international affairs (Phase IV). Additional discussion of this approach to synthesizing knowledge of global relations is presented and illustrated by Hollist and Guetzkow.[54]

Hopefully it is apparent even from this brief statement of our ongoing research strategy that we indeed have learned to seek an eclectic mix of deductive and inductive knowledge concerning international relations. By exploring alternative explanations of varying phenomena and subjecting each to empirical analysis as a further basis for deciding on its theoretical significance, we endeavor to expand existing all-computer statements of theories of global affairs. More than ever before, perhaps, we can fruitfully bring together fragmented "theories" and data-based research findings into complex networks of interrelated variables. Now may be the time to mount these "variable systems" as computer simulations, the operation of which may highlight unexpected interaction effects among variables. As more and more scholars advocate and employ all-computer simulation in their own social science research on international affairs,[55] it may become increasingly beneficial to work collaboratively. Given the magnitude of the task, it is imperative that more and more of us work integratively with others in the years ahead.

NOTES

1. Randall L. Schultz and Edward M. Sullivan, "Developments in Simulation in Social and Administrative Science," in Simulation in Social and Administrative Science: Overviews and Case-Examples,

edited by Harold Guetzkow, Philip Kotler and Randall L. Schultz (Englewood Cliffs: Prentice-Hall, 1972), pp. 3-47.

2. Harold Guetzkow, "Some Correspondences between Simulations and 'Realities' in International Relations," in New Approaches to International Relations, edited by Morton A. Kaplan (New York: St. Martin's Press, 1968), pp. 202-69.

3. Paul L. Smoker, "An International Processes Simulation: Development, Usage, and Partial Validation" (Ph.D. diss.: Lancaster, England: University of Lancaster, 1968), Part I.

4. Stuart A. Bremer, "National and International Systems: A Computer Simulation" (Ph.D. diss.: Michigan State University, 1970), and Stuart A. Bremer, Simulated Worlds: A Computer Model of National Decision-Making (Princeton: Princeton University Press, forthcoming).

5. Harold Guetzkow, "Structured Programs and Their Relation to Free Activity Within the Inter-Nation Simulation," in Simulation in International Relations: Development and Teaching, edited by Harold Guetzkow, Chadwick F. Alger, Richard A. Brody, Robert C. Noel, and Richard C. Snyder (Englewood Cliffs: Prentice-Hall, 1963), p. 105.

6. Rudolph J. Rummel, "Dimensions of Conflict Behavior Within and Between Nations," General Systems Yearbook 8 (1963): 1-50.

7. Ibid., p. 17.

8. Paul L. Smoker, "International Relations Simulations," Peace Research Reviews 3, no. 6 (1970): 45-52.

9. Harold M. Schroder, Michael J. Driver, and Siegfried Streufert, Human Information Processing: Individuals and Groups Functioning in Complex Social Situations (New York: Holt, Rinehart and Winston, 1967), p. 99 and Chapters 5-7.

10. Harold Guetzkow, "Simulation in International Relations," in Proceedings of the IBM Scientific Computing Symposium on Simulation Models and Gaming (White Plains, N.Y.: International Business Machines Corporation, 1966), pp. 261-67.

11. Bremer, Simulated Worlds, op. cit., and William Ladd Hollist and Harold Guetzkow, "Cumulative Research in International Relations: Empirical Analysis and Computer Simulation of International Armament Processes" (Evanston: Northwestern University, 1975), mimeographed.

12. Charles D. Elder and Robert E. Pendley, "A Test and Reconstruction of the Economic Model in an Inter-Nation Simulation" (Evanston, Ill.: Northwestern University, 1970), p. 33, mimeographed. Programmed Assumptions 11 and 12 are described in Guetzkow, "Structured Programs," op. cit., pp. 123-26.

13. Robert E. Pendley and Charles D. Elder, "An Analysis of Political Constraints in an Inter-Nation Simulation: A Critique in Terms of Contemporary Theory and Data on the Stability of Regimes and Governments" (Evanston, Ill.: Northwestern University, 1970), p. 21, mimeographed.

14. Smoker, "An International Processes Simulation," op. cit., pp. 53-54.

15. Charles D. Elder and Robert E. Pendley, in "Simulation as Theory Building in the Study of International Relations" (Evanston: Northwestern University, 1970), mimeographed, sketch the heuristics of work with prototypic variables. This essay is an overview of their more detailed work in Elder and Pendley, "Test and Reconstruction of the Economic Model," op. cit., and Pendley and Elder, "Analysis of Political Constraints," op. cit., which are specifically in the economic and political domains of the INS.

16. Charles F. Hermann, "Validation Problems in Games and Simulations with Special Reference to Models of International Politics," Behavioral Science 12, no. 3 (1967): 216-31.

17. Dorothy L. Meier, "Progress Report: Event Simulation Project," Simulated International Processes Project (Evanston, Ill.: Northwestern University, 1963).

18. Terry Nardin and Neal E. Cutler, "Reliability and Validity of Some Patterns of International Interaction in an Inter-Nation Simulation," Journal of Peace Research 6, no. 1 (1969): 1-12.

19. Ibid., p. 5.

20. Hermann and Hermann, "An Attempt to Simulate," op. cit., Table 2.

21. Ibid., pp. 409-10.

22. John R. Raser, Donald T. Campbell and Richard W. Chadwick, "Gaming and Simulation for Developing Theory Relevant to International Relations," General Systems 15 (1970): 188-91.

23. Hermann and Hermann, "An Attempt to Simulate," op. cit., pp. 410-12.

24. Industrial College of the Armed Forces, World Politics Simulation III-1969 (Washington, D.C.: Simulation and Computer Directorate, 1969), p. 20.

25. Bernard P. Ziegler, "A Conceptual Basis for Modeling and Simulation," International Journal of General Systems 1, no. 2 (1974): 213-28.

26. Guetzkow, "Some Correspondences between Simulations and 'Realities,'" op. cit., pp. 224, 235, and 250.

27. Susan D. Jones and J. David Singer, Beyond Conjecture in International Politics: Abstracts of Data Based Research (Ithaca: F. E. Peacock, 1972); Paul J. Rossa, "Classification of Jones and

Singer Abstract," Northwestern University Memorandum, Evanston, Ill., August 13, 1974, p. 2

28. George Modelski, "Simulations, 'Realities' and the International Relations Theory," Simulation and Games 1, no. 2 (1970): 131.

29. Imre Lakatos, "Falsification and the Methodology of Scientific Research Programmes," in Criticism and Growth of Knowledge, edited by Imre Lakatos and Alan Musgrave (Cambridge: Cambridge University Press, 1970), pp. 91-197.

30. Guetzkow, "Collaboration in Computer Simulation," op. cit.; Wm. Ladd Hollist and Harold Guetzkow, "Cumulative Research in International Relations: Empirical Analysis and Computer Simulation of International Armament Processes" (Evanston: Northwestern University, 1975), mimeographed.

31. William J. McGuire, "Some Impending Reorientations in Social Psychology: Some Thoughts Provoked by Kenneth Ring," Journal of Experimental Social Psychology 3, no. 2 (1967): 124-39.

32. Paul L. Smoker, "Social Research for Social Anticipation," American Behavioral Scientist 12, no. 6 (1969): 11.

33. Paul L. Smoker, "Simulating the Human World," Science Journal 6, no. 7 (1970): 53.

34. Harold Guetzkow, "Long Range Research in International Relations," The American Perspective 4, no. 4 (1950): 421-40, reprinted in International Politics and Foreign Policy: A Reader in Research and Theory, edited by James N. Rosenau (New York: Free Press, 1961), pp. 53-59.

35. Nigel Howard, The Field of Nations: An Account of Some New Approaches to International Relations (London: Little, Brown and Company, 1971), p. 100.

36. Guetzkow, "Simulation in International Relations," op. cit.

37. Charles A. Powell, "Simulation: The Anatomy of a Fad; A Critique and a Suggestion with Respect to its Use in the Study of International Conflict," Acta Politica 3, no. 3 (1969): 313-14.

38. Jones and Singer, Beyond Conjecture, op. cit.

39. Harold Guetzkow, "Final Report: Simulated International Project, Advanced Research Projects Agency, Contract no. SD 260," (Evanston, Ill.: Northwestern University, 1972).

40. Hayward R. Alker, Jr., "Decision-Makers' Environments in the Inter-Nation Simulation," in Simulation in the Study of Politics, edited by William D. Coplin (Chicago: Markham Publishing Company, 1968), pp. 31-58.

41. William D. Coplin, "Inter-Nation Simulation and Contemporary Theories of International Relations," American Political Science Review 40, no. 3 (1966): 562-78.

42. Karl W. Deutsch and W. Deiter Senghass, "Towards a Theory of War and Peace: Propositions, Simulations and Reality," paper presented at the meetings of the American Political Science Association, September 1969.

43. Modelski, "Simulations, Realities, and the International Relations Theory," op. cit.

44. Robert L. Pfaltzgraff, Jr., "Simulation and International Relations Theory: A Comparison of Simulation Models and International Relations Literature" (Medford: Tufts University, 1972), mimeographed.

45. Bremer, "National and International Systems," op. cit.

46. Reimund Seidelmann, <u>Simulation in Internationaler und Auswartiger Politik: Die Inter-Nation Simulation (INS) und ihre Verwertbarkeit fur Analyse und Prognose</u> (Frankfurt: Verlag Anton Hain, Meisenheim am Gian, 1973).

47. Industrial College of the Armed Forces, <u>World Politics Simulation</u> (Washington, D.C.: Simulation and Computer Directorate,

48. Industrial College of the Armed Forces, <u>International Relations Exercise</u> (Washington, D.C.: Simulation and Computer Directorate, 1971).

49. William D. Coplin, Michael K. O'Leary and Stephen L. Mills, "Analytical Description of PRINCE" (Syracuse: Syracuse University, 1971).

50. Robert C. Noel, "Inter-University Gaming and Simulation Through the POLIS Network," paper presented at the meetings of the American Political Science Association, September 1971.

51. Smoker, "An International Processes Simulation," op. cit., Chapters 6-10.

52. Bremer, "National and International Systems," op. cit., p. 146.

53. Richard A. Brody, "Some Systematic Effects of the Spread of Nuclear Weapons Technology: A Study Through Simulation of a Multi-Nuclear Future," <u>Journal of Conflict Resolution</u> 7, no. 4 (1963): 663-753.

54. Hollist and Guetzkow, "Cumulative Research in International Relations," op. cit.

55. Nazli Choucri and Robert C. North, <u>Nations in Conflict: National Growth and International Violence</u> (San Francisco: W. H. Freeman, 1975); J. David Singer, "The Historical Experiment as a Research Strategy in the Study of World Politics," <u>Political Inquiry</u> 2, no. 1 (1974): 41-44; Jeffrey S. Milstein, <u>Dynamics of the Vietnam War: A Quantitative Analysis and Predictive Computer Simulation</u> (Columbus: Ohio State University Press, 1974); Francis W. Hoole, "The Simulation of Alternative Budgetary Futures for the

World Health Organization," in The United Nations: Problems and Prospects, edited by Edwin Fedder (St. Louis: Center for International Studies, University of Missouri, 1971), pp. 143-64; Jay W. Forrester, World Dynamics (Cambridge: Wright-Allen, 1971); Donella H. Meadows, Dennis L. Meadows, Jorgen Panders, and William W. Behrens, III, Limits to Growth (New York: Universal Books, 1972); Mihajlo Mesarovic and Eduard Pestel, Mankind at the Turning Point: The Second Report to the Club of Rome (New York: E. P. Dutton, 1974); Barry B. Hughes, "Computer Simulation of Political Decision-Making: A General Approach and Prototype" (Cleveland: Case Western Reserve University, 1974).

PART V

THE 1914 PROJECT (STANFORD STUDIES IN INTERNATIONAL CONFLICT AND INTEGRATION)

CHAPTER

17

**THE STANFORD STUDIES
IN INTERNATIONAL
CONFLICT AND
INTEGRATION**
Robert C. North

Since their inception in 1958, the Stanford Studies in International Conflict and Integration have been involved in crisis studies and investigations into some of the longer-term antecedents of war. The intent from the start was to develop partial theories, or proto-theories, and test them as "scientifically" as possible. By this we meant that the investigations should advance from explicit assumptions, observe recognized canons of inquiry, and yield findings that could be accepted or rejected according to some rational criteria and that would tend to be cumulative. To date, no investigations have been made into cases of integration, but from the early days of the project, the concept of integration has been inherent in the efforts that have been made toward the development and testing of theory. In the course of the research we have encountered many more difficulties than were initially anticipated, but despite much trial-and-error experimentation, several blind alleys, and the expenditure of vastly more time than we had foreseen as necessary, we are generally pleased with our progress so far. It is rewarding, moreover, that such high professional criteria are invoked by our critics in this volume for the assessment of our work.

The research enterprise—both the crisis studies and the investigation of the longer-term antecedents of war—has proceeded from a number of fundamental assumptions. Our study of international conflict has been undertaken in terms of nesting systems and subsystems involving complicated interactivity of variables throughout: both "horizontally," between systems, and "vertically," within a single system. Through a shift in perspective, a subsystem may be viewed as a system with subsystems of its own. It is assumed that any substantial change in one component of a system, whatever its causes, is likely to affect other components of the system and thus the system as a whole. Moreover, any substantial change in one system, whatever its causes, may be expected to affect any other system with which the first system is interacting.

Living systems and systems of living components, as well as some nonliving systems, share certain general characteristics. Each system encompasses an information or signal subsystem, which includes the capability of making choices or decisions. Each system also encompasses an energy-processing system; that is, it is capable of acquiring energy from the environment; processing it in various ways; and using it, through some effector system, to act or perform work.

All human activity involves energy. Inside the individual every cognition, every feeling and every decision involves some release of biological energy. And every human activity in the external environment involves some release of biological energy, or a combination of biological energy and mechanical energy impounded from the environment.

Living systems and systems of living components display allometry, which refers to the tendency of a more efficient system, one that can metabolize or otherwise transform energy more effectively than others, to control a greater share of the available energy-rich resources than a less efficient system. The concept of allometry is relevant to studies of national power, expansion, domination, and conflict. Living systems are also characterized by equifinality, which means that different systems can reach comparable states by different paths of activity or development. This latter consideration has complicated the formulation and testing of theoretical propositions at almost every step.

Using content analysis and interaction analysis, the crisis studies focused primarily upon the information, or signal, system. We were concerned with the ways in which the leaders of one country perceived and responded to the actions of other countries in a situation of crisis. A major challenge was the measuring of the intensity of affect, or emotion, associated with the quantifying of perceptions, the various levels of conflict on which actions were taken, and the analysis of relationships between the two.

The study of the longer-term antecedents of war involved causal modeling, simulation, and "retrospective forecasting." The data included levels and rates of change in "home" population, domestic territory, colonial territory, national income, military expenditures, trade, alliances, and the like, together with interaction, or event data. The causal modeling involved a system of simultaneous equations.

When the overall project was begun, the intent was to complete the World War I study in a few months and then move on to another crisis. That was in the autumn of 1958. By the early 1960s we were still plowing our way through the six weeks between the assassination of Francis Ferdinand in late June 1914 and the outbreak of war in early August. It was a vastly larger undertaking than we had anticipated. Having decided upon content analysis as a methodology, we discovered that the translation of pertinent documents from the various languages into English was a formidable task to begin with and that the coding of materials was a task of Herculean proportions. As we experimented with machine-content analysis, Ole R. Holsti made a successful adaptation of the General Inquirer, which Philip Stone and others had developed at the Massachusetts Institute of Technology. When he began teaching at the University of British Columbia, Holsti took this part of the research with him. Over the years, the graduate students who worked on the project became the sustaining asset. Numbers of them rose above the drudgery to make contributions of the greatest importance.

By 1964 it was possible to assess in a general way what the yields and limitations of the crisis studies were going to be. The limitations were largely unavoidable, at least for the time being. Some of them stemmed from the methodology, which despite automation was still enormously expensive, in terms of time and human patience and effort as well as of money. Thousands of hours still had to be spent in the collection and hand preparation of documents before any analysis could be undertaken. We experimented with simplified "high speed" programs of analysis that required less manual work and had some success, but with considerable losses of information, precision, and nuance. Perhaps when the technology of optical scanning is further developed, some of this massive preliminary drudgery can be eliminated, but in the meantime the efficient application of content analysis is limited to relatively small amounts of documentation. The other limitation emerged from the nature of the crisis phenomenon itself.

In some respects, a crisis is like the tip of an iceberg. It is a critical part, but still only a small part, of a much larger reality "down below." A crisis does not merely erupt: it is the outcome of powerful antecedent and ongoing processes. From our studies of crisis, moreover, it appears that the intense, escalatory processes that characterize the phenomenon are so unstable that successful "crisis management" is likely to be chancy at best. Disturbing also was the fact that our investigations had so far been confined almost wholly to the informational, signal, decision-making aspect of the systems under study. Where did the energy acquisition, energy transformation, and energy application aspects of the system fit in? There was very little systematic work in political science, social psychology, or sociology to provide any precedent. What about allometry? Was there not something in the concept of allometry that might clarify some important tendencies in human behavior generally, as well as the relative growth and exercise of power among nations and differences in their ability to acquire, control, and exploit territory and a wide range of critical resources?

Our conclusion was not that the study of crises should be discontinued. Certainly there are "better" and "worse" ways to make decisions in crises, and it is highly desirable that statesmen and their advisers know as much as possible about their dynamics. In a nuclear age, however, it is probably of equal importance to learn as much as possible about what "drives" nations to behave the way they do and about how crises might be avoided.

In the early 1960s we began searching a number of standard works, such as the Cambridge ancient, medieval, and modern history series; Toynbee's A Study of History; and a number of other studies, reading rapidly and keeping a list of the "causes" of various wars as they were identified by distinguished historians. Suddenly history began to make sense. The undertaking was so fruitful that we continued the search through a number of anthropology books and appropriate ethnologies.

In the course of this reading we found many references to the "nature of man," to his greed, ambitions, love of power, reactions to uncertainty, fear and threat, and so forth; yet overall, our list of "causes" turned out to be considerably shorter than might have been expected. What caught our particular attention were scattered references to population growth, the effect of new technologies, and the unrelenting search for resources. Again and again it was noted that ample resources often contributed to increased populations. Increased populations, in turn, generated demands for more resources. Also, a technological advance often enabled a people to reach out for more resources. Some technologies made it possible to uncover domestic resources that had previously been unattainable or to put old resources to new uses; but often a relatively advanced technology, in the sense of applied knowledge and skills, gave a people the capabilities, organizational cohesion, and political as well as military power to conquer their neighbors or threaten them into submission, enslave them, drive them off, or exploit them in any number of ways and thus gain access to new resources. Frequently they invaded sparsely settled, low capability regions that were rich in needed resources.

This was explosive history, but the historians, while making frequent, if widely scattered, references to all these phenomena, seemed never to have related them systematically or to have perceived the theoretical potentials inherent in them. To the extent that these propositions "tested out" when used in other modes of analysis, a certain cumulativeness might be achieved. Nazli Choucri began collecting and preparing demographic, economic, military, and political data for a series of trend analyses.

Again the task was far more difficult and time-consuming than we had initially imagined. The months were extended into years. Completing her doctorate at Stanford, Nazli moved on to Queens University, and thence to M.I.T. In Cambridge she began working with the TROLL system, which brought a whole array of rigorous statistical controls to bear upon time series analysis. By this time she was using econometric techniques and had begun developing a system of simultaneous equations that was an enormous advance over the arrangement of equations we had been using. Although we were still dissatisfied with several aspects of what we had done, the work began to look almost respectable. It was none too soon; 14 years had now elapsed since the inception of the project. Fortunately, Holsti's book was in press.

Since the beginning of the project, we have used three broad types of data: attribute data, cognitive data, and action data. The attribute data fall into two main categories of variables: fundamental "master variables," such as population, technology, territory, and energy and other resources; and allocational data, such as investments in agriculture, industry, and services and expenditures for the military and for health, education, and welfare. The cognitive data include perceptions, attitudes, and decisions, the affects or emotions that influence attitudes and decisions, statements of goals and interests, policies, and the like. The action data include imports and exports, troop movements, currency flows between nations, and the like; and also metricized or scaled action data, such as those data produced by Charles McClelland, by the Lincoln Moses-Richard Brody scale, by Edward Azar, and others.

In the long run the development and refinement of new tools and methodologies should make it feasible to use all three types of data simultaneously and interactively in computerized modeling, simulation and forecasting. These capabilities, we believe, will make possible a whole range of rigorously controlled historical and futuristic studies that even a few years ago could not have been seriously proposed. We expect the late 1970s and early 1980s to be extremely fruitful in this regard.

CHAPTER

18

A PHILOSOPHY-OF-SCIENCE ASSESSMENT OF THE STANFORD STUDIES IN CONFLICT AND INTEGRATION

James A. Caporaso

SCOPE OF A PHILOSOPHY OF SCIENCE ASSESSMENT

When asked to contribute this section on philosophy of science, I confess I had a certain amount of confusion about the nature of the task. This led to several questions, of which the most fundamental were the following. What is a philosophy of science evaluation? What kinds of issues does it expose? What kinds of evaluative criteria does it suggest? In particular, how would such an evaluation differ from a "substantive" evaluation? I hope the editors of this volume will forgive me for doing violence to their categories, but looking back, it now appears that this lack of a clear distinction in my mind was a healthy thing. In what follows, I enumerate five "philosophy of science" criteria, but these criteria should be part of any sound evaluation, not just one based on special philosophy of science principles. A philosophy of science evaluation is merely an evaluation with certain universal scientific principles in mind. Ideally, we should not have to talk about philosophy of science, nor about methodology for that matter. When our own research practices become sufficiently informed by sound philosophical principles and

---

I would like to express my thanks to Gordon Hilton, Mark Levine, Raymond Duvall, and Rob Mahoney, as well as to the editors of this volume, for their helpful comments. I would also like to express my gratitude to the Carnegie Foundation for International Peace (Geneva) for providing facilities used in writing this paper.

when these principles cease to be "principles" and become "research habits," talk of them will be unnecessary.

THEORY AND ITS EVALUATION

The central focus of the philosophy of science is the critical evaluation of scientific theory, particularly the logical structure of theory. At times the philosophy of science almost merges with its sister disciplines of sociology of science, as with Thomas Kuhn;[1] history of science, as with Paul K. Feyerabend;[2] and epistemology of science, as with Campbell and Popper.[3] Despite this, it retains a distinctive focus in its concern with the grounds for scientific knowledge in general and the scrutiny of scientific theory more specifically.

Given the crucial role of "theory" in what is to follow, a brief discussion of this term is in order. I define a theory as a deductively organized, logically interrelated set of hypotheses that serves as an explanation for some specified behavior.[4] A theory has three components: (1) A series of empirically uninterpreted concepts, some of which are variables, rather than object concepts such as Napoleon, West Germany, or the Democratic Party; (2) rules of relations among these concepts that provide a determinate structure for the hypotheses;* and (3) some empirical interpretation of these concepts. The first two components represent the "modeling" stage of theory. The world is represented and rehearsed in symbolic form, but is not yet tested against experience. The first two components correspond to what is often called "theory construction," while the third, assuming it proceeds from the prior two stages, corresponds to "theory testing." The third and last step is provided by a set of rules of correspondence that assign definite empirical content to the variables in the theory. At the lowest level this is a problem of finding operational definitions of a concept. At another level it is a problem of concept validity; and at still another level it is a question of assigning a magnitude (scale value) to the indicators of the concepts.

There are also some auxiliary concepts that need to be defined. A hypothesis is a single statement of relationship among variables.

---

*These rules are logical terms such as "if", "then," "not" (that is, if a then b), which provide syntactical invariance for the system. Sometimes these rules are very weak, as in "if a is sufficiently strong, then b," or "if a, then sometimes b."

A model is a set of uninterpreted concepts and their relationships. A conceptual framework, or approach, is merely a set of concepts to orient inquiry without either specified relations or empirical interpretation.

CRITERIA FOR THEORY EVALUATION

The criteria that are useful in evaluation of theory are somewhat more varied than is normally assumed. I will suggest five criteria: deductiveness, scope, parsimony, falsifiability, and empirical fit.

<u>Deductive Power</u>. A theory is usually thought of as highly deductive if, with the help of a few general statements (axioms), a large number of more concrete propositions (theorems) can be derived. This could be measured roughly by comparing the number of theorems to axioms, a theory being more deductive the higher the theorem-to-axiom ratio. A "theory" with no theorems would be a collection of ad hoc statements.

There are several reasons why a deductively formulated theory may be desirable.[5] Arranging the hypotheses in a deductive way encourages the researcher to tease out all the logical consequences of a few basic ideas. By doing this it is possible to generate testable consequences of a theory that are quite different on substantive grounds.* Also, deductive organization should facilitate the identification of those strategic hypotheses that, if tested, will maximize the implicative strength of the results. By "implicative strength" I mean the number of sentences in the theory for which a particular test will serve as evidence, that is, "have implications."

<u>Scope or Generality</u>. Theories that have broad scope are to be preferred over those that are more limited. There are two aspects to the generality criterion. First, a theory may offer a general explanation that applies to a large number of units (unit generality), nation-states, cities, or formal organizations. Such a theory would have no terms in it referring to the proper names of units. Second, a theory may provide an explanation that extends to a larger number of variables; that is, it explains a greater range of phenomena (variable generality) as opposed to explaining a constant range of phenomena in more places.

---

*For example, Durkheim tested his theory of suicide across religious groups, different family categories, and various occupational categories.

Parsimony. Hopefully the earlier discussion made it clear that
theories are more than extended descriptions and summaries of
data; rather, theories attempt to reduce large amounts of data to
order by appealing to simplifying principles. Parsimony is a variation of the simplifying functions of theory. In concrete terms,
parsimony means "fewness of parameters" and uncomplicated functions
in the analysis of the data.

Falsifiability. What this criterion requires is very simple; it
requires that a theory be refutable in principle. The greater the
number of independent ways a theory can be refuted, the better the
theory. Of course, a theory can be falsified by failure to reject the
null hypothesis or to conform to a desired r^2 or by showing that a
supposed relationship is really spurious. What I have in mind,
however, is closer to Karl Popper's notion of falsifiability.[6] For
Popper a theory is falsifiable to the extent that its predictions are
risky or improbable. "The international system will have some
violence in the 1980s" has a high probability of being true. "The
international system will have more violence in the 1980s than in
the 1970s" is less probable. "There will be a world war in 1984
involving the United States, Japan, France, the Soviet Union, and
Sweden" is still less likely. It is possible that each of these predictions* was drawn from a deductive and parsimonious theory. What
makes the last statement preferable to the other two is its riskiness
or low a priori probability. In the evaluation of theory, then, we
are interested in predictions that, if "unenlightened by the theory
in question, we should have expected an event which was incompatible
with the theory."[7]

Fit, or Empirical Adequacy. Any political theorist will be anxious
for his theory to "fit the facts" or to "account for the observations."
The primary reason for constructing a theory is to explain a particular field of behavior. Three classes of criteria are suggested:
(1) measures of improbability of relationships (How likely is it that
this relationship is non-random?); (2) measures of strength of relationships; and (3) statements about the form of the relationship.

One standard measure of improbability is the statistical test
of significance. We utilize the significance test by testing parts
(hopefully theorems) of our theory against experience and ask to

---

*As stated, these three assertions are not really predictions,
since there is no "if . . . then" structure. They come closest to
forecasts. The assumption here is that the occurrences of these
specific events were deduced from a theory.

what extent the relations we find are less likely than the ones we would expect from the laws of probability.* This baseline underlies a good deal of our statistical practice. It supplies our expectations about the null hypothesis and its critical limits, and it serves as the denominator of the analysis of variance ratio.[8] Measures of the strength of association are less controversial. The square of the product-moment correlation coefficient, r^2, provides a commonly accepted measure of strength. The form of the relationship is the functional relationship among the variables, such as the linear, cubic, or step change variables.

THE STANFORD STUDIES IN CONFLICT AND INTEGRATION

The Stanford Studies in Conflict and Integration is an extensive project under the central direction of Robert C. North. However, since important contributions to the project have been made by numerous people, many of whom have left Stanford, it is important to delimit the literature under review here.[9] Basically, I see the project taking place in two stages: the crisis stage and the long-term conflict stage (from 1870 to 1914), in which the underlying political, economic, and geographic causes of the conflict spiral are seen to rest. I will proceed by examining these two phases separately.

EVALUATION OF THE CRISIS STUDIES

The Stanford Studies in Conflict and Integration began as an intensive examination of the events leading up to World War I. The major research goal was to understand the general processes of hostility, threat perception, and decision-making under crisis conditions.[10] The two crises that the authors† study are the 1914 crisis leading up to World War I and the Cuban Missile Crisis of 1962. Both of these "events" describe what the authors would call

---

*Strictly speaking, there is not one, single set of "laws of probability." These laws differ slightly if the probability distribution is generated by assumptions about sampling error as opposed to "urn randomization" or any number of other assumptions.

†There are various authors involved in this part of the project. These include Robert C. North, Ole R. Holsti, Richard A. Brody, Dina A. Zinnes and Howard E. Koch, Jr.

"a situation of unanticipated threat to important values in restricted decision time." (emphasis in original).[11] In their effort to understand crisis behavior, the authors adopted a two step, mediated stimulus-response model and applied it at the level of national decision makers. This is a simple, closed-loop model, as depicted in Figure 18.1

S is thought of as a stimulus from the environment that may or may not be perceived by another actor.[12] A response (R) is a reaction of an actor to some stimulus initiated by another actor. Both S and R are behavioral and provide no information about either perceptions or intentions. This is where r and s come in: the "r" term stands for the perception of S (stimulus input) by the target country, and s suggests the way this perception is translated into a set of vicarious "plans" about how to respond to S. As Holsti, North, and Brody point out, r corresponds to the "definition of the situation" by a national actor,[13] while s corresponds to the complex ways in which the external environment is modeled, "rehearsed," and vicariously played out with various plans functioning as "decision sets."[14] This model is considerably richer than an unmediated S-R model, in which any stimulus is automatically translated into a response. Under this general S-r:s-R rubric, the authors test a variety of propositions having to do with the conflict spiral, the relationship between military mobilization and the perception of hostility, and the effects of crisis on decision making.

Let me turn first to the paper by North, Brody, and Holsti on the conflict spiral leading to the outbreak of World War I.[15] In many ways this is an important article, in that it provides for the first systematic empirical testing within the proposed conceptual framework. Starting within the basic S-r:s-R model, the authors proceed to ask under what conditions a crisis leads to the reaction process of reciprocal hostility, perception, and the escalating conflict spiral. Initially they are interested in the r:s part of the model, that is, the perceptions by one state of another's actions and the formulation of "plans," intentions, and courses of action toward the other state. The authors find contradictory results for the Dual Alliance and the Triple Entente. There is a correlation (Pearson's r) of .87 between the Dual Alliance's perception of the Triple Alliance. However, the coefficient for the Triple Alliance's perceptions of the hostility of the Dual Alliance with their own expressions of hostility is only .33 and not statistically significant.

Since the S-r:s-R model is a general model of unrestricted scope, this inconsistent evidence poses some problems in evaluation. One interpretation of the results is that there is a standoff between accepting or rejecting the theory, since one set of results was supportive and another unsupportive. The difficulty with this view

FIGURE 18.1

Stimulus-Response Model of Crisis Decision Making

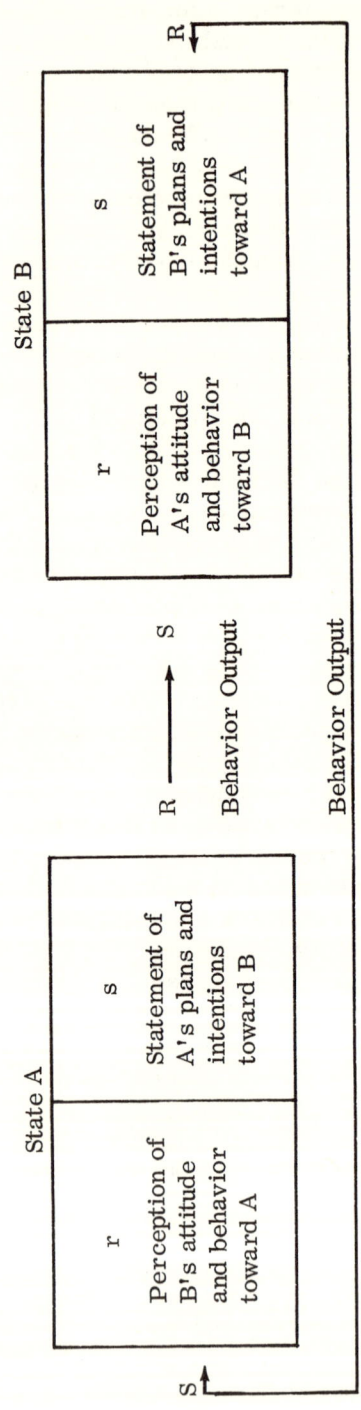

Source: Ole R. Holsti, Robert C. North and Richard A. Brody, "Perception and Action in the 1914 Crisis," in Quantitative International Politics: Insights and Evidence, edited by J. David Singer (New York: The Free Press, 1968), p. 133.

is that supportive and unsupportive evidence have an entirely different status in the logic of theory testing. If a test is confirmed by the data, we merely mean that it has not been disproved, that it is consistent with observation, as many other theories may also be; but if a test of a theory produces negative results, we are compelled by the canons of logic to reject the theory. It has been pointed out that it is this asymmetry between the logical inconclusiveness of confirmation and the logical "certainty" of disconfirmation that lies at the basis of Popper's attachment to falsification.[16] If one accepts these arguments, it is not defensible to count positive and negative evidence equally.

There are other possible responses. The theory may be rejected, or special circumstances may be appealed to in the form of an ad hoc explanation, or the different coefficients may be described without any attempt to reconcile contradictions. The route the authors chose was to introduce an ad hoc explanation. During the period under examination, England was involved in a domestic conflict situation and allegedly "for much of the six week period was not focusing on the Continental situation."[17] If we accept this specially tailored explanation, the anomaly disappears and the theory is preserved. If we reject ad hoc explanations as inherently inadmissable, then the theory must be rejected or at the very least reformulated to include the new variable.

From these initial tests the authors go on to test the same hypothesis (perception of hostility is related to intentions of hostility), using data on the frequency of perceptions rather than on the intensity of perceptions. That is, they looked at how many (frequency) hostile perceptions there were as opposed to how hostile (intensity) the perceptions were. Though there seems to me to be a fundamental conceptual difference between these two measures, they are nevertheless used to test the "same" hypothesis. This time the correlation coefficients are statistically significant for both the Dual Alliance and the Triple Entente.[18] This leaves us with some unanswered questions: (1) Why do we have an inconsistency between the results for the two alliances? (2) Why do we have different results for the frequency and intensity measures of hostility? (3) If the answer to the first question is the special hypothesis concerning England, why does this not also affect the results based on the frequency measures? Concerning this last point, I would expect that an additional burden on the attention span of a government would have a greater effect on its quantity of communication than the affective content of that communication. (4) Finally, what are the conceptual differences between the frequency and intensity measures? What concepts are we tapping with these two measures? An approach to these questions within an explicit measurement framework would have been very helpful. In the absence of an explicit measurement discussion informing the reader about the ways in which the abstract concepts were coordinated with operational indicators, it is difficult to make a disciplined choice between the two measures.

One of the drawbacks of the 1914 crisis studies was that it focused only on a crisis that had a known outcome—war. Thus it was not really defensible to conclude that decision-making under crisis conditions leads to war. For this reason Holsti, Brody, and North attempted to examine the Cuban missile crisis.[19] In this study the authors attempted to link up all four variables in the S-r:s-R model. They used the actions of the United States and the Soviet Union during the October Crisis and scaled these actions from one to ten on the dimension of "degree of violence." This served as the information on the S and R components. Then they content-analyzed all the publicly available documents relevant to certain Soviet and U.S. decision makers and utilized this as the perceptual data (s and r). The data analysis showed that the pattern of Soviet and U.S. perceptions corresponded very closely with the actual violence as reflected in the action data. This indicated that both the Soviet Union and the United States perceived each others' actions accurately. Similarly, as the actual level of violence in the behavioral data declined (S and R), perception of it declined, as did the statements of intent toward the respective crisis partner. The result of all this was that both countries responded (R) at the "appropriate" level, that is, roughly at the level of the input stimulus.[20] This, at least, is the language provided by the authors. At a more specific level the results seem more equivocal. Spearman rank order correlations are used to describe the fit of the data. No significance tests are provided. Though the coefficients are very high, they are based on a limited number of observations (six and seven) and are therefore likely to be unstable.

Let us assume that the theory does fit the data: then what does it confirm, and how do we incorporate the results of this research into the 1914 studies? It may at first seem strange that the model can be confirmed in both World War I and the Cuban Missile Crisis, since one crisis terminated in war while the other did not; but oddly enough, war is not really part of the theory. In one strict interpretation of the S-r:s-R model, there is nothing stated about where the action-reaction process will lead. The major predictions of the theory are only that certain of the terms will be linked. However, another interpretation is that violent actions will lead to the perception of hostility, to reciprocal violence, and to hostile perceptions in an escalating positive feedback process. This interpretation is supported by the authors, as follows:

PHILOSOPHY OF SCIENCE ASSESSMENT 363

The general proposition can be stated in somewhat more detail as follows: If state A—either correctly or incorrectly—perceives itself threatened by state B, there is a high probability that A will respond with threats of hostile action. As state B begins to perceive this hostility directed toward itself, it is probable that B, too, will behave in a hostile (and defensive) fashion. This threatening behavior by B will convince A that its initial perceptions were correct, and A will be inclined to increase its hostile (and defensive) activity. . . . Thereafter, the exchanges between the two parties will become increasingly negative, threatening and injurious.21

From this it appears that the S-r:s-R model is asserting more than covariations among the four variables in the model. However, an additional hypothesis is needed to produce escalation, the conflict spiral, and war. This is a hypothesis about how one actor (or both) overreacts to another's behavior, either in terms of perceptual distortions (r), exaggerated threats (s), or responses (R) at a level of violence that is greater than the original hostile stimulus (S).

Thus in evaluating the model we really have at least three substantive interpretations. First, we could interpret the S-r:s-R model as a model of international escalation as described previously. If this interpretation is accepted, the Cuban missile crisis invalidates the model, since continued escalation did not occur. Second, we could adopt the position that a nation will perceive and respond to hostility at exactly the same level as the original violence. This model would seem to lead to an equilibrium at whatever level the violence is initiated. However, a slight relaxation of the assumptions of this model would allow for small changes in acceleration or deceleration of hostility. Third, we could say that the S-r:s-R model provides no guidance to questions of this sort, that is, whether escalation, deescalation, or equilibrium is predicted, and that all it does do to orient inquiry is to provide a general framework or set of categories for talking about the subject matter. If this interpretation is adopted, then we merely have two descriptions of crisis behavior and no empirical tests relevant to the refutation of any theory at the grand level. We still have a series of important middle-range propositions that can be evaluated independently of the S-r:s-R model, however.

There are other important articles dealing with crisis behavior,22 but these are superseded for the most part by the more recent and comprehensive book by Ole Holsti, Crisis, Escalation, War.23 This book is important not only because it is the most coherent statement of the findings of the first phase of the project to date, but also because it involves a real addition to and elaboration of the assumptions of the S-r:s-R model as originally stated. Prior to this book, peculiar as it sounds, "crisis" was not really a variable in the Stanford Project. Though it was on the minds of the researchers and though, indeed, crises were chosen as the object of investigation, they nevertheless functioned as constants during the actual research process. Recall the definition of crisis as "a situation of unanticipated threat to important values and restricted decision time."[24] None of the key concepts in this definition—"unanticipated threat," or surprise and threat if these are viewed as separate; "importance of values being threatened"; and "amount of decision time"—enter into the S-r:s-R model, and consequently, none enter into the empirical tests.* The closest one can come to these concepts is "the perception and expression of hostility," but even hostility seems conceptually quite independent of threat. A nation might perceive itself as an object of hostility but not feel threatened because of its greater strength or physical isolation. All this is not to say that a crisis was not present in 1914 or 1962 but only that it was not built into the theory as a measured variable.

It is one of the virtues of Holsti's book that he partially replaces this constant with variable terms such as "crisis-induced stress" and "perceived time pressure." The overall model is presented in Figure 18.2, in which there are ten causal arrows that link together and give coherence to a set of individual propositions. However, of the ten arrows, only two can be deleted while still preserving all the information (lines B to F and B to G). In other words, these arrows represent the only real deductions in the model. The others remain as basic hypothetical statements. Nevertheless, while the theory is not powerfully deductive, it is certainly not ad hoc either. Furthermore, there are a number of implicit deductions in the model that have not been spelled out. For example, one could easily draw arrows from "crisis-induced stress" to variables C, D, and E.

From this general model Holsti proceeds to test two sets of hypotheses, the first concerning time perception and the second related to the perception of decisional alternatives. Overlooking

---

*For example, Zinnes writes about "hostility" and "perception of hostility," while Holsti, North, and Brody write about "violent behavior" and "perceived hostility." See Dina A. Zinnes, "The Expression and Perception of Hostility in Pre-War Crisis: 1914," and Ole R. Holsti, Robert C. North, and Richard A. Brody, "Perception and Action in the 1914 Crisis," both in <u>Quantitative International Politics: Insights and Evidence</u>, edited by J. David Singer (New York: Free Press, 1968).

FIGURE 18.2

Stress, Time, and Decision Making

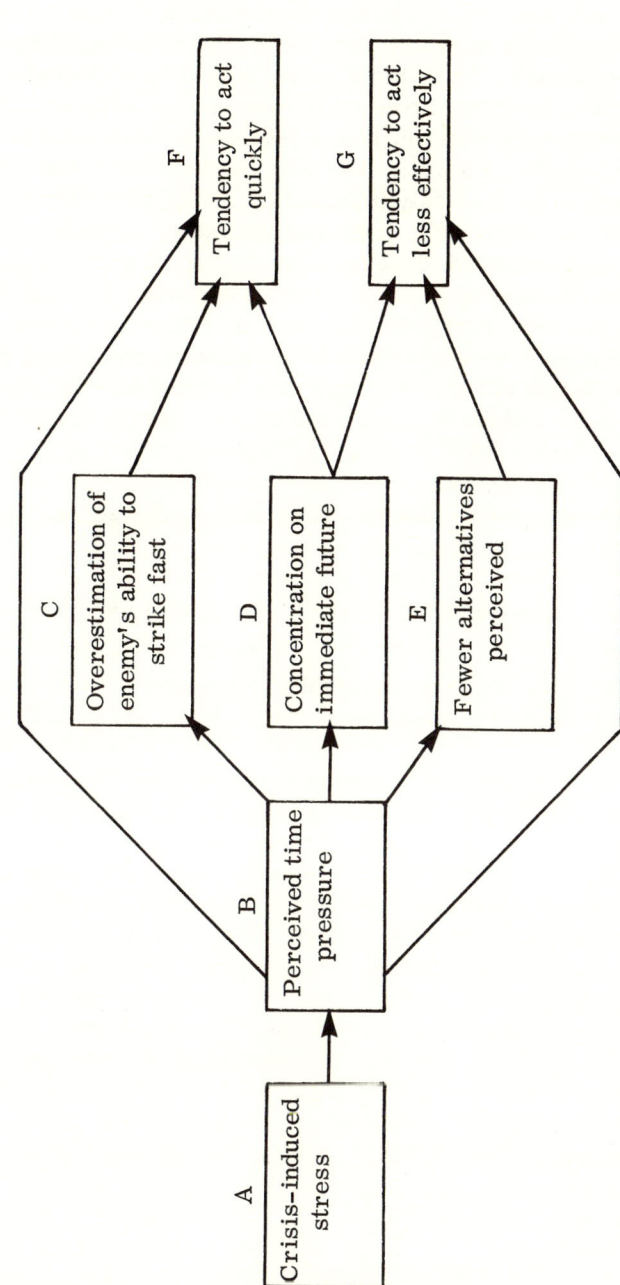

Source: Ole R. Holsti, Crisis, Escalation, War (Montreal: McGill-Queens University Press, 1972), p. 122.

nuances from hypothesis to hypothesis, Holsti tested each proposition by providing nonparametric measures of association and tests of significance (Goodman-Kruskal gamma). The results showed that the tests were almost uniformly significant.[25] Holsti does not rest content with demonstrating statistical significance, but also takes care to eliminate the most plausible of the rival hypotheses.

In summary, then, this book fares well by philosophy of science standards. Though not powerfully deductive, the theory is clear, parsimonious, falsifiable, and of potentially broad scope, and it seems to fit the data well. The only reservation is that the laws of the theory are stated only in terms of the improbability of the relationships and their strength; nothing is said about the form of the relationship, although it would seem that the form of relationship is crucial in relation to the reciprocal behavior of decision makers under stressful conditions. As Dean G. Pruitt points out, in the study of joined reaction systems, the function describing each party's reaction is one of the most important determinants for the outcome.[26] Since we are ultimately interested in whether decision making under these conditions leads to an upward spiral and war or deescalation and peace, it seems necessary to ask more than whether stress is related to perception of time, alternatives, and so on.

GENERAL EVALUATION OF CRISIS STUDIES

In addition to the more detailed commentary, some general questions should be raised about the status of the stimulus-response framework. My interpretation of this framework is that it is not a theory at all in any strict sense but rather a meta-language, a language within which one can intelligently discuss other languages, such as sets of propositions. This meta-language is used to launch the testing of a series of more specific propositions that are in no sense logical deductions of the framework, but merely statements that fit loosely under some generic labels and that can therefore be talked about in a standardized vocabulary. It is even questionable whether the generic terms "stimulus" and "response" are given independent empirical interpretation, that is, whether the rules of correspondence are logically independent of the rules specifying the relationships between stimulus and response. Such independence would be a minimum requirement for an empirical test of the stimulus and response terms; yet it is unlikely that we will identify activities in the environment as stimuli that do not have a very high probability of eliciting a response. Similarly, a response is not just any kind of undirected behavior, or even one the causal antecedents of which we are unlikely to trace out easily; rather it is an activity that is responding to some stimulus. B. F. Skinner seems to accept this openly when he argues that portions of behavior are called stimulus and response only if they are lawfully related; in Chomsky's paraphrase, "if the dynamic laws relating them show smooth and reproducible curves."[27] Though the authors conceptualize stimulus and response as independent occurrences, they are not independent except in the most restricted sense.

My final criticism of the crisis phase is perhaps the most fundamental and applies to the bulk of the crisis literature, with the important exception of the Holsti book. This concerns the ambiguity with which the linkages among the key terms have been specified. Recall the basic S-r:s-R model outlined in Figure 18.1. We can see that there is a relationship among the component terms so that S→r→s→R. However, we are not told anything more about the nature of this relationship, such as how much of a unit change in r there is for every change in S; and we are not told whether the perception of the stimulus will be at the same intensity level as the stimulus itself, higher than the stimulus or lower than the stimulus. If answers to questions of this sort had been supplied by the general model, the structure of relationships would have been more determinate and hence more readily falsifiable. To put it differently, a theory that specifies the level at which each term reacts to every other term would make for a theory that is potentially compatible with a greatly reduced range of empirical outcomes, and thereby a riskier theory. This not having been done, the structure of the theory becomes permissive and agreement with observation is possible under a variety of substantively quite different outcomes. It is consistent with an escalation; with a conflict spiral resulting in war; with a dampening of tension-hostility and deescalation; and with static equilibrium, in which a response is met at the exact level of the stimulus, with this exchange going on indefinitely. It may also be consistent with different mixes of these, such as a response pattern that is sometimes above the stimulus level and sometimes below it. In fact, the only constraint the model places on the data is that there be some relationship between each successive pair of terms (S-r, r-s, s-R).

The absence of more specific links among the concepts is especially troubling in that our primary substantive interest is with the kind of reaction process. We want to know if escalation, deescalation, or equilibrium will occur, and on what these different processes depend.

In sum, a weakness of the links among the theoretical concepts makes for a permissive theory, one that is at ease with diverse empirical outcomes. This makes the theory less corrigible, less sensitive to error, and less prone to rejection or reformulation. As a consequence, the different substantive outcomes of the Cuban Missile Crisis and the crisis before World War I have no effect on the theory, simply because the theory specifies nothing relevant to these differences.

THE DETERMINANTS OF VIOLENCE STUDIES

Moving from the crisis studies to the second phase, in which Choucri and North focus on the broader determinants of international expansion, conflict, and violence, involves a fundamental switch in perspectives.[28] While the crisis studies gave us a close-up, detailed picture of the psychological, political, and organizational pressures involved in decision making under stressful conditions, in this phase we are presented with an aerial view of the structural dynamics of a much longer period and with a less neatly bound subject matter. The crises of 1914 and 1962 lasted approximately six weeks and ten days respectively, as defined by the researchers. In contrast, the period focused on by Choucri and North lasted 45 years, from 1870 to 1914.* The transition is not only an abrupt one in terms of the length of the time period and the neatness of the organizational boundaries, but it also demands a switch from an analysis based on the psychological variables of perception, motivation, hostility, and threat to a more structural account of behavior in which our eye is trained on the consequences, intended and

---

*The authors' choice of 1870 as the initial year of their time frame is an excellent one, if we are to judge by the economic history literature of the period. In his excellent survey, Hobsbawn notes that while the first phase of the industrial revolution, the textile period, had taken root in England as early as the middle of the eighteenth century, the second phase, based on coal, iron and steel, did not gather steam until the latter half of the nineteenth century. See E. J. Hobsbawn, <u>Industry and Empire</u> (Middlesex, England: Penguin Books, 1968). Similarly, David Landes puts the beginnings of industrial expansion in 1750, but these early stirrings of growth were confined to England. However, "the period from 1850-1873 was Continental industry's coming-of-age." See: David S. Landes, <u>Unbound Prometheus: Technological Change and Industrial Development in Western Europe from 1750 to the Present</u> (Cambridge, England: University Press, 1972), p. 193.

PHILOSOPHY OF SCIENCE ASSESSMENT   369

unintended, of variables such as population growth, technology, military expenditure, and colonial expansion.

The theory of violence that Choucri and North offer rests on three general sets of variables, the "dynamics" of which may radically shift from one stage of development of the conflict to the next. The first step of the theory is based on the distribution of attributes and capabilities among nations.

> The crucial variables are population, resources, and technology, where technology refers to the general level and rate of development of human knowledge and skills in a society. A combination of growing population and developing technology imposes rapidly increasing demands upon resources. To meet these demands a society tends to develop specialized capabilities. The greater the unsatisfied demands and needs in a society and the greater the capabilities, the higher is the likelihood that national activities will be extended outside territorial boundaries.[29]

There is a three-way interaction here of population, technology, and capabilities. As population grows and interacts with technological advances, new demands are created for food, resources, manufactured goods, and so on. These demands may be met internally, particularly with large and thinly populated countries. However, if a population is large and rapidly growing, this option will also eventually be exhausted and attention will be directed toward external sources. This occurrence the authors write of as lateral pressure, a general term denoting an expansiveness associated with the search for sources of energy. Once lateral pressure has come about, we encounter what the authors call a "breakpoint" or "phase shift," in which the system moves out of its previous set of dynamics (that is, relations among variables)* into another phase in which a new set of relations becomes important. This is the phase of interstate rivalry, competition, and conflict. As soon as two or more states exert lateral pressure, this possibility is opened up.

This, then, is the two-stage process by which the nation-state system moves from industrial-demographic growth to lateral pressure and external expansion. The first stage focuses on the attributes of the states themselves, and the second focuses on interstate rivalries, comparisons, alliances, arms races, and conflict. The third step

---

*The authors use the term "dynamics" frequently; I have translated this for my own understanding as meaning "set of relationships."

in this ambitious but sequentially coherent theory involves providing the linkage between the dynamics of external rivalry and the occurrence of crisis, escalation, and war. The concept of "crisis" retains its importance, but its position in the overall theory is much more modest. It is now seen as the tip of the iceberg, the tail end of the long conflict spiral, the exposure of which is made possible by the existence of its bulkier submerged portion.

The switch to the project's second phase is also a significant one on methodological grounds. From mostly nonparametric statistical analysis on judgmentally scaled data culled from content analysis and military actions, we move to the most powerful and innovative of the hypothesis-testing and parameter estimation techniques adopted from econometrics, which include multiple regression analysis, path analysis, and recursive modeling. Part of this shift involves moving from a tradition in which hypotheses are tested for significance in a bivariate way, to one in which many variables are treated simultaneously as both dependent and independent variables and in which the estimation of the parameters (coefficients) of previously specified models may be substituted for tests of significance. Finally, in the newer approach more emphasis is placed on the form of the relationship given by the slope.

The following analysis will focus mostly on the book Nations in Conflict, since this is the most comprehensive and recent statement of this phase of the project. Instead of proceeding with a point-by-point evaluation, I will try to highlight some salient dilemmas. The problems center mostly on the three-way tug of war between empirical fit, parsimony, and falsification. As the theory is stated, it fulfills all these criteria; but after repeated confrontations with observation, compromises are made that affect the generality, parsimony, and refutability of the original theory. This is the line of thought that will be developed below.

The Dilemma Between Fit and Parsimony.* Although there is a wealth of material presented in Nations in Conflict, the basic procedure was the same across all empirical tests. The authors provided a diagram of the hypothetical relationships, wrote an equation to match the diagram, presented the data analysis, and interpreted the results. As an example, the procedure for testing the lateral pressure hypothesis is presented in Figure 18.3.

---

*In my discussion of the data analysis I will have to be very selective. The amount of evidence the authors provide is far too great to be adequately summarized here.

FIGURE 18.3

Hypothesized Lateral Pressure Dynamics

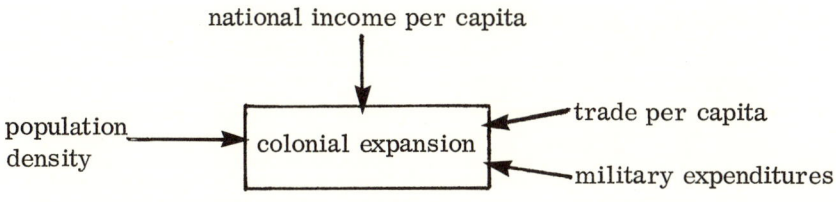

Note: These dynamics can be represented by the following equation:

colonial area = α_1 + B_1 population/area + B_2 national income/population + B_3 imports + exports/population + B_4 (army expenditures + navy expenditures) + u_1.

where α refers to the intercept
B refers to the coefficients to be estimated
u_1 refers to the error term.

Source: Adapted from Nazli Choucri and Robert C. North, Nations in Conflict: National Growth and International Violence (San Francisco: W. H. Freeman and Company, 1975), p. 179.

Since I cannot begin to summarize all the tests of the theory, I will focus on patterns of response to the evidence. Fitting the equation to the British data, the authors find that for the 1871-1914 period only population density and the constant (α) were statistically significant, but that these accounted for over 99 percent of the variance in colonial expansion. The authors add that while no other variables were significant for the period as a whole, 96 percent of the variance in the colonial area from 1871 to 1890 can be explained by the technology variable (national income per capita) and the constant term. Conversely, though density is significant for the period as a whole, it is not significant for the period 1871-90.[30]

Moving to the other countries on which the equation was tested, we find various results. For France, over the entire period, 97 percent of the variance in colonial expansion can be accounted for by the variables in the equation. Population density and national income per capita (technology) were the most significant variables.[31] This seems puzzling too, in light of the following assertion, which appears earlier in the manuscript:

> France . . . was characterized by a relatively stable home population and, aside from the loss of Alsace-Lorraine, a constant home territory in combination with comparatively high levels of technological advancement. At the same time, France's overseas expansion was spectacular.[32]

The German data also provided strong fits, with population and technology also the most important variables here. Though these two variables are significant for the period as a whole, the strength of the fit increases considerably if applied from 1884 to 1914, since 1884 was the year Germany first acquired colonial territory.[33] For Russia the authors report that the "constant term best explains Russian lateral pressure,"[34] which I presume means that the Russian expansion was due to variables outside the equation, or to variables outside the equation that cause the initial level, which may then have an independent impact. The population density of Russia was statistically significant throughout, but defense expenditures were significant only from 1871 to 1890.

Italy presents a contrasting picture, with trade explaining most of the variance in Italian colonial expansion, although both population density and defense expenditures had some impact for shorter periods of time.[35] Austria-Hungary presented difficulties for the analysis, since her territorial acquisitions were very limited during this period. The authors plead the special circumstances, as follows:

> In view of the very limited extent of her colonial acquisitions, this indicator of lateral pressure was not adequate for capturing the expansion of Austrian-Hungarian activities and interests, which were expressed largely through commercial, trade and quasi-military activities in the Balkans.[36]

Let us pause for a moment and attempt to assess this evidence. The percentage of variance explained is extremely high from equation to equation. My first reaction to R^2 values of .90 and above in the social sciences is to suspect that some artifact is responsible for this. Most of the variables are growing at various rates, so one might expect high correlations; however, the authors have carefully checked for autocorrelation using the Durbin-Watson statistic and have made corrections when appropriate.* In light of this, the strength of the relationships is impressive. Not quite so persuasive is the number of variables in the equations, which were not statistically significant. Therefore, one should not interpret the high percentages of variance explained as indicating that the authors have a complete theoretical system.

There are problems of a more serious nature. The analysis and interpretation are laced with idiosyncratic reformulations and singular statements. The results are statistically unstable from one equation to the next, and the coefficients change from one country to another and across different time periods. Are a series of statements of the following kind to be viewed as theory? "For Russia population density was statistically significant for the whole period,"[37] while "defense expenditures were significant from 1871 to 1890,"[38] but "in Italy trade per capita was important for the whole period,"[39] while "1889 to 1914 is explained well by defense expenditures."[40] All interpretations were not so gratuitous, with population density performing fairly consistently, but again we are forced back to the essential asymmetry of confirmation and falsification.

The way the authors handle Austria-Hungary further debilitates the parsimony of the theory. They first note that Austria-Hungary underwent considerable growth in population and production, the two variables that were most consistently related to colonial expansion. We should therefore expect that a strong relationship will exist in this case, too, but instead the authors assert that the colonial expansion variable does not adequately "capture" the lateral pressure concept in this context.[41]

This interpretation comes dangerously close to neutralizing the legitimacy of disconfirming evidence. What this special argument amounts to is that there is a set of indicators of lateral pressure, some of them relevant in some cases and different ones relevant in others. This is not an unreasonable suggestion in principle, but its persuasiveness rests on a very sophisticated measurement model that has not been demonstrated, a measurement model for which there are substitutable indicators or equivalent indicators. Since there is no attention to problems of measurement, relationships among indicators, or equivalent indicators, this appeal seems groundless. Besides this point, there seems to be an internal inconsistency. "Trade" is asserted to be a substitutable indicator of lateral expansion; but if we go back to Figure 18.3, we see that trade is entered into

---

*They have also checked for second-order auto-correlation using moving averages.

the equation as an independent variable to explain the dependent variable rather than as a conceptually independent regressor, this amounts to a specification error. The final result of this will be to increase the strength of the relationships (R^2), but in a way that can only be theoretically confusing, since it would indiscriminately lump two kinds of covariance together, the former because of the lawful connections between variables, the latter because of between-indicator associations.

There are several ways in which the authors might reconcile these diverse results, two in particular. These are found in the notion of "breakpoints" and the introduction of ad hoc hypotheses.

A "breakpoint" refers to a point or region in a time series that signals a shift in the relations of the variables to one another. After a certain value of a variable is reached, a "critical point" is passed and the system moves into a new family of equations. Obviously this concept is relevant to theory testing in general. It is sometimes assumed that relations among variables are the laws of nature and do not change, that only the values of the variables change; but the breakpoint formulation suggests that these laws themselves are subject to change and are therefore, presumably, subject to inquiry and explanation. This viewpoint is not inherently objectionable, but its utility greatly depends on how the notion is introduced, applied, and executed. As a tool in the hands of a curve-fitter, it is just one more device to segment the data base, apply a new designation to it, and proclaim that a new set of dynamics has been ushered in. Fortunately Choucri and North have a theory that can admit, and perhaps indirectly implies, that breakpoints exist. They specifically assert that there will be an initial period during which population pressure, technology, and the search for raw materials will predominate, but that once lateral pressure has occurred a new set of relationships emerges. Thus when the authors find much closer fits between the independent variables of population growth and technological growth and the dependent variable of colonial expansion for the earlier part of the 1870-1914 period, this seems roughly consistent with the theory.

A second way to reconcile the results is to introduce ad hoc hypotheses, but this will increase the fit of the theory only at the expense of its testability. What it leads to in the extreme is the construction of a list of singular statements to accommodate a set of observations. This list amounts to a compendious way of describing the data by linking together a series of descriptive summaries, and as such it fails to fulfill the inferential, predictive, and conditional requirements of good theory. As Ernest Nagel so aptly put it,

> The primary function of such statements [that is, scientific laws] is to explain and predict. But if a scientific state-

ment asserts no more than what is asserted by the evidence for it, we are being slightly absurd when we employ the statement for explaining or predicting anything included in this evidence, and we are being inconsistent when we use it for explaining and predicting anything not in that evidence. To call a statement a law is therefore to say more than that it is a presumably true unrestricted universal. To call a statement a law is to assign a certain function to it, and therefore to say in effect that the evidence on which it is based is assumed not to constitute the total scope of its predication.42

The Dilemma Between Fit and Falsifiability[43]

As originally stated, the present theory has many potential falsifiers. If lateral pressure increased when population and technology decreased, or stayed constant, this would falsify the initial stage of the theory. Similarly, if violence increased while "intersections" decreased, this would count as negative evidence. There are many things that are incompatible with the theory. What is disturbing is that a greater number of falsifiers exist in the earlier stages of its "development." For example, in the article on "The Dynamics of International Conflict," the authors were clearer about the manner in which variables were combined to produce certain effects and about the relative importance of "rate" versus "levels" variables.[44] In the manuscript <u>Nations in Conflict</u>, the authors put forward the proposition that "when demands are high and current activities are insufficient to meet them, these demands combine with established capabilities to produce the extension of a society's activities to meet its goals and preferences."[45]

This hypothesis does not provide information about how demands combine with capabilities to produce lateral pressure. Thus the hypothesis is compatible with a marginal or zero effect of demands and a large effect of capabilities, with a co-occurrence of both capabilities and demands as main, additive effects, with capabilities and demands as an interactive effect, or with a joint interaction and additive effect. Contrast this permissive, and hence not readily falsifiable, hypothesis with an earlier one: "The demands and specialized capabilities of a society combine multiplicatively to produce what might be called lateral pressure."[46]

In this earlier hypothesis the combination rules are provided, thus giving a prediction for a more specific and less probable outcome. The number of basic data statements that this may contradict is greater than the later hypothesis, and for this reason it has more empirical content. It may be that as the authors moved from the earlier to the later stages of the project their theory acquired increasing fit with observations, but it may have done so by suffering a loss of falsifiability.

There are other weaknesses in this context, too. The authors deal for the most part with "growth" variables, at least in the first set of dynamics concerning population and technology. Most variables that are monotonically increasing will probably show a sizable correlation with these growth variables. This is not to say that the theory is wrong, or trivial in any sense, but that there are likely to be many other phenomena that are consistent with the same occurrences, such as the growth of industrial cartels, to take just one important case.

Another weakness is that the authors shifted their approach between rate variables and levels, between lagged and unlagged models, between additive and multiplicative terms, and between alternative model specifications in terms of included and excluded variables. As the authors themselves admit, the final data analysis was preceded by "considerable experimentation with preliminary data sets and alternative combinations of the explanatory variables in this study, and earlier formulations were discarded because of weak statistical findings."[47] However, it is important to note from Nations In Conflict itself that this experimentation was done only on the British data set and that the results of this analysis were then used in independent tests on the other five countries. Still, this preliminary sensitivity analysis and tuning of the theory, especially to the extent that it took place before the writing of the Nations In Conflict manuscript itself on the entire data set, must not be seen as a series of technical adjustments that are neutral with respect to theory-testing. Rather, they must be interpreted as resulting in the progressive elimination of data that could falsify the theory.

There are several ways in which the theory's empirical content, and hence its falsifiability, might be improved. First, trend could be removed from the variables that show sustained growth, and an analysis could be performed on residuals. This will show how closely the variables move around a trend-free line. It is a riskier approach. Second, the authors could try to predict breakpoints, not in terms of the exact year of occurrence or the precise value of the threshold point, but simply by identifying which countries and which variables are likely to experience breakpoints. This will reduce the temptation of the more opportunistic, retroactive interpretations of these "phase shifts." Third, they might try to deduce the empirical consequences of the theory that distinguish it from related theories. What does the theory predict in the first set of dynamics that Lenin's theory of imperialism does not predict or that the balance of power does not predict in the theory's second stage. Discrimination with Leninist theories could be obtained by looking at a control group of noncapitalis

countries. Finally, I think the authors need to spend more time
evaluating the negative evidence. Often an equation will produce a
high R^2 at the same time that several variables in the equation are
insignificant. Do we accept the equation as a whole because of high
R^2, or do we reject it because of component predictive failures?
In a logically connected theory, is it possible to accept some parts
and reject others? How do we treat rejected parts of the theory if
they are "conditions" for moving on to a further stage in the dynamics?
To the extent that a theory is loosely stated and its logical connections
are weak, parts of that theory become modularized as they relate to
evidence. It then becomes possible to selectively eliminate parts of
the theory rather than the entire structure. However, to the extent
that a theory is tightly connected, evidence for a part of it may
spread through the whole theory and have a more widespread impact.

IN LIEU OF A CONCLUSION: A PROGRESSIVE ROLE FOR THE AD-HOC HYPOTHESIS[48]

Evaluation of a research project in terms of criteria supplied
by philosophy of science presumes a fixed faith in the latter; yet
I confess to having had some nagging doubts throughout this exercise
about the appropriateness of standards passed on to the social
sciences by philosophers who have for the most part taken physics
and classical astronomy as their subject matter. Indeed, according
to recent evidence[49] it appears that philosophers of science have
not even accurately reconstructed classical astronomy.* As Feyerabend notes, "Contemporary philosophy of science not only fails to
describe accurately some of the most exciting episodes in the history
of thought, it would also have given extremely bad advice to the
participants."[50]

I am not quarreling with such general criteria as generality,
parsimony, or agreement with observations; the problem is what
to do in the face of limited failures. A rigorous application of the
falsificationist perspective would lead us to reject a theory if it
"fails" in the face of evidence, and failure would occur if a theory
stood up 90 or 99 percent of the time, given the asymmetry between

---

*By this I don't mean to say that it is the task of the philosopher
of science to reconstruct historically. That is for the history of
science to worry about. It is the task of the philosopher of science
to reconstruct logically, in the sense of abstracting those principles
and activities on which the progress of science depends.

confirmation and rejection. Such rigorous standards would only seem to be appropriate under at least the following list of conditions: (1) the theory being tested is complete (includes all variables) and closed (is insulated from all disturbing influences); (2) there are no important data weaknesses, such as unreliable or incorrect reporting of data or coding errors; (3) the indicators of a concept remain constant across entities and time units (the correspondence rules are temporally and spatially invariant); (4) there are no threshold effects in any of the variables that would cause the relationships with other variables to change after a certain magnitude is passed; (5) there are no interaction effects between any variable in the theory and any variable left out; and (6) there are no one-shot interventions into the theory of an occurrence so unique that it cannot be smoothly incorporated into the model. What all this amounts to, in short, is a demand for "perfect knowledge" in an erratic, noise-filled world.[51]

Since we are nowhere near fulfilling these conditions, perhaps we should relax our interpretation of the falsificationist perspective and the use of the ad hoc hypothesis. To do otherwise could easily lead to the rejection of a perfectly good theory for the wrong reasons. This does not mean that data no longer performs its winnowing role in acting as evidence for or against a theory, but only that we should give the same critical scrutiny to negative results as to positive results. Adopting this viewpoint, we interpret the responses of Choucri and North to their data analysis in a different light. They sometimes flatly ignore inconsistent, uneven agreement of theory with observation, as when entirely different slopes, R^2s, and significance tests are reported for different countries, and they occasionally remove data from the theory, as by proclaiming "colonial expansion" to be an inadequate indicator of "lateral pressure" in the case of Austria-Hungary.[52] They sometimes introduce ad hoc hypotheses to bring anomalous results in line with theory, and they shore up temporal inconsistencies through the introduction of the notion of "breakpoints" and "phase shifts." Nevertheless, in light of the generality of this theory, its incorporation and synthesis of other important theories, and its remarkable success in explaining a large number of important variables, this may be a much more "rational" response than rejection of the theory.

As I look back over this entire project, I am dissuaded from making any summary comment that attempts to distill the worth of this effort into a few basic thoughts. North and his collaborators have cut themselves a large task indeed. This task involves an understanding of the laws that translate national characteristics into international behavior in the form of lateral pressure. It requires a study of how this pressure interacts with other variables in that system in such a way that many traditional forms of internatio rivalry such as arms races, alliances, compensations, and divide and rule strategies are produced and how these forms of rivalry and competition lead to violence. Finally, the authors are seeking to understand how the dynamics of interstate rivalry served as background factors or as parameters of the crisis behavior in 1914. Thus the proposed theory addresses itself to a broad range of important substantive concerns in an integrative fashion. In addition, it dovetails and selectively co-opts portions of attribute theories of violence, in which the nation-state is the relevant focus, as well as more systemic theories, such as the balance of power, and theories that crisscross this traditional distinction, such as theories of imperialism. To my mind, the work of the project as a whole, but in particular the epic book by Choucri and North, goes a long way toward making irrelevant the persistent argument over "where the causes of war reside"—in the characteristics of nation-states; in the structure of the international system; or in the "minds of men." The project, in a complicated way, is saying "all three." There are inexorable national pressures, amoral systemic forces, and pathological psychic processes. Perhaps such a synthesis in itself will justify a close look at this theory in the years to come.

NOTES

1. Thomas Kuhn, The Structure of Scientific Revolutions, (Chicago: University of Chicago Press, 1962).
2. Paul K. Feyerabend, "Against Method: Outline of an Anarchistic Theory of Knowledge," in Minnesota Studies in Philosophy of Science, vol. 4 (Minneapolis: University of Minnesota Press, 1970), pp. 17-130, and Paul K. Feyerabend, "Problems of Empiricism, Part II," in The Nature and Function of Scientific Theories, edited by Robert G. Colodny (Pittsburgh: University of Pittsburgh Press, 1970), pp. 275-353.
3. Donald T. Campbell, "Evolutionary Epistemology," in The Philosophy of Karl Popper, edited by Paul Schlipp (LaSalle, Ill.: Open Court Publishing, 1974), pp. 413-63, and Karl R. Popper, Conjectures and Refutations: The Growth of Scientific Knowledge (New York: Harper and Row, 1963).
4. While I have not taken this definition from any one source, I believe it is consistent with the general views of Ernest Nagel, The Structure of Science (New York: Harcourt, Brace and World, 1961); Arthur Stinchcombe, Constructing Social Theories (New York: Harcourt, Brace and World, 1968); R. B. Braithwaite, Scientific Explanation: A Study of the Function of Theory, Probability and Law in Science (Cambridge: Cambridge University Press, 1968).

5. For a general discussion of axiomatic and deductive theories, see Hans L. Zetterberg, On Theory and Verification in Sociology (Totowa, N.J.: Bedminster Press, 1966), and Hubert M. Blalock, Jr., Theory Construction: From Verbal to Mathematical Theory (Englewood Cliffs: Prentice-Hall, 1969), pp. 10-26.

6. Popper, Conjectures and Refutations, op. cit.

7. Ibid., p. 36.

8. Stinchcombe, Constructing Social Theories, op. cit., p. 5.

9. There are various authors involved in this part of the project. They include Robert C. North, Richard A. Brody, Ole R. Holsti, and Dina A. Zinnes. The relevant works are Dina A. Zinnes, "The Expression and Perception of Hostility in Pre-War Crisis: 1914," in Quantitative International Politics: Insights and Evidence, edited by J. David Singer (New York: Free Press, 1968), pp. 85-119; Ole R. Holsti, Robert C. North, and Richard A. Brody, "Perception and Action in the 1914 Crisis," in Quantitative International Politics: Insights and Evidence, edited by J. David Singer (New York: Free Press, 1968), pp. 123-58; Robert C. North, Richard A. Brody, and Ole R. Holsti, "Some Empirical Data on the Conflict Spiral," Papers, Peace Research Society (International) 1 (1964): 1-14; Ole R. Holsti, Richard A. Brody, and Robert C. North, "Measuring Affect and Action in International Reaction Models: Empirical Materials from the 1962 Cuban Crisis," Papers, Peace Research Society (International) 2 (1965): 170-90; Ole R. Holsti, Crisis, Escalation, War (Montreal: McGill-Queens University Press, 1972). I have intentionally not included Dina A. Zinnes, Robert C. North and Howard E. Koch, Jr., "Capability, Threat and the Outbreak of War," in International Politics and Foreign Policy, edited by James N. Rosenau (New York: Free Press, 1961), pp. 469-82. This was one of the earliest reports of the project and is most vulnerable to criticism. However, its main line of conceptual argument and the accompanying methodology were substantially changed and enriched subsequently. The major works I will consider under the second part of the project's research are Nazli Choucri and Robert C. North, "The Determinants of International Violence," Papers, Peace Research Society (International) 12 (1968): 33-63; Nazli Choucri and Robert C. North, "In Search of Peace Systems: Scandinavia and the Netherlands, 1870-1970," in Peace, War, and Numbers, edited by Bruce M. Russett (Beverly Hills: Sage Publications, 1972), pp. 239-74; Nazli Choucri and Robert C. North, "Dynamics of International Conflict: Some Policy Implications of Population, Resources, and Technology," in Theory and Policy in International Relations, edited by Raymond Tanter and Richard H. Ullman (Princeton: Princeton University Press, 1972), pp. 80-122; Robert C. North and Nazli Choucri, "Population, Technology, and Resources in the Future International

System," Journal of International Affairs 25, no. 2 (1971): 224-37; Nazli Choucri and Robert C. North, Nations in Conflict: National Growth and International Violence (San Francisco: W. H. Freeman, 1975).

10. Since the relevant literature here is extensive and does not lend itself to grouped analysis, I will comment only on the most important works. These are: North, Brody, and Holsti, "Some Empirical Data," op. cit.; Holsti, Brody, and North, "Measuring Affect and Action," op. cit.; and Holsti, Crisis, Escalation, War, op. cit.

11. Holsti, Crisis, Escalation, War, op. cit., p. 9.

12. Holsti, North, and Brody, "Perception and Action," op. cit., p. 132.

13. Ibid.

14. Richard A. Brody, "Cognition and Behavior: A Model of International Relations," in Experience, Structure, and Adaptability, edited by O. J. Harvey (New York: Springer Publishing, 1966), p. 341.

15. North, Brody, and Holsti, "Some Empirical Data," p. 9.

16. John R. Raser, Donald T. Campbell, and Richard W. Chadwick, "Gaming and Simulation for Developing Theory Relevant to International Relations," General Systems 15 (1970): 184.

17. North, Brody, and Holsti, "Some Empirical Data," op. cit., p. 9.

18. Ibid.

19. Holsti, Brody, and North, "Measuring Affect and Action," op. cit., pp. 170-90.

20. Ibid., pp. 177-78.

21. North, Brody, and Holsti, "Some Empirical Data," op. cit., p. 1.

22. For example, Dina A. Zinnes, "Expression and Perception," op. cit., pp. 85-119; Ole R. Holsti, "The 1914 Case," American Political Science Review 59, no. 2 (1965): 365-78; and Ole R. Holsti and Robert C. North, "Perceptions of Hostility and Economic Variables," in Comparing Nations, edited by Richard Merritt and Stein Rokkan (New Haven: Yale University Press, 1966), pp. 169-90.

23. Holsti, Crisis, Escalation, War, op. cit.

24. Ibid., p. 9.

25. For results concerning the first set of hypotheses, see Holsti, North, and Brody, "Perception and Action," op. cit., p. 137. For results concerning the second set, see Ibid., pp. 158-59.

26. See Dean G. Pruitt, "Stability and Sudden Change in Interpersonal and International Affairs," in International Politics and Foreign Policy, edited by James N. Rosenau (New York: Free Press, 1969), pp. 294-95.

27. Noam Chomsky, "Review of B. F. Skinner's Verbal Behavior," Language 35, no. 1 (1959): 31.
28. Choucri and North, Nations in Conflict, op. cit.
29. Choucri and North, "In Search of Peace Systems," op. cit., p. 241.
30. Choucri and North, Nations in Conflict, op. cit., pp. 392-93.
31. Ibid., p. 396.
32. Ibid., p. 84.
33. Ibid., p. 398.
34. Ibid., p. 394.
35. Ibid., p. 399.
36. Ibid.
37. Ibid., p. 395.
38. Ibid.
39. Ibid., p. 399.
40. Ibid.
41. Ibid.
42. Nagel, Structure of Science, op. cit., p. 63.
43. In this section I am heavily indebted to Karl Popper, The Logic of Scientific Discovery (New York: Harper and Row, 1959).
44. Choucri and North, "Dynamics of International Conflict," op. cit.
45. Choucri and North, Nations in Conflict, op. cit., p. 373.
46. Choucri and North, "Dynamics of International Conflict," op. cit., p. 90.
47. Choucri and North, Nations in Conflict, op. cit., p. 373.
48. In this section I am indebted to Paul K. Feyerabend's writings. See Feyerabend, "Against Method," op. cit., and Feyerabend, "Problems of Empiricism," op. cit.
49. See the discussion in Feyerabend, "Problems of Empiricism," op. cit., pp. 301-19, concerning the "methods" used by Galileo in introducing his revolutionary thoughts.
50. Ibid., p. 276.
51. May Brodbeck, "Explanation, Prediction and 'Imperfect Knowledge'," in Readings in the Philosophy of the Social Sciences, edited by May Brodbeck (New York: Macmillan, 1968), pp. 363-98.
52. Choucri and North, Nations in Conflict, op. cit., p. 399.

CHAPTER

19

AN APPRAISAL OF THE METHODOLOGICAL AND STATISTICAL PRACTICES USED IN THE 1914 PROJECT

Karen Ann Feste

The objective of this essay is to provide a critical examination of the studies resulting from the 1914 project at Stanford University, which focused on an analysis of the documentation produced by some of the parties prior to their entrance into the first world war. In particular, attention will be given to the forms of data collection, compilation, and techniques of statistical analysis employed in these research endeavors. The central question underlying the investigation is to what extent these studies have appropriately and correctly employed statistical methods on the available data? The overall design of the project and the subsequent findings from the extensive research on the materials will be noted insofar as these two aspects are related to matters of methodology. Various aspects of data handling are divided into the following sections in the critique: (1) data collection, (2) coding procedures, (3) variable definitions and uses, and (4) tests used in hypothesis testing. In the conclusion we will draw together some suggestions and recommendations and an overall evaluation of these studies regarding proper methodological applications.[1]

DATA COLLECTION

An important aspect of social science research is the procedure used in gathering information once a problem has been defined for study. The methods utilized in bringing together materials for the 1914 studies may be evaluated along several dimensions, on which the principal criterion for review is the completeness of the data set. The reliability, validity, and comparability of the materials are also central in this assessment. We are interested in ascertaining whether the researchers have selected appropriate data sources and units of analysis that capture all of the significant variation and richness in the observation field. After a brief description of the data sources and collecting procedures, some deviations from data-gathering standards will be discussed.

The sources used for analyzing the 1914 crisis were drawn from the national archives of some of the participant states for the period between the assassination of the Archduke, heir to the throne of Austria-Hungary, on June 28, 1914, and the outbreak of general war on August 4, 1914.[2] The selection of almost 6,000 documents, totaling some 1.4 million words, was governed by questions of availability and by the need for authenticity.[3] The scope was limited to the following:

> data that was [sic] directly relevant to the conflict, or to Balkan politics, military affairs or other matters that clearly affected the conflict. The types of documents included statements on policy (diplomatic and military), diplomatic instructions and reports, consular reports, intelligence and military reports, departmental memoranda, records of cabinet and council meetings, parliamentary debates, memoirs, and diaries.[4]

The perceptual data constructed from these sources were wholly derived from documents authored by selected British, French, Russian, German, and Austro-Hungarian decision makers, that is, persons filling key roles, such as heads of state, heads of governments, or foreign ministers, unless "there was clear indication that the person had no part whatever in the formulation of decisions."[5] All of these documents were subjected to a content analysis. Which key documents were actually content analyzed? In three published works where the list is given, there seem to be some differences about the identity of the "key decision makers" and whether or not written materials produced by these individuals were included in the subsequent perceptual-data evidence.* In the Zinnes article,

---

*See Dina A. Zinnes, "The Expression and Perception of Hostility in Pre-War Crisis: 1914," and Ole R. Holsti, Robert C. North, and Richard A. Brody, "Perception and Action in the 1914 Crisis," both in Quantitative International Politics: Insights and Evidence, edited by J. David Singer (New York: Free Press, 1968), pp. 88, 135, and Ole R. Holsti, Crisis, Escalation, War (Montreal: McGill-Queens University Press, 1972), pp. 38-29. The number of key decision makers included in the Zinnes study is 29 (6 from Austria-Hungary,

METHODOLOGICAL AND STATISTICAL PRACTICES 385

communications from 6 different Austro-Hungarian leaders were content analyzed; in the article by Holsti, North, and Brody, there were 8 Austro-Hungarian decision makers included; and in Holsti's Crisis, Escalation, War, only 3 leaders from Austria-Hungary are in the data set. For each of the remaining countries in the 1914 project, the list of key decision makers is differently identified in the specific analyses and the extent of disagreement among the authors is considerable. This is particularly true of the French and Austro-Hungarian data sets, and to a lesser extent, there is a lack of agreement in identifying and selecting the key decision makers in Germany and Great Britain.

The actual effect of these differences on any data set is unknown. The reader of these published studies is not supplied with a frequency distribution table giving the amount of information produced by any of the individuals whose documents were included in one research piece while excluded from another.* It is entirely possible that using any collection of documents from selected decision makers produces substantially the same set of perceptual findings. The only way to resolve the matter would be a replication of these studies and others in which different data bases were used, interchanging the actual data sets and then comparing the results for the hypotheses that were tested. This is an empirical matter and not necessarily a major limitation of the research results that have emanated from the 1914 studies.

---

4 from Germany, 4 from Great Britain, 9 from France, 3 from Russia, and 3 from Serbia). In the Holsti, North, and Brody piece, the total number of decision makers is 28 (8 from Austria-Hungary, 6 from Germany, 5 from Great Britain, 6 from France, and 3 from Russia). The Holsti report includes a list of 17 key decision makers (4 from Austria-Hungary, 3 from Germany, 3 from Great Britain, 3 from France, 2 from Russia, and 2 from Serbia). Across these three studies, there is agreement on the identity of the key decision makers in only 13 cases. Although Serbian data were used in two of the published articles, in neither work is the reader provided with a description of these special data.

*In Ole R. Holsti, Crisis, Escalation, War (Montreal: McGill-Queens University Press, 1972), pp. 239-60, a breakdown of crisis actions, hostile perceptions, and message frequencies is given by country in a chronological order throughout the six-week period. In almost all of the publications resulting from this project, however, we are not provided with any list of particular key decision makers, thus making it impossible to adequately evaluate the extent of bias introduced into the data set.

The research workers involved in the 1914 studies made a concerted effort to assure the authenticity of the items of documentary evidence that were included in the final data set. A variety of secondary sources were consulted to cross-check information, and while it is never claimed that the total universe of existing documentation has been examined, the researchers indicate that they have made an effort to utilize all of the relevant, authentic data brought to their attention.[6]

These documents cover a very substantial record of the relevant communications of the five countries that participated in the 1914 conflict, yet it cannot be said that the record is complete. The potential magnitude of the missing data can be estimated, but never known precisely. Some of the more obvious sources of lost information are the direct communications between the leaders of the states themselves, either on a face-to-face basis, in telephone conversations, or in informal meetings at which minutes were not kept. Missing data may also be attributed to misfiling in foreign offices or deliberate suppression of particular pieces of information. The project workers also admit that the exclusion of Serbian and Italian documents because of inaccessability posed some difficulties for defining the final data set.[7]

Is the problem of missing data a serious one? This matter is addressed in several of the published pieces, but after amply documenting the authentic nature of the actual data set and suggesting sources for lost information, these scholars clearly do not believe any major bias has been created in their data by the exclusion of information derived from the settings mentioned above. The magnitude of this information loss is unknown and potentially represents a large error; whether such information is likely to be distributed randomly is debatable. We have no reason to assume that data that originate in direct personal confrontation form are necessarily identical or even highly similar to the contents of written documents. Conversely, it cannot be said that such information is completely different. We may only speculate, moreover, that the suppressed documents might contain certain patterns of information that are not revealed to the same extent in the set of preserved documents.

In almost any situation in which the primary source of materials is documentary evidence, it will be improbable that the totality of evidence can be brought together. It is a moot point, therefore, to question the universality of the data set. However, some issues can be raised with regard to the actual sample that the data represent. A number of published articles pay attention to the problem of the completeness or representativeness of the data collection. Holsti admits that the 1914 data, while a rich set of information, represent only a <u>sample</u> (Holsti's emphasis), rather than the entire universe of communications within and between the foreign offices of the five European states.[8] He goes on to state that "it appears reasonable to assume that the available data are a representative sample."[9]

In the Robert C. North, Ole R. Holsti, M. George Zaninovich, and Dina A. Zinnes handbook on content analysis techniques, it is noted that social scientists must reduce a research area to manageable size by "sampling the total universe of available data by selecting appropriate cases and countries to be studied and in choosing persons and documents from which content analysis data are to be extracted."[10] This is the only valid method for gathering and analyzing data; yet, several questions may be considered regarding the nature of the sampling procedure utilized in these studies.

First of all, we might legitimately ask whether the data are to be regarded as a sample or a universe. If the data are actually considered to be a sampling of the entire set of communications between and within the five major states in the 1914 crisis, or a sample of all communications between the decision makers of all warring countries at this time, then some of the features of drawing good samples might be worthy of mention. Two kinds of samples are generally recognized: nonprobability and probability types. In nonprobability samples, the selection of elements is governed by design; a case may be chosen for the sample accidentally, purposefully, or to meet the specifications of a quota scheme. While some generalizations may be inferred from these data, it is improper to base such conclusions on statistical tests of significance, since specific criteria for selecting data, randomness and independence, must be met if sample statistics are to be appropriately applied in data analysis. The laws of sampling distribution, from which theoretical distribution tables are derived, provide a basis for drawing inferences to the population from the results of sample data analysis.

It is difficult to say whether the 1914 documents were selected randomly. In specifying the criteria for inclusion, the researchers were intent on collecting a set of documents for the time period in question that was as authentic and complete as possible. By selecting the communications of the key decision makers of five countries, the independence criterion governing sample selection was violated. The probability for each item in the selection process was either 1.0 or 0.0, since the desire of the project directors was to formulate a complete set of the key decision makers' documents rather than to sample the existing documentation. This aspect of the data collection does not pose major limitations, provided the appropriate statistical tests and the interpretations that apply to such tests do not include assumptions of probability sampling techniques.

CODING PROCEDURES

The entire set of documents from the key decision makers of the five major states involved in the 1914 conflict was subjected to a thematic content analysis. This meant that 5,078 themes were extracted from the documents, using a thematic construction as the basis for coding perceptions. Each time, the textual materials specified the perceiving party, the perceived state, a verbal connector (an action or attitude), and a target state. These four components were isolated in a piece of documentary evidence, and the coders were instructed to rearrange the materials to this format and record the information. The resulting materials, or perceptions, were catalogued, counted, ranked on intensity scales, and used in the subsequent hypotheses testing.

Perhaps I ought to mention some of the assumptions and features of a content analysis of textual materials before evaluating the sampling or representativeness of these data. An analysis of the content of verbal materials is an examination and evaluation of the language used to express attitudes and actions. Emphasis is placed on the creation of classification schemes for categorizing language elements systematically. The data are subjected to a set of rules and procedures, which are used to define the categories and units of language.[11]

One of the uses of content analysis as a technique for analyzing data is to measure attitudinal variables by examining the perceptions and images expressed by a message sender on a specific topic. When this technique is employed to discover patterns within textual data, some implicit assumptions are made about the role of language. The developed classification scheme must be theoretically meaningful for the purposes of study and in concert with our general understanding of the way language is used. This serves to establish validity in the data set. Another aspect of the content categories is the matter of reliability in an analysis of textual data. Here it is important that the analysis be structured in a way that is amenable to replication.

The scholars involved in the 1914 project have been careful and concerned that the perceptual data meet these requirements of validity and reliability. It is usually an easier task to develop ways of analyzing textual materials capable of replication. This requires a simple, straightforward set of rules for coding verbal data, of which the reliability is measured by the consistency of agreement in coding information between the recorders. Several reliability coefficients are given in the published results, and problems of achieving an acceptable coefficient of intercoder agreement are noted in the articles about the project.[12] The use of such coefficients indicates the concern of those involved in the project for developing good data.

Even if the data are reliable, the problem of validity, and hence, interpretation of the 1914 materials remains. Assumptions about the structure and meaning of language, about the comparability of perceptions among individuals, and about aggregating those perceptions when analyzing the data are central concerns in this matter. In content analysis the presumption is made that an underlying structure of word usage exists and that all individuals conceptualize and express their thoughts in a relatively consistent manner. Thoughts that are identical will be expressed in nearly identical language, which implies that the meanings of words enjoy agreement among all individuals. There are no conclusive empirical tests of these premises. In content analytic studies, these assumptions form the basis for establishing comparability in the data set and provide a justification for aggregating individual attitudes. Hence we can only operate as if the variation among the cases is representative of actual differences and similarities characterizing the data, recognizing that our standards for measuring discrepancies may be completely wrong.

Another assumption regarding the function of language as a symbol system for expressing attitudes concerns the operationalized attitudinal variables. Verbal statements are regarded as an accurate reflection of an individual's attitudes or perceptions. Two related types of error may exist in the 1914 data set containing perceptual information. First, there may be individual variation in perceptions and in the variance of defining the set of perceptions aggregated across all key decision makers for a single country. Second, individual and aggregate variances of perceptions may not be transferred analogously to the variance parameters actually measured in the verbal statements. The connection between attitudinal variance and variation in the verbal statements designed to assess attitudinal variance may not produce a perfect match. The key to operationalizing perceptions through verbal statements is generally the assumption that language functions as a representation of the feelings individuals have about particular subjects and ideas.[13] By use of this premise, it is believed that the estimated error variance in the data is minimized. If, on the contrary, language does not operate this way but is employed instrumentally, whereby individuals express messages in a strategic manner in order to manipulate their interactions in certain directions, then inferences cannot be drawn about individual attitudes from an evaluation of verbal messages because of differences in variance parameters. In the literature on diplomatic techniques used in international relations, it is often asserted that the instrumental use of language is dominant.[14]

In the 1914 studies, the research workers do not explicitly discuss the representative or the instrumental model of language usage in these communication data. It seems evident that an isomorphic variance between perceptions and verbal statements is accepted, thereby approximating the representational function of language.

The researchers are admittedly aware of limitations in the 1914 perceptual data. Dina A. Zinnes provides an excellent description of the compromising choices that had to be made in locating an acceptable "mix" of coding procedures that produced reliable as well as valid results.[15] In the North, et al., handbook, adequate discussion is accorded to this matter.[16] Nonetheless, we feel it is appropriate to bring attention to several potential weaknesses in the data set, since these characteristics ultimately determine which statistical tests may be legitimately used in analyzing this information.

Several conclusions can be drawn that provide an overall evaluation of the data set used to test hypotheses in the 1914 crisis. Since the data collection is incomplete, it should not be treated as a universe. There are too many sources of missing data, making the effects of the bias introduced difficult to estimate systematically. On the other hand, the data do not meet the requirements of a probability sample, but may be properly labeled a purposive sample. The basic assumption governing this form of sample gathering is that, with good judgment, one can hand pick the cases and assure representativeness in the data that span the variance existing in the population. Purposive samples are more commonly used, however, whenever information about the information is known. By matching universe and sample characteristics, a small data set, that is, the sample, is legitimately used as a basis for making predictions. The effects of the missing data on the 1914 studies remain unknown, and this limits the predictive capability of applied statistical tests.

We have noted a variety of points where measurement error entered into the coding of these data. The data may not meet the requirements of validity, partially because of the missing information and partially because of differences in individual coding practices. Reliability in these data does not present a problem, provided we accept the extent of intercoder agreement reflected in the coefficients. The matter of isomorphic variances between attitudes and verbal statements was also noted as a factor that may reduce the scope of generalizability of the hypotheses that are examined. This is basically a question of research design and therefore beyond the concern of this essay.

Another aspect of the coding procedures used in these studies focuses on the types of scales created to measure the variables specified in the hypotheses. In the following section, scale construction will be discussed and evaluated.

VARIABLE DEFINITIONS

There are two sets of variables used in testing hypotheses in the 1914 studies; these sets of variables divide into perceptual and action variables. Some of the measurements of action variables are straightforward, aggregate interval data, and we will dispense with any discussion of these factors. The perceptual data and some of the action variables, however, were evaluated along scales of intensity, and here a critical assessment is in order.

The major perceptual variables include hostility, capability, stress, coalition, alternatives, power, frustration, satisfaction, friendship, and a desire to change the status quo. In coding the documentary materials, a list of "tip-off" words brought the recorder's attention to a particular statement and served as a guideline for categorizing a perception. These word lists are not provided in an appendix to any of the published articles dealing with the 1914 studies, so we can only assume that this technique enabled the coders to catalogue the perceptions into each of the categories appropriately. The set of perceptions consisted of statements that were evaluated along intensity continuums. Using two methods of scalar construction, paired comparisons, on a final 12-point scale, and the Q sort technique, on a final 9-point scale, were created for some of the variables.

The paired comparison technique requires a group of judges to rank order pairs of masked statements along a specified dimension, after which the ranked scores are aggregated for all judges and an ultimate scale is derived. The Q sort technique consists of an arrangement of statements into nine groups along a normal distributive format, in which higher proportions of statements are placed into the middle categories and proportionately smaller numbers of statements are contained at each end of the continuum.

Such techniques are well known in the field of attitudinal measurement in psychology. The procedure is basic: assemble a group of judges who are supposed to understand what the dimension under discussion is all about, and ask them to order cases on that dimension.[17] The method has difficulties, though. By the aggregation of judgments, individual variances may tend to be canceled out. Methods of standardization, such as ranking and percentaging, can help make the differing perspectives more comparable. What, however, is the precise purpose of this type of scale construction: a high degree of agreement among judges, or a representation of all biases and points of view? Both aspects are important, but achieving one may mean compromising the other.

The 1914 researchers carefully describe the scale-building procedures used on the perceptual data. High coefficients of agreement among the judges are reported. In a number of instances these scales are assumed to meet the requirements of an interval-level measurement, meaning that statistical tests appropriate for interval data can be applied. The question of concern here is whether such scales do conform to the interval measurement requirement.

The essential characteristic of an interval scale is that a unit of measurement differentiating points along the scale be identified. Some measurement theorists disagree about whether scales created from the paired comparison or Q sort techniques are properly considered as ordinal or interval measurement devices. Clyde Coombs has stated that the scales used in psychology are regarded as interval scales because the unit of measurement is assumed to be constant. He cautions, however, that this type of scale should be used only if by manipulation of the objects it can be experimentally demonstrated that the numbers assigned to the objects obey the laws of addition. The problem of measurement in attitudinal scaling is in measuring the intensity function empirically, where the unit selected for differentiating the items must be invariant.[18]

The conceptualization of scaling procedures is viewed differently by Bernard S. Phillips, who defines scales as "a method for assigning numbers to a property of objects in order to impart some of the characteristics of numbers to the properties in question."[19] The phenomena are organized by humans, who measure the properties of phenomena in such a way that the characteristics may be imparted to these properties. Since it is a specific human intervention to arrange items in an ordered manner, it is also up to the researcher to determine whether the phenomena should be treated in either an ordinal or interval manner. With specific reference to the equal interval claims in certain attitudinal scales, Phillips concludes, however, that "it seems this method does not allow definite criteria for deciding whether or not a given scale has certain characteristics of number systems and hence it is difficult to decide whether interval measurement should be used."[20]

Hubert M. Blalock holds a more conservative position, specifying two essential criteria for treating items along an interval measurement dimension: (1) there must be a physical unity that can be agreed upon as a common measurement standard and (2) it must be possible to replicate the scale-building procedures and reach the same results.[21] Whether or not it is possible to attain interval scales in the area of attitudinal measurement, Blalock concludes that most techniques yield very poor approximations to interval scales and that many probably should not even be considered to give legitimate ordinal scales.*

It is not always a simple matter to decide what type of scale can be used, and there is disagreement among measurement theorists on this point. An ordinal scale results only if the judges are able to rank individual statements along some dimension. If the judges are required to place a group of statements into a definite rank order, this can be accomplished, whether or not a judge believes it is achievable. The 1914 studies have used methods of attitudinal scaling procedures to create intensity measures of the perceptual data; yet we have no empirical demonstration that the intensity of perceptions is actually distinguished in the manner they specify. One must assume that the intensity dimension accurately reflects differentiation of the phenomena.†

If there is reason to believe that a unit of intensity on the scale has been defined and delimited invariantly, then the analyst is justified in making use of interval-level statistical tests. Whether

---

*With regard to the Thurstone equal-appearing interval scales, Blalock writes: "If there is a high degree of consensus among the judges, then an interval scale can be legitimately used. The argument seems to be legitimate provided there is a high degree of consensus among judges and provided judges are given a large number of piles. Thurstone's method still represents difficulties in conceptualizing the concept concerned. It becomes necessary to postulate that it is the existence of such a unit which makes agreement among judges possible." Hubert M. Blalock, Social Statistics (2nd ed., New York: McGraw-Hill, 1972), p. 20.

†The use of a particular mathematical model presupposes that a certain level of measurement has been attained. Responsibility for this choice rests with the researchers in the 1914 studies, who determine whether or not their data permit the use of arithmetic operations when performing analyses. When the operations by which objects are placed on a scale involve direct comparison of the items in terms of the extent to which they possess the attribute in question, it is relatively easy to see that the scale reflects the order of positions but not necessarily the distances between them. The statistics applicable to data measured along such scales permit nominal and ordinal tests. Strictly speaking, the analysis should be limited to computations of medians, percentiles, and rank order correlations, such as Spearman's rho and Kendall's tau.

various techniques used to create attitudinal scales in the social sciences yield data corresponding to interval measurement assumptions has been the subject of considerable controversy. In a review of attitudinal measurement methods, Harry S. Upshaw concluded that the accumulated evidence suggests that the scale model for categorized data leads to an ordinal rather than an interval scale.[22]

Whether we select the purist's position on matters of statistical application or not, each approach to measurement theory involves a possible gain and a possible loss. If we choose to perfect instruments for measurement before using them, the results of the investigation may be more impressive within the context of justification. The possible loss here is the delay involved in perfecting the instruments and possibly the neglect of the kinds of phenomena for which it is difficult to develop reliable, precise, and valid measures. If the investigator proceeds before the instruments have been perfected, erroneous findings may result, but the possible gain is an immediate increase in knowledge and the opportunity to utilize this knowledge to improve the instruments. Whichever choice is made by the investigator, the possible losses involved ought to be taken into account.

By providing this background to the controversy over the level of measurement in attitudinal scaling, we simply wish to emphasize that it is not clear whether the perceptual variables can be analyzed using interval-level statistical tests. This is a caution, not a criticism of the 1914 studies, inasmuch as the lack of agreement among measurement theorists prevents us from drawing any conclusions about measurement level. In the next section of the paper, in which the tests used in analyzing these data will be discussed, these comments about the characteristics of ordinal and interval scales should be kept in mind.

HYPOTHESIS TESTING

The process of measurement in data analysis involves two operations: the development of an instrument to do the measuring and the collection of data. Several deficiencies in the measurement procedures employed by the 1914 project have been noted and discussed. These aspects of measurement serve to limit the range of statistical manipulations that may be appropriately used in testing hypotheses with these data. We are often tempted to presume that data meet the assumptions required for particular tests in order to enable ourselves to make use of more powerful statistical techniques. It is also true that such tests discriminate variable differences in a finer manner, making it more likely that meaningful relations will be delineated. If higher-level statistics are applied as a method for hypothesis testing when the data do not meet the assumptions or the proper sampling and measurement levels, a severe problem in interpreting the results is created. We shall proceed to examine the set of tests actually used in analyzing the 1914 data and then evaluate their appropriateness in light of these comments.

It has been argued here that the 1914 data specifications are as follows: (1) a nonprobability sample, (2) ordinally measured perceptual variables, and (3) interval data for the behavioral variables. As such, the range of appropriate statistics to analyze these data is necessarily limited. Table 19.1 lists some statistical computations that are applicable for the 1914 data and indicates whether or not these procedures were employed. Table 19.2 contains a set of statistical operations used in analyzing the 1914 materials in which actual data specifications may not have met the assumptions of the statistic.

TABLE 19.1

A Selection of Statistics Appropriate for
Analyzing the 1914 Data

Appropriate Measures	Applied in Published Studies	
	Yes	No
Univariate		
Frequency counts	x	
Cumulative frequencies	x	
Proportions and percentages	x	
Medians		x
Quartiles		x
Range		x
Bivariate		
Phi	x	
Gamma	x	
Spearman's rho	x	
Lambda		x
Contingency coefficient		x
Cramner's V		x
Kendall's tau		x
Partial rank-order correlation		x

Source: Compiled by the author.

TABLE 19.2

Application of Inappropriate Statistics to the 1914 Data

Statistical Operation	Assumption Violated	
	Measurement Level	Sampling
Computing mean intensity of attitudinal measurement	x	
Aggregating intensity mean scores and computing total mean	x	
Computing the Product Moment Correlation	x	
Setting confidence levels for Product Moment Correlation		x
Computing and interpreting Chi Square		x
Computing and interpreting Analysis of Variance		x
Computing and interpreting Mann-Whitney		x
Computing and interpreting Kruskal-Wallis		x

Source: Compiled by the author.

There are two related points to be summarized from these tables, which are that a number of applicable statistical operations for these data were not employed and that the use of several of the tests was inappropriate, given the data specifications. It cannot be argued, necessarily, that ruling out statistical procedures of questionable applicability would have severely restricted the amount of information that could have been derived from the data set, given the non-use of other available tests. The specifics of knowledge gained about the 1914 crisis would be altered, since the criteria for measurement-level and sampling procedures delimit the range of legitimate generalizations. Which statistical operations were inappropriately applied on these data, and why?

Perhaps the most frequent violation concerns the calculations of mean intensity scores on the perceptual variables. Where perceptual variable measurement is properly considered interval, such statistics may be used. However, if measurements of perceptual variables are at best ordinal, then the arithmetic procedures, such as adding and dividing scores, are invalid for deriving a central tendency measure. The median and other positional measures (quartile, quintile, decile) might have been used to draw interpretations of differences and similarities within these data. To be sure, the mean uses more information than the median, because all the exact scores are involved in the computation and whenever data correctly conform to interval measurement, the mean is preferred. However, as we have argued earlier, these perceptual data do not appear to be in conformity with interval-level measurement.

The second most common error in statistical application committed by the investigators studying the 1914 data crisis has been that of computing the product-moment correlation coefficient to establish bivariate relationships if the perceptual variable measurement only met requirements of ordinality.[23] Although a correlation model is certainly the appropriate one for testing most, if not all, of the hypotheses of interest to these scholars, data limitations might rule out the use of a Pearson's r. The appropriate tests would be confined to Spearman's rho and Kendall's tau, the equivalent measures of association for rank-order data. Recently, however, some methodologists have contended that the Product Moment Correlation does not assume interval-level data. Their reasoning is that numbers are ignorant and that statistical measures do not discriminate: any set of numbers, regardless of their empirical referents, can be used with the operations of adding, subtracting, multiplying, and dividing.*

Like the dispute concerning measurement level in attitudinal scaling, the controversy over the use of the Product Moment Correlation revolves around the meaning and properties (inherent or ascribed) of ordinal- and interval-level data. Given these differences of opinion among social science analysts and members of the statistical community, it might be a wiser strategy to rely

---

*Perry E. Jacobson, Jr., in "Applying Measures of Association to Nominal-Ordinal Data," Pacific Sociological Review 15, no. 1 (1972): 59, argues that Spearman's rho is essentially Pearson's product-moment correlation coefficient, where the only difference is that rho is based on ranks, not scale values. Moreover, he suggests that a set of ranks in and by itself is an interval scale, since ranks refer to the relative positions within a set of cases and are obtained by numbering the cases. This numbering process is at the same time a counting process, thus making cases the common unit of measurement. Therefore, computing the mean for a set of ranks does not distort the underlying dimension.

on those tests that all agree are appropriately applied to a set of data in the context of examining a particular problem. This would have resulted in greater use of the Spearman's rho, even if the test were applied in a number of articles. (Most of Ole R. Holsti's published pieces and some of the work of Dina A. and Joseph Zinnes do use Spearman's rank-order association measure.)

Tests of significance are widely used in analyzing the 1914 data. Certainly the use of Chi Square, Mann-Whitney, Kruskal-Wallis, and the Analysis of Variance, while representing creativity on the part of the investigators in making sense out of the information collected, should not have been used because the assumptions of sample selection are violated.[24] All of these tests require a data set characterized by independent and random sample selection. It was demonstrated earlier that the 1914 data in no way meet the assumptions of a probability sample. Moreover, sample statistics are applied to determine whether or not a relationship found in the sample also exists in the population. These tests, unless accompanied by appropriate correlational measures, say nothing about the form of bivariate associations. The difficulty here concerns the manner of drawing inferences from the data results to a specified population.*

---

*Various significance tests require a probability sample, a certain measurement level, a grouping in the data, and a given sample size. The chance factor refers to the risk of finding the contrary result in the population, given the existence of a relationship in a sample. Other justifications for using significance tests on population data, as suggested by J. David Singer and Melvin Small, "Alliance Aggregation and the Onset of War, 1915-1945," in Quantitative International Politics: Insights and Evidence, edited by J. David Singer (New York: Free Press, 1968), pp. 275-76, as a "benchmark" to differentiate real and random relations seem unwarranted. As noted in the text, there is no way to interpret the statistical inference when significance tests are performed on population data. Stephen Brown, "Intensive Analysis in Political Research," Political Methodology 1, no. 1 (1974): p. 9, has argued that nonprobability samples should occupy an important position in exploratory social science research. Until we establish a greater number of social behavior laws, he suggests examining a set of "behavioral specimens" rather than selecting a sample. This still means, however, that the analysis is not conducted as if one were working with a probability sample, meaning that statistical significance tests do not form the basis for interpreting results.

Because the 1914 data do not comprise a probability sample, none of the significance tests that have been applied can be appropriately interpreted. Even if a probability sample of the data set were selected, the problems of statistical inference would not be eliminated. In reviewing the data collecting procedures, we concluded that error variance is not necessarily randomly distributed, because of the exclusion of certain information. Therefore the testing of hypotheses through the method of significance tests cannot be claimed as an appropriate statistical application. What general evaluation of hypothesis-testing procedures may be accorded the 1914 studies? We shall attempt to pull together various strands of the arguments presented in these pages in light of the overall technical applications and appropriateness.

CONCLUSION

In a 1972 publication, Dina A. Zinnes has arrayed the set of correlational results from some of the content analysis studies in the context of the stimulus-response model, which provided one theoretical basis for analyzing these materials.[25] Significance tests were applied in nearly all of the analyzed data and reported in research reports. Problems of data interdependence or contamination, because of compilation procedures in the content-analytic methods used on these materials, are noted by Zinnes.[26] We have not listed this matter as a limiting feature of the hypothesis testing, even though it violates one of the critical assumptions of correlational analysis.

Correlational studies between perceptual data and action or behavioral data were conducted in several published works. The action data were coded through a content analysis of materials and also included such aggregate variable measurement as the flow of gold in and out of London, changes in the gold reserves of national banks, securities of prospective belligerents, securities of prospective neutrals, wheat futures, exchange rates, and market money rates.[27]

In one paper Holsti and North noted that substantial support can be given to the premise that content analysis of what the decision makers say may be fruitfully used as a research tool in the study of international relations.[28] They noted that analysis of the perceptual data and the independently drawn action data, when measured independently, described a similar picture of the escalation of the 1914 crisis into general war. Why, they ask, should we bother with the content analysis data at all, if the aggregate variables appear to be sensitive to the crisis? This suggests two important criteria: first, that the economic indicators respond to a variety of stimuli, some economic, some political, and some social; and second, that the analysis of economic indicators alone may not tell us much about why the actors are behaving the way they are.29

The overall evaluation of several tests used in analyzing these 1914 data ultimately reduces the sources of difficulty to the failure to address problems of sampling and attitudinal measurement directly. Obviously, the investigators recognize these problems. The alternative is not to avoid working with attitudinal data, or arriving at properly-based probability samples, but rather to solve some of these methodological hang-ups. This is undoubtedly a very difficult task, but because it is at the core of much of the research endeavor and has continually cropped up in these studies, it cannot be avoided.

In social research, one must be careful not to apply assumptions that are too restrictive, such as the equivalence of attitude intensity across a set of individuals, and then to continue applying that model. There may well be ways of handling individual differences that would reduce the need for employing this assumption. Perhaps these types of studies could best be improved if comparisons between different kinds of attitudinal scale measurements could be made. As long as many of the variable concepts are measured indirectly with an unobserving measuring unit like intensity, it is difficult to accept the validity or reliability of data if the values are founded on these scales. Establishing agreement among judges is one way to handle the problem, and the realm of possibilities of combining judgmental evaluations seems almost endless.*

The zest of these scholars for testing hypotheses has resulted in a misuse of some statistical operations. Their attempts to uncover relationships in the phenomena should be lauded, however, and in many instances the statistical usage is by and large correct;

---

*In Robert C. North, Ole R. Holsti, M. George Zaninovich, and Dina A. Zinnes, <u>Content Analysis: A Handbook with Application for the Study of International Crisis</u> (Evanston, Ill.: Northwestern University Press, 1963), evaluative assertion analysis, pattern analysis, and factor analysis are the methods suggested for scaling perceptions. The advent of computer technology has provided the opportunity for undertaking complex semantic distance analysis. Another approach that has been suggested for the weighting and aggregating of subjective judgments is contained in Merlyn E. Nightengale, "The Value Statement," <u>Naval Research Logistics Quarterly</u> 17, no. 1 (1970): 1-18.

METHODOLOGICAL AND STATISTICAL PRACTICES

I have not listed all of the appropriate applications, since they are obvious to the reader of these studies. If a central objective of the 1914 project was to build a set of coherent relationships between the attitudes and the behavior of the decision makers of states during the prewar crisis, then some deficiencies in these studies as discussed in these pages remain. If, however, the primary purpose was to establish the causes of World War I, that is a different problem entirely: the boundaries of that issue are limitless. Some of the later studies have focused on this larger question.[30] Because these works did not seem to fit with the bulk of the 1914 content analysis studies, I have excluded them from the discussion.

SOME FURTHER THOUGHTS ON THE 1914 DATA ANALYSES

The problem of sampling that was cited in the preceding pages does not seem to be a major limiting feature characterizing the 1914 data set. However, the use of significance tests as a means of determining the existence of bivariate relationships in these data is still incorrect. The statistical analyses should have been confined to appropriate associational measures developed for hypothesis testing with ordinal data, in which description, rather than inference, is the basis for interpreting results. As we have argued, it is difficult to clarify the nature of relationships among variables if the data set contains too many departures from the assumptions underlying certain statistical tests.

We would like to propose several paths of analyses that the researchers in the 1914 project have not considered in published reports. By and large, the perceptual variables have been treated as categorically separate concepts, regarding which the researchers' attention was focused primarily on perceived and expressed hostility. While we have no reason to assume that hostility is a unidimensional variable, it has been treated as such in these studies. Both the Q sort and paired comparison techniques of scale analysis, as applied to the hostility concept, assume a common singular dimension in defining the variable. This approach, which is frequently employed in social science research, is a legitimate method for conceptualizing variables. The 1914 investigators, however, appear to be interested in first exploring the content and form of the decision makers' perceptions and then examining the linkages between these attitudes and the policies (behavior) undertaken by the states. The structure and form of perceptions have not been studied in the thorough, comprehensive manner that would seem to be suggested by a number of the hypotheses proposed.

What types of analyses would be appropriate to deal with this issue? We shall briefly outline two methods for examining the existence of multidimensions within a data set: scaling and nonmetric factor analysis.

Scale analysis, as developed by Guttman, Torgerson, and Mokken, is based on the notion that pairs of items can be arranged into a ranking scheme that is determined by the frequency and content of item response in the data.[31] The properties of monotonicity and item difficulty define the location of any item in the ranking structure. If the analysts in the 1914 project had examined the relationships between different statements, which in the context of the analysis implied difference perceptions, the pairwise association among all statements (or items) would be established and linkages among larger sets of statements or perceptions might have been developed. Such an approach would not necessitate making assumptions about the dimensional, distributional, or metric properties of the data, which, we argued, are difficult to support for the 1914 data set. The scale analysis would be limited to establishing variable associations on the basis of the presence or frequency of different statements, as opposed to assessing the intensity of perceptions directly. In short, the analysis would entail an exploratory search of the structural relationships among the decisions makers' statements, designed as a method for evaluating the perceptual form of the variables.

A more or less standard criticism of scale analysis is that it presupposes that a single dimensionality characterizes much of the data. If the items are not scalar, it may mean that they are completely unrelated or that they form parts of different dimensions that are common to a broadly conceptualized variable. Scaling, however, does establish the form of association between the unit elements on which the analysis is performed, and it might be a useful device for determining the dimensional nature of perceptions in the 1914 data.* This procedure could provide another way of measuring intensity with nominal and ordinal variables.

Factor analysis is another technique that is often suggested for searching for underlying dimensions in a data set, to compress or reduce the number of different variables or categories. For the most part, factor analysis programs require interval-level data and would be inappropriate for the 1914 data. The Guttman-Lingoes

---

*Robert J. Mokken, in <u>A Theory and Procedure for Scale Analysis</u> (the Hague: Moulton, 1972), recommends the H coefficient for assessing the monotonic relationship between two items. It is seen as far more stable than the Guttman coefficient of reproducibility.

nonmetric factor analysis is a reformulation of the factor problem. It is designed to represent a factor solution capable of reproducing only the rank order pattern of the data matrix, which means that the assumptions may be relaxed.[32] Moreover, the nonmetric solution, which reflects order relations, is also helpful when there is a lack of linearity in the input data and is applicable when one is interested in examining the co-occurrence, affinity, or association between two items. Establishing the clusterings of perceptions in spatial representation might give a better indication of how attitudinal structures are connected and what is the relational nature between perceptions and behavior.*

With regard to the actual testing of hypotheses in the 1914 studies, it would seem that a major criterion for prediction would suggest relationships between rates of change in variables interlocked in associational propositions. This is not only a correlational problem, but a matter of regression analysis. Regression has not been, and cannot be, appropriately used on these data; yet the nature of the question posed in many hypotheses would seem to imply the regressional statistical model. We might wonder, therefore, whether or not the stated hypotheses have in fact been tested. Because regression analysis is inapplicable, the possibilities for building causal models incorporating more than two variables are thwarted. Relatively simpler notions in which perceptual variables are included, such as the mapping of communications networks during the 1914 crisis, become more difficult to handle without the aid of regression, which is the core of measuring connections between rates of change among variables. For these reasons, the techniques of scaling and nonmetric factor analysis would be useful.

The problem of assessing the precise connections between attitudes and behaviors in the context of the outbreak of war is an important issue in the analysis of international politics. The 1914 studies have shed light on some of the forms these relationships may take. As research on the various methodological aspects of data analysis continues, the resulting findings should be even more solid and impressive.

---

*Roger N. Shepard, A. Kimball Romney, and Sara Beth Nerlove, eds., <u>Multidimensional Scaling: Theory and Applications for the Behavioral Sciences</u> (New York: Seminar Press, 1972), contains a wealth of scaling possibilities that could conceivably be applied to the 1914 content-analyzed data dealing with perceptual variables. We have isolated only two quite simple possibilities by which further analyses might proceed.

NOTES

1. The specific set of studies to be reviewed include Howard E. Koch, Jr., Robert C. North, and Dina A. Zinnes, "Some Theoretical Notes on Geography and International Conflict," Journal of Conflict Resolution 4, no. 1 (1960): 4-14; Dina A. Zinnes, Robert C. North, and Howard E. Koch, Jr., "Capability, Threat and the Outbreak of War," in International Politics and Foreign Policy, edited by James N. Rosenau (New York: Free Press, 1961), pp. 469-82; Dina A. Zinnes, "Hostility in International Decision-Making," Journal of Conflict Resolution 6, no. 3 (1962): 236-43; Robert C. North, Ole R. Holsti, M. George Zaninovich, and Dina A. Zinnes, Content Analysis: A Handbook with Application for the Study of International Crisis (Evanston, Ill.: Northwestern University Press, 1963); Robert C. North, Richard A. Brody, and Ole R. Holsti, "Some Empirical Data on the Conflict Spiral," Papers, Peace Research Society (International) 1 (1964): 1-14; Ole R. Holsti, Richard A. Brody, and Robert C. North, "Violence and Hostility: The Path to World War," paper presented at the American Psychiatric Association Conference, Los Angeles, Calif., 1964; Ole R. Holsti, "The 1914 Case," American Political Science Review 59, no. 2, (1965): 365-78; Ole R. Holsti and Robert C. North, "The History of Human Conflict," in The Nature of Human Conflict, edited by Elton B. McNeil (Englewood Cliffs: Prentice-Hall, 1965), pp. 155-71; Ole R. Holsti and Robert C. North, "Perceptions of Hostility and Economic Variables in the 1914 Crisis," in Comparing Nations, edited by Richard L. Merritt and Stein Rokkan (New Haven: Yale University Press, 1966), pp. 169-90; Dina A. Zinnes, "A Comparison of Hostile Behavior of Decision-Makers in Simulate and Historical Data," World Politics 18, no. 3 (1966): 474-502; Robert C. North, "Perception and Action in the 1914 Crisis," Journal of International Affairs 21, no. 1 (1967): 103-22; Dina A. Zinnes, "The Expression and Perception of Hostility in Prewar Crisis: 1914," in Quantitative International Politics: Insights and Evidence, edited by J. David Singer (New York: Free Press, 1968), pp. 85-119; Ole R. Holsti, Robert C. North, and Richard A. Brody, "Perception and Action in the 1914 Crisis," in Quantitative International Politics: Insights and Evidence, edited by J. David Singer (New York: Free Press, 1968), pp. 123-58; Ole R. Holsti, "Individual Differences in 'Defining the Situation'," Journal of Conflict Resolution 14, no. 3 (1970): 303-10; Ole R. Holsti, "Time, Alternatives and Communications: The 1914 and Cuban Missile Crises," in International Crisis: Evidence from Behavioral Research, edited by Charles F. Hermann (New York: Free Press, 1972), pp. 58-80; Ole R. Holsti,

Crisis, Escalation, War (Montreal: McGill-Queens University Press, 1972); Dina A. Zinnes "Some Evidence Relevant to Man-Milieu Hypotheses," in The Analysis of International Politics: Essays in Honor of Harold and Margaret Sprout, edited by James N. Rosenau, Vincent Davis, and Maurice East (New York: Free Press, 1972), pp. 209-51; and Dina A. Zinnes, Joseph Zinnes, and Robert McClure, "Hostility in Diplomatic Communications: A Study of the 1914 Crisis," in International Crisis: Evidence from Behavioral Research, edited by Charles F. Hermann (New York: Free Press, 1972), pp. 139-62.
  2. Zinnes, North, and Koch, "Capability, Threat," op. cit., p. 472.
  3. Different numbers of actual documents that defined the data set are reported in Zinnes, North, and Koch, "Capability, Threat," op. cit., p. 473, and Holsti, Crisis, Escalation, War, op. cit., p. 39. The statement in the text uses Holsti's numerical report, as the most recently published study.
  4. Zinnes, North and Koch, "Capability, Threat," op. cit., p. 472.
  5. Holsti, North and Brody, "Perception and Action," op. cit., p. 134.
  6. See Zinnes, North, and Koch, "Capability, Threat," op. cit., p. 472, and Holsti, Crisis, Escalation, War, op. cit., pp. 42-43.
  7. Zinnes, "Expression and Perception," op. cit., p. 89; Holsti, North, and Brody, "Perception and Action," op. cit., p. 134; and Holsti, Crisis, Escalation, War, op. cit., pp. 38-39.
  8. Holsti, Crisis, Escalation, War, p. 42.
  9. Ibid., p. 43.
  10. North et al., Content Analysis Handbook, op. cit., p. 39.
  11. Ole R. Holsti, Content Analysis for the Social Sciences and the Humanities (New York: Addison-Wesley, 1969), p. 2.
  12. North, et al., Content Analysis Handbook, op. cit., pp. 49, 51-64; Zinnes, "Expression and Perception," op. cit., pp. 90-92; and Holsti, Crisis, Escalation, War, op. cit., p. 46.
  13. Ithiel de Sola Pool, Trends in Content Analysis (Urbana: University of Illinois Press, 1959), Chapter 2.
  14. Robert Jervis, The Logic of Images in International Relations (Princeton, N.J.: Princeton University Press, 1970), and Thomas Schelling, The Strategy of Conflict (New York: Oxford University Press, 1963).
  15. Zinnes, "Expression and Perception," op. cit., pp. 90-92.
  16. North, et al., Content Analysis Handbook, op. cit., pp. 17-41.
  17. John E. Mueller, "The Use of Judges to Generate Quantitative Data," in Approaches to Measurement in International Relations: A

Non-Evangelical Survey, edited by John E. Mueller (New York: Appleton-Century-Crofts, 1969), p. 249.

18. These comments are drawn from Clyde Coombs, "Psychological Scaling without a Unit of Measurement," Psychological Review 57, no. 1 (1950): 145-58, in which he introduces the idea of an "ordered metric" scale on which the magnitude of intervals could be ordered.

19. Bernard S. Phillips, Social Research Strategy and Tactics (2nd ed., New York: The Macmillan Company, 1971), p. 206.

20. Ibid.

21. Hubert M. Blalock, Social Statistics (2nd ed., New York: McGraw-Hill, 1972), pp. 20-23.

22. Harry S. Upshaw, "Attitude Measurement," in Methodology in Social Research, ed. Hubert M. Blalock, Jr., and Ann B. Blalock (New York: McGraw-Hill, 1968), p. 90.

23. North, Brody, and Holsti, "Conflict Spiral," op. cit., pp. 6, 9, and Zinnes, "Expression and Perception," op. cit., pp. 106, 114.

24. Zinnes, Zinnes, and McClure, "Hostility in Diplomatic Communications," op. cit., pp. 149-61; Holsti, "The 1914 Case," op. cit., pp. 236, 241-44; and Holsti, Crisis, Escalation, War, op. cit., Chapters 2 and 6.

25. Zinnes, "Man-Milieu Hypothesis," op. cit., p. 237.

26. Ibid.

27. Such correlational studies are conducted in Holsti, North, and Brody, "Perception and Action," op. cit.; Holsti and North, "Perceptions of Hostility," op. cit.; and Holsti, Crisis, Escalation, War, op. cit.

28. Holsti and North, "Perceptions of Hostility," op. cit., p. 189.

29. Ibid., p. 190.

30. Nazli Choucri and Robert C. North, Nations in Conflict: National Growth and International Violence (San Francisco: W. H. Freeman and Co., 1975); Holsti, "Individual Differences," op. cit.; and Gordon Hilton, "A Closed and Open Model Analysis of Expression of Hostility in Crisis," Journal of Peace Research 8, nos. 3-4 (1971): 249-62.

31. For an overview of this field see Robert J. Mokken, A Theory and Procedure for Scale Analysis, (The Hague: Moulton, 1972).

32. David Napior, "Nonmetric Multidimensional Techniques for Summated Ratings," in Multidimensional Scaling: Theory and Applications for the Behavioral Sciences, edited by Roger N. Shepard A. Kimball Romney, and Sara Beth Nerlove (New York: Seminar Press, 1972), pp. 158-80.

CHAPTER

20

AN EVALUATION OF
THE SUBSTANTIVE
CONTRIBUTION OF THE
STANFORD STUDIES
IN CONFLICT AND
INTEGRATION
Mark S. Levine

A project with the chronological length and conceptual breadth of the Stanford Studies in Conflict and Integration cannot be adequately summarized. Indeed, because of the high quality of research that forms the corpus of this project, it should not be summarized; new entrants into the field of quantitative international politics should have to read this research in the original. There is much to be learned by simply following the articulation, elaboration, and alteration of the Stanford Studies from the early papers to the most current output. Rather than trying to summarize the project's substantive results, I will use this chapter as a vehicle for my reactions to the project, first indicating what I consider the major issues the project addressed; the assumptions underlying the various models; the interplay of substantive concerns and operational decisions; and finally, the implications of the results for the development of theory in international relations. At the outset I assure the reader that my comments are based on a subset of the full bibliography of the project emphasizing those pieces that I consider most instructive.[1] I will not deal explicitly with the intellectual history of the project or the project participants, nor will I dwell on the obvious facts that (1) the Stanford Studies have made a major impact on the technological development of political science through the application and

---

I would like to express my thanks to James Caporaso and Gordon Hilton for their suggestions. I also thank Richard J. Lamb of W. H. Freeman and Co., the publishers of Nazli Choucri and Robert C. North, <u>Nations in Conflict: National Growth and International Violence</u> (San Francisco, 1975), for providing me with a copy of the page proofs of that long-awaited manuscript.

popularization of content analysis and event-data analysis; (2) the Stanford Studies and Stanford University have been the training ground of several of the most innovative and productive scholars in theoretical-empirical international relations; (3) according to his collaborators, much of the responsibility for the coherence and vision of the project is Robert C. North's; and (4) the funds invested by Stanford University and other sources have been well spent and should continue to be invested to support additional analyses of the interwar period.

DOMINANT THEMES IN THE HISTORY OF THE PROJECT

For a research project to be characterized as "major," it seems to be necessary, if not sufficient, that it ask large, nontrivial questions and that it not focus its energies on the solution of intriguing, yet transitory, puzzles. Although the primary focus of the project has shifted from the early crisis studies to the more recent studies by Ole R. Holsti and Nazli Choucri and Robert C. North, the questions central to the research have been questions central to our understanding of the international system and the pathology of war.

Early Crisis Studies

The early crisis studies seem to have begun from the observation that World War I was the war that nobody seemed to want or expect.[2] The basic question, then, is what happened in the interval of time following the assassination of the archduke that made war increasingly unavoidable. The answer that is suggested is twofold: (1) the nature of the environment within which the decision makers found themselves after the assassination was that of a crisis; and (2) decision making in crisis environments has distinctly pathological characteristics. Most importantly, decision makers respond to their perceptions of hostility in the environment. In crises, the link between this perception and the actual level of hostility becomes weak; that is, reality and perceptions of reality become less congruent. Certainly perceptions are the basis of day-to-day noncrisis decision making; but the authors argue that the more deeply involved in a crisis, the more likely the decision maker is to over-perceive the level of hostility in the environment and the more likely he or she is to respond with hostility to the perception of hostility. This

SUBSTANTIVE CONTRIBUTION 409

propensity to over-perceive hostility and then react in a hostile manner produces an accelerating spiral of conflict-laden behavior. There is such deviation-amplifying feedback in the process that the further into the process one moves, the less important the actions of the perceived opponents become and the more important one's perceptions of them.

The early crisis papers express these notions in the convenient vocabulary of a two-step mediated stimulus-response model, symbolized by S-r:s-R. The frequently reproduced schematic diagram is shown in Figure 20.1, where S represents a stimulus from the environment, r is the perception of internal representation of the stimulus, s is the internal expression of some planned response to the stimulus, and R is the actual behavioral response to S. The act R then becomes part of the environment of the other actor; that is, it becomes an S, which then may be perceived, and so on. This vocabulary helps organize the hypotheses by focusing attention on the important linkages in the model: how accurately do decision makers perceive their environments (s-r)? to what extent are plans of action functions of the perceptions of the decision makers (r:s)? to what extent are decision makers capable of selecting policies for implementation that accurately represent their intentions (s-R)? Finally, each of these links may be expected to vary with involvement in a crisis situation. No deductions follow from the adoption of the mediated S-R formulation, but it does alert the reader to the central role of the psychological states of decision makers.

Although the authors of the early papers were interested in the effects of the crisis environment on decision making, their design precluded serious consideration of the dynamics within crises. In these papers it is noted that Germany and Austria-Hungary, the Dual Alliance, became quickly involved in the events following the assassination, whereas France, Great Britain, and Russia, the members of the Triple Entente, were far less involved during the first month after the assassination (June 27 to July 27, 1914). The Triple Entente seemed to be deeply involved only in the immediate prewar days, July 28 to August 4. Thus in the first month's data a contrast is shown between one alliance that was crisis-involved and one that was not. Crisis may be treated as a variable, but only a simple dichotomous variable. Since one can easily conceptualize degrees of severity of crisis, these early studies seem to miss the important issue of what happens to the decision-making process as a crisis progresses and/or intensifies. Indeed, some of the early studies entirely lose crisis as a variable by pooling the data across alliances and/or across time for the Triple Entente.[3]

FIGURE 20.1

The S–r:s–R Model

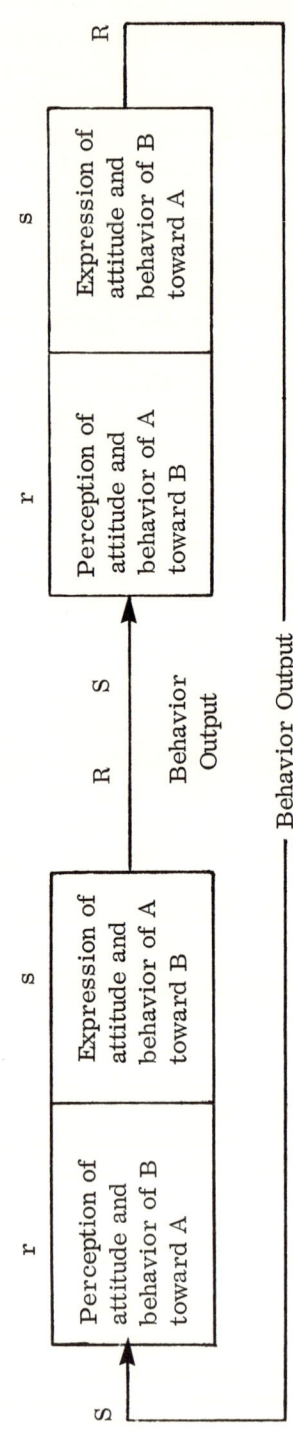

Source: Robert C. North, Richard A. Brody, and Ole R. Holsti, "Some Empirical Data on the Conflict Spiral," Papers, Peace Research Society (International) 9 (1968): 125–37.

Ole R. Holsti's Reformulation

Fortunately the volume that ties together the crisis studies recognizes this issue and seeks to build crisis into the design as a multi-valued variable.[4] Holsti poses the following question:

> The more general question is how crisis—defined here as a situation of unanticipated threat to important values and restricted decision time—is likely to affect policy processes and outcomes. What are the probable effects of crisis upon abilities which are generally considered essential to effective decision making?[5]

The answer to these questions comes from the analysis of a crisis byproduct, which is stress. He argues that sudden threatening situations requiring immediate attention, that is, crises, will produce stress. Stress becomes a continuously varying (at least in principle) product of the occurence of a crisis event. In a sense crisis does not vary; it merely happens; but its consequent, stress, varies as the participants to the situations feel more or less threatened, more or less fatigued, more or less constrained as further events unfold and their perceptions change.

The question that is never addressed directly, although the Cuban missile crisis studies help, is, How do the dimensions of crisis itself, <u>degree</u> of threat, surprise, and limitation on decision time, affect the production of stress and thus the conduct of the postevent period? I consider this important, since every situation involving decision that one is confronted with has a finite decision time, is to some degree unanticipated, and is in some way threatening; that is, it can be placed in the definitional three-space of crisis. Stress is more than a simple surrogate for crisis, since stress can be produced by situations that would not normally be classified as crises. Although Holsti's approach introduces a continuously varying correlate of crisis into the design, crisis itself or any of its several defining dimensions is not an aspect of his research.

Crisis-induced stress becomes the driving factor in Holsti's model. Although the earlier mediated stimulus-response formulation is no longer present, the theoretic focus remains on the effects of a hostile environment on the psychological states of decision makers. Holsti's model attempts to specify more precisely how misperceptions, errors, suboptimal policies, and the like enter into the decision process. His model represents a series of hypotheses that could account for the inconsistencies between S and r, r and s, and s and R in the earlier formulation. The model, as represented in Figure

20.2, is unidirectional, with the perception of constrained decision time being the crucial intervening variable.

Although one can sympathize with Holsti's attempt to keep his model parsimonious, unfortunately there seem to be several lacunae. For the paths among the variables that carried the causal flow, little attention was paid to the form of the functional dependency. By default Holsti adopts unspecified monotones for these functions with his utilization of nonparametric, associational statistics. The verbal discussion of the hypotheses at several points suggested nonlinearities, limiting behaviors, and the like that would have enriched the model and increased its falsifiability had they been built in. Clearly the author had some hesitation about the ability of the data to withstand such analysis.

The absence of feedback in the model is bothersome when combined with the loss from the earlier model of the interactional basis of crisis decision making. One would think that acting too quickly and ineffectively are likely to produce results that increase the stress-level on the actor. Further, the opponent's behavior will also be less predictable, making it more difficult for the actor to plan his or her next actions, thereby increasing the uncertainty and stress. The "joined behavior" characteristic of the earlier formulation is an important aspect of the explanation of the escalatory property of crises. Indeed, I wonder whether, without either feedback or interaction, this model could account for exponential growth in the behavior modeled without stipulating that stress must grow explosively. Finally, it is unfortunate that stress is exogenous, since it precludes answering why some crises wind down rather than escalate. According to the model, should a crisis wind down, as in the Cuban case, that must happen because of a lessening of stress, but any explanation of that process is outside the model. Indeed, as Holsti ends up doing, only ad hoc conjectures can be presented to account for the different results of the crises in 1914 and 1962.[6]

Dynamics of Conflict Studies

The final set of studies was generated by Nazli Choucri and Robert C. North, published in a series of articles that seemed to be strategically placed in journals to expose different groups of readers to the findings.[7] The often revised manuscript of <u>Nations in Conflict</u> represents the state-of-the-art report on this portion of the Stanford Studies. In terms of chronological focus, type of data analyzed, statistical methodology, and complexity of model,

FIGURE 20.2

Ole R. Holsti's Model: Stress, Time, and Decision Making

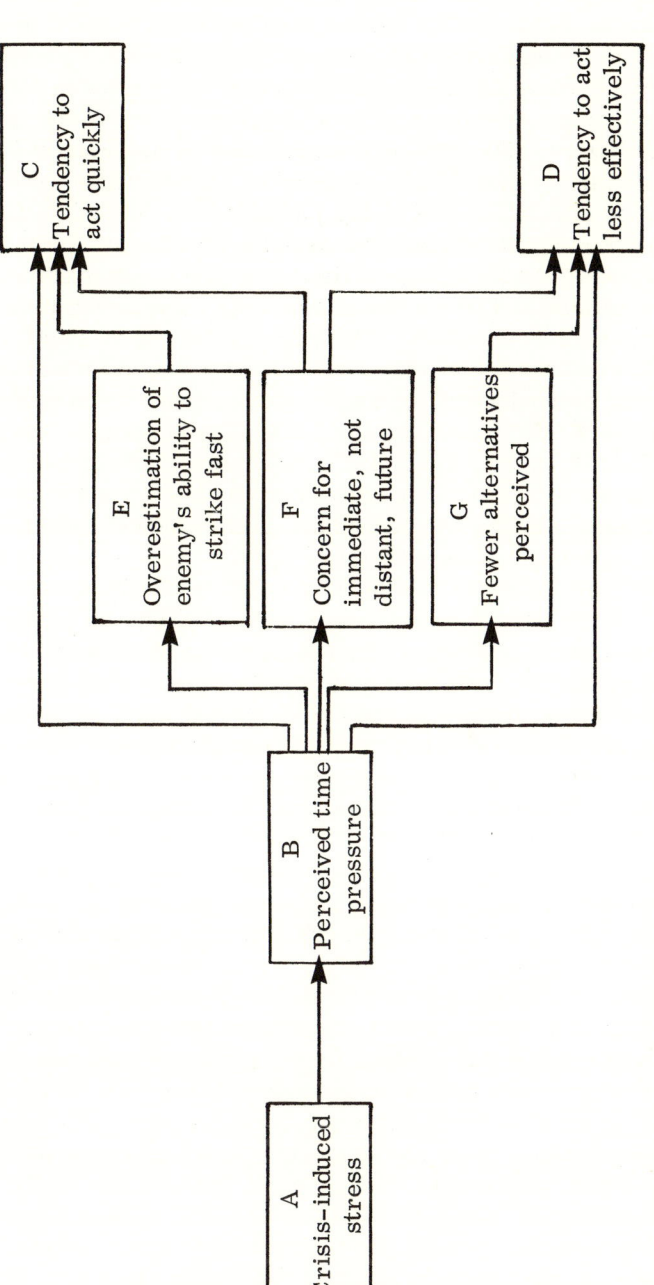

Source: Ole R. Holsti, Crisis, Escalation, War (Montreal: McGill-Queens University Press, 1972), p. 122.

these studies diverge from the crisis studies. Whereas the crisis studies focused on the weeks between the assassination of the archduke and the outbreak of large-scale hostilities during the late summer of 1914, these studies examine the 45-year period prior to the assassination. The earlier studies relied heavily on data on perceptions and sentiments drawn from content analyses of the official documents, while these studies use aggregate data on the demographic, economic, and political attributes of the major European powers. The bivariate nonparametric analyses of links in rather simple models are replaced by simultaneous equation estimation and simulation of a richly joined, nonrecursive model.

Whereas the earlier studies dealt with the dynamics of crises, the Choucri-North studies address the problems of national growth and technological development and their relationship to international competition and conflict. Their model, as represented in Figure 20.3, begins with the assertion that a growing population and a growing technological base will produce demands on a nation that may exceed the resources available. Given adequate capabilities, a nation faced with unfulfilled demands may manifest lateral pressure: "the process of extending national activities beyond a nation's border," for example by the acquisition and exploitation of colonial territories. Such extensions of the domain of activity of the nation must be protected, implying the expansion of military capabilities. If there are several nations simultaneously dealing with increasing demands through lateral pressure, there is a strong likelihood of increased competition for resources and resulting conflictory intersections among the expanding nations. Such growth may lead to an environment in which a crisis event might escalate to war.[8]

It is at this point that one can see the strong theoretical dovetailing of these studies with the earlier crisis analyses. One of the questions raised in the crisis studies, the question that motivated the Cuban investigation, was why some crises escalate while others wind down. One response is that some property of the crisis event or the crisis participants is such that there is variance in the rate of production of stress or the ability to cope with stress.[9] An alternative approach is contextual, suggesting that the nature of the international system within which the crisis event occurs will affect the way in which the event is finally processed and will determine whether the event instigates an explosive conflict spiral. As one may interpret Choucri and North, it is not particular systemic variable values, such as the number of actor nations participating in a crisis, that matter, but rather it is the nature of the causal links among variables that indicates whether a nation, and thereby the international system within which that nation operates, is war-prone. As presented by Choucri and North, the nature of the theory

FIGURE 20.3

The <u>Nations in Conflict</u> Model

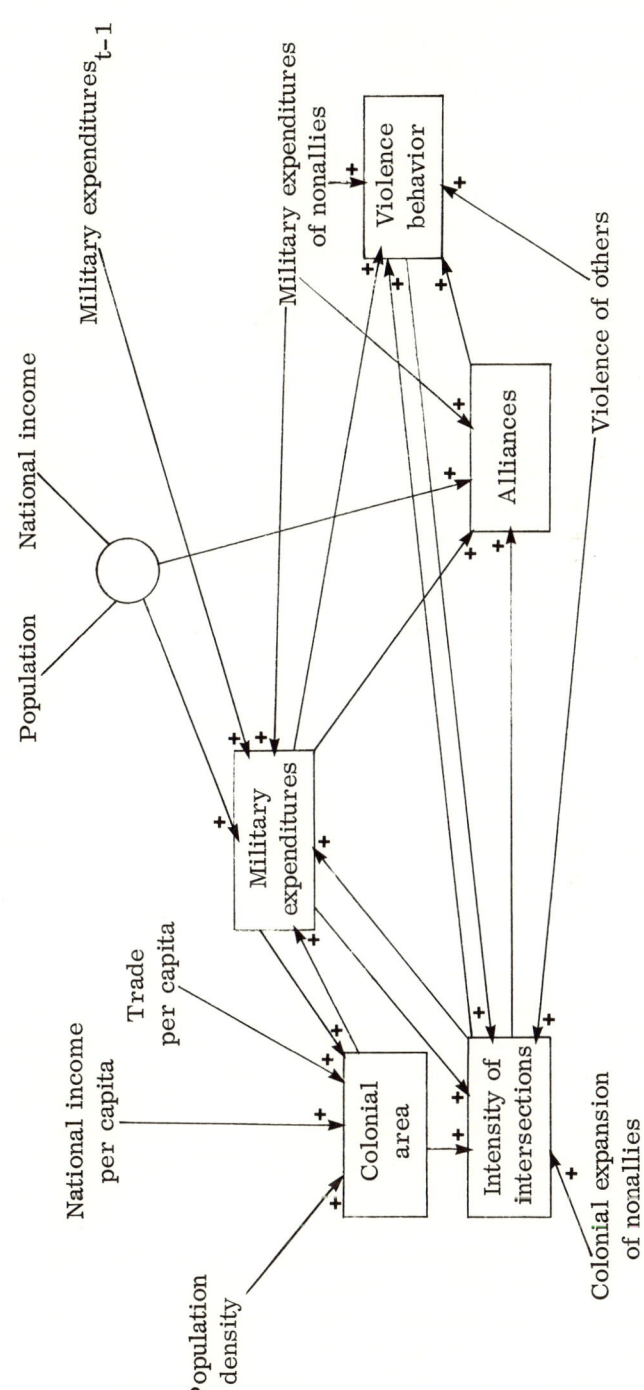

Source: Nazli Choucri and Robert C. North, <u>Nations in Conflict: National Growth and International Violence</u> (San Francisco: W. H. Freeman and Company, 1975), p. 170.

that characterizes the mapping of demographic and economic growth processes onto international interactions determines whether nations are war-prone or are able to deal with competition and conflict without resort to the use of force. This distinction is developed most clearly in their article on peace systems.[10] Again, it is not an attribute of a nation or of the international system that determines the propensity to become involved in war; rather it is the structure of causality governing the dynamics of the nation that is crucial. The Choucri-North work represents an empirical investigation of a structural model of explanation.

One may note that this particular model, as pictured in Figure 20.3, has the alarming property of being explosive. All of the links in the model are characterized by hypothesized positive coefficients, including the feedback loops. Since the principal exogenous variables of population, technology, capabilities, and demands all are likely to be characterized by strong positive trend components, the model predicts concurrent expansion in the endogenous variables. Because of the joint dependencies among the endogenous variables, their growth should be explosive. Thus the structural properties of the model are consistent with a system that is driven and that drives itself to higher and higher levels of violent conflict.

Choucri and North recognize that their model seems to represent a shift from the level of analysis centering on the decision maker, or the individual, that characterized the crisis studies. They argue that the aggregate variables represent the "traces" of the multitude of individual decisions and argue as follows:

> Presumably, a firm policy of restraint or other firm exercise of political will in Vienna, Belgrade, St. Petersburg, or Berlin might have prevented the outbreak of war during the summer of 1914—as firmness had served to constrain the Balkan crises in 1908-1909 and in 1912-1913. But larger populations, advancing technologies, and greater industries had created seemingly insatiable demands that required more resources, more commerce, more markets, more sea routes, more colonies, more bases, vastly larger navies, and alliances tying together countries in competing camps.[11]

They seek to maintain the conceptual thread of a decision-making approach to international relations in the tradition of the crisis studies and of the work of Richard C. Snyder, H. W. Bruck, and Burton Sapin,[12] focusing on the interplay on the internal and external settings and the constraints on decision making that these settings generate.

In discussing Russian reactions to the actions of Austria-Hungary towards Serbia and the subsequent joint sensitivity to arms increments, North and Choucri argue that "such competition becomes salient only to the extent that basic differentials in population growth, technological advancement, and access to resources have already become considerable and are perceived as such by all sides."[13] In other words, for the causality suggested in this earlier version of the model to work, that is, for the structure to produce the particular pattern of responses to the set of inputs, a prior dynamic is required. The system had to be conditioned to receive the inputs by the growth of sufficient status differentials among nations and by the perception of these differentials by the relevant actors. Thus variation in the attributes of nations and in the distribution of value in the international system becomes crucial to the implementation of the war-prone model. Although there is strong emphasis on the economic, demographic, and technological bases of international behavior, that is, on attribute theory, Choucri and North continually reinforce the position that the systemic, structural, and contextual properties of the phenomena being modeled govern the particular form the actions will assume.

The most intellectually provocative aspect of the Stanford studies comes from the conjunction of the Choucri-North and the crisis models, which provide conceptualization of the history of the international system that is temporally partitioned. The partitions derive not from historical events nor from particular attributes of nations or decision makers but rather from the structure of interdependency among social processes. One starts with the benign peace-system pattern of interdependency in which the demands for resources do not have such a causal impact on other social processes that conflict escalates. Should certain crucial causal links change, this peace system may be transformed into a war-prone system, with the explosive property described above. Should certain events occur, perhaps as unpredictable as the event in June 1914, a second transition will carry the system into its crisis configuration. Thus there are three noncompetitive theories of international behavior, each representing an alternative structure of action, all of which in principle could be supported by empirical investigation of either different periods of time in the history of a single set of nations or of different sets of nations at one point in time.

Holsti and North used the imagery of a whirlpool in one of the earliest articles on the project, as follows:

> Thus, like a series of separate eddies, the various nations were at first linked in a number of local situations as described by the conflict model. But as eddies, when

> they come in contact, form a whirlpool, so the major
> powers of Europe were drawn into a general conflict
> which none had desired and few had even foreseen, at
> least consciously.[14]

It would seem that it was an early insight of the project researchers that the nature of the conflict spiral is to link things together, achieving a disasterous economy of scale. It is not the separate dynamics of single nations that matters as much as it is the fact that such dynamics co-occur in a finite environment.

What we are denied, however, is a discussion of the nature of the transition processes, those crucial variables and/or events that carry the system from peace-prone to war-prone to crisis and war, and are perhaps even capable of reversing this ordering. Choucri and North are sensitive to the issue: "We do not seek to predict discrete events, such as the outbreak of WW I. We are concerned, rather, with changes in the system, changes that are conducive to crisis and war."[15] They do not, however, deal with either the conceptualization of system change or its measurement. They do look at changes in the estimates of their model's parameters for different periods for each nation, but these represent change within a system, not change of system. Indeed, nothing in their analysis tells us when the European system was ripe for war, that is, whether had the assassination occurred in 1913 there would have been war. Their notion of transformation is fuzzy and seems to be little more than a descriptive property of the data. What is required is a theory of transformation or transition that would locate those mechanisms of the deeper structure that drives the system through its various manifest structures. Consider the following observation:

> From our evidence, however, it is not possible to infer
> any clear snow-balling process whereby conflicts of lower
> intensity necessarily give rise to conflicts of higher
> intensity. A period of high-intensity conflict can be,
> and often is, followed by a period of relative tranquility.[16]

This observation, which seems to falsify the inherent explosive property of the Choucri-North model, tantalizes us with the question of why previous conflicts did not escalate. Is it the restraint or lack of it among decision makers, the stress and fatigue levels, or other aspects of the situation that decide when events become war-productive crises, or is it that the structure has yet to pass through the transformation to its crisis state and thus events could not become crises? Might the slow moving, trend-dominated variables in the model be pushing the system inexorably to a point at which war is a virtual certainty, requiring only a small stochastic perturbation to catalyze it, or are more volatile variables required? Can the dynamics of a system give rise to its own transformation, as would be consistent with Marxist thought, or must the source of the transformation lie outside the system being modeled? "We need a more specific theoretical statement of when and how changes are expected and what forms they may take."[17] Agreed, but the fact that the authors have even raised the issue of system transformation explicitly is a notable achievement.

METHODOLOGICAL ISSUES AFFECTING THE SUBSTANTIVE FINDINGS

One approach to an evaluation of the substantive contribution of the Stanford Studies would be to employ methodological criteria to winnow out the empirical results that do not stand up under rigorous scrutiny. The Stanford Studies have already benefited from methodological suggestions and reanalyses.[18] Thus I will focus only on a few of the methodological and operational decisions that seem crucial to substantive evaluation. The first set of issues is more stylistic than methodological. Many of the project reports have been characterized by inadequate clarity of presentation of the operational decisions made in the course of the empirical investigations. Whereas the conceptual and theoretical portions are typically precise, some operational presentations are opaque, as in an early Choucri-North paper called "The Determinants of International Violence."[19] In at least one case there is inconsistency between the specification of a model in equation and path diagramatic form.[20] The lack of presentation of intermediate statistical results, such as bivariate correlations, especially in the Choucri-North work, makes it difficult for the careful reader to consider other formulations and/or rival hypotheses. The scant publication of the project's raw data may be understood on the basis of publishers' antipathy to data handbooks, but it does stand in the way of reanalysis and replication, especially when no version is available through the Inter-University Consortium for Political Research at the University of Michigan.

Occasionally index values do not seem to be properly calculated from the intermediate values presented,[21] or verbal conclusions seem to be inconsistent with previously reported statistics. The most glaring example of this is a summary comment that the S-R correlation was higher for the Triple Entente than the Dual Alliance, when earlier the opposite had been shown.[22] At other times, calculations are not reported that would have been inconsistent with the authors' hypotheses, had they been presented.[23]* In the Choucri-North volume, references are made to the constant term in an equation accounting for variance in the dependent variable, such as, "For the full period the constant term best explains Russian colonial area,"[24] and partial correlations are run involving the constant. Errors and inconsistencies such as these are probably unavoidable, and my mentioning them may well be considered a cheap shot; they become bothersome only because they intrude into a consideration of the substantive implications of the research.

To the extent that an issue is stylistic or not pervasive in a body of research, it can be easily ignored, but pervasive methodological problems must be addressed. The existence of strong trend components in many of the data series analyzed, both in the crisis studies and in the later Choucri-North work, is an issue that has serious debilitating implications. Consider the following as examples:

1. Holsti reports a set of correlations (gamma's) between level of stress and communication volume, but stress is dominated by trend.[25]

2. As an attempt to validate his measure of stress, which is perceived hostility, Holsti correlates it with other measures that are supposedly sensitive to level of stress, such as prices of stocks and bonds, gold flows, and interest rates. Although he obtains some relatively strong correlations, it is clear that the correlations are based on a strong common trend, while in general the daily fluctuations around the trend component are not well picked up.[26]

3. An early paper relates hostility with mobilizations of troops. The correlations are .78 and .86 for the Alliance and Entente, respectively. The mobilization data are a monotonic, nondecreasing series, since there were no demobilizations and the perceptions and expressions of hostility "rise uniformly through time as measured by frequency."[27]

4. In the Choucri-North volume, most of the exogenous variables and several of the endogenous variables are dominated by trend, at least as well as I can determine from the graphs of the series. They make observations like "German colonial expansion was closely related to domestic growth; correlations between home population and colonial empire, and, between national income and colonial empire were at or above .85."[28] All three variables have strong trends, population and colonial area seeming to be strict monotones. The essential questions that emerge here are (1) What interpretation

---

*Dividing each series into late and early segments, I find no significant difference between the Entente and the Alliance in either period.

can one give to a correlation between variables with strong trend
components? (2) What is the effect of trend on estimation? (3)
How does the existence of trend interact with one's biases toward
confirmation and the consideration of plausible rival hypotheses?

The presence of trend in the independent variables implies
that they will be highly correlated and that the resultant effect of
this multicollinearity will be that estimates of the autonomous
contribution of the individual independent variables will be impossible.
Trend in the dependent as well as the independent variables will
produce estimates of variance explained that may well be considered
artificially inflated. Since any variable with trend will correlate
strongly with any other trend-dominated variable, the research
design adopted must be sensitive to the exclusion of plausible rival
hypotheses that contain variables that share the property of trend.
Conventional procedures are available for coping with this problem,
such as the use of differenced variables or of a preliminary regression on time, to remove the linear trend component. The analysis
of differences or detrended residuals is based on the realization
that if there is a true causal dependency between variables, their
bumps, or deviations from their trend lines, will be correlated in
addition to the correlations of the raw series. This will not be true
for variables that are characterized by trend but have no causal
connection. Since a substantively provocative aspect of the Stanford
models is the explicit adoption of dyadic reaction processes, their
results should have been protected by more care paid to the rival
explanation of simple within-nation processes that happen to share
trend with the endogenous variables. This is especially true of the
Choucri-North work, in which confirmation of the plausibility of
the postulated model takes precedence over the exhaustion of rival
explanations; the existence of trend makes this an unfortunate choice.

As a simple example, I reanalyzed the U.S. and Soviet data
from one of the early studies of the Cuban missile crisis.[29] Rather
than assume that the behaviors of the superpowers were linked, I
"postulated" that both nations simply cooled off as a result of
unspecified domestic processes, perhaps having to do with the
desire to maintain the basic structure of the international system,
or any of a broad variety of verbal conjectures. The point is, my
"model" predicts that both series will have negative trend, but that
the stochastic fluctuations about the trends in the series will be
unrelated. Whereas the correlation (tau) between the two raw level
of violence series is .73, the partial correlation controlling for
time, that is, trend, is .07, a negligible value with only ten observations. Results such as this must be considered as substantial
threats to the authors' models and represent the intrusion of
methodological-design flaws in important substantive discourse.

The nature of the measurement model and the resultant operationalizations of the concepts in the various models is another point at which methodological issues obfuscate potential substantive contributions. The Stanford group has been notably creative in its development of data bases and has provided an example of the feasibility of mixing of different types of data, such as action (event) and perception (content analytic), in order to model a verbal theory adequately. They have been admirably honest in admitting to mistakes in their operationalizations, as in the discussion of the use of the total trade variable in <u>Nations in Conflict</u>.[30] On the other hand, there is a generally cavalier attitude toward the issues of reliability, validity, and composition rules.

An extreme example of this can be drawn from two versions of the Choucri-North operationalization concerning the use of raw or level variables versus first differences, as follows:

> Our use of delta or change variables ($X_t - X_{t-1}$) is based on the consideration that changes tend to delineate international dynamics more precisely than do absolute levels.[31]

> In an earlier stage of our analysis we focused exclusively on rate of change for all the variables; however, our estimated coefficients tended to wash out, yielding few statistically significant coefficients. Subsequently, we found that more robust (and statistically significant) estimates of the endogenous variables could be obtained by using only levels. The results of this analysis, using levels only, are presented here.[32]

Authors are certainly allowed to change their minds about the face validity of particular measures, but it seems that issues other than validity motivated the shift from differences to raw scores. Especially since the Stanford group tends to use single-variable manifestations of distal constructs, rather than multiple operationalization and scale construction with attendent calculations of reliability estimates, they have little ammunition to justify such radical changes in the measurement model. Holsti's validity experiments, despite the existence of trend-related problems, represents a healthy concern about the appropriateness of his measures that is sorely missing elsewhere.[33] Holsti's volume is based on the assumption that the perception of international hostility may be used as a surrogate measure for stress. Since the epistemic link is not obvious, his validity experiments are well justified.

At one point at least, Choucri and North attempt to justify the choice of a variable with an assertion that runs in the face of empirica reality. They discuss the use of national income as the measure for technology as follows: "Nations with comparatively high levels of national income (gross national product) do tend to have comparatively high levels of technology."[34] This assertion runs in the face of the frequently observed weak relationship in the cross-section between measures of technology-economic development and GNP or NI. Conventionally GNP has been viewed as a measure of size. It discriminates between large and small nations but not between advanced and backward. More frequently, GNP per capita is selected as a technological-economic development indicator. Since the growth patterns of GNP and population may not coincide, one cannot assume that GNP will behave as GNP per capita in time series. Again, this is simply an example of a more general attitude toward measurement.

The need for creative instrumentation was most acute in Choucri and North's development of the concept of lateral pressure, which "can be manifested in many different types of activity, depending on the nature of the demands that are not being satisfied domestically and on the capabilities that are available."[35] They claim that colonial expansion was "the dominant mode" of expression of lateral pressure in the period before World War I; but clearly a disjunctive composition rule spanning alternative potential modes of expression would be required to generate the necessary isomorph.[36] At another point these authors note that a nation may react to the growth of another nation "by increasing its own strength and effectiveness in a wholly different area."[37] Here again, a disjunctive rule might be required to capture this relationship, or a statistical treatment that permits a multidimensional dependent variable, such as canonical correlation. The form of this relationship is an improvement over Lewis F. Richardson's unnecessarily simplified assumption,[38] and it requires more careful consideration.

One final issue may be raised in this discussion of the relationship between their methodology and their substantive contribution, and that is whether the studies have been able to extract a single finding from a body of findings. Whereas in the crisis studies the statistical procedures were bivariate, single-equation correlations, the Choucri-North studies are based on simultaneous estimation of a multi-equation system. The focus of the studies that culminate in <u>Nations in Conflict</u> is not to increase our correlational knowledge base, but rather to begin to develop systematic theories of international behavior. The kind of results that emerges from such a simultaneous estimation procedure is fundamentally different from that from studies that are basically correlational, like the crisis studies of COW, or single-equation multiple correlation and canonical, like DON. The result of the decision to go after theory is that most of the results in Nations in Conflict cannot be taken out of context. By this I mean that these results are inexorably imbedded in the remainder of the model and any single bit of information is contingent on all the other bits by virtue of the joint determinacy and feedback throughout the model. Thus if the basic theory is wrong, that is, misspecified, or if at least some decomposable segment is wrong, then unless one can isolate those erroneous portions and determine that a particular result of interest is not conditional on the former, then one cannot use that interesting result. In this context one should recall that the procedures used by Choucri and North do not test their model, but simply estimate the parameters of the model under the strong assumption that the model is appropriately specified.*

THE ABSENCE OF INVARIANCE ISSUE

The next set of issues that have an impact on the substantive interpretability of the Stanford Studies stems not from methodological matters but from a property of the empirical results. Lacking an adequate philosophy-of-science catch phrase, I term this the "absence of invariance" cluster. It stems from findings like the following:

1. For the Dual Alliance, the correlation between perception of the Entente as hostile and the expression of hostility toward the Entente was .87, while the parallel correlation for the Entente was only .33.[39]

2. In summarizing and attempting a synthesis of the various results in Nations in Conflict, the authors use the following language:

> On balance [in the British case], however, at least one distinct path to violence-behavior emerges . . . that originates in the dynamics of domestic growth. In the case of France . . . unlike the case of Britain. . . a clear path can be traced from domestic growth . . . to expansion . . . through military expenditures and alliances, to violence-behavior. For Germany . . . the situation is quite different. . . . In the case of Italy . . . four distinct paths. . . . In the case of Russia . . . there is a direct (but negative) path. . . . Finally, for Austria-Hungary . . . three distinct paths to violence, but with many contributing factors.[40]

---

*I will grant their point, however, that the notable success of their simulations should be considered support for the model.

In the figures containing the statistically significant paths for each nation or, even better, in the parameter estimates for each nation, there is very little overlap to be found in the graphs and little agreement across the parameter estimates. In Figure 20.4 I have indicated those paths in the original model (Figure 20.3) that were statistically significant in at least three of the six analyses. These consistently appearing links are relatively few, especially among the jointly determined variables.

3. In their consideration of breakpoints, Choucri and North estimate their model for subsets of years for each of the nations, as follows:

> Certain relationships proved much stronger than others, depending on the period and country examined . . . and even the paths for a single nation vary according to which period (the full period or a subperiod) was analyzed.[41]

These within-nation temporal shifts of parameters can be rather noticeable, as seen in Figure 20.5, the comparison of the early and late period for Great Britain.

The nature of findings such as these suggests some consideration of the nature of the scientific laws that are likely to emerge out of multiple case diachronic studies. If we are dealing with dynamic processes in which we have several spatiotemporal units observed over some period of time with a series of measures taken on each unit at each time point, we may observe, or believe that in principle we may observe, regularities of the following forms:[42]

1. $Y_i = F(X_i, p)$

where i subscripts a case; Y and X are the endogenous and exogenous variables, respectively; p is a vector of parameters that are constant across cases; and the only differences across cases are the values of the exogenous variables that produce different realizations for the dependent processes;

2. $Y_i = F(X_i, p_i)$

where now we allow idiosyncratic parameters for each case, which implies that cases with the same values for X may have different Y's and that, conversely, cases with different X's may have identical Y's;

3. $Y_i = F_i(X_i, p_i)$

FIGURE 20.4

Frequently Appearing Links in the Nations in Conflict Analyses

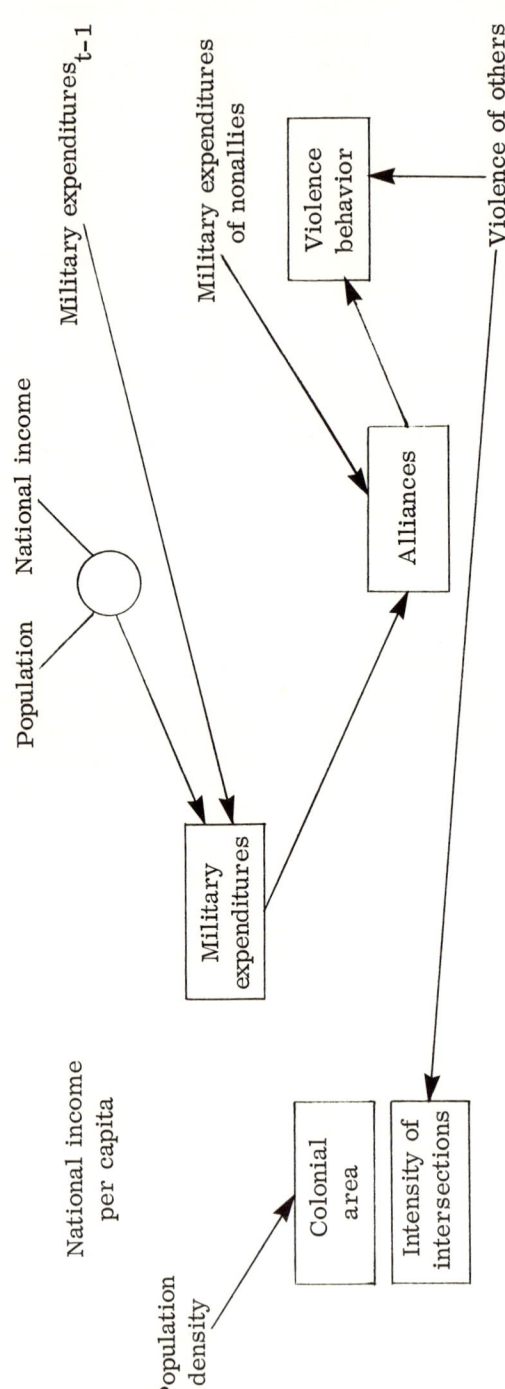

Note: The numbers above the arrows refer to the number of analyses out of the total of six in which the particular link was found to be statistically significant. Only links found significant in three or more cases are shown.

Source: Adapted by the author from Nazli Choucri and Robert C. North, Nations in Conflict: National Growth and International Violence (San Francisco: W. H. Freeman and Company, 1975), p. 170, on the basis of ibid., pp. 248-53.

FIGURE 20.5
Links Appearing in the British Subperiod Analyses

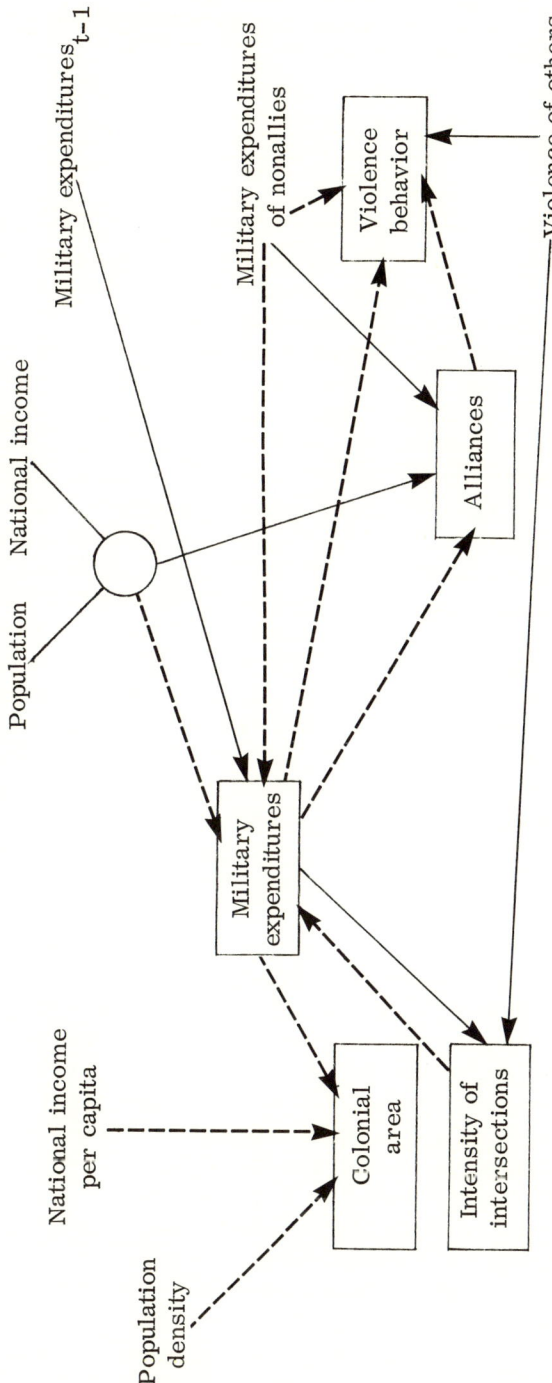

Note: Solid arrows represent links found in both the 1871-90 and 1891-1914 analyses; broken arrows represent links found in either period, but not in both.

Source: Adapted by the author from Nazli Choucri and Robert C. North, Nations in Conflict: National Growth and International Violence (San Francisco: W. H. Freeman and Company, 1975), p. 170, on the basis of ibid., p. 248.

where in this form we allow the X's to be mapped onto the Y's by different functions across cases, that is, spatially varying structures;

4. $Y_i = F [X_i, p_i(t)]$

5. $Y_i = F_i [X_i, p_i(t)]$

where, in these final forms, not only do we allow the parameters and, in the last, the function to vary across cases, we also allow the parameters to vary within a case over time.

It seems obvious that as one moves from laws of the first type toward those of the last type, one loses generality and parsimony but gains accuracy. One may be tempted to build a supratheory to account for the idiosyncracies of parameters and functions that emerge from the last three forms, in the manner of Zvi Griliches.[43] Without some clear theory to account for the idiosyncracies, the adoption of one of the last forms for the laws in a theory may make that theory nonrefutable. By this I mean that without some constraints on functions and parameters, any Y can be made to fit any, and all, X's.

Although the matter is not explicitly treated, the crisis studies seem to be based on models of the first two types. Zinnes makes an explicit assumption of a common model underlying all cases in order to justify her decision to pool the data from all countries.[44] Holsti's work, with its separate estimates of strengths of relationships for the two alliances but a common statistical model, seems to fit the second formulation. Choucri and North have adopted the fourth form, assuming a constant specification of the theory but allowing national and time-specific estimation of parameters. Their claim is that they are evaluating a single general model, but their combination of space and time variation in parameters with no attempt beyond ad hoc conjecture to deal with these differences makes me question whether the notion of lawlike regularity is getting lost in the econometrics. The only invariance that is left is the supposed invariance of the specification of the causal structure, but there is no adequate procedure to test against the null hypothesis of misspecification. I have no difficulty in dealing with parameters that vary from place to place, such as the gravitational "constant"; nor is it difficult to adjust to parameters that vary over time as a function of changes in the dynamics of the system under observation. I can deal sequentially with either over-time or over-place variation in the parameters of a theory, but the combination of the two makes me worry that we are approaching a theory of "Russia, 1891".

SUBSTANTIVE CONTRIBUTION 429

The adoption of forms other than the first permits the explicit anticipation of situations of multifinality and equifinality, that is, one-to-many and many-to-one mappings of initial conditions onto terminal states of systems. Indeed it is only by the invocation of equifinality that the heterogeneity of the results for the six nations can be combined with the common conclusion of entrance into World War I: "Different countries can move toward the same outcome—the outbreak of war in 1914, for example—by different 'paths', i.e. by different sequences of events."[45] The comparison of the Cuban crisis with the 1914 crisis may represent an example of multifinality, at least to the extent that there were common attributes across the two initial events. The parallel does not seem all that strong, in that in the 1914 case one pair of actors had committed itself to war, that is, war was a part of the decision-making environment, while in the Cuban case war was not desired by any of the actors.

The most puzzling extension of the invariance issue comes from Choucri and North's development of the peace-system model as follows:

> Thus, a model of peace systems will be one in which the greatest number of links in a war-prone conflict model appear to be non-significant or provide negative effects on conflict-related variables. . . . Such relations are characterized not by positive feedback and explosive dynamics but by inverse effects and negative feedback loops at some critical junctures. . . . Therefore, theoretically at least, the underlying structure of variables in a war-prone conflict system is similar to that of peace systems; the difference lies in initial values, coefficients, and levels and rates of change.[46]

The positive signs linking the terms in the Nations in Conflict model become the crucial factor: peace system nations may generate internal pressures to expand externally, but either lateral pressure is not generated by this or the mode of expression of lateral pressure is such that violent conflict is avoided. If it is not the structure that differentiates peace- and war-prone nations, but rather the trajectories of the exogenous variables and the parameters, then a causal explanation of parameters becomes crucial to conflict avoidance. The attention to the variance in parameter estimates across time and space in Nations in Conflict and the peace system article is cursory and ad hoc, which is a very unfortunate choice of research resource allocation. Without attention to this issue, it becomes impossible to reason in a meaningful way from the results of the analysis, since there are several sets of results. Since the procedures employed provide only parameter estimates and not tests of the appropriateness of the model, and since the variance in the estimates precludes pooling or averaging the results, one cannot generalize from these results without a theory of the parameters. If the variation in the parameters cannot be explained, then I would question the appropriateness of the specification of the model that generated the parameters.

A CONCLUDING SCENARIO

If I attempt to weave together the various results of the Stanford Studies, perhaps being a bit more generous than I have been up to this point, I get the following scenario. The basically uncontrolled, if not uncontrollable, tendencies of populations to grow and technologies to expand produce ever-increasing demands for resources. The historical residuals of uneven development and unequal distribution of value combine with demands to create conflict arenas, in which potentially or actually violent events among competing nations or groups of nations become more likely and more frequent. For a finite period, "a firm policy of restraint or other firm exercise of political will"[47] on the part of the relevant decision makers may keep such events from escalating into major warfare, but eventually, despite "universal intentions to the contrary,"[48] some situation will get out of hand; that is, a crisis environment will emerge. The more involved the nations get in the crisis, the more likely will be overestimations of threat and hostility and overly hostile responses to acts by other nations.[49] Eventually, perceived hostility will grow of its own accord, independent of the reality of the others' actions.[50] War becomes, in the limit, unavoidable. In this scenario I have combined the inexorable, nonmanipulable pressures, derived from the dynamics of demography and technological advancement, that are the focus of the Choucri-North studies, with the asymmetric response to amicable and hostile stimuli that emerges in the early crisis studies and the observation from Holsti's work on the trajectory of stress in crisis situations. When combined, these authors collectively paint a rather gloomy picture of the prospects for peace in a non-zero-growth world, a picture that becomes only gloomier when the systemic, structural sources of conflict discussed by Johan Galtung are introduced.[51]

If the dynamics of international behavior were congruent with this scenario, then one might expect a constant state of war. Although structural violence may be everywhere at all times, war as conceptualized by the Stanford group is not. It is possible that the act of having a war does something to the dynamics of the total process that so fundamentally shifts the values of some critical variables or so alters the parameters that the total system is set back to an earlier state. But then the dynamics begin again.

If one accepts the scenario, there is a clear policy consequence. Since it is rather unlikely that the aspects of human nature that intrude on rationality in crises can be changed, then in order to avoid periodic war one must control population and technological growth and the resultant drain on resources. The worm turns, and the discipline is advised that "theories of war will have to take into account domestic socioeconomic processes as well as foreign relations."[52]* With increased attention to the parameters, one may find them to be manipulable; if they are manipulable, the decision makers may be able to keep the total system from exploding by controlling the parameters. If the parameters cannot be controlled, then social policies must be constructed to control the trajectories of the exogenous variables. Such seem to be the choices that emerge if one accepts the basic thrust of the findings of the Stanford group.

My mind does not come to rest after reading the Stanford Studies papers. Probably it should not, since the questions raised require constant attention. Certainly the book has not been closed on the origins of the first world war nor on the behavior of decision makers under stress. There is a distinct, aesthetically pleasing property to the project's papers, with the consistent intermingling of theory formulation and empirical investigation. I find hints of Washington's rejection of entangling alliances, Eisenhower's warnings about the military-industrial complex, Frederick Jackson Turner's recognition of the social role of the frontier, and a substantial dose of Hobson and of Lenin. When it is mixed with creative data-making and statistical sophistication, the result is heady brew.

NOTES

1. The articles and books on which this chapter is based, in order of publication, are Dina A. Zinnes, Robert C. North, and Howard E. Koch, Jr., "Capability, Threat and the Outbreak of War,"

---

*When the first edition of the World Handbook came out, the common criticism was the plethora of socioeconomic-demographic variables and the relative paucity of political measures. See Bruce M. Russett, et. al., World Handbook of Political and Social Indicators (New Haven: Yale University Press, 1964).

in International Politics and Foreign Policy, edited by James N. Rosenau (New York: Free Press, 1961), pp. 469-82; Robert C. North, Richard A. Brody, and Ole R. Holsti, "Some Empirical Data on the Conflict Spiral," Papers, Peace Research Society (International) 1 (1964): 1-14; Ole R. Holsti, Richard A. Brody, and Robert C. North, "Measuring Affect and Action in International Reaction Models: Empirical Materials from the 1962 Cuban Crisis," Papers, Peace Research Society (International) 2 (1965): 170-90; Ole R. Holsti and Robert C. North, "The History of Human Conflict," in The Nature of Human Conflict, edited by Elton B. McNeil (Englewood Cliffs: Prentice-Hall, 1965), pp. 155-71; Ole R. Holsti, "The 1914 Case," American Political Science Review 59, no. 2 (1965): 365-78; Ole R. Holsti, "Perceptions of Time and Alternatives as Factors in Crisis Decision-Making," Papers, Peace Research Society (International) 3 (1965): 79-120; Ole R. Holsti, Robert C. North, and Richard A. Brody, "Perception and Action in the 1914 Crisis," in Quantitative International Politics: Insights and Evidence, edited by J. David Singer (New York: Free Press, 1968), pp. 123-58; Dina A. Zinnes, "The Expression and Perception of Hostility in Pre-War Crisis: 1914," in Quantitative International Politics: Insights and Evidence, edited by J. David Singer (New York: Free Press, 1968), pp. 85-119; Nazli Choucri and Robert C. North, "The Determinants of International Violence," Papers, Peace Research Society (International) 12 (1969): 33-63; Robert C. North and Richard Lagerstrom, War and Domination: A Theory of Lateral Pressure (New York: General Learning Press, 1971); Robert C. North and Nazli Choucri, "Population, Technology, and Resources in the Future International System," Journal of International Affairs 25, no. 2 (1971): 224-37; Nazli Choucri with Robert C. North, "In Search of Peace Systems: Scandinavia and the Netherlands, 1870-1970," in Peace, War, and Numbers, edited by Bruce M. Russett (Beverly Hills: Sage Publications, 1972), pp. 239-74; Nazli Choucri and Robert C. North, "Dynamics of International Conflict: Some Policy Implications of Population, Resources, and Technology," World Politics 24, Supplement (1972): 80-122; Ole R. Holsti, Crisis, Escalation, War (Montreal: McGill-Queens University Press, 1972); and Nazli Choucri and Robert C. North, Nations in Conflict: National Growth and International Violence (San Francisco: W. H. Freeman and Company, 1975).

2. The early crisis studies are North, Brody, and Holsti, "Some Empirical Data," op. cit.; Holsti, Brody, and North, "Measuring Affect," op. cit.; Zinnes, North, and Koch, "Capability, Threat," op. cit.; Holsti, North, and Brody, "Perception and Action," op. cit.; Zinnes, "Expression and Perception," op. cit.; Holsti, "The 1914 Case," op. cit.; and Holsti, "Perceptions of Time," op. c

3. See, in particular, Zinnes, "Expression and Perception," op. cit.
4. Holsti, Crisis, Escalation, War, op. cit. See also Holsti's earlier "Perceptions of Time," op. cit.
5. Holsti, Crisis, Escalation, War, op. cit., p. 9.
6. Ibid., pp. 192-97.
7. Choucri and North, "The Determinants," op. cit.; North and Choucri, "Population Technology," op. cit.; Choucri and North, "In Search of Peace Systems," op. cit.; Choucri and North, Nations in Conflict, op. cit.; Choucri and North, "Dynamics of International Conflict," op. cit.
8. See the excellent development of the theory in Choucri and North, Nations in Conflict, op. cit., Chapter 1.
9. Holsti, Crisis, Escalation, War, op. cit., pp. 192-97.
10. Choucri with North, "In Search of Peace Systems," op. cit.
11. Choucri and North, Nations in Conflict, op. cit., p. 156.
12. Richard C. Snyder, H. W. Bruck and Burton Sapin, Foreign Policy Decision-Making (New York: Free Press, 1962). See the discussion in Zinnes, "Expression and Perception," op. cit., pp. 85-86, and Holsti, Crisis, Escalation, War, op. cit., p. 51.
13. North and Choucri, "Population, Technology," op. cit., p. 234.
14. Holsti and North, "History of Human Conflict," op. cit., p. 170.
15. Choucri and North, Nations in Conflict, op. cit., p. 9
16. Ibid., p. 202.
17. Ibid., p. 280.
18. For example, Gordon Hilton, "The 1914 Studies—A Re-Assessment of the Evidence and Some Further Thoughts," Papers, Peace Research Society (International) 13 (1969): 117-141. See also the broader, more conceptual paper by Richard C. Snyder and Hayward R. Alker, "Stanford International Studies Presidential Visiting Committee Internal Review of the Stanford Studies in Conflict and Integration," (Stanford: Stanford University, 1968).
19. Choucri and North, "The Determinants," op. cit.
20. Choucri and North, "In Search of Peace Systems," op. cit., pp. 258-59.
21. Holsti and North, "The History of Human Conflict," op. cit., pp. 164-65.
22. Holsti, North, and Brody, "Perception and Action," op. cit., pp. 152, 157.
23. Ibid., p. 153.
24. Choucri and North, Nations in Conflict, op. cit., p. 181.
25. Holsti, Crisis, Escalation, War, op. cit., p. 93.
26. Ibid., pp. 51-70.

27. North, Brody, and Holsti, "Some Empirical Data," op. cit., pp. 10-11.
28. Choucri and North, Nations in Conflict, op. cit., p. 38.
29. Holsti, Brody, and North, "Measuring Affect," op. cit., p. 177.
30. Choucri and North, Nations in Conflict, op. cit., p. 34.
31. Choucri and North, "In Search of Peace Systems," op. cit., p. 259.
32. Choucri and North, Nations in Conflict, op. cit., p. 173.
33. Holsti, Crisis, Escalation, War, op. cit., pp. 51-80.
34. Choucri and North, Nations in Conflict, op. cit., p. 166.
35. Ibid., p. 17.
36. See the discussion of composition rules in Philip J. Runkel and Joseph E. McGrath, Research on Human Behavior: A Systematic Guide to Method (New York: Holt, Rinehart and Winston, 1972), pp. 329-35.
37. Choucri and North, Nations in Conflict, op. cit., p. 22.
38. Lewis F. Richardson, Arms and Insecurity (Pittsburgh, Pa.: The Boxwood Press, 1960).
39. North, Brody, and Holsti, "Some Empirical Data," op. cit., pp. 6, 9.
40. Choucri and North, Nations in Conflict, op. cit., p. 246.
41. Ibid., pp. 244-45.
42. Hayward R. Alker, Jr., alerted me, after I had written the preliminary version of this section, to a similar discussion in P. G. Herbst, Behavioural Worlds: The Study of Single Cases (London: Tavistock, 1970). My first three forms correspond to Herbst's Type A, Type B, and Type C laws, respectively.
43. Zvi Griliches, "Hybrid Corn: An Exploration in the Economics of Technological Change," Econometrica 25, no. 4 (1957): 501-22.
44. Zinnes, "Expression and Perception," op. cit., p. 117.
45. Choucri and North, Nations in Conflict, op. cit., p. 27.
46. Choucri and North, "In Search of Peace Systems," op. cit., pp. 241, 243.
47. Choucri and North, Nations in Conflict, op. cit., p. 156.
48. Holsti, North, and Brody, "Perception and Action," op. cit. p. 124.
49. Ibid., p. 152.
50. Holsti, Crisis, Escalation, War, op. cit., p. 46.
51. For example, see Johan Galtung, "A Structural Theory of Aggression," Journal of Peace Research 1, no. 2 (1964): 95-119.
52. Choucri and North, Nations in Conflict, op. cit., p. 254.

CHAPTER

21

A REEVALUATION OF
THE RESEARCH PROGRAM
OF THE STANFORD
STUDIES IN
INTERNATIONAL CONFLICT
AND INTEGRATION

Robert C. North
Ole R. Holsti
Nazli Choucri

THE BACKGROUND OF THE PROJECT

Since the overall critique of the Studies in International Conflict and Integration has indicated a number of ambiguities and obscurities in the reporting of our work to date, we are taking this opportunity to clarify some of the important assumptions, philosophy of science interpretations, central strategies, and investigation sequences that constitute our long-range research program. In undertaking this task, we shall not only address ourselves to the issues raised by our critics, but also identify a few of the more difficult problems that still confront us.

When the crisis research was undertaken in 1958 and the growth-expansion-competition analysis in 1965, there were no precedents for either type of research design. Large-scale investigations of this kind amount to an ongoing learning process. It is therefore often considerably easier to identify what should have been done after the results are in than when the strategy is being designed.

THE EQUIFINAL NATURE OF THE SOCIAL SCIENCES

Some of the difficulties presented by the research stem from the nature of human affairs and from some fundamental uncertainties that plague the social sciences. If we had known at the beginning what we know now, we might have done many things quite differently. It is true that a certain amount of trial-and-error experimentation took place, and that after going down some blind alleys it was entirely

possible to back out again. But it is also true that some early
decisions were essentially irreversible, and thus we were locked
into certain procedures that, if we had it to do over again, we would
certainly modify or avoid. Of course, we accept full responsibility
for what we did and the way we did it. It should be noted, however,
that in no instance involving statistical analysis, either in the content
analysis or in the aggregate studies, did we proceed beyond the first
stages of tentative probing without consultation with statisticians,
psychologists, social psychologists, economists, or other appropriate
specialists. What we learned was that even eminent consultants
differ among themselves and sometimes offer contradictory advice.
Under such circumstances, one is thus ultimately left with better,
but not decisively better, information with which to make the critical
methodological decision.

This difficulty has been underscored once more by the comments
of Karen Ann Feste, James A. Caporaso, and Mark S. Levine in
Chapters 18 to 20 of this volume. In Chapter 19, Feste questions
the use of analysis of variance, as reported upon in Chapter 3 of
Crisis, Escalation, War.[1] On the other hand, in Chapter 18 Caporaso
wrote that he considered it both appropriate and helpful of the project
to have done so in that context. We are not prepared to conclude
that he is right and Feste wrong; we merely accept this consideration
as further evidence that well-trained persons can disagree on this
issue. Perhaps the important question is, can a particular type of
analysis help us to understand something worth knowing from the
data?

With respect to several of the dilemmas noted and criticisms
raised by Caporaso and Levine in Chapters 18 and 20, respectively,
we believe that much of the difficulty resides in the equifinal nature
of the subject matter itself: in human affairs there is no getting
around the fact that the same outcome is often reached by different
"paths" or causal sequences and that the same or closely similar
causal sequences often lead to different outcomes. In the past this
pernicious aspect of human reality has led scholars to the conclusion
that each event is so inescapably unique that causal analyses and
prediction are a waste of time, if not a travesty. We do not go this
far, of course, or we would not be spending time, energy, and
resources on the kind of research we are doing. In fact, we believe
that modern techniques can settle once and for all some of the more
traditional strictures on research evaluation.

A philosophy of science that is derived from the investigation
of problems of finality, but adapted to the study of problems of
equifinality, may need to be reexamined. If some of the bootless
controversies can thus be gotten rid of, the social science community
can then get on with the respectable but extremely difficult and

usually discouraging job of finding out how and why human beings behave in the curious, often incomprehensible, and sometimes self-destructive ways they do.

Social scientists are often accustomed to testing narrow hypotheses that are easily falsifiable. We, however, are working with an entire framework comprising numerous interconnected hypotheses. Thus we are not seeking early closure but are still experimenting with the simultaneous equations we have developed and are still quite willing to modify them. We are considerably less concerned with the "preservation" of our overall "theory," especially the growth-expansion-competition aspects of our theory, than our critics seem to think we are or should be. We regard a theory as a tool that can be tested only by its application. Thus, its fitness must be judged, as the research progresses, by the results of its application.[2]

LIMITS TO THE DEFENSE OF A GIVEN THEORY

Since the publication of Klauss Knorr and James N. Rosenau's Contending Approaches to International Politics,[3] quantitative methods have become more widely accepted in the field. Unfortunately, however, expectations about the ease with which they can be incorporated into the international relations discipline are often unrealistic. The task involves more than merely the construction of a promising theory, the gathering together of readily available data, and the application of some statistical package. In practice the data are normally hard to get, incomplete, inconsistently selected and aggregated by gathering agencies, often all but incomparable between one country and another, and almost always full of errors in their raw state. In practice, also, there are relatively few guidelines for the selection or construction of indicators; there is little or no precedent for the selection of levels over rates of change, or vice versa; and there are few criteria for determining when or if a model can legitimately be adjusted, modified, or changed. If a hypothesis does not survive an empirical test, or if it is sustained for one country but not for another, one is often at a loss to conclude whether the theory is wrong, the data were in error, the selection of indicators was faulty, or the analytic tool misapplied. Under such circumstances it is difficult to avoid a certain amount of experimentation; reiterative, almost trial-and-error analysis; consideration of auxiliary ad hoc hypotheses; and adjustment and even readjustment of theory.

In the social sciences, at least, there are limits beyond which the defense of a theory may diminish its generative powers. From the start we have presented our theory explicitly as a prototypical and partial theory. To have done otherwise during this stage of its development would have been dysfunctional for the long and painful process of theory revision and refinement that the extremely difficult subject matter requires. Nowhere have we interpreted high percentages of variance as indicating that we have anything like a complete theoretical system. While we retain confidence in the general thrust, we expect many more years of thought and trial-and-error investigation and a great deal more modification, revision, and refinement of the theory to take place before anything like a viable overall theory emerges. In short, we view this type of investigation as a long and necessarily painful learning process, during which parts of the overall theory, as we envision it, will almost certainly be modified or even discarded. What the overall theory may look like a few years hence is not much more than a matter of speculation and not worth a great deal of serious discussion at this point, although we agree that the issues raised by our critics are important ones.

Within a broad philosophy-of-science approach, there are two contrasting perspectives that are relevant here. According to one viewpoint, the empirical criterion for a satisfactory theory is agreement with observed facts. Within this perspective, once a theory has been falsified, and in spite of the risks involved, it must be eliminated.[4] According to another viewpoint, however, "the empirical criterion for a series of theories is that it should produce new facts. The idea of growth and the concept of empirical character are soldered into one."[5] In these terms, "no experiment, experimental report, observation statement or well-corroborated low-level falsifying hypothesis alone can lead to falsification. There is no falsification before the emergence of a better theory."[6] Within this latter perspective a model is "a set of initial conditions (possibly together with some of the observational theories) which one knows is bound to be replaced during the further development of the programme, and one even knows more or less how."[7]

It may be that with respect to Germany and several other countries over a given period of time, $a + b + c + d$ leads to X, whereas for France the same combination of variables yields Z. How can we account for this discrepancy? One way of confronting this discrepancy might be to assume that in the case of France an unidentified variable (e) intervenes and thus precludes the expected outcome X. Although we do not know what e is, a number of candidates might be put forward in the form of initial propositions or hypotheses that can be tested in subsequent iterations as a preliminary step toward an understanding of the anomalous behavior of the French variables. Under such circumstances it would be seriously counter-productive to reject the overall theoretical thrust prematurely merely because the behavior of X in the French case is not accounted for by the initial formulation. In terms of progress within a given research enterprise, therefore, it may be dysfunctional to throw the whole theoretical baby out with the bath water of early empirical tests.

Caporaso may be correct in his assertion that the fact that Austria-Hungary underwent considerable growth but did not obtain substantial colonies appears to damage our theory. However, this seeming inconsistency may lead us, or others, into a useful reformulation and refinement of the theory, although this may not be achievable without first going through a stage of initial candidate explanations: perhaps potential Austro-Hungarian colonial expansion was blocked by the expansionist activities of more powerful states or by states or combinations of states not represented in the analysis, since lateral pressure is not inexorable but is subject to potentially identifiable external as well as internal constraints, and/or perhaps Austro-Hungarian expansionism was expressed in another mode, such as trade or foreign investment, since lateral pressure is subject to equifinality, that is, it can be manifested in more than one mode.

THE USE OF AUXILIARY HYPOTHESES

Auxiliary hypotheses can always be used in an effort to harmonize theories and factual propositions. The problem is how to distinguish between scientific and purely semantic adjustments and between rational and irrational modifications of theory. In the terms put forward by Karl Popper, the saving of a theory through the use of auxiliary hypotheses that satisfy certain well-defined conditions tends to serve scientific progress, whereas the saving of a theory through the use of auxiliary hypotheses that do not serve such conditions, such as ad hoc hypotheses or mere linguistic devices, contributes to degeneration.[8]

Unfortunately, also, it is often considerably easier to provide an ad hoc explanation than to test it. One reason for this is that the data for such testing may not be readily available or may not exist at all. Thus we used colonial territory as an indicator because it was relatively available. We would have liked to use foreign investment also, as an indicator of lateral pressure manifested in a different mode of behavior; but most unfortunately for the adequate testing of the model in various times and places, reliable foreign investment data are extremely uneven and next to impossible to obtain for the time series analysis of most countries year in and year out. We have identified foreign trade as still another critically important indicator of lateral pressure, but we failed to incorporate it into the model successfully. There are good reasons for this difficulty. In terms of lateral pressure, imports and exports have quite different implications—expansion of activities for obtaining raw materials versus expansion of activities in the securing of markets—that involve extremely complicated inter-nation patterns, (including elusive feedback) of input and output of goods, currency, and credit. Thus it is much easier to identify trade as a critical variable than to incorporate it successfully into a model, the objective of which is substantially different from that of a purely economic model, and to prepare and analyze the data effectively.

The building and testing of adequate theory on the different manifestations of lateral pressure presents major difficulties. Depending upon its capabilities and other considerations, a society has possibilities for "choosing" among various types of activities beyond its borders: occupying territory, acquiring colonies, importing, exporting, investing, concluding alliances, establishing military bases, blockading, invading, extending aid, supporting coups, and so forth. Except in very crude ways, the current state of the growth-expansion-competition theory provides no coherent way of predicting, in any particular set of circumstances, what mode or manifestation of lateral pressure a given society will tend to exert, or under what conditions it will be likely to switch emphasis from one to another. As in the case of the demand-capability function, such "choices" may be made on a variety of levels and may well involve extremely complex feedbacks.

A great deal more work needs to be done on the relationship between demand and capability. A major difficulty here is that demands are generated and capabilities provided on different levels and in quite different sectors of society—with banks of feedbacks within feedbacks. The problem of identifying appropriate levels of aggregation is therefore not easily solved. A second difficulty is that many capabilities are not merely capital, available stocks, or resource and manpower reserves, but involve "pools" of knowledge and skills. Some critical capabilities are complex hierarchies of ongoing activities and standard operating procedures. It is often very difficult to obtain manageable indicators of such elusive capabilities.

Since the publication of <u>Nations in Conflict</u>,[9] we have developed the theoretical underpinnings of the demand-capability determinants of lateral pressure by formulating these relationships in dynamic nonlinear terms. This theoretical expansion was then tested against data for the United States from 1930 to 1970, and on this basis experimental forecasts of U.S. lateral pressure were undertaken to the year 2000. Similar experiments are currently being undertaken with data for Japan from 1870 to 1941. This extension, development, and formal respecification of our prototheory could not have been undertaken without the experience reported in <u>Nations in Conflict</u>.[10] In this fashion we have regarded our theory as worthy of ongoing respecification and reformulation in the light of experience, data availability, and overall results.[11]

In order for us to ascertain in practice by what sort of change any particular scientific theory has been brought about, we must appraise it "together with its auxiliary hypotheses, initial conditions, and, especially, together with its predecessors." In following this procedure, however, "what we appraise is a series of theories rather than isolated theories."[12]

THE PROGRESSIVE TESTING OF THEORY

Against this background, if we take a series of theories within which each subsequent theory emerges from the adding of auxiliary clauses to the previous theory, or from semantical reinterpretations of the previous theory, then such a series represents a theoretically progressive problemshift (1) "if each new theory has some excess empirical content over its predecessor, that is, if it predicts some novel, hitherto unexpected fact."[13] Such a series also represents an empirically progressive problemshift if (2) "some of this excess empirical content is also corroborated, that is, if each new theory leads us to the actual discovery of some new fact."[14] Finally, such a problemshift is itself progressive, (3) "if it is both theoretically and empirically progressive, and degenerating if it is not."[15] In these terms, an ongoing research program involves continual adjustment, readjustment, and even replacement of theoretical statements, a theory in the series being "falsified" at whatever point it is superseded "by a theory with higher corroborated content."[16]

In classical logic, the <u>modus tollens</u> is a falsifying mode of inference whereby the falsification of a conclusion entails the falsification of the system from which it is derived.[17] All scientific programs, from the perspective of Lakatos, can be characterized by their "hard core." If the negative heuristic is employed, the <u>modus tollens</u> is not directed at this "hard core." Instead, "we must use our ingenuity to articulate or even invent 'auxiliary hypotheses' which perform a <u>protective belt</u> around this core, and we must redirect the <u>modus tollens</u> to <u>these</u>."[18] Thus, the brunt of tests must be borne by "this protective belt of auxiliary hypotheses,"[19] which are "adjusted and re-adjusted, or even completely replaced, to define the thus-hardened core. A research programme is successful if all this leads to a progressive problemshift; unsuccessful if it leads to a degenerating problemshift."[20]

No doubt it would be extremely useful to look at a control group of noncapitalist countries in order to enhance discrimination between the growth-expansion-competition theory and Leninist theories. In fact, we have collected appropriate data for the USSR and the People's Republic of China and have undertaken some preliminary analyses. It must be pointed out, however, that because of noncomparability of data (different ways of calculating Gross National Product, for example), inadequacies of data, and so forth, this undertaking is far easier to suggest than to accomplish. In the meantime, as indicated in Nations in Conflict,[21] it must be emphasized that "lateral pressure" is not synonymous with "imperialism," as defined by Lenin or even by noncommunist writers. It is not only that a socialist country with appropriate combinations of population, technology, resources, and so forth may exhibit lateral pressure; even more important, a country may exhibit lateral pressure without necessarily dominating or exploiting any other country; and while manifesting lateral pressure, it may suffer domination and exploitation by another country. From this, we might conclude that imperialism is a special case or subset of the broader concept of lateral pressure.

In these terms we envision research, in this problem area, at least, as an iterative process of building and testing. Such a process describes both our theory and our methods. Indeed, the building and testing of theory at initial stages in this type of research cannot be easily separated except as an artificial construct. The "refinement" of a model means that evaluations of it have produced new insights into ways of making the model more representational of the phenomenon under study. For the kind of research under discussion here, any such iterative process of building and testing requires many levels, for individual data, indicators, equations, and even the larger system model itself. It becomes difficult to separate the building from the testing.

COMMENTS ON THE CRISIS STUDIES

There are a number of factual errors in Feste's chapter—for example, product moment correlation coefficients appear nowhere in Crisis, Escalation, War[22]—but she does raise a number of interesting and important issues. It is to some of these problems, as well as to the general tone of her discussion, that we shall address these further comments.

Feste has an unfortunate tendency to present a viewpoint as proven when in fact she has merely raised an interesting question. We would fully agree with the value of bringing such questions to the attention of others who might wish to engage in studies of crisis decision making; indeed, most if not all of the points raised in her chapter were discussed in Crisis, Escalation, War,[23] with detailed efforts to indicate why certain research choices were made. However, we question the value or appropriateness of Feste's somewhat dogmatic assertions, which imply that she has demonstrated her thesis beyond all doubt. For example, she points to some potential sources of difficulty in the opening pages of her chapter and is shortly prepared to conclude that she has identified points at which "measurement error entered" into the coding of these data. This judgment is of course premature, given the fact that Feste has only raised questions and has not really demonstrated the existence of any measurement errors.

THE "INSTRUMENTAL" VERSUS "REPRESENTATIONAL" MODELS OF COMMUNICATION

The relative merits of the "instrumental" and "representational" models of communication are indeed an important question for those who use documentary materials as a source of data. There is an extensive literature on this question, and one would have no difficulty in citing eminent authorities in support of one position or the other. Thus it is perhaps more fruitful to rephrase the "instrumental versus representational" controversy to ask under what circumstances it might be most appropriate to adopt one viewpoint or the other.

If the 1914 data had consisted mostly of public speeches, direct messages between foreign or prime ministers, and the like, then there would be strong reason to believe that an instrumental model would be most appropriate for the content analysis. That is, in such circumstances we could assume that a significant purpose of communication would be to persuade, cajole, threaten, or otherwise influence the behavior of those receiving the communication. However, as is made clear in Crisis, Escalation, War,[24] as well as in other studies of the 1914 crisis, the great bulk of the documentary information consisted of intragovernmental communication, private memoranda circulated within foreign offices, instructions to ambassadors stationed abroad, marginal notations or extended comments

on incoming telegrams, and the like. In short, the materials
selected for coding consisted largely of messages written by officials
of a given nation to their colleagues for the purpose of information.
Moreover, the authors of these messages had no reason to suspect
that their words would be made public during their lifetimes. It
was only the willingness of the post-1918 governments in Russia,
Germany, and Austria-Hungary to make these confidential documents
public (in part because they would tend to discredit the diplomacy
of the prewar regimes) that led ultimately to the publication of major
document collections by the five leading nations in the crisis. Thus,
although internal communications may not be devoid of instrumental
qualities, we would argue that the choice of a representational model
in the particular circumstances surrounding the 1914 data is a
defensible one. Without direct access to the leaders in question,
it is not possible to prove beyond all doubt that a representational
model is most appropriate; it is equally impossible to prove that
the alternative instrumental model would have been preferable.
The question, then, comes down to this: Do the results in <u>Crisis,
Escalation, War</u> seem plausible? Do they have important normative
implications for the crucial problem of decision making under stress?
In the absence of any possibility of settling some questions beyond
all doubt, each reader will have to assess the answers in the light
of broader considerations than purely methodological ones.

RELIABILITY OF CODING

In questioning the results of the coding, Feste writes, "By the
aggregation of judgments, individual variances may tend to be canceled out." The reliability coefficients calculated for the content
analysis data in fact take the judgment of each coder and assess
the level of agreement among the coders on each item. Every time
the coders disagreed, the reliability coefficient declined, and the
more they disagreed, that is, the further apart their judgments were
on the 9-point scale, the sharper the drop in the reliability coefficient.
Indeed, because the distance between coders was squared, a disagreement of three points on the scale resulted in a penalty nine
times greater than a disagreement of only a single point. Put
somewhat differently, there could be no canceling-out effect because
reliability coefficients were computed item-by-item and coder-by-coder, rather than on an aggregated basis. Finally, we are puzzled
by Feste's assertion that reliability is not a problem, "provided we
accept the extent of intercoder agreement reflected in the coefficients.
We trust that she does not mean to imply that the reliability data were
somehow falsified.

MEASUREMENT AND SCALES

At various points Feste acknowledges that social science methodology does not constitute a rigid set of prescriptions but rather that eminent scholars can be cited in support of various viewpoints on many key questions; yet in the later parts of her chapter she continues her critique as if a particular viewpoint had been demonstrated beyond any reasonable doubt. For example, she points out, quite appropriately, that "measurement theorists disagree about whether scales created from the paired comparison or Q sort techniques are properly considered as ordinal or interval measurement devices." On the next page she adds, "there is disagreement among measurement theorists on this point" [scaling]; yet in later parts of her chapter she is prepared to use in unqualified form such terms as "misuse," "frequent violations," and "deficiencies": none of these terms seems appropriate in light of the fact that there are disagreements among the most qualified specialists on the issues at hand and in light of Feste's failure to demonstrate that specific methodological choices resulted in inappropriate inferences from the data. Thus, unless one is prepared to assume that Feste is the final arbiter on such matters, Table 19.2 of her chapter should only be regarded as representing her preferences, not as a definitive judgment.

Feste strongly insists on the inapplicability of parametric statistics, although, as we would remind the reader, in Crisis, Escalation, War nonparametric statistics were used in every instance save one, which was the analysis of variance in Chapter 3. Even in that case the data were reanalyzed using nonparametric equivalents.[25] Moreover, in view of her disapproval of using parametric statistics, her conclusion recommending the use of regression is somewhat puzzling.

In conclusion, we applaud Feste's diligence in undertaking a review of some significant problems in our quantitative research, and we agree that it is highly appropriate that studies of the kind we have undertaken be subjected to the most careful critical scrutiny. Indeed, one of the advantages of quantitative research is that such critiques can be undertaken far more easily than in the case of less systematic studies; but we do question the somewhat dogmatic manner in which Professor Feste presents her thesis and especially her tendency to take as demonstrated fact what is in reality one position among many on a series of issues. In view of the fact that many of the raw data are presented in an appendix of Crisis, Escalation, War,[26] perhaps Professor Feste would have made a more valuable contribution had she chosen the admittedly more difficult task of demonstrating better ways of analyzing the data and, even more importantly, addressing the most significant question, that of whether alternative statistical or other methods would have resulted in significantly different substantive and theoretical conclusions.

ISSUES EMERGING FROM THE GROWTH-EXPANSION-COMPETITION STUDIES

The investigation of the major European powers for the period 1870 to 1917 involved a time-series study of attribute and interaction data. The book Nations in Conflict amounts to a progress report on this undertaking.[27] We are still improving the concepts, the methodology, and the indicators involved in this type of research. Our partial or "proto" theory involves strong links and feedback between domestic growth and international violence. According to the main thrust of this prototheory, a combination of a growing population (growing relative to home territory and readily accountable resources) and an advancing technology leads to the expansion of a country's activities and interests beyond its borders; to intersections with the activities and interests of other countries; and to the aggravation of international competitions, conflicts, and levels of violence behavior. In turn, the competitions, conflicts, and violence tend to affect domestic growth. Over time these processes produce conditions that are conducive to international crises and war. The dynamic aspects of these tendencies emerge in large part from differentials in the levels and rates of change of the major variables both within and between countries.

Some Relatively Trivial Issues

The Chapter 18 and Chapter 20 reviews of Nations in Conflict by Caporaso and Levine touch on many important issues that need further clarification. Our observations fall into two categories: first, clarifications that bear on fairly trivial matters or that involve some misunderstanding occasioned by our own explanations of what we have done and, second, an explanation of some of the more fundamental issues and objectives. Among the more trivial issues that need clarification is the fact that we have interpreted the constant term, which is statistically significant in the colonial expansion equation, as capturing the impact of variables that were operating prior to the starting date of the equation and that generate the initial level of the dependent variable and may then have independent effects as well. These are factors that our theoretical specification of lateral pressure has not incorporated; nor have we attempted to do so in this volume, although we have done so elsewhere.

Thus the finding that the constant term may in some cases be the best explanatory term for a nation's expansion is in no way an "inconsistency" or an "error," as Levine suggests. His statement that the partial correlations are run involving the constant is also incorrect. In the context of our theoretical framework, the constant acquires specific substantive meaning. To exclude it from our statistical analysis would not make any sense theoretically. In our experimentation with the British data, however, we have observed that the statistical patterns are remarkably similar for the other explanatory variables when the constant term is not included in the equation. The major differences are (1) that explanatory power drops substantially and (2) that the serial correlation in the error or disturbance term is so strong that the effects of such a misspecification cannot be adequately corrected. These two consequences reinforce our theoretical reasons for incorporating the constant term in the equation.

The high R^2 values for several of the colonial expansion equations are indeed problematic. We seriously believe that some artifact is responsible for them. However, we have checked for serial correlation in the disturbances and for the structure of the underlying errors by using the Durbin-Watson statistic, which is appropriate only for testing first order autoregressive processes, and also by using correlograms of the residuals. We do not interpret the high percentage of variance explained as indicating that we have a complete theoretical system,[28] but we do point to the successes and failures of our simulations of colonial expansion to provide some clues about the missing theoretical specifications.

Over the years we have frequently been called upon to produce tables of bivariate correlation coefficients. In our earlier reports we have complied; but as our investigations proceeded, it became increasingly clear that bivariate correlations can be, and often are, misleading. Indeed, we note this as follows in Appendix B of <u>Nations in Conflict</u>:

> Correlation gives no indications concerning cause and effect; it gives only <u>one</u> number as an aid towards understanding a complex relationship, rather than the estimation of a mathematical function yielded by regression techniques; it demands more restrictive assumptions concerning the distribution of the data than does regression; and unlike regression, it does not tell us <u>how</u> two

variables move together. For those interested in correlations, however, the partial correlations between the statistically significant independent variables and the dependent variables are reported in the tables in Chapters 11 to 15.[29]

Correlation matrices are available from the authors or, alternatively, can be obtained directly by a reanalysis of the data.

We strongly disagree with Professor Levine's statement that the strong trend components in the aggregate variables have debilitating implications. Indeed, our theory derives very strongly from the consequences of trends. Perhaps we should have made it more clear than we have done in <u>Nations in Conflict</u> that we are concerned with trends as well as with causal relationships. To de-trend the variables would amount, in our view, to brute empiricism. This is why we sought to protect the data from any contamination by a substantive trend component by artificially de-trending them, while at the same time seeking to reduce the distorting effects of serial correlation among the observations of independent variables by correcting for systematic bias in the disturbances. For this reason, too, we have taken great care to identify the structure of serial correlation in the disturbances and to correct appropriately through the use of generalized least squares. We also performed an experiment which was designed to determine what changes in coefficients might result from estimation procedures.[30]

With respect to the reaction processes of arms race dynamics, the existence of trend itself constitutes an important aspect of the "real world," which needs to be accounted for directly rather than through the removal of the linear component.

The use of absolute levels rather than rates of change in reporting our results reflects more than a simple change in measurement, as Levine argues. It is also a shift in underlying theoretical concerns. His point is well taken, but it is largely incomplete.

We are not in accord with Caporaso's statement that our "analysis and interpretation are laced with idiosyncratic formulations and singular statements." We have developed one general theoretical statement, from which we have derived a specific model that has been tested for the six major European powers and at all subperiods throughout the 45 years we examined. Our results indicate that some specifications and indicators are more appropriate for some countries than for others and for some periods rather than others. This is an important set of findings that provides a check against our theory and the data and indicators employed for these tests. In <u>Nations in Conflict</u> we have tried to disentangle the more idiosyncratic interpretations from those that could provide a broader theoretical structure.[31] No theory can be specific enough and yet remain sufficiently parsimonious to provide a satisfactory explanation for every individual parameter estimate in each individual equation.

We are indeed somewhat uncomfortable with some of our indicators. As Caporaso correctly notes, the colonial expansion variable for the Austro-Hungarian case is particularly problematic. We referred to this case earlier. Although this variable does not adequately represent the underlying latent construct of lateral pressure, we cannot infer from the results that lateral pressure did not occur or that pressures for expansion were not present. This situation in no way debilitates the parsimony of theory, but it does point to some important problems of specification and indication problems that as yet remain unresolved.

The care with which we have developed our metric as well as nonmetric data series, the operationalization of key concepts, and the development of reliability checks[32] hardly justifies Levine's observation that we have exhibited a "cavalier attitude toward the issues of reliability, validity, and composition rules." Indeed, it is this very care that prevented us from publishing Nations in Conflict several years earlier.

Since the concept of lateral pressure encompasses many different possible activities, it is indeed our argument that there is a set of indicators of lateral pressure, some of which are relevant in some cases and different ones relevant in others. We consciously take note of this factor as an important input into our analysis. In our preliminary analysis trade was used as an exogenous variable. This treatment of it was not successful, however, since imports and exports perform more complex functions than we provided for. Among these complexities is the fact that imports, and exports, too, in a different way, may be a manifestation of lateral pressure, but may also contribute to it or reduce it. It is all too easy to confuse the concept, modes, manifestations, and indicators of lateral pressure.

We do agree, however, that we have not explicitly incorporated technology into our formulation of lateral pressure, as was reported in Nations in Conflict.[33] In our more recent work we have specified explicitly how the technological variable combines with other factors in the production process to contribute to a nation's lateral pressure.

Levine takes issue with our observation that "Nations with comparatively high levels of national income (gross national product) do tend to have comparatively high levels of technology" and points to the observed weak relationship in cross-sectional data between measures of technological-economic development and GNP or national income. This observation reflects a fundamental misunderstanding of the relationship among technology, economic growth, and GNP measures on the part of Levine. Economists often remind us that technology is a necessary input in the production process and that output (GNP or national income) is fundamentally dependent upon the technological input into production.[34] Theories of economic development and models of growth all—with one exception—accord technology a paramount role in the production process. Indeed, as Simon Kuznets observed in 1966, "Whatever the source, the increase in the stock of useful knowledge and the extension of its application are of the essence in modern economic growth; and the rate and the locus of the increase in knowledge markedly affect the rate and structure of economic growth. . . . No matter where these technological and social innovations emerge, . . . the economic growth of any given nation depends upon their adoption."[35]

Breakpoints signal changes in the relationship among variables. We initially employed the same breakpoints for all equations in all countries; but on theoretical grounds we expected different breakpoints for different countries. It is precisely when we expected a break on theoretical grounds that we have tested for its existence; this procedure in no way reflects ad hoc hypotheses. However, Caporaso is correct in pointing to the distinction between testing ideas and describing what is seen. We have done both, and we have taken great care to describe what we have seen when the results of the tests were inconsistent with our hypotheses and the theory upon which they are based.

What is indeed required, and what we have not provided, is a theory of transformation or transition to locate the mechanisms leading to system change. Levine takes note of our observation that "it is not possible to infer any clear snow-balling process"[36] whereby conflicts of lower intensity necessarily give rise to conflicts of higher intensity. "A period of high intensity conflict can be, and often is, followed by a period of relative tranquility."[37] Our findings indicate that the likelihood of war is not created by a simple incremental process but that two types of dynamics, the conflictual and the cooperative, can occur simultaneously. These are not opposites; each tends to be closely associated with the other. In the case of World War I, we have been able to obtain clues into the nature of the underlying process: the mean of the general conflict distribution need not necessarily reflect increasing implications for violence, yet peak values may simultaneously indicate greater conflict content. We suspect, although we have as yet not tested this hypothesis, that it is certain patterns of interaction between the conflict and cooperation factors, as reflected in the mean and peak statistics, that yield clues about why certain conflicts escalate into war and others do not. The current work on conflict patterns among the United States, the Soviet Union, and China is providing precisely the type of evidence called for by Levine.

There is no theoretical reason why the coefficients would be identical or why an identical set of linkages should be found. In explaining the discrepancies between expectations and empirical findings, we have drawn on our theory. There are theoretical reasons why we would expect Austria-Hungary to have exhibited a set of statistically significant linkages that were somewhat different from those for Great Britain. Our theory is not specific enough to allow us to express the differences in terms of the precise magnitude of the coefficients, but it does provide some important guidelines for articulating our general expectations and our explanations of deviations from a set of stimulated linkages.

We have indeed undertaken considerable experimentation with preliminary sets of data and alternative combinations of the explanatory variables, but only on the British data. We did not seek to eliminate data that could falsify the theory, but rather to employ only data for which the known measurement error was within some tolerable bounds. Data of known poor quality were eliminated. For example, there were simply too many missing observations in the series for merchant marine ships; the observations that were recorded were not standardized in terms of ship size or carrying capacity; and there were too many discrepancies within each series and among the series for different countries. Similarly, we decided not to employ colonial population as an indicator of lateral pressure since the recorded observations included a natural birth rate component, the magnitude of which we could not ascertain. Our theory says nothing about natural increases in the native populations in the colonies, since including such increases as part of the lateral pressure indicator is simply not acceptable on either theoretical or empirical grounds. We certainly did not eliminate "parts of the theory," as Caporaso maintains, but we did take care not to contaminate the empirical analysis with measures that clearly included extraneous factors. Nonetheless, there are aspects of our theory, or partial theory as we term it, that are less rigorously specified than are some others. There are also aspects of our findings that we feel greater confidence in than others.[38] Thus Caporaso's observations regarding criteria for rigorous applications of falsification perspective are extremely important: clearly we have succeeded in meeting these only partially, at best.

In presenting his critique, Levine has intertwined his discussions of the crisis studies and the attribute analyses in such a way that a criticism of one may seem to apply to the other. This is potentially misleading, since the two approaches are quite different: seldom if ever is a methodological criticism of one likely to pertain to the other. It is difficult to respond to his assertion that we "do not test" the model, since he does not define the term and hence we do not know what it means to him. Increasingly, our analyses are raising serious questions in our minds about the appropriateness of applying the more traditional philosophy-of-science criteria to problems in the social sciences. Certainly we have not achieved any ultimate test; if it were achievable at all, that would require its use in a much wider variety of times and places. We are somewhat surprised, on the other hand, that Levine's comment upon our simulations and "retrospective forecasts," which we consider a very promising type of "test," is not very extensive.

Also puzzling is Levine's observation that we do not "test" our model but "simply" estimate the parameters. Estimation is a form of testing. A nonsignificant coefficient may result from a variety of sources, including misspecification, and our task is to determine which. Years of testing, retesting, specifying, and respecifying are hardly consistent with his statement that we have simply estimated the parameters of the model. Our earlier papers report comparisons of alternative specifications. <u>Nations in Conflict</u> reports a recent stage.

In view of the complexities of the processes we are seeking to capture, it would be surprising if we came up with a simple discrete result. It is indeed correct to note, as Professor Levine does, that there are different sets of results. This is the whole point. The expectation that one "answer" can be found to the question of war is untenable to say the least. We take heart in the fact that we have a "series of results" and would have been deeply suspicious of anything else.

Some Fundamental Issues

Such are some of the more trivial observations to be made by way of clarifying several of the queries raised by Caporaso and Levine; but there are more fundamental issues. First, the use of a particular statistical technique is in itself a theory about the structure of data, and there are some implicit assumptions about the impact of the findings of alternative data structures. Indeed, the data themselves reflect an implicit or underlying theory that has guided their initial compilation. The theory of data is an area that yet remains insufficiently investigated. In some cases functional form needs to be established by data, while in others it is specified by theory. The interaction between the investigator's theory, the data themselves, their structure, the selection of indicators, and the theory underlying the compilation of the data in the original sources themselves raise important problems that social scientists have barely begun to investigate.

Second, the whole issue of "negative results" is also problematic. It should be made clear that a result that is not statistically significant is not a negative result but merely a result of which one cannot say, with any certainty, that it could not have been achieved by chance. If the n were increased, then a result that is not statistically significant might become so. Particularly in cases in which the correlations are in the expected direction, the lack of statistical significance provides no information at all about the hypothesis. Certainly it does not provide "inconsistent results."

Third, our purpose, at this stage of the research program at least, is not to present a tight theory that can be readily refuted in its entirety but to develop a general prototheory and to observe how generally it applies, and to what extent, among countries and across time periods. This is where the blend of econometrics and history comes in: history was employed to try to explain the reasons for specific deviations from theory, or from expected significance of parameters. We do not expect to find the same coefficients with exactly the same magnitudes for all countries in all periods; that would mean that all countries were exactly alike, which is a manifest absurdity and most unlikely in a field characterized by equifinality. Even science allows for a range of values. It is our belief that at the current stage in the study of international relations this type of general prototheory will enable scholars with quite different perspectives to relate their work in a more orderly way and thus to enhance the development of the field as a whole.

Fourth, perhaps we should reiterate what it is that we have done. We have developed a system of simultaneous equations, estimated the parameters, and then simulated the behavior of the system over time. Our objective has been to develop a model that would assist in raising queries regarding the impact of possible policy interventions in a conflict process. From the start our study of growth-expansion-competition phenomena has been characterized by work with a system of simultaneous equations. We have not employed single-equation estimation procedures, such as regression analysis using ordinary least squares, but instead we have used a combination of two-stage least squares and generalized least squares. A preoccupation with problems of "fit" in single equations simply distracts from some of the real complexities of such problems in the simultaneous equation case.[39]

The entire estimation exercise we have undertaken was employed as an input into the simulations. Admittedly we have spent so much time and effort in model building and estimation that we have not made as full a use of the estimation results for simulation purposes as we might have made; nor have we undertaken as extensive policy experiments as we would have wished. Unfortunately, neither Caporaso's nor Levine's review addresses itself to problems of simulation and forecasting or to the implications of estimation procedures; data problems; or difficulties with indicators and attendant measures, specifically for simulation and forecasting.

The underlying or ultimate objective of our analyses was to develop some confidence in theoretical bases and in methodological procedures for exploring alternative system behaviors and eventually for modeling alternative futures. The work that has been subsequent to <u>Nations in Conflict</u> has placed greater emphasis on simulation that is undertaken largely for forecasting purposes. Some of our recent work on forecasting lateral pressure in the United States over the next 30 years is illustrative of these more recent investigations.

Against this background, we regret that neither reviewer gives any attention to the simulation and forecasting exercises, each choosing instead to emphasize basic statistical issues and difficulties. We consider our simulation of international processes[40] as a fundamental and critical aspect of this work, and we regard the simulation as a major objective of our research program on the dynamics of internation conflict. Employing simulation techniques and quantitative data to see how accurately the model could predict known data on colonial area, intensity of intersections, military expenditures, alliances, and violent behavior is in our view a necessary prerequisite for systematic analysis of alternative future. We view the problems associated with simulation and forecasting as more important, both theoretically and methodologically, than more routine problems of statistical analysis, parameter estimation, or model testing. For too long, quantitative analyses of international relations have focused exclusively upon statistical issues rather than on simulation or forecasting. This is largely because of the general state of the art in the field, but it is also because most quantitative scholars are still all too concerned with comparatively routine methodological problems. We now need to move in a more exploratory fashion in the relatively unknown areas of simulation, forecasting, and investigation into the structure of alternative futures.

SOME REMARKS IN CONCLUSION

The preceding pages expose a central issue that underlies the research program and involves relationships between quality and quantity—cognitions, affects, and decisions on the one hand and such factors as levels and rates of change of population, technology, resources, investments, budgetary distribution, and colonial territories on the other. Our colleagues are sometimes confused by what appears to have been a sudden shift from one type of study to the other and troubled by a seeming lack of attention in growth-expansion-competition studies to the "human" aspects of international affairs. In fact, the switch from cognitive-affective-decision studies to attribute studies was not as abrupt as it may have seemed from the outside. It was far from being a capricious change, but was forced upon us by the logic underlying the research program from the start. Reduced to capsule form, this logic asserts in all human affairs the following are true:

    1. Individuals and groups are utterly dependent upon the earth and its resources.

    2. Any substantial change in the physical, as well as the social, environment affects the cognitions, feelings, values, decisions, and activities of component groups and individuals.

    3. Any substantial activity on the part of individuals, groups, or whole societies affects the physical and social environment.

    4. Quality and quantity are interactive and inseparable, in that any substantial change in the level or rate of change of population, technology, available resources, investment structure, or allocation of resources and benefactions will affect human values, feelings, and expectations. Conversely, substantial changes in human values, feelings, and expectations will affect the future levels and rates of change of critical attribute variables.

The "scenario" that Professor Levine derives by combining the implications of the crisis studies with the implications of the growth-expansion-competition studies has occurred to us as well; but since we have not yet made a formal attempt to link the two, a warning is in order. Levine writes, "If the dynamics of international behavior were congruent with this scenario, then we might expect a constant state of war." The crucial comment here is that the two sets of implications have not yet been systematically linked.

The problem is not only that crisis dynamics have not been integrated with the dynamics of growth-expansion-competition; the difficulty lies deeper. As suggested above, a full-blown model must deal with cognitive phenomena, attribute (including distribution) phenomena, and action phenomena, all of which are interwoven almost beyond unraveling. The crisis studies proceeded almost as if the attribute phenomena did not exist, whereas the growth-expansion-competition studies were carried out almost as if cognitive phenomena did not exist; yet it is fully manifest that both phenomena, and also action phenomena, are operating all the time, intensely interactively, over the long sweep and also in crisis. It is partly for this reason that Nations in Conflict purposely stops short of the initiation of crisis and the outbreak of war. This is also one of the reasons we have presented the book as a progress report rather than a conclusive study. Thus, although we believe that the growth-expansion-competition variables, which are themselves in large part the outcome of human feelings, perceptions, and decisions, affect cognitions in powerful ways, we are nevertheless profoundly aware that the outbreak of war is the outcome of human evaluations, risk assessments, and choice. This awareness is a constant reminder of how much remains to be done, both theoretically and substantively, before anything like a sufficient understanding or adequate theory of the behavior of states and empires is achieved.

Levine's comments about the "strong theoretical dovetailing" of the attribute analyses with the crisis studies require one important caution. In our own minds we see the cognitive data of the crisis studies and the attribute data of the "growth and expansion" studies as capable of combining, along with action data, into a single model. In theoretical terms, we foresee the weaving together of three partial theories, growth and expansion theory, competition and conflict theory, and crisis theory, into a full-blown theory. To date, however, we have barely begun to undertake this essential task of "weaving," or integration. Indeed, the mere linking of the longer-range growth-expansion-competition variables with the short-term crisis variables presents some extremely perplexing problems.

In this connection, great caution must be exercised in drawing inferences about "war-prone" systems and "peace-prone" systems. Our investigation of "peace systems" has so far been exploratory and highly tentative, and the book <u>Nations in Conflict</u> does not attempt to deal with this issue in any explicit way. Up until now, at least, we have discussed this distinction only in the longer-term framework of growth, expansion, and competition, but not at all in a crisis context. In the course of the research program so far, we have only recently begun to devote serious attention to combining the cognitive attribute and distribution and action variables in a systematic way. There are many frustrating difficulties involved in this effort, but a few moments' reflection will provide some initial clues.

"DRY STATISTICS" AND HUMAN VALUES

As indicated in <u>Nations in Conflict</u>,[41] each datum of population, technology, resource transfer or transformation, trade or national expenditure, budgetary allocation, and so forth, amounts to a trace, so to speak, left by some individual or group decision. Thus the size or rate of change of a country's population at any given time is the outcome of millions of private decisions, "conscious" or "unconscious," to have or not to have children. So, too, a nation's general level of technology and the advances made are the outcome of large numbers of research and production enterprises undertaken by individuals working singly, in private firms or in agencies of government. Even the "decision" of 10 million Germans to drink an additional cup of coffee each day or of 20 million Americans to consume a gallon of gasoline more each day (or a gallon less) will affect relations between their respective states and countries in South America, Africa, or the Middle East. Furthermore, different contributions to national defense are taken simultaneously by dozens or hundreds of research and planning centers in and out of government, large numbers of suppliers and contractors, and others, most of whom are in imperfect communication with each other. Thus a country's military budget can be as much the outcome of expectations and pressures from the private sector and of the personal ambitions and interests of bureaucrats in the war and navy departments as it is of interactions with major powers. Often the accumulation of countless individual decisions creates tendencies that were not planned or foreseen. Much of these hidden dynamics tend to be captured, although they may not be neatly specified, in the attribute and distribution data that are often dismissed as "dry," "dead," and "nonhuman."

Whatever changes in the natural, social, political, or economic environments are brought about by aggregations of decisions by rank and file members of the populace, governmental bureaucrats, national leaders, and others, these changes will tend to alter perceptions of what is, what ought to be and what can be. In many different sectors of society such changes will also create perceptual "gaps" between what is and what ought to be and thus generate demands for closing them. If the appropriate capabilities are present, such demands will give rise to further decisions and actions, many of which in turn will bring about further environmental change, and hence new sequences of cognitions, decisions, and actions. In the longer-run perspective of the research program, it is these dynamics and the various linkages involved that we shall be trying to elucidate.

THE USEFULNESS OF THE CRITIQUE

In conclusion, we want to underscore the usefulness of this type of critique, not only to our own research program, but also to the discipline at large. Addressing ourselves to issues raised by these critics has proved valuable to us in formulating our approach to a number of current and upcoming conceptual and testing problems. In addition, we are confident that interchanges of this kind will be helpful to our colleagues and especially to younger scholars who are just getting started in the field. It seems self-evident that the viability of any research program must depend upon frequent reassessment and the generation of further lines of investigation.

NOTES

1. Ole R. Holsti, Crisis, Escalation, War (Montreal: McGill-Queens University Press, 1972).
2. Karl R. Popper, The Logic of Scientific Discovery (New York: Basic Books, 1961), p. 108.
3. Klaus Knorr and James N. Rosenau, eds., Contending Approaches to International Politics (Princeton: Princeton University Press, 1969).
4. Popper, Logic, op. cit., p. 33.
5. Imre Lakatos and Alan Musgrave, eds. Criticism and the Growth of Knowledge (Cambridge: The University Press, 1970), p. 119.
6. Lakatos and Musgrave, Criticism, op. cit., p. 119.
7. Ibid., p. 136.
8. Popper, Logic, op. cit., pp. 78-84.
9. Nazli Choucri and Robert C. North, Nations in Conflict: National Growth and International Violence (San Francisco: W. H. Freeman and Company, 1975).
10. Ibid.
11. Nazli Choucri and Marie Bousfield, "Alternative Futures: Forecasting Sources of Foreign Expansion" (Cambridge: M.I.T. Center for International Studies, 1975).
12. Lakatos and Musgrave, Criticism, op. cit., p. 118.
13. Ibid.
14. Ibid.
15. Ibid.
16. Ibid.
17. Popper, Logic, op. cit., p. 76.
18. Lakatos and Musgrave, Criticism, op. cit., p. 133.
19. Ibid.
20. Ibid.
21. Choucri and North, Nations in Conflict, op. cit.
22. Holsti, Crisis, Escalation, War, op. cit.
23. Ibid.
24. Ibid.
25. Holsti, Crisis, Escalation, War, op. cit.
26. Ibid., Appendix
27. Choucri and North, Nations in Conflict, op. cit.
28. See ibid., Chapter 18, for our own assessments.
29. Ibid., p. 302.
30. These processes are described in ibid., Appendix B; Appendix C reports the results of an experiment comparing nine alternative estimation procedures.

31. Ibid., Chapter 16.
32. See ibid., Appendix A.
33. Ibid.
34. Paul A. Samuelson, <u>Economics: An Introductory Analysis</u> (6th ed., San Francisco: McGraw-Hill Book Company, 1964), p. 737.
35. Simon Kuznets, <u>Modern Economic Growth: Rate, Structure, and Spread</u> (New Haven: Yale University Press, 1966), pp. 286-87.
36. Choucri and North, <u>Nations in Conflict,</u> op. cit., p. 202.
37. Ibid., p. 202.
38. See ibid., Chapter 18, for our assessments.
39. For a description of the methods employed, see ibid, Appendix B; for a comparison of alternative estimation procedures, see Appendix C.
40. As reported in ibid., Chapter 17.
41. Ibid.

PART VI

SUMMARY, CONCLUSIONS, AND IMPLICATIONS

CHAPTER 22

SUMMARY, CONCLUSIONS, AND IMPLICATIONS

Francis W. Hoole
Dina A. Zinnes

The assessment of four major projects in the field of quantitative international politics that is reported in this volume was undertaken to identify applied research lessons and gain perspective on the progress being made in the field. A primary goal of the evaluation was to learn from past efforts so that current and future research can be improved. In this chapter we will summarize the highlights of the essays in the book and draw together some general conclusions and implications for the field of quantitative international politics. We will begin by presenting an overview of the comments regarding philosophy of science, methodology, and substance. Next we will state some general conclusions; and finally, we will discuss the implications of the assessment for the field of quantitative international politics.

PHILOSOPHY OF SCIENCE

The philosophy of science evaluations represent an intriguing mix of different approaches. In Chapter 3, Brian L. Job and Charles W. Ostrom, Jr., write about what they view as the sequence in the research process of the Correlates of War (COW) project. Gordon Hilton, on the other hand, in Chapter 8 is interested in how scientific research has proceeded in the field of quantitative international politics. Using the ideas of three philosophers of science, he attempts to judge which of three explanations for the way science proceeds best accounts for the evolution of the Dimensionality of Nations project. Cheryl Christensen and Robert Butterworth, writing in Chapter 13, share Hilton's orientation by looking at the

Inter-Nation Simulation project through the eyes of the same philosophers of science, but they are less concerned about deciding which philosopher of science appears to provide the best account of the process of science; rather, these authors build on the ideas of Imre Lakatos to emphasize their view of the research enterprise contained in the INS project. James A. Caporaso's approach in Chapter 18 is similar to the Job-Ostrom approach. Like Job and Ostrom, Caporaso is concerned with specifically evaluating a project utilizing criteria derived from philosophy of science; but whereas Job and Ostrom focus primarily on the overall research strategy of the COW project, Caporaso's critique is more related to the evaluation of theory and to specific theoretical statements found in the 1914 studies. Although the evaluators interpret their tasks somewhat differently, it is nevertheless possible to identify similar concerns in the four essays.

One of the major topics discussed in these essays is that of criteria for theory evaluation. The authors are unhappy with what seems to be the predominant practice of relying exclusively on empirical fit in evaluating theories. While it was agreed that empirical fit is an important criterion, the evaluators feel that multiple criteria are needed. Unfortunately, they do not neatly agree on the exact set of criteria that should be used.

Caporaso builds directly on the logical positivist approach in the philosophy of science, identifying five criteria for the evaluation of theory: fit, or empirical adequacy; parsimony; deductive power; scope; and falsifiability. By fit he means the theory accounts for the facts, and he discusses measures of improbability, of strength, and of the form of relationships between variables. By parsimony he means simplicity: a theory should be a concise abstraction of reality. By deductive power he means the possibility of making systematic derivations of theorems (propositions, hypotheses) from axioms. By scope he means the range of application, or domain, of the theory. By falsifiability he means the capability of a theory of being refuted. He accepts the Karl Popper notion that "a theory is falsifiable to the extent that its predictions are risky or improbable. For Caporaso the greater the fit, parsimony, deductive power, scope and falsifiability, the better the theory. He also notes dilemmas involved in developing theories that are high in fit and parsimony or fit and falsifiability. He gives the 1914 project high marks for theory development, after using these criteria to evaluate the work of the project.

While Job and Ostrom, in Chapter 3, are basically concerned with the research process in their assessment of COW, they nevertheless discuss three criteria for theory evaluation: fit, falsifiability and plausibility. Their conceptions of fit and falsifiability are simila

SUMMARY, CONCLUSIONS, AND IMPLICATIONS

to Caporaso's, and we will not discuss them further. Their concept of plausibility is based upon Wesley Salmon's ideas and is concerned with the "credibility of the hypothesis apart from its support in the data." According to Job and Ostrom, plausibility considerations must logically precede empirical investigation and involve delimiting the inquiry to hypotheses that are theoretically plausible. They suggest that not all possible hypotheses should be examined; the investigation should be confined to plausible hypotheses, thus reducing the chances of confirming a hypothesis that only coincidentally accounts for a prediction.

Both Chapter 13, by Christensen and Butterworth, and Chapter 8, by Gordon Hilton, suggest multiple criteria for the evaluation of theory, but they use a considerably different approach from that found in the Caporaso and Job-Ostrom papers. The Christensen-Butterworth and Hilton chapters, as well as Chapter 21, by Robert C. North, Ole R. Holsti, and Nazli Choucri, suggest the utility of Lakatos' concept of sophisticated methodological falsificationism. They urge the comparative testing of theories, emphasizing that theory evaluation is a three-cornered fight between a theory, alternative theories and data. This is in contrast to the Caporaso and Job-Ostrom orientation, in which theory evaluation is a two-cornered struggle between theory and data. The Christensen-Butterworth, Hilton and North-Holsti-Choucri chapters emphasize falsifiability vis-a-vis another theory and suggest theory evaluation criteria of excess empirical content and empirical confirmation. Excess empirical content means that novel facts can be predicted by one theory but not by another theory. Empirical confirmation means data fit by the new theory and its excess empirical content. In the Lakatos tradition a new theory must be theoretically and empirically progressive if it is to be accepted as falsifying another theory. Thus a theory is falsified only when replaced by a better alternative.

The philosophy of science evaluators emphasize eight different criteria for the evaluation of theories: fit, parsimony, deductive power, scope, falsifiability, plausibility, theoretical progression (excess empirical content), and empirical progression (corroborated excess empirical content). The criterion of utility (theoretical utility, educational utility and policy utility) is also mentioned in passing by Christensen and Butterworth. In addition, in Chapter 11, Rudolph J. Rummel, agreeing with the evaluators that multiple criteria are needed for evaluating theory, suggests eight criteria that overlap with, but are not necessarily identical to, those proposed by other writers: specificity, elegance, richness, validity, operationalizability, testability, confirmation, and importance. Although the authors do not always agree on the specific criteria, it is clear that they share the common conviction that the use of some set of multiple criteria will enhance the efforts to build empirical theory.

The second major issue to emerge in the philosophy of science essays concerns the research process. Job and Ostrom are concerned primarily with the temporal ordering of data collection, data analysis, and theory construction. They disagree with the temporal priority given to data collection and description in the Correlates of War Project. Building on the ideas of Hempel, they categorize the orientation of COW as a "narrow inductivist conception of scientific inquiry," and point out the limitations of that approach. They propose instead the use of Hempel's "wide inductivist conception of scientific inquiry," which calls for theory construction and generation of hypotheses, then operationalization of concepts, collection of data, and testing of hypotheses. Job and Ostrom feel that scientific inquiry should emphasize the "rigor of justification" rather than the "purity of discovery." Singer disagrees with Job and Ostrom concerning the way researchers ought to proceed in the contemporary field of quantitative international politics, especially in regard to the temporal ordering of the research process. He also feels that Job and Ostrom have not correctly interpreted the research of the Correlates of War Project.

Both the Christensen-Butterworth and Hilton papers present the research process in a slightly different light than Job and Ostrom. They discuss the orientation to the research process of Thomas C. Kuhn and of Popper and Lakatos. Both papers find the ideas of Lakatos especially exciting and urge serious consideration of his orientation. They emphasize that theory testing is a kind of cybernetic process involving constant feedback and change. They see a research program as specifying the paths of research to avoid (negative heuristics) and paths of research to pursue (positive heuristics). Of particular importance is Lakatos' rational, rather than sociological or psychological, orientation, which suggests when a progressive problem shift takes place and how anomalies should be handled. The significance of the Lakatos orientation lies, according to Christensen and Butterworth, in the fact that such a perspective "makes the researcher more capable of learning in [a] problem-fraught environment."

Although the various writers suggest new ways of thinking about how research ought to proceed and how theory can be evaluated, no consensus emerges regarding the proper manner in which research ought to proceed or the exact criteria to be used for the evaluation of theory. However, they agree that the research enterprise should be theoretically focused in the beginning and proceed in as flexible and pragmatic a manner as possible, avoiding any rigidity that might not allow for changes or feedback. There is also considerable agreement that the role of data is important but limited, that some form of falsification should be emphasized in the empirical aspect of

SUMMARY, CONCLUSIONS, AND IMPLICATIONS 467

research, and that the development of empirical theory in the field of international politics requires a systematic research program yielding a progression of studies that build on one another. The overall philosophy of science assessment appears to be that, generally speaking, the project researchers have struggled admirably, if not always successfully, to cope with complex research problems.

METHODOLOGY

If one resorts to evidence from the empirical world to examine a given generalization, then the means by which evidence is gathered, assigned values, and evaluated is important. The methodology papers indicate that a wide variety of techniques have been used in the projects examined. In this section we will attempt to summarize the highlights of the discussion on research design, measurement rules, data collection, and data or statistical analysis.

The basic design of the Dimensionality of Nations Project was correlational, cross-sectional, exploratory, and then hypothesis-testing in nature. It focused primarily upon the nation-state and the dyad as units for analysis, and it utilized data from secondary sources. The general design of the Correlates of War Project was correlational, time-series, and exploratory in nature. The basic unit of analysis was the international system. The data came from secondary sources. The 1914 project essentially has been engaged in hypothesis testing, utilizing data that have been collected from unpublished archival and secondary sources. The nation-state and the coalitions of that historical period serve as the basic units for analysis. The orientation is correlational and time-series in nature. The Inter-Nation Simulation Project was based primarily upon a hypothesis-testing, experimental, cross-sectional format that utilized laboratory data and focused upon the individual, nation-state, and international systems as units of analysis.* The validity studies of INS also involved cross-sectional correlational analysis utilizing data from secondary sources. Although only general comments on research design are made by the evaluators, it appears they find no major faults in the basic designs of the projects.

The evaluators identify a number of the measurement techniques that were used, the principal ones being factor analysis, paired

---

*Stuart J. Thorson, writing in Chapter 14, is especially intrigued by the possibilities for examining policy and design questions within the INS research framework.

comparisons, Q sort, frequency count indices, and straightforward aggregate data indicators. In general the evaluators feel that the most serious methodological problems lie in the area of measurement, and a number of difficulties are specified. It is felt that the relationship between measurement rules and theoretical concepts is not always carefully delineated. For example, Karen Ann Feste, in Chapter 19, is concerned about the ambiguity involved in measurement of unobserved items like intensity. In Chapter 9, Leo Hazlewood worries about the use of exploratory rather than confirmatory factor analysis and the use of atheoretical scaling criteria like variance explained. Raymond Duvall suggests in Chapter 4 that there is a lack of conceptual clarity in the Correlates of War studies that has led to less than satisfactory measures of some items. Stuart J. Thorson discusses the validity problems of the INS Projects, in Chapter 14. Both Feste and Duvall feel that there is confusion over the level of measurement actually achieved and that in some instances the level of measurement has been less than that claimed by the researchers. Duvall also raises a question concerning the entity to which measured properties have been attributed. Hazlewood argues that some of the factor analyses that he studied suffered from the use of ratio or proportional variables, an improper ratio of cases to variables, a lack of stability of space and factors, and a decomposition problem. The evaluators make a number of measurement-related suggestions, including multiple operationalism, confirmatory factor analysis, scaling, and nonmetric factor analysis.

The evaluators also identify a variety of different data collection techniques. The primary ones involve the direct collection of aggregate data from secondary sources and content analysis of historical documentation. On the whole the projects are praised for their data collection efforts, and the methodological essays indicate that data collection is the methodological strong suit of the projects. The data sources are assessed as adequate, and their rules for the collection of data are considered to be sufficiently clear to allow replication. However, the evaluators do point to five sources of potential error in the data collection process. Hazlewood reported a concern about the way the types of data to be collected were selected in the DON project, specifically in the atheoretical selection of variables. Feste and Duvall raise the question of sampling, that is, the manner in which the data have been selected from the larger population. Feste and Hazlewood raise the question of missing data, and Duvall raises the question of the comparability of data over time for a variable. Feste argues that there is also a problem when the entities being compared change from one analysis to another.

The statistical and data analytic techniques used in the projects have included numerous nonparametric bivariate measures, bivariate

SUMMARY, CONCLUSIONS, AND IMPLICATIONS

and multivariate correlation analysis, canonical correlation, polynomials, causal modeling and spectral analysis. The predominance of linear techniques was overwhelming. While the evaluators give the projects adequate marks for the use of data analytic techniques, the statistical and data analytic facets are not considered to be the most sophisticated aspects of the projects.

The evaluators identify four major problems in the use of statistical and data analytic techniques. Hazlewood and Duvall express a concern over a lack of adequate theoretical guidance in the use of data analytic techniques: Hazlewood questions the appropriateness of certain specific uses of canonical analysis, while Duvall is concerned about the implications of the linear assumption when using regression models. Both writers suggest the importance of theoretically specifying the relationship between variables. A second problem is raised by Feste and Duvall. These evaluators express concern over the use of tests of significance in examining hypotheses when the data cannot be assumed to be a random sample. Feste also points to a third difficulty: the application of statistics that assume one level of measurement to data that in fact are measured at a different level. Finally, Duvall sensitizes the reader to the requirements for the proper use of regression analysis, suggesting ways to obtain more adequate estimates of parameters in structural equation models.

In sum, the evaluators feel that the methodological aspects of the projects have been adequately handled, although some aspects appear to be considerably stronger than others. Specifically, the evaluators suggest that the data collection efforts have been the most outstanding characteristic of the projects from a methodological standpoint, followed by research design, statistical and data analysis, and then measurement. Although the evaluators suggest that the methodological practices of the projects, particularly in the area of measurement, might be improved, most of their critical comments can be seen as suggestions for refining what are essentially adequate methodological practices.

On the whole the reaction to the methodological evaluations is one of agreement, although some take issue with specific criticisms and indicate that at times the evaluators lack perspective or are too dogmatic and purist in their orientation. In Chapter 11, Rudolph J. Rummel strongly disagrees with Hazlewood regarding the handling by the DON project of confirmatory factor analysis, ratio variables, ratio of variables to cases, stability of factors, and missing data and about whether theory guided the use of canonical correlation. In the forward, Bruce Russett worries that some evaluators of methodology focus on such minor issues as the use of specific statistical techniques while ignoring more important items such as the level of analysis. Robert C. North, Ole R. Holsti and Nazli Choucri, in discussing in Chapter 21 the use of statistics by the 1914 project, note the controversial nature of certain types of criticism in their comment that "even eminent consultants differ among themselves and sometimes offer contradictory advice." J. David Singer, in his rejoinder in Chapter 6, disagrees with a great many of the measurement and data analysis points raised by Duvall. There also appears to be some feeling that there has been too little discussion by the evaluators of what substantive difference the discussed methodological concerns really make. The overall discussion of the methodological aspects of the projects seems to be captured by Robert C. North's comment in Chapter 17 that "In the course of the research, we have encountered many more difficulties than were initially anticipated, but despite much trial-and-error experimentation, several blind alleys, and the expenditure of vastly more time than we had foreseen as necessary, we are generally pleased with . . . progress so far."

SUBSTANTIVE CONSIDERATIONS

As we indicated in the first chapter, the questions regarding the substantive contributions of the projects are the crucial ones. Unless quantitative international politics research is able to make a substantive contribution, it is failing to meet its basic commitment. In this section we will summarize the comments of the substantive evaluators on the questions that were asked by each project and the results that have been reported and their overall significance, and we will attempt to assess the extent to which the projects under review have been successful in moving toward the goal of developing empirical theory about international political phenomena.

Chapter 10, by Richard H. Van Atta and Dale B. Robertson, and Chapter 7, by Rudolph J. Rummel, observe that the major substantive focus of the Dimensionality of Nations Project has been the linkage between national attributes and international behavior by the governmental representatives of nation-states. The first phase of the DON Project involved empirical identification of the major dimensions of nations in regard to national attributes and international behavior and locating the nations on these dimensions. During this phase the major questions were related to these concerns. During the second phase, questions were asked about how attribute and behavior dimensions are related. This second phase has so far consisted of formulating and evaluating two different field theory models that relate national attributes and behavior.

SUMMARY, CONCLUSIONS, AND IMPLICATIONS

With a primary concern for understanding the causes of war, the Correlates of War project has focused on describing the attributes of the international system and identifying the variables that correlate with war. In Chapter 5, Harvey Starr notes a series of specific questions that have been addressed by the COW Project, including an examination of the relationships between national alliance experiences and war, between international organizations and war, between status and violence, between power distribution and war, and between status inconsistency and alliance aggregation. Starr observes that alliances, balance of power models, and Galtung's status theory have been systematically analyzed by the project. The second phase of the COW project, which has only recently begun, is focusing on multivariate models and emphasizing theory construction and testing.

The original research goal of the 1914 project was to understand the general process of decision making under crisis conditions and the effect of this process on hostility and threat perception. In the early period of the project a general stimulus-response orientation was utilized, and a number of specific propositions having to do with the conflict spiral and the effect of crisis on decision making were examined. The second phase of the project has involved, so far, a broadening of the decision-making concerns to noncrisis situations and has focused on the long-term antecedents of war, examining the distribution of attributes and capabilities among nations. Here the interactions among population, technology, and capabilities have been a major focus, as have been interstate rivalries, arms races, alliances and international conflict. (See Chapters 17 and 20.) One specific indication of the substantive focus is found in North's classification in Chapter 17 of the data examined by the project into three types: attribute, cognitive, and action.

The Inter-Nation Simulation Project pursued an eclectic research strategy involving concerns that are traditionally associated with several disciplines, in an effort to develop a macrotheory of international relations. Among the earlier concerns of the project that Stuart A. Bremer identifies in Chapter 15 were such issues as the effects of nuclear proliferation; the relationships among personality variables, stress, and aggression; the relationships among hostile communication, threat perception, and armament production; the effect of cognitive rigidity; the differences between crisis and noncrisis decision making; the consequences of the capacity to delay response; the impact of ethnocentric perceptions on behavior; the causes and consequences of strategic doctrines; the factors determining alliance cohesion; and the applicability of the theory of collective goods for alliance behavior. During the later phases of the project a major effort was made to test, or validate, the INS as a theory and to develop and test refined theoretical statements of international politics in the form of man-computer and all-computer simulation models.

It is thus easy to conclude that the substantive concerns of the projects being reviewed are important, varied, and interesting; let us now consider the research findings and their significance.

During the first phase of the Dimensionality of Nations project a number of descriptive findings regarding the dimensions of national attributes and behavior were identified. Van Atta and Robertson report some of these findings in detail in Chapter 10, labeling them an empirical taxonomy. Rummel notes in Chapter 7 that this phase has established, among other things, that "International Relations is highly structured: the treaties, trade, aid, threats, GNP per capita, defense expenditures, literacy, riots, and other attributes and behaviors of nations are organized into very stable and clear patterns." He also observes that "the major dimensions accounting for national variation in attributes concern wealth, politics and power." In the second phase, the major substantive finding has been that Model II provides impressive empirical fits to data from a variety of countries.* (See Chapter 10.) Model II views the behavior of nation j on behavior dimension k as a linear function of the distance between i and j on all attributes. Model II differs from Model I in that the parameters are allowed to differ from nation to nation. More recently field theory has been expanded by the incorporation of status theory, and Model II is considered to be the operational interpretation of status-field theory. Van Atta and Robertson summarize their view of the impact the DON project has had on the field in the following way: "There is no question that because of the DON Project we know much more about relationships between attributes and behaviors, and know how to ask more pointed and specific questions regarding their relationships."

The Correlates of War project has been particularly successful in providing measures that describe war, the diplomatic importance of states, status inconsistency, alliances, intergovernmental organizations, and the power distribution in the international system. Starr's list of 52 different findings of the COW project in Chapter 5 indicates that considerable success has also been achieved in the testing of hypotheses linking these variables. Furthermore, the COW project has built upon and extended Lewis F. Richardson's original work, and Starr provides a comparison of what he identifies as the 21 major findings of the COW Project and the 16 major findings of Richardson. While Starr feels COW has made an important con-

---

*At the most general level Rummel offers, in Chapter 11, five propositions that he feels contain the general conclusions of the DON project to date.

SUMMARY, CONCLUSIONS, AND IMPLICATIONS 473

tribution to the field, he also feels that the project has yet to develop what he calls a "causal" knowledge. He reports no attempt to develop and test a general theory of the causes of war and concludes that the "greatest strength of the enterprise rests in the development of the data base from which we may test speculation with reproducible evidence."

The first phase of the 1914 project analyzed hypotheses regarding crisis decision making that were developed from the stimulus-response framework. (See Chapter 20.) The findings of these analyses then became the basis for the second phase of the project, which has involved the development and successful testing of a general theory of violence. This theory, stated as a multiequation model, focuses on the violent behavior of nations. Among the key exogenous variables are population density, military expenditures for the prior year, and national income per capita. The model assumes that increasing population and technology place severe pressure upon resources, and create unsatisfied demands. The greater the unsatisfied demands and the greater the capacity of a country, the greater the propensity for the extension of international activities. When international activities and external expansion become important, a new set of relationships develops that focuses on interstate rivalries, arms races, and conflict. This may then lead to a crisis syndrome focusing on escalation and war. In his overall evaluation of the project, Mark S. Levine concludes, "the funds invested . . . have been well spent and should continue to be invested to support additional analyses."

Bremer notes in Chapter 15 that the initial work of the Inter-Nation Simulation Project produced a partial, yet tremendously complex, macrotheory of international relations with the INS man-machine simulation model; but he argues that the wide variety of questions addressed by the project precluded the development of a coherent body of knowledge. The second phase of the project saw the development and successful testing of a revised, and even more complex, partial theory of international relations in the form of the man-machine International Processes Simulation. This work was followed by a series of all-computer simulation models of various aspects of international politics. Bremer concludes that the INS Project has made a limited substantive contribution to the field of international politics, but on the other hand he applauds the project's contribution in teaching international relations scholars to "think differently" and identifies seven ways in which he feels this reorientation was facilitated by the INS Project.

Thus the substantive evaluators have alerted us to the wide variety of concerns addressed by the projects, identified the significant substantive findings, and in general praised the progress made toward the goal of developing substantive knowledge in the form of an empirical theory of international political phenomena. It is clear that the writers feel that important and difficult questions have been and are being asked and that, on balance, satisfactory progress is being made in the development of answers to those questions.*

GENERAL CONCLUSIONS

Generally speaking, the projects reviewed in this volume have received praise from the evaluators. Beyond this we can further identify three general conclusions that seem to emerge from these essays. First, there is no single best way to pursue quantitative research in the field of international politics. Indeed, many legitimate ways exist for doing this type of research. Furthermore, since quantitative research is both time-consuming and expensive, it is especially important that projects be carefully planned and monitored in order to maximize the likelihood of success. The ideas of philosophers of science like Hempel, Kuhn, Popper, and Lakatos could be used to help scholars plan long-range research strategies, and many of the suggestions contained in this volume could be of assistance in the development of both long- and short-range research efforts. However, there is no obvious alternative to a theoretically focused research program that proceeds in a flexible and creative manner. We would emphasize that philosophy of science issues, empirical evidence, and methodological considerations are of great importance, but they should be kept in proper perspective, with the primary focus on substantive matters and the development of empirical theory.

Second, we conclude that while the methodological practices being employed in the field are essentially adequate, there is room for improvement. More attention should be given to novel research designs, perhaps of an experimental or quasi-experimental nature. Although their measurement procedures are adequate, the researchers need to focus carefully on several measurement issues. More attention should be paid to the relationship between measurement rules and the level of measurement obtained and to the relationship

---

*One of the more interesting issues raised was the degree to which it is reasonable to expect a theoretical statement in international politics to contain the same parameter values for all cases for all years. This issue is of potential interest for all scholars in the field of quantitative international politics, and we have not previously seen so much importance attached to it in regard to the development of theory in the international politics field. See Chapters 7, 8, 10, 11, 17, 18, 20, and 21.

SUMMARY, CONCLUSIONS, AND IMPLICATIONS 475

between the level of measurement and the statistical analysis. More awareness is also needed of the limitations of factor analysis. Finally, some consideration should be given to multiple operationalism. In addition to research design and measurement issues, it appears that more attention should be devoted to such problems as the selection of the types of data to be collected, sampling, missing data, and comparability of data. Data analysis could be improved by relating analysis techniques more closely to theoretical statements and by checking to determine that the assumptions of the data analytic or statistical techniques are met. Finally, it seems obvious that methodological concerns should be kept in a proper perspective and research techniques should be evaluated in regard to their effect on substantive findings.

Third, it seems fair to conclude that the projects under review in this volume have made a major contribution to the international politics literature. The substantive findings identified by the project evaluators reflect this contribution in part. In addition, the prominence, if not predominance, of these projects in the contemporary international politics field is a clear indication of their value as assessed by the field. When they were begun ten and fifteen years ago these projects were high-risk ventures being tried in a field solidly based on another research paradigm. The projects demonstrated that the new research paradigm could also make a significant substantive contribution to the literature. Through this demonstration the projects helped transform the paradigm within which international politics scholars work. Finally, these projects have trained a large number of individuals to do research and teach at the graduate and undergraduate level within the new paradigm.

We think it appropriate to conclude that the major overall contribution of this assessment has been to make us more sensitive to research problems in the field of quantitative international politics. Having gone through this "sensitivity training," perhaps scholars will be in a better position to identify problems and to propose solutions to the numerous difficulties that each of us faces in our research endeavors. At least we hope so, because even though significant progress has been made, we still have a long way to go in the development of theoretical explanatory knowledge in the field of quantitative international politics.

IMPLICATIONS

In this section we would like to consider what we feel are the most important implications of the assessment reported in this volume; but before doing that, let us note that the ideas contained in this section are our own and do not necessarily reflect the thoughts of other contributors.

First, we feel that more emphasis should be placed on theory development and testing, and less on exploratory studies. In no way do we mean to fault the many excellent and legitimate exploratory studies that have been undertaken in the past: obviously, both exploratory and theory-testing studies are needed, and the research process must be one of interaction between theory and data. However, in the past the emphasis seems to have been placed on exploratory studies, and we would like to urge that more attention be given to theory development before data are collected and analyzed. We see this trend as having already started, and it is probably fair to say that the QIP research of the 1960s was primarily concerned with data collection and analysis, while QIP research of the 1970s is moving towards model building and testing.*

Second, we feel that the current temptation in the international politics field to place emphasis upon and commit huge amounts of resources to the development of new data banks should be resisted. We feel that an attempt should be made to obtain agreement on basic data needs, that cooperative efforts for the systematic collection and dissemination of appropriate data sets should be developed, and that collected data, such as General Assembly roll-call votes, COW data, DON data, and World Handbook data, should be kept up to date. However, we are dubious about the benefits in relation to costs that data collection has for the field as a whole. Data-bank enterprises are expensive, and as resources begin to dwindle we feel it is increasingly necessary that researchers be able to demonstrate theoretical justifications for collecting additional data sets. In general we feel that all data-collection efforts, whether interview, aggregate, observational, content analytic, or laboratory, should be related to specific theoretical concerns. All of this, of course, does not mean that existing data sets should be abandoned; indeed, more use should be made of existing data, and once data have been collected they should be saved and made available for analysis by others. The International Relations Data Archive of the Inter-University Consortium for Political Research at the University of Michigan performs a valuable service in this regard, and we encourage scholars to support its efforts by continuing to send collected data to the archive headquarters. Our argument concerns future data collection efforts. It is our hope that new efforts in this

---

*We note that Harold Guetzkow and Wm. Ladd Hollist in Chapter 16 and Rummel in Chapter 11 project their own research as essentially theoretical work.

SUMMARY, CONCLUSIONS, AND IMPLICATIONS

regard will be carefully evaluated with respect to the anticipated theoretical contribution that a new data set will make.

Third, we feel that suggestions concerning the education of graduate students are implicit in the evaluations. Clearly the emphasis on the substantive problems of the field and on the techniques of data collection and data analysis must be continued. However, we must supplement these with more training in research design and measurement and more exposure to subjects like philosophy of science, epistemology, formal logic, and mathematics by advising graduate students to enter summer programs like the one at the Inter-University Consortium for Political Research and encouraging students to develop theoretical skills through outside minors. In this way we believe that the quality of research in the international politics field will be improved.

Fourth, there is an implication that a theoretical clearinghouse is needed in the international politics field. Perhaps Bruce Russett identifies the need most clearly when he writes in the foreword to this volume, "I . . . find it a bit surprising that the major projects generally seem to have learned so little from one another. Although there is some cross-referencing, there is sometimes a lack of any systematic effort to exploit or build upon the findings of other projects." A theoretical clearinghouse would facilitate communication among the scholars working on the development of empirical theory in the field of international politics by promoting newsletters, meetings, and other similar activities. It appears that the Interpolimetrics Section of the International Studies Association is starting to perform a clearinghouse function, and we urge all interested scholars in the international politics field to join and participate in the activities of this organization. However, we acknowledge that in the final analysis it is the responsibility of each individual scholar to be more conscientious in consulting the work of others.

Fifth, we feel that the discussion in this volume contains implications for the decisions of funding agencies. Specifically, we feel that such agencies should demonstrate a greater willingness to support theoretical studies by scholars, even though some of these may appear to be high-risk ventures. Small grants providing for more released time for young professors and more graduate student assistance would be one approach. For example, ten faculty grants at $3,000 for a summer and ten graduate student grants at $1,500 for a summer over a five-year period would permit an agency to support 100 high-risk theoretically oriented projects for the five years with the relatively small investment of $225,000. We also feel that Russett's suggestions for cross-fertilization should be seriously considered by funding agencies: We quote these suggestions from the foreword to this volume as follows:

Perhaps special mini-conferences would help; they could
be arranged around particular topics such as arms races
or status inconsistency and carefully organized to bring
together across projects people who are working at different levels of analysis. Another valuable kind of mini-conference might be one in which the data set from one
or more of the big projects was made available to users
in an interactive computer mode and in which a variety
of people with different methodological and theoretical
orientations met to generate and immediately test hypotheses.

Indeed, it appears to us that there are many common substantive threads in the projects discussed in this volume, and it may be that closer analysis would lead to tests, as described in Lakatos, that compare the theoretical statements articulated by these, or other, projects or alternatively to a merging of the theoretical findings of the researchers associated with these, or other, projects.

We feel that the field of quantitative international politics has come a long way since its beginning in the 1950s. However, we also believe that great challenges remain. Given the strides that have already been made, we are both optimistic and enthusiastic about its prospects. We see in the projects reviewed in this volume the promise of more theoretical efforts and greater analytical sophistication. If this trend continues we are confident that even greater progress will be made in the next decade of research.

While the primary goal of this interpolimetrics project has been to stimulate careful and thoughtful evaluations of specific research in the QIP field, there was in addition a secondary purpose to this enterprise, which was to improve the quality of criticism in the international politics field: to move to broadly-based critiques and to provide more careful and constructive criticism than is found in the quickly prepared and verbally presented critiques given at professional meetings or the all too brief book reviews and exchanges that usually appear in professional journals. Perhaps it is useful, then, to consider whether this subsidiary goal has been met. Although it is clear from the dialogue between evaluators and project heads that disagreements, some important, exist, it seems to us that one cannot but be impressed with the overall high quality of the discussion. Regardless of whether one agrees with the criticisms or with the rebuttals, the conclusion that the dialogue, on balance, has been useful and productive seems to us, at least, inescapable.

PART
VII
BIBLIOGRAPHIES

THE CORRELATES OF WAR PROJECT

Principal Investigator:
J. David Singer
Prepared by:
J. David Singer

Bennett, Robert. "Composition of the Global/International System, 1816-1970: Inclusion Criteria and a Revised Population." Ann Arbor: University of Michigan, Mental Health Research Institute, 1975.

Bremer, Stuart A. "Formal Alliance Clusters in the Interstate System: 1816-1965." Paper presented at the American Political Science Association annual meeting, Washington, D.C., September 1972.

_____. "A Sociometric Analysis of Diplomatic Bonds, 1817-1940." Paper presented at the Events Data Conference, Michigan State University, 1971.

_____. "The Trials of Nations: An Improbable Application of Probability Theory." Ann Arbor: University of Michigan, Correlates of War Project, 1975.

_____; Singer, J. David; and Luterbacher, Urs. "The Population Density and War Proneness of European Nations, 1816-1965." Comparative Political Studies 6, no. 3 (1973): 329-48.

_____ and Stuckey, John. "The Powerful and the War-Prone: Relative National Capability and War Involvement, 1820-1964." Ann Arbor: University of Michigan, Correlates of War Project, 1975.

Bueno de Mesquita, Bruce. "The Effects of Systemic Polarization on the Probability and Duration of War: Toward an Early Warning Indicator of War." Paper presented at the International Studies Association annual meeting, Washington, D.C., February 1975.

_____. "The Impact of Alliance on Industrial Development." East Lansing: Michigan State University, 1973.

_____. "Measuring Polarity in the Major Power System." Rochester: University of Rochester, 1974.

_____. "Measuring Systemic Polarity." Journal of Conflict Resolution 19, no. 2 (1975): 187-216.

_____. "Systemic Polarity and the Occurence and Duration of War, 1900-1965." Paper presented at the meetings of the International Studies Association, 1975.

_____ and Singer, J. David. "Alliance, Capabilities, and War: A Review and Synthesis." Political Science Annual 4, edited by Cornelius Cotter (Indianapolis: Bobbs-Merrill, 1973): 237-80.

Cannizzo, Cynthia A. "The Costs of Combat: Predicting Deaths, Duration and Defeat in Interstate War, 1816-1965." Paper presented at the International Studies Association annual meeting, Washington, D.C., February 1975.

_____. "The Costs of Combat: Predicting Deaths, Duration, and Defeat in Interstate War, 1816-1965." Doctoral dissertation, Ann Arbor: University of Michigan, 1975.

Deutsch, Karl W., and Singer, J. David. "Multipolar Power Systems and International Stability." World Politics 16, no. 3 (1964): 390-406.

Gochman, Charles. "Status, Conflict, and War: The Major Powers, 1820-1970." Ph.D. dissertation, Ann Arbor: University of Michigan, 1975.

_____. "Status, Power, and Interstate Conflict: The Major Powers, 1820-1970 (A Research Note and Some Preliminary Findings)." Paper presented at the meetings of the International Studies Association, Washington, D.C., 1975.

Jones, Susan, and Bennett, Robert. "Civil Wars, 1816-1970: A Typology and Tentative Population." Ann Arbor: University of Michigan, Mental Health Research Institute, 1975.

Leng, Russell J. "The Future of Events Data Marriages: A Question of Compatibility." International Interactions, forthcoming.

_____. "When Will They Ever Learn? A Study of Inter-Nation Behavior in Chronic Dyadic Conflict." Paper presented at the meetings of the American Political Science Association, Chicago, Illinois, 1974.

_____ and Goodsell, Robert. "Behavior Indicators of War Proneness in Bilateral Conflicts." In Sage International Yearbook of Foreign Policy Studies, vol. 2. Edited by Patrick McGowan. Beverly Hills: Sage Publications, 1974, pp. 191-266.

_____ and Singer, J. David. Coder's Manual for Identifying and Describing International Actions. Middlebury, Vt.: Middlebury College, mimeographed.

Luterbacher, Urs. "Continuite et Indetermination dans les Conflits Internationaux: Une Analyse Mathematique et Statistique." Schweizerisches Jahrbuch fur Politische Wissenschaft, no. 13 (1973), pp. 147-62.

_____. "Dimensions Historiques de Modeles Dynamiques de Conflits: Application aux Processus de Course aux Armements 1900-1965." Ph.D. dissertation, Geneva: Graduate Institute of International Studies, 1972.

Mihalka, Michael. "Interstate Conflict in the European State System, 1816-1970." Ph.D. dissertation, Ann Arbor: University of Michigan, 1975.

Ray, James Lee. "Aggregation and Confusion: The Levels Problem Revisited." Ann Arbor: University of Michigan, Correlates of War Project, 1975.

_____. "Status Inconsistency and War Involvement among European States, 1816-1970." Ph.D. dissertation, Ann Arbor: University of Michigan, 1974

_____. "Status Inconsistency and War Involvement in Europe, 1816-1970." Papers, Peace Science Society (International) 23, (1974): 69-80.

_____ and Singer, J. David. "Measuring the Concentration of Power in the International System." Sociological Methods and Research 1, no. 4 (1973): 403-437.

Russett, Bruce M.; Singer, J. David; and Small, Melvin. "National Political Units in the Twentieth Century: A Standardized List." American Political Science Review 2, no. 3 (1968): 932-51.

Sabrosky, Alan. "Commitments, Capabilities, and the Expansion of Interstate War, 1816-1965." Ph.D. dissertation, Ann Arbor: University of Michigan, 1975.

_____. "From Bosnia to Sarajevo: A Comparative Discussion of Interstate Crises." Journal of Conflict Resolution 19, no. 1 (1975): 3-24.

_____. "The War Performance of Peacetime Allies." Paper presented at the meetings of the International Studies Association, 1975.

Singer, J. David. "The 'Correlates of War' Project: Interim Report and Rationale." World Politics 24, no. 2 (1972): 243-70.

_____. "Data-Making in International Relations." Behavioral Science 10, no. 1 (1965): 68-80.

_____. Deterence, Arms Control and Disarmament: Toward a Synthesis in National Security Policy. Columbus: Ohio State University Press, 1962.

_____. "Escalation and Control in International Conflict: A Simple Feedback Model." General Systems 15 (1970): 163-73.

_____. "From a Study of War to Peace Research: Some Criteria and Strategies." Journal of Conflict Resolution 14, no. 4 (1970): 527-42.

_____. "A General Systems Taxonomy for Political Science." Morristown, N.J.: General Learning Press, 1971.

_____. "The Historical Experiment as a Research Strategy in the Study of World Politics." Political Inquiry 2, no. 1 (1974): 23-52.

_____. "The Incomplete Theorist: Insight without Evidence." In Contending Approaches to International Politics. Edited by Klaus Knorr and James N. Rosenau. Princeton: Princeton University Press, 1969, pp. 62-86.

_____. "Inter-Nation Influence: A Formal Model." American Political Science Review 57, no. 2 (1963): 420-30.

_____. "Knowledge, Practice, and the Social Sciences in International Politics." In A Design for International Relations Research. Edited by Norman D. Palmer. Philadelphia: American Academy of Political and Social Science, 1970, pp. 137-49.

_____. "Modern International War: From Conjecture to Explanation." In The Search for World Order: Essays in Honor of Quincy Wright. Edited by Albert Lepawsky, Edward Buehrig, and Harold Lasswell. New York: Appleton-Century-Crofts, 1971, pp. 47-71.

_____. "The Outcome of Arms Races: A Policy Problem and A Research Approach." Proceedings IPRA 3, no. 2 (1970): 137-46.

_____. "The Peace Researcher and Foreign Policy Prediction." Papers, Peace Science Society (International) 21 (1973): 1-14.

_____. "The Political Science of Human Conflict." In The Nature of Human Conflict. Edited by Elton B. McNeil. Englewood Cliffs: Prentice-Hall, 1965, pp. 139-54.

_____. The Scientific Study of Politics: An Approach to Foreign Policy Analysis. Morristown, N.J.: General Learning Press, 1972.

_____. "Stable Deterrence and Its Limits." Western Political Quarterly 15, no. 3 (1962): 449-64.

_____. "Theorists and Empiricists: The Two-Culture Problem in International Politics." In The Analysis of International Politics. Edited by James N. Rosenau, Vincent Davis, and Maurice A. East. New York: Free Press, 1972, pp. 80-95.

_____. "Threat Perception and the Armament-Tension Dilemma." Journal of Conflict Resolution 2, no. 1 (1958): 90-105.

_____; Bremer, Stuart; and Stuckey, John. "Capability Distribution, Uncertainty, and Major Power War, 1820-1965." In Peace, War, and Numbers. Edited by Bruce M. Russett. Beverly Hills: Sage Publications, 1972, pp. 19-48.

_____ and Small, Melvin. "Alliance Aggregation and the Onset of War, 1815-1945." In Quantitative International Politics: Insights and Evidence. Edited by J. David Singer. New York: Free Press, 1968, pp. 247-86.

_____ and Small, Melvin. "The Composition and Status Ordering of the International System: 1815-1940." World Politics 18, no. 2 (1966): 236-82.

_____ and Small, Melvin. "Foreign Policy Indicators: Predictors of War in History and in the State of the World Message." Policy Sciences 5, no. 3 (1974): 271-96.

_____ and Small, Melvin. "Formal Alliances, 1815-1939: A Quantitative Description." Journal of Peace Research 3, no. 1 (1966): 1-32.

_____ and Small, Melvin. "National Alliance Commitments and War Involvement, 1815-1945." Papers of the Peace Research Society (International) 5 (1966): 109-140.

_____ and Small, Melvin. "Patterns in International Warfare, 1816-1965." Annals of the American Academy of Political and Social Science 391 (1970): 145-55.

_____ and Small, Melvin. The Wages of War, 1816-1965: A Statistical Handbook. New York: John Wiley and Sons, 1972.

_____ and Wallace, Michael. "Inter-governmental Organization and the Preservation of Peace, 1816-1964: Some Bivariate Relationships." International Organization 24, no. 3 (1970): 520-47.

Skjelsbaek, Kjell. "Shared Membership in Intergovernmental Organizations and Dyadic War, 1865-1964." In The United Nations: Problems and Prospects. Edited by Edwin Fedder. St. Louis: Center for International Studies, 1971, pp. 31-61.

Small, Melvin. "The Applicability of Quantitative International Politics to Diplomatic History." The Historian, forthcoming.

_____ and Singer, J. David. "The Diplomatic Importance of States, 1816-1970: An Extension and Refinement of the Indicator." World Politics 25, no. 4 (1973): 577-99.

_____ and Singer, J. David. "Formal Alliances, 1816-1965: An Extension of the Basic Data." Journal of Peace Research 6, no. 3 (1969): 257-82.

_____ and Singer, J. David. "Historische Tatsachen und Wissenschatliche Daten am Beispiel der Erforschung von Kriegen." In Soziologie und Sozialgeschichte: Aspekte und Probleme. Edited by Peter C. Ludz. Opladen: Westdeutscher Verlag, 1973, pp. 221-41.

_____ and Singer, J. David. "The War Proneness of Democratic Regimes." Jerusalem Journal of International Relations, forthcoming.

Stuckey, John, and Singer, J. David. "The Powerful and the War-Prone: Ranking the Nations by Relative Capability and War Experience, 1820-1964." Paper presented at the conference on Poder Social: America Latine en El Mundo, Mexico City, May 1973.

Thompson, James. "Energy Consumption as an Indicator of Industrial Growth and National Capabilities: World Trends, 1870-1970." Paper presented at the meetings of the International Political Science Association, Montreal, Canada, 1973.

Von Riekhoff, Harald. "Status Inconsistency and the War Behavior of Major Powers, 1815-1965." Paper presented at International Relations Theory Conference, Toronto, 1973.

Wallace, Michael. "Alliance Polarization, Cross-cutting, and International War, 1815-1964: A Measurement Procedure and Some Preliminary Evidence." Journal of Conflict Resolution 17, no. 4 (1973): 575-604.

_____. "Power, Status, and International War." Journal of Peace Research 8, no. 1 (1971): 23-35.

_____. "Status, Formal Organization and Arms Levels as Factors Leading to the Onset of War, 1820-1964." In Peace, War and Numbers. Edited by Bruce M. Russett. Beverly Hills: Sage Publications, 1972, pp. 49-69.

_____. War and Rank Among Nations. Lexington, Mass.: D. C. Heath, 1973.

_____ and Singer, J. David. "Intergovernmental Organization in the Global System, 1816-1964: A Quantitative Description." International Organization 24, no. 2 (1970): 239-87.

_____ and Singer, J. David. "Large Scale Violence in the Global System: Definition and Measurement." Paper presented at the International Political Science Association Congress, Montreal, August 1973.

Wheeler, Hugh. "Effects of War on Industrial Growth." Society 12, no. 4 (1975): 48-52.

_____. "The Effects of War on Industrial Growth, 1816-1965." Ph.D. dissertation, Ann Arbor: University of Michigan, 1975.

_____. "The Effects of War on National Power, 1860-1965: Postwar Changes in Energy Consumption." Paper presented at the International Studies Association annual meeting, Washington, D.C., February 1975.

Yamamoto, Yoshinobu. "Probability Models of War Expansion and Peacetime Alliance Formation." Ph.D. dissertation, Ann Arbor: University of Michigan, 1974.

____ and Bremer, Stuart. "Major Power Intervention in Ongoing War: A Probability Model, 1816-1965." Ann Arbor: University of Michigan, Correlates of War Project, 1975.

**DIMENSIONALITY OF
NATIONS PROJECT**
Principal Investigator:
Rudolph J. Rummel
Prepared by:
Rudolph J. Rummel

Chadwick, Richard W. "International Involvement: Steps toward the Quantitative Measurement and Explanation of International Policies." Dimensionality of Nations Project, Research Report No. 37. Honolulu: University of Hawaii, 1972.

Choi, Chang-Yoon. "The Contemporary Foreign Behavior of the U.S. and U.S.S.R.: An Application of Rummel's Status-Field Theory." Dimensionality of Nations Project, Research Report No. 68. Honolulu: University of Hawaii, 1973.

_____. "The Contemporary Foreign Behavior of the U.S. and U.S.S.R.: An Application of Rummel's Status-Field Theory." Ph.D. dissertation, Honolulu: University of Hawaii, 1973.

Denton, Frank H., and Phillips, Warren R. "Some Patterns in the History of Violence." Journal of Conflict Resolution 12, no. 2 (1968): 182-95.

Firestone, Joseph. "Concept Formation, System Analysis and Factor Analysis in Political Science." Dimensionality of Nations Project, Research Report No. 23. Honolulu: University of Hawaii, 1969.

_____. "National Motives and Domestic Planned Violence: An Examination of Time-Lagged Correlational Trends in Cross Time Regressions." Dimensionality of Nations Project, Research Report No. 26. Honolulu: University of Hawaii, 1969.

_____ and McCormick, David. "An Exploration in System Analysis of Domestic Conflict." Dimensionality of Nations Project, Research Report No. 24. Honolulu: University of Hawaii, 1969.

_____ and Oliva, Gary. "National Motives and National Attributes: A Crosstime Analysis." Dimensionality of Nations Project, Research Report No. 25. Honolulu: University of Hawaii, 1969.

Gleditsch, Nils Petter. "Rank Theory, Field Theory and Attribute Theory: Three Approaches to Interaction in the International System." Dimensionality of Nations Project, Research Report No. 47. Honolulu: University of Hawaii, 1970.

Hall, Dennis. "Computer Program Profile." Dimensionality of Nations Project, Research Report No. 14. Honolulu: University of Hawaii, 1968.

―――― and Rummel, Rudolph J. "The Patterns of Dyadic Foreign Conflict for 1963." Multivariate Behavioral Research 5, no. 3 (1970): 275-94.

Hannah, Herbert. "Some Dimensions of International Conflict Settlement Procedures and Outcomes." Dimensionality of Nations Project, Research Report No. 11. Honolulu: University of Hawaii, 1968.

――――. "Some Dimensions of International Conflict, 1914-1965: The Prediction of Outcomes." Ph.D. dissertation, Honolulu: University of Hawaii, 1968.

Keim, Willard, and Rummel, Rudolph J. "Dynamic Patterns of Nation Conflict, 1955-1963." Dimensionality of Nations Project, Research Report No. 27. Honolulu: University of Hawaii, 1969.

Kent, George. "The Application of Peace Studies." Journal of Conflict Resolution 15, no. 1 (1971): 47-53.

――――. "The Evaluation of Policy Alternatives." Dimensionality of Nations Project, Research Report No. 55. Honolulu: University of Hawaii, 1971.

――――. "Foreign Policy Analysis: Middle East." Papers, Peace Research Society (International) 14 (1969): 95-112.

――――. "Plan for Designing the Future." Dimensionality of Nations Project, Research Report No. 60. Honolulu: University of Hawaii, 1972.

――――. "Policy Analysis for Action Recommendations." Dimensionality of Nations Project, Research Report No. 51. Honolulu: University of Hawaii, 1971.

――――. "Political Design." Dimensionality of Nations Project, Research Report No. 63. Honolulu: University of Hawaii, 1972.

――――. "Prescribing Foreign Policy." Dimensionality of Nations Project, Research Report No. 59. Honolulu: University of Hawaii, 1972.

_____. "Teaching Practical Policy Analysis." Dimensionality of
Nations Project, Research Report No. 56. Honolulu: University
of Hawaii, 1971.

McCormick, David. "A Field Theory of Dynamic International
Processes." Dimensionality of Nations Project, Research
Report No. 30. Honolulu: University of Hawaii, 1969.

Oliva, Gary, and Rummel, Rudolph J. "Foreign Conflict Patterns
and Types for 1963." Dimensionality of Nations Project,
Research Report No. 22. Honolulu: University of Hawaii, 1969.

Park, Tong-Whan. "Asian Conflict—Systemic Perspective: Application of Field Theory (1955 and 1963)." Dimensionality of Nations
Project, Research Report No. 35. Honolulu: University of
Hawaii, 1969.

_____. "Asian Conflict in Systemic Perspective: Application of Field
Theory (1955 and 1963)." Ph.D. dissertation, Honolulu:
University of Hawaii, 1969.

_____. "Measuring Dynamic Patterns of Development: The Case of
Asia, 1949-1968." Dimensionality of Nations Project, Research
Report No. 45. Honolulu: University of Hawaii, 1970.

_____. "Peaceful Interactions in Asia: The Delineation of Nation
Groups." Dimensionality of Nations Project, Research Report
No. 32. Honolulu: University of Hawaii, 1969.

_____. "The Role of Distance in International Relations: A New
Look at the Social Field Theory." Behavioral Science 17, no. 4
(1972): 337-48.

Phillips, Warren R. "The Conflict Environment of Nations: A
Study of Conflict Inputs to Nations in 1963." In Conflict Behavior
and Linkage Politics. Edited by Jonathon Wilenfeld. New York:
David McKay, 1972, pp. 124-47.

_____. "Dynamic Patterns of International Conflict." Dimensionality
of Nations Project, Research Report No. 33. Honolulu: University of Hawaii, 1969.

_____. "Dynamic Patterns of International Conflict: A Dyadic
Research Design." Dimensionality of Nations Project, Research
Report No. 17. Honolulu: University of Hawaii, 1968.

_____. "Dynamic Patterns of International Conflict." Ph.D. dissertation, Honolulu: University of Hawaii, 1969.

_____. "The Dynamics of Behavioral Conflict." Dimensionality of Nations Project, Research Report No. 49. Honolulu: University of Hawaii, 1970.

_____. "International Communications." Dimensionality of Nations Project, Research Report No. 46. Honolulu: University of Hawaii, 1970.

_____. "Investigations into Alternative Techniques for Developing Empirical Taxonomies: The Results of Two Plasmodes." Dimensionality of Nations Project, Research Report No. 15. Honolulu: University of Hawaii, 1968.

_____. "A Mathematical Theory of Conflict Dynamics." Dimensionality of Nations Project, Research Report No. 39. Honolulu: University of Hawaii, 1970.

_____. "Research Proposal Submitted to the Arms Control and Disarmament Agencies." Dimensionality of Nations Project, Research Report No. 38. Honolulu: University of Hawaii, 1970.

_____ and Hall, Dennis R. "The Importance of Government Structure as a Taxonomic Scheme for Nations." Comparative Political Studies 3, no. 1 (1970): 63-89.

_____ and Rummel, Rudolph J. "Forecasting International Relations: Some Views on the Relevancy of The Dimensionality of Nations Project to Policy Planning." Dimensionality of Nations Project, Research Report No. 36. Honolulu: University of Hawaii, 1969.

Pratt, Richard, and Rummel, Rudolph J. "Issue Dimensions in the 1963 United Nations General Assembly." Multivariate Behavioral Research 6, no. 3 (1971): 251-86.

Rhee, Sang-Woo. "China's Cooperation, Conflict and Interactive Behavior; Viewed from Rummel's Field Theoretic Perspective." Dimensionality of Nations Project, Research Report No. 64. Honolulu: University of Hawaii, 1973.

_____. "Communist China's Foreign Behavior: An Application of Field Theory Model II." Dimensionality of Nations Project, Research Report No. 57. Honolulu: University of Hawaii, 1971.

____. "Communist China's Foreign Behavior: An Application of Field Theory Model II." Ph.D. dissertation, Honolulu: University of Hawaii, 1971.

____. "Themes of North Korea's Unification Messages: A Study on Pattern Shifts, 1948-1968." Dimensionality of Nations Project, Research Report No. 66. Honolulu: University of Hawaii, 1973.

____; Omen, George; and Rummel, Rudolph J. "Attributes of Nations: Data and Codes 1950-1965." Dimensionality of Nations Project, Research Report No. 65. Honolulu: University of Hawaii, 1973.

____; Omen, George; and Rummel, Rudolph J. "Behaviors of Nation-Dyads: Data and Codes 1950-1965." Dimensionality of Nations Project, Research Report No. 67. Honolulu: University of Hawaii, 1973.

Rummel, Rudolph J. *Applied Factor Analysis*. Evanston: Northwestern University Press, 1970.

____. "Attribute and Behavioral Space of Nations: Variables and Samples for 1950." Dimensionality of Nations Project, Research Report No. 13. Honolulu: University of Hawaii, 1968.

____. "The Dimensionality of Nations Project." In *Comparing Nations*. Edited by Richard Merritt and Stein Rokkan. New Haven: Yale University Press, 1966, pp. 109-130.

____. "Dimensions of Conflict Behavior Within and Between Nations." *General Systems* 8 (1963): 1-50.

____. "Dimensions of Conflict Behavior Within and Between Nations." In *Macro-Quantitative Analysis*. Edited by John V. Gillespie and Betty A. Nesvold. Beverly Hills: Sage Publications, 1971, pp. 49-84.

____. "Dimensions of Conflict Behavior Within Nations, 1946-59." In *Macro-Quantitative Analysis*. Edited by John V. Gillespie and Betty A. Nesvold. Beverly Hills: Sage Publications, 1971, pp. 39-48.

____. "Dimensions of Dyadic War, 1820-1952." *Journal of Conflict Resolution* 11, no. 2 (1967): 176-83.

_____. "Dimensions of Error in Cross-National Data." In <u>Handbook of Method in Cultural Anthropology</u>. Edited by Raoul Naroll and Ronald Cohen. Garden City, N.Y.: Natural History Press, 1971, pp. 946-61.

_____. "Dimensions of Foreign and Domestic Conflict Behavior: A Review of Empirical Findings." In <u>Theory and Research on the Causes of War</u>. Edited by Dean G. Pruitt and Richard C. Snyder. Englewood Cliffs: Prentice-Hall, 1969, pp. 219-28.

_____. <u>The Dimensions of Nations</u>. Beverly Hills: Sage Publications, 1972.

_____. "DON Project: A Five-Year Program." Dimensionality of Nations Project, Research Report No. 9. Honolulu: University of Hawaii, 1967.

_____. "The DON Project: Policy Relevance and Overview." Dimensionality of Nations Project, Research Report No. 34. Honolulu: University of Hawaii, 1969.

_____. <u>The Dynamic Psychological Field</u>. Beverly Hills: Sage Publications, 1975.

_____. "Field and Attribute Theories of Nation Behavior: Some Mathematical Interrelationships." Dimensionality of Nations Project, Research Report No. 31. Honolulu: University of Hawaii, 1969.

_____. "Field Theory and the 1963 Behavior Space of Nations." Dimensionality of Nations Project, Research Report No. 44. Honolulu: University of Hawaii, 1970.

_____. "Field Theory and Indicators of International Behavior." Dimensionality of Nations Project, Research Report No. 29. Honolulu: University of Hawaii, 1969.

_____. "A Field Theory of Social Action with Application to Conflict within Nations." <u>General Systems</u> 10 (1965): 183-211.

_____. "Forecasting International Relations: A Proposed Investigation of Three Mode Factor Analysis." <u>Technological Forecasting</u> 1, no. 2 (1969): 197-216.

_____. "Indicators of National and Cross-National Patterns." <u>American Political Science Review</u> 63, no. 1 (1969): 127-47.

_____. "International Patterns and National Profile Delineation."
In <u>Computers and the Policy-Making Community</u>. Edited by
Davis Bobrow and Judah L. Swartz. Englewood Cliffs: Prentice-
Hall, 1969, pp. 154-202.

_____. "Measures of International Relations." Dimensionality of
Nations Project, Research Report No. 8. Honolulu: University
of Hawaii, 1967.

_____. "Progress in Understanding International Relations: The
DON Project." <u>East-West Center Review</u> 4 (1968): 15-25.

_____. "The Relationship Between National Attributes and Foreign
Conflict Behavior." In <u>Quantitative International Politics:
Insights and Evidence</u>. Edited by J. David Singer. New York:
Free Press, 1967, pp. 187-214.

_____. "Social Time and International Relations." <u>General Systems</u>
17 (1972): 145-58.

_____. "Some Attributes and Behavioral Patterns of Nations."
<u>Journal of Peace Research</u> 4, no. 2 (1967): 196-206.

_____. "Some Empirical Findings on Nations and Their Behavior."
<u>World Politics</u> 21, no. 2 (1969): 226-41.

_____. "Status-Field Theory and International Relations." Dimensionality of Nations Project, Research Report No. 50. Honolulu:
University of Hawaii, 1971.

_____. "A Summary and Annotated Bibliography of Research by the
Dimensionality of Nations Project, 1967-1973." Dimensionality
of Nations Project, Research Report No. 69. Honolulu: University of Hawaii, 1973.

_____. "Understanding Factor Analysis." <u>Journal of Conflict Resolution</u> 11, no. 4 (1967): 444-80.

_____. "U.S. Foreign Relations: Conflict, Cooperation, and Attribute
Distances." In <u>Peace, War, and Numbers</u>. Edited by Bruce M.
Russett. Beverly Hills: Sage Publications, 1972, pp. 71-113.

Sawyer, Jack. "Dimensions of Nations: Size, Wealth, and Politics."
<u>American Sociological Review</u> 73, no. 2 (1967): 145-72.

Van Atta, Richard, and Rummel, Rudolph J. "Testing Field Theory on the 1963 Behavior Space of Nations." Dimensionality of Nations Project, Research Report No. 43. Honolulu: University of Hawaii, 1970.

Vincent, Jack E. "Comments on Social Field Theory." Dimensionality of Nations Project, Research Report No. 58. Honolulu: University of Hawaii, 1972.

_____. "An Examination of Voting Patterns in the 23rd and 24th Sessions of the General Assembly." Dimensionality of Nations Project, Research Report No. 54. Honolulu: University of Hawaii, 1971.

_____. "Testing Some Hypotheses About Delegate Attitudes at the United Nations and Some Implications for Theory Building." Dimensionality of Nations Project, Research Report No. 52. Honolulu: University of Hawaii, 1971.

_____; Baker, Roger; Gagnon, Susan; Hamm, Keith; and Reilly, Scott. "Empirical Tests of Attribute, Social Field, and Status Field Theories on International Relations Data." International Studies Quarterly 17, no. 4 (1973): 405-443.

Wall, Charles. "Code ∅991 Procedure." Dimensionality of Nations Project, Research Report No. 62. Honolulu: University of Hawaii, 1972.

_____ and Kam, Alan C. "DYNA: Dynamic Storage and Allocation in FORTRAN for the IBM/360 Operation System." Dimensionality of Nations Project, Research Report No. 53. Honolulu: University of Hawaii, 1971.

_____ and Rummel, Rudolph J. "Estimating Missing Data." Dimensionality of Nations Project, Research Report No. 20. Honolulu: University of Hawaii, 1969.

INTER-NATION SIMULATION PROJECT

Principal Investigator:
Harold Guetzkow
Prepared by:
Doreen R. Ellis

Alger, Chadwick F. "Use of the Inter-Nation Simulation in Undergraduate Teaching." In Simulation in International Relations. Edited by Harold Guetzkow, Chadwick F. Alger, Richard C. Brody, Robert C. Noel, and Richard C. Snyder. Englewood Cliffs: Prentice-Hall, 1963, pp. 150-89.

Alker, Hayward R., Jr. "Decision-Makers' Environments in the Inter-Nation Simulation." In Simulation in the Study of Politics. Edited by William D. Coplin. Chicago: Markham Publishing Company, 1968, pp. 31-58.

_____. "Highly Programmed Political-Military Simulations: Developments in Holestic, All-Computer Models." Paper presented at a seminar on Simulated International Processes. Washington, D.C.: Industrial College of the Armed Forces, 1969.

_____. "The Uses of Simulation for International Relations Theory-Building: Some Reflections and Research Possibilities." New Haven: Yale University, 1965.

_____ and Brunner, Ronald D. "Simulating International Conflict: A Comparison of Three Approaches." International Studies Quarterly 13, no. 1 (1969): 70-110.

Bailey, Gerald C. "Utilizing Simulation of International Behavior in Political Military Affairs—A Preliminary Analysis." McLean, Va.: Human Resources Research, Inc.

Beach, P.; Brody, Richard A.; and Driver, Michael J. "Chronologies of the INS-8 Series." Evanston, Ill.: Northwestern University, 1962.

Bonham, G. Matthew. "Relations of Validator Satisfaction to Some External Perceptions of Decision Makers." Cambridge: Massachusetts Institute of Technology, 1965.

_____. "Simulating International Negotiation." Journal of Conflict Resolution 15, no. 15 (1971): 299-315.

_____. "A Computer Simulation of Non-Crisis Information Processing by Foreign Policy Decision Makers." Mimeographed. Berkeley: University of California, 1970.

Bremer, Stuart A. "National and International Systems: A Computer Simulation." Ph.D. dissertation, East Lansing: Michigan State University, 1970.

_____ and Ross, David Scott. "SIPER Simulated International Processes (Version III)." Evanston, Ill.: Northwestern University, 1970.

Brody, Richard A. "Some Systematic Effects of the Spread of Nuclear Weapons Technology: A Study through Simulation of a Multi-Nuclear Future." Journal of Conflict Resolution 7, no. 4 (1963): 663-753.

_____. "The Spread of Nuclear Weapons and Alliance Stability: The Model." Evanston, Ill.: Northwestern University, 1963.

_____. "Varieties of Simulations in International Relations Research." In Simulation in International Relations. Edited by Harold Guetzkow, Chadwick F. Alger, Richard A. Brody, Robert C. Noel, and Richard C. Snyder. Englewood Cliffs, N.J.: Prentice-Hall, 1963, pp. 190-223.

Busse, Walter E. "Northwestern Simulation Archives—Man Computer Models of International Relations." Evanston, Ill.: Northwestern University, 1969.

Campbell, Donald T. "Inter-Nation Simulation as a Laboratory for the Teaching of Theories Relevant to International Relations." Evanston, Ill.: Northwestern University, 1967.

Caspary, William. "The Causes of War in INS-8." Evanston, Ill.: Northwestern University, 1962.

Chadwick, Richard W. "Developments in a Partial Theory of International Behavior: A Test and Extension of Inter-Nation Simulation Theory." Ph.D. dissertation, Evanston, Ill.: Northwestern University, 1966.

_____. "Relating Inter-Nation Simulation Theory with Verbal Theory in International Relations at Three Levels of Analysis." Evanston, Ill.: Northwestern University, 1966.

_____. "An Empirical Test of Five Assumptions in an Inter-Nation Simulation, About National Political Systems." General Systems 12 (1967): 177-92.

_____. "An Inductive, Empirical Analysis of Intra and Inter-national Behavior, Aimed at a Partial Extension of Inter-Nation Simulation Theory." Journal of Peace Research 6, no. 3 (1969): 193-214.

_____. "A Partial Model of National Political-Economic Systems." Journal of Peace Research 7, no. 2 (1970): 121-32.

_____. "Theory Development through Simulation: A Comparison and Analysis of Associations Among Variables in an International System and an Inter-Nation Simulation." International Studies Quarterly 16, no. 1 (1972): 83-127.

_____ and Smoker, Paul L. "Some Research Problems and Proposals for Continuing and Extending SIP Validity Operations." Evanston, Ill.: Northwestern University, 1966.

Christensen, Cheryl. "A User's Observation of the Benson Model." Evanston, Ill.: Northwestern University, 1969.

Coplin, William D. "Inter-Nation Simulation and Contemporary Theories of International Relations." American Political Science Review 40, no. 3 (1966): 562-78.

_____. "Comparison of State Department and High School Runs in the World Politics Simulation." Detroit: Wayne State University, 1968.

Dawson, Richard E. "Simulation in the Social Sciences." In Simulation in Social Science: Readings. Edited by Harold Guetzkow. Englewood Cliffs: Prentice-Hall, 1962, pp. 1-15.

Deutsch, Karl W. "Simulation of International Politics: A Provisional Assessment." Mimeographed. New York, 1969.

_____ and Senghass, W. Deiter. "Toward a Theory of War and Peace: Propositions, Simulations and Realities." Paper presented at the meetings of the American Political Science Association, September 1969, New York.

Driver, Michael J. "Conceptual Structure and Group Processes in an Inter-Nation Simulation." Ph.D. dissertation, Princeton: Princeton University, 1962.

──── . "European Perceptions of Nations—A Multidimensional Analysis of National Points of View." Evanston, Ill.: Northwestern University, 1972.

──── . "The Perception of Simulated Nations—A Multidimensional Analysis of Social Perception as Affected by Situational Stress and Characteristic Levels of Cognitive Complexity in Perceivers." Evanston, Ill.: Northwestern University, 1961.

──── . "A Structural Analysis of Aggression, Stress, and Personality in an Inter-Nation Simulation." Mimeographed. West Lafayette, Ind.: Purdue University, 1965.

Druckman, Daniel. "Ethnocentrism in the Inter-Nation Simulation." Journal of Conflict Resolution 12, no. 1 (1968): 45-68.

Elder, Charles D. "Moderately Programmed Political-Military Simulations: The World Politics Simulations—Transformation of the Inter-Nation Simulation into a Man-Machine Exercise in an Interactive Mode." Washington, D.C.: Industrial College of the Armed Forces, 1969.

──── . "Some Conceptual and Statistical Problems in the Treatment of Iterated Systems—Runs in the Inter-Nation Simulation." Evanston, Ill.: Northwestern University, 1966.

──── and Pendley, Robert E. "Simulation as Theory Building in the Study of International Relations." Mimeographed. Evanston, Ill.: Northwestern University, 1970.

──── and Pendley, Robert E. "A Test and Reconstruction of the Economic Model in an Inter-Nation Simulation." Mimeographed. Evanston, Ill.: Northwestern University, 1970.

Fabri, D. "Structural Theory of Aggression, Galtung." Computer module, Lancaster, England: Peace Research Centre, 1968.

Fischer, Lucas R. "The RAND/MIT Political-Military Exercise and International Relations Theory." In Simulationen Internationaler Prozesse, Politische Vierteljahreschrift. Edited by Lucien Kern and Horst-Dieter Ronsch. Opladen: Westdeutscher Verlag, 1972, pp. 219-38.

Forcese, Dennis. "Power and Military Alliance Cohesion: Thirteen Simulation Experiments." Ph.D. dissertation, St. Louis: Washington University, 1968.

Gleditsch, Nils Petter. "Report on the Reliability of the Message from Coding in International Processes Simulation." Evanston, Ill.: Northwestern University, 1967.

Gomer, Louise C. "Master List of Variables in the Simulation of International Processes." Evanston, Ill.: Northwestern University, 1967.

Gorden, Morton. "Burdens for the Designer of a Computer Simulation of International Relations: The Case of TEMPER." In Computers and the Policy-Making Community. Edited by Davis B. Bobrow and Judah L. Schwartz. Englewood Cliffs: Prentice-Hall, 1969, pp. 222-45.

_____. "International Relations Theory in the TEMPER Simulation." Simulated International Processes Project. Evanston, Ill.: Northwestern University, 1967.

Gotthail, Diane L. "An Approach to a Comparison of Verbal Theories of International Relations with Inter-Nation Simulation Theory: Examples from Wolfers on Alliances." Urbana: University of Illinois, 1966.

Guetzkow, Harold. "Collaboration in Computer Simulation for Decision-Making in International Affairs." International Studies Notes 1, no. 1 (1974): 8-9.

_____. "A Decade of Life with the Inter-Nation Simulation." In The Process of Model Building in the Behavioral Sciences. Edited by Ralph M. Stogdill. Columbus, Ohio: Ohio State University Press, 1970, pp. 31-53.

_____. "Final Report: Simulated International Processes Project, Advanced Research Projects Agency, Contract No. SD 260." Evanston, Ill.: Northwestern University, 1972.

_____. "General Strategy in the Incremental Development of International Processes Simulation through PLATO." Evanston, Ill.: Northwestern University, 1965.

———. "Joining Field and Laboratory Work in Disaster Research." In Man and Society in Disaster. Edited by George W. Baker and Dwight H. Chapman. New York: Basic Books, 1962, pp. 337-55.

———. "Long Range Research in International Relations." The American Perspective 4, no. 4 (1950): 421-40.

———. "Planning Research on the Utilization of Simulation." Evanston, Ill.: Northwestern University, 1965.

———. "Prospects for Developments in International Relations in the 1970's through Simulation." Washington, D.C.: Industrial College of the Armed Forces, 1969.

———. "Report on a Decade of Activity." Evanston, Ill.: Northwestern University, 1969.

———. "Simulation in International Relations." In Proceedings of the IBM Scientific Computing Symposium on Simulation Models and Gaming. White Plains, N.Y.: International Business Machines Corporation, 1966, pp. 249-78.

———. "Simulations in the Consolidation and Utilization of Knowledge about International Relations." In Theory and Research on the Causes of War. Edited by Dean G. Pruitt and Richard C. Snyder. Englewood Cliffs: Prentice-Hall, 1969, pp. 284-300.

———. "Some Correspondences between Simulations and 'Realities' in International Relations." In New Approaches to International Relations. Edited by Morton A. Kaplan. New York: St. Martin's Press, 1968, pp. 202-269.

———. "Structured Programs and Their Relation to Free Activity within the Inter-Nation Simulation." In Simulation in International Relations: Development and Teaching. Edited by Harold Guetzkow, Chadwick F. Alger, Richard A. Brody, Robert C. Noel, and Richard C. Snyder. Englewood Cliffs: Prentice-Hall, 1963, pp. 103-149.

———. "Toward the Acceleration of Research in Simulating International Processes." Evanston, Ill.: Northwestern University, 1964.

———. "A Use of Simulation in the Study of Inter-Nation Relations." Behavioral Science 4, no. 3 (1959): 183-91.

____; Brody, Richard A.; Driver, Michael J.; and Beach, Philip F. "An Experiment on the N-Country Problem Through Inter-Nation Simulation." In Proceedings of the Seminar on International Conflict and Peace. Edited by R. C. Hunt. New Haven: Yale University Press, 1962.

____ and Cherryholmes, Cleo. Inter-Nation Simulation Kit. Chicago: Science Research Associates, 1966.

____; Hermann, Charles F.; and Hermann, Margaret G. "Pilot Simulation of World War II." China Lake, Calif.: U.S. Naval Ordnance Test Station, 1964.

____ and Jensen, Lloyd. "Research Activities on Simulated International Processes." Background 9, no. 4 (1966): 261-74.

Hermann, Charles F. "Crises in Foreign Policy-Making: Simulation of International Politics." Ph.D. dissertation, Evanston, Ill.: Northwestern University, 1965.

____. "Validation Problems in Games and Simulations with Special Reference to Models of International Politics." Behavioral Science 12, no. 3 (1967): 216-31.

____. "A Validity Problem: Crisis in Simulated Foreign Policy Organizations." Paper presented at the meetings of the American Political Science Association, 1964.

____ and Guetzkow, Harold. "Prediction Considerations of Possible Relevance in Validating Inter-Nation Simulation." China Lake, Calif.: U.S. Naval Ordnance Test Station, 1962.

____ and Hermann, Margaret G. "An Attempt to Simulate the Outbreak of World War I." American Political Science Review 61, no. 2 (1967): 400-416.

____ and Hermann, Margaret G. "The Potential Use of Historical Data for Validation Studies of the Inter-Nation Simulation: The Outbreak of World War I as an Illustration." China Lake, Calif.: U.S. Naval Ordnance Test Station, 1962.

____ and Hermann, Margaret G. "Validation Studies of the Inter-Nation Simulation." China Lake, Calif.: U.S. Naval Ordnance Test Station, 1963.

Hermann, Margaret G. "Stress, Self-Esteem, and Defensiveness in an Inter-Nation Simulation." Ph.D. dissertation, Evanston, Ill.: Northwestern University, 1965.

_____. "Testing a Model of Psychological Stress." Journal of Personality 34, no. 3 (1966): 381-96.

Hicks, Bruce H. "Potential Use of PLATO for Simulation of International Processes." Evanston, Ill.: Northwestern University, 1965.

Hoole, Francis W. "Societal Conditions and Political Aggression: The Examination of Selected Hypothesis Derived from Frustration-Aggression Theory." Bloomington: Indiana University, 1972.

Jensen, Lloyd. "American Foreign Policy Elites and the Prediction of International Events." Papers, Peace Research Society (International) 5 (1966): 199-209.

_____. "Predicting International Events." Peace Research Reviews 4, no. 6 (1972): 1-65.

_____. "United States Elites and Their Perceptions of the Determinants of Foreign Policy Behavior." Paper presented at the meetings of the Midwest Political Science Association, 1966.

_____ and White, Michael J. "Selected Abstracts Related to the Simulation of International Military Processes." Evanston, Ill.: Northwestern University, 1966.

Krend, Jeffrey A. "A Comparison of Guetzkow-Modelski Correspondence Ratings." Evanston, Ill.: Northwestern University, 1969.

_____. "Computer Simulations of International Relations as Heuristics for Social Status, Action and Change." Simulated International Processes Project. Evanston, Ill.: Northwestern University, 1972.

_____. "A Documentation of Paul Smoker's IPS." Evanston, Ill.: Northwestern University, 1971.

_____. "A Reconstruction of Oliver Benson's 'Simple Diplomatic Game'." Simulated International Processes Project. Evanston, Ill.: Northwestern University, 1970.

____. "War and Peace in the International System—Deriving an All-Computer Heuristic." Paper presented at the Summer Simulation Conference, 1972.

Kress, Paul. "On Validating Simulation with Special Attention to Simulation of International Politics." <u>International Interactions</u> 1, no. 1 (1974): 41-50.

Kriesberg, Louis. "Aspects of International Collective Decision-Making." Evanston, Ill.: Northwestern University, 1968.

____ and Leavitt, Michael R. "A Simulation of International Negotiations with Trade-Offs in Objectives." Evanston, Ill.: Northwestern University, 1969.

Leavitt, Michael R. "Allyl—Description of the Model." Evanston, Ill.: Northwestern University, 1970.

____. "A Comparison of Four War Models in Man-Computer Simulations." Evanston, Ill.: Northwestern University, 1967.

____. "A Computer Simulation of International Alliance Behavior." Ph.D. dissertation, Evanston, Ill.: Northwestern University, 1971.

____. "A Computer Simulation of International Relations." Madison: University of Wisconsin, 1970.

____. "Four Man-Computer War Calculation Routines." Computer module, Evanston, Ill.: Northwestern University, 1968.

____. "International Communications." Computer module, Evanston, Ill.: Northwestern University, 1968.

____. "Markov Processes in International Crisis: An Analytical Addendum to 'An Event-Based Simulation of the Taiwan Straits Crises.'" In <u>Experimentation and Simulation in Political Science</u>. Edited by J. A. Laponce and Paul L. Smoker. Toronto: University of Toronto Press, 1972, pp. 280-92.

____. "MULTYP/Multiple Typal Analysis: A Clustering Program." <u>Behavioral Science</u> 16, no. 4 (1971): 417-18.

____. "Partial Annotated Bibliography on Military Operations/Defense Systems Simulations." Washington: Industrial College of the Armed Forces, 1969.

____. "Thoughts on Computer Simulation of International Relations."
Paper presented at the meetings of the American Political
Science Association, Los Angeles, September 1970.

____. "Three-Man Bargaining Model." Computer module, Evanston,
Ill.: Northwestern University, 1970.

____. "Transition to the 1970's: The Development of Computer
Simulation Modules for the Study of International Relations."
Evanston, Ill.: Northwestern University, 1969.

____ and Kriesberg, Louis. "Two-Man Bargaining Model."
Computer module, Evanston, Ill.: Northwestern University,
1968.

Licklider, Roy E. "Simulation and the Private Nuclear Strategies."
Simulation and Games 2, no. 2 (1971): 163-71.

McGowan, Patrick J. "Some External Validities of the Inter-Nation
Simulation." Mimeographed. Evanston, Ill.: Northwestern
University, 1972.

____. "Studies in Inter-Nation Simulation Validity." Evanston,
Ill.: Northwestern University, 1967.

Meier, Dorothy L. "Progress Report: Event Simulation Project."
Simulated International Processes Project. Evanston, Ill.:
Northwestern University, 1964.

____. "Progress Report: Event Simulation Project." Simulated
International Processes Project. Evanston, Ill.: Northwestern
University, 1965.

____. "Simulation Techniques in a 'Realistic' Policy Context."
Journal of Human Resources 13, no. 3 (1965): 356-71.

____ and Stickgold, Arthur. "Progress Report: Analysis Procedures.
Event Simulation Project. St. Louis: Washington University,
1965.

Meyers, Mary Lee. "Bibliographic and Abstracted Sources:
An Annotated Listing of Sources which include Materials Dealing
with Simulation in the Social Sciences, Especially Those Concerned with the Simulation of International Processes."
Evanston, Ill.: Northwestern University, 1968.

Modelski, George. "Simulations, 'Realities' and International Relations Theory." Simulation and Games 1, no. 2 (1970): 111-34.

Nardin, Terry. "An Inquiry into the Validity of a Simulation of International Relations." Evanston, Ill.: Northwestern University, 1965.

_____. "Integrative Behavior in a Simulated International System." Evanston, Ill.: Northwestern University, 1965.

_____. "Uses of Threats in Strategic Interaction: An Experiment in International Politics." Ph.D. dissertation, Evanston, Ill.: Northwestern University, 1967.

_____ and Cutler, Neal E. "Reliability and Validity of Some Patterns of International Interaction in an Inter-Nation Simulation." Journal of Peace Research 6, no. 1 (1969): 1-12.

_____ and Cutler, Neal E. "A Seven Variable Study of the Reliability and Validation of Some Patterns of International Interaction in the Inter-Nation Simulation." Evanston, Ill.: Northwestern University, Simulated International Processes Project, 1967.

Noel, Robert C. "Evolution of Inter-Nation Simulation." In Simulation in International Relations: Developments for Research and Teaching. Edited by Harold Guetzkow, Chadwick F. Alger, Richard A. Brody, Robert C. Noel, and Richard Snyder. Englewood Cliffs: Prentice-Hall, 1963, pp. 69-102.

_____. "Inter-Nation Simulation Participants' Manual." In Simulation in International Relations: Developments for Research and Teaching. Edited by Harold Guetzkow, Chadwick F. Alger, Richard A. Brody, Robert C. Noel, and Richard C. Snyder. Englewood Cliffs: Prentice-Hall, 1963, pp. 43-68.

_____. "A Simplified Political-Economic System Simulation." Ph.D. dissertation, Evanston, Ill.: Northwestern University, 1963.

Park, Tong-Whan. "A Guide to Data Sources in International Relations: Annotated Bibliography with Lists of Variables." Evanston, Ill.: Northwestern University, 1968.

Pelowski, Allan L. "An Event-Based Simulation of the Taiwan Straits Crisis." In *Experimentation and Simulation in Political Science*. Edited by J. A. Laponce and Paul L. Smoker. Toronto: University of Toronto Press, 1972, pp. 259-79.

———. "A Global Eco-Tactic-Population Control as a Multinational Business Proposition." In *The Politics of Ecosuicide*. Edited by Leslie L. Roos, Jr. New York: Holt, Rinehart and Winston, 1970, pp. 370-92.

———. "International Business Growth." Computer module, Evanston, Ill.: Northwestern University, 1969.

———. "National Attributes and Cross-National Business: A Combined Regression-Simulation Study." Evanston, Ill.: Northwestern University, 1970.

———. "One Approach to Simulation Module Construction in International Relations." Evanston, Ill.: Northwestern University, 1969.

Pendley, Robert E. "INSCAL: A Fortran Program for Performing the Calculations for the Inter-Nation Simulation." Evanston, Ill.: Northwestern University, 1966.

——— and Elder, Charles D. "An Analysis of Political Constraints in an Inter-Nation Simulation: A Critique in Terms of Contemporary Theory and Data on the Stability of Regimes and Governments." Mimeographed. Evanston, Ill.: Northwestern University, 1970.

Pfaltzgraff, Robert L., Jr. "Simulation and International Relations Theory: A Comparison of Simulation Models and International Relations Literature." Mimeographed. Medford: Tufts University, 1972.

Pirro, Ellen B. "Frustration-Aggression: A Causal Model Analysis." Evanston, Ill.: Northwestern University, 1972.

Pool, Ithiel de Sola. "Comparison of a Human Game and a Computer Simulation." Cambridge: Massachusetts Institute of Technology, 1969.

Raser, John R. "Personal Characteristics of Political Decision-Makers: A Literature Review." *Papers, Peace Research Society (International)* 5 (1966): 161-81.

_____; Campbell, Donald T.; and Chadwick, Richard W. "Gaming and Simulation for Developing Theory Relevant to International Relations." General Systems 15 (1970): 183-204.

Remy, Richard C. "Trade and Defense in the IPS—International Processes Simulation—and Selected Referent Systems." Evanston, Ill.: Northwestern University, 1967.

Rennagel, William C. "A Report on the International Systems Simulation Seminar at O.S.U." Paper presented to the Simulated International Processes Project. Evanston, Ill.: Northwestern University, 1969.

Robinson, James A. "Simulating Crisis Decision-Making." Paper presented at the joint meetings of the Institute of Management Sciences and the Operations Research Society of America, 1964.

_____; Anderson, Leroy; Hermann, Margaret G.; and Snyder, Richard C. "Teaching with Inter-Nation Simulation and Case Studies." American Political Science Review 60, no. 1 (1966): 53-65.

_____; Hermann, Charles F.; and Hermann, Margaret G. "Studies of Crisis Decision-Making." China Lake, Calif.: U.S. Naval Ordnance Test Station, 1964.

_____; Hermann, Charles F.; and Hermann, Margaret G. "Search Under Crisis in Political Gaming and Simulation." In Theory and Research on the Causes of War. Edited by Dean G. Pruitt and Richard C. Snyder. Englewood Cliffs: Prentice-Hall, 1969, pp. 80-94.

Rosenband, Larry. "Comparisons Between an Inter-Nation Simulation and a Real World of 1955." Evanston, Ill.: Northwestern University, 1968.

Sager, Alan M. "Comparative Politics and the National Political Model of the Inter-Nation Simulation: A Test of Five Hypotheses Across Four Groups of Nations." Evanston, Ill.: Northwestern University, 1967.

_____. "The Internal Validity of the Inter-Nation Simulation: A Comparison of the WINSAFE II and INS-8 Simulations." Austin: University of Texas, 1972.

Schwartz, David C. "Experimental Studies in Alliance Behavior." Evanston, Ill.: Northwestern University, 1966.

Seki, Hiroharu. "Toward an N-Generation Model of International Process Simulation Theory." Evanston, Ill.: Northwestern University, 1967.

———. "The Use of PLATO in Inter-Nation Simulation." Evanston, Ill.: Northwestern University, 1966.

Shapiro, Michael J. "Cognitive Rigidity and Moral Judgments in an Inter-Nation Simulation." Evanston, Ill.: Northwestern University, 1966.

Sherman, Allen William. "The Social Psychology of Bilateral Negotiations." Masters thesis, Evanston, Ill.: Northwestern University, 1963.

Smoker, Paul L. "Analyses of Conflict Behavior in an International Processes Simulation and an International System, 1955-1960." Simulated International Processes Project. Evanston, Ill.: Northwestern University, 1968.

———. "The Arms Race as an Open and Closed System." Papers, Peace Research Society (International) 7 (1967): 41-62.

———. "Feierabend Frustration/Aggression Theory." Computer module, Lancaster, England: Peace Research Centre, 1968.

———. "An International Processes Simulation, Conflict Theory and Analysis." Evanston, Ill.: Northwestern University, 1968.

———. "International Processes Simulations: A Description." In Experimentation and Simulation in Political Science. Edited by J. A. Laponce and Paul L. Smoker. Toronto: University of Toronto Press, 1972, pp. 315-65.

———. "An International Processes Simulation: Development, Usage, and Partial Validation." Ph.D. dissertation, Lancaster, England: University of Lancaster, 1968.

———. "International Processes Simulation: An Evaluation." Paper presented at the Events Data Conference. Michigan State University, East Lansing, Mich., 1970.

———. "International Processes Simulation: Notes on Step-Change from Inter-Nation Simulation." Evanston, Ill.: Northwestern University, 1967.

_____. "An International Processes Simulation–Theory and Description." Lancaster, England: University of Lancaster, 1967.

_____. "International Relations Simulations." Peace Research Reviews 3, no. 6 (1970): 1-84.

_____. "IPS Research and Development." Computer module, Lancaster, England: Peace Research Centre, 1968.

_____. "Nation-State Escalation and International Integration." Journal of Peace Research 4, no. 1 (1967): 60-75.

_____. "Participant's Manual–International Processes Simulation." Evanston, Ill.: Northwestern University, 1968.

_____. "Report on International Processes Simulation." Evanston, Ill.: Northwestern University, 1967.

_____. "Richardson Arms Race Dynamics." Computer module, Lancaster, England: Peace Research Centre, 1968.

_____. "Simulating the Human World." Science Journal 6, no. 7 (1970): 49-53.

_____. "Social Research for Social Anticipation." American Behavioral Scientist 12, no. 6 (1969): 7-13.

_____. "Tanter/Midlarsky Theory of Revolution." Computer module, Lancaster, England: Peace Research Centre, 1968.

_____. "A Time Series Analysis of Sino-Indian Relations." Journal of Conflict Resolution 13, no. 2 (1969): 172-91.

_____. "Working Electoral Theory." Computer module, Lancaster, England: Peace Research Centre, 1969.

Snyder, Richard C. "Some Perspectives on the Use of Experimental Techniques in the Study of International Relations." In Simulation in International Relations: Development for Research and Teaching. Edited by Harold Guetzkow, Chadwick F. Alger, Richard A. Brody, Robert C. Noel, and Richard C. Snyder. Englewood Cliffs: Prentice-Hall, 1963, pp. 1-23.

_____. "Some Recent Trends in International Relations Theory and Research." In Proceedings of the Conference of the International

Political Science Association. Urbana: University of Illinois Press, 1963.

Soroos, Marvin S. "Crisis Behaviors in the International Processes Simulation and the Berlin Reference System." Raleigh: North Carolina State University, 1971.

_____. "An Interpretation of Patterns of Discrepancies Between the International Process Simulation and an International Reference System." In The Simulation of Inter-societal Relations. Edited by Joseph D. Ben-Dak. New York: Gordon and Breach, 1973, pp. 1-28.

_____. "Patterns of Cross-National Activities in the International Simulation and a Real World Reference System." In International Interactions: a Reader. Edited by Edward Azar. New York: Gordon and Breach, 1975.

Steinbrunner, John D. "Relatively Unprogrammed Political-Military Simulations: The RAND/MIT Political Military Exercise and Developments for Data-Based Operations." Washington, D.C.: Industrial College of the Armed Forces, 1969.

Streufert, Siegfried. "The Components of a Simulation of Local Conflict: An Analysis of the Tactical and Negotiations Game." Evanston, Ill.: Northwestern University, 1968.

Sullivan, Denis G. "The Concept of Power in International Relations." Paper presented at the meetings of the Midwest Political Science Association, 1960.

_____. "Towards an Inventory of Major Propositions Contained in Contemporary Textbooks in International Relations." Ph.D. dissertation, Evanston, Ill.: Northwestern University, 1963.

Targ, Harry R., and Nardin, Terry. "The Inter-Nation Simulation as a Predictor of Contemporary Events." Mimeographed. Evanston, Ill.: Northwestern University, 1965.

Van Atta, Richard. "A Simulation Test of the Balance of Power." Evanston, Ill.: Northwestern University, 1969.

Walbeck, Norman V. "Aspects of International Interaction in the Referent System and the International Processes Simulation: Cooperation and Conflict." Evanston, Ill.: Northwestern University, 1968.

Winter, Ernest Florian. "Perception Problems in International Relations Research." Evanston, Ill.: Northwestern University, 1967.

Wright, George D. "Inter-Group Communication and Attraction in Inter-Nation Simulation." Ph.D. dissertation, St. Louis: Washington University, 1963.

Zinnes, Dina A. "Coalition Formation in Simulation and International Systems." Princeton: Princeton University, 1966.

———. "A Comparison of Hostile Behavior of Decision Makers in Simulate and Historical Data." World Politics 18, no. 3 (1966): 474-502.

———; Van Houweling, Douglas E.; and Van Atta, Richard H. "International System Structure and the Balance of Power Propositions: A Computer Simulation Study." Bloomington: Indiana University, 1972.

STANFORD STUDIES IN INTERNATIONAL CONFLICT AND INTEGRATION
Principal Investigator:
Robert C. North
Prepared by:
Robert C. North

Brody, Richard A. "Cognition and Behavior: A Model of Inter-Unit Relation." In Proceedings of the ONR Conference on Cognition and Development. Edited by O. J. Harvey. Washington: U.S. Office of Naval Research, 1965.

_____. "Deterrence." International Encyclopedia of the Social Sciences. Vol. 4. New York: Crowell-Collier, 1968, pp. 130-33.

_____. "International Relations as a Behavioral Science." In Psychology and International Relations. Edited by Gerald Sperrazzo. Washington: Georgetown University Press, 1965, pp. 53-61.

_____. "Spread of Nuclear Weapons and the Survival of the Cold War System." In Proceedings of the World Affairs Institute. San Diego: San Diego State College, 1962.

_____. "Three Conceptual Schemes for the Study of International Relations." In Foreign Policy Decision-Making. Edited by Richard C. Snyder, R. W. Bruck and Burton Sapin. New York: Free Press, 1962.

Choucri, Nazli. "International Conflict Processes: A System View." In Beitrage zu einer Ethik des Friedens. Vienna: Herder, 1973.

_____. "International Non-Alignment: Quantitative Perspectives on the Afro-Asian Variant." In Behavioral International Relations. Edited by Michael Haas. San Francisco: Chandler Publishing, 1973.

_____. "The Nonalignment of Afro-Asian States." Canadian Journal of Political Science 2, no. 1 (1969): 1-17.

_____. "The Perceptual Basis of Nonalignment." Journal of Conflict Resolution 13, no. 1 (1969): 57-74.

_____. "Political Implications of Population Dynamics: A Synthesis and Critical Review." New York: United Nations, Population Policy Division, 1973.

_____. Population Dynamics and International Violence: Propositions, Insights and Evidence. Cambridge: Massachusetts Institute of Technology, Center for International Studies, 1973.

_____. "Population, Resources and Technology: Political Implications of the Environmental Crisis." International Organization 26, no. 2 (1972): 175-212.

_____; Laird, Michael; and Meadows, Dennis. Resource Scarcity and Foreign Policy: A Simulation Model of International Conflict. Cambridge: Massachusetts Institute of Technology, Center for International Studies, 1972.

_____ and North, Robert C. "Causes of World War I: A Quantitative Analysis of Longer-Range Dynamics." In Grossmachtrivalitat und Weltkrieg: Sozialwissenschaftliche Studien zum Historikerkommentare. Edited by Klaus Jurgen Gartzel, Giesela Kress, and Volker Rittberger. Gutersloh: Bertelsmann Universitatsverlag, 1972.

_____ and North, Robert C. "The Determinants of International Violence." Papers, Peace Research Society (International) 12 (1968): 33-63.

_____ and North, Robert C. "Dynamics of International Conflict: Some Policy Implications of Population, Resources, and Technology." In Theory and Policy in International Relations. Edited by Raymond Tanter and Richard H. Ullman. Princeton: Princeton University Press, 1972, pp. 80-122.

_____ and North, Robert C. Nations in Conflict: National Growth and International Violence. San Francisco: W. H. Freeman and Company, 1975.

_____ with North, Robert C. "In Search of Peace Systems: Scandinavia and the Netherlands: 1870-1970." In Peace, War, and Numbers. Edited by Bruce M. Russett. Beverly Hills: Sage Publications, 1972, pp. 239-74.

_____ and Ross, D. Scott. "A Preliminary Report on a Forecasting Model of Energy Imports and International Political Costs, Resistance and Conflict." Cambridge: Massachusetts Institute of Technology, Center for International Studies, 1973.

Ekman, Paul; Tufte, Edward R.; Archibald, Kathleen; and Brody, Richard A. "Coping with Cuba: Divergent Policy Preferences of State Political Leaders." Journal of Conflict Resolution 10, no. 2 (1966): 180-97.

Fagen, Richard R. "The Behavioral Scientist and International Relations." American Behavioral Scientist 4, no. 8 (1961): 29-30.

———. "Calculation and Emotion in Foreign Policy: The Cuban Case." Journal of Conflict Resolution 6, no. 3 (1962): 214-21.

———. "Some Assessments and Uses of Public Opinion in Diplomacy." Public Opinion Quarterly 24, no. 3 (1960).

Haas, Michael. "Some Societal Correlates of International Political Behavior." Ph.D. dissertation, Stanford, Calif.: Stanford University, 1964.

Hardyck, Jane Allen, and Braden, Marcia. "Prophecy Fails Again: A Report of a Failure to Replicate." Journal of Abnormal and Social Psychology 64, no. 2 (1965): 382-87.

Holsti, Ole R. "An Adaptation of the 'General Inquirer' for the Systematic Analysis of Political Documents." Behavioral Science 9, no. 4 (1964).

———. "The Belief System and National Images: A Case Study." Journal of Conflict Resolution 6, no. 3 (1962): 244-52.

———. "The Citizen, the Scholar, and the Policy Maker: Some Dissenting Views." Background 8, no. 2 (1964): 93-100.

———. "Computer Content Analysis as a Tool in International Relations Research." In Proceedings of the Yale-IBM Conference on Computers for the Humanities. New Haven: Yale University, 1965.

———. Crisis, Escalation, War. Montreal: McGill-Queen's University Press, 1972.

———. "East-West Conflict and Sino-Soviet Relations." Journal of Applied Behavioral Science 1, no. 2 (1965): 115-30.

———. "Individual Differences in 'Defining the Situation.'" Journal of Conflict Resolution 14, no. 3 (1970): 303-310.

———. "The 1914 Case." American Political Science Review 59, no. 2 (1965): 365-78.

_____. "Perceptions of Time and Alternatives as Factors in Crisis Decision-Making." Papers, Peace Research Society (International 3 (1965): 79-120.

_____. "Private Perceptions and Public Policy." In The Grand Design: Proceedings of the Institute of World Affairs. Los Angeles: University of Southern California, 1964.

_____. "Research in International Crisis." In Proceedings of the Rocky Mountain-Great Plains Peace Research Conference. Fort Collins: Colorado State University, 1963.

_____. "Time, Alternatives and Communications: The 1914 and Cuban Missile Crises." In International Crisis: Evidence from Behavioral Research. Edited by Charles F. Hermann. New York: Free Press, 1972, pp. 55-80.

_____. "The Value of International Tension-Measurement." In Weapons Management in World Politics. Edited by J. David Singer. Ann Arbor: University of Michigan Press, 1963.

_____; Brody, Richard A.; and North, Robert C. "International Relations as a Social Science: A Research Approach." International Social Science Journal 17, no. 3 (1965): 442-53.

_____; Brody, Richard A.; and North, Robert C. "Measuring Affect and Action in International Reaction Models: Empirical Materials from the 1962 Cuban Crisis." Papers, Peace Research Society (International) 2 (1965): 170-90.

_____; Brody, Richard A.; and North, Robert C. "Violence and Hostility: The Path to World War." Paper presented at the American Psychiatric Association Conference, Los Angeles, Calif., 1964.

_____ and North, Robert C. "The History of Human Conflict." In The Nature of Human Conflict. Edited by Elton B. McNeil. Englewood Cliffs: Prentice-Hall, 1965, pp. 155-71.

_____ and North, Robert C. "Perceptions of Hostility and Economic Variables." In Comparing Nations. Edited by Richard Merritt and Stein Rokkan. New Haven: Yale University Press, 1966, pp. 169-90.

_____; North, Robert C.; and Brody, Richard A. "Perception and Action in the 1914 Crisis." In Quantitative International Politics:

Insights and Evidence. Edited by J. David Singer. New York: Free Press, 1968, pp. 123-58.

Koch, Howard E., Jr.; North, Robert C.; and Zinnes, Dina A. "Some Theoretical Notes on Geography and International Conflict." Journal of Conflict Resolution 4, no. 1 (1960): 4-14.

Korten, David C. "Situational Determinants of Leadership Structure." Journal of Conflict Resolution 6, no. 3 (1962): 222-35.

Nomikos, Eugenia V., and North, Robert C. International Crisis: The Outbreak of World War I. Montreal: McGill-Queen's University Press, 1975.

North, Robert C. "Conflict." In International Encyclopedia of the Social Sciences, vol. 3. New York: Crowell-Collier Publishing, 1968, pp. 226-32.

———. "Decision-Making in Crisis." Journal of Conflict Resolution, 6, no. 3 (1962): 197-200.

———. "Fear, Anxiety and the Behavior of States." Alabama Mental Health, 15, no. 1 (1963).

———. "International Conflict and Integration: Problems of Research." In Intergroup Relations and Leadership. Edited by Muzafer Sherif. New York: John Wiley and Sons, 1962, pp. 190-203.

———. "International Relations: Putting the Pieces Together." Background 8, no. 3 (1963): 119-30.

———; Brody, Richard A.; and Holsti, Ole R. "Some Empirical Data on the Conflict Spiral." Papers, Peace Research Society (International) 1 (1964): 1-14.

——— and Choucri, Nazli. "Background Conditions to the Outbreak of the First World War." Papers, Peace Research Society (International) 9 (1968): 125-37.

——— and Choucri, Nazli. "Population, Technology, and Resources in the Future International System." Journal of International Affairs 25, no. 2 (1971): 224-37.

———; Holsti, Ole R.; and Brody, Richard A. "Perception and Action in the Study of International Relations: The 1914 Crisis." In

STANFORD STUDIES 519

    Quantitative International Politics: Insights and Evidence. Edited by J. David Singer. New York: Free Press, 1966, pp. 123-58.

____; Holsti, Ole R.; Zaninovich, M. George; and Zinnes, Dina A. Content Analysis: A Handbook with Application for the Study of International Crisis. Evanston, Ill.: Northwestern University Press, 1963.

____; Koch, Howard E., Jr.; and Zinnes, Dina A. "The Integrative Functions of Conflict." Journal of Conflict Resolution 4, no. 3 (1960): 355-74.

____ and Lagerstrom, Richard. War and Domination: A Theory of Lateral Pressure. New York: General Learning Press, 1971.

Raser, John R. "Capability to Delay Response: Explication of a Deterrence Concept and Research Employing Inter-Nation Simulation." Ph.D. dissertation, Stanford, Calif.: Stanford University, 1964.

Zaninovich, M. George, "An Empirical Theory of State Response: The Sino-Soviet Case." Ph.D. dissertation, Stanford, Calif.: Stanford University, 1964.

____. "Pattern Analysis of Variables within the International System: The Sino-Soviet Example." Journal of Conflict Resolution 6, no. 5 (1962): 253-68.

Zinnes, Dina A. "The Expression and Perception of Hostility in Pre-War Crisis: 1914." In Quantitative International Politics: Insights and Evidence. Edited by J. David Singer. New York: Free Press, 1968, pp. 85-119.

____. "Hostility in International Decision-Making." Journal of Conflict Resolution 6, no. 3 (1962): 236-43.

____; North, Robert C.; and Koch, Howard E., Jr. "Capability, Threat and the Outbreak of War." In International Politics and Foreign Policy. Edited by James N. Rosenau. New York: Free Press, 1961, pp. 469-82.

____; Zinnes, Joseph; and McClure, Robert. "Hostility in Diplomatic Communications: A Study of the 1914 Crisis." In International Crisis: Evidence from Behavioral Research. Edited by Charles F. Hermann. New York: Free Press, 1972, pp. 139-62.

ABOUT THE CONTRIBUTORS

Stuart A. Bremer, Assistant Professor, Political Science Department, University of Michigan

Robert Butterworth, Assistant Professor, Political Science Department, University of Pittsburgh

James A. Caporaso, Associate Professor, Political Science Department, Northwestern University

Cheryl Christensen, Assistant Professor, Department of Government and Politics, University of Maryland

Nazli Choucri, Associate Professor, Political Science Department, Massachusetts Institute of Technology

Raymond Duvall, Assistant Professor, Political Science Department, Yale University

Karen Ann Feste, Assistant Professor, Graduate School of International Studies, University of Denver

Harold Guetzkow, Professor, Political Science Department, Northwestern University

Leo Hazlewood, Manager, Projections and Plans Department, Policy Sciences Division, CACI, Inc.

Gordon Hilton, Assistant Professor, Political Science Department, Northwestern University

William Ladd Hollist, Research Associate, Political Science Department, Northwestern University

Ole R. Holsti, George V. Allen, Professor, Political Science Department, Duke University

Francis W. Hoole, Assistant Professor, Political Science Department, Indiana University

Brian L. Job, Assistant Professor, Political Science Department, University of Minnesota

Mark S. Levine, Assistant Professor, Political Science Department, Northwestern University

Robert C. North, Professor, Political Science Department, Stanford University

Charles W. Ostrom, Jr., Assistant Professor, Political Science Department, Michigan State University

Dale B. Robertson, Doctoral Candidate, School of International Service, American University

Rudolph J. Rummel, Professor, Political Science Department, University of Hawaii

Bruce Russett, Professor, Political Science Department, Yale University

J. David Singer, Professor, Political Science Department, University of Michigan

Harvey Starr, Assistant Professor, Political Science Department, Indiana University

Stuart J. Thorson, Associate Professor, Political Science Department, Ohio State University

Richard H. Van Atta, Senior Associate, Policy Sciences Division, CACI, Inc.

Dina A. Zinnes, Professor, Political Science Department, Indiana University

RELATED TITLES
Published by
Praeger Special Studies

MATHEMATICAL MODELS OF INTERNATIONAL
RELATIONS
Edited by Dina A. Zinnes
and John V. Gillespie

CONTROL THEORY AND INTERNATIONAL
RELATIONS RESEARCH
Edited by John V. Gillespie
and Dina A. Zinnes

QUANTITATIVE TECHNIQUES IN FOREIGN POLICY
ANALYSIS AND FORECASTING
Michael K. O'Leary and William D.
Coplin, with the assistance of
Howard B. Shapiro

POLITICS OF DIVISION, PARTITION, AND
UNIFICATION
Edited by Ray Edward Johnston

INTERNATIONAL ADMINISTRATION AND
GLOBAL PROBLEMS: An Analysis of the
World Food Conference
Thomas G. Weiss and Robert S.
Jordan

Augsburg College
George Sverdrup Library
Minneapolis, Minnesota 55404